Street by Str...

C000076446

GLOUCESTERSHIRE
PLUS BRISTOL, CHEPSTOW,
CRICKLADE, SHIPSTON-ON-STOUR
Enlarged Areas Cheltenham, Gloucester

1st edition May 2001

© Automobile Association Developments
Limited 2001

This product includes map data licensed from
Ordnance Survey® with the permission of the
Controller of Her Majesty's Stationery Office.
© Crown copyright 2000. All rights reserved.
Licence No: 399221.

Published by AA Publishing (a trading name of
Automobile Association Developments
Limited, whose registered office is Norfolk House,
Priestley Road, Basingstoke, Hampshire, RG24 9NY.
Registered number 1878835).

Mapping produced by the Cartographic
Department of The Automobile Association.

A CIP Catalogue record for this book is
available from the British Library.

Printed by in Italy by Printer Trento srl

Key to map pages ii-iii

Key to map symbols iv-1

Enlarged scale pages 2-5

Street by Street 6-381

Index – towns & villages 382-386

Index – streets 387-433

Index – featured places 433-442

ii

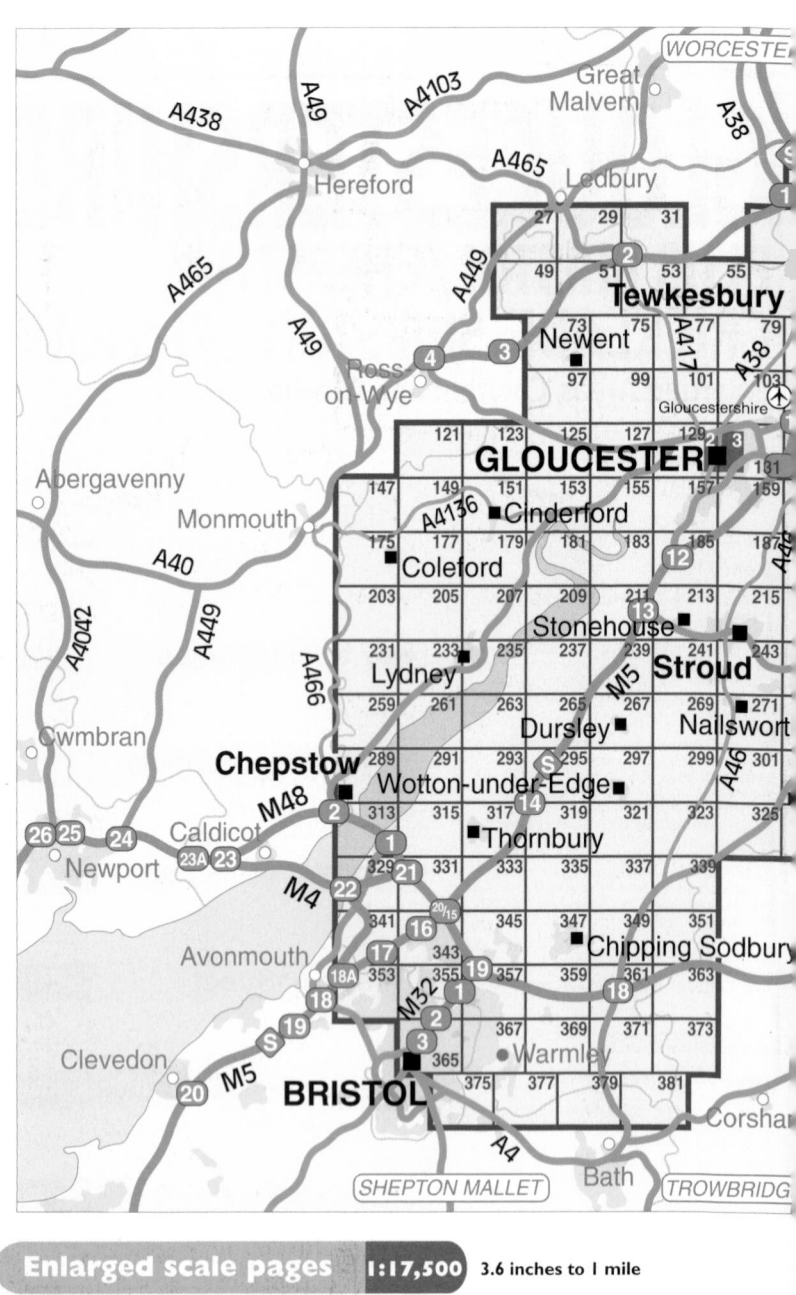

Enlarged scale pages 1:17,500 3.6 inches to 1 mile

```
0                    1/2          miles                    1
0          1/2              1      kilometres      1 1/2
```

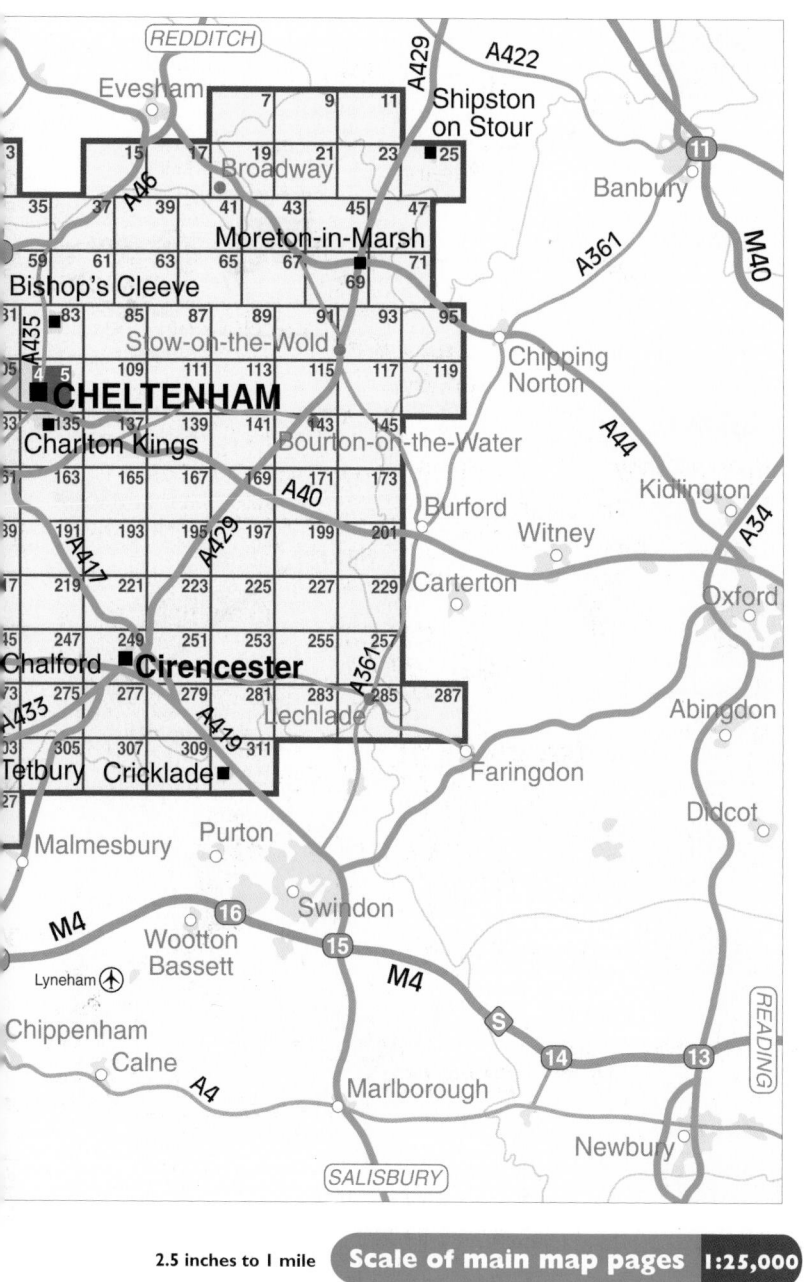

2.5 inches to I mile   **Scale of main map pages**   **1:25,000**

| 0 | 1/2 | miles | I | 1 1/2 |
| 0 | 1/2 | I kilometres | 1 1/2 | 2 |

iv

Symbol	Description
Junction 9	Motorway & junction
Services	Motorway service area
	Primary road single/dual carriageway
Services	Primary road service area
	A road single/dual carriageway
	B road single/dual carriageway
	Other road single/dual carriageway
	Restricted road
	Private road
← ←	One way street
	Pedestrian street
=========	Track/footpath
	Road under construction
]==={	Road tunnel
P	Parking

Symbol	Description
P+	Park & Ride
	Bus/coach station
	Railway & main railway station
	Railway & minor railway station
⊖	Underground station
⊖	Light railway & station
+++++++++	Preserved private railway
LC	Level crossing
•—•—•—	Tramway
- - - - -	Ferry route
....	Airport runway
— · — · — ·	Boundaries- borough/ district
ᵛᵛᵛᵛᵛᵛᵛ	Mounds
93	Page continuation 1:25,000
7	Page continuation to enlarged scale 1:17,500

	River/canal lake, pier	&#9855;	Toilet with disabled facilities
	Aqueduct lock, weir		Petrol station
465 ▲ Winter Hill	Peak (with height in metres)	PH	Public house
	Beach	PO	Post Office
	Coniferous woodland		Public library
	Broadleaved woodland	*i*	Tourist Information Centre
	Mixed woodland	✗	Castle
	Park		Historic house/ building
	Cemetery	Wakehurst Place NT	National Trust property
	Built-up area	M	Museum/ art gallery
	Featured building	†	Church/chapel
⊓⊔⊓⊔⊓	City wall	Y	Country park
A&E	Accident & Emergency hospital		Theatre/ performing arts
	Toilet		Cinema

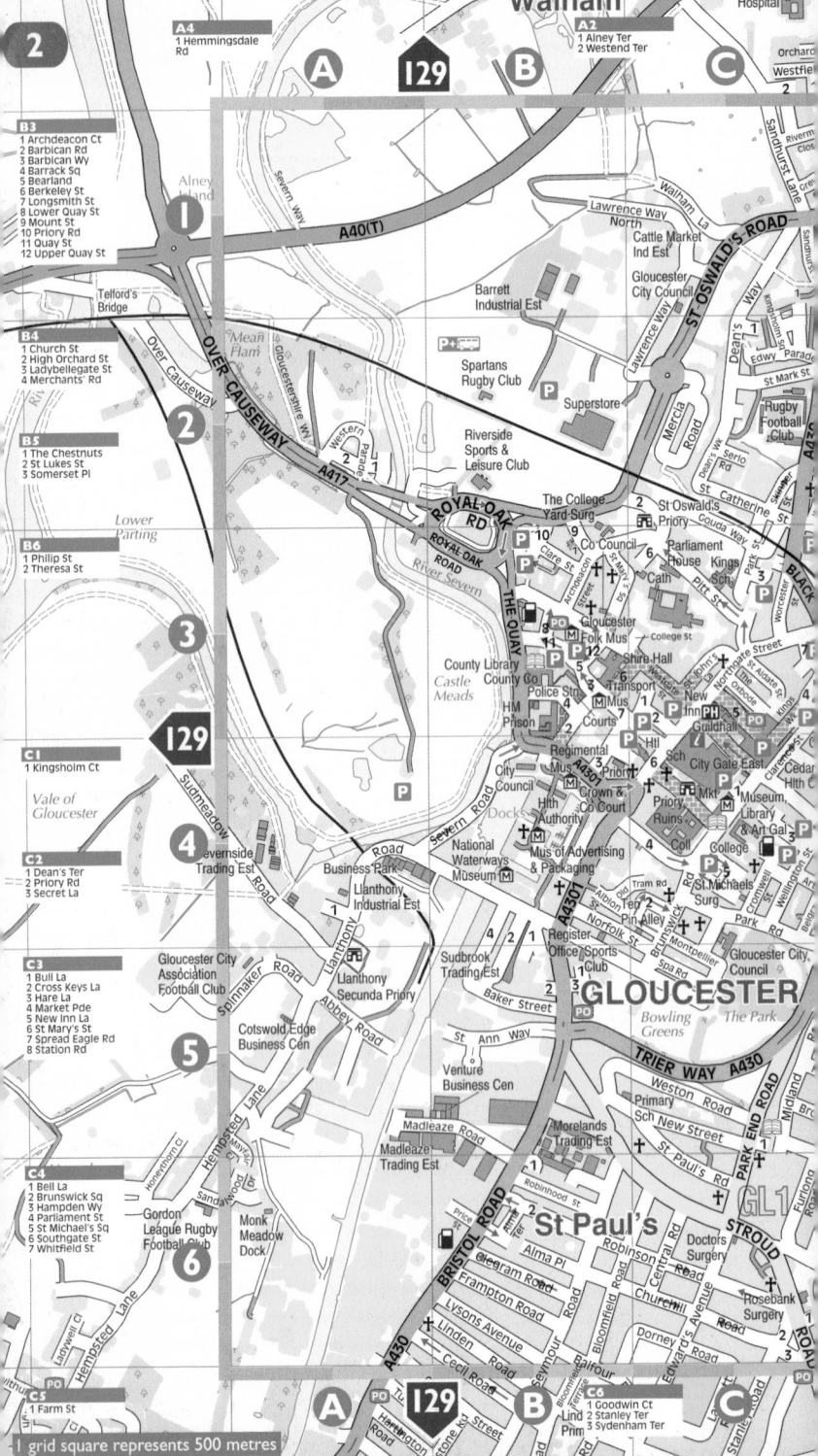

Central Gloucester 3

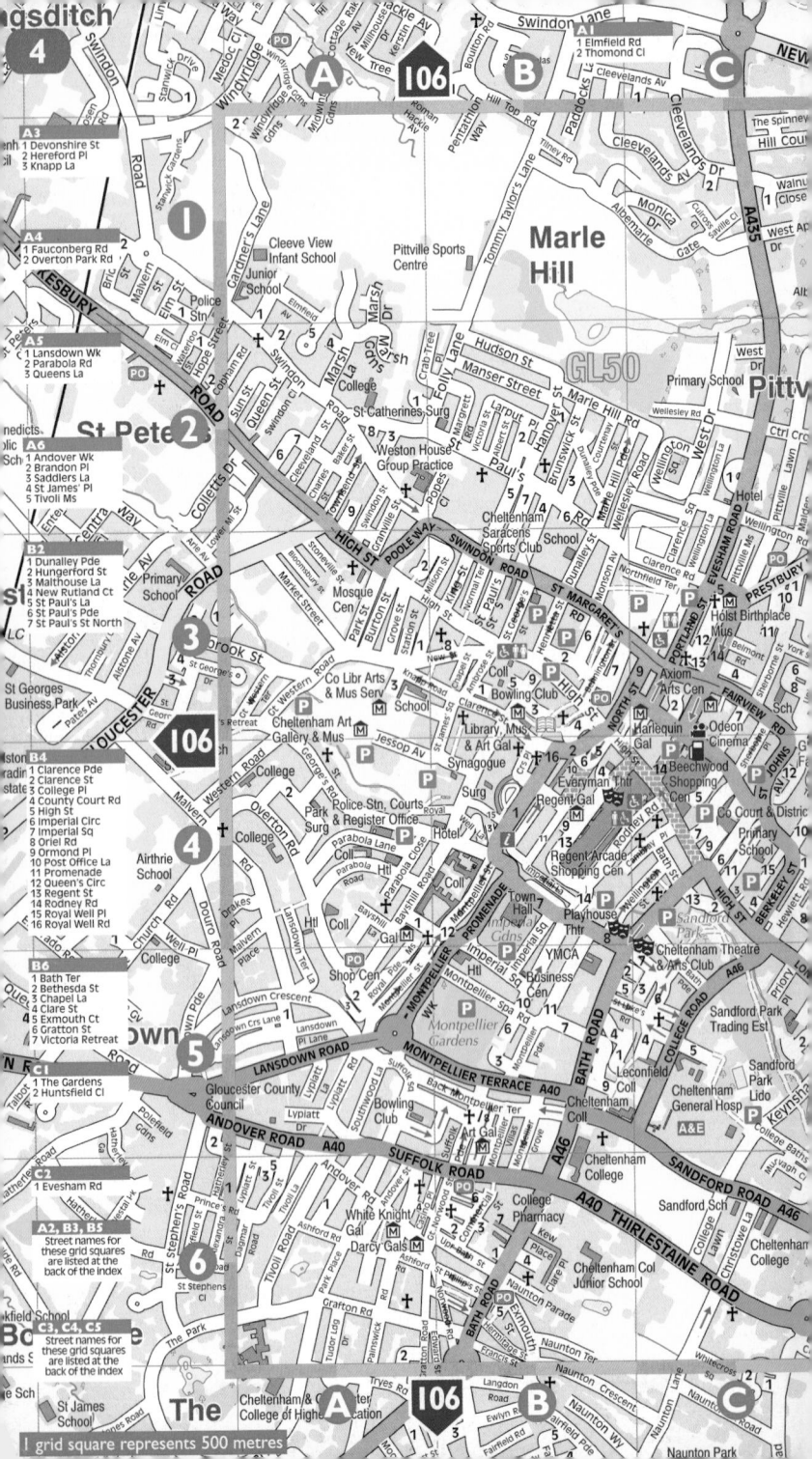

G2
1 Corner Farm Dr
2 Manor Cl

Honeybourne Station

Grove Farm

F G H J K

Domestic Fowl Trust

Honeybourne

Wyatt Avenue

Beaufort End

Stratford Road

Cemetery

Mickleton Road

I

Green Close

1

First School

PO

2

Gloster Ades Road

Manor Farm

Poden

Poden Lane

3

Weston Road

4

Worcestershire County
Gloucestershire County

8

Honeybourne Airfield
Industrial Estate

5

B4035

Honeybourne Road

6

B4632

Weston-
sub-Edge

7

Buckle Street

PO

Dover View

Parsons Lane

Chapel Lane

B4632

8

The Lynches

F G H 19 J K

F G H J K

Upper Clopton

Coleman's Hill

Meon Road

Granbrook Lane

Cedar Road

STRATFORD

B4632

GRANBROOK LANE

B4632

Mickleton

Old Mnr Gdns

Warwickshire County
Gloucestershire County

Mickleton Wood Farm

Hidcote Combe

Chapel Lane

Back Lane

Cotswold Edge

Arbour Close

Ballard Close

Cemetery

AY ROAD

Baker's Hill

Kiftsgate Gardens

Hidcote Manor Garden (NT)

Hidcote Bartrim

10

Niniveh Farm

CAMPDEN ROAD

B4081

Monarch's Way

Heart Of England Way

Hidcote Boyce

Longlands Farm

Furze Lane

Hidcote Road

GL55

Mickleton Hills Farm

Monarch's Way

F G H **21** J K

Eb

Campden Road

York Farm
G3
1 Nellands Cl

H2
1 Cross Leys

Caleys
Fields

F G H J K

1

Mansill Farm

Ilmington Road

Mickleton

Road

Armscote   Road

2

New Bridge Farm

Street

Bennett Place

Keyte

Rd

PO PH

Ilmington School

Centenary   Way

Ilmington

Centenary Way

3

Fern Close

Tennery Way

Back

Street

Middle St

Valanders

La

Bellards Lane

Campden Street

Frog La

Crump Street

Foucote Hill

Foxcote Hl

Harolds Farm

4

Darlingscott

5

Potters

La

Southfield
Farm

Cathole

6

Longdon
Manor

7

Compton
Scorpion Manor

8

Holt Farm

F G **23** J K

Far
Longdon

I2

E8
1 Brockeridge Rd

D8
1 Hill End Rd
2 Nut Orchard La

D7
1 Freemans Cl

A B C D E

Manor Farm

Strensham Service Area N

Lo
St

M5

Bourne Road

Hill Croome ✝

Moat Fa

Hill Vw Rd

1

Upper
Strenshan

2

Green Lane

Court Rd

Ley
Farm

3

A38(T)

Stratford

4

Phelp's
Farm

M50

5

A38(T)

Brockeridge
Common

6

Gubberhill

Hill E

Hill End Road

✝

M50

7

Junction 1

The
Twittocks

Brockeridge Road

Hill End Road

Hillview
Lane

Paxhill
Lane

Goschen Cl

The
Mayalls

Twynin

Brook

Unworth
Lane

Orchard Dr

Fleet Lane

8

Puckrup

Lane

Cherry Orchard Lane

Twyning

Twyning
CP School

Fleet
Lane

Fleet Road

Bow Lane

Puckrup
Lane

A38

Filmore Lane

A **33** B C D E

Bow
Farm

Church
End

Abbots

K8
1 Bricknell Av
2 The Croftlands
3 Glebeland Dr
4 Gravel Pits Cl
5 Homestead Cl
6 Plantation Crs
7 Russet Cl

F **G** Strensham **H** **J** **K** Eckington Field Farm

I

2

Mill Lane

3

Bredon Field Farm

Junction 8

Worcestershire County
Gloucestershire County

4 Bredon's Norton

Showborough House

Rectory Farm

5

6

Moreton Lane

Mill End

Severn Sailing Club

7

green

Manor House

First School

PH PO

Back La

Church St

Bredon Barn (NT)

KEMERTON ROAD

HIGH ST

College Road

Bredon

8

F **G** **H** **34** **J** **K**

River Avon

Mill Lane

B4080

TEWKESBURY

ROAD

M5

CHELTENHAM

14

A B C D E

Netherton

Kersoe

Wychavon Way

Wychavon Way

The Dingle

W... Way

Ashton Wood

Holcomb Nap

Wychavon Way

Cotton's Lane

Elmley Road

Baker's Lane

Cornfield W...

Hillside

PO

Ashton under Hill

Ashton under Hill Primary School

station

Brickford Road

Willow Cl

Grafton

Wychavon Way

A46(T)

Carrant Brook

A46(T)

A46(T)

Wychavon Way

...ton Road

A B **37** C D E

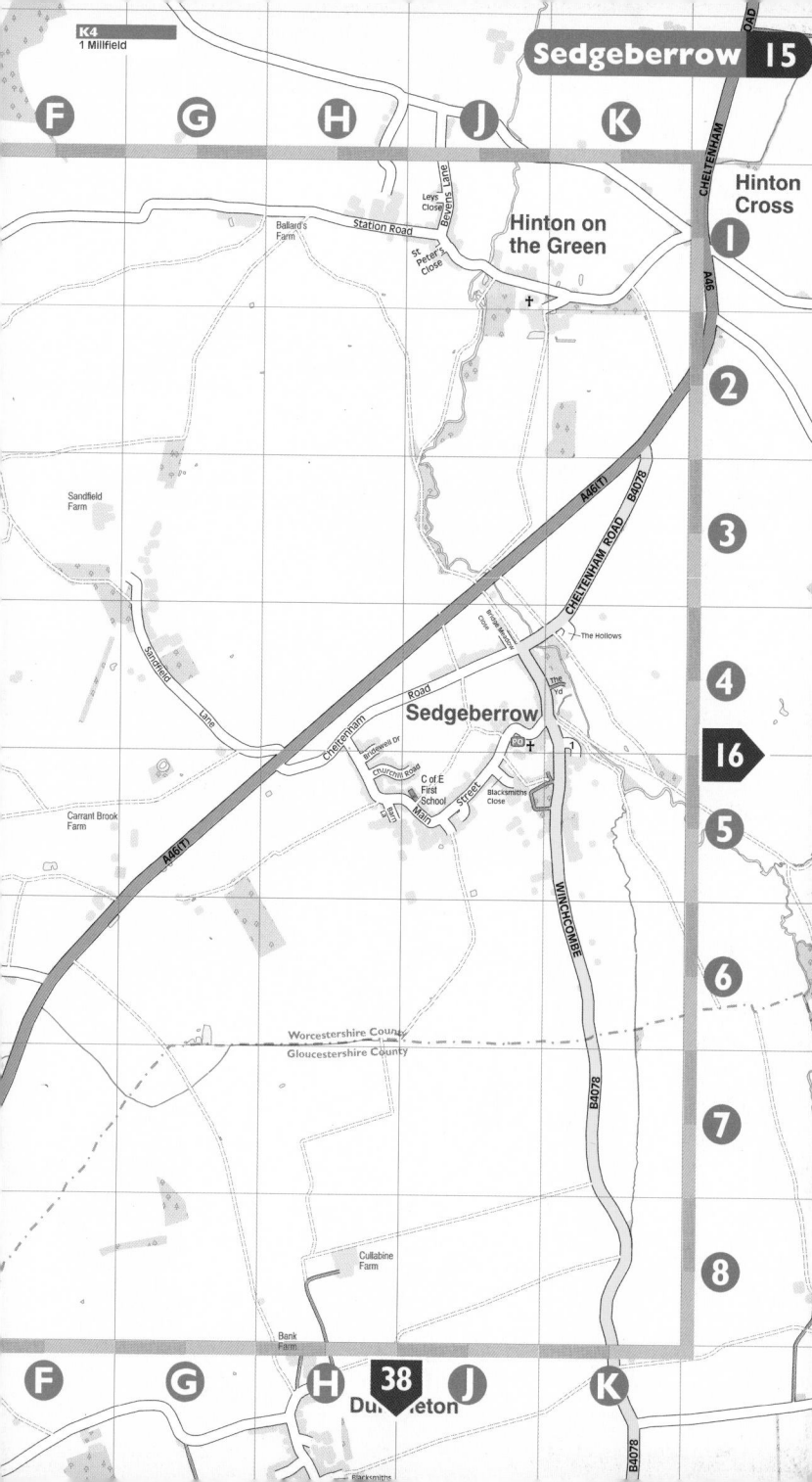

16

D5
1 Woodland Cl

C5
1 Old Hall Cl

A   **B**   **C**   **D**   **E**

CHELTENHAM ROAD

A46

Hinton
Cross

Greville Hall
Farm

1

2

A46 (T)

B4078

CHELTENHAM ROAD

3

Mount
Pleasant

The Hollows

4

15

5

WINCHCOMBE

Aston
Somerville

School Rd

Broadway Road

Church Rd

6

B4078

River Isbourne

7

Worcestershire County
Gloucestershire County

8

A   **B**   **39**   **C** rmington   **D**   **E**

78

1 grid square represents 500 metres

J4
1 Blacksmiths La

K4
1 The Squires

F G H J K

Whitfurrows

Bond
Industrial
Estate

Gallipot
House

I

2

3

Murcot

Murcot Road

Old Well
Farm

EVESHAM ROAD

A44

Evesham Road

Hinton Road

Childswickham

Broadway Road

Green Cl

New St

Farmers La

Atkinson St

Chapel La

Vicarage

Childswickham
School

4

Pennylands

Bank

18

5

Tuck Mill
Farm

6

Buckland
Fields

7 CHELTENHA

Peasebrook
Farm

B4632

WR12

8

Little
Buckland

Worcestershire Co
Gloucestershire Count

F G H 40 J K

Buckland

Rectory

House

F G H 7 J K

1

2

3

4

20

5

6

7

8

Saintbury

Willersey

PO

Top Farm

The Lynches

Park Farm

Weston Park

County

County

Foxhill Manor

Golf Course

Farncombe House

Hotel

Campden Lane

Buckle Street

Cotswold Way

Buckle Street

FISH HILL

FISH

Tilbury Hollow

Campden House

Coombe Farm

B4632

B4632

B4632

F G H 42 J K

Broadway Tower

Penn Farm

A44

20

E2
1 Weigh Bridge Ct

D4
1 Izod's Cl

D3
1 Coronation Cl

Attlepin Farm

A   **B**   **8**   **C**   **D**   **E**

The Lynches

Top Farm

1

Kingcomb

The Bratches

ASTON ROAD

E3
1 Leysbourne
2 Seymour Ga

2

Cotswold Way

Kingcomb Lane

Chippin
Campde
School

E4
1 Pear Tree Cl

The Hoo

**Chipping
Campden**

3

Cotswold Way

Kingcomb

Weston
Park

Dyer's Lane

The Medical Centre

The
Primary
School

Back
Ends

Hotel
Hotel

Town
Hall

HIGH ST

Police
Stn

Littleworth

4

The Narrows

Cotswold Way

Blind Lane

Westington

Park Road

**SHEEP
STREET**

Federated Primary
Ebrington & St Jar

The
Green

19

5

CONDUIT HILL

Swimm

6

Campden
House

7

Monarch's Way

Tilbury
Hollow

B4081

8

Coombe
Farm

Campden Hill
Farm

A   **B**   **43**   **C**   **D**   **E**

e Farm

I grid square represents 500 metres

F G H **II** J K

I

Holt Farm

Compton
Scorpion Manor

Far
Longdon

Portabello
Farm

2

B4035

B4035

orth

3

Charingworth
Grange

Newborough

Gloucestershire County
Warwickshire County

A429

4

Cottage
Farm

Tankards Hill

24

Carson
CI

Church
Green

Bencon

**Stretton-
on-Fosse**

5

Blackdowns

6

Paddle Brook

A429

Middle
Ditchford

7

Ditchfc
Frary

Ditchford
Hill

A429

Lower Ditchford
Village

8

Knee Brook

A429

The Ellen Badger

1 A3400
2 Green Lane Cl
3 Orchard Cl
4 South Lynn Gdns
5 Stour Ct

WEST ST

NEW STREET

OLD RD

LONDON ROAD

CHURCH ST

Fell Mill Lane

River Stour

B4035

Barcheston

Cemetery

Willington

CV36

River Stour

Farnington Farm

North Farm

Burmington

Main Street

The Lane

A3400

Burmington Grange

Cherington Butts

Mitford Bridge

County

Wolford Fields

Weston Mill

F **G** **H** **J** **K**

I **2** **3** **4** **5** **6** **7** **8**

A8
1 Monks Meadow

Ayllton
Court

Lillends

Brook
Farm

Ice
Marcle

A B C D E

I

The
Court

2

Laddin
Farm

3

White
House

Pre

A449

Preston Brook

4

Huntley's
Farm

Velcourt

A449

5

Ryemeadows

Gloucestershire County
Ceuniq of Herefordshire

6

Hallwo
Green

PH

7

Hellen's
House

Much Marcle
C of E Primary
School

Much
Marcle

8

Bridges
Farm

A B C D E

48

B4024

F

G Rowland's Green

H

J

Old Wharf Industrial Es

K Wharf

LEADON

Old Lilly Hall

Hill House

Lilly Hill Lane

A449

Robinscroft

Orlham Lane

A449

Ludstock

Orlham Farm

Siddington Farm

Orlham Lane

River Leadon

Hazel Farm

B4216

I

2

Argu Farm

3 B4216

County of Herefordshire
Gloucestershire County

Oldfields

Henberrow

Dinchall Farm

4

Leddington

Mirabels Farm

Poets Path

Parm

28

5 †

B4215

Tillputsend Cott

B4216

6

Rosehill

Poets Path

Donnington Hall

Greenw 7

Poets Path

B4215

Great Netherton

Tillers' Green

Weston Brook

Poets Path

8

Ockingto Farm

F

B4024

G

Windcross Farm

H 49

J

K

F **G** **H** **J** **K**

Eastnor
Castle

Wayend
Street

A438

Gold Hill
Farm

Hillend

I

2

Howler's
Heath

High
Wood

County of Herefordshire
Gloucestershire County

3

Clencher's
Mill

Toney's
Farm

4

30

Pepper
Mill

Clench Brook

Bromsberrow
Place

5

Bromsberrow

Albright Lane

**Brown's
End**

Brookend

Bromsberrow
C of E School

Albright Lane

Aubreys
Farm

6

Court
†

Albright Lane

Grove
House

Dyke House Lane

Wood End Street

A417

A417

7 2
Ju

Russell's
End

M50

8

A417

M50

Bell Lane

Sandfield

Bromsberrow Heath
ss Park

M50

**Bromsberrow
Heath**

Lintridge

Fairfields

F **G** **H** **51** **J** **K**

Ptera
Hall

F **G** **H** **J** **K**

1
2
3
4
5
6
7
8

Miller's Court
Miller's Court Road

rts Street

PH

Rye
Street

A438

Birtsmorton

The
Hill

A438

A438

Whiting
Farms

White
End

Berrow

M5

rtway

Netherley Lane

Grovefield

Underhill
Farm

Pendock
C of E
School

M50

M50

Cleeve Ho

B4208

ndock

PO

Grafton Lane

Hill Court
Farm

Frogsmarsh

53

Marsh
Court

F **G** **H** **J** **K**

D5
1 Crofts Fld

Queenhill

A B C D E

M50

Bredon School

River Severn

Bow Farm

Severn Way

Gunnice

Fuller's End

Hill House

Worcestershire Way Link

Windmill Tump

Worcestershire Way

Slades Green

Worcestershire Way Link

Bushley Green

Bredon School

The Rampings

Green Street

Wood Street

Bush

Sam Hill Wood

Wood Street

Stokes Road

Green Street

Massey Farm

A438

A438

A438

Bushley Park

Forthampton

Church Lane

PO

Alcock's Farm

Worcestershire County
Gloucestershire County

A B 56 C D E

Home Farm

BISHOP'S

F   G   H   J   K

I

2

3

4

36

5

6

7

8

Kinsham

CHELTENHAM

ROAD

B4079

Kinsham Lane

Kinsham Lane

Queensmead

Worcestershire County

Gloucestershire County

Carrant Brook

Carrant Brook

Casemore Lane

Aston on Carrant

Aston
Cross

A46(T)

A46(T)

North Av

South Av

Austin
Road

St Barnabas Ct

Pamington

Tirle Brook

Ellenborough
Dr

B4079

A335

Te

F   G   H **59** J   K

B4079

Tirle Brook

A B C D E

1

2

3

4

35

5

6

7

8

A B 60 C D E

Crashmore Lane

Silk Mill

Main Street PO

Manor House

Little Beckford

A46(T) CHELTENH

Cheltenham Road

Blacksmiths La

A46(T)

Crashmore Lane

The Elms

Teddington Hands

A46(T)

B4077

A46(T)

Alstone Farm

A435

Walnut Row

Gander La

St Nicholas

Manor

Teddington

Bengrove

A435

Worcestershire County
Gloucestershire County

Carrant Brook

Ashton Road

Station

Back Lane

F G H 14 J K

I
2
3
4
38
5
6
7
8

Beckford

A46(T)

A46(T)

Worcestershire County
Gloucestershire County

Didcot Farm

Hill Farm

Great
Washbourne

Little
Washbourne

B4077

Beckford Road

Primary
School

School

Blenheim Cl

Dibden Lane

St Margarets Rd

Willow Bank Road

St Margarets

Alderton

B4077

Alstone

F G H 61 J K

Alderton
Fields

F G H 16 J K

1 Leasow House

2

3

4

40

5

6

7

8

Wormington

Mill Farm

Cotton's Farm

Raymeadow Farm

Wormington Grange

Berry Wormington

B4632

Lydes Farm

Manor

Stanway Grounds

Church Lane

Toddington

B4652

BROADWAY ROAD

B4077

Toddington Primary School

New Town

B4652

B4077

B4632

Stanway

WR12

**West
End**

End

End

Snowshill Road

Snowshill Lane

F G H **18** J K

Buckland

Rectory

Hotel

Cotswold Way

Manor Farm

Gloucestershire County

Buckland
Wood

Coneygree La

Kite's
Nest

Dor
Knap

Middle
Hill House

Dulverton
Wood

I

2

3

4

42

5

Cotswold Way

Great Brockhampton
Farm

Snowshill

Snowshill
Manor (NT)

Hill Barn
Farm

6

7

8

F G H **65** J K

Stan
Ash
Wood

Upper
Slatepits

Buckle Street

I

Peter's
Farm

A44

Cotswold Way

Broadway
Tower

Broadway Tower
Country Park

Spring
Industrial
Estate

2

Dor
Knap

Kite's
Nest

Buckle Street

3

Middle
Hill House

Heath Farm

Gloucestershire County

Worcestershire County

Bulverton
Wood

4

Broadway
Wood

Seven
Wells

41

Buckle Street

5

Spring Hill

Hill Barn
Farm

6

Buckle Street

7

Snowshill
Hill

8

Upper
Slaughte

Street

Hornsleasow
Farm

1 grid square represents 500 metres

F G H 20 J K

Campden Hill

I

Hangman's Hall
Farm

2

Lapstone Farm

Northwick
Hill

3

B

Holt
Farm

Dovedale Farm

4

Upton Wold
Farm

44

5

Campden
Ashes

6

7

Far Upton
Wold Farm

A44

8

Highland
Lodge

Bourton
Far Hill Farm

Kidlones

F G H 67 J K

Bourton
Hill House

44

C3
1 The Dell

A　B　**21**　C　D　E

Northwick Business Centre

Well Farm

John Brooke

I
Hangman's Hall Farm

Monarch's Way

Northwick Park

STATION

Not

2

B4479

STATION ROAD

3
Blockley

C of E School

Winterway

Monarch's Way

Park Road

Greenway Road

Police Station

Cem

Summerfield

Summerway Cl

Sleepy Hollow Farm Park ●

Dovedale Farm

PO

Bell Bank

Hotel

Chapel Lane

PH

High Street

School Lane

Pasture Lane

LOWER ST

B4479

Pasture Farm

4

43

Day's Lane

Brook Ln

Donkey La

Park Farm

Monarch's Way

Dovedale

Downs Farm

5

6

Hailstone Farm

7
Bourton Woods

A44

B4479

8

A424

A44

Bourton-the-Hill

1 †

A　B　**68**　C　D　E

1 grid square represents 500 metres

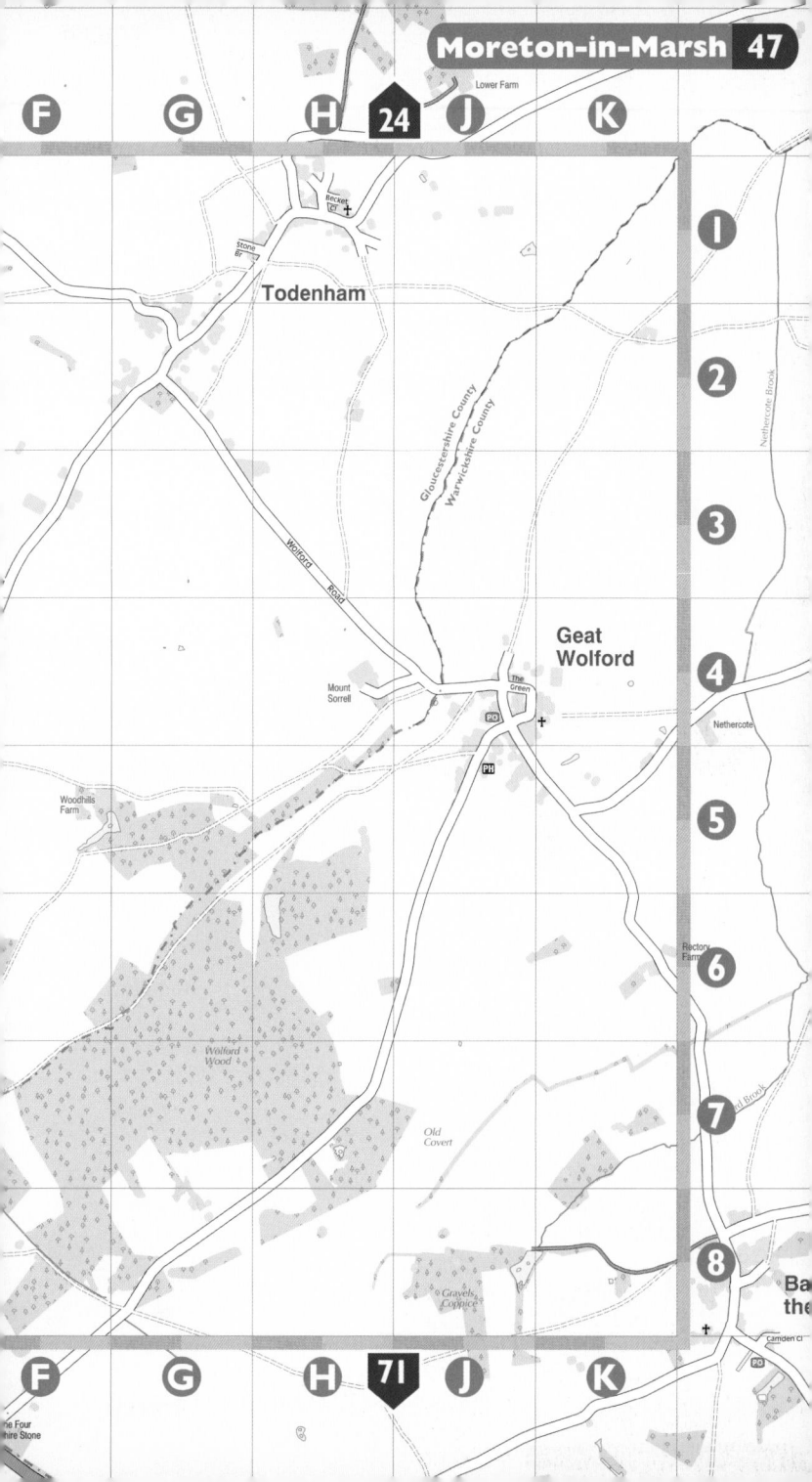

F G H **24** J K

I
2
3
4
5
6
7
8

Lower Farm

Becket
Ct

Stone
Br

Todenham

Wolford Road

Gloucestershire County
Warwickshire County

**Geat
Wolford**

The
Green

Mount
Sorrell

PO

PH

Nethercote

Nethercote Brook

Woodhills
Farm

Wolford
Wood

Rectory
Farm

Brook

Old
Covert

Ba
the

Camden Cl

PO

Gravels
Coppice

he Four
hire Stone

Much
Marcle

A

B

26

C

D

E

C of E Primary
School

B4024

1

B4024

Bridges
Farm

Friar's
Court

Stonehouse
Farm

Awnells

1

2

3

Kempley Brook

St Mary's
Church

County of Herefordshire

Gloucestershire County

4

Kempley
Court

Bickerton
Court

5

Brookland

Daffodil Way

Whittocks
End

6

Daffodil Way

Kempley

7

Fishpool

Kempley Green

Woodhouse
Farm

8

Daffodil Way

A

B

C

D

E

Daubies
Farm

Upton
Court

I grid square represents 500 metres

F G H 31 J K

I

B2ge End

3

4

54

5

6

7

8

F G H 76 J K

Grafton Lane

1 Johnstone Cl

ndock

Frogsmarsh

Marsh Court

Lime Street

Cole's Farm

Gadfield Elm

B4208

Eldersfield

Lime st

Worcestershire County
Gloucestershire County

shill

The
Hill

The Hawthorns

Moorend Road

**Pillows
Green**

The
Moat

Moat Lane

B4208

Pillows Green Road

Staunton

A417

Ledbury Road Crescent

MALVERN ROAD

B4213 **STRAIGHT LANE**

Staunton & Corse C of E
Aided School

Staunton Court
Business Park

Staunton
Court

Prince Crescent

Police Station

Corse
Surgery

WORCESTER

Walker's
Farm

GLOUCESTER RD

The Stone Rd

Corse

School Crescent

**Snig's
End**

Bayliss'
Farm

Pitt's
Mill

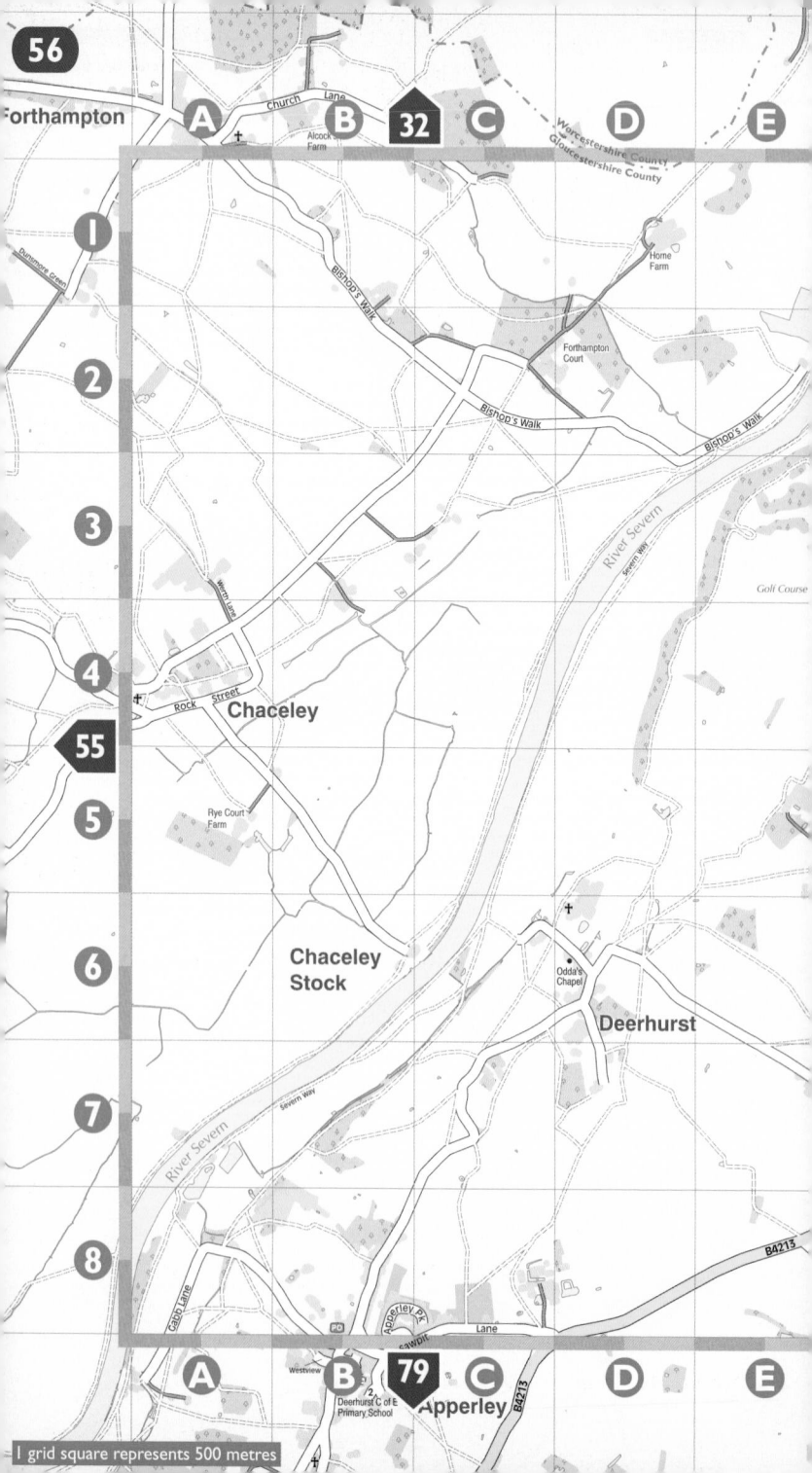

Forthampton

A   Church   Lane   B   32   C   Worcestershire County   D   Gloucestershire County   E

Duthmere Green

1

Bishop's Walk

2   Bishop's Walk   Home Farm

Forthampton Court

3   River Severn   Golf Course

Severn Way

Watts Lane

4   Rock   Street   Chaceley

55

5   Rye Court Farm

6   Chaceley   Odda's Chapel   Deerhurst
Stock

7   Severn Way
River Severn

8   B4213

Cabb Lane   Apperley Rd   Lane

A   Westview   B   79   C   D   E
PO   Sawpit
Deerhurst C of E   Apperley   B4213
Primary School

TEWKESBURY

Priors Park

Walton Cardiff

wer Lode

Tredingto

Deerhurst Ilton

33

80

58

F G H J K

I

1

2

3

4

5

6

7

8

G2
1 Theocs Cl

H2
1 Hastings Pl

H3
1 Gupshill Cl

J2
1 Coventry Cl
2 Devonshire Pl
3 Ted Preston Cl

J3
1 Abbey Meadow
2 Holme Rd
3 Manor Pl
4 Somerset Pl
5 Woodville Rd

K2
1 Cormorant Av

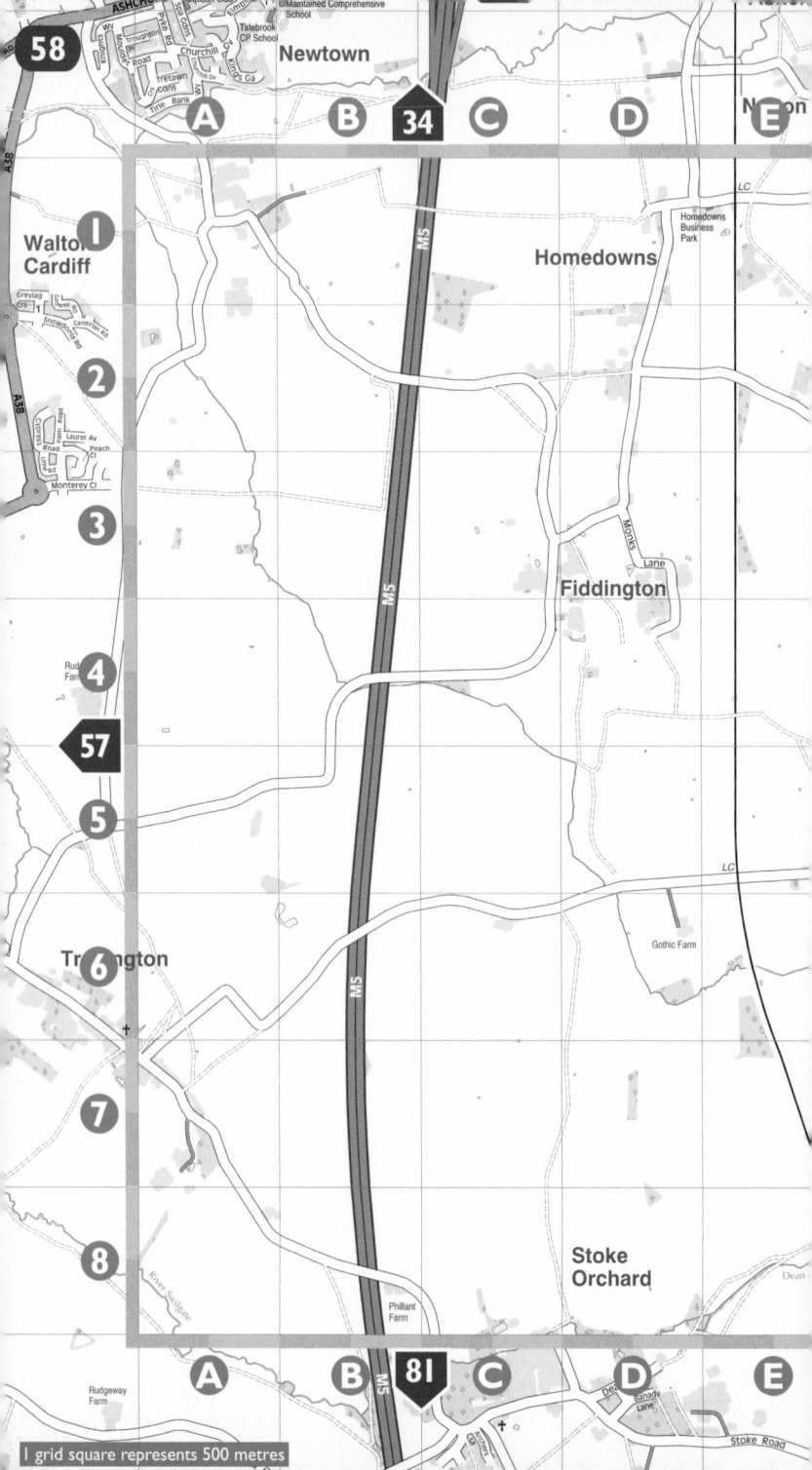

F G H 35 J K

I

2

Oxenton ✝

3

4

60

5

6

7

8

Claydon

A4079

A435

Tirle Brook

Bozard's Farm

Woodstone La

Malleson Road

Shutter La

Gotherington Fields

Gotherington Field Farm

Long Furlong

Glebe Farm

Court Farm

Dean Farm

A435

A   B   **42**   C   D   E

I
Slatepits

Buckle Street

2   Half Moon
Plantation

3

Scarborough
Farm

4

◀ 65

5   Ford Hill
Farm

Gloucestershire Way   Gloucestershire Way

6

Trafalgar
Farm

7

8   B4

Snowshill
Hill

Hornsleasow
Farm

B4077

A   B   **89**   C   D   E

F G H 43 J K

Highland

Kildanes Bottom

Bourton Far Hill Farm

I

2

Waverton Stud

Bourton Hill House

3

Sezincote Warren

4

Hinchwick Hill Barn

68

The Warren

5

Hinchwick

6

...rthire Way

7

Guitinghill Farm

Hinchwick Manor Farm

8

Condicote

F G H 90 J K

K1
1 Jameson Ct
2 University Farm

K2
1 Bowes Lyon Cl
2 St Edwards Ct
3 St James Ct
4 St Pauls Ct
5 St Peters Ct

GL56

A44

BOURTON ROAD

STOW ROAD

A429

Monarch's Way

OXFORD ST

HIGH ST

Moreton-in-Marsh
Moreton-in-Marsh Station

St Davids Primary School

Upper Fields Farm

Fosseway Farm

Redesdale Place Hotel

Fosseway Avenue

Lower Rye Farm

Frogmore Farm

Little Barrow

Heath Barn

North Rye House

ngborough

Donnington

F G H **47** J K

Ba
the

I
2
3
4
5
6
7
8

The Four
Shire Stone

A44

Kitebrook

A44

Brookend
House

Salter's Well
Farm

Middle Brookend
Farm

Grove Farm

Chasleton
Glebe

Oxfordshire County
Gloucestershire County

The
Lane

Chastleton
House (NT)

Chastleton

Hill Farm

Horn Farm

Horn   Lane

Macmillan Way

Peasewell
Wood

Chastleton
Barrow

A B 49 C Four D ks E le
Gree

1

2

Shaw
Common

3

Peter's Farm

Hay
Wood

Hawthorne Hill
White House

4

Whitehouse Lane

5

ORTY'S PITCH
Cockatoos
Lover's Walk

B4221

Lower House

6 Gorsley †

3 Prospect Row   Linton Road   Old Lane (Simmonds Lane)

B4221

Kew Lane

7

Ford Farm

Ford Lane

Kilcot

Kilcot Wood

Little
Gorsley

8

Briery Hill

Beavan's
Hill

Gypsy Lane   Mill — Lane

A B 96 C D E

Ravenshill

Acorn
Wood

I grid square represents 500 metres

G6
1 Bradfords Ct

H5
1 Greenaways

F G H **50** J K

Botloe's Green

1
H6
1 Gardeners Wy

Newbarn Farm

The Scarr

GL18

2
H7
1 Connemara Cl

Ford House Road

3
J5
1 Friar's Wk

Littlefor

4

74

5
J6
1 America Gdns
2 Peacock Cl
3 Peacock Gdns
4 St Bartholomews

6
J7
1 Cherry Bank

7
K5
1 Croft Cl

8

The Parks

Birches Lane

B4215

Scarr Road

Orchard Rd

Holder's Farm

Coldharbour Lane

Three Ashes Lane

Hilter Farm

B4215 LAMBS BARN PITCH

Three Ashes

Hopyard Lane

Cottage Pitch

Furnace Lane

orne Hill

✝

Oxenhall

Ell Brook

Old Station Rd

Horsefair Lane

Tewkesbury Road

Texwon Wy Road

Hill Top Lane

Cleev

Cleeve Mill Lane

Picklenash

ROSS ROAD

Glebe Infant School

BRIDGE ST

B4215

Lake

Court Rd

Holts Road

Glebe Cl

HIGH ST

side

Holts Health Centre

Shambles Museum

Gloucester street

Cowdy Gallery

Foley Road

Onslow Road

Police Stn

Watery Lane

NEWENT

Akermans Orch

The Tythings

Johnstone Road

Brookside

Craddock Rd

Foley Rd

Conigree Court

Bradfords La

Taughall

Knights Way

Cemetery

Newent Town Council

CULVER STREET

Newent Sports Centre

Newent Community School

Common Fields

Warren Lane

Southend

Southend Farm

Lane

B4216

Boulsdon

F G H **97** J K

K6
1 Ayland Cl
2 Blenheim Dr
3 Cleeve Ri
4 The Crease
5 Pippin Cl

74

Compton Green

A B **51** C D E

Brand Green

Newbarn Farm

I

2

3

Ford House Road

Ford House Farm

Tewkesbury Road

Littleford

Stream Lane

Tewkesbury Road

Carswalls Manor

Upleadon

Collinpark Wood

Eden Trail

Gloucester

4

73

Hill Top Lane

Hook's Lane

5

Cleeve Mill

Cleeve Mill Lane

B4215

Court Rd

Gloucester Street

6

Road

Onslow Rd

Brass Mill

Newent Town Associated Football Club

Ell Brook

Okle Clifford

7

Nelfields

Coxmore Farm

B4215

Malswick

8

Rymes Place Farm

B4215

A B **98** C D E

Pauntley Court

I grid square represents 500 metres

Caerwents

F G H 52 J K Grange

Everess Farm

I Pitt's Mill

2 Corse H Farm

Stanbrook Farm

Oridge Street

Grove Farm

3 The Tailors

Forge Lane

✝

Upleadon Court

4

76

Middletown

5

River Leadon

Hill House Farm

6

Buttersend

7

Ell Brook

Limbury

Butts Lane

8

The erleys

F G H 99 J K

Red Hill Farm

Highleadon Court

✝

53

Corse

Snig's End

Brierley Grange

A B C D E

Stanbrook Farm

Pitt's Mill

1

Corse House Farm

School Crescent

Prince Crescent

Corse Surgery

Police Station

Lawn Farm

Oridge Street

2

Oridge Street

Oridge Street

Grove Farm

Oridge Street

Old Field Top

3

Crosshands Farm

The Tailors

Stone End House

4

Foscombe

Corse Court Farm

5

Prestberries Farm

Hill House Farm

6

Blackwells End Green

7

Corsend Farm

Corsend Road

Hartpury

Limbury

Buttersend Lane

Fuller's La

Broad St

8

Foley Rd

Baker's Rd

Danford Lane

A B C D E

WORCESTER ROAD

B4211

GLOUCESTER

A417

1 grid square represents 500 metres

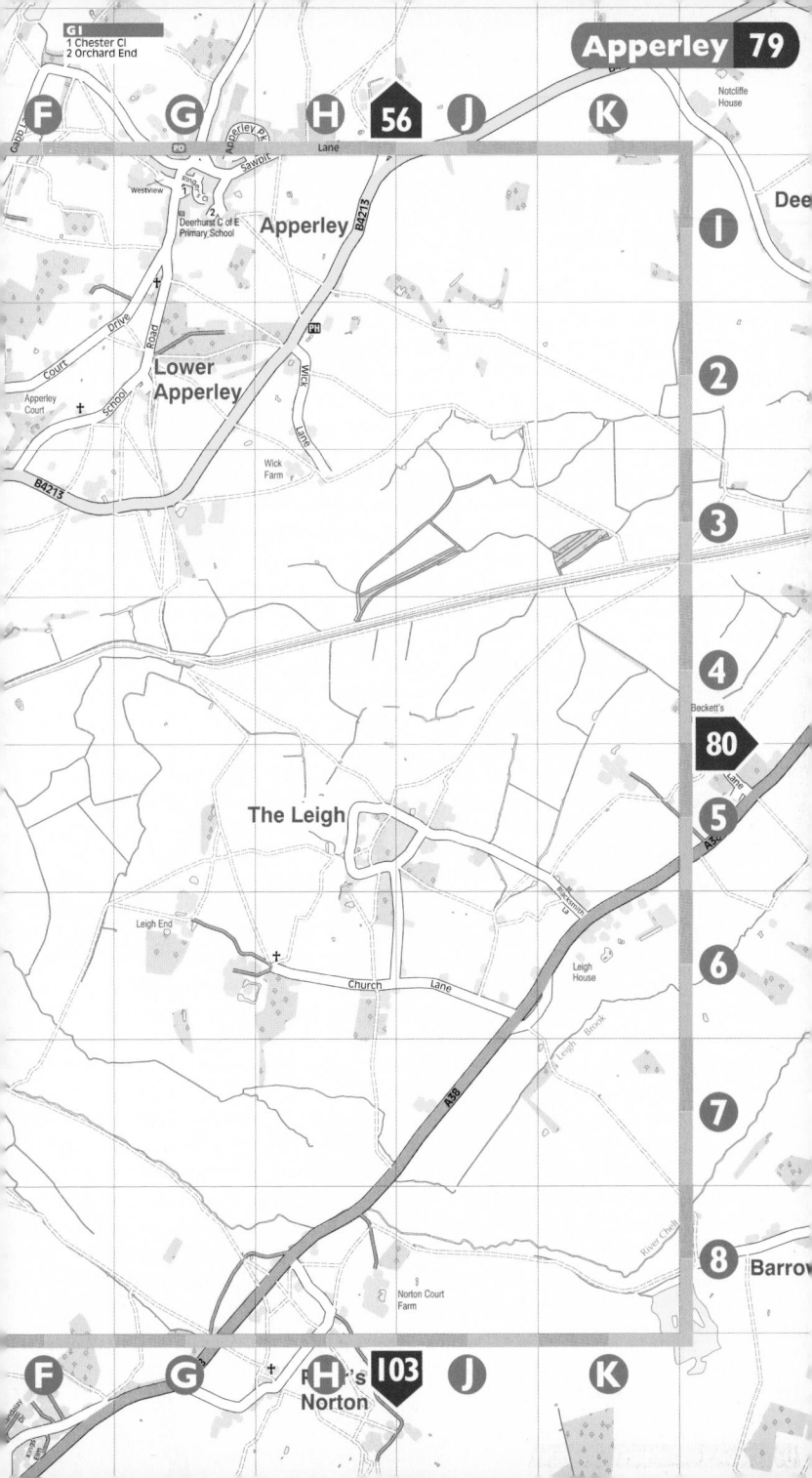

Stoke Orchard

58

F G H J K

Dean Brook

Phillant Farm

Dean Lane

Banady Lane

Stoke Road

1

Cursey Lane

2

rdwicke

Mill Lane

The Park

3

Colman's Farm

4

82

Barn Farm

Villa Farm

Lowdilow Lane

5

Elmstone Hardwicke

Lowdilow La

6

ne Gardens

Chestnut Farm

7

Stanton Drive

TEWKESBURY

Moat Lane

ROAD A4019

8

Uckington

105

F G H J K

Pilgrove Farm

HAYDEN ROAD

Cheltenham Retail Park

Civil Service Sports Club

Manor Park Business Cen

Kingsditch Retail Park

King

GLOUCESTER ROAD B4634

Blaisdon Wy

Barley Ct

82

A   **B**   **59**   **C**   **D**   **E**

I

Stoke Road

2

Dean Brook

Dean Farm

Glebe Farm

Court Farm

Stoke Road

Hayfield Way

Malvern View
Business Park

Cheltenham North
Rugby Club

Bishop's Cleeve

Stoke

A435

3

The Park

Wingmoor
Farm

4

81

Home Farm

Mead

Norton Dr

5

Brockhampton

Hyde Brook

LC

Hyde
Farm

6

Hyde Lane

7

Copse

Swindon

Swindon Village
Primary School

Evesham

Dark Lane

Gilbert
Dr

Stemco
Drive

Rosehip Rd

Church
Road

Manor
Road

8

LC

**Wymans
Brook**

Hunting
Butts

Wymans La

Swindon La

Cheltenham
Retail Park

Civil Service
Sports Club

Manor Park
Business Cen

Ashville
Trading Est

Shaftesbury
Industrial Est

Rumbolds Rd

Cotswold
Chelten

A   **B**   **106**   **C**   **D**   **E**

Kingsditch

Kingsditch
Retail Park

Swindon Lane

St Nicholas
Terrace

Swindon

F1
1 Murray Cl

F2
1 Buckland Cl
2 Gilders Paddock
3 Pullar Cl
4 Roberts Cl
5 St John's Cl
6 Shipway Ct
7 Stoke Park Cl
8 Streamside
9 Willow Park Dr

F   G   H   60   J   K

279
▲ Nottingham Hill
(Fort)

I

F3
1 Hisnams Fld
2 Icombe Cl
3 Tobyfield La

2

F4
1 Cantors Ct
2 Holder Rd
3 Mayfield Cl

3

G2
1 Birchfield Rd
2 Bootenhay Rd
3 Cares Cl
4 Huntsmans Cl
5 Owls End Rd
6 Ward Cl

4

84

5

G3
1 Bishops Cl

6

H2
1 Celandine Bank
2 Longlands Cl

7

H3
Street names for this grid square are listed at the back of the index

8

Woodmancote

Southam

F   G   H   107   J   K

Prestbury

J3
1 Hillside Cl
2 Pear Tree Cl

H2
1 Tobacco Cl

J1
1 Gillett Cl
2 Malthouse La
3 Mill La

Winchcombe

F   G   H   62   J   K

1 Tobacco Cl

North St

Hailes Street

Police Station

Town Hall

Winchcombe C of E
Infant School

Winchcombe Junior
School

B4632

Gloucester Street

Castle Street

I

2

Sudeley Castle

Gloucester Street

B4632

Cheltenham Road B4632

Postlip
House

Postlip

River Isbourne

Corndean
Farm

Corndean
Hall

Cotswold Lane

Cotswold Way

Wadfield
Farm

Cotswold Way

3

4

86

5

6

7

8

Cotswold Way

Belas Knap

Humblebee

Wontley
Farm

West
Down

F   G   H   109   J   K   Charlton
Abbots

West
Wood

86
Footbridge

Stancombe La
Puck Pit La
Stancombe La
Gloucestershire Way

A **B** Stanc Wood **63** **C** **D** **E**

Little Farmcote

Station

Town Hall

Castle Street

I

2

Sudeley Castle

3

Sudeley Lodge

4

Parks Farm

85

Wardens Way

Wadfield Farm

5

6

Waterhatch

7

Spoonley Farm

8

Goldwell Farm

Charlton Abbots

A **B** Hott Farm **110** **C** **D** **E**

1 grid square represents 500 metres

F G H 64 J K

Slade Barn
Farm

1

Pinnock
Farm

2

3

4

88

Wardens' Way

5

Cluting
Wood

Manor
House

Lynes Barn
Farm

mcote Wood

Wardens' Way

6

Camden Ln

7

Roel Hill
Farm

Roel
Farm

Camden Line

8

F G H III J K

88

Slade Barn
Farm

A

B

65

C

Temple
Guiting

D

E
B4077
B4077

Hyde

1

Manor
Farm

2

Temple Guiting
School

The Sherry
PH
+

Leigh
Wood

3

4

87

Kineton

Wardens Way

5

Manor
House

Critchford Lane

6

Castlett
Farm

Barton

7

Wardens Way

Castlett St

8

PH
+
Piccadilly
PH
The Sq

A

B

112

C

Wardens Way

Guiting
Power

G
St

Guiting Rd
Billy Ho Lane

+

D

E

1 grid square represents 500 metres

F G H 66 J K

B4077

1
2
3
4
90
5
6
7
8

Kinetonhill
Farm

Bemborough
Farm

Cotswold
Farm Park

Summerhill

F G H 113 J K

Grange Hill
Farm

Wardens' Way

A B **67** C D E

E1
1 Church Vw
2 Close Gdns

Condic

B4077

Fox Farm

B4077

Cotricote Lane

Kinetonhill
Farm

Swell Wold
Farm

89

Swell Hill
Farm

Eyford Hill
Farm

Eyford
Park

Rockcliffe

A B **114** C D E

Wardens' Way

Wardens' Way

Eyford
Knoll

B4068

1 grid square represents 500 metres

1 Whittlestone Cl

Luckley
Fa..
1 Stonehouse Ct

F G H 68 J K

I

Banks Fee
Farm

Duncombe House

2

Flagstone Farm

3

B4077

Upper Swell

4

Gloucestershire Wy

92

TEWKESBURY

Swell Buildings
Farm

Bowl Farm

Abbotswood

5

6 8

St Mary's
Close
Whittlestone
Hollow

Lower Swell

Condicote Lane

Swell
Primary School

1

B4068

Rectory
Cl

Mill Lane

7

Nether Swell
Manor

8

F G H 115 J K

Monarch's Wy

Macmillan Way

Hyde Mill

F G H J K

Hill Farm
Greypoose Lane
A436
A44

I

Chastleton
Barrow

A436

2

Park
Farm

Glebe
Farm

3

Cornwell
Cornwell
Manor

Daylesford
Hill Farm

4

...shire County
...ordshire County

Kingham Hill
Farm

5

Kingham Hill
School

6

Slade
Farm

Kingham Hill
School

7

**Sarsden
Halt**

8

F G H 119 J K

Ki... ...ry
Prim... ...ool
Churchill Road

Hastings
Hill

Kingham Road

The Moor
West Street
The Green
Chapel Lane
Langston Road

Chu

F **Boul** G **on** H **73** J K

I

2

3

4

98

5

6

7

GL19

8

The Moat

Anthony's Cross

Anthony's
Cross

Normans

National Birds
of Prey Centre

The
Green

Woodgate

Cugley

Ploddy
House

Judge's Lane

Black House Farm

Taynton House

Taynton

Jewent
Woods

Moat Lane

Judge's Lane

Clifford Manor

Byfords Farm

Mote
Lane

sshouse

Castle Hill
Wood

Mote
Farm

Prestbury
Farm

Huntley
Manor

Northend
Farm

F G H **125** J K

A B **74** C D E

I

Rymes Place Farm

Caerwents

2

Normans

Kent's Green

3

Taynton Pound Farm

Taynton Court Farm

4

97

Drews Farm

5

Haynes Farm

Taynton

6

Mork Lane

The Grove

7

Moor Lane

Molu Farm

GL19

8

Morse's Farm

Prestbury Farm

A B **126** C D E

Poplar Farm

F G H 75 J K

1
2
3
4
100
5
6
7
8

I
+

The Alderleys
Red Hill Farm
Highleadon Court
Moat Farm
B4215
Park Road
Drews Farm
Highleadon
River Leadon
B4215
New Hall
Bovone
Tibberton Primary School
Orchard
Phelps Way
Rise
Bovone Lane
Old Ct. Dr.
Muzzle Patch
Tibberton
Meredith
Rudford
B4215
Birdsend
Whitehall Farm
Whitehall Lane
ller's Elm
Rundlesshill

F G H 127 J K

Woodgreen

Ell Brook
uttersend Lane

Croft

Longridge Lane

F   **G**   **H**   **77**   **J**   **K**

Rudford Lane

Lane

Longridge End

olridge

Brawn Farm

I

2

Long Reach

Spring Hill

Sandhurst

3

PO

Moat Farm

Old Moat

4

Gardiner's Farm

102

Bengrove Farm

Maisemore Park

River Severn

5

Ease Lane

Abbot's Lodge

6

Old Road

The Rudge

A417

† Steadings Business Centre Maisemore Court

Maisemore

Blacksmiths Lane

Church Rise

The Ridings

Stanleigh Ter

Persh Lane

Bridge Farm

Abloads Court

7

Persh Farm

Maisemore Ham

West Channel

East Channel

Sandhurst Lane

8

A417

F   **G**   **H**   **129**   **J**   **K**

Walham

Winfield Hospital

Westfie

Orcha

A40(T)

A   **B**   **78**   **C**   **D**   **E**

E8
1 Durand Cl
2 Falcon Cl

B8
1 Hayes Ct
2 Longford Ms
3 Meadvale Cl

Bishop's Norto

Wainlode La

Wainlode L

Nor

Brawn Farm

1

2

Willington Court

Sandhurst Lane

Wallsworth

dhurst

3

St Lawrence Cl

PO

Moat Farm

4

Old Moat

Lane

Gardiner's Farm

101

Bengrove Farm

Wallsworth Hall

Sandhurst Lane

5

A38

Twigworth

PO

Brock Lane

6

Abbot's Lodge

Lane

7

Abloads Court

Twigworth C of E School

A38

Tewkesbury Road

Pludberie Brook

Drymeadow Farm

Dry Meadow La

Innsworth Technology Park

8

East Chan

Sandhurst Lane

Abloads Court

Austin Dr

LEWIS AV

Stafflecroft Ct

Longford

Police Station

Victoria Rd

Longford La

A40(T)

Way

Lacy Cl

Fleming Cl

Simon Rd

Crispin

A   **B**   **130**   **C**   **D**   **E**

Walham

Winfield Hospital

PLOCK CT

Fairmile Gdns

Beauchroft Road

The Milestone School

Longford Special School

Longlevens RFC

F7
1 Bullfinch Wy
2 Chaffinch Cl
3 Robins End

G7
1 Campbell Cl
2 Middleton Lawn

F **G** **H** 79 Court **J** **K**

Prior's
Norton

A38

Vale of Gloucester

I
H6
1 Glendower Cl

2
H7
1 Aragon Wy
2 Armada Cl
3 Drake Cl
4 Parr Cl

3
H8
1 Heathdean Rd

Wood Farm

4

Hatherley Manor
Hotel

104

Down Hatherley

Down Hatherley Lane

Frog Furlong Lane

Hatherley Brook

Down Hatherley Lane

5
J6
1 Compton Cl
2 Essex Cl
3 St Vincent Wy
4 Thomas Moore Cl
5 Victory Cl

Gloucestershire
Aviation Museum

6

Grenville
Close

Brickhampton Court
Golf Club

J7
1 Apple Tree Cl
2 Buckingham Dr
3 Japonica Cl
4 Leacey Ct
5 Marleyfield Cl

Minstrel
Wy

Innsworth

Snowdon

Westover Ct

7

J8
1 Berryfield Gld
2 Forsythia Cl
3 Gardiners Cl
4 Kilminster Ct

Orchard
Way

Holtham

Roberts
Rd

Field End

Gray Cl

Gibson Rd

Nicholson Close

Parton Road

Innsworth County
Primary School

Larkfield Infant
School

Zinnia Cl

Shamrock Cl

Police Station

St Marys RC
Primary School

Crayen Drive

Parton Manor
Infant School

8

Parton Manor
Junior School

A40(T)

Parton Lane

A40(T)

Churchdown
School

Trubshaw Ct

K8
1 Andorra Wy
2 Chadbournes
3 Hazelcroft
4 Quinton Cl

CHELTENHAM   A40(T)

K7
1 Meadow Wy

Bush
Hay

Churchdown Village
Infant School

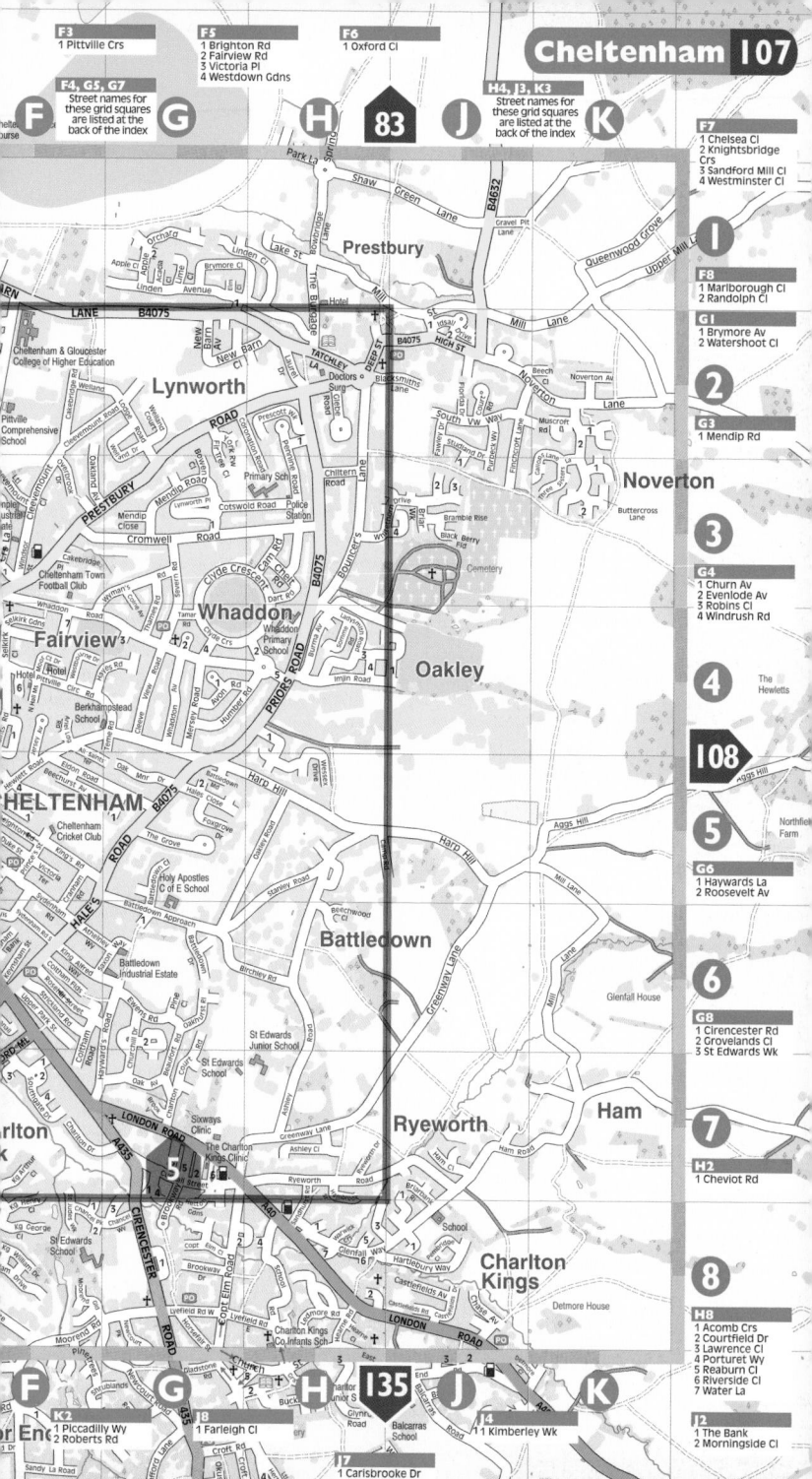

108

A   B   84   C   D   E

1

Queenw...
Upper Mill Lane
Lane

Cotswold Way

Lower Hill
Farm

Upper Hill
Farm

2

Noverton Av
TON
Lane
Mulcroft
ed
2

Noverton

Cotswold Way

Drypo
Farm

3

Buttercross

Piccadilly
Farm

4

The
Hewletts

5

107

Aggs Hill

Aggs Hill

Northfield
Farm

Puckham
Farm

6

Mill Lane

Lane

Glenn... House

Cotswold Way

7

Ham

Ham
Hill

Ham Road

Wil
Fal

8

Detmore House

Colgate
Farm

Woodlands

Dowdeswell
Wood

A   B   136   C   D   E

1 grid square represents 500 metres

Goldwell
Farm

A   B   86   C   D   E

Charlton
1 bots

Holt
Farm

2

Whitehill
3   Farm

Cotehay

4   Brockhampton
Park

109   PO   Oxleaze

Park Lane   Brockhampton

5

PO

6

Church Lane   Sevenhampton

7   Soundborough

8

Syreford

A   B   138   C   D   E   A436

A436

F G H 87 J K

1
2
3
4
112
5 B4068
6 A436
7
8

Roel Hill
Farm

Roel
Farm

Windrush Way

Windrush Hill

Hawling Lodge

Hawling

Southdown
Farm

A436

A436

Slade Barn
Farm

F G H 139 J K

Salperton

Gloucestershire Way

A B **88** C D E

I

2

Hawling
Lodge

Windrush Way

3

Windrush Way

B4068

B4068

4

Naunton
Downs

III

5

B4068

Windrush Way

6

A436

Westfield

Windrush Way

7

A436

STANBOROUGH LANE

Notgrove

8

GL54

New
Covert

Salperton

A B **140** C D E

Guiting
Power

PH
The Sq
Piccadilly
Tally HO Lane
PO
Cheltenham

Warden's Way

Tally
House

B4068

F   G   H   89   J   K

I
2
3
4
114
5
6
7
8

Warden's Way

Naunton

Grange Hill
Farm

PO   PH

VILLAGE
AV

Warden's Way

Dale St

Naunton Downs
Golf Club

Brockhill
Barm

B4068   Harford Bridge

Lower
Harford Farm

Windrush WAY

Windrush Way

Roundhill Farm

Iworth

Windrush Way

Windrush Way

Hill Farm

Upper
Harford

A436

Folly
Farm

114

A   B   **90**   C   D   E

Rockcliffe

1   Wardens' Way
Wardens' Way   Wardens' Way
Eyford Knoll   Sw
He
B4068

2

3

68   Harford Bridge

4   Lower Harford Farm   Harfordhill Farm   Wagborough Bush   Manor Farm

Windrush Way   **◄113**

5   River Windrush

Windrush Way

6

7   Upper Harford   **A436**   Windrush Way   Aston Farm   Gloucestershire Way   Windrush Way

Windrush Farm

8   **A436**

Camp Farm

A   B   **142▼**   C   D   E

Gloucester

1 grid square represents 500 metres

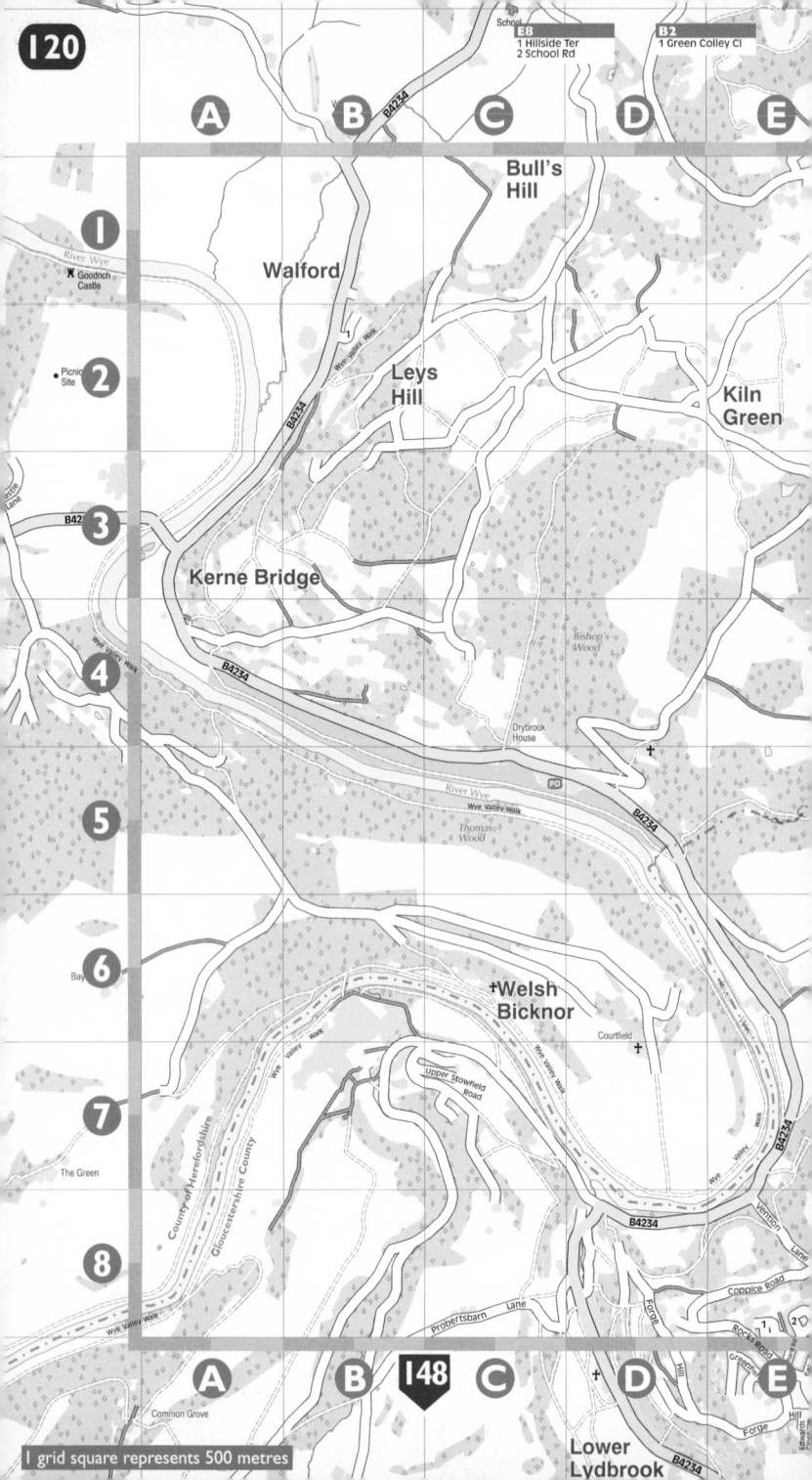

H6
1 Caudle Cl

J6
1 Belle Vue Rd
2 Boxtree Cl

F G H J K

I

K6
1 Crooked End Pl

2

K8
1 Roebuck Mdw

3

4

122

5

6

7

8

Great Howle
Farm

The
Dam

Great Marstow
Farm

Deep
Dean

Hope
Mansell

Cowles
House

County of Herefordshire
Gloucestershire County

Vain
Farm

Cash Hill
Cinderhill
St
High St
Townsend
Cander Lane
School Lane
Harvey
Normans
Way
St John's Rd
Kenyan Lane
Highfield Road
St Margaret's
Road
Varnister Road
Park Vw

Crooked
End

Ruardean C of E
Primary School
Pettycroft
Meend Lane

Ruardean

Turner's
Tump

Ruardean
Hill

Ruardean
Woodside

Smithers
Cross

Bakers Piece Road
Barn Lane
The Patches
Forest
Walker's Lane
Farm Road

brook

Newtown

Mor
Mor

PO

F Readings G The
Plu H 149 J K

Highbeech Road
High Street
Ash Dene
Aston Bridge Road

Woodside
CP School

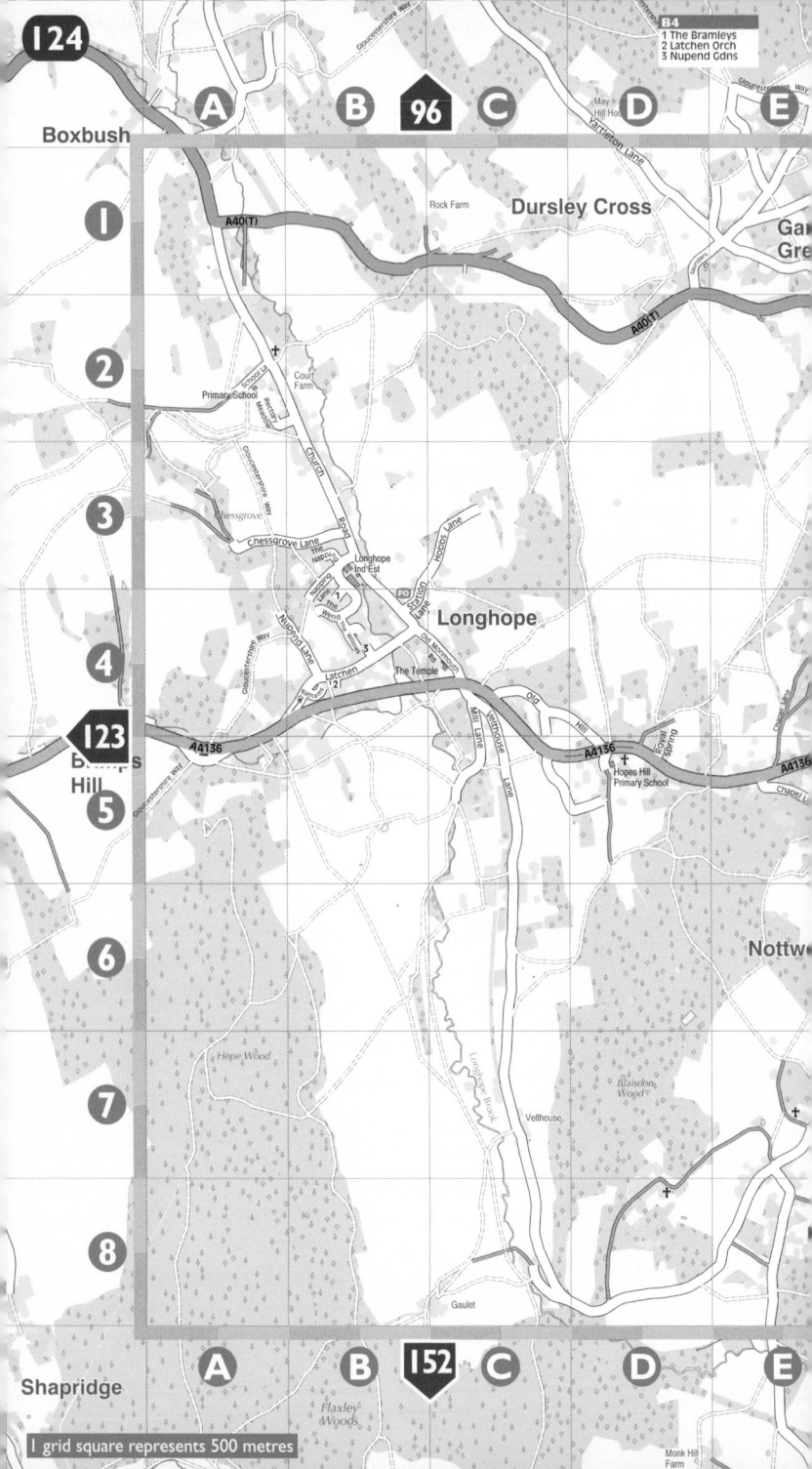

124

Boxbush

A   **B**   **96**   **C**   **D**   **E**

1
A40(T)
Rock Farm
Dursley Cross
Ga
Gre

2
Primary School
Court Farm

3
Chessgrove
Chessgrove Lane
Longhope Ind Est
Hobbs Lane
Church Road

4
Gloucestershire Way
Nupend Lane
Latchen
The Temple
Longhope
Old Monmouth Rd
Barton Lane

123
A4136
Mill Lane
Velthouse Lane
Old Hill
Royal Spring
A4136
Hopes Hill Primary School
A4136

5
B---'s
Hill
Gloucestershire Way
Chapel L

6
Nottw

7
Hope Wood
Longhope Brook
Blaisdon Wood
Velthouse

8
Gaulet

Shapridge

A   **B**   **152**   **C**   **D**   **E**

Flaxley Woods
Monk Hill Farm

B4
1 The Bramleys
2 Latchen Orch
3 Nupend Gdns
May Hill Hou
Tarrleton Lane
Gloucestershire Way

1 grid square represents 500 metres

E1
1 Clayburn Cl
2 Gordon Cl
3 Peters Fld
4 Popes Meade
5 Stoney Fld

D1
1 Blacksmiths Gnd
2 Cottage Fld
3 Mickle Mead
4 Pipers Gv
5 Poole Gnd

Lassington

A   B   **100**   C   D   E

I

Highnam
Green

Highnam
Business
Centre

Highnam

Highnam
School

Highnam
Woods

Pinetum

2

Claw

Two Mile Lane

3

A40(T)

Linton
Farm

A40(T)

Beauchamp
House

4

127

A48(T)

Gloucestershire Way

Upper Moorcroft
Farm

5

Hygrove Lane

6

Hygrove
House

The
Redlands

A48(T)

Moorcroft
House

7

A48(T)

Watery Lane

Minsterworth
School

Lane

Calcott's
Green

Gloucestershire Way

Highcross
Farm

8

Gloucestershire Way

Severn Way

A   B   **156**   C   D   E

Minst   ham

River Severn

I grid square represents 500 metres

Walham

I

Winfield Hospital

J5
1 Hemmingsdale Rd

West Channel

A417

A40(T)

Sandhurst Lane

Alney Island

Over

A40(T)

Alney Island

Telford's Bridge

River Severn

OVER CAUSEWAY

Over Causeway

A417

2

Cattle Market North
Ind Est

ST OSWALD'S ROAD

Gloucester City Council

3

St Mary St
St Mark St

Rugby Football Club

Barrett Industrial Est

Spartans Rugby Club

Superstore

Riverside Sports & Leisure Club

K5
1 Church St
2 High Orchard St
3 Ladybellegate St
4 Merchants' Rd

House Kings
Cath Sq

Black

ROYAL OAK RD

ROYAL OAK ROAD

The College Yard Sqn

Co Council

4

Gloucester Folk Mus

Shire Hall

Port Ham

Lower Parting

Vale of Gloucester

Sudmeadow

THE QUAY

County Library

Castle Meads

County Gaol

Police Stn

HM Prison

Courts

Shire Hall

Regiments

130

Crown Court

City Council

Museum

Priory

5

Museum of City Library & Art Gal

College

K6
1 The Chestnuts
2 St Lukes St
3 Somerset Pl

Business Park

Llanthony Industrial Est

Severnside Trading Est

Seymour Road

National Waterways Museum

Mus of Advertising & Packaging

Dock

Gloucester City Council

GLOUCESTER

Bristol Road

Llanthony Road

Gloucester City Association Football Club

Llanthony Secunda Priory

Cotswold Edge Business Cen

Sudbrook Trading Est

Baker Street

Norfolk St

Office Sports Club

The Park

Bowling Green

6

TRIER WAY A430

WESTGATE A430

K7
1 Philip St
2 Theresa St

Venture Business Cen

St Ann Way

Madleaze Road

Madleaze Trading Est

Morelands Trading Est

STROUD ROAD

Paul's Rd

PARK

Newark

Gordon League Rugby Football Club

Monk Meadow Dock

BRISTOL ROAD

Graham St

Alma Pl

Frampton Road

St Paul's

Robinson

Linden Road

7

GL1

K8
1 Talbot Ms

Hempsted School

Hempsted Lane

Rea Lane

Rectory La

Court Comm

Hempsted

Newark Road

Linden Avenue

Lysons Avenue

Linden Primary Sch

Granville Street

Seymour Road

Tuffley Avenue

8

K4

Street names for this grid square are listed at the back of the index

Ribston Hall Girls High Sch

BRISTOL ROAD

STROUD ROAD

Century Ind Est

157

Rd

Industrial Estate

Trading Est

Mansell

Linden Road

Stanley Road

Cromwell

Turley Avenue

Tredworth Road

Laburnum Rd

F   G   H   J   K

Linden

F1
1 Ballinska Ms
2 Calspick Wy
3 Clomoney Wy
4 Cotswold Gdns
5 Lacca Cl
6 Miller Cl
7 Sandstar Cl
8 Sheevaun Cl

F6
1 Ebrington Cl
2 Julian Cl
3 Steeple Cl

F5, F7, G2
Street names for these grid squares are listed at the back of the index

H1, J5, K1
Street names for these grid squares are listed at the back of the index

F8
1 Trygrove

G1
1 Bradshaw Cl
2 Canning Rd
3 Foxleigh Crs
4 Melody Wy
5 Mutsilver Ms
6 Patseamur Ms
7 Saylittle Ms

G6
1 Woodgate Cl

G7
1 Claudians Cl
2 The Copse
3 Crasby Cl
4 Marefield Cl
5 The Orangery
6 Pinery Rd
7 Whitewell Cl

G8
1 Benson Cl
2 Centurion Cl
3 The Maples
4 Pilgrim Cl
5 Spartan Cl
6 Thorn Stock Gdns
7 Wigmore Cl

H6
1 Ellesmere Cl
2 St Margarets Rd

H8
1 Augustine Wy
2 Dianas Cl
3 Henry Ryder Cl
4 Minster Gdns
5 Neptune Cl
6 Remus Cl
7 Trajan Cl

J6
1 St Philip's Cl

J7
1 Mogridge Cl

K8
1 Grierson Cl
2 Montgomery Cl
3 Varley Av
4 Waterton Cl

K7
1 Hampton Cl

J8
1 Bramley Ms
2 Ellison Cl
3 Pippin Cl

Elmbridge

Barnwood

Hucclecote

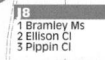

132

104

A2
1 Barnhay
2 Chapel Hay Cl
3 Drews Cl

A1
1 Bader Av
2 Barnes Wallis Wy
3 Cochran Cl
4 Dowding Wy
5 Lysander Ct
6 Sunderland Ct
7 Swordfish Cl

A B C D E

B1
1 Tynings Ct

1

2

B8
1 St Annes Cl

3

4

131

5

6 A417(T)

Junction 11a

7

8

A B C D E

160

Churchdown

Trubshaw Ct
Chosen Hill Former Pupils Rugby Football Club
Albemarle Rd
Chosen Hill School
Chosen Hill Rd
Anne Hathaway Dr
Churchdown Village Infant School
The Av
The Piece
Church Road
White House Farm
Crittycraft Lane
Barrow Hill
Brockworth Road
Chosen Hill House
Woodlands Farm
Hucclecote Lane
GL3
Dean Farm
Hunt Court Farm
Stump Lane
M5
Brockworth Court
Brockworth
Junction 11a
Cedar Road
Hucclecote Road
Brockworth Comprehensive School
Boverton Av
Ermin St
County Primary Infant School
Brockworth

1 grid square represents 500 metres

Reddings Farm

Churchdown School

Parton Manor Junior School

A40(T)

Station Road
Brockhampton Lane
Brookfield Road
M5

Churchdown Lane

A417(T)

A46 SHURDINGTON

136

Detmore House

A

Colgate Farm

B **108** **C**

D

Woodlands

E

1

A40

2 London Road

River Chelt

Cotswold Way

Dowdeswell Reservoir

A40

Dowdeswell Wood

Low
Dow

3 Rossley Manor

Cotswold Way

Lineover Wood

4

Cotswold Way

135

A436

A436

St Pa
Epist

5 A436

Pegglesworth

6

Chatcombe Wood

7

Foxcote Hill Farm

Ratshill Bank

Pinchley Wood

8 Needlehole

Gloucestershire Way

A

B **164** **C**

D

E

Hilcot Wood

Hilcot

1 grid square represents 500 metres

J2
1 Huntsmans Meet

J3
1 Crossfields

F   G   H   109   J   K

Syreford

1

Sandywell Park

Hunter's Way

PO

Station

A40

Waterside Close

Ossage

PH

Andoversford

2

Primary School

Sports Club

Temple Mills

GLOUCESTER ROAD

Andoversford Industrial Estate

Andoversford Industrial Estate

A40

3

A436

A436

swell

y

PH

4 Shipton Solers

138

Foxcote

A436

5

PH

A40(T)

6

7

Northfield Farm

Thorndale

8

F   G   H   165   J   K

Thornhill Farm

Upcote Farm

F **G** **H** **III** **J** **K**

Salperton

I

Salperton
Park

2

Gloucestershire Way

Penhill
Farm

3

Canon's
Barn

Hill
Barn

Hazleton
Grove

4

140

5 Hazleton

6

Manor
Farm

7

A40(T)

8

Compton
Abdale

F **G** **H** **167** **J** **K**

Shipton
Farm

GL.54

(A) (B) **112** (C) (D) (E)

New Covert

140

Salperton

1

Salperton Park

2

Gloucestershire Way

Farhill Farm

Gloucestershire Way

3

Canon's Barn

Hazleton Grove

4

139

Milkwell Covert

5

Hazleton

6

The Downs Brake

7

Hill Barn

Castle Barn Farm

8

(A) (B) **168** (C) (D) (E)

A40(T)

F G H 113 J K

Folly Farm

I

Notgrove

Gloucestershire Way

Cold Aston

Cold Aston C of E Primary School

2

PH

Chase Lane

Lane

Macmillan Way

Bangup Barn

Bangup

Grove Farm

3

Pountwell

Aston Grove

4

142

Shewhill Barn

5

Macmillan Way

Smith's Barn

6

Broadwater Bottom

Turkdean

7

A429

8

F G H 169 J K

Leygore Manor

A429

142

A   B   **114**   C   D   E

I

Cold Aston
Cold Aston C of E
Primary School

2

Macmillan Way

3   Grove

4

141

5

6

Fox Hill
Farm

Sweetslade
Farm

Gloucestershire Way

A429

Monarch's Way

7   Broadwater
Bottom

Furzehill
Wood

8

A   B   **170**   C   D   Farming E
Grove

Camp Farm

Starvall

A436

I grid square represents 500 metres

116

143

172

E2
1 Blenheim Cl
2 Harris Gdns
3 Snipe Rd

D7
1 Orchard Bank

C2
1 Manor Farm

Wyck
Beacon

A   B   C   D   E

1

Bobble
Barn

2

Sandy   Lane

Pound
Lane

The Pound

Little Rissington

3

4

5

Leasow Lane

6

The Barn
Business
Centre

Lane End

Green's
Cl

PH

1

Great
Rissington
CP School

7

Great
Rissington

8

Sherborne Lane

A   B   C   D   E

I grid square represents 500 metres

F G H 117 J K

Church Westcote

Cemetery

Nether Westcote

Upper Rissington

Smith Barry Crescent
Smith Barry Rd
Kirby Road
Road
Randall

Little Rissington Airfield

Gloucestershire County
Oxfordshire County

Warren Farm

Tangley Woods

The Follies

Barrington Bushes

A424

Merrym

1
2
3
4
5
6
7
8

F G H 173 J K

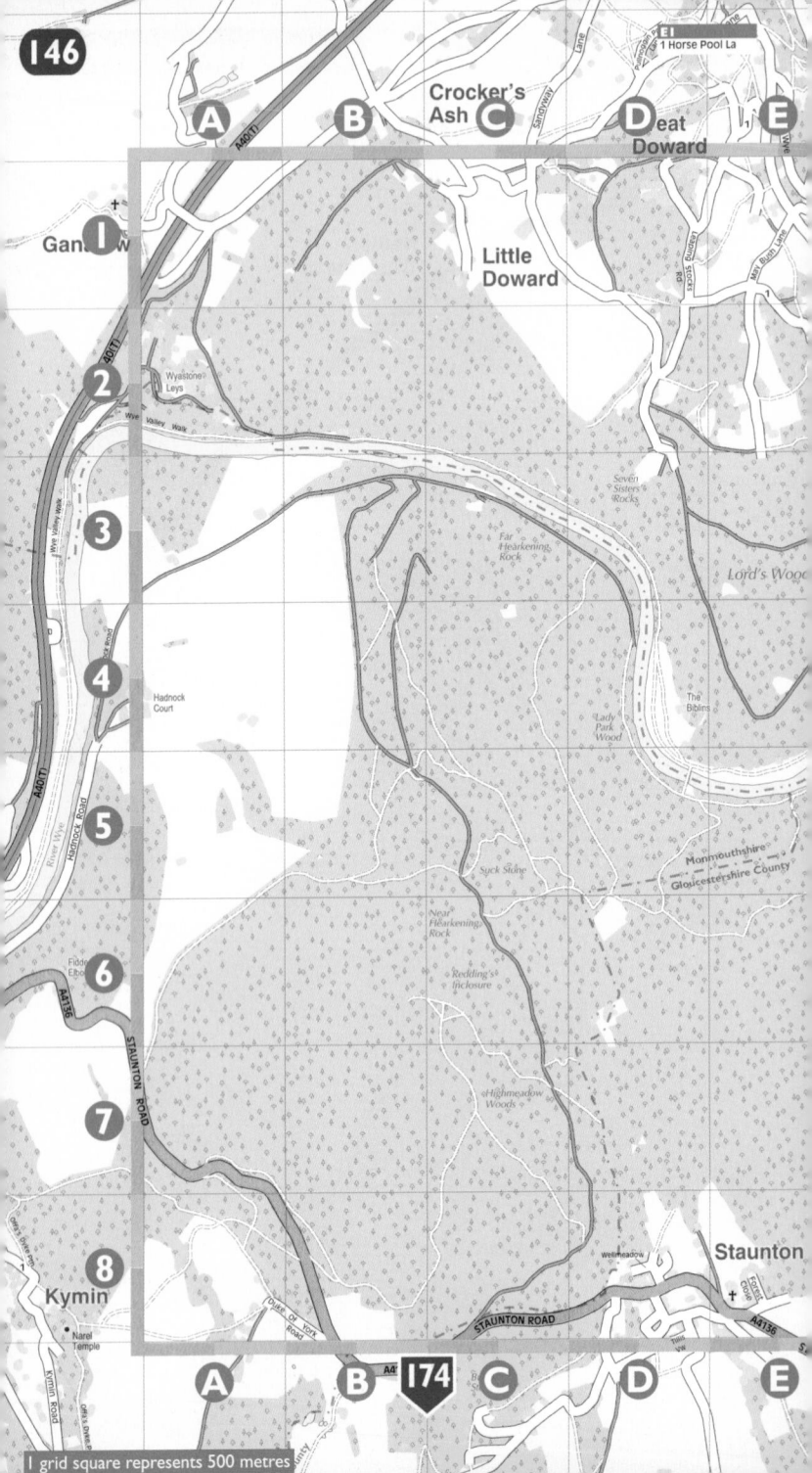

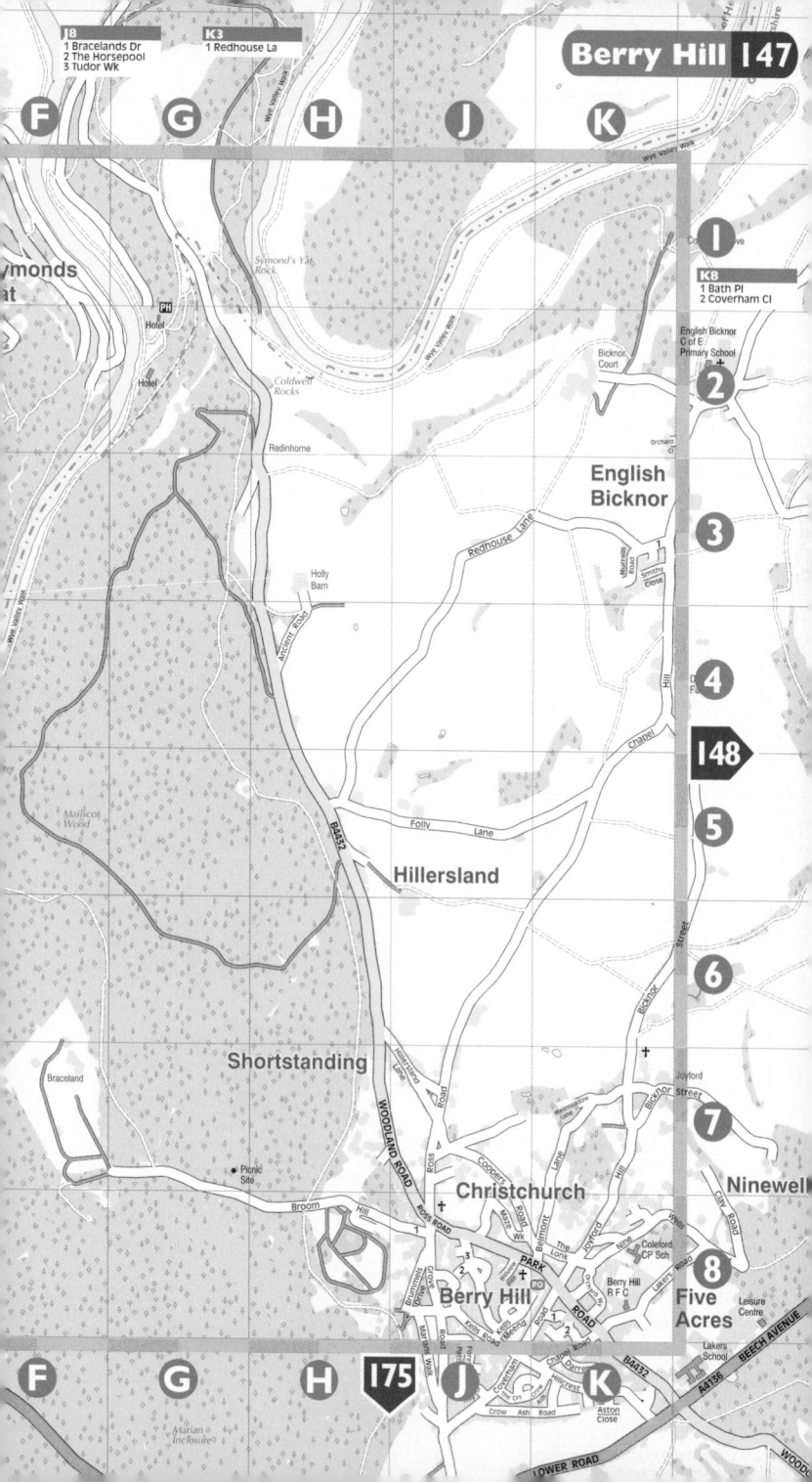

F G H J K

J8
1 Bracelands Dr
2 The Horsepool
3 Tudor Wk

K3
1 Redhouse La

K8
1 Bath Pl
2 Coverham Cl

Wye Valley Walk

Symonds Yat

Symond's Yat Rock

Hotel

Hotel

PH

Coldwell Rocks

Redinhorne

Holly Barn

Bicknor Court

English Bicknor C of E Primary School

Orchard Cl

English Bicknor

Redhouse Lane

Upper Lydbrook Road

Smithy Close

Maillscot Wood

B4432

Folly Lane

Hillersland

Chapel Hill

I48

Bicknor Street

Shortstanding

Braceland

Picnic Site

Broom Hill

Hillersland Lane

Ross Road

Coopers Road

Belmont Road

Joyford Lane

Joyford Street

Joyford

Ninewell

Christchurch

Wellington Lane

Coleford CP Sch

Berry Hill RFC

Five Acres

Leisure Centre

City Road

Berry Hill

Ross Road

Park Road

The Links

Brailsford Road

Grove Road

Martian Way

Kings Meadow

Coverham Road

Hillcrest

Crow Ash Road

Forest Road

Lakers School

Bakers Road

Aston Close

Beech Avenue

Dockham Road

B4432

A4136

F G H **I75** J K

Marian Inclosure

LOWER ROAD

WOODS

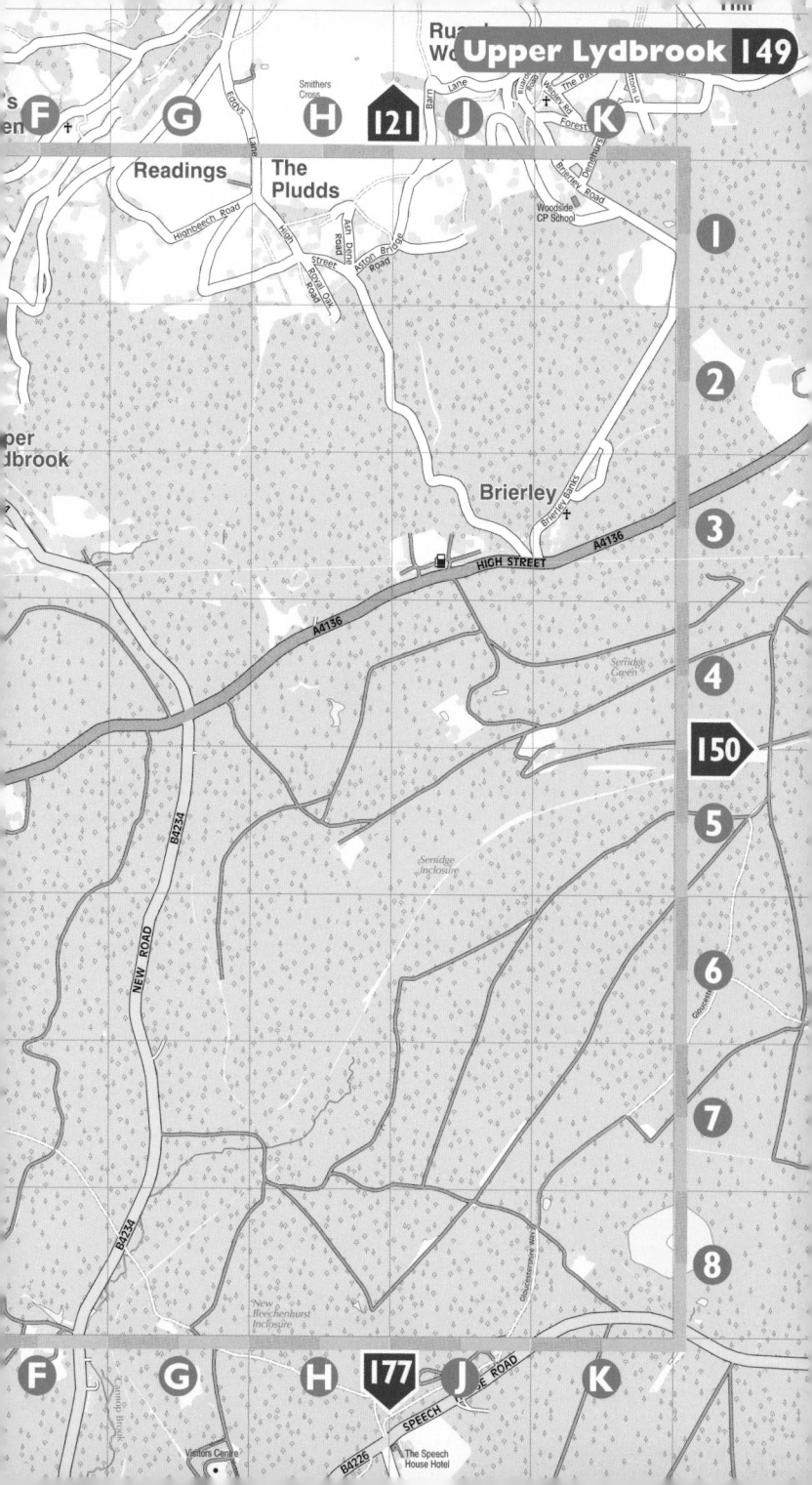

Ruar
wo

Smithers
Cross

F

G

H

121

J

K

Readings

The
Pludds

Highbeech Road

High
Street

Ash Dene
Road

Aston Bridge
Road

Joyce Clk

Eddy's Lane

Barn Lane

The Park

Forest

Brierley Road

Woodside
CP School

I

per
dbrook

2

Brierley

Brierley Lands

3

HIGH STREET

A4136

A4136

Serridge
Green

4

150

B4234

5

NEW ROAD

Serridge
Inclosure

6

Goosewell

7

B4234

8

New
Beechenhurst
Inclosure

F

G

H

177

J

ROAD

SPEECH

K

GLOUCESTERSHIRE WAY

Visitors Centre

B4226

The Speech
House Hotel

Cannop Brook

Cinderford 151

F5
1 Edge Hills Cl
2 Ferndale Cl
3 Market St
4 Marshall's La
5 Moorland Cl
6 Mountjoy's La
7 Mountjoy's Lane End
8 Oakwood Cl

F7
1 Double Vw
2 West Vw

G5
1 Beacons View Rd
2 Uplands Cl

G6
1 Highview Rd

Shapridge

Green Bottom

Collafield

Littledean Hill

Heywood Sports Centre
The Heywood School
Forest View Primary School
Forest View Upper Sch
Oakdene School
Forest Hill Care
Forest of Dean District Co

The Palace Theatre

Littledean Primary School

Littledean

Little Dean Hall

CINDERFORD

Plump Hill County Primary School

The Rookery

Welshbury Wd

The slad

ELTON ROAD

A4151

The Grove

GL14

Little Hyde

nge Village

Stears

F G H 125 J K

1
2
3
4
154
5
6
7
8

Wintles Lane

Northwood
Green

Grange
Court

LC

Longcroft
Farm

Morwents
Farm

Church Lane

Brook
Farm

Adsett

Adsett
Court

Grange Court Road

A48(T)

HIGH ST

Elton
Court

Westbury-on-Severn
C of E Primary School

Westbury-on-Severn

Colchester

Westbury
Surgery
Medical
Surgery

Westbury Court
Garden (NT)

A48(T)

WINTLES HILL

Stantway

Rock Lane

Stamp...
Lane

Ga

Strand Lane

Strand

Moys Hill
Farm

Cleeve

Arlingham
Warth

Gravel
Farm

Severn Way

F G H 181 J K

Hayden
Farm

F A48(T) G H 127 J Elmore Back K

Dun Farm

River Severn

Severn Way

Gloucestershire Way

Severn Way

Lake Street

Severn Way

I

2

Elmore Court

3

Farleys End

Bridgernacote

Barhouse

Kenton Green

4

156

Severn

Wicks Green Farm

Velthouse Farm

5

Downend

6

Castle End Farm

Clarke's Farm

7

Madam's End Farm

Ellis's Farm

8

Longney

Longney Primary

Manor Farm

Laynes Farm

F G H 183 J K

Severn

156

E4
1 Brockeridge Cl
2 Longfield

Highcross
Farm

D6
1 Bekdale Cl
2 Waterdale Cl

D5
1 Ferry Gdns
2 Kingfisher Ri
3 Merchants Mead
4 Millers Dyke
5 Sandpiper Cl
6 Watermans Ct
7 Waterside Cl

Gloucestershire Way

Gloucestershire Way

A   B   128   C   D   E

Severn Way

1

E5
1 Blackthorn Gdns
2 Camellia Wk
3 Magnolia Wk
4 Pendock Cl
5 Silver Birch Cl

GL2

River Severn

Severn Way

Minsterworth Ham

Corn Ham

2

E6
1 Ashleworth Gdns
2 Cheviot Cl
3 Goss Wood Cnr
4 Mendip Cl

Weir
Green

Elmore
Court

Elmore

3

E7
1 Catkin Cl
2 Chestnut Cl

Lov
Rea

Barhouse

Kenton
Gr   4

Elmore   Lane

Severn Way

Stonebench

155

Whimbrel

The
Meadow
Ct

Severnvale

Highclere

Mallard
Ct

Teal   Causeway

Moorhen
Ct

Dunlin

Sheldrake   Road

5

E8
1 Ploughmans Wy

Hollow
Farm

Pintail
Close

Ardea

Millers
Dyke

Quedge

Copper
Beech Gv

Severn Vale
Secondary Sc

6

Chiltern

Pennine

Brecon

Quantocks

Stroudwater Dr

Pirton

7

Clarke's
Farm

Hardwicke
Farm

Wharfedale Wy

Longney
Road

Ribble
West

Mendip
Close

Dimore Cl

Oak Tree

Dart
Elmbridge
Road

Kingsholm

Madam's End
Farm

School
Farm

Millers Green

Orchard
Close

Hardwicke Parochial
Primary School

Cornfield

8

Stank   Lane

Church   Lane

Green   Lar

Hardwic

A   B   184   C   D   Quedgeley
                                                     Estate We   E

Laynes
Farm

Southfield
Farm

Pound   Lane

Sticky   Lane

1 grid square represents 500 metres

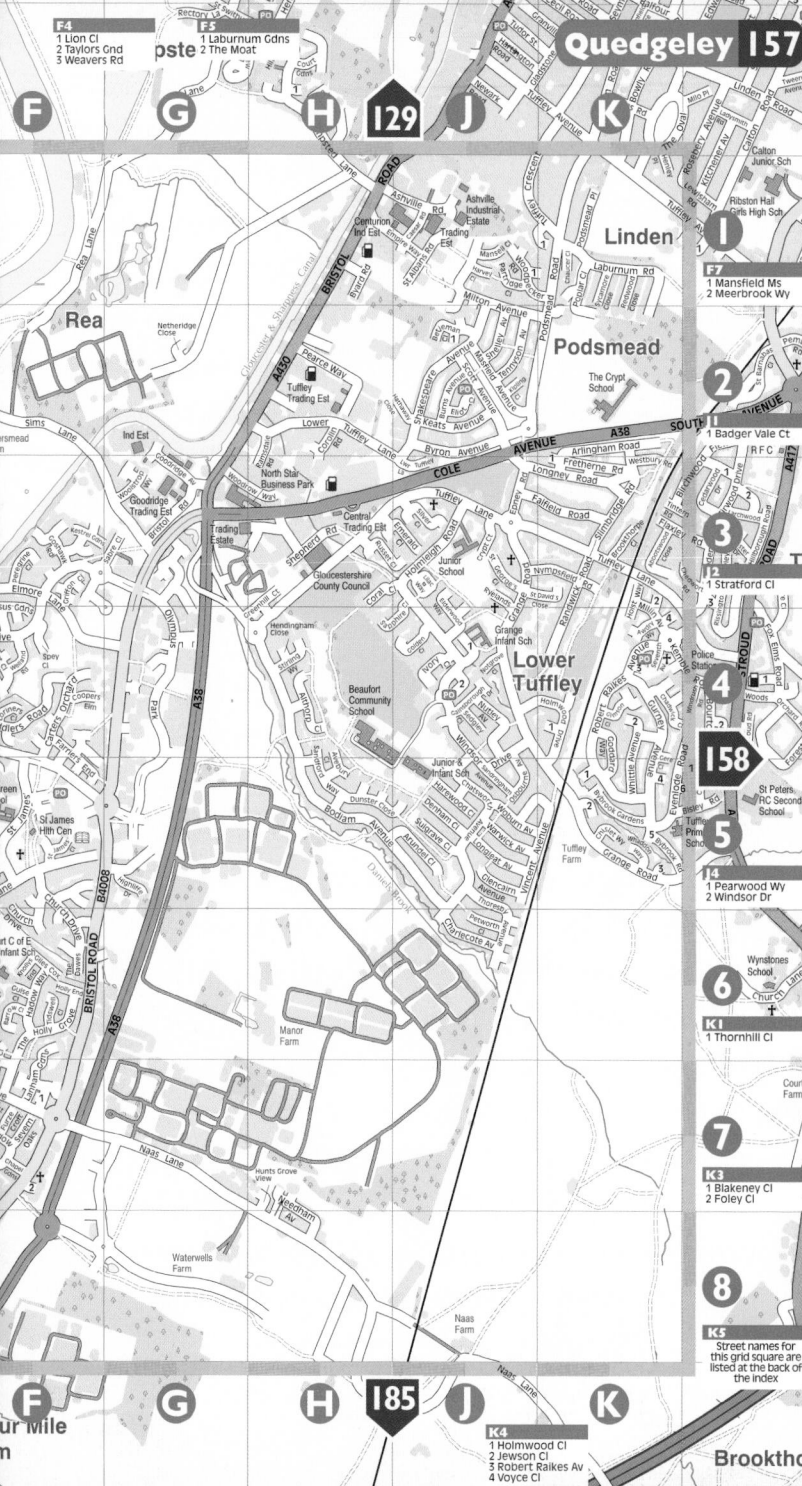

F4
1 Lion Cl
2 Taylors Gnd
3 Weavers Rd

F5
1 Laburnum Gdns
2 The Moat

F **G** **H** **129** **J** **K**

1

Linden

F7
1 Mansfield Ms
2 Meerbrook Wy

Rea

Podsmead

2

1 Badger Vale Ct

3

J2
1 Stratford Cl

Lower
Tuffley

4

158

5

J4
1 Pearwood Wy
2 Windsor Dr

6

K1
1 Thornhill Cl

7

K3
1 Blakeney Cl
2 Foley Cl

8

K5
Street names for
this grid square are
listed at the back of
the index

F **G** **H** **185** **J** **K**

K4
1 Holmwood Cl
2 Jewson Cl
3 Robert Raikes Av
4 Voyce Cl

Brookthorp

A5
1 Tetbury Rd

A4
1 Eardisland Rd
2 Winchcombe Rd

130

A3
1 Beechwood Gv
2 Cherrywood Gdns
3 Coberley Rd

A1
1 Lime Tree Ct
2 Sunnycroft Ms

Saintbridge

Cemetery

A   B   C   D   E

Linden Priman Sch

Railway

Calton Junior Sch

Ribston Hall Girls High School

Central Technology College

Saintbridge Sports Centre

FINLAY ROAD

Li---m **1**

B1
1 Dickens Ms
2 Finlay Pl
3 Northfield Sq

Reservoir

Beaufort

The Moat Infant Sch

Police Station

PAINSWICK

Podsmead

The Crypt School **2**

B2
1 Elmira Road

Arlingham Road
Fretherne Rd
Westbury Rd

SOUTHERN   AVENUE

Old Cryptians RFC

Arrowhead Close

3

Tuffley

Country Park

Robins Wood Hill

Dry Ski Slopes

Matson

Matson Council Offices

C1
1 Broom Bungalows
2 Melick Cl

Matson Rugby Clubhouse

wer fley

4

Police Station

Woods

Larkham

Fox Elms

Bazeley Rd

MATSON AVENUE

157

5

St Peters RC Secondary School

Tuffley Primary School

Tuffley Farm

C2
1 Charlock Cl
2 Primrose Cl

Sneedham's Green

Sneedhams Rd

6

Whaddon

Wynstones School

Church Lane

Pound Farm

D1
1 Amberley Rd
2 Chatcombe Rd
3 Saintbridge Pl

M5

7

Court Farm

Chilgers Lane

Upton Lane

D2
1 Evans Wk
2 School Ms

Ongers Farm

8

Brentlands

A   B   **186**   C   D   E

Brookthorpe

Maisemore

Upton Lane

Hilles House Farm

E2
Street names for this grid square are listed at the back of the index

E3
1 Gatmeres Rd
2 Matson Av
3 Oaktree Gdn

131

F **G** **H** **J** **K**

I

2

3

Abbotswood Farm

Bondend

Bowden Hall
(Hotel)

Whitley
Court

4

160

5

Pincott Farm

Upton St Leonards

6

Prinknash
Abbey

7

Moorend

GL4

Bird
Park

8

Mill Lane

Pope's
Wood

Kimsbury
House

Sevenleaze Lane

187

F **G** **H** **J** **K**

Fort

F
G
H
137
J
K

I

2

Withington
C of E School
Withington

Withington
Primary School

PH

3

Shornhill
Farm

Upcote
Farm

High Street

Withington
Woods

Staple
Farm

4

166

5

Little
Colesbourne

The Call
Scrubs

6

7

Woodlands

Boy's
Grove

Pinswell

8

Monkham
Wood

F
G
H
193
J
K

Ilicomb
Wood

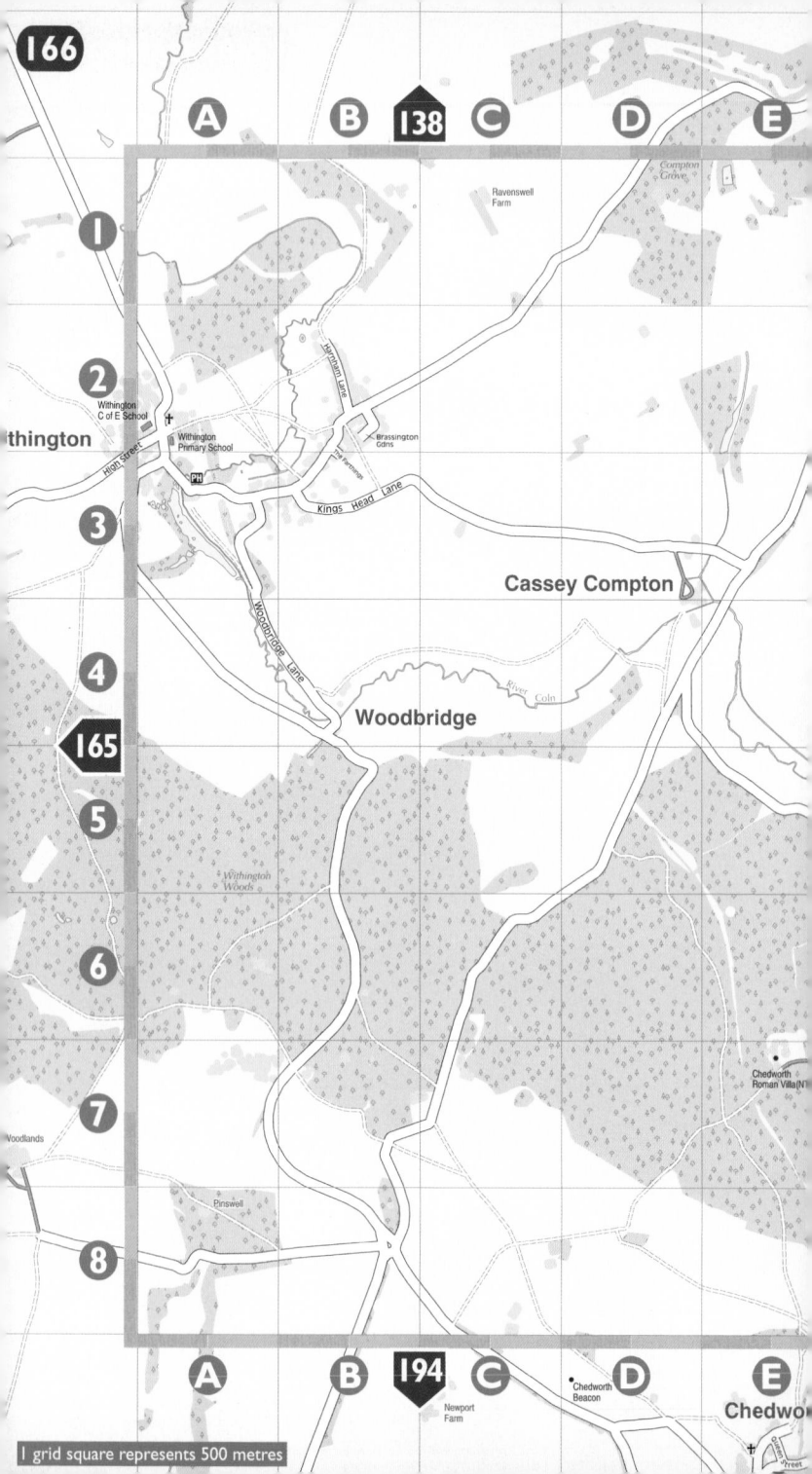

166

A B **138** C D E

165

1

Compton Grove

Ravenswell Farm

2
Withington
C of E School
Withington
Primary School

thington

High Street

Brassington Gdns

Kings Head Lane

3

Cassey Compton

Hyndham Lane

Woodbridge Lane

4

River Coln

Woodbridge

5

Withington Woods

6

Chedworth Roman Villa (N)

7

Woodlands

Pinswell

8

A B **194** C D E

Chedworth Beacon

Newport Farm

Chedwo

1 grid square represents 500 metres

G4
1 Barnett Wy
2 Bettenson Ri
3 Hammond Dr

H4
1 Farmington Ri

F G H 141 J K

I
H5
1 Short Hedges Cl

2

3

4

170

5

6

7

8

Leygore
Manor

Northleach
Downs

A429

A40(T)

Prison
Copse

Hill House
Farm

Monarch's Way

Monarch's

Heritage
Centre

A429

Old Coalyard
Farm Est

Gracie

Forey Road

Shepherds Wy

Antelope
Paddock

Police Stn

Hotel

Farmington Road

MacArthur Rd

Northleach

High St

Mill View

East End

Walters Garden

Church End

Arthur Rd

Nostle Rd

Eastington Rd

Fallows Rd

Bassett Road

Mill End

All Alone

Cats Abbey
Farm

Upper End

Eastington

well

Crickley
Barrow
Farm

Trinder's
Barn

F G H 197 J K

F G H **143** J K

I

2

3

4

172

5

6

7

8

The Fork

Upper Broad

Sandy Hill Farm

Crookmoor Ash

Northfield Barn

Sherborne Common

Sherborne Brook

Cemetery

Sherborne
PO

Oranges

Sherborne Park

Home Farm

A40(T)

A40(T)

Snowbottom

Camp Barn

F G H **199** J K

F G H **145** J K

Tayton Busbes

I

2

Coalesterbrook

3

Miletree Clump

4

Oxfordshire County
Gloucestershire County

5

6

7

Great Barrington

River Windrush

8

Minnow Lane

Middle

Road

Home Farm

Little Barrington

F G H **201** J A40(T) K

A40(T)

Christchurch

F G H 147 J K Five Acres

Ivy Hill

Lakers School

Leisure Centre

BEECH AVENUE

Marian Inclosure

I

I5
1 The Links

Lower Road

Lower Berry Hill

STAUNTON ROAD A4136

2

Forest Hills Golf Clu.

K3
1 Wynols Hill La

Crossways

Lark Rise

Baker Hill

3

K4
1 The Crescent
2 Kings Meade
3 Market Pl
4 Poolway Ct
5 Prospect Pl
6 Vicarage Ct

Scowles

St Johns School

Cemetery

GLOUCESTER ROAD

Police Stn

Bells Place

Bells Hotel
Royal
Forest of Dean
Golf Club

4

176

COLEFORD

Willow Tree Surgery

The Great Western Railw

Gloucestershire Co Council
Forest of Dean
District Council

Coleford Health Centre

High Meadow Farm

High Nash

Brunston Surg

5

The Links

OLD STATION WAY

K5
1 Bessemer Cl
2 Centurions Wk
3 Copley Dr
4 Fairfield Cl
5 Fairways Av
6 Nash Wy
7 Tufthorn Av

Whitecliff

Rock Lane

Newland Street

6

Tufthorn Industrial Estate

7

Millend

Pingry Farm

Puzzle Wood

PERRYGROVE ROAD

B4228

Edenwall Road
Forest Road
Station Road

LAMBSQUAY ROAD

Scatterford Farm

Minnie Lane

Pingry Lane

8

wland

Inwood

F G H 203 J Clearwell Caves K

Hotel
PH
Hotel

OAKWOOD ROAD

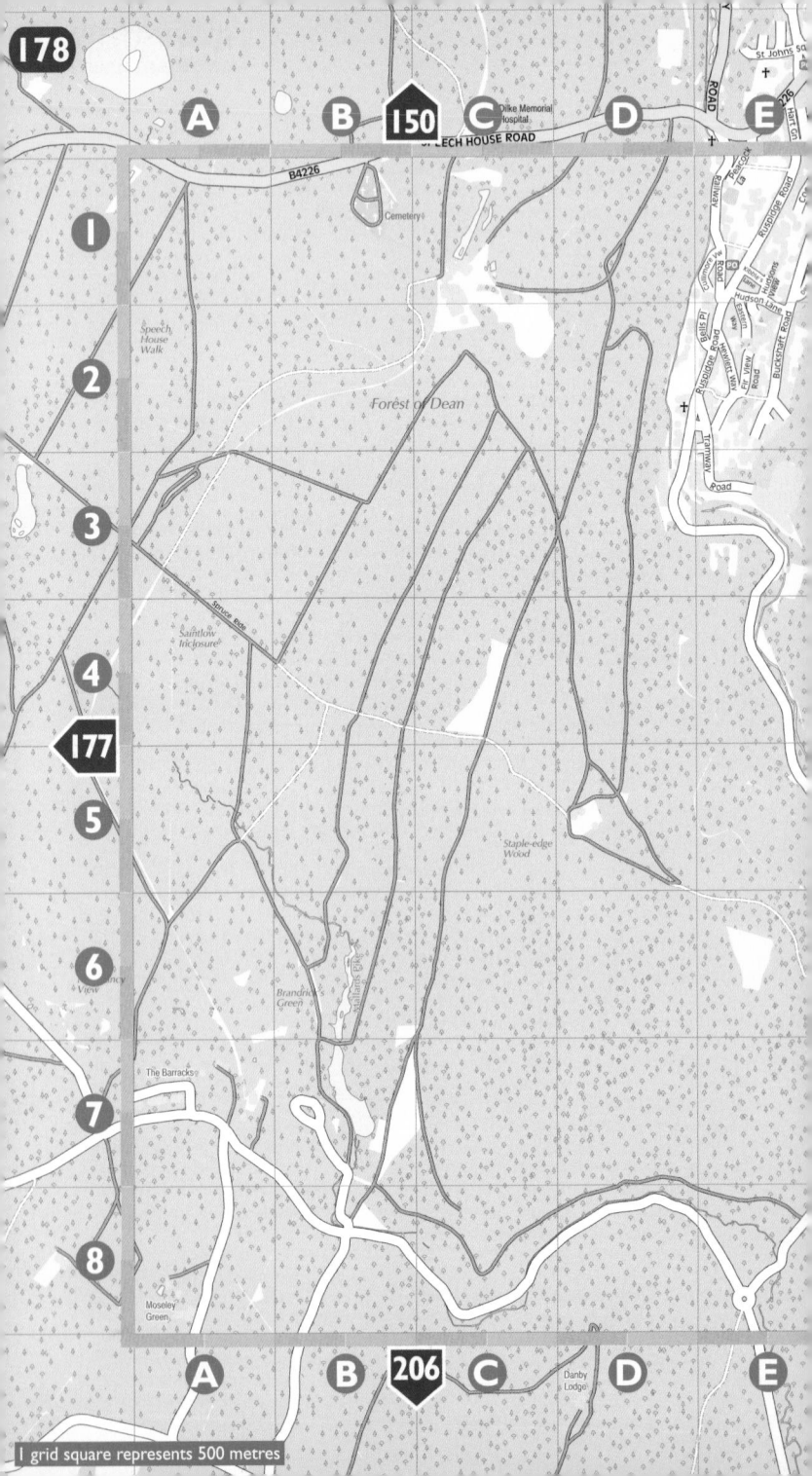

178

A   B   150   C   Dike Memorial Hospital   D   E

SPEECH HOUSE ROAD

St John's sq

ROAD

RAILWAY

B4226

Cemetery

Roscoign Road

Buckshaft Road

1

Speech House Walk

Hudson Lane

2

Forest of Dean

Alloway Road
Betts Pl
Alloway Road
Hereford New
Fir View Road

3

Spruce Ride

4

Saintlow Inclosure

Tramway Road

177

5

Staple-edge Wood

6

View

Brandrick's Green

Valley Brook

The Barracks

7

8

Moseley Green

A   B   206   C   Danby Lodge   D   E

1 grid square represents 500 metres

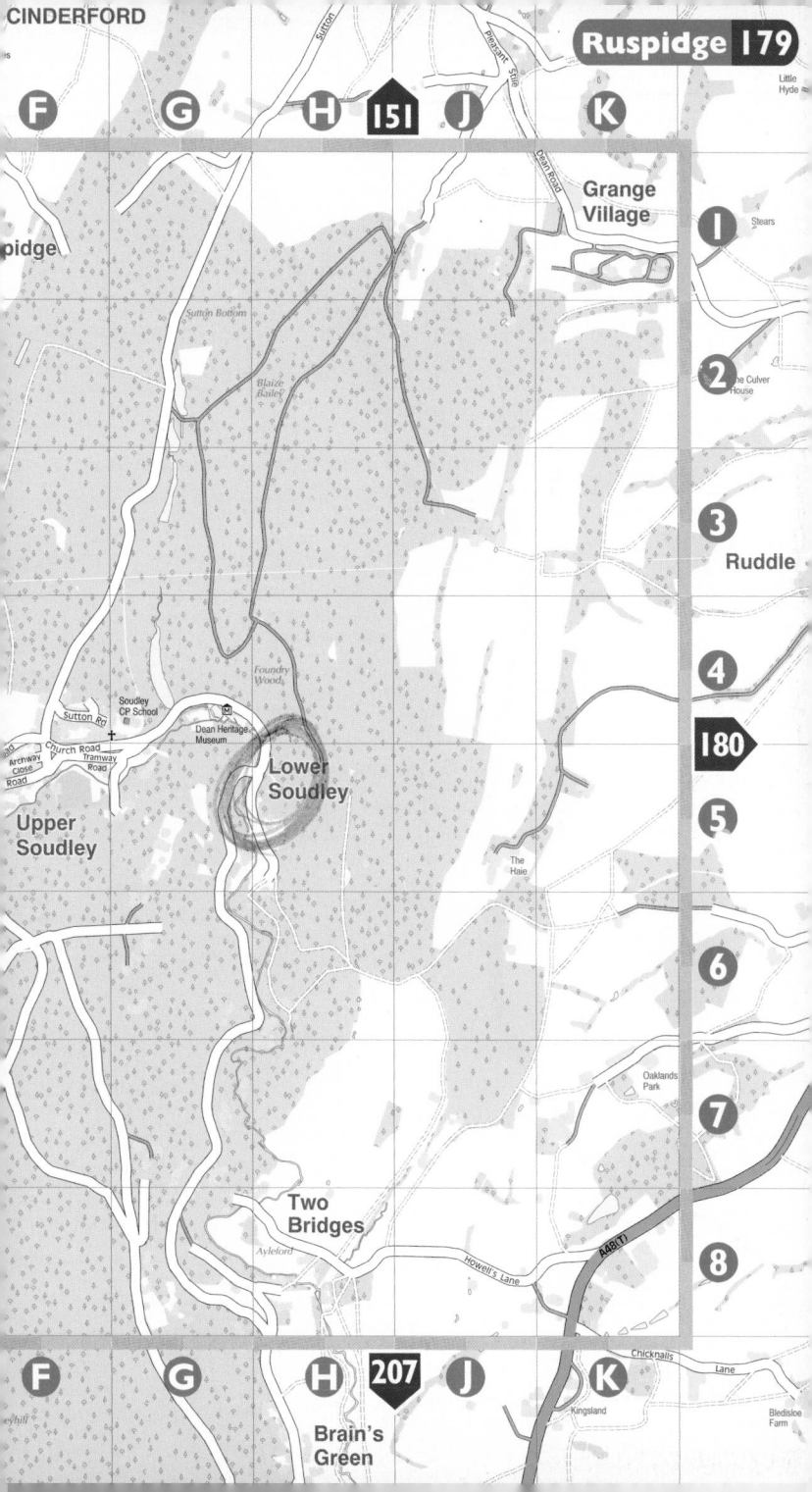

F G H 151 J K

Little
Hyde

pidge

Grange
Village

1 Stears

2 The Culver
House

Sutton Bottom

Blaize
Bailey

3 Ruddle

4

180

Foundry
Woods

Soudley
CP School

Dean Heritage
Museum

Sutton Rd

Lower
Soudley

5

Church Road
Archway
Close
Road
Tramway
Road

Upper
Soudley

The
Haie

6

Oaklands
Park

7

Two
Bridges

Ayleford

Howell's Lane

A48(T)

8

Chicknalls
Lane

F G H 207 J K

eyhill

Brain's
Green

Kingsland

Bledisloe
Farm

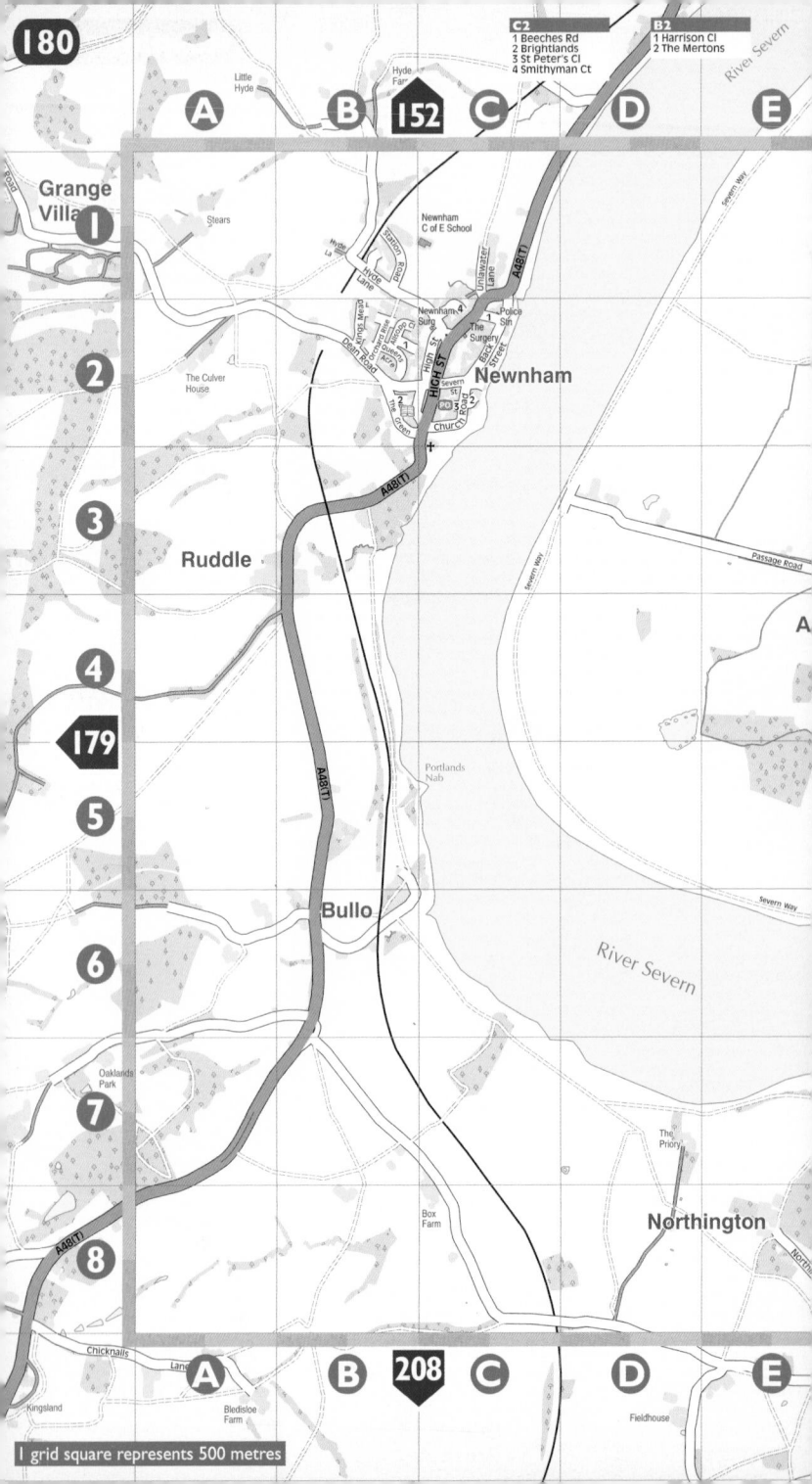

A   B   152   C   D   E

C2
1 Beeches Rd
2 Brightlands
3 St Peter's Cl
4 Smithyman Ct

B2
1 Harrison Cl
2 The Mertons

River Severn

Little
Hyde

Hyde
Farm

Severn Way

Grange
Villa

1

Stears

Newnham
C of E School

Hyde La

Larton Road

Hyde Lane

Dean Road

A48(T)

2

The Culver
House

Long Mead

Newnham
Surg

Newnham
4

Police
Stn

High St

The
Surgery

Back Street

3

Ruddle

A48(T)

Newnham

Severn
St
2
PO
2
Church

The Green

Severn Way

Passage Road

4

A

179

5

Portlands
Nab

Severn Way

6

Bullo

River Severn

Oaklands
Park

7

The
Priory

Box
Farm

Northington

8

A48(T)

North

Chicknails   Lane

A   B   208   C   D   E

Kingsland

Bledisloe
Farm

Fieldhouse

1 grid square represents 500 metres

Cleeve

F Artingham Warth

G

H 153

J Gravel Farm

K

1 Haydon Farm

Lower Dumball

2

River Severn

Severn Way

3

Slowwe House

Silver Street

Woodthorpe Ln

High Street

Friday Street

Vale Bank

Bell Orch

The Ct (PO)

Church Road

Podms Lane

Milton End

4

Overton Lane

182

Overton

5

6

Overton Farm

Severn Way

The Reddings

7

Hock Cliff

Severn Way

8

F

G

H 209

J

K

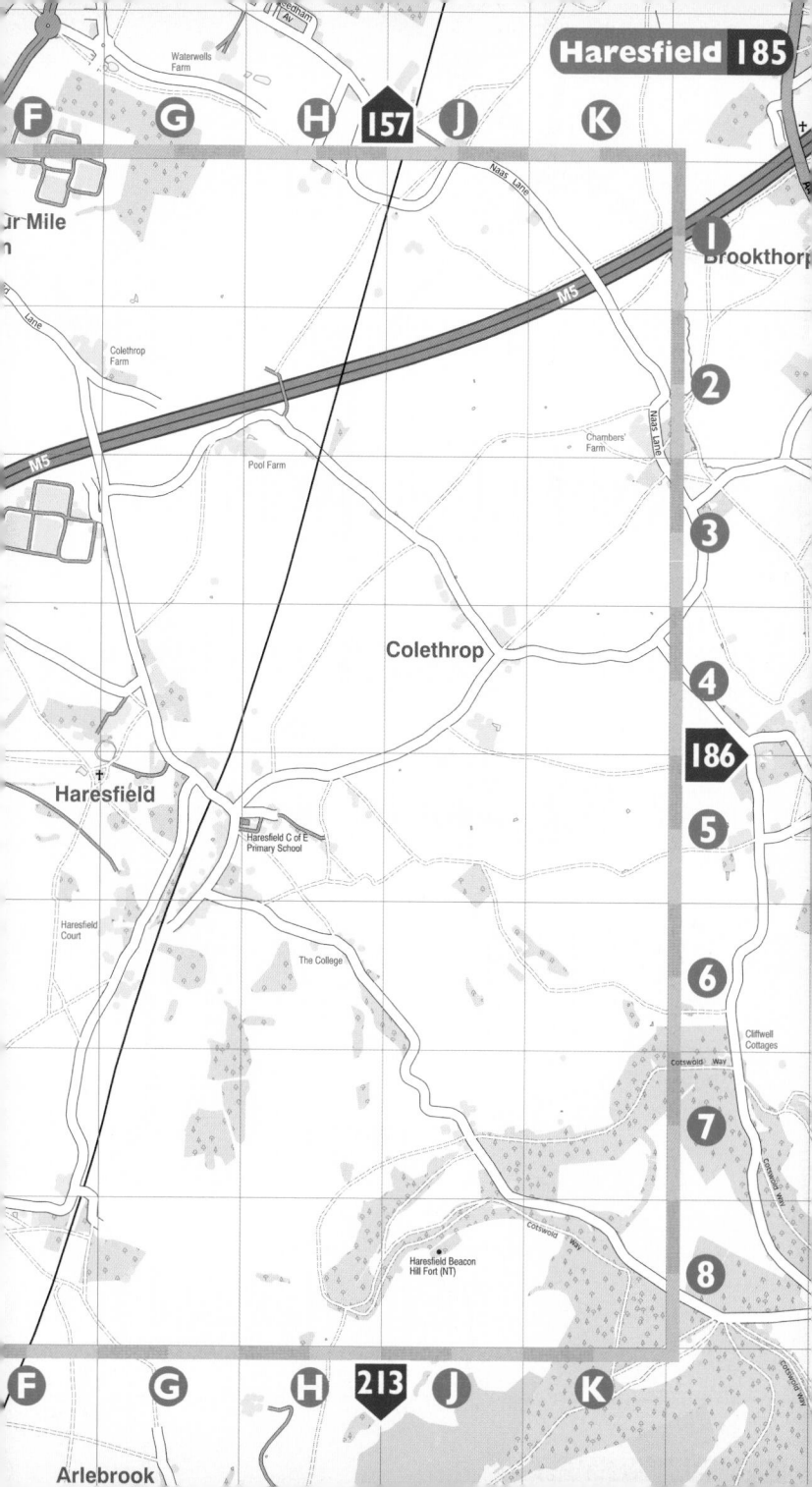

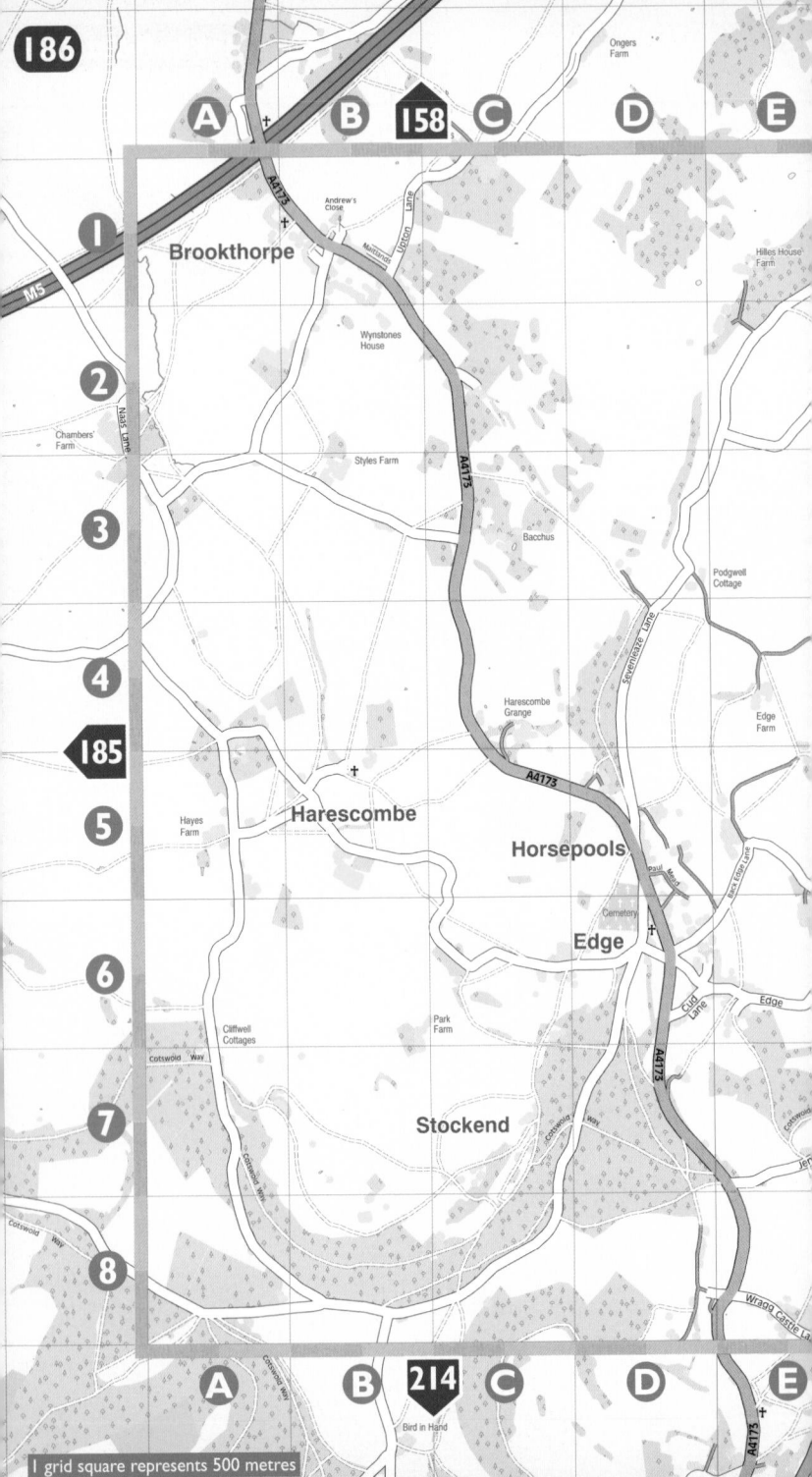

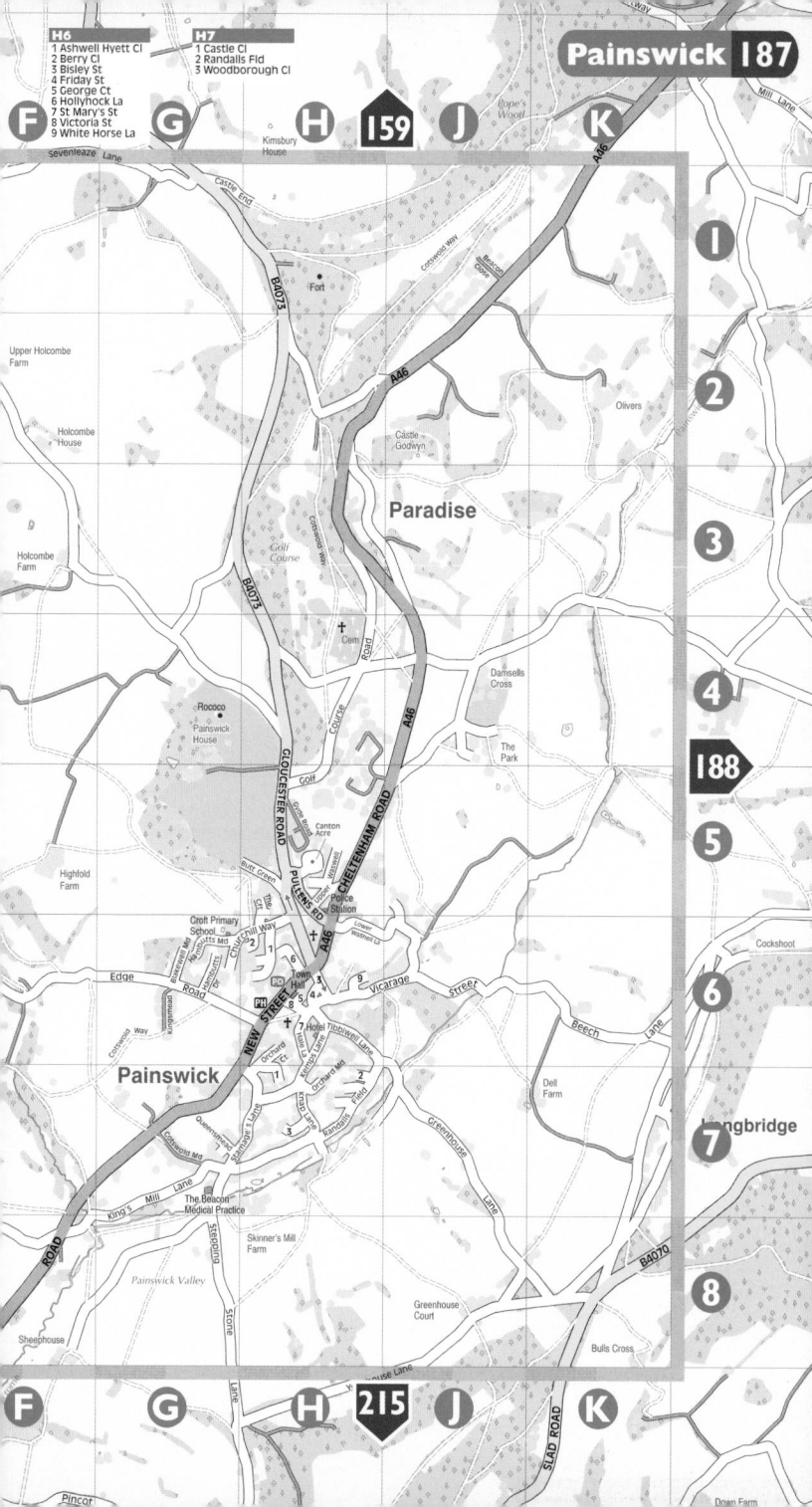

H6
1 Ashwell Hyett Cl
2 Berry Cl
3 Bisley St
4 Friday St
5 George Ct
6 Hollyhock La
7 St Mary's St
8 Victoria St
9 White Horse La

H7
1 Castle Cl
2 Randalls Fld
3 Woodborough Cl

F G H 159 J K

I
2
3
4 188
5
6
7 Longbridge
8

F G H 215 J K

Seventeaze Lane
Castle End
B4073
Fort
Kimsbury House
Pope's Wood
A46
Cotswold Way
Beacon Corner
Mill Lane
Upper Holcombe Farm
Holcombe House
Olivers
A46
Holcombe Farm
Castle Godwyn
Paradise
Golf Course
Cem
Course Road
Damsells Cross
The Park
Rococo
Painswick House
B4073
GLOUCESTER ROAD
Golf Course
CHELTENHAM ROAD
PULLENS RD
A46
Canton Acre
Cockshoot
Highfold Farm
Croft Primary School
Churchill Way
Butt Green
The
Town Hall
PH
Police Station
Lower Washwell La
Vicarage Street
Beech Lane
Edge Road
Cotswold Way
Kingsmead
Blackness Mill
Hotel Tibbiwell Lane
Dell Farm
Painswick
Orchard Rd
Orchard Rd
Stepping Stone Lane
New Street
Kings La
Randalls Fld
Greenhouse Lane
Cockshoot
The Beacon Medical Practice
King's Mill Lane
Skinner's Mill Farm
B4070
ROAD
Painswick Valley
Stone Lane
Greenhouse Court
Sheephouse
Bulls Cross
SLAD ROAD
Pincot
Yokehouse Lane
Down Farm

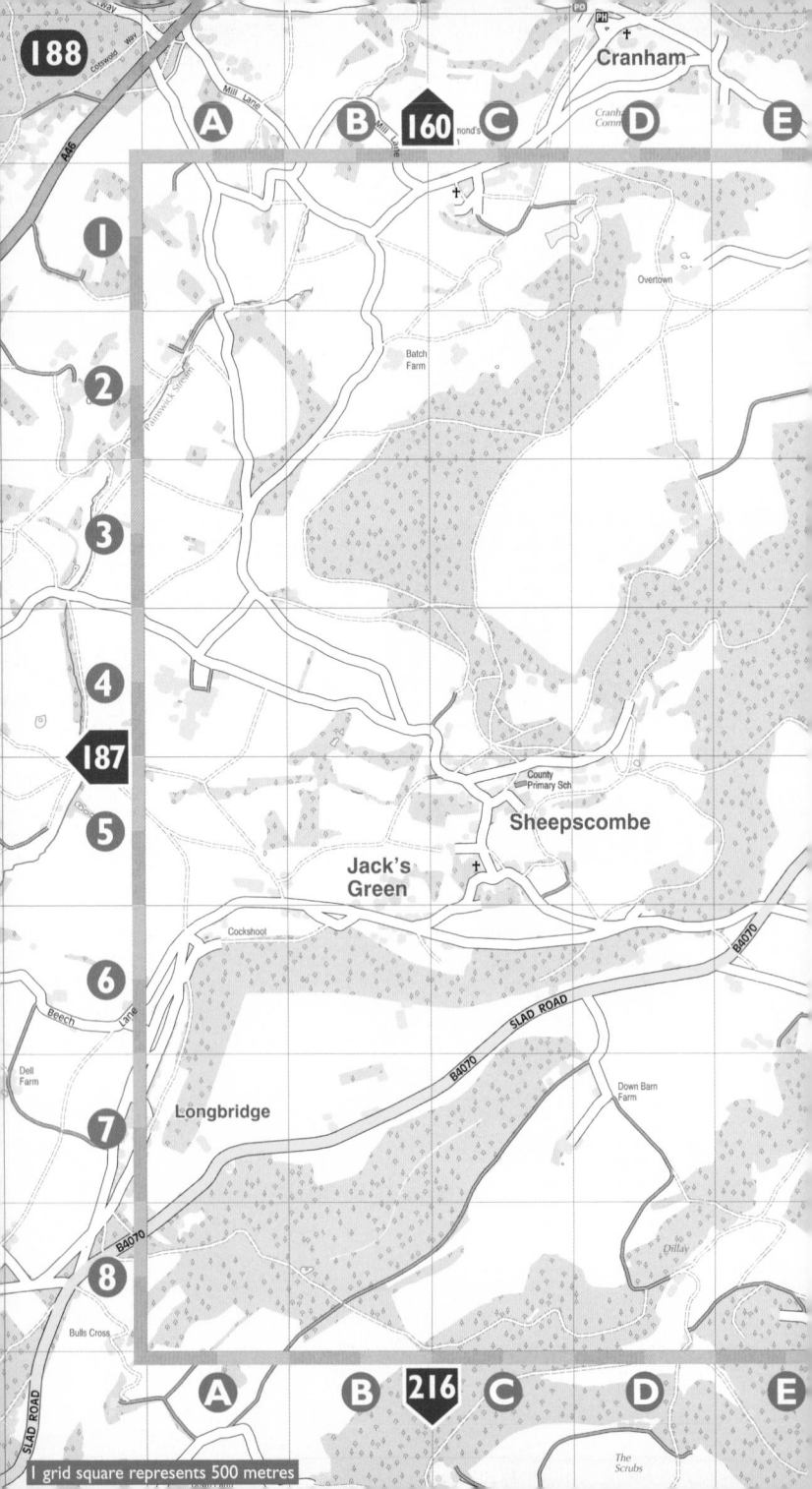

Cranham

PO
PH

Cranham
Common

A
B
160
C
D
E

mond's

Mill Lane
Mill Lane

1

Overtown

2

Batch
Farm

Pinswell School

3

4

187

County
Primary Sch

5

Sheepscombe

Jack's
Green

Cockshoot

6

Beech Lane

SLAD ROAD

B4070

Down Barn
Farm

Dell
Farm

7

Longbridge

B4070

8

B4070

Dillay

Bulls Cross

A
B
216
C
D
E

SLAD ROAD

The
Scrubs

1 grid square represents 500 metres

F G H **161** J K

I
2
3
4
190
5
6
7
8

Longdole
Barn

Cranham
Wood

Hazel Hanger
Wood

Climperwell
Farm

B4070

Calf Way

B4070

Moor
House

Morcombe

Wateredge
Farm

Bidfield
Farm

Whiteway

Hazle
Manor

Wishanger

The Camp

Calf Way

Henley
Farm

Honeycombe
Farm

Miserden C of E
Primary School

Lypiatt

F G H **217** J K

Sudgrove

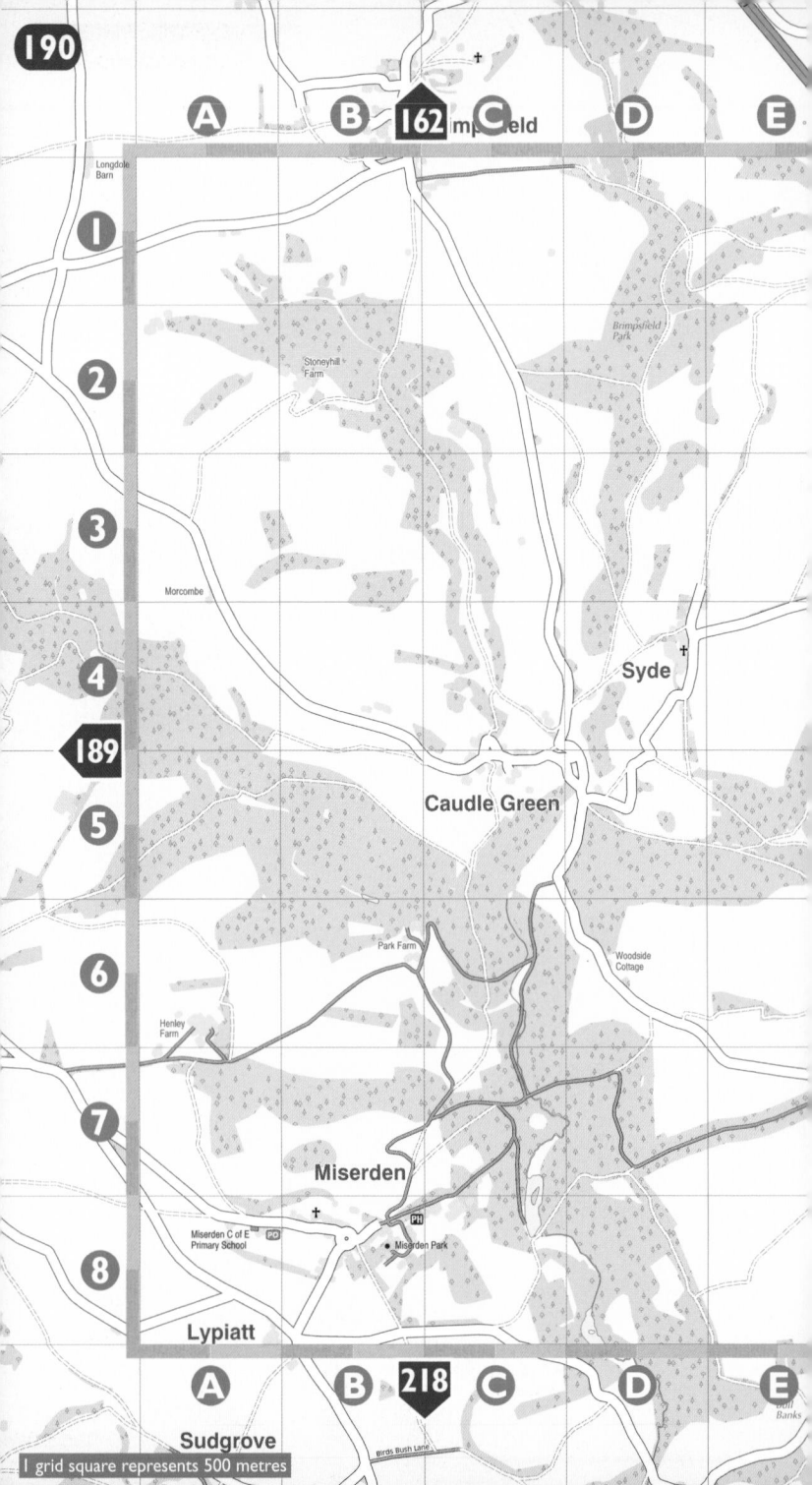

A B 162 mp C eld D E

Longdole
Barn

1

2
Stoneyhill
Farm

3
Morcombe

Brimpsfield
Park

4
Syde

189

5
Caudle Green

6
Park Farm
Woodside
Cottage

Henley
Farm

7
Miserden

8
Miserden C of E
Primary School
Miserden Park
PH

Lypiatt

A B 218 C D E

Sudgrove
Birds Bush Lane
1 grid square represents 500 metres

Elkstone

F G H 163 J K

I

2

3

4

192

5

6

7

8

Highgate Farm

Slutswe

Gloucester Beeches

Sadlers Farm

Combend Manor

Elkstone Farm

Harcombe Farm

Watercombe Farm

Fosse Farm

Beechpike

Winstone

Jackbarrow Road

Pike Road

Fosse Fld

Back Lane

School Rd

Notch Road

Croft Lane

Manor Farm

Cotswold

Rectory Farm

F G H 219 J K

Duntisbourne Abbo

Burrowthorn

Slutswell

A · B · **164** · C · D · E

I

Sadlers
Farm

Hall's
Grove

2

Combend
Manor

3

Rapsgate
Park

Eycot
Wood

Watercombe
Farm

4

191

Shewel
Wood

5

6

Cotswold
Park

Cotswold
Farm

7

Hobbs Lane

Burcombe La

8

Burcombe   Lane

Field's
Farm

Moor
Wood

A · B · **220** · C · D · E

Voxhills
Farm

F G H 165 J K

I
2
3
4
194
5
6
7
8

Monkham Wood

Hicomb Wood

Marsden

Shawswell

Cliterline Wood

River Churn

Rendcomb Park

Green Meadow Farm

Rendcomb College

Rendcomb

Rendcomb Buildings

Old Park

odmancote

Nordown

White Way

White Way

Morton's Way

Morton's Way

F G H 221 J K

Primary School

Churn Hill

Chapel Lane

Dark Lane

A435

194

A   B   166   C   D   E

1

Newport
Farm

• Chedworth
Beacon

Chedwo

Chedworth

PH

2

Chedworth
Laines

Sells
Farm

3

Pinkwell

Macmillan Way

4

Chittlegrove

Monarch's Way

193

E OW

5

White Way

Ashwell
Lodge

6

Monarch's Way

White Way

Rendcomb
Buildings

7

8

Nordown

White Way

Calmsden

Dark Lane

Dark La

A   B   222   C   D   E

I grid square represents 500 metres

F G H **169** J K

Trinder's
Barn

I

Crickley Barrow
Farm

*Broadfield
Covert*

Trowel

2

Broadfield
Farm

3

Calcot Peak
Farm

4

198

5

River Leach

Oldwalls
Farm

6

Prehistoric
Monument

7

Kilkei
Farm

8

F G H **225** J K

198

A   B 170 C   D   E

1   Lodge
                                      Park

Trowel
Covert
2   Larkethill
                               Wood   Conygree
                                           Farm

Broadfield
Farm
3

4

197

River Leach
5   Cocklebarrow
                               Farm

6

7   Kilkenny
               Farm

                               B4425
8   Swy
                                                       Farm

A   B 226 C   D   E
                  Kilkenny
                  Cott

1 grid square represents 500 metres

F G H **171** J K

I

2

3

4

200

5

6

7

8

Camp Barn

Snowbottom Belt

Budgehill Wood

Rabbit Ground Plantation

Blackpits Copse

Aldsworth

B4425

B4425

Ladbarrow Farm

Dean Farm

Ⓐ A40(T) Ⓑ 172 Ⓒ Ⓓ Ⓔ

1

Camp Barn

dgehill oh

2

3

Hill Barn

4

199

5

B4425

6

Barrington Downs Farm

7

8

No Man's Land Plantation

Ⓐ Ⓑ 228 Ⓒ Ⓓ Ⓔ

A40(T)

PH

Eastleach Downs Farm

1 grid square represents 500 metres

acaroni Downs Farm

Church Lane

Milkwall

E5
1 Sun Green Cl

A2
1 Michaels Wy

A1
1 Gorse La

A   B   176   C   D   E

Clearwell
Caves

I

E6
1 Ironstone Cl
2 Pine Crest Wy
3 Puzzle Cl

Ellwood

Ellwood County
Primary School

Ellwood
Football Club

2

Orepool

Sling

Marsh
Lane

Shophouse   Road

3

Little
Drybrook

Clements End

Trow
Green

4

203

Noxon
Farm

Noxons
Park

5

Mill
Hill

Bream's
Meend

BREAM

6

AVENUE
B4231

New   Road

Bream
Sports Club

Bream

COLEFORD ROAD

Bream
Cross

7

Roads
Farm

Farewell   Lane

Prior's
Lodge

Close Turf
Farm

8

The
Hoggins Farm

Willsbury
Farm

A   B   232   C   D   E

Priors
Mesne

I grid square represents 500 metres

F5
1 Admirals Cl
2 Badgers Wy
3 Whitechapel Rd

F6
1 Acacia Cl

Fancy Road

F   **G**   **H**   177   **J**   **K**

Moseley Green

HOP ROAD

Parkend

I

J5
1 Morcroft Pl

B4234

Hughes Terrace

Crown La

2

Church Wy

Parkend School

Church Drive

Dean Forest Railway

3

Oakenhill Wood

NEW ROAD

Parkhill Inclosure

B4234

Knights Parchy

4   York

Captains Green Road

Crown Road

Bowson Road

Crown Road

School Road

Main Road

Upper

206

Crown Road

Woodland Road

Whitecroft Road

Gresley Dr

High Beech Crs

Pillowell

Whitecroft Road

Pillowell

5

The Eaves

Park Hill

Park Cl

Corner Rd

James Wk

Hillside Cl

Pillowell CP School

Knockly

B4234

Hilsnail Rd

6

Brockhollands Road

The Ivy

B4234

Kidnalls

Brockhollands

7

5

B4234

Dean Forest Railway

BREAM ROAD

NEW ROAD

8

F   **G**   **H**   B4231   233   **J**   **K**   New Mills

A **B** 178 **C** **D** **E**

1

Danby
Lodge

2

Cockshoot
Wood

Oakenhill Wood

3

Yorkley
Slade

Ridgeway

Trubshot Road

Morse Lane

Danby Way

Kings View

Woodland

Yorkley Hlth Cen

Severn View
Road

Cartway Green

Coopers Hill

Bailey's Hill

New Road

Palmers Flat

Dockham Road

4

Yorkley
County
School

Yorkley

St Swithins

Cut And
Fry Rd

Kears Rd

205

*Pillowell
CP School*

School Road

5

James St

Herberts Way

Pillowell

Yorkley Wood Road

Yorkley Wood Road

Yorkley
Lane

Philip's
Cl

James Wy

Cburch
Walk

Stephins Road

Oldcrof

6

Yorkley
Court

Soilwell

Kidnalls

7

Old
Dam
Road

8

Dean Forest Railway

B4234

NEW
ROAD

Grove
Lane
Road

Allaston
Road

Windsor
Road

Oak
Meadow

Allaston

Highfield Lane

A
New
Mills

Lancaster Close

Court Road

Berkeley Cl

Dean

Primrose Wy

B 234 **C** **D** **E**

1 grid square represents 500 metres

208

Northington

A   B   180   C   D   E

Chicknails
Lane

Kingsland

1

Bledisloe
Farm

Box
Farm

Fieldhouse

2

Hawfield

3

Little
Box

LC

Hall Farm

4

Poulton
Court

Hagloe

207

5

Hagloe House

Oatfield
Farm

6

Gatcombe

7

8

Tites
Point

A   B   236   C Curton   D   E

1 grid square represents 500 metres

F G H 181 J K

I
2
3
4
210
5
6
7
8

River Severn

Woodend Lane

PD
PH

Middle Point

The Dumbles

The Wildfowl Trust

New Grounds

Newgrounds Lane

Severn Way

F G H 237 J K

The Warth

Shepherd's Pat

210

A B **182** C D E

1

Severn Way

Saul
Warth

Gloucester and Sharpness Canal

B4071

Frampton on Severn
C of E School

Lake Lane

Oval
Rd

The Oval

BRIDGE ROAD

Framp

PO

Frampton
Court

Whitminster Ln

Whitles Lane

The Street

Water Lane

2

3

Severn Way

4

Splatt
Bridge

Vicarage Lane

Cedar Close

**Church
End**

◀**209**

5

6

**New
Grounds**

7

The
Marshes

Gloucester and Sharpness Canal

River C

8

Severn Way

Hope House
Farm

Longbatton Lane

Wickaters

Hillhouse
Farm

A B **238** C D E

Shepherd's Patch

Ryalls Lane

1 grid square represents 500 metres

F5
1 Glenthorne Cl

Haresfield Beacon
Hill Fort (NT)

185

Arlebrook

Oxlynch

Standish Park
Farm

Stroud
Green

B4008

Standish
Hospital

Arrowsmith
Drive

Horsemarling
Farm
Maidenhill
School

Woodcock
Lane

Robin's
Lane

Stonehouse

Robbers Road

Ash Lane

The Ryelands

Sandpits Lane

Far Westrip Lane

Westrip

Foxmoor
Lane

The Bassetts

The Bridle

Cotswold Way

Foxmoor
CP School

Cotswold Way

Pearcroft Rd

Brown's Lane

Wycliffe
College

Ryeford

Ebley Road B4008

Ryeford
Industrial Estate

B4008

A419

Cashes
Green

The Tynings

Cashes Green
CP School

Cashes Green
Road

The Stirrup

Hunters Way

Hospital

Cross Ct

The Beagles

Foxmoor CP School

Ebley

Orchard
Road

Cainscross
Parish
Council

Westward Road

WESTWARD ROAD

Cedar Rd

Ebley
Industrial
Estate

Stroud
District
Council

Ruscombe

Randwick

Randwick C of E
Primary School

The Stocks

Brimbledge Road

214

Ruscombe

Puck

Cashes Green
CP School

Whiteshill
Parish
School

H & L
Trading
Est

Fort Ter

B4008

Dudbridge

A419

A419

I
F7
1 Aldergate St
2 Kestrel Ct
3 Laburnum Wk
4 St Cyril's Rd
5 Upper Queen's
  Rd

2
Standish
K6
1 Hawthorn Ri
2 Perry Orch
3 St Michael's Pl
4 Springfield Rd
5 The Wordens

3
K7
1 The Brush

4

5
K8
1 Holly Tree Gdn
2 Huntingdon Cl

6
F6
Street names for
this grid square are
listed at the back of
the index

7

8

F

G

H

187

J

K

1

2

3

Nature Reserve

4

216

5

Fennells

6

7

8

Slad

Wick Street

Uplands

Bowbridge

F

G

H

243

J

K

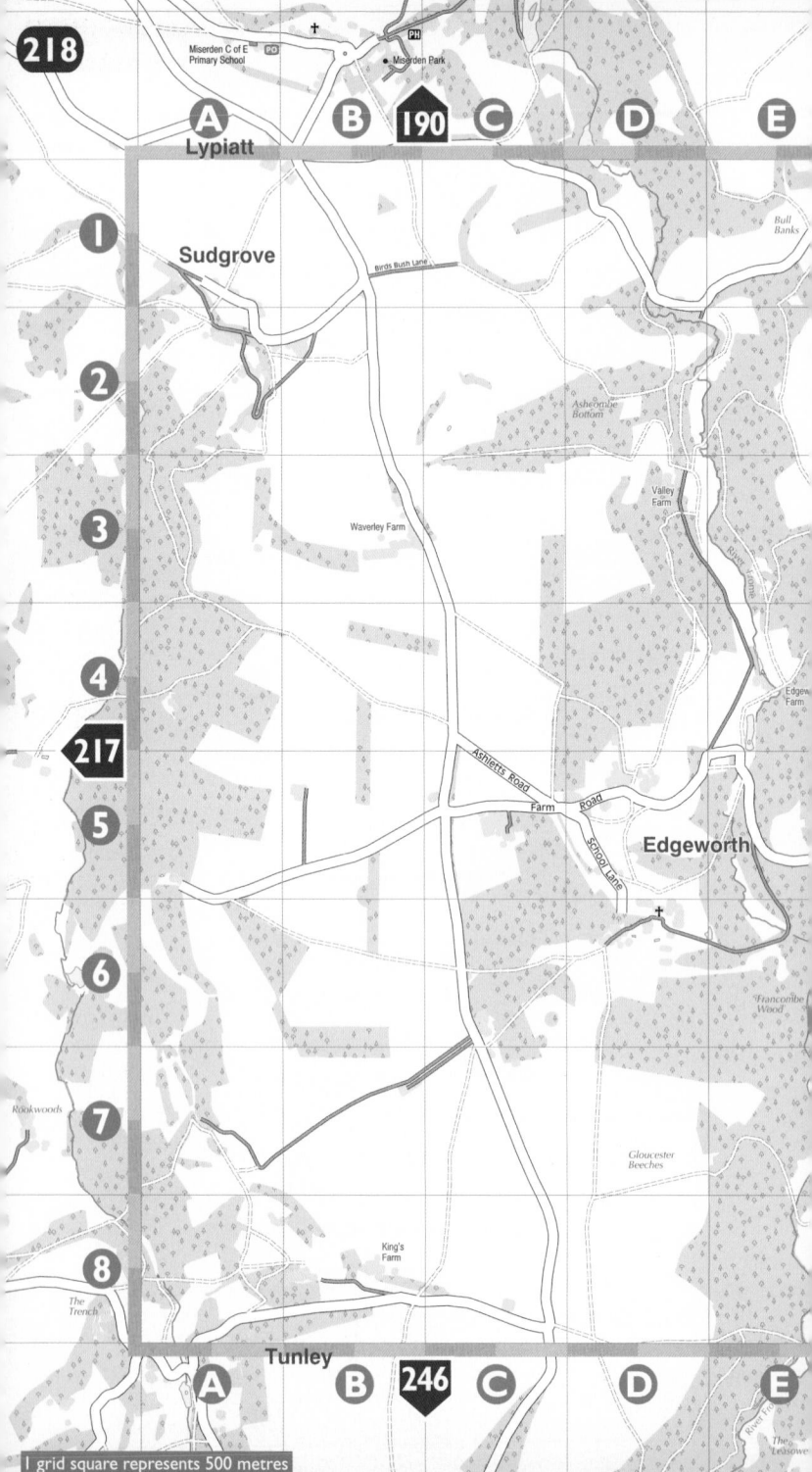

218

A   B   190   C   D   E

Lypiatt

1   Sudgrove

Birds Bush Lane

Bull Banks

2   Ashcombe Bottom

3   Waverley Farm   Valley Farm

River Frome

4

217   Edge Farm

5   Ashletts Road   Farm Road   Edgeworth

School Lane

6   Francombe Wood

7   Rookwoods   Gloucester Beeches

8   King's Farm

The Trench

Tunley

A   B   246   C   D   E

The Leasowe

River Frome

1 grid square represents 500 metres

F G H 191 J K

**Duntisbourne
Abbots**

A417(T)

1

2

**Duntisbourne
Leer**

Nutbeam
Farm

3

Jackbarrow
Farm

New Barn
Farm

...isbourne
...mon

Craptree Lane

Hoar
Stone

4

Weigh

220

...urne

Macmillan Way

5

Longhill Road

**Duntisbourne
Rouse**

...swoode
...on

Longhill
Farm

6

Overley
Wood

Longhill Road

7

Overley
Farm

8

F G H 247 J K

Park
Corner

Overley Road

Winson

224

196

223

252

A   B   C   D   E

1

2

3

4

5

6

7

8

Pool House

Fosscross Lane

Potato Barn

Hay Lane

Meadowlands Farm

Cadmoor Copse

River Coln

Pc
Pollicker's Lane

B4425

Quarry Hill Farm

rnsley

Welsh Way

Poultmoor Farm

PH

Barnsley House Gardens

Welsh Way

Re
To

Ampney Knowle

B4425

F G H **197** J K

1
2
3
4
226
5
6
7
8

Ablington

Bibury
Farm

B4425

Arlington
Police
Station
The Quarry
PH
Arlington Mill
Museum
Hotel
B4425
Awkward Hill
Hawkers
The Diane
Breen Gallery
Rack Isle
Bibury
Cemetery Lane
Bibury C of E
Primary School
Hotel

Bibury

The
Grove

River Coln

Furzey
Barn Farm

Coneygar
Farm

Coneygar
Wood

Kelroy

F G H **253** J K

Hartwell
Farm

A B **198** C D E

1

B4425

2

B4425

Kilkenny
Cottages

Bratch
Copse

3

4

Knoll
Barn

225

5

Salt Way

Moor's
Farm

6

Salt Way

Willia
Park

7

Coneygar
Farm

Coln
St Aldwyns

PO

PH

Hotel

Hathero
Castle S

River Coln

8

Coneygar
Woods

Coneygar Road

Fowler's Hill

Ne

A B **254** C D E

Springfield Road

Coring
Gardens

Church

Mawley Road

Victoria Road

Road

Quenington

I grid square represents 500 metres

F G H 199 J K

I

2

3

4

228

5

6

7

8

Dean Farm

River Leach

Lappingwell Wood

Coltsmoor Farm

Tyning Wood

Williamstrip Farm

East Leach Folly

Macaroni Farm

The Old Estate Sawmill Workshops

rop School

Hatherop

Macaroni Wood

F G H 255 J K

Barrow Elm Farm

Homeleaze Farm

Hammeroniu Barton

228

A   B   **200**   C   D   E

I

No Man's Land
Plantation

Eastleach
Downs Farm

Macaroni Downs
Farm

2

River Leach

Lappingwell
Wood

3

4

◄227

5

East Le
Folly

Beer Furlong
Buildings

6

7

Macaroni
Farm

BUTTS

PO

Eastleach
Turville

8

Mac
Wo

A   B   **256**   C   D   E

Hammersmith

Homeleaze
Farm

1 grid square represents 500 metres

F G H 201 J K

I
2
3
4
5
6
7
8

Westwell
Copse

Holwell Downs
Farm

Oxfordshire County
shire County

Filkins Down
Farm

Broughtondowns
Plantation

Furze
Ground

Sheephouse
Farm

College
Farm

Locombe Hill

Oxleaze
Farm

Filkins
Farm

tleach
tin

Shire
Gate

The
Pills

F G H 257 J K

The Great
Hoggins Farm

Close Turf
Farm

Gloucestershire Way

Willsbury
Farm

Prior's
Lodge

A Bre **B** **204** **C** **D** **E**

Severn View
Farm

1

Priors
Mesne

Gloucestershire Way

The Warren

2

Old Bangs
Wood

Rodmore
Farm

3

Glebe
Farm

4

Clanna
Lodge

Cottage
Farm

231

Gloucestershire Way

5

Collier's Pitch

Lower
Common

Royle
Reddings

Clanna

6

Park
Farm

Gloucestershire Way

7

**Woolaston
Common**

Clanna Lane

Nupper

Beanhill

Woolaston Common

Scout Hill

Errands Rd

Woodside

Sandtumps

Smallbrook

8

**Woolaston
Woodside**

Severn View

Long Fence

Glewstone
Rocks

The
Post PO

A48(T) MAIN ROAD

Knapp Lane

Church

A **B** **260** **C** **D** **E**

Netherend
Road

Netherend Chs

Netherend

Woolaston
1 grid square represents 500 metres

234

A5
1 Chantry Cl
2 Vicarage Cl

A4
1 Darters Cl
2 Herbert Howells Cl
3 Steeple Vw

A3
1 The Springs

A **B** st **206** **C** **D** **E**

B1
1 Charnwood Ct

New Mills

1

Highbury

2

B2
1 Alderdale

Lydney & District Hospital

Stonebury Day Hospital

3

Lydney C of E School

Newerne

Highfield Lane

Highfield

Cross Hands

Hurst Farm

B3
1 The Folders

Police Station

Lydney Hlth Cen

Seven Banks Primary School

4

Town Hall

Whitecross School

Whitecross Business Park

Lydney Cricket Club

Lydney Rugby Football Club

Lydney

Steel

Tutnalls

Pylers Way

Rushyleaze

Seven Road

Orchard

Mount Pleasant

Lakeside

Lydney Golf Club

233

Swimming Pool

Cemetery

5

C2
1 Caesars Cl

Naas Court

A48(T)

Mead Lane

6

Ward Industrial Estate

Lydney Station

Lydney Industrial Estate

Naas House

Lydney Yacht Club

Harbour Road

Lydney Harbour

7

New Grounds

8

A **B** **262** **C** **D** **E**

236

A B **208** C D E

1

2

3 Hinton

4

235

5 Brookend

Newtown

6

7 Wanswell

8

A B **264** C D E

Purton

Titel Point

Severn Way

Severn Way

Kingshill Farm

Pool Farm

Simbridge Ln

Halmore

Acton Hall

Church La

The Crescent

Bays Hill Sharpness Primary School

Stambourne Lane

Hainses

Halmore Lane

Oldlands Farm

Pitbrook

Berkeley Vale Community School

Berkeley Leisure Centre

Rookery La

Wanswell Court Farm

Bushy Grove

Gloucester and Sharpness Canal

Quarry Way

Road

Station Road

Ridgeside Industrial Estate

Wickselm

1 grid square represents 500 metres

F   G   H   **209**   J   K

1
Shepherd's Pa

2

3
The Moors

Moorend

4

238

5

6
Horns Hill

7
Woodend

8

Severn Way

Newgrounds Lane

Kingston Road

Uptherbrook Lane

The Warth

Gloucester and Sharpness Canal

Vale of Berkeley

Red Wood

Perry Lane

Hurst Farm

Old Hurst Farm

Billow Brook

Tumpy Green

Billow Farm

Marlpool Farm

adstone

Whitehall Farm

A38

Leathern Bott

Clingre House

F   G   H   **265**   J   K

B4066

A38   Hotel   **Berkeley Road**

Cross

F G H 211 J Middle Street K

I
Osborne House

2
Elmtree Farm

3

4

240

5

6

Silver Street

7
Peak Lane

8

F G Green Street H 267 J Far Green K

Capehall Farm

Downton Farms

Peter's Street

Elmcote Farms

River Cam

Waterend Farm

Westfield Farm

Lapley Farm

Corner Farm

Coaley

The Street

Pinnells End Farm

River Cam

Field Lane

Field Farm

Hamshill

Trenley House

Trenley Road

Green Street

lothorpe

Ashmead House

Cress Green

240

A B 212 C D E

Bridgend

1

Stanl Down

Osborne House

2

Elmtree Farm

Bath Road

Peter's Street

3

† Frocester

PH

Court Road

Frog Lane

Bath Road

Church

Rom

Cem

4

239

5

Frocester Hill

Sandiford's Knoll

Cotswold W

Gipsy Lane

6

Hill Farm

Silver Street

7

Trenley House

Haw Street

Peak Lane

Silver Street

Trenley

Road

Cotswold Way

B4066

Lever's Hill

Benton Court

Tinkley Lane

8

Ham Farm

Coaley Peak

The Ham

Far Green

A B 268 C D E

Ashmead House

Knapp Lane

Cotswold Way

Uley Long Barrow

Hetty Pegler's Tump

Ny sf

PO

Church Street

From Street

1 grid square represents 500 metres

1 grid square represents 500 metres

Bowbridge

Thrupp

The Heavens

Claypits Lane

Claypits Lane

Thrupp Primary School

Far Thrupp

Phoenix Trading Est

Kingfisher Business Park

LONDON ROAD

Brimscombe

Brimscombe Mills Estate

Brimscombe Port Business Park

Quarhouse

Bourne Lane

Bourne

Cemetery

Hotel

Knapp Lane

Burleigh

Burleigh

Cirencester Road

Besbury Park

Cirencester Road

Old Common

Dr Brown's Cl

Windmill Road

Cambridge Way

Police Station

Trinity Drive

The Bulwarks

West End

Box

Minchinhampton

Common Road

Woefuld-

Bubblewell

F1
1 Weyhouse Cl

F5
1 Shepherds Well

G3
1 Silvertree Gdns

H4
1 Brimscombe La

H5
1 The Roundabouts
2 Spinney Ct

H7
1 Burleigh Tor

H8
1 Dr Crawfords Wy
2 Southfield

J5
1 Claire's Cl

J7
1 Blue Boys' Pk

J8
1 Bell La
2 High St
3 Kings St
4 Parsons Ct

K8
1 Eastfield Rd
2 Glebe Rd
3 Syon Rd

K7
1 The Tynings

K5
1 Cotswold Cl

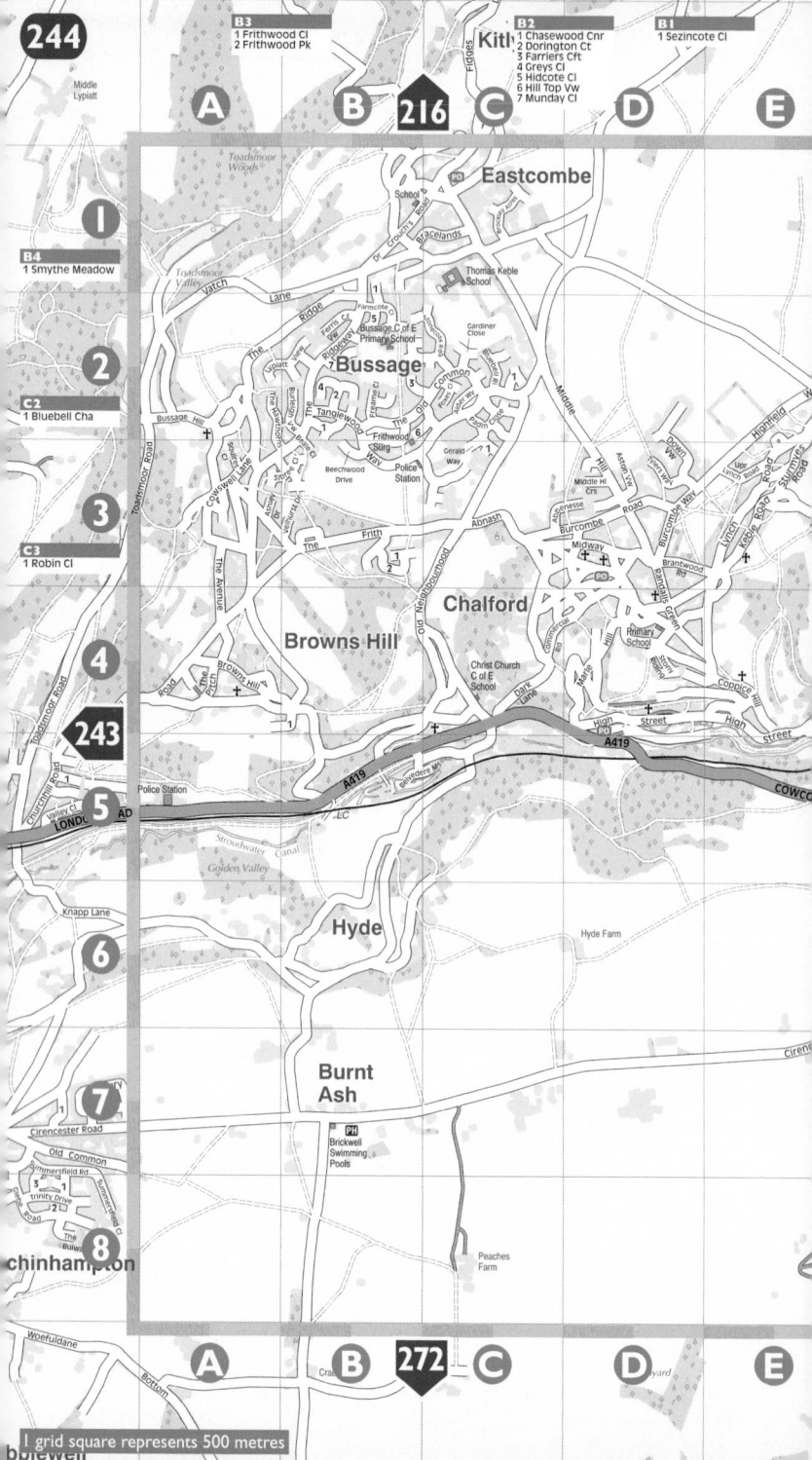

B3
1 Frithwood Cl
2 Frithwood Pk

Kitl

B2
1 Chasewood Cnr
2 Dorington Ct
3 Farriers Cft
4 Greys Cl
5 Hidcote Cl
6 Hill Top Vw
7 Munday Cl

B1
1 Sezincote Cl

B4
1 Smythe Meadow

C2
1 Bluebell Cha

C3
1 Robin Cl

Middle
Lypiatt

A B C D E

Eastcombe

School

Bracelands

Thomas Keble
School

Gardiner
Close

Bussage C of E
Primary School

Bussage

The Old

Tanglewood

Frithwood
Surg

Gerald
Way

Police
Station

Beechwood
Drive

Chalford

Midway
PO

Brantwood
Rd

Primary
School

Christ Church
C of E
School

Browns Hill

The Frith

Neighbourhood

Park
Lane

High
PO

A419

High
Street

High
Street

Coppice

Commercial

COWCC

London Rd

LC

Stroudwater Canal

Golden Valley

Knapp Lane

Hyde

Hyde Farm

Burnt
Ash

Cirencester Road

Old Common

Trinity Drive

The Bulw

PH
Brickwell
Swimming
Pools

Peaches
Farm

chinhampton

Woefuldane

Bottom

Cirence

yard

A B C D E

1 grid square represents 500 metres

bbiewen

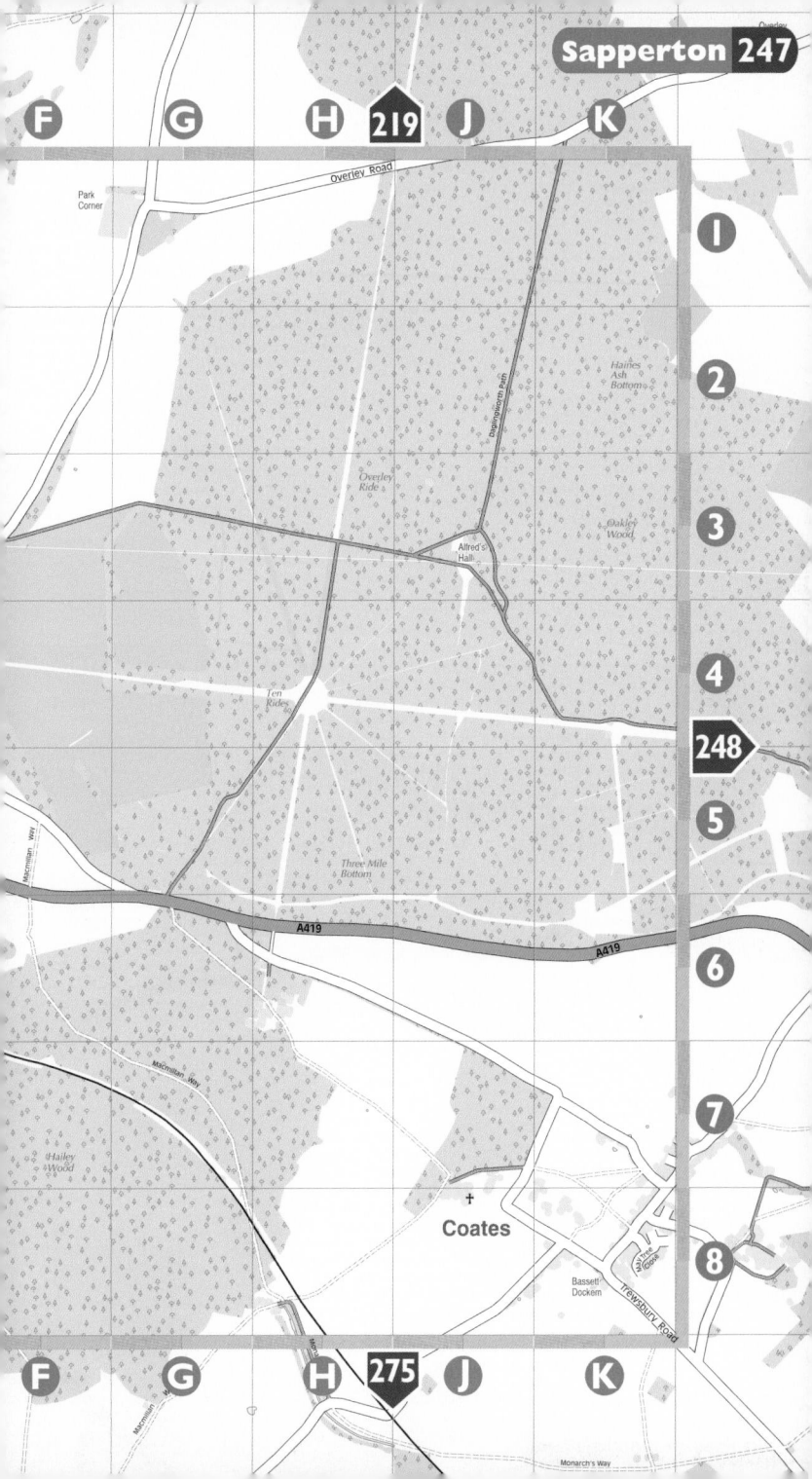

G7
1 Smith's Fld

G8
1 Reeves Cl

Cirencester Golf Club

F   G   H   **221**   J   K

Baunton

I
H2
1 Elphick Rd
2 Glebe Cl

Stratton

2
H7
1 Apsley Cl
2 Shalford Cl

3
H8
1 Foxes Bank Dr
2 Greyfriars Wk
3 Linacre Crs
4 Masefield Rd
5 Michaels Mead
6 Morestall Dr
7 Somerville Ct

Bowling Green

4

250 ▶ BURFOR

5
LONDON R

J4
1 Gooseacre La
2 Trafalgar Rd

6

J5
1 Black Jack St
2 Gosditch St
3 Hakeburn Rd
4 Park St
5 Silver St
6 West Market Pl

Water

7   A429   CI

J6
1 Ashcroft Gdns
2 North Wy
3 Phoenix Wy
4 Querns La

8
Southmead

J8
1 Countess Lilias Rd

Chesterton

F   G   H   **277**   J   K

K8
1 Bridge Cl

K7
1 Bridge End
2 Mercian Cl
3 Sperringate
4 Watermoor Wy

K6
1 Carpenters La
2 Dyer St
3 Purley Av

H6, J7
Street names for these grid squares are listed at the back of the index

250

A **B** **222 C** **D** **E**

A7
1 The Smithy

A6
1 Abbots Rd
2 Akeman Rd
3 Austin Rd
4 Golden Farm Rd
5 Hersta Cl
6 Queen Anne's Rd
7 St Mary's Rd

Wiggold
A5
1 Blue Quarry Rd
2 Churchill Rd
3 Tudor Rd

redhedge
Covert

1

A8
1 Kingsmead
2 North Hill Rd
3 Nursery Rd

2

B7
1 Crabtree La

3

Whiteway
Farm

HI Crs

Yellow School
Copse

Hare
Bushes

B4425

Bowling **4** een

Norcote

249

GROVE LANE

5

BURFORD ROAD

A429

Arnold's
Way

LONDON ROAD   A417

Lyndon Rd

The Beeches

Cirencester Kingshill
School

Whiteway
Business Centre

Whitesands
Road
The
Green

Archery Road

Pheasant Way

Park

6

SWINDON ROAD

Queen Elizabeth

Golden Farm Road

New Mills

A417

Cirencester County
Junior School

Watermoor

Kings Hill

7

North Home Road

A429

Prospect
Place
Queen
Street

CIRENCESTER

Kingshill Lane

Witpit Lane

Witpit Lane

Primary
School

School Lane

8

BRISTOL ROAD

Love Lane
Industrial Estate

Crickage Road

SWINDON ROAD

loucestershire
county Council

Bridge Road

Southmead

Kingsway

B Tech
Business
Park

Siddington

Preston

Love Lane
Trading Estate

Cirencester
Business Estate

Elliott
Road

A **B** **278 C** **D** **E**

Siddington House

H5
1 The Pleydells

F Barnfields
G
H 223
J
K

I
1

Ampney Knowle

2 Lower Field Farm

Brookfield Farm

Glebe Farm

Ampney Riding

3

Bown's Farm
B4425
Ampneyfield

Long Furlong

Park Farm

4

252

Hilcot End

5

Ampney Park

School Lane

Allotment Lane

The Downs Field

Ampney Crucis

LONDON ROAD

A417

PH Hotel
A417
Ampney Brook

6

Eastington House

A417

Waterton House

7

Ampney St Pete

ugustine

8

F
G
H 279
Church Lane
J
K

Manor House

Harnhill

A B **224** C D E

Re
o

Welsh Way

Ampney
Knowle

1

2

Lower Field
Farm

Brookfield
Farm

Poulton
Grange

Long Furlong

3

GL7

4

◀ **251**

5

Hilcot
E

Ampney
St Mary

Betty's
Grave

6

Bell Lane

Ampney Brook

7

A417

Eastington
House

Ampney
St Peter

ASHBROOK LA

LONDON R

Stonel
Poun

8

Crickade Street

Poulton

A B **280** C D E

Priory
Farm

F G H 225 J K

I
2
3
4
254
5
6
7
8

Welsh Way

Hartwell
Farm

Poulton
Fields

Sunhill

Welsh Way

Honeycomb
Leaze Farm

Toms
Copse

Manor
Farm

Verge
Farm

A417

A417

F G H 281 J K

Grove
Elizabeth
Gardens

St Mary's
Fie
Meysey
Close

High Street

Gloucestershire County
Wiltshire County

A   B   226   C   D   E

Hotel

Ne

Coneygar
Wood

Conegyar Road   Fowler's Hill

old arch   Spring
Gardens

1

Church Mawley Road

Quenington

2

Donkeywell
Farm

3

4

253

Hon
Leaze

5

6

Welsh Way

Broad Water

7

Welsh Way

FAIRFC

Park
Coln Gat
Police St

Milton End

Mill Lane

The
Green

MILTON   BRIDGE
STREET   STREET

PO   Hotel

Coln House
Special School

8

Horcott

Horcott
Road
Industrial Estate

A417

A   B   282   C   D   E

Courtbro

Horcott
Industrial
Estate

F7
1 Barker Pl
2 Beauchamp Cl
3 Keble Lawns
4 Manor Cl

F8
1 Beaumoor Pl

F G H **227** J K

I
2
3
4
256
5
6
7
8

Macaroni Wood

Barrow Elm Farm

Homeleaze Farm

Leafield Farm

Lea Wood

Farhill Farm

South Farm

Snowstorm Gorse

Crabtree Pk

Marys Dr

Aldsworth Cl

The Quarry

Churchill

Fairford FC

LONDON ROAD

A417

East End

Thornhill Farm

F G H **283** J K

...worth ...er Park

A

B

228

C

D

E

D3
1 Wadham Cl

Homeleaze
Farm

Macaroni
Wood

Hammersmith Bottom

Tiltup

Southrop C of E
Primary School

South

Lechlade Road

Quarry
View

Dawes
Close

PO

South Farm

255

Stanford
Hall

Snowstorm
Gorse

Claydon
Fields

Thornhill Farm

Brixworth Lane

Claydon
House

A

B

284

C

D

E

I grid square represents 500 metres

I

2

3

4

5

6

7

8

H8
1 Swansfield

F   G   H   229   J   K

1
2
3
4
5
6
7
8

Shire Gate

The Pils

fyield

A361

Langford Downs Farm

Gloucestershire County
Oxfordshire County

Common Barn Farm

Hulse Ground Farm

Great Lemhill Farm

Little Faringdon

Langford House

Little Lemhill Farm

A361

Horseshoe Lake

Briary Road
Kingsmead
Kingsfield Circus
Kingsfield West
Kingsfield South
Gassons Road
Lane

STATION ROAD

Butler's Field

Cuthwine Place

Butler's Court

Cemetery

F   G   H   285   J   K

F G H **231** J K

Woolaston
Woodside

I

Oakhill Wood

East Wood

Chase House

Keynsham

Woolaston Slade

2

Park Hill Road

Park Hill

Park Hill Road

Nature Reserve

B4228

PARK HILL LANE

Gloucestershire Way

Little Common

Gloucestershire Way

3 Woolasto

High Woolaston

Ashwell Grove

Braves Road

St

Beacon Ash

Gloucestershire Way

Kelva Lane

Ashwell Grange

4

260

Rosemary Lane

5

A48(T)

Stroat

6

Rosemary Lane

7

Wibdon

Hanley Lane

8

A48(T)

Hanley House

Philpots Court

F G H **289** J K

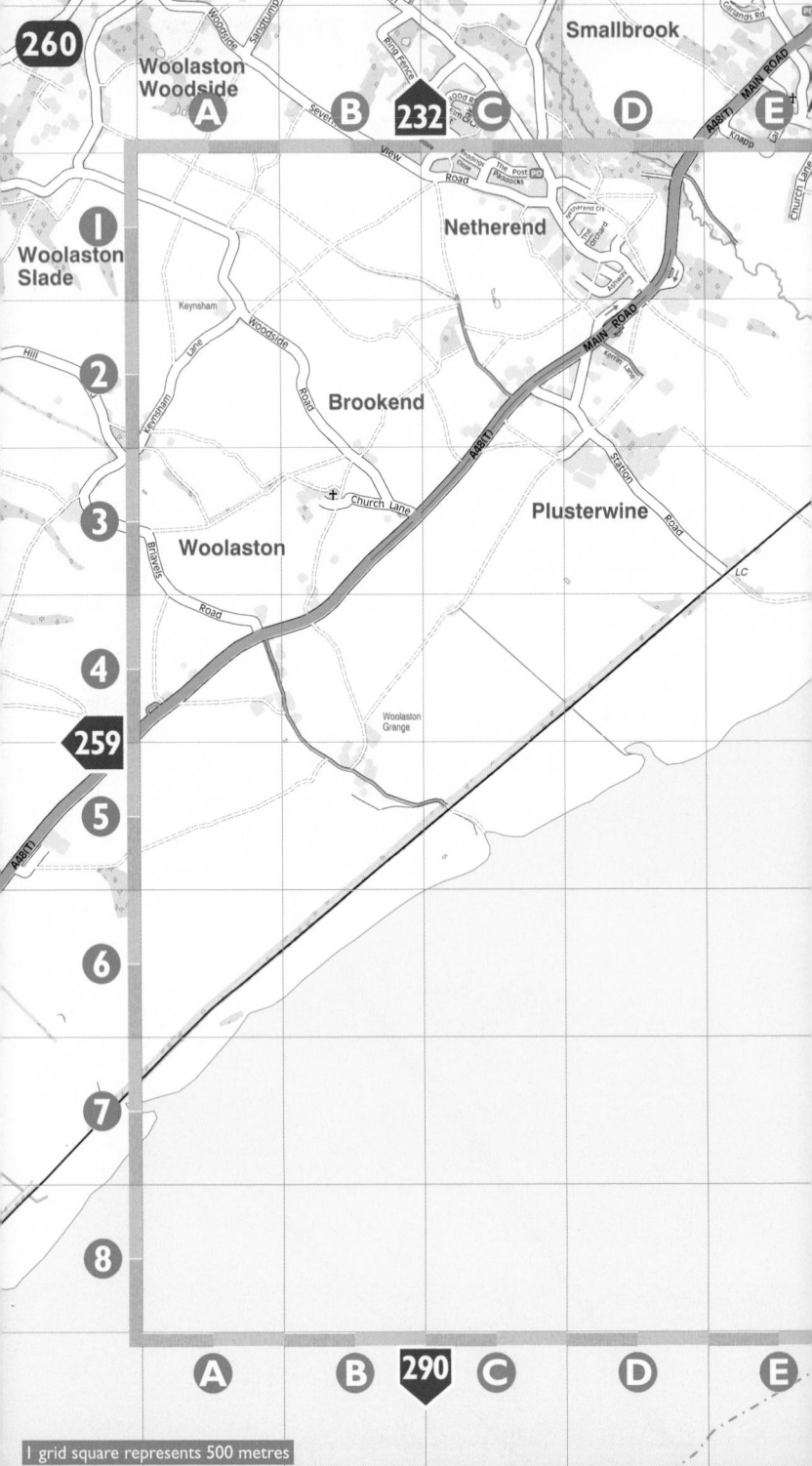

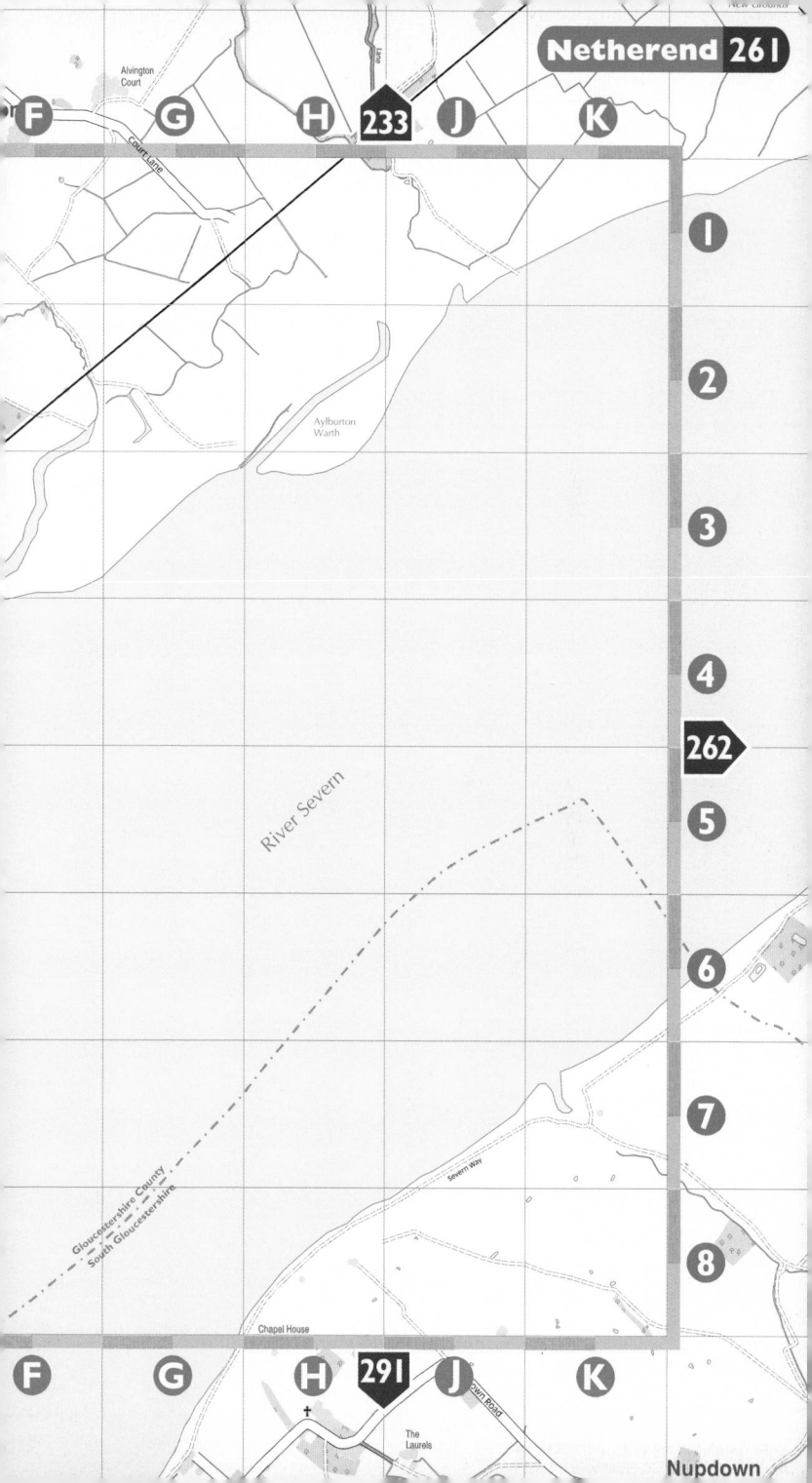

Alvington
Court

Court Lane

F **G** **H** 233 **J** **K**

New Grounds

1

2

Aylburton
Warth

3

4

262

River Severn

5

6

7

Severn Way

Gloucestershire County
South Gloucestershire

8

Chapel House

F **G** **H** 291 **J** **K**

The Laurels

Down Road

Nupdown

262

A   B   234   C   D   E

1

2

3

4

261

5

Severn Way

Severn House Farm

Severn Lane

6

Worldsend

County of Gloucestershire
South Gloucestershire

7

Worldsend Farm

8

A   B   292   C   D   E

Day...

Up

Nupdown

1 grid square represents 500 metres

Hook Street

Ham

Hystfield

The Paddock

Severn Way

Berkeley Pill

Oakhunger Ln

Hamfield Farm

Severn Way

Hamfield Lane

Floodgates Farm

Hamfield Lane

Woodlands Lane

Woodlands Farm

Blackhall Cott

Willis Elm

Park Farm

Park House

Whitcliff Park (Deer Park)

Pedington Elm

Pedington Farm

Oakhunger Farm

Westfield Brake

Forest View Road

Cemetery

Berkeley Primary School

Berkeley Hospital

Salter St

Lantern Cl

Jumpers Lane

Marybrook Medical Centre

Brownsmill Farm

ton

235

264

293

GL13

Leathern
Bottle

Clingre
House

Whitehall
Farm

B4066
A38
Hotel **Berkeley Road**
B4066
TAIT'S HILL

New Clingre
Farm

Lorridge
Farm

Clingre
Farm

B4060

Kitts Green
Farm

Standle
Farm

Standle Lane

M5

266

Stinchcombe

Blanchworth

Goldwick
Farm

Crossways

Hogsdown
Farm

M5

Fortune
Farm

Maycroft Lane

Lower Wick

**Upper
Wick**

295

Middle Wick

**Nibley
Green**

Isle
of Rhe

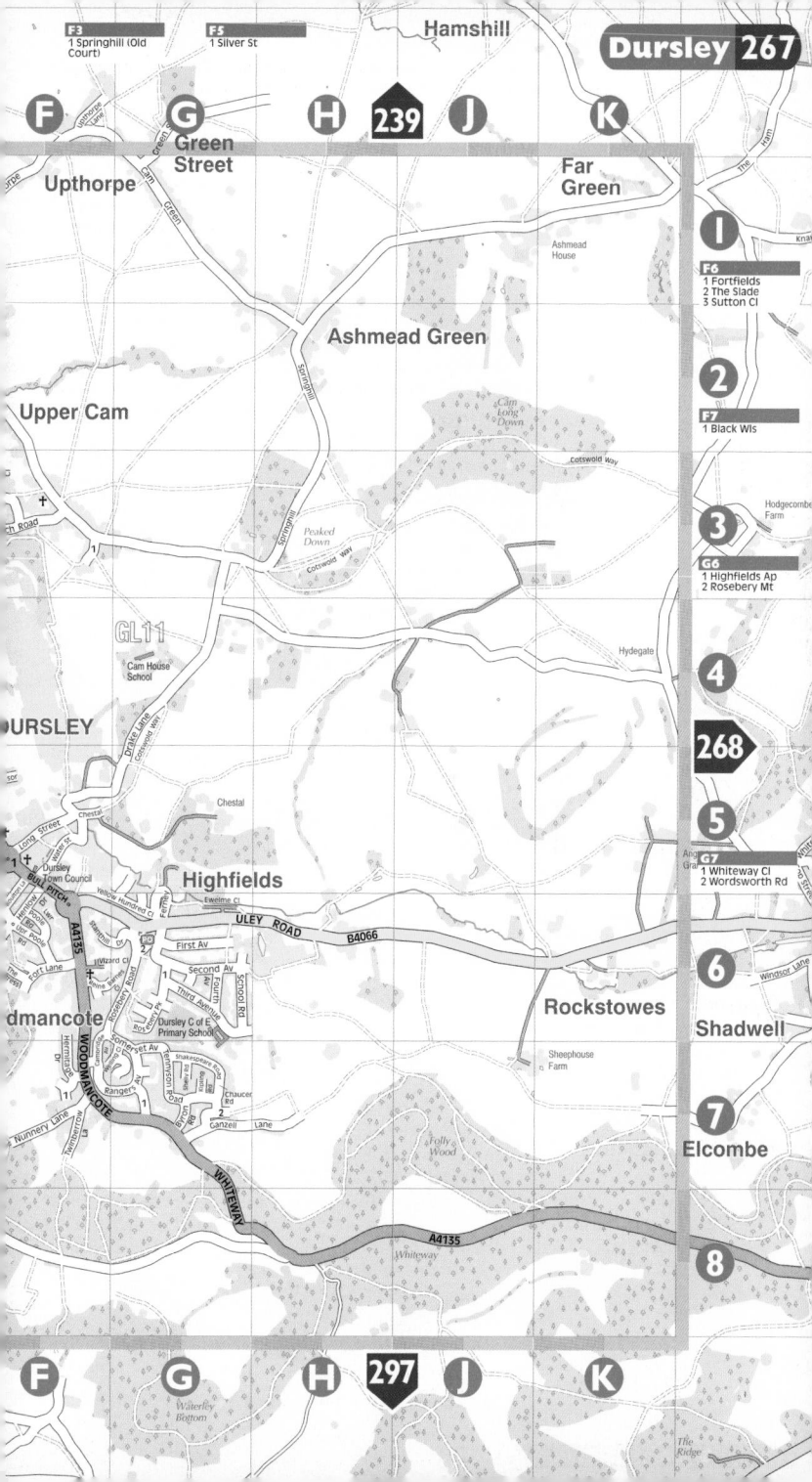

F G H **241** J K

I

Collier's
Wood

Tinkley Lane

Tinkley
Farm

Nympsfield Road

2 High Wood

Bewlas Wood

Lower Lutheredge
Farm

Field Farm

3

dcock

Upper Lutheredge
Farm

Sallywood
Farm

4

270

B4058

Nupend

5

Boscombe Lane

Woodleaze
Farm

6

Kingscote
Wood

7

Binley
Farm

8

F G **299** J K

Kingscote

Ashel Barn

Lower
Hazelcote

Cherington

Black
Covert

Lowesmoor
Farm

Hazelton
Covert

Macmillan Way

Hazelton
Manor Farm

Oatfi

Windmill
Tump
Long Borrow
•

Tump
Plantation

Wickfield
Wood

Grove
Farm

Trull
House

A433

Holt
Farm

Culkerton

Chesterton

249

Upper
Siddington

278

Ewen

Shorncote

307

F G H **251** J K

1

2

3

4

280

5

6

7

8

Harnhill

Church Lane

Manor House

Driffield

Manor Farm

A417(T)

Cirencester Road

Driffield Cross Roads

Northmoor Lane

Northmoor

A419(T)

Manor Farm

Vines Brake

Sisters Farm

Fosse Farm

Cirencester Road

Dukes Brake

Churn

Wildmoorway Lane

Station Road

Cirencester Road

Manor Farm

Dove

Station Road

SPINE ROAD (EAST)

Cerney Wick Lane

B4696

Cerney w

F G H **309** J K

Meysey Hampton 281

F | A417 | G | H | 253 | J | K | A417

Verge Farm

Gloucestershire County

1

Hampton Grove
Elizabeth Gardens
St Mary PIB
High Street
Meysey Close
Hampton Croft
Church Street
School
School La
PIB
PH
Beech Lea
Strawberry
High Street

Meysey
Hampton

2

Marston
Hill

3

Wiltshire County
Gloucestershire County

4

282

5

Castle Hill
Farm

6

The Street

7

Marston
Meysey

pney

8

The Street

F | G | H | 311 | J | K

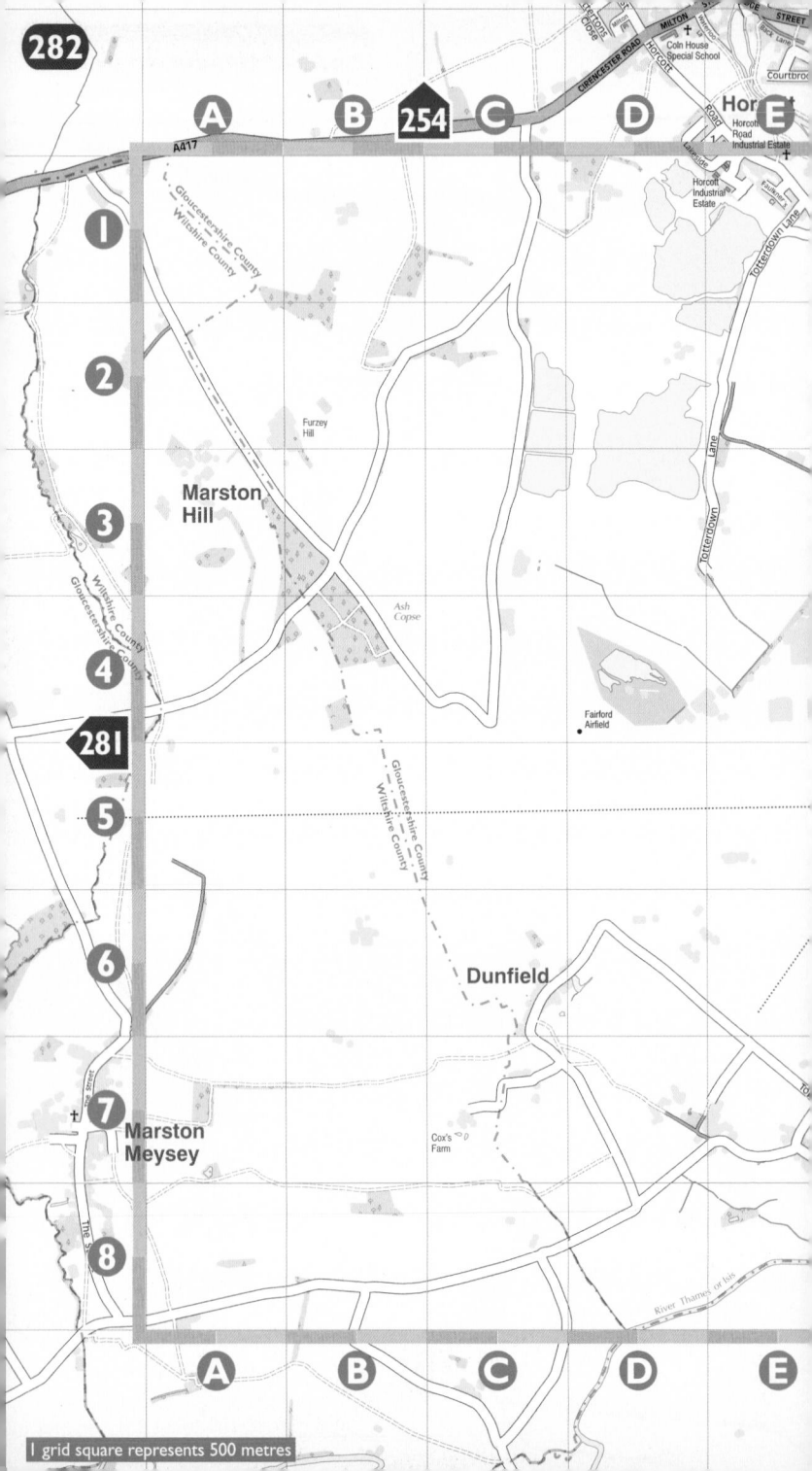

F8
1 Swynford Cl
2 Wakefield Cl

End

F G H **255** J K

Thornhill Farm

1

2

3

Cotswold
Water Park

Whelford

4

284

5

6

Ham
Barn

7

8

Whelford Road

John of
Gaunt Rd

npsford

F G H J K

Gloucestershire County
Swindo

Hannington
Bridge

A Thornhill Fa

B

256 laydon
elds

C

D

E Brynworth Lane

I

Claydon
House

Warren's Cross
Farm

A417

Brynworth Lane

2

Cotswold
Water Park

3

4

River Coln

283

Inglesha

5

Dudgrove
Farm

Gloucestershire County
Swindon

6

Ham
Barn

7

8

River Thames or Isis

A

B

C

D

Thames Pat

E

Thames Farm

F G H J K

Grafton

Langley Lane

A4095

I

2

Radcot
Bridge Farm

3

Thames Path

4

River Thames or Isis

Camden Farm

Thames Path

✝

5

**Eaton
Hastings**

6

Crabtree Farm

7

Stud Farm

Northfield
Farm

HLADE ROAD A417

8

Manor Farm

LECHLADE ROAD A417

Eaton Wood

F G H J K

Step Farm

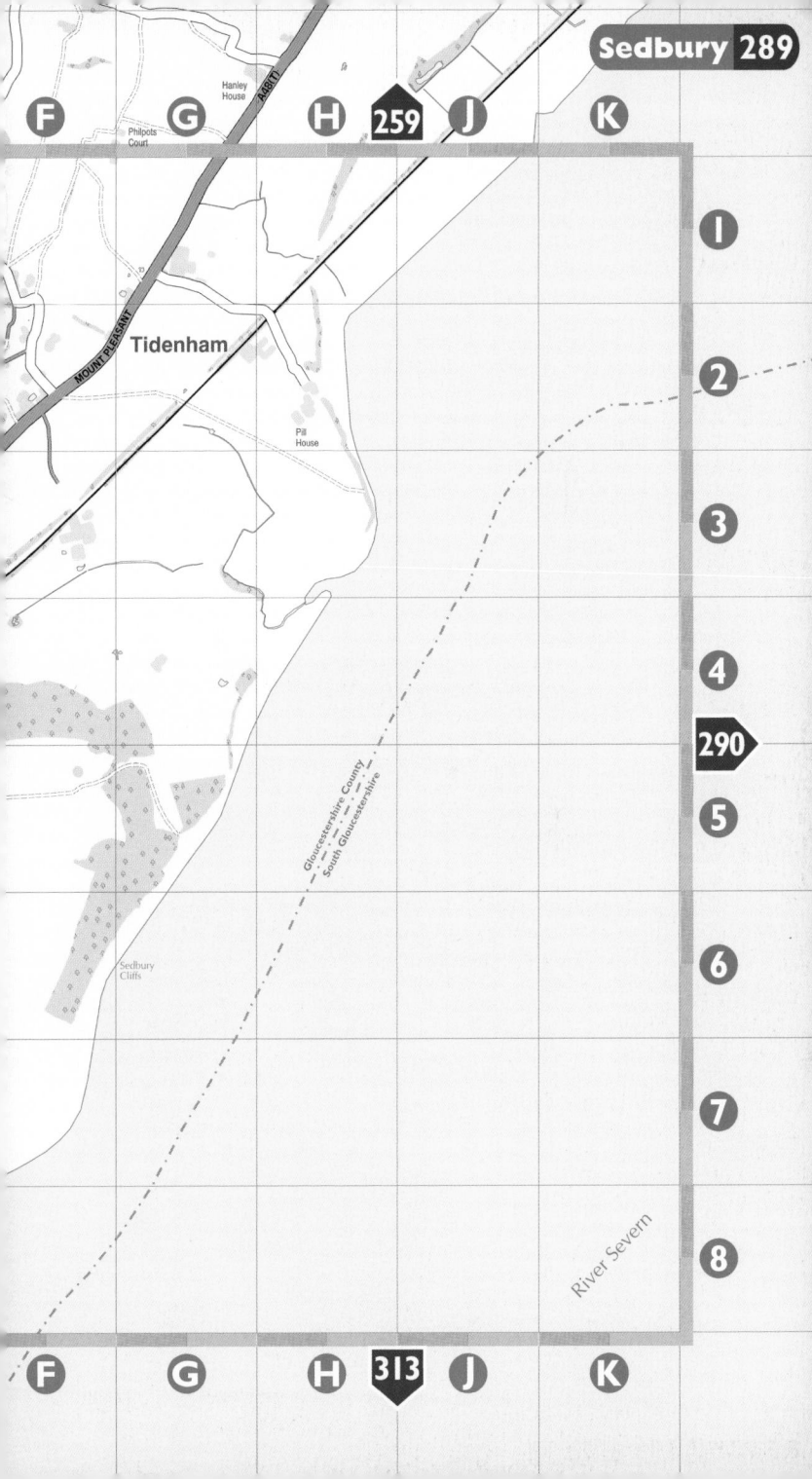

Hanley House

Philpots Court

A48(T)

MOUNT PLEASANT

Tidenham

Pill House

I

2

3

4

290

5

6

7

8

Gloucestershire County
South Gloucestershire

Sedbury Cliffs

River Severn

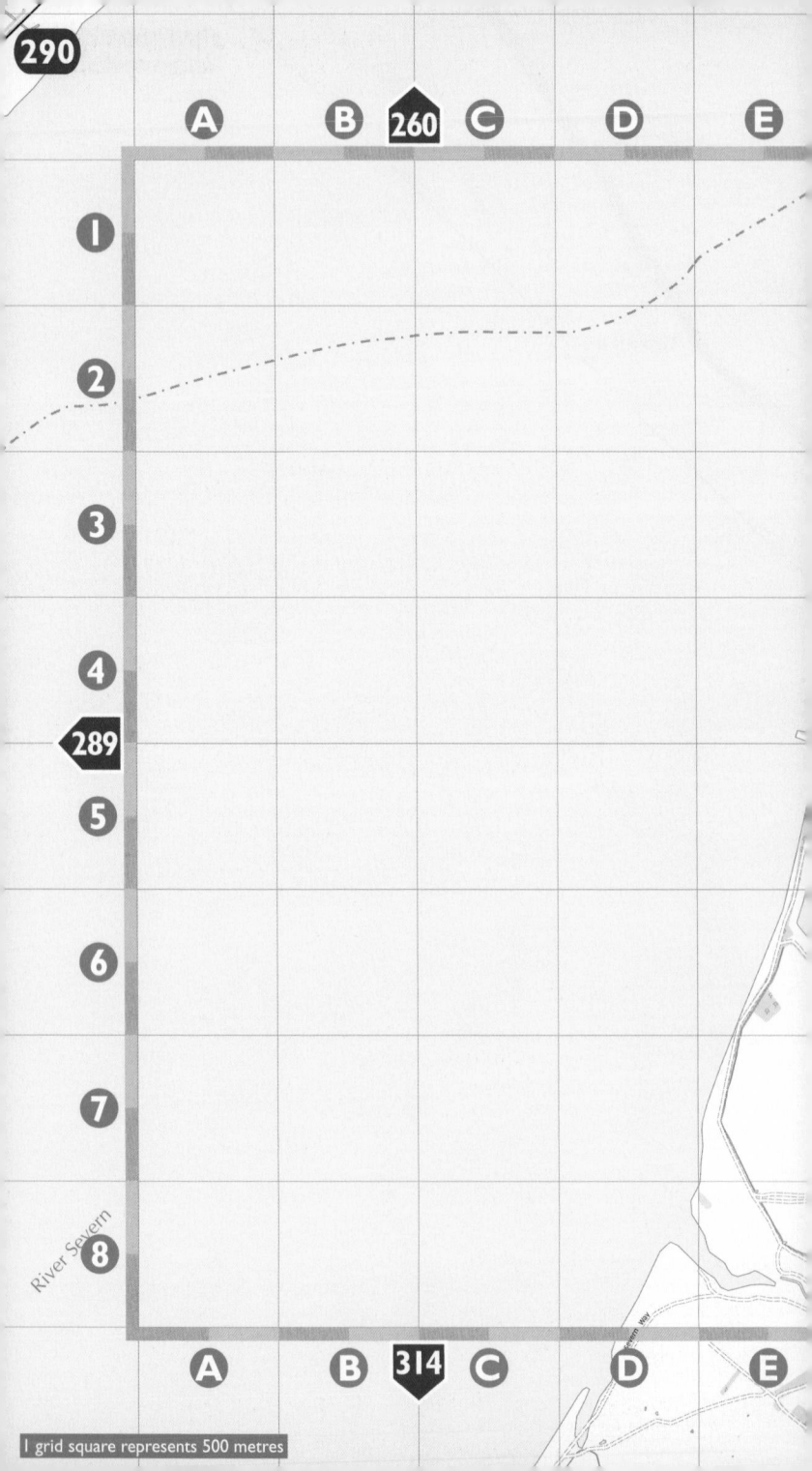

260

A   B   C   D   E

1

2

3

4

289

5

6

7

River Severn

8

A   B   314   C   D   E

1 grid square represents 500 metres

F G H 261 J K

I
Nupdown
2
3
4
292
5
6
7
8

Chapel House
Nupdown Road
The Laurels

Shepperdine
Shepperdine Road

Jobsgreen Farm
Shepperdine Road
Knight's Farm

Power Station
s Centre

Hill Lane

Oldbury Naite

The Naite
Fost Lane

Oldbury House

W. End
Westend Lane
Camp Road
Ham Lane

estend

Featherbed Lane
PO

Oldbury-on-Severn

F G H 315 J K

Chapel Road
Pickeamoor Lane

PH

Marsh Lane

Pullens Green

Oldbury-on-S...

Gloucestershire Cou...
South Gloucestershire

292

A   B   **262**   C   D   E

B

I

Nupdown

Dayhouse Farm

Tranton Lane

Upp

2

Upp

3

Hill Lane

Nupdown Road

Scotlands Farm

Hill Court

Hill

4

Woodend Lane

Church Hill Wood

291

5

Lane

6

Rockhampton Rhine

7

Lodge Farm

Lane

8

Lane

Duckhole   Newton

A   B   **316**   C   D   E

Horse Lane

F G H 263 J K

I

2

3

4

294

5

6

7

8

F G H 317 J K

Hystfield

Appleridge Farm

Appleridge Lane

Gloucestershire County
South Gloucestershire

Newpark Farm

Lower Stone

Moorslade

The Elms

Sundayshill Lane

Sundayshill

H M Young Offender Institute

Sundayshill Lane

Stone

Stone with Woodford C of E Primary School

Meadow

A38

Falfield

Mill La

Church Av

PO

A38

Eastwood Park

Rockhampton

Pound House Farm

Pedington

Gambri

Lane

294

A   B 264 C   D   E

I   Swanley

Swanley La

2   Mitford La

Woodford
Damery Lane

Stone with
Woodford C of E
Primary School   Michael Wood Service Area

3   Damery La

Middle Mill Farm

Stone
Court   Damery Lane
Mead

4

293

Moorslade   Green Farm

5   Damery Lane

Moorslade Lane

6
Heneage Cl

Heneage La   Old
Court
Farm

7 Falfield
Sundayshill Lane   Mill La

Eastfire Cl   Brook Farm

Church Rd   B4509
H M Young Offender
Institute   PO

Junction 14   Tortworth
VC Primary School

8

Eastwood
Park

A   B 318 C   D   E

Cambrill
Lane   Leyhill

1 grid square represents 500 metres

F7
1 Chipping Cl
2 Dyersbrook
3 High St
4 Tabernacle Pitch

G7
1 Cotswold Wy
2 Durn's Rd
3 Ludgate Hl
4 Manor La
5 Mitre Pitch

G8
1 Shepherd's Leaze
2 Shepherds Wk
3 Turnpike Av

H6
1 Beechwood Gv

F   G   **267**   H   J   K

I

2

3

4

298

5

6

7

8

Whiteway

Waterley
Bottom

The Ridings

Cotswold
Edge
Golf Club

The Ridings

B4058

Tyley Bottom

Old London Road

B4058

Park Lane

Coombe Road

Holywell   Coombe

Coombe Lane

Blackquarries Hl

Blackquarries Hill

Newmark
Park

Synwell

Cotswold Wy

Cotswold Way

Parklands

CULVERHAY

COOMBE ROAD

Valley
Road

Court Orchard

Culverhay
Surgery

The Chipping

Cotswold Wy

OLD TOWN

The Studio
Gallery

Long Street

Orchard Road

Synwell

Jay's
Mead
Cemetery

Cherry
Orchard

London Road

Market

Clarence
Rd

Water Lane

WOTTON-UNDER-EDGE

The
British
School

Mill Hill Rd

Pitman Place

Wortley Rd

Bradley Rd

Henbury
Tor

Wotton Court

Cotswold Way

Bearlands

Leys
Farm

Ⓐ Ⓑ **268** Ⓒ Ⓓ Ⓔ

I

A4135

B4058

The Ridge

Bowcott Farm

Symonds Hall Farm

2

Cotswold Edge Golf Club

3

4

Ashcroft Road

Ashcroft House

Tyley Bottom

297

Sawcombe Farm

5

6

Ferney Farm

Ozleworth

Park Lane

Blackquarries Hill

7

Newark Park

Ozleworth Park

Blacksmith Hill

8

West

Ozleworth Bottom

Ⓐ Ⓑ **322** Ⓒ Ⓓ Ⓔ

Mill Lane

olwell

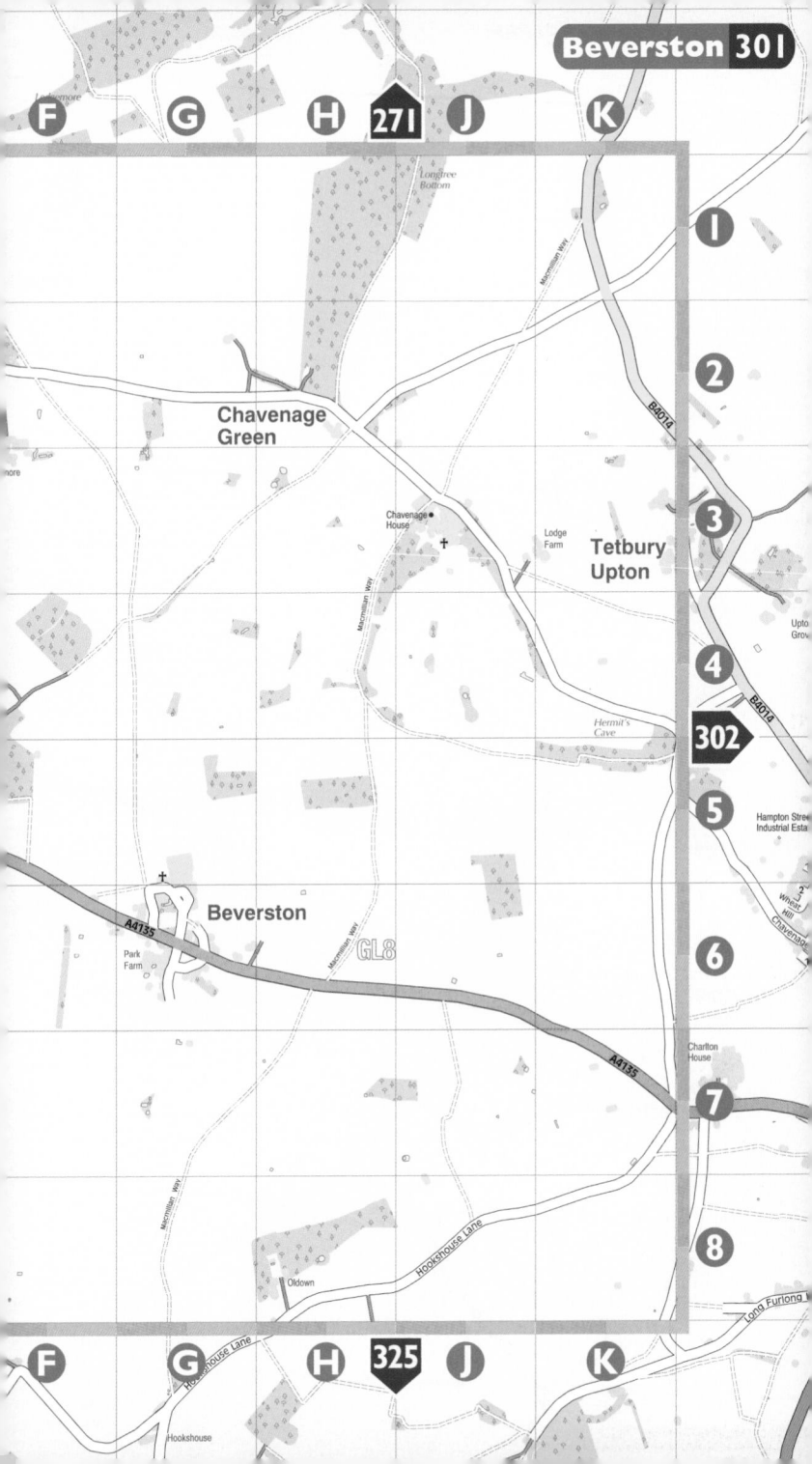

302

B5
1 Woodward Cl

A6
1 Newleaze Gdns
2 Romney Rd

A5
1 Webb Rd

Star Farm

A   B   272   C   D   E

I

B6
1 Alexander Gdns
2 Chestnut Cl
3 Elizabeth Gdns
4 Five Trees Ct
5 London Rd
6 Malthouse Wk

Summerwell Farm

2

B7
1 Monarch's Wy
2 Old Brewery La

Colly Farm

3   Tetbury

Lodge Farm

C5
1 Jacobs Cl
2 Suffolk Cl

Lowfield Farm

Upton Grove

4

301

Highfield Farm

5

Hampton Street Industrial Estate

Sir William Romneys School

Ryland Close

C6
1 Cherry Orchard Rd
2 Cookspool
3 Cotswold Cl

A433   Ilsom

LONG

6

St Marys C of E Primary Sch

Priory Industrial Estate

Tetbury Industrial Estate

C7
1 Chantry Ct
2 Gumstool Hl
3 Long St
4 Market Pl
5 Silver St

Charlton House

HAMPTON STREET   LONG LANE

CIRENCESTER   Herd Lane

7   A4135   CHARLTON ROAD   NEW CHURCH ST

Romney Ho Surgery   Connoisseur Gal

The Clinic   Tetbury Gal

TETBURY

Eight Bells Gal

FOX HILL

Monarch's Wy   The Folly Farm

Old Quarries Industrial Estate   NEWNTON ROAD   B4014

8

Long Furlong Lane

BATH ROAD

A   B   326   C   D   E

Slads Farm

I grid square represents 500 metres

Tetbury 303

E8
1 Brookside

274

Monkerton Way

A433

I

Holt
Farm

Culkerton

Road

2

Manor
Farm

New
Barn

3

Morgans
Tynings

4

Manor
Farm

Ashley

Gloucestershire County
Wiltshire County

Monkerton Way

303

5

Fosse
Gate

Stadborough
Copse

6

**West
Crudwell**

7

Davis
Ct

Chedglow

Tuffleys Lane

Hobt

The
Ridgeway

Crudwell Lane

8

Tetbury

The
Pattance
Lane

PO

STREET

THE

The
Butts

The

Goods Lands

A429

A429

F G H 275 J K

I

2

Kemble Wood

Gloucestershire County
Wiltshire County

3

Woodlands

Dean Plantation

4

306

5

Laynes Farm

The Grove

Dean Farm

Chelworth

Chelworth Lawns

A429

6

Oaksey Wood

Crudwell La

7

Flintham House

of E School

8

Eastcourt

F G H J K

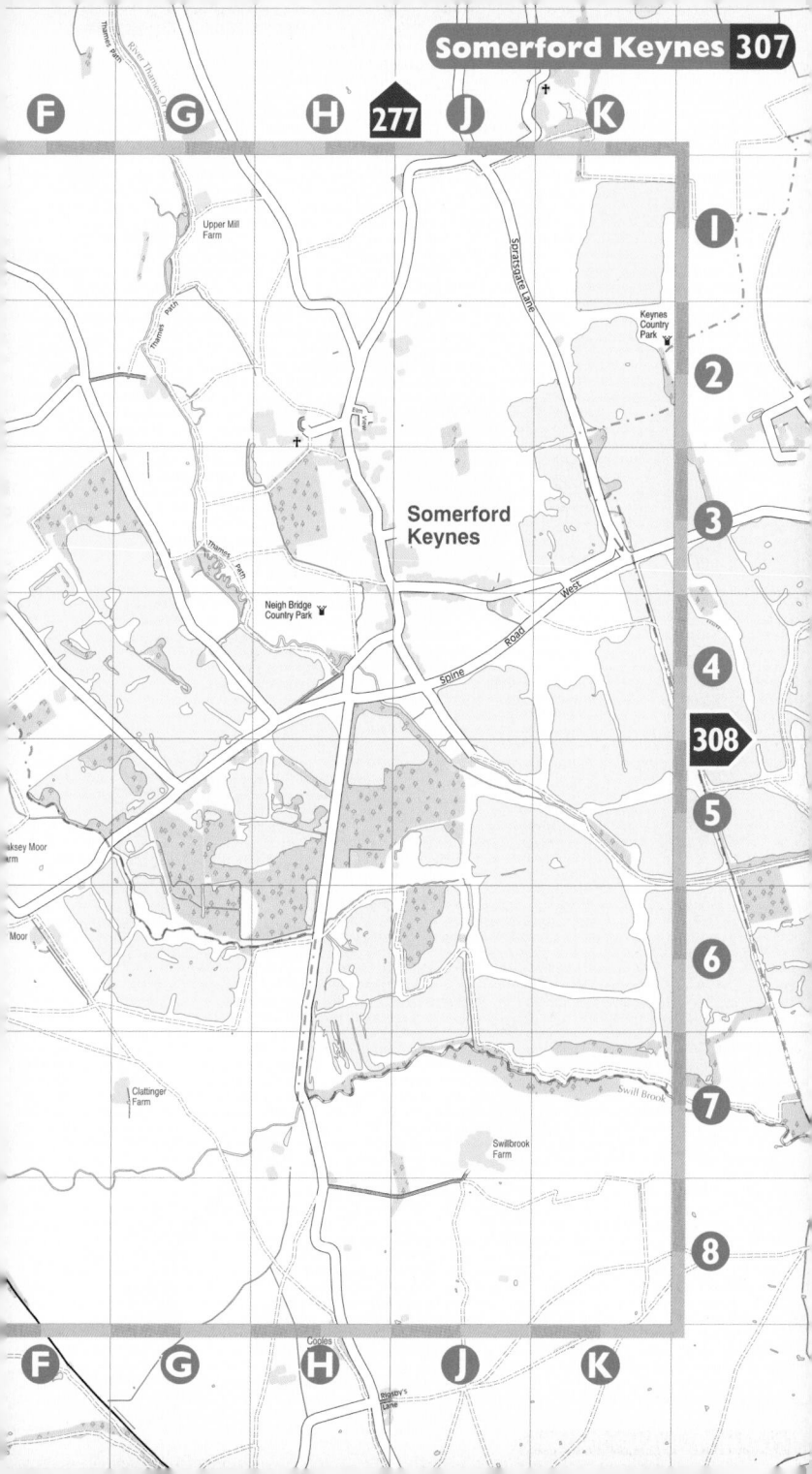

F   G   H   277   J   K

I

Upper Mill
Farm

Thames Path

Keynes
Country
Park

2

3

Somerford
Keynes

Neigh Bridge
Country Park

Spine   Road   West

4

308

5

aksey Moor
Farm

Moor

6

Swill Brook

7

Clattinger
Farm

Swillbrook
Farm

8

F   G   H   Coples   J   K

Bigsby's
Lane

F G H 279 J K

279

I

Cerney Wick Lane

Spine Road (East)

Cerney Wick Lane

B4696

Broadway Lane

Wickwater Lane

Cerney Wick

Riding School

2

Friday's Ham Lane

Cleveland Farm

Gloucestershire County
Wiltshire County

3

Ham Lane

Thames

4

310

Hailstone Hill

5

6

Thames or Isis

Waterhay Bridge

Manor Farm

Bournelake Farm

7

Waterhay

Malmesbury Road

Archer's Farm

Bourne Lake Park

B4040

8

Chelworth Lower Green

F G H J K

Leigh

Malmesbury Road

Braydon Lane

Leigh C of E School

Chelworth Industrial Estate

310

A B **280** C D E

D5
1 Bailiffe Piece

C7
1 Bishopsfield

C6
1 Cliffords

Manor
Farm

Down Ampney Rd

1

D6
1 Kitefield
2 Pleydells

Westfield
Farm

Cirencester Road

Latton

Cerney W 2

Riding
School

D7
1 Parsonage Farm
2 Portwell

A419(T)

The Street

Croft Lane

Goody

Sheeppen Bridge

3

E6
1 Hammonds

4

Thames Path

North
Meadow

Thames Path

Nature
Reserve

A419(T)

309

5

Hailstone
Hill

Stones Lane

Horse
Pond

6

Stones Lane

Lady Mead

Horsey Down

Cricklade Leisure
Centre

Fullers Av

Bath

Infants
School

Junior
School

Prior Park
Preparatory School

**CALCUTT
ST**

Golf Course

COMMON HILL

Golf Club

The Forty

Cricklade
Town Council

HIGH STREET

B4040

CRI

7

Bournelake
Farm

Cricklade Hotel &
Country Club

The Forty

B4553

Dance
Common

MALMESBURY ROAD

**Chelworth Upper
Green**

Chelworth Road

8

**Chelworth Lower
Green**

A B C D E

Chelworth Industrial
Estate

Broadleaze
Farm

A **B** **288** **C** **D** **E**

Pembroke Junior & Infant School

1

Bulwark

Thornwell Junior School

2

M48

3

Junction 2

Army Apprentices College

Beachley

4

M48

5

Beachley Point

6

7

Gloucestershire County
South Gloucestershire

8

A **B** **328** **C** **D** **E**

Monmouthshire
Gloucestershire

1 grid square represents 500 metres

J7
1 Orchard Dr

F G H 289 J K

River Se

I

2

3

4

314

5

6

Double
Farm

7

8

B4461

Severn Bridge

Severn Way

Severn Way

Severn View Service Area

Toll

M48

B4461

Manor
Farm

Severn Way

Junction 1

A403

Saniol
the Rw

PH

Old Passage

Severn Way

Aust

F G H 329 J K

Cake Pill
Gout

A403

Old Splatt Rhine

F Westend

G

H

291

J

K

Oldbury-on-Severn

I

2

3

4

316

5

6

7

8

Westend Lane
W End
Oldbury House
W End
The Naite
Camp Road
Sherbed Lane
PO
PH
Chapel Road
Pickedmoor Lane
Pullens Green
Oldbury-on-Severn C of E School
Church Road
Kington Road
Parkmill Farm
Churchmead Farm
Kington House
St Arild's House
Slock Farm
Stock Hill
Hotel
St Marys C of E Se
Sheil Scho
St Glo
Kington
Kington Lane
Kington Lane
Westwing School
Mumbleys Lane
Hay Wood
BS35
Jubilee Way
Jubilee Way
Club House
Golf Course
Gate Farm
Mumbleys Lane
Marlwood Gr
ALVESTON HILL

F

G

H

331

J

K

Alveston Down

VATTINGSTONE LANE
Marlwood School
Alveston
DOWN ROAD
Strode Com
Rode Common

316

B6
1 Dart Cl
2 St Mary St
3 Tyndale Vw
4 Upper Bath Rd

C3
1 Pittville Cl

C4
1 Cossham Cl
2 Hawthorn Crs
3 Howard Rd
4 North East Rd
5 Whitfield Rd

C5
1 Chestnut Dr
2 Sycamore Dr
3 Thicket Wk

C6
1 Ladden Ct
2 Springfield

C7
1 Cherwell Cl
2 Medina Cl

D4
1 Campion Cl
2 Foxglove Cl
3 Fulmar Cl
4 Kestrel Cl
5 Kingfisher Cl
6 Nightingale Cl

D6
2 Hillbrook Rd
3 Homefield
3 Meadowside
4 Shannon Ct
5 Sibland Way

B5
1 Crispin La
2 Quaker La
3 Saw Mill La

B4
1 Coombe Av
2 Kensington Cl
3 Orchard Gra

B3
1 Kempton Cl

D7
1 Armstrong Cl
2 Bockerem Cl
3 Brookmead
4 Solent Wy
5 Tamar Cl

E5
1 Cleveland Cl

A B 292 C D Newton E

Lower Morton

Upper Morton

GLOUCESTER ROAD

Morton

THORNBURY

315

Alveston

DOWN ROAD

332

1 grid square represents 500 metres

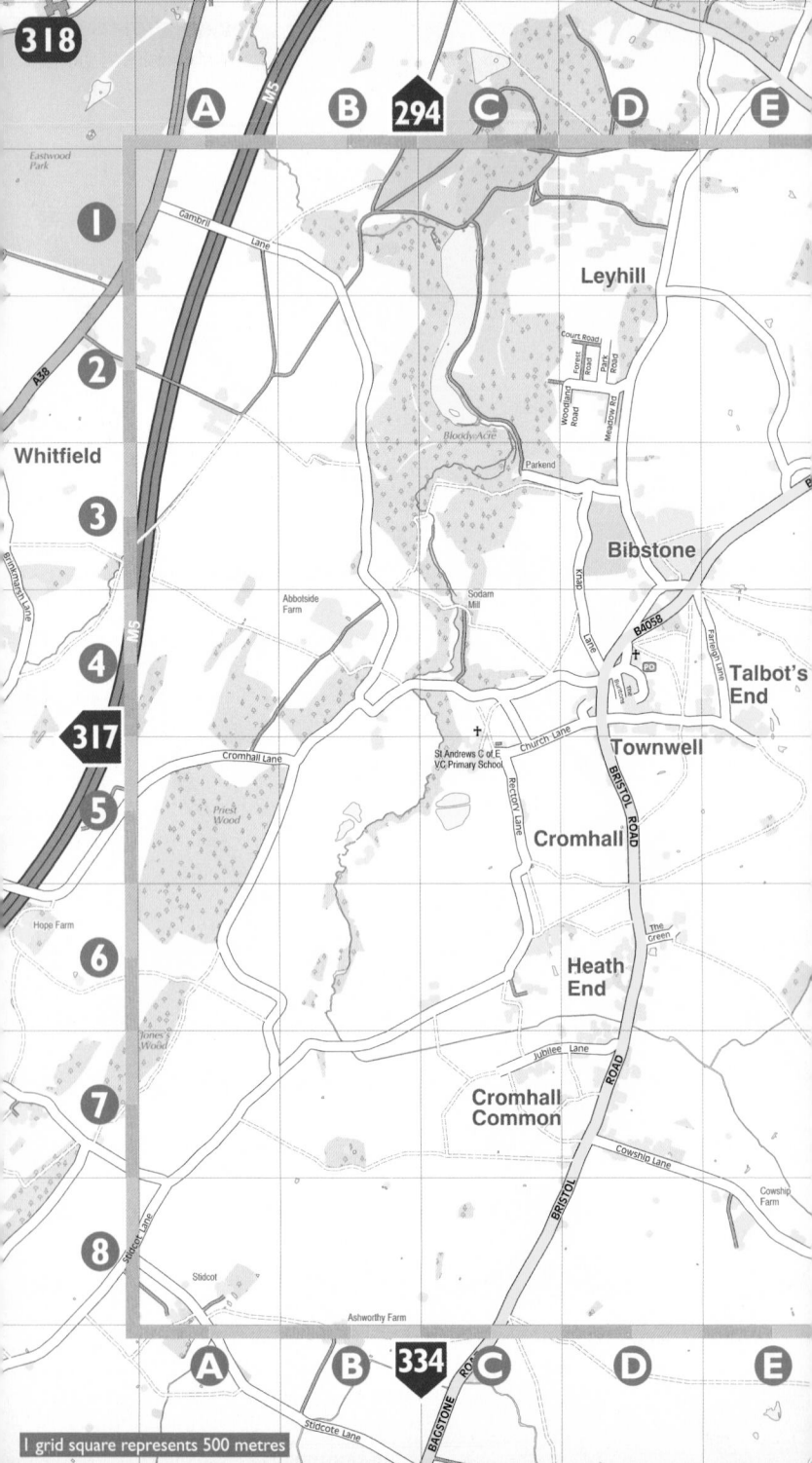

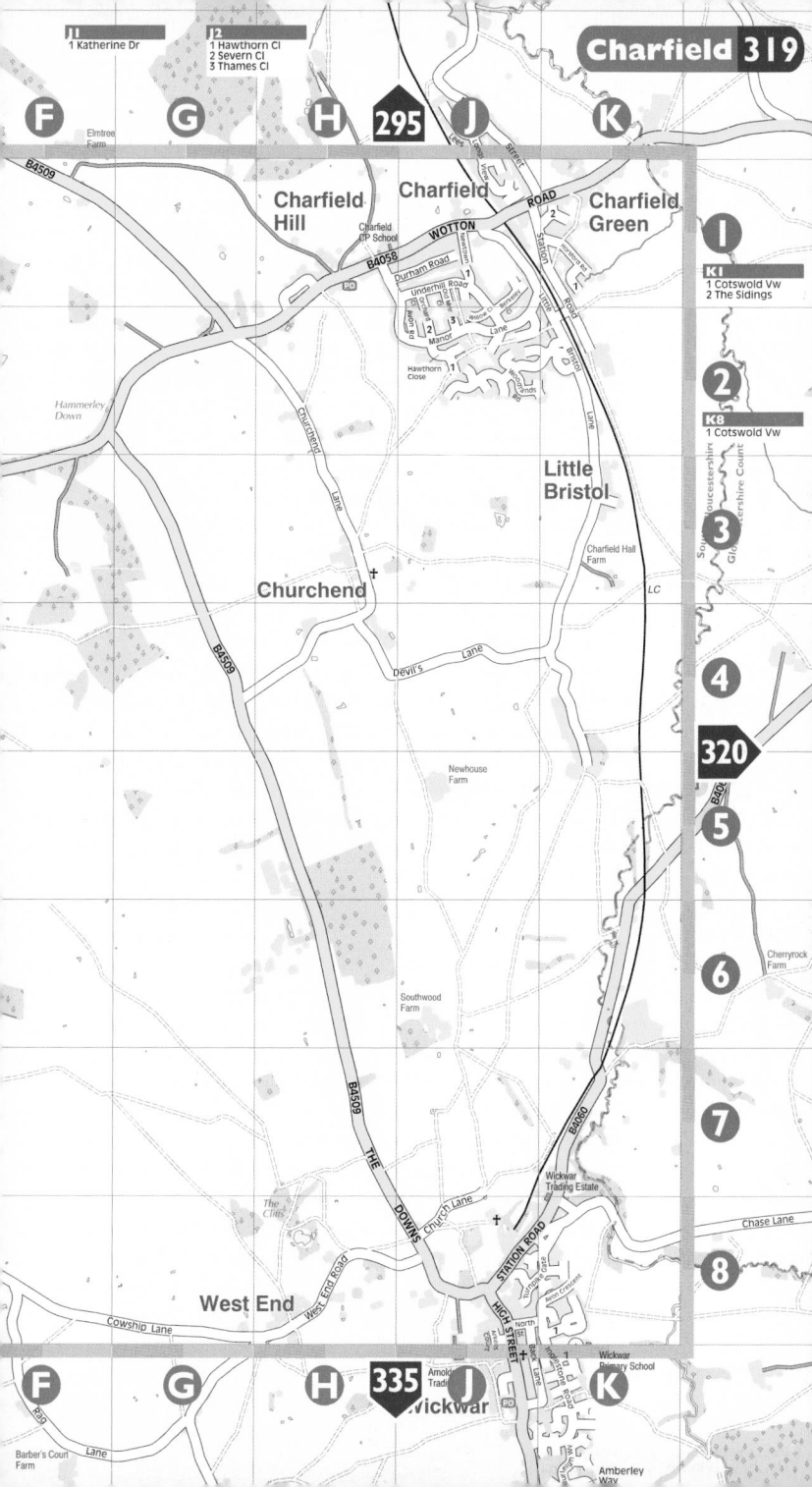

J1
1 Katherine Dr

J2
1 Hawthorn Cl
2 Severn Cl
3 Thames Cl

F   G   H   `295`   J   K

B4509

Charfield
Hill

Charfield

Charfield CP School

WOTTON   ROAD

Charfield
Green

B4058

Durham Road

Underhill Road

Manor   Lane

Hawthorn
Close

Elmtree
Farm

I

K1
1 Cotswold Vw
2 The Sidings

2

K8
1 Cotswold Vw

Hammerley
Down

Churchend Lane

Little
Bristol

Charfield Hall
Farm

LC

3

Churchend

B4509

Devil's   Lane

4

`320`

5

Newhouse
Farm

6

Cherryrock
Farm

B4509

THE   DOWNS

Southwood
Farm

7

The
Cliffs

Church Lane

Wickwar
Trading Estate

Chase Lane

8

West End

Cowship Lane

West End Road

STATION   ROAD

HIGH   STREET

Wickwar
Primary School

F   G   H   `335`   J   K

Wickwar

Barber's Court
Farm

Amberley
Way

A B **296** C D **D3** E

D3
1 Weavers Cl

D2
1 Orchard Wk
2 Russet Ct

B4058 NEW ROAD

B4058

HARFIELD ROAD

Katerine Lady
Berkeley
School

WOTTON ROAD B4060

Sports
Centre

Hawpal
Farm

Charfield Gre
1

B4062

Vineyard Lane

Dye House

Kingswood
County Primary School

Abbey
Gate

Grange
Farm

OLD RECTORY RD

Kingswood

Bristol Road

2

GL12

WICKWAR ROAD

Sir Stanley
School

Cross
Meadow

Highlees
Road

Little
Bristol

3

Charfield Hall
Farm

LC

Neathwood
Farm

B4060

Cemetery

Upper Barns
Farm

4

◀ **319**

Highwood
Farm

Folly
Farm

5

B4060

Cherryrock
Farm

Haroldsfield
Farm

Lower Witheymore
Farm

6

B4060

Mounteney's
Farm

Gloucestershire County

South Gloucestershire

7

Wickwar
Trading Estate

Kites
Farm

Mounteney's
Lane

Inglestone
Farm

Chase Lane

8

Chase Hill

South Moon
Ridings

Wickwar
Primary School

Way

A B ▼ **336** C D E

Lower Woods
Lodge

1 grid square represents 500 metres

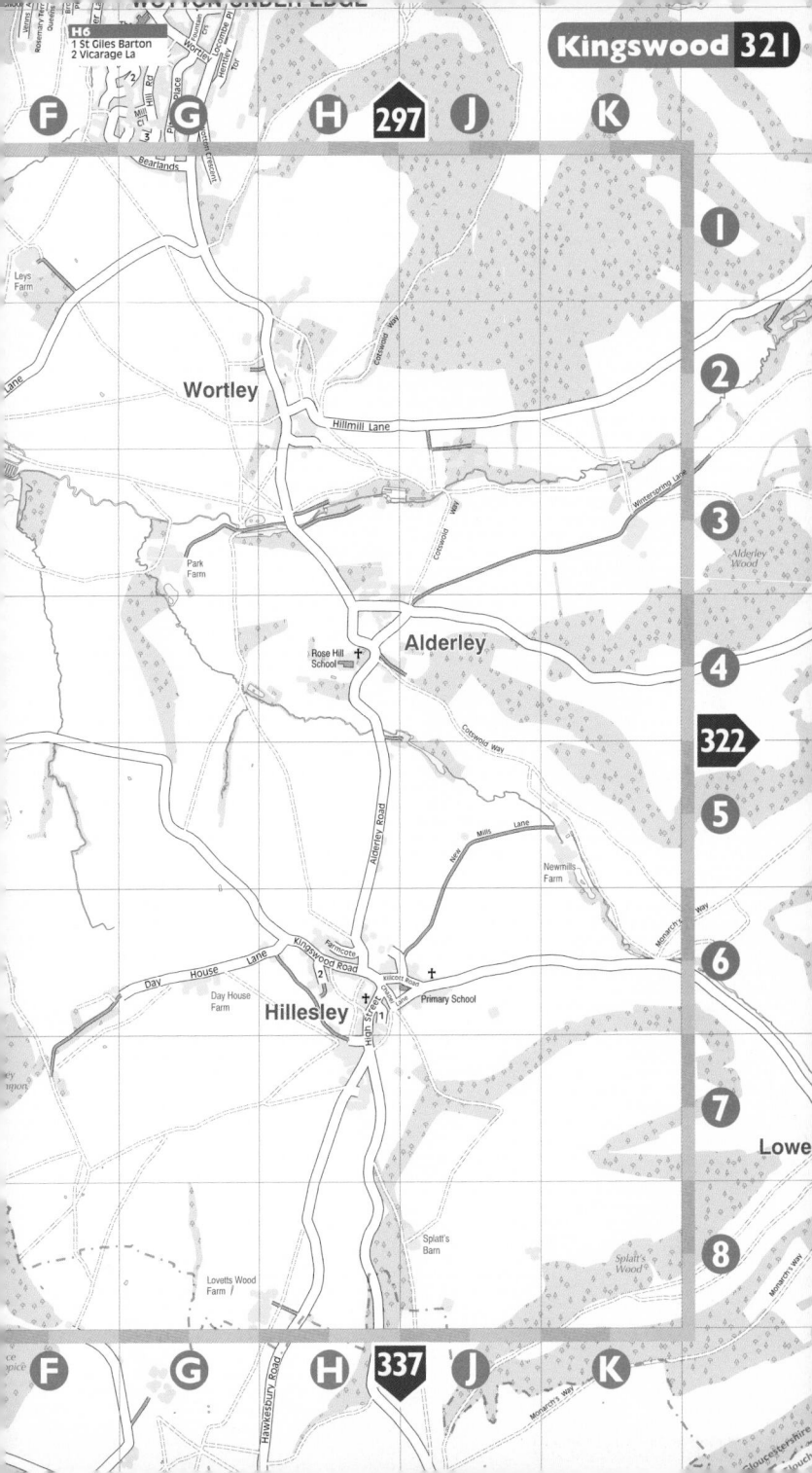

324

A B 300 C D E Nesley Farm

Bowldown Road

1

Twymead Lane

2

Bowldown Wood

3 Leighterton

Cem

Monarch's Way

4

Down Farm

323

Monarch's Way

5

6 Visitor Centre ●

Waste Barn

Magnum Way

7 Silk Wood

Gloucestershire County
Wiltshire County

8

A Knockdown B A433 C D E

1 grid square represents 500 metres

F7
1 Jackson Cl

Old Passage

Aust

F　**G**　**H**　**313**　**J**　**K**

severn Way
A403

Cake Pill
Gout

I

Old Solah Rhine

Valley Farm
Road

2 ngst

Severn Way

Bilsham Lane

Bilsham
Farm

3

A403

Aust
Rd

Northwick

Redwick &
Northwick
C of E School

Bilsham Lane

Holm
Farm

Holm Lane

4

330

M4

Walning
Farm

Greenditch
Farm

Greendi

5

Redham Lane

SEVERN ROAD

NORTHWICK ROAD

Pear Tree
Farm

treet

6

Ostbridge
Manor Farm

Pilning

Bank Road

HANDS ROAD

Pilning
Farm

7

Torrs Farm

Pilning
CP School

Bank Road

Rookery Lane

8

Rookery Farm

MARSH COMMON

Ellinghurst
Farm

Pilning
Station

nend
arm

F　**G**　**H**　**341**　**J**　**K**

330
B4461
330

A
B
314
C
REDHILL
LANE
D
E
1 Daldry Gdns

Elberton

Aust Road
Priestpool

1

Ingst Road

2
Valley Farm
Ingst
New Leaze

Ingst Road

3
Rhyne, Ingst
Olveston Common
Olveston & Elberton Primary School

Church Hill

The Green

The Surger

4
Mead Lane
Mead Farm

Catherine Hill

329
M4

Greenditch St
Awkley Ln

Junction 21

5
Greenditch Farm
Greenditch Street
Awkley Lane

Redham Lane

6
Pear Tree Farm
Pilning street
Awkley
Hardy Lane

Ostbridge Manor Farm

7
Pilning Farm
The Naith

Moor Lane

8

Marshwall Lane
Cemetery

A
B
342
C
D
E

Lower Knole Farm

Lower Court

The Pound
Surgery

K2
1 Hazel Gdns
2 Olive Gdns

F G H 315 J K

B4461 VATTINGSTONE LANE

Martwood School

Alveston Down

Alveston I

Hazel Farm

Oldown Country Park

Stroud Common

Underwood Close Primary School

Old Down

The Loans

Lower Hazel

GLOUCESTER ROAD

Sheepcombe Farm

Tockington Manor School

Washingpool Hill Road

Rudgeway 332 H ROAD

The Roundabout

Oakleaze

Tockington Park Farm

Tockington Park Lane

Harts

Woodhouse Down

Fernhill Farm

M4

Hortham Wood

Hortham Farm

GLOUCESTER ROAD

F G 343 J K

Hortham Lane

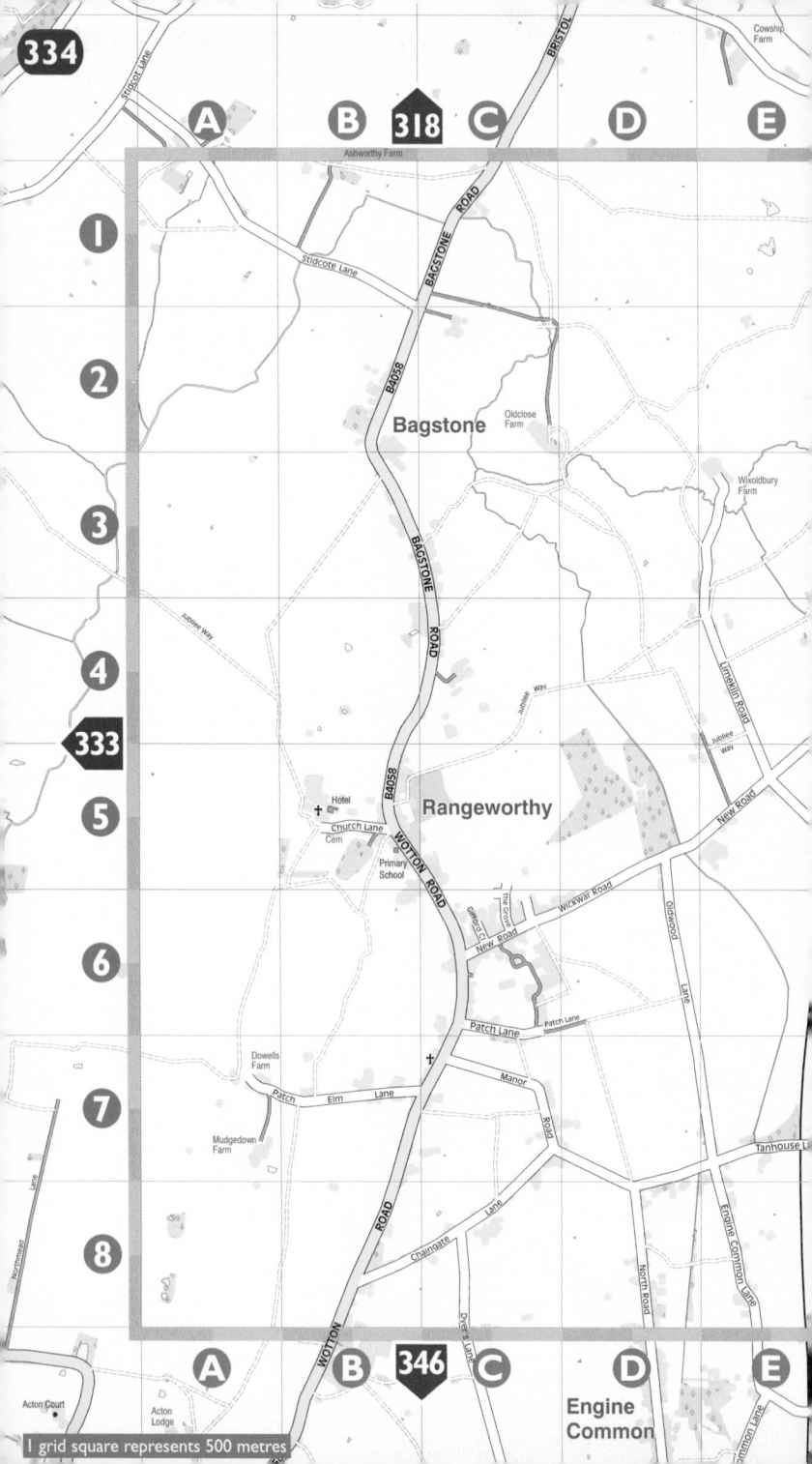

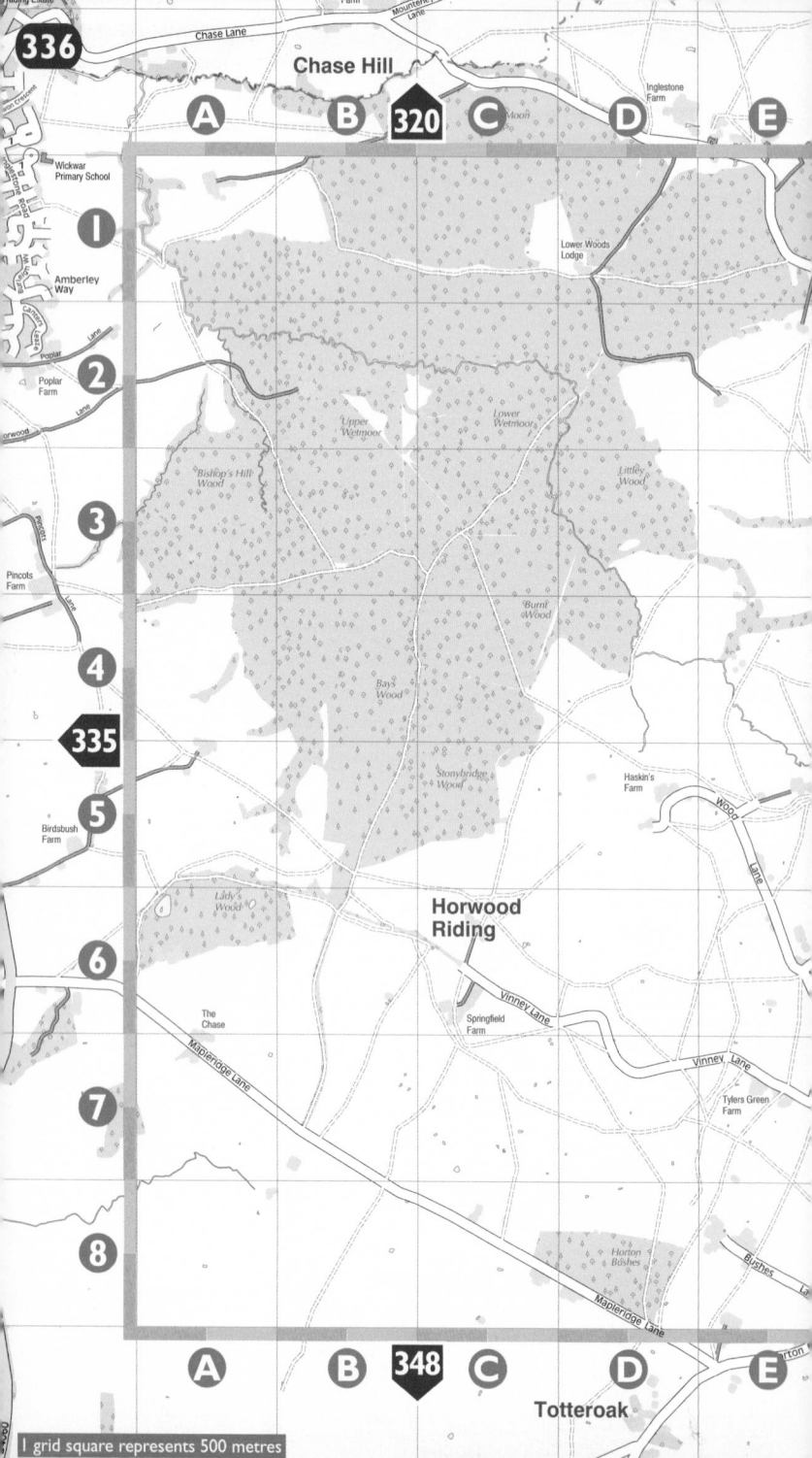

336

Chase Lane

Chase Hill

A **B** **320** **C** **D** **E**

Wickwar Primary School

I

Amberley Way

Lower Woods Lodge

Poplar Farm

2

Upper Wetmoor

Lower Wetmoor

Bishop's Hill Wood

Littley Wood

3

Pincots Farm

Burnt Wood

4

Bays Wood

335

Haskin's Farm

5

Birdsbush Farm

Stonybridge Wood

Wood Lane

Lidy's Wood

Horwood Riding

6

The Chase

Vinney Lane

Springfield Farm

Vinney Lane

7

Maplendge Lane

Tyers Green Farm

8

Horton Bushes

Bushes La

Maplendge Lane

A **B** **348** **C** **D** **E**

orton

Totteroak

I grid square represents 500 metres

322

337

350

A B C D E

1
2
3
4
5
6
7
8

Upper
Kilcott

Starveall

Beech Lane
Farm

Milly
Wood

Bangel
Wood

Gloucestershire County
South Gloucestershire

Hennel
Bottom

Splatt's
Wood

Barley
Ridge

Hawkesbury Upton
Primary School

High Street

Bath Street

Park Street

Hunters Mead

PO

Hawkesbury
Upton

France Lane

Birgage

Sandpits Lane

Highfield Lane

Highfield
Farm

Britain
Bottom

Dunkirk
Farm

A46

A433

Folly Farm

Swangrove

Dunkirk

Petty
France

Hotel

Hotel

Bodkin
Wood

Bodkin
Hazel
Wood

GL9

A46

A B C D E

American
Barn

Church La

L
E
E

Knock

Oldbury on
the Hill

Woodhayes
House

A433

Creephole

Didmarton

St Arild's
Rd

PH

THE STREET

A433

A433

Hinnegar

Bullpark
Wood

PO

Church La

Sopworth

Badminton
Down

South Gloucestershire
Wiltshire County

Gloucestershire County
Wiltshire County

Luckley
Farm

Wick
Farm

nton

North End
Farm

Cherry
Orchard

Cherry Orchard Lane

Primary
School

SHERSTC

SOPWORTH

F G H 323 J K

I
2
3
4
5
6
7
8

F G H 351 J K

342

330

341

354

E1
1 Chestermaster Cl
2 Walnut Tree Cl

D5
1 Newnham Pl

C7
1 Spruce Wy

A B C D E

I

E6
1 Thirlmere Rd

2

3

4

5

6

7

8

A B C D E

Marshwall Lane

Cemetery

Lower
Court Farm

Lower Court Rd

Church Road

The Pound

Surgery

Almondsbury C of E
VC Primary School

Monmouth   Hill

Townsend

Church
Lw

Sundays Hill

Over   Lane

Lower
Knole Farm

Cattybrook
Farm

North Bristol
Rugby Football Club

Knole Pk

Over Lane

Ash   Lane

Badger L

Lane

Over

Over Lane

Aztec
West

Park   Avenue

Park Avenue

PAT

Coniston Primary
School

South
Gloucestershire Council

Coniston

Coniston

Wintermere Road

MS

Patchway
Trading Estate

Superstore

Junction 17

Hollywood
Tower

BLAKE HILL

CRIBBS CSWY

BS CAUSEWAY

Highwood Lane

Highwood
Lane

Highwood Road

Pegasus Road

Vulcan Rd

Lysander Road

Merlin Road

Martin Road

Lysander

Cribbs Causeway
Shopping
Centre

The Mall

Highwood Road

Patchway
Junior School

Callicroft
Infant
Sch

Patchway
Town Council

Patchway
Health Clinic

Rodway   Road

Coniston Road

Callicroft Road

Coldharbour Ln

Courtheath Road

Catbrain

Filton Airfield

I grid square represents 500 metres

F
G
H **331**
J
K

Almondsbury

BS32

Junction 16

Junction 20/15

BRADLEY STOKE

Little
Stoke

BS34

E7
1 Dawley Cl
rst Farm

Oldfi
Farm
D8
1 Holmwood Cl

A8
1 Goose Acre

A

B

332

C

D

E

Hortham
Farm

M5

1

Gaunt's
Earthcott
Lane

Gaunt's Earthcott

Old Gloucester Road

2

**Frogland
Cross**

Perrinpit Road

3

North
Woods

Gloucester Road
Farm

Old Gloucester Road

St Mary
Rugby
Club

ter
k

4

Trench Lane

343

B4427

Hotel

5

Swan Lane

Bradley Brook

6

B4427

Green Lane

Silverhill
School

Junior Way

M4

B4058

Watley

7

Bluebell

Great Meadow Road

Primary
School

8

Church Lane

Church Lane

High Street

Parkside
Ridings High
School

Robbins

Ot

Winterbourne

St Michaels C of E
VC Primary School

4057

WINTERBOURNE ROAD

Bakers

LANE

B4057

Flower Gallery

Flaxpits

Heat
C

A

Gr
Stoke

B

356

C

BEACON

WINTER

Green

Bradley

D

E

F6
1 Prospect La

F7
1 Common Rd
2 Crossley Cl

F **G** **H** **333** **J** **K**

Latteridge

B4059

Acton Court

Iron Acton

YATE ROAD

I
Acton Lodge

G6
1 Thornhayes Cl

Hill House

2
Police Stn

G7
1 Nightingale La
C of E School

Sheephouse Farm

Folly Road

B4058

Laddenside Farm

Elm Farm

BRISTOL ROAD

Frome Valley Walkway

Cog Mill Farm

Perrinpit Farm

Latteridge Rd

Park Rd

High Street

Station Road

Cem

Holly Hill

Algars Manor

3

H6
1 Barley Cl
2 Downfield Dr
3 Winchcombe Rd

4
Frome Valley Walkway

346
's Bottom

5

H7
1 The Spinney

rth Corner

BRISTOL ROAD

Church Road

Conifer Cl

Western Av

School

Rylestone Close

Mount Cl

Fernbrook Road

Morley

Foxe Rd

Rockside Dr

Mill Lane

Meadow and

Church Cl

Church Road

PO

Frampton End Rd

Frampton End

6

A432

J7
1 Gladstone La
2 Hillside La

Frampton Cotterell

Frampton Cotterell C of E School

Doctors Surg

Rectory Rd

Clyde Rd

Park Row

Park Lane

Rockside Gardens

Highcroft Junior School

Infant School

The Csw

Meadow Crew

7

J8
1 Church La
2 Willow Wy

Watley's End

BS36

Nightingale Road

Park Lane

Frome Valley Walkway

Heather Av

Beesmoor Road

Woodend

West End

South View

Bell

Manor Rd

The Rd

Rose Cl

Coalpit Road

Doctors Surg

Coalpit Heath

8

Saint Francis Drive

The Gully

North Road

York Lane

River Frome

BADMINTON ROAD

Manor C of E School

Roundways

Vicarage Rd

Heath

K7
Street names for this grid square are listed at the back of the index

Road

F **G** **H** **357** **J** **K**

Park Lane

Ratns Close

Henfield

Ram Hill

Broad La

icks Common

I grid square represents 500 metres

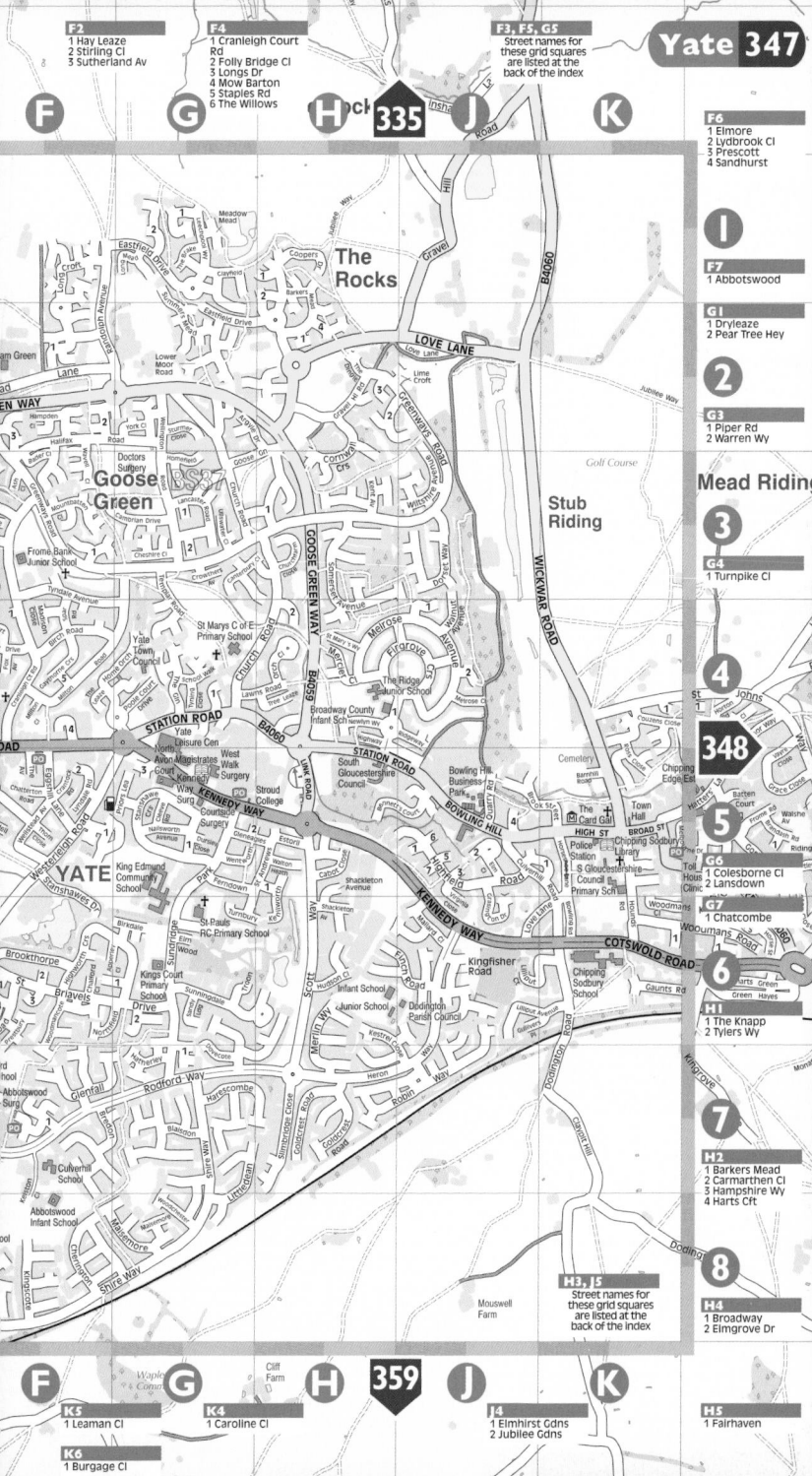

Mapleridge

Horton

Horton Primary School

Horton Hill

Horton Hill

Widderhill Farm

Horton Court (NT)

Highfield Lane

Hall Lane

New Tyning Lane

Crowshall Barn Farm

Mc;auch's Way

bury

Grickstone Farm

A46

Seven Mile Plantation

Beech Copse

Cotswold Way

Lyegrove House

Lyegrove Farm

Old Sodbury County Primary School

Church Lane

Old Sodbury

Hill Lane

B4040

A46

BATH ROAD

F **G** **H** **337** **J** **K**

I

2

3

4

350

5

6

7

8

F **G** **H** **361** **J** **K**

Henbury 353

F3
1 Coombe Cl
2 Cousins Cl
3 Gleneagles Dr
4 Green Dell Cl
5 Greenside Cl
6 Ison Hill Rd

F4
1 Kings Weston Rd

F7
1 Dinglewood Cl

F8
1 Ebenezer La
2 Poplar Av

G2
1 Nettlestone Cl

G3
1 Scandrett Cl

G4
1 Dundas Cl
2 Gray's Cl
3 Henbury Rd

G7
1 Hammond Gdns

H3
1 Champneys Av
2 Dolman Cl
3 Dowdeswell Cl
4 Langfield Cl
5 Lowlis Cl
6 Modecombe Gv
7 Tratman Wk
8 Trevelyan Wk

H6
1 Westover Gdns

H8
1 Stoke Hamlet
2 Stoke La

I3
1 Ardenton Wk
2 Fane Cl
3 Machin Gdns
4 Passage Rd
5 Priestwood Cl
6 Stoulton Gv

J4
1 Ellinghurst Cl
2 Fennell Gv
3 Roselarge Gdns
4 Thornmead Gv

K8
1 Blandford Cl
2 Grange Cl North
3 Waterford Rd

K4
1 Concorde Dr

H5, J7
Street names for these grid squares are listed at the back of the index

J6
1 Elmfield Rd
2 Greystoke Gdns
3 Watkins Yd

341
354

Catbrain

Brentry

Southmead

Eastfield

Henleaze

Henbury

Westbury on Trym

Stoke Bishop

A8
1 Croft Vw

A7
1 Bredon Nook Rd
2 Evelyn Rd
3 Whiteleaze
4 Woodchester Rd

A6
1 Alexandra Rd
2 Falfield Wk
3 Francis Rd

A4
1 Burneside Cl
2 Keswick Wk
3 Lowther Rd
4 Mardale Cl
5 Millard Cl
6 Standon Wy
7 Twenty Acres Rd

B2
1 Charlton Pl

Catbrain

A **B** 342 **C** **D** **E**

I

B3
1 Northwoods Wk

A5, B4, B7
Street names for
these grid squares
are listed at the
back of the index

Filton Airfield

2

B5
1 Greenfield Rd
2 Westleigh Cl

Brentry Primary
School

3

Knole Lane

B6
1 Greenfield Av
2 Greenway Dr
3 Greenway Pk
4 Kelston Gdns

Brentry

Brentry
Hospital

4

353

Fairway Industrial
Centre

Golf
Course

Charborough Road CP School

Filton
Police
Stn

5

St Teresas
RC School

The Craft Gallery

Portfolio
Gallery

Northville

C5
1 Greenpark Rd
2 Kenmore Gv

Badocks Wood
Primary School

Bristol
City
Council

Monks
Park School

Eden Grove

C6
1 Sherston Rd

6

Southmead
Health
NHS Trust

Monks
Park Surgery

C7
1 Canvey Cl
2 Greenwood Cl

Police
Station

Southmead
Hospital

Horfield
Sports
Centre

Eastf

7

The Lake
Surgery

Horfield
C of E
School

C8
1 Druetts Cl
2 Kellaway Av
3 Somerton Rd
4 Tayman Cl

Henleaze

Horfield

Filton Avenue
Junior School

Horfield
Health
Centre

8

Golden
Hill

Bristol
Rovers FC

Bristol
RUFC

Bristol Civil Service
Sports Club

BS7

D7
1 Caine Rd

A

D6, E7
Street names for
these grid squares
are listed at the
back of the index

B 364 **C** **D** **E**

D8
1 Crofton Av

Henleaze Infant School

E5
1 Cropthorne Rd

E5
1 Austen Gv
2 Cropthorne Rd
South
3 St Gregory's Wk
4 Thackeray Wk

C5
1 Cropthorne Rd

HM Prison

E3
1 Glebelands Rd

1 grid square represents 500 metres

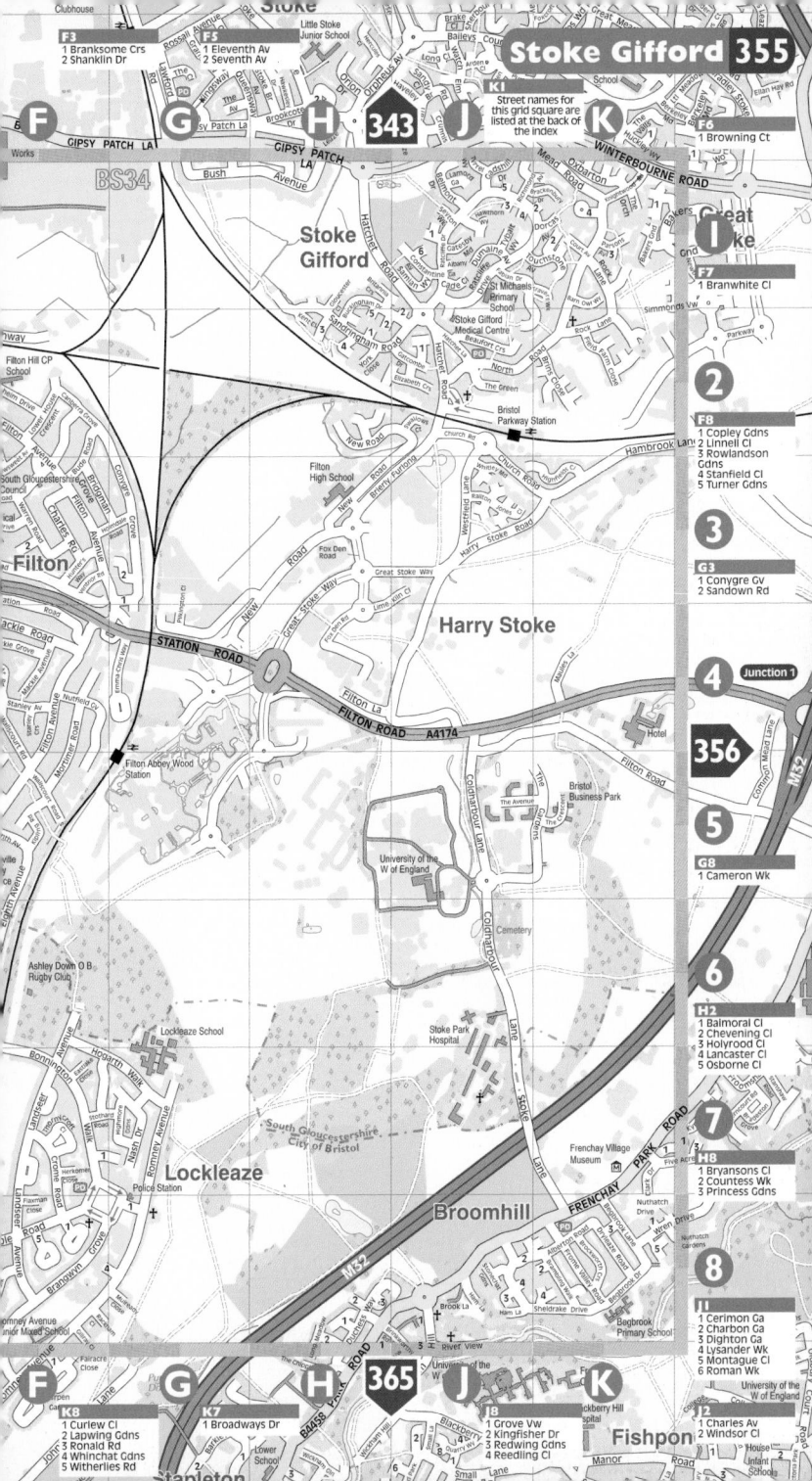

Stoke Gifford 355

BS34

Clubhouse

Little Stoke Junior School

Stoke

Stoke Gifford

GIPSY PATCH LA

GIPSY PATCH LA

Works

Bush Avenue

Filton Hill CP School

South Gloucestershire Council

St Michaels Primary School

Stoke Gifford Medical Centre

The Green

Bristol Parkway Station

Hambrook Lane

Great Stoke

Filton High School

New Road

Fox Den Road

Great Stoke Way

Harry Stoke

Filton

STATION ROAD

New Road

Great Stoke Way

Filton La

FILTON ROAD A4174

Hotel

Filton Road

Filton Abbey Wood Station

University of the W of England

Colthurst Lane

Bristol Business Park

The Avenue

The Greens

Ashley Down O B Rugby Club

Lockleaze School

Cemetery

Stoke Park Hospital

Stoke Lane

South Gloucestershire City of Bristol

Lockleaze

Police Station

Broomhill

FRENCHAY

M32

PARK ROAD

Frenchay Village Museum

Nuthatch Drive

Begbrook Primary School

University of the W of England

Fishpon

Stanleton

River View

Sheldrake Drive

Blackberry Hill

Blackberry Hill Hospital

Manor Road

356

344
355
366

B8
1 Lanaway Rd
2 Little Hayes
3 Oldbury Court Dr

B7
1 Churchside

B5
1 Beaufort Pl
2 Berkeley Gn

A7
1 Blenman Cl
2 Probyn Cl
3 Scott Lawrence Cl
4 Stourden Cl

C5
1 Bryants Cl

C6
1 Beckspool Rd

C7
1 Quarry Rd
2 Tuckett La

C8
1 Bracey Dr
2 Bridges Dr
3 Grangewood Cl
4 Shimsey Cl
5 Urfords Dr

D1
1 Bradstone Rd
2 Hazelgrove
3 Ludwell Cl

D5
1 Bampton Dr

D7
1 Cleeve Wood Rd
2 Heath Ct

D8
1 Chestnut Rd
2 Conifer Cl
3 Edmund Cl

E2
1 Cairn Gdns
2 Prospect Cl

E5
1 Greystones
2 Queensholm Av

A D6, E1, E6
Street names for
these grid squares
are listed at the
back of the index

C
1 Oakdale Ct

D
1 Buckingham Pl
2 Westerleigh Rd
3 Woodlands

1 grid square represents 500 metres

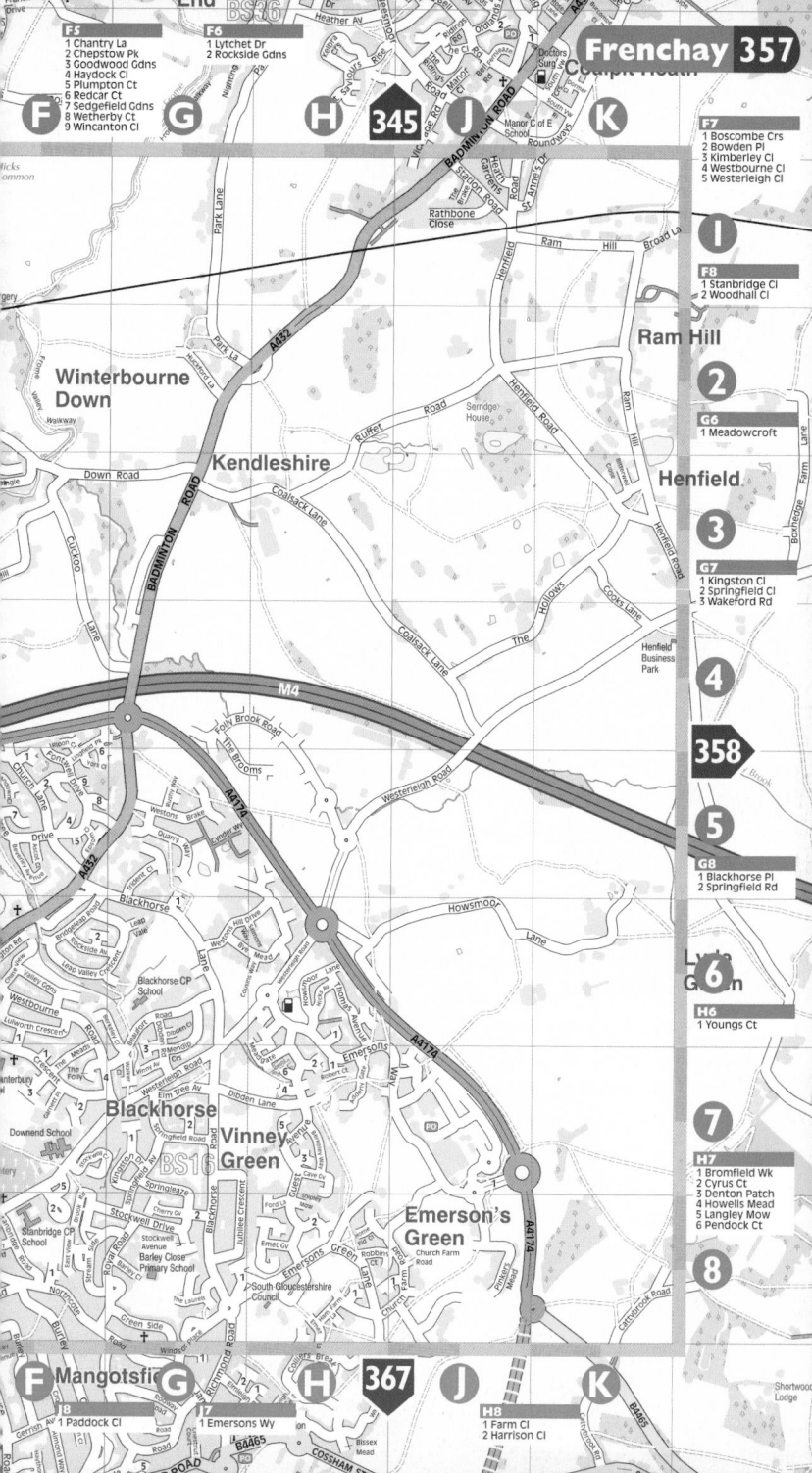

F5
1 Chantry La
2 Chepstow Pk
3 Goodwood Gdns
4 Haydock Cl
5 Plumpton Ct
6 Redcar Ct
7 Sedgefield Gdns
8 Wetherby Ct
9 Wincanton Cl

F6
1 Lytchet Dr
2 Rockside Gdns

F7
1 Boscombe Crs
2 Bowden Pl
3 Kimberley Cl
4 Westbourne Cl
5 Westerleigh Cl

F8
1 Stanbridge Cl
2 Woodhall Cl

G6
1 Meadowcroft

G7
1 Kingston Cl
2 Springfield Cl
3 Wakeford Rd

G8
1 Blackhorse Pl
2 Springfield Rd

H6
1 Youngs Ct

H7
1 Bromfield Wk
2 Cyrus Ct
3 Denton Patch
4 Howells Mead
5 Langley Mow
6 Pendock Ct

H8
1 Farm Cl
2 Harrison Cl

H8 (Mangotsfield)
1 Paddock Cl

I7
1 Emersons Wy

Cockpit Heath

Ram Hill

Henfield

Lyde Green

Winterbourne Down

Kendleshire

Mangotsfield

Blackhorse

Vinney Green

Emerson's Green

345 358 367

F G H **349** J K

1
2
3
4
362
5
6
7
8

B4040

BATH ROAD

Sheepcot
Barn

Sheepcot
Barn

A46 ROAD

BATH ROAD

✝
Tormarton

PH
Hotel

ington Ash

RIVER LANDROIT

M4

Junction 18

Lower Lapdown
Farm

MARSHFIELD ROAD

Shire Hill

West Littleton
Down

Rownham
Farm

Tormarton Road

Wolvenot Lane

Lane

F G H **371** J K

362

Newhouse Farm

B4040

Acton T

350

A   B   C   D   E

Tormarton

1

Warren Barn

Oakes Lane

Old Warren

2

Sheepcot Barn

Parks Farm

South Glouceste

Wiltshire C

3

4

We Fa

361

South Gloucestershire

Wiltshire County

5

Kington Down Farm

6

Holloway Hill

Shire Hill

7

Down Farm

Rownham

8

Broadmead Brook

A   B   C   D   E

Tormarton

372

Shir Far

Broadmead Brook

F G H 351 J K

Hollybush Cl

Trinity
C of E
School

BURTON ROAD

B4053

Littleton Drew I

M4

Marsh Lane

B4039

M4 2

B4039

Burton

The Meads

Horsedown 3

Edgecorner Lane

4

Nettleton Road

Macmillan Way

Nettleton
Green

5

Lugbury
Farm

6

Wood Lane

Macmillan Way

Nettleton
Shrub

7

Hill

Smith Street

ton

8

West Kington
Wick

F E2
1 Bankside

Stanbrid School

G E3
1 Chestnut Rd

South Glouce Council

H

357

J

K

Mangotsfield

Police Station

B4465

Mangotsfield United FC

COSSHAM STREET

Bissex Mead

MANGOTSFIELD ROAD

POMPHREY HILL

MAIN ROAD

SHORTWOOD

Shortwood

Mangotsfield School

Golf Course

Lodge Farm

STATION ROAD

Primary School

Hot Water La

New Cheltenham

Fisher Road

Siston Common

Goose Green

Goose Green

Webbs Heath

Webb Heath

Warmley Hill

DEANERY ROAD

Kingsfield School

DEANERY ROAD

HIGH STREET

A420

LONDON ROAD

Station Close

Warmley

Grimsbury Park School

Warmley Tower

Parsons Walk

ROAD

BATH ROAD

Cadbury Heath CP School

Warmley C of E School

North Comm

St Stephens Business Centre

Close Farm Surgery

372

Rownham
Farm

A   **B**   **362**   **C**   **D**   **E**

Breadmead Brook

1

Shirehill
Farm

Tormarton Road

2

3

Downthorns
Farm

Down Road

Marfor
Industrial
Est

4

Culverslade

371

5

Marshfield
Cemetery

South Gloucestershire
Wiltshire County

A420

Star
Farm

Robbins Close

Hay Street

Chippenham
Rd

Withymead Rd

arshfield   Marshfield Primary
School   Church Lane   **East End**

Market Place

6

7

8

Fuddlebrook

Alford Lane

Kenwicke Rd

A   **B**   **381**   **C**   **D**   **E**

The
Raizes

I grid square represents 500 metres

F8
1 Holly Dr

West Kington
Wick

363

F **G** **H** **J** **K**

I

2

3

Fosse
Farm

Mountain
Bower

4

Old Coach Road

North Wraxall

A420

5

The
Shoe

Bury Camp

6

7 Hall
Farm

8

Lucknam
Park

Hotel

Woodlane

Thickwood Lane

Thickwood

F **G** **H** **J** **K**

Larch Road

Doncombe Lane

PO

Euridge
Manor
Farm

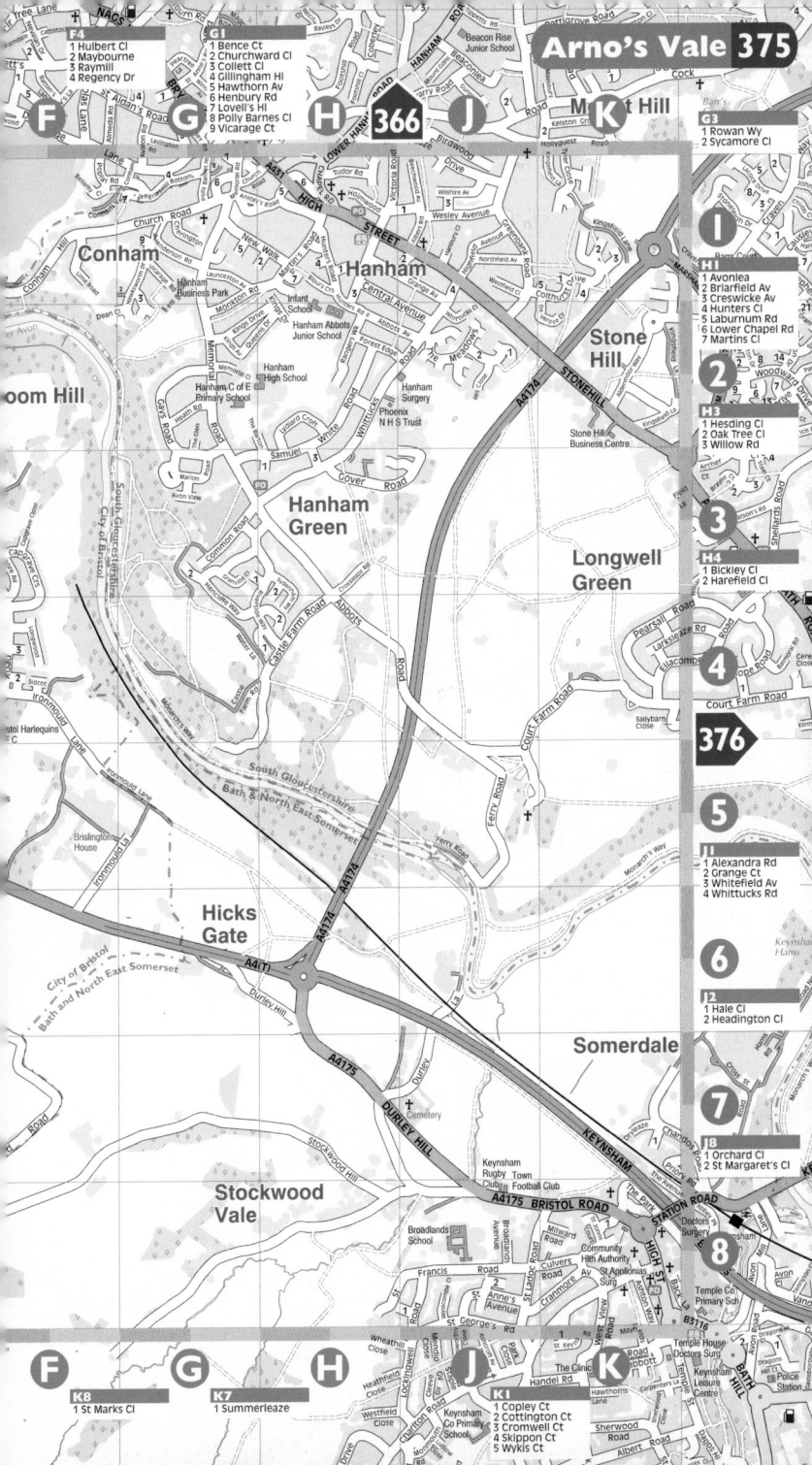

F4
1 Hulbert Cl
2 Maybourne
3 Raymill
4 Regency Dr

G1
1 Bence Ct
2 Churchward Cl
3 Collett Cl
4 Gillingham Hl
5 Hawthorn Av
6 Henbury Rd
7 Lovell's Hl
8 Polly Barnes Cl
9 Vicarage Ct

G3
1 Rowan Wy
2 Sycamore Cl

H1
1 Avonlea
2 Briarfield Av
3 Creswicke Av
4 Hunters Cl
5 Laburnum Rd
6 Lower Chapel Rd
7 Martins Cl

H3
1 Hesding Cl
2 Oak Tree Cl
3 Willow Rd

H4
1 Bickley Cl
2 Harefield Cl

J1
1 Alexandra Rd
2 Grange Ct
3 Whitefield Av
4 Whittucks Rd

J2
1 Hale Cl
2 Headington Cl

J8
1 Orchard Cl
2 St Margaret's Cl

K8
1 St Marks Cl

K7
1 Summerleaze

K1
1 Copley Ct
2 Cottington Ct
3 Cromwell Ct
4 Skippon Ct
5 Wykis Ct

Conham

Hanham

Hanham Green

Stone Hill

Longwell Green

Hicks Gate

Somerdale

Stockwood Vale

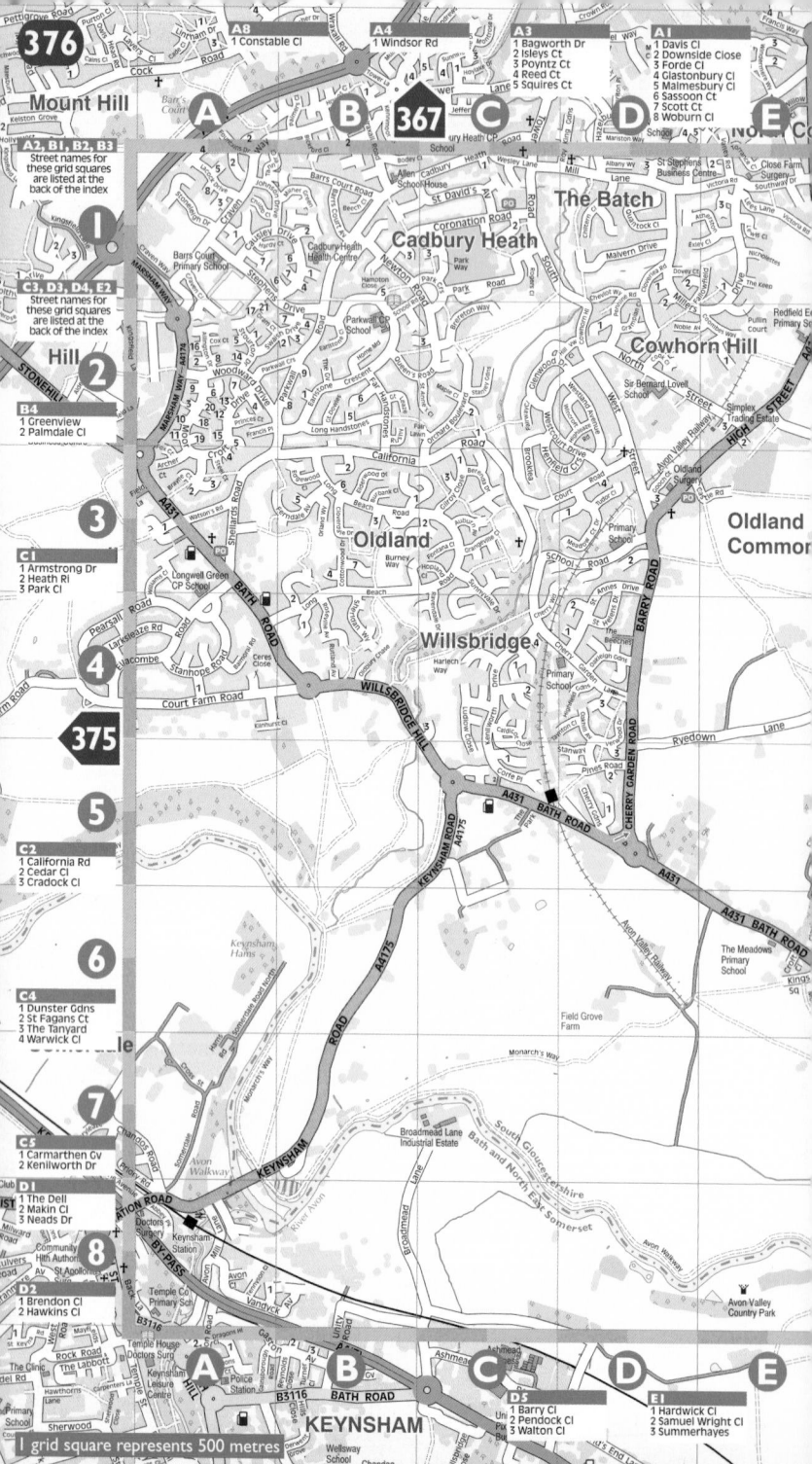

F G H **370** J K

The Folly

Ashton

I

2

Limestone Link

Limestone Link

Nimlet

Henley Tyning Farm

Leigh Lane

3

Bankswood Servior

Hall Lane

Hall Lane

Torney Court Farm

4

380

Hartley Farm

Tadwick

A46(T)

5

Tadwick Lane

South Gloucestershire

Wiltshire County

Cotswold Way

Langridge

Langridge Lane

Ashcombe House

A46(T)

6

GLOUCESTER

7

ROAD

Upper Langridge Farm

8

A46(T)

Woolley

High Street

Church St

Blacksmith Lane

Tadwick Lane

Swainswick Sch

F G H J **BA1** K

Walcot Rugby Club

Upper Swainswick

F G H **372** J K

I
2
Barracks
3
Coleme Rugby
Football
Club
4
5
6
7
8

The Raizes

Ashwicke
Hall (Sch)

Ashwicke
Grange

Airfield

Ashwicke Road

Oakford Lane

The
Rocks

Hunters
Hall

South Gloucestershire
Wiltshire County

Bath Road

Westwood
Farm

Oakford
Farm

Three Shire Stones

Road Hill

Road Hill

Alcombe

South Gloucestershire
Bath and North East Somerset

Rodney
Farm

Stewry Lane

Bannerdown Road

Wiltshire County
Bath & North East Somerset

Shockerwick
House

Banner
Down

Spackwick Lane

F G H J K

Northend

The
Mount

BATH ROAD A4

Abbeydale	158	E2
Abenhall	123	J7
Ablington	225	F2
Abson	369	F4
Acton Turville	350	E8
Adlestrop	94	D4
Alcombe	381	K6
Alderley	321	J4
Alderton	37	K7
Alderton Fields	61	K1
Aldsworth	199	F5
Alkerton	211	J7
Allaston	206	B8
Almondsbury	343	G2
Alstone	61	F1
Alstone	106	A4
Alveston	331	K1
Alveston Down	331	H1
Alvington	232	E8
Amberley	242	E7
Ampney Crucis	251	H5
Ampney St Mary	252	B5
Ampney St Peter	252	A7
Andoversford	137	K2
Andrews Corner	203	F8
Anthony's Cross	97	J2
Apperley	79	H1
Arle	106	A2
Arlebrook	213	F1
Arlingham	180	E4
Arlington	225	F4
Arno's Vale	374	A2
Ashchurch	34	E7
Ashleworth	77	G6
Ashley	304	A4
Ashley Down	364	D2
Ashmead Green	267	H2
Ashton Keynes	308	C5
Ashton under Hill	14	B6
Aston Cross	35	H6
Aston Ingham	96	B2
Aston Magna	45	H2
Aston on Carrant	35	J4
Aston Somerville	16	B5
Aston Subedge	8	C6
Aust	313	K8
Avening	272	A6
Avening Green	295	G6
Awkley	330	B6
Awre	208	E1
Aylburton	233	H6
Aylburton Common	233	F5
Aylworth	113	F5
Aztec West	342	E4
Badgeworth	133	F3
Bagendon	221	G4
Bagpath	242	E4
Bagpath	299	F4
Bagstone	334	B2
Baker's Hill	176	A3
Ball's Green	271	H2
Bamfurlong	104	C6
Barcheston	25	G2
Barnsley	223	K7
Barnwood	131	G5
Barrow	80	A8
Barton	3	E5
Barton	88	D6
Barton End	270	E6
Barton Hill	365	G8
The Batch	376	C1
Batsford	45	G6
Battledown	5	F5
Battlescombe	217	H5
Baunton	221	J8
Beach	377	K4
Beachley	312	D3
Beckford	37	F2
The Beeches	250	B5
Beechpike	191	H5
Bencombe	268	C6
Bengrove	36	D8
Benhall	105	J6
Bentham	161	H1
Berkeley	264	B3
Berkeley Heath	264	C3
Berkeley Road	265	H1
Berrow	31	H5
Berry Hill	147	J8
Berwick	341	F8
Beverston	301	G6
Bevington	262	E8
Bibstone	318	D3
Bibury	225	J4
Bilson Green	150	D5
Birdlip	161	K5
Birdwood	126	C4
Birtsmorton	31	K2
Birts Street	31	F1
Bishop's Cleeve	82	D3
Bishop's Norton	78	D8
Bishopston	364	B2
Bisley	217	F5
Bitton	377	G6
Blackhorse	357	F7
Blaisdon	124	E8
Blaise Hamlet	353	F4
Blakeney	207	J4
Bledington	118	C5
Blockley	44	A3
Boddington	80	C7
Bollow	154	D6
Bondend	159	J3
Botloe's Green	73	J1
Boughspring	258	E7
Bould	118	C8
Boulsdon	73	G8
Bournes Green	245	F1
Bournside	106	A7
Bournstream	296	D4
Bourton-on-the-Hill	44	E8
Bourton-on-the-Water	115	F8
Bowbridge	243	F1
Bowling Green	249	K4
Box	271	G1
Boxbush	154	D7
Boxwell	323	G1
Bradley	296	D6
Bradley Green	296	D7
Bradley Stoke	343	J6
Brain's Green	207	H1
Brand Green	74	B1
Breadstone	237	F8
Bread Street	214	B5
Bream	204	E6
Bream's Meend	204	D5
Bredon	13	J8
Bredon's Hardwick	34	B3
Brentry	353	K4
Bretforton	6	C1
Bridge End	54	A2
Bridgend	212	E8
Bridge Yate	368	A7
Brierley	149	J3
Brimpsfield	162	C8
Brimps Hill	123	K5
Brimscombe	243	H4
Brislington	374	D3
Bristol	364	E6
Britain Bottom	338	B5
Broad Campden	21	F6
Broad Moor	150	E3
Broadoak	152	E7
Broadrock	288	D1
Broadway	18	C3
Broadwell	93	G2
Broadwell	176	C3
Brockham End	378	B6
Brockhampton	82	C5
Brockhampton	110	B5
Brockhollands	205	F7
Brockweir	230	C7
Brockworth	160	A1
Brokenborough	327	G7
Bromley Heath	356	C4
Bromsberrow	29	H5
Bromsberrow Heath	29	F8
Brookend	236	A5
Brookend	260	B2
Brookthorpe	186	A1
Broomhill	355	J8
Broom Hill	375	F2
Broom's Green	28	B8
Brown's End	29	J5
Browns Hill	244	B4
Bubblewell	271	J1
Bubb's Hill	163	H7
Buckland	41	F1
Buckover	317	G4
Bulley	127	G2
Bullo	180	B6
Bull's Hill	120	C1
Bulwark	312	C1
Burleigh	243	G7
Burmington	25	C5
Burnt Ash	244	B7
Burton	363	H3
Bury End	18	D7
Buscot	286	A6
Bushley	32	E5
Bushley Green	32	B4
Bussage	244	B2
Butterrow	243	F2
Cadbury Heath	376	B7
Cainscross	214	B7
Calcot	196	C5
Calcott's Green	128	A8
Calcutt	311	G7
Calmsden	194	D6
Cam	266	C2
Cambridge	238	E2
Camer's Green	30	E3
The Camp	189	G7
Cannop	177	F2
Carterspiece	148	C5
Cashes Green	213	K6
Cassey Compton	166	C3
Castletump	50	B7
Catbrain	341	K8
Caudle Green	190	C5
Cerney Wick	309	K2
Chaceley	56	A4
Chaceley Hole	55	H4
Chaceley Stock	56	B6
Chalford	244	C4
Chapel Hill	233	G6
Charfield	319	K6
Charfield Green	319	K6
Charfield Hill	319	K6
Chargrove	133	K3
Charingworth	22	E2
Charlton Abbots	109	K1
Charlton Kings	107	J8
Charlton Park	5	D6
Chase End Street	30	B3
Chase Hill	320	B8
Chastleton	71	H8
Chavenage Green	301	G2
Chaxhill	154	D5
Chedglow	304	D3
Chedworth	194	E7
Chedworth Laines	194	B2
Cheltenham	5	D4
Chelworth	305	J3
Chelworth Lower Green	309	K8
Chelworth Upper Green	310	B8
Cherington	273	F4
Chesterton	249	G8
Childswickham	17	K4
Chipmans Platt	211	K5
Chipping Campden	20	D2
Chipping Sodbury	348	B5
Christchurch	147	J8
Churcham	127	H5
Church Down	104	B8
Churchdown	132	C2
Church End	33	J7
Church End	210	C4
Churchend	212	A8
Churchend	319	H3
Church Westcote	117	J8
Cinderford	151	F1
Cirencester	250	A3
Clapton-on-the-Hill	143	H1
Claydon	59	F3
Clay Hill	365	K4
Claypits	211	H5
Clearwell	203	H4
Cleeve	153	J1
Cleeve Hill	84	B4
Clements End	204	B4
Clencher's Mill	29	F1
Clifford's Mesne	96	E4
Coaley	239	J4
Coaley Peak	240	B1
Coalpit Heath	345	K4
Coalway	176	C5
Coates	247	J2
Cobb's Cross	30	B3
Coberley	163	F2
Cockleford	163	G5
Codrington	359	J4
Cold Ashton	370	E5
Cold Aston	141	J2
Coldharbour	230	C2
Coleford	175	H4
Colethrop	185	J4
Collafield	151	H4
Coln Rogers	196	A3
Coln St Aldwyns	226	C2
Coln St Dennis	196	B4
Colt's Green	348	C3

Compton Abdale	139 G8
Compton Green	51 G8
Compton Greenfield	341 G6
Condicote	67 K8
Coney Hill	130 E7
Conham	375 F1
Coombe	297 H6
Coombe Dingle	352 E6
Coomb's End	348 E8
Cornwell	95 H3
Corse	53 G8
Corse Lawn	55 F4
Cotham	364 A5
Cotswold Community	308 B2
Cowhill	314 E3
Cowhorn Hill	376 D2
Cowley	163 G4
Cranham	160 D8
Cress Green	212 A8
Crew's Hole	365 K7
Cribbs Causeway	341 H8
Cricklade	310 E7
Cromhall	318 C5
Cromhall Common	318 C7
Crooked End	121 K6
Cross Hill	288 E1
Crossways	175 G3
Crossways	317 F4
Crudwell	304 E8
Culkerton	304 A1
Cutsdean	65 G5
Daglingworth	220 C7
Damery	295 G5
Dancing Green	122 B1
Daneway	246 B3
Darlingscott	11 K5
Daylesford	94 D6
Deerhurst	56 D6
Deerhurst Walton	80 A1
Derry Fields	308 C6
Didbrook	64 A3
Didmarton	339 G2
Dixton	61 F5
Dodington	360 C1
Donnington	28 B6
Donnington	92 B1
Dorn	46 A5
Doughton	325 K3
Down Ampney	280 E7
Downend	270 B5
Downend	356 D7
Down Hatherley	103 G4
Doynton	369 H5
Draycott	45 F2
Draycott	238 D6
Driffield	279 J2
Drybrook	122 D7
Duckhole	292 C8
Dudbridge	214 A8
Dumbleton	38 C1
Dunfield	282 C6
Dunkirk	338 B6
Duntisbourne Abbots	219 H1
Duntisbourne Leer	219 H3
Duntisbourne Rouse	219 K5
Dursley	267 F4
Dursley Cross	124 C1
Dyer's Common	340 E3
Dymock	49 J3
Dyrham	370 A2
Earthcott Green	333 F7
Eastcombe	244 C1
Eastcourt	305 K8
East End	255 F8
East End	372 B6
Easter Compton	341 H5
Eastfield	353 K7
Eastington	170 A7
Eastington	211 K6
Eastleach Martin	229 F7
Eastleach Turville	228 C7
Easton	365 G5
Eastville	365 G3
Eaton Hastings	287 F5
The Eaves	205 G5
Ebley	213 J8
Ebrington	22 A1
Edge	186 D6
Edge End	148 C7
Edgeworth	218 D5
Elberton	330 E1
Elcombe	268 A7
Eldersfield	53 K3
Elkstone	163 J8

Ellwood	204 C1
Elmbridge	131 F3
Elmore	156 B3
Elmore Back	127 J8
Elmstone Hardwicke	81 J5
Elton	152 E5
Emerson's Green	357 J8
Engine Common	346 D1
English Bicknor	147 K3
Epney	183 G3
Etloe	207 J6
Evenlode	70 D8
Ewen	277 F7
Fairfields	51 J1
Fairford	254 E7
Fairview	5 D3
Falfield	294 A7
Far Green	267 K1
Farleys End	155 H3
Farmcote	64 B7
Farmington	170 B3
Far Oakridge	245 K2
Far Thrupp	243 H3
The Fence	202 D6
Fiddington	58 C3
Fiddler's Green	105 G4
Filton	355 F3
Fishponds	365 K1
Fishpool	48 C7
Five Acres	148 A8
The Flat	154 E2
Flaxley	152 C3
The Folly	370 D8
Footbridge	63 F8
Ford	65 G7
Forest Green	270 C1
Forthay	266 C8
Forwood	271 H1
Foscot	118 D6
Fossebridge	195 J3
Four Mile Elm	185 F1
Four Oaks	49 J8
Foxcote	137 G5
Frampton Cotterell	345 G7
Frampton End	345 J6
Frampton Mansell	245 J4
Frampton on Severn	210 E1
France Lynch	245 F3
Frenchay	356 B6
Fretherne	182 B7
Frocester	240 B3
Frogland Cross	344 C2
Fromebridge	211 H3
Fyfield	257 F2
Gadfield Elm	53 F3
Ganborough	68 C7
Ganders Green	124 E1
Gatwick	154 A6
Gaunt's Earthcott	344 B1
Gawcombe	117 G7
Geat Wolford	47 K4
Glasshouse	96 E7
Gloucester	2 B5
Golden Hill	354 B8
Golden Valley	104 E4
Goose Green	347 F3
Goose Green	367 J5
Gorsley	72 A6
Gossington	238 B5
Gotherington	60 B6
Grafton	14 A7
Grange Village	179 K1
Great Badminton	351 F4
Great Barrington	173 G6
Great Rissington	144 C3
Great Stoke	356 A1
Great Washbourne	37 G5
Great Witcombe	161 F4
Green Bottom	151 J3
Green Street	160 C3
Green Street	239 G8
Greenway	27 K7
Greet	62 E5
Gretton	62 B5
Gretton Fields	61 K2
Grovesend	317 F7
Guiting Power	88 D8
The Hacket	317 F6
Hagloe	208 B4
Hailes	63 K5
Hallen	352 E1
Hall End	335 F3
Hallwood Green	26 E7
Halmore	236 D5

Ham	107 K7
Ham	263 K5
Hambrook	356 C4
Hampen Manor	138 C2
Hampnett	168 C2
Hampton Fields	272 B2
Hamshill	239 J8
Hanham	375 H1
Hanham Green	375 H3
Hardwicke	81 F2
Hardwicke	156 E8
Hardwicke	184 B1
Harescombe	186 B5
Haresfield	185 F5
Harleywood	270 D4
Harnhill	279 H1
Harrow Hill	122 E8
Harry Stoke	355 J4
Hartpury	76 C7
Hasfield	77 J3
Hatherley	105 H8
Hatherop	227 F7
Hawcross	52 B5
Hawkesbury	337 H4
Hawkesbury Upton	338 A4
Hawling	111 G3
Hayden	104 E3
Hazleton	140 A5
Heath End	318 D6
Heathfield	264 E5
Hempsted	129 G8
Henbury	353 G4
Henfield	357 K3
Henleaze	354 A8
Henley	160 E1
Hester's Way	105 J3
Hethelpit Cross	52 D6
Hewelsfield	231 H5
Hewelsfield Common	231 F4
Hicks Gate	375 G6
Hidcote Bartrim	9 K4
Hidcote Boyce	9 K6
High Brotheridge	160 C6
Highfield	234 C2
Highfields	267 G5
Highleadon	99 J3
Highnam	128 C3
Highnam Green	128 C1
High Nash	175 J5
High Woolaston	259 J3
Hilcot	164 D1
Hilcot End	251 K5
Hill	292 D3
Hill Croome	12 A1
Hill End	12 E6
Hillend Green	49 K8
Hillersland	147 J5
Hillesley	321 H6
Hillfields	366 B3
Hinchwick	67 J5
Hinnegar	339 F4
Hinton	236 A3
Hinton	360 A8
Hinton Cross	16 A1
Hinton on the Green	15 J1
Holbrook Common	368 C7
Holywell	297 G6
Homedowns	58 C1
Honeybourne	7 G1
Hook Street	263 J2
Hope Mansell	121 K2
Horcott	254 E8
Horfield	354 D7
Horsedown	363 K3
Horsepools	186 C5
Horsey Down	310 B6
Horsley	270 B5
Horton	349 F1
Horwood Riding	336 C6
Houndscroft	242 D5
Howley	296 C5
Hucclecote	131 H7
Hudnalls	230 C2
Huntingford	295 H6
Huntley	125 J3
Hyde	65 G8
Hyde	244 B6
Hystfield	293 H1
Icomb	117 H4
Ilmington	11 H2
Inchbrook	242 B8
Inglesham	284 E4
Ingst	330 A2
Innsworth	103 J6

Iron Acton 345 K2
Itchington 333 F4
Jackaments Bottom 275 G7
Jack's Green 188 B5
Joy's Green 120 E8
Kelmscot 286 D3
Kemble 276 C7
Kemble Wick 306 B2
Kempley 48 D6
Kempley Green 48 D8
Kempsford 283 F8
Kendleshire 357 G3
Kenton Green 155 K4
Kent's Green 98 C2
Kerne Bridge 120 A3
Kersoe 14 C2
Ketford 50 E4
Kilcot 72 D7
Kilkenny 136 E4
Kiln Green 120 E2
Kineton 88 C4
Kingham 119 G2
Kingscote 299 G1
Kingscourt 242 D5
Kingsditch 106 A1
King's Green 30 C6
Kings Hill 250 B6
Kingshill 266 E4
Kingsholm 3 D2
King's Stanley 241 F2
Kingswood 320 C2
Kingswood 366 E6
Kington 315 J5
Kinsham 35 F2
Kitebrook 71 J3
Kitlye 216 C8
The Knapp 317 F3
Knightsbridge 80 C4
Lane End 122 C2
Langley 84 E1
Langridge 379 G6
Lansdown 106 A6
Lansdown 378 E8
Lasborough 299 J5
Latteridge 333 H8
Latton 310 D2
Laverton 40 E3
Lawrence Weston 352 C5
Leathern Bottle 265 K1
Lechlade 285 H2
Leckhampton 134 C2
Leddington 27 H4
Leighterton 323 K3
The Leigh 79 G5
Leonard Stanley 241 F3
Leyhill 318 D1
Leys Hill 120 B2
Lightpill 242 B2
Lime Street 54 B5
Linden 157 K1
Linkend 54 E3
Lintridge 29 H8
Little Badminton 350 E1
Little Barrington 173 F8
Little Barrow 69 K7
Little Beckford 36 D3
Little Bristol 319 K3
Littledean 151 J6
Littledean Hill 151 H5
Little Doward 146 C1
Little Drybrook 204 C3
Little Faringdon 257 K6
Littleford 74 A4
Little Gorsley 72 C8
Little Haresfield 184 E7
Little Herbert's 135 J2
Little London 124 E5
Little Rissington 144 C2
Little Shurdington 133 J6
Little Sodbury 348 E3
Little Sodbury End 348 C2
Little Stoke 343 H7
Littleton Drew 363 K1
Littleton-upon-Severn 314 C5
Little Washbourne 37 H6
Little Witcombe 161 G2
Littleworth 20 C3
Littleworth 242 E6
Lockleaze 355 G7
Longborough 69 F7
Longford 102 A8
Longhope 124 C4
Long Newnton 327 G1
Longney 155 G8

Longridge 188 A7
Longridge End 101 F1
Longwell Green 375 K3
Lowbands 52 D3
Lower Apperley 79 G2
Lower Berry Hill 175 H2
Lower Cam 266 C1
Lower Chedworth 195 H4
Lower Dowdeswell 136 E2
Lower End 220 D8
Lower Hamswell 378 E3
Lower Hazel 331 J3
Lower Kilcott 322 A7
Lower Lemington 46 C5
Lower Ley 154 D2
Lower Lode 57 F2
Lower Lydbrook 148 D1
Lower Meend 230 D1
Lower Morton 316 D2
Lower Oddington 93 K6
Lower Rea 156 E3
Lower Slaughter 115 H4
Lower Soudley 179 H5
Lower Stone 293 J4
Lower Swell 91 K7
Lower Tuffley 157 J4
Lower Wick 265 C8
Luckington 351 K2
Ludstock 27 G2
Luxley 96 A6
Lyde Green 358 A6
Lydney 234 B4
Lynworth 5 E1
Lypiatt 190 A8
Maisemore 101 G7
Malswick 74 C7
Mangotsfield 367 F1
Marle Hill 4 B1
Marsden 193 G2
Marsh Common 341 G2
Marshfield 371 J4
Marsh Lane 204 B2
Marston Hill 282 A3
Marston Meysey 281 K7
Matson 158 E3
Mayshill 346 A5
Mead Riding 348 A3
Meysey Hampton 281 J2
Mickleton 9 G2
Middle Duntisbourne 220 B4
Middle Street 211 J8
Middle Wick 295 H1
Middle Yard 241 H3
Milbury Heath 317 H5
Mile End 176 C2
Milkwall 176 B7
Mill End 169 F5
Millend 175 H7
Millend 212 A7
Millend 296 E1
Mill Hill 204 E5
Milton End 181 H4
Milton End 254 C7
Minchinhampton 243 J8
Minsterworth 127 J7
Miserden 190 B7
Mitcheldean 123 F4
Mitton 34 A6
Montpelier 364 C4
Moor End 135 F1
Moorend 159 G6
Moorend 237 K4
Moorend 356 E4
Moreton-in-Marsh 46 B8
Moreton Valence 184 B6
Mork 203 F7
Morton 316 D4
Mountain Bower 373 F2
Mount Hill 366 E8
Mount Pleasant 16 D3
Much Marcle 26 A8
Murcot 17 G1
Murrell's End 51 H5
Murrell's End 100 B5
The Mythe 33 H5
Nag's Head 272 C5
Nailbridge 150 D1
Nailsworth 270 E3
Nashend 216 E7
Nastend 212 B5
Natton 34 E8
Naunton 113 H2
Nebsworth 10 D4
Netham 365 G8

Netherend 260 C1
Netherton 226 E8
Nether Westcote 145 J1
Nettleton 162 C6
Nettleton Green 363 G5
Nettleton Shrub 363 H6
New Cheltenham 367 F5
Newent 73 H6
Newerne 234 A3
New Grounds 209 K6
Newington Bagpath 299 H4
Newland 175 F6
Newmarket 270 B2
New Mills 234 A1
New Mills 250 B6
Newnham 180 C2
New Passage 328 C5
Newport 264 D6
Newtown 292 D8
Newtown 34 B8
New Town 63 H1
Newtown 212 B6
Newtown 235 K5
Nibley 207 G4
Nibley 346 C5
Nibley Green 296 A1
Nimlet 379 H3
Ninewells 148 A7
Norcote 250 D4
Norman Hill 266 E3
North Cerney 221 J2
North Common 367 K8
North Corner 345 F5
North End 308 D4
Northington 180 D8
Northleach 169 H4
North Nibley 296 B5
North Stoke 377 K7
Northway 34 D4
Northwick 329 G4
Northwood Green 153 H1
North Wraxall 373 K4
Norton 102 E1
Notgrove 141 G1
Nottwood Hill 124 E6
Noverton 107 K3
Nupdown 291 K1
Nupend 212 B4
Nupend 270 A5
Nuppend 232 E7
Nympsfield 268 E1
Oakle Street 127 F6
Oakley 107 J4
Oakridge 245 H3
Oaksey 306 B6
Okle Green 75 F6
Oldbury Naite 291 H7
Oldbury-on-Severn 291 G8
Oldbury on the Hill 339 G1
Oldcroft 206 E6
Old Down 331 G3
Oldend 212 D5
Oldland 376 B3
Oldland Common 376 C3
Old Passage 313 H8
Old Sodbury 349 F7
Olveston 330 E3
Oridge Street 76 B2
Over 129 G2
Over 342 B4
Overton 181 K5
Owlpen 268 E5
Oxenhall 73 G4
Oxenton 60 A3
Ozleworth 298 C6
Paganhill 214 C6
Painswick 187 G7
Palmer's Flat 176 A6
Pamington 35 G7
Pancakehill 195 H3
Paradise 187 J3
Parkend 184 C4
Parkend 205 H1
Parkfield 358 C7
Park Hill 259 H2
The Park 106 B8
Parkway 28 C2
Patchway 342 E5
Paxford 22 B2
Pendock 31 F8
Pennsylvania 370 D7
Perrott's Brook 221 H6
Petty France 338 A3
Picklenash 73 G5

Piff's Elm 80 E5
Pilley 134 E2
Pillowell 205 K5
Pillows Green 53 J6
Pilning 329 F7
Pinfarthings 242 D8
Pitchcombe 214 E2
Pitt Court 296 E1
Pittville 4 C2
Playley Green 52 B2
The Pludds 149 H1
Plump Hill 123 G7
Plusterwine 260 C3
Podsmead 157 K2
Poole Keynes 306 E3
Poolhill 51 F7
Pope's Hill 152 B4
Portway 31 F6
Postlip 85 F3
Poulton 252 E8
The Pound 50 A4
Prescott 61 G7
Prestbury 107 H1
Preston 26 D3
Preston 250 D8
Prior's Norton 103 H1
Priors Park 57 J1
Pucklechurch 368 C1
Puckrup 12 A8
Puckshole 214 A6
Pullens Green 315 G1
Purton 207 H8
Putloe 184 A6
Pye Corner 356 D3
Quarhouse 243 J4
The Quarry 266 B2
Quedgeley 156 E5
Quenington 254 C1
Ram Hill 357 K2
Randwick 213 J4
Rangeworthy 334 C5
Rea 157 F2
Readings 149 G1
Ready Token 224 E8
Redbrook 174 B5
The Reddings 104 E7
Redland 364 A3
Redmarley D'Abitot 52 A3
Redwick 328 D6
Rendcomb 193 H6
Ridgeway 365 K3
Rockhampton 293 F7
Rockness 270 C4
The Rocks 347 H1
Rockstowes 267 K6
Rodborough 214 B8
Rodley 182 D2
Rodmarton 274 C6
Rooksmoor 242 C4
Rowanfield 105 K4
Ruardean 121 J7
Ruardean Hill 122 A7
Ruardean Woodside 121 J8
Ruddle 180 A3
Rudford 99 J7
Rudgeway 331 K5
Ruscombe 214 A3
Ruspidge 178 E1
Ryeford 213 G8
Rye Street 31 F2
Ryeworth 107 J7
Ryton 50 E1
St Anne's Park 365 J8
St Briavels 203 G8
St Briavels Common 230 C5
Saintbridge 130 D8
Saintbury 19 G2
St Catherine 380 D5
St Chloe 242 D6
St George 366 A7
St Mark's 105 K5
St Paul's 2 B6
St Peter's 106 B3
Salperton 139 K1
Salperton Park 139 K2
Sandhurst 101 J3
Sandpits 55 F6
Sapperton 246 D3
Sarsden Halt 95 K8
Saul 182 D7
The Scarr 73 J2
Scowles 175 G4
Sedbury 288 D7
Sedgeberrow 15 J4

Selsley 242 A2
Sevenhampton 110 B6
Seven Springs 135 G7
Severn Beach 328 D8
Sezincote 68 D3
Shab Hill 162 B3
Shadwell 268 A6
Shakesfield 49 H2
Shapridge 151 K1
Sharpness 235 H4
Shaw Common 72 C2
Sheepscombe 188 C5
Shepherd's Patch 237 K1
Shepperdine 291 H3
Sherborne 171 J4
Shipton 138 A4
Shipton Moyne 326 C6
Shipton Oliffe 138 C4
Shipton Solers 138 A4
Shirehampton 352 A7
The Shoe 373 C5
Shorncote 277 K8
Shortstanding 147 G7
Shortwood 270 B3
Shortwood 367 K2
Shurdington 133 H4
Shuthonger 33 G2
Siddington 278 B2
Silver Street 240 A7
Siston 368 B3
Siston Common 367 G5
Slad 215 J2
Sladbrook 52 C8
Slimbridge 238 C2
Sling 204 A2
Smallbrook 232 D8
Snig's End 53 H8
Snowshill 41 H6
Somerdale 375 K7
Somerford Keynes 307 J3
Sopworth 339 K5
Soundwell 366 E3
Southam 83 H6
South Cerney 278 D7
Southend 296 C3
Southmead 353 K5
Southrop 256 E3
Speedwell 366 A4
Springbank 105 H3
Standish 212 E1
Stanley Downton 240 E1
Stanley Pontlarge 61 J5
Stanton 40 D5
Stantway 153 K6
Stanway 64 A1
Staple Hill 366 E2
Stapleton 365 G1
Starveall 338 D2
Staunton 53 F7
Staunton 146 E8
Staverton 104 C2
Steam Mills 150 D2
Stinchcombe 265 K5
Stockend 186 B7
Stockwell 162 B5
Stockwood 374 C6
Stockwood Vale 375 G8
Stoke Bishop 353 F8
Stoke Gifford 355 H1
Stoke Orchard 58 D8
Stone 294 A3
Stone Hill 375 K2
Stonehouse 213 G6
Stowe 203 G4
Stowe Green 203 H4
Stowell 168 A7
Stow-on-the-Wold 92 B6
Strand 153 H7
Stratford 12 A4
Stratton 249 G2
Stretton-on-Fosse 23 H5
Stroat 259 J6
Stroud 214 C5
Stroud Green 213 F2
Stub Riding 347 K3
Stumps Cross 64 E5
Sudgrove 218 A1
Sundayshill 293 J6
Sunhill 253 G4
Swanley 294 E1
Swindon 82 B7
Swineford 377 H7
Syde 190 D4
Symonds Yat 147 F1

Synwell 297 G7
Syreford 137 K1
Taddington 65 F3
Tadwick 379 H5
Talbot's End 318 E4
Tarlton 275 F2
Taynton 97 K6
Teddington 36 A8
Teddington Hands 36 C6
Temple Guiting 88 C1
Tetbury 302 C7
Tetbury Upton 301 K3
Tewkesbury 57 G1
Thames Head 276 B3
Thornbury 316 B5
Througham 217 J2
Thrupp 243 G2
Tibberton 99 F6
Tickmorend 270 B4
Tidenham 289 G2
Tidenham Chase 258 E4
Tidmington 24 E5
Tillers' Green 27 H8
Tilsdown 266 D2
Tiltups End 270 D7
Tirley 55 G8
Tirley Knowle 54 D6
Tockington 330 E5
Toddington 39 G8
Todenham 47 H1
Tormarton 361 J4
Tortworth 294 E7
Totteroak 348 C1
Town Street 55 G7
Townwell 318 D5
Tredington 57 K6
Tredworth 3 D6
Tresham 322 C3
Triangle 230 D6
Trow Green 204 A4
Tuffley 158 A3
Tumpy Green 237 J6
Tunley 246 A1
Turkdean 141 F7
Tutnalls 234 C4
Tutshill 288 B5
Twigworth 102 C5
The Twittocks 12 B7
Two Bridges 179 H8
Two Mile Hill 366 B5
Twyning 12 D8
Twyning Green 12 E8
The Tynings 133 K4
Tytherington 333 J1
Uckington 81 H8
Uley 268 B5
Up Hatherley 133 H1
Uplands 215 G5
Upleadon 74 D4
Upleadon Court 75 H4
Upper Cam 267 F2
Upper Coberley 164 A2
Upper Dowdeswell 136 E3
Upper End 169 J6
Upper End 221 F4
Upper Framilode 182 C5
Upper Hill 292 E1
Upper Kilcott 338 D1
Upper Ley 126 A6
Upper Lode 33 F7
Upper Lydbrook 149 F2
Upper Morton 316 E2
Upper Oddington 93 J7
Upper Rissington 145 F2
Upper Siddington 277 K2
Upper Slaughter 115 F2
Upper Soudley 179 F5
Upper Strensham 12 E2
Upper Swell 91 K4
Upper Up 278 C8
Upper Wick 265 H8
Upper Wraxall 372 E5
Upthorpe 267 F1
Upton Cheyney 377 J6
Upton St Leonards 159 H4
Viney Hill 207 F5
Vinney Green 357 G7
Walford 120 A1
Walham 129 K1
Wallow Green 270 B3
Wallsworth 102 C3
Walton Cardiff 57 K1
Wanswell 235 K7
Wapley 359 G2

Warden Hill	133 K1	Wheatenhurst	183 G8	Withington	165 J2
Warmley	367 H7	Whelford	283 J4	Woodbridge	166 B4
Warmley Hill	367 F6	Whitebrook	202 B4	Woodchester	242 B4
Warmley Tower	367 H8	Whitecliff	175 H5	Woodcroft	288 D2
Waterend	154 E5	Whitecroft	205 H5	Woodfield	266 C3
Waterhay	309 G7	White End	31 G5	Woodford	294 C2
Waterlane	217 H8	Whitehall	365 G5	Woodhouse Down	331 H7
Watermead	160 C2	Whiteleaved Oak	30 B2	Woodmancote	83 H3
Watermoor	249 K7	Whiteshill	214 C2	Woodmancote	193 F7
Watledge	270 E1	Whiteshill	356 C3	Woodmancote	266 E6
Watley's End	345 G7	Whiteway	189 J5	Wood Stanway	64 C3
Webb's Heath	368 A6	Whiteway	270 B4	Woolaston	260 A3
Welsh Bicknor	120 C6	Whitfield	317 K3	Woolaston Common	232 B7
Westbury-on-Severn	153 F6	Whitminster	211 H1	Woolaston Slade	259 K1
Westbury on Trym	353 G8	Whittington	109 G7	Woolaston Woodside	232 A8
West Crudwell	304 D7	Wibdon	259 H7	Woolley	379 J8
West End	18 C8	Wick	369 F8	Woolridge	101 F2
Westend	211 K4	Wickridge Street	77 G3	Woolstone	60 B5
West End	271 K6	Wick Street	215 H2	Worley	270 C2
Westend	291 F8	Wickwar	335 J1	Wormington	39 H1
West End	319 G8	Wiggold	222 D8	Worrall Hill	148 E4
Westerleigh	358 C2	Willersey	19 F2	Wortley	321 G2
Westerleigh Hill	359 F3	Willesley	324 E8	Wotton	3 F3
Westington	20 C4	Willington	25 J3	Wotton-under-Edge	297 G7
West Kington	362 E7	Willsbridge	376 C4	Wyck Rissington	116 B6
West Kington Wick	363 H8	Winchcombe	62 C8	Wyegate Green	202 D5
West Littleton	371 G3	Windrush	172 D8	Wymans Brook	82 C8
Westonbirt	325 F6	Windsoredge	270 B1	Yanworth	168 A6
Weston-sub-Edge	7 K7	Winson	196 B8	Yate	347 F5
Westrip	213 J6	Winstone	191 G6	Yate Rocks	335 H8
Westwell	201 J5	Winterbourne	344 D8	Yorkley	206 A4
Whaddon	5 E3	Winterbourne Down	357 F2	Yorkley Slade	206 C3
Whaddon	158 B6	Wishanger	189 H6		

USING THE STREET INDEX

Street names are listed alphabetically. Each street name is followed by its postal town or area locality, the Postcode District, the page number, and the reference to the square in which the name is found.

Example: **Abbey Ct** *BRSG/KWL/STAPK* BS4 .... **374** E1 ▯

Some entries are followed by a number in a blue box. This number indicates the location of the street within the referenced grid square. The full street name is listed at the side of the map page.

GENERAL ABBREVIATIONS

ACC	ACCESS	CTRL	CENTRAL	GTWY	GATEWAY
ALY	ALLEY	CTS	COURTS	GV	GROVE
AP	APPROACH	CTYD	COURTYARD	HGR	HIGHER
AR	ARCADE	CUTT	CUTTINGS	HL	HILL
ASS	ASSOCIATION	CV	COVE	HLS	HILLS
AV	AVENUE	CYN	CANYON	HO	HOUSE
BCH	BEACH	DEPT	DEPARTMENT	HOL	HOLLOW
BLDS	BUILDINGS	DL	DALE	HOSP	HOSPITAL
BND	BEND	DM	DAM	HRB	HARBOUR
BNK	BANK	DR	DRIVE	HTH	HEATH
BR	BRIDGE	DRO	DROVE	HTS	HEIGHTS
BRK	BROOK	DRY	DRIVEWAY	HVN	HAVEN
BTM	BOTTOM	DWGS	DWELLINGS	HWY	HIGHWAY
BUS	BUSINESS	E	EAST	IMP	IMPERIAL
BVD	BOULEVARD	EMB	EMBANKMENT	IN	INLET
BY	BYPASS	EMBY	EMBASSY	IND EST	INDUSTRIAL ESTATE
CATH	CATHEDRAL	ESP	ESPLANADE	INF	INFIRMARY
CEM	CEMETERY	EST	ESTATE	INFO	INFORMATION
CEN	CENTRE	EX	EXCHANGE	INT	INTERCHANGE
CFT	CROFT	EXPY	EXPRESSWAY	IS	ISLAND
CH	CHURCH	EXT	EXTENSION	JCT	JUNCTION
CHA	CHASE	F/O	FLYOVER	JTY	JETTY
CHYD	CHURCHYARD	FC	FOOTBALL CLUB	KG	KING
CIR	CIRCLE	FK	FORK	KNL	KNOLL
CIRC	CIRCUS	FLD	FIELD	L	LAKE
CL	CLOSE	FLDS	FIELDS	LA	LANE
CLFS	CLIFFS	FLS	FALLS	LDG	LODGE
CMP	CAMP	FLS	FLATS	LGT	LIGHT
CNR	CORNER	FM	FARM	LK	LOCK
CO	COUNTY	FT	FORT	LKS	LAKES
COLL	COLLEGE	FWY	FREEWAY	LNDG	LANDING
COM	COMMON	FY	FERRY	LTL	LITTLE
COMM	COMMISSION	GA	GATE	LWR	LOWER
CON	CONVENT	GAL	GALLERY	MAG	MAGISTRATE
COT	COTTAGE	GDN	GARDEN	MAN	MANSIONS
COTS	COTTAGES	GDNS	GARDENS	MD	MEAD
CP	CAPE	GLD	GLADE	MDW	MEADOWS
CPS	COPSE	GLN	GLEN	MEM	MEMORIAL
CR	CREEK	GN	GREEN	MKT	MARKET
CREM	CREMATORIUM	GND	GROUND	MKTS	MARKETS
CRS	CRESCENT	GRA	GRANGE	ML	MALL
CSWY	CAUSEWAY	GRG	GARAGE	ML	MILL
CT	COURT	GT	GREAT	MNR	MANOR

MS	MEWS
MSN	MISSION
MT	MOUNT
MTN	MOUNTAIN
MTS	MOUNTAINS
MUS	MUSEUM
MWY	MOTORWAY
N	NORTH
NE	NORTH EAST
NW	NORTH WEST
O/P	OVERPASS
OFF	OFFICE
ORCH	ORCHARD
OV	OVAL
PAL	PALACE
PAS	PASSAGE
PAV	PAVILION
PDE	PARADE
PH	PUBLIC HOUSE
PK	PARK
PKWY	PARKWAY
PL	PLACE
PLN	PLAIN
PLNS	PLAINS
PLZ	PLAZA
POL	POLICE STATION
PR	PRINCE
PREC	PRECINCT
PREP	PREPARATORY
PRIM	PRIMARY
PROM	PROMENADE
PRS	PRINCESS

PRT	PORT
PT	POINT
PTH	PATH
PZ	PIAZZA
QD	QUADRANT
QU	QUEEN
QY	QUAY
R	RIVER
RBT	ROUNDABOUT
RD	ROAD
RDG	RIDGE
REP	REPUBLIC
RES	RESERVOIR
RFC	RUGBY FOOTBALL CLUB
RI	RISE
RP	RAMP
RW	ROW
S	SOUTH
SCH	SCHOOL
SE	SOUTH EAST
SER	SERVICE AREA
SH	SHORE
SHOP	SHOPPING
SKWY	SKYWAY
SMT	SUMMIT
SOC	SOCIETY
SP	SPUR
SPR	SPRING
SQ	SQUARE
ST	STREET
STN	STATION
STR	STREAM

STRD	STRAND
SW	SOUTH WEST
TDG	TRADING
TER	TERRACE
THWY	THROUGHWAY
TNL	TUNNEL
TOLL	TOLLWAY
TPK	TURNPIKE
TR	TRACK
TRL	TRAIL
TWR	TOWER
U/P	UNDERPASS
UNI	UNIVERSITY
UPR	UPPER
V	VALE
VA	VALLEY
VIAD	VIADUCT
VIL	VILLA
VIS	VISTA
VLG	VILLAGE
VLS	VILLAS
VW	VIEW
W	WEST
WD	WOOD
WHF	WHARF
WK	WALK
WKS	WALKS
WLS	WELLS
WY	WAY
YD	YARD
YHA	YOUTH HOSTEL

POSTCODE TOWNS AND AREA ABBREVIATIONS

ALMDB	Almondsbury
AVONM	Avonmouth
BAD	Badminton
BDWAY	Broadway
BRKLY	Berkeley
BRSG/KWL/STAPK	Brislington/Knowle/St Anne's Park
BRSTK/PCHW	Bradley Stoke/Patchway
BUR/CRTN	Burford/Carterton
BWTH/CHD	Brockworth/Churchdown
CBATH/BATHN	Central Bath/Bath north
CBRIS/FH	Central Bristol/Floating Harbour
CBRISNE	Central Bristol north & east
CFTN/FAIL	Clifton/Failand
CHCAM	Chipping Campden
CHELT	Cheltenham
CHELTE/BC	Cheltenham east/Bishop's Cleeve
CHELTS	Cheltenham south
CHELTW	Cheltenham west
CHEP	Chepstow
CHNTN	Chipping Norton
CHPMW/MSHF	Chippenham west/Marshfield
CIND	Cinderford

CIR	Cirencester
CLFD	Coleford
COR/BOX	Corsham/Box
COTS	Cotswolds
DSLY	Dursley
EVE	Evesham
EVILLE/WHL	Eastville/Whitehall
FGDN	Faringdon
FRCTL/WBN	Frampton Cotterell/Winterbourne
GL	Gloucester
GLE	Gloucester east
HGHW	Highworth
HGRV/WHIT	Hengrove/Whitchurch
HNBRY/STHM	Henbury/Southmead
HNLZ/SM/SNYPK/WT	Henleaze/Sea Mills/Sneyd Park/Westbury-on-Trym
HORF/LLZ	Horfield/Lockleaze
KEYN	Keynsham
KGWD/HNM	Kingswood/Hanham
LED	Ledbury
LYD	Lydney
MALM	Malmesbury
MANG/FISH	Mangotsfield/Fishponds

MIM	Moreton-in-Marsh
MONM	Monmouth
MTCHDN	Mitcheldean
NWNT	Newent
OLD/WMLY/WICK	Oldland/Warmley/Wick
PER	Pershore
PTSHD/EG	Portishead/Easton-in-Gordano
RDLND/MONT	Redland/Montpelier
RGTMLV	Rural Great Malvern
RSTROUD/NAIL	Rural Stroud/Nailsworth
RTEWK/TIB	Rural Tewkesbury/Tibberton
RWYE	Ross-on-Wye
SHPSTR	Shipston-on-Stour
STNHO	Stonehouse
STRAT	Stratford-upon-Avon
STROUD	Stroud
TET	Tetbury
TEWK	Tewkesbury
THNB/SVB	Thornbury/Severn Beach
UUSV	Upton upon Severn
VGL	Vale of Gloucester
WUE	Wotton-under-Edge
YATE/CS	Yate/Chipping Sodbury

Index - streets

Aar - Alb

A

Aaron Rd *CIR* GL7	278 D2
Abbenesse *RSTROUD/NAIL* GL6	244 C3
Abbey Ct *BRSG/KWL/STAPK* BS4	374 E1 🔟
Abbeydale *FRCTL/WBN* BS36	344 E8
Abbey La *THNB/SVB* BS35	316 D8
Abbeymead Av *GLE* GL4	131 F7
GLE GL4	159 G2
Abbey Meadow *TEWK* GL20	57 J3 🔟
Abbey Pk *KEYN* BS31	376 A8
Abbey Rd	
HNLZ/SM/SNYPK/WT BS9	353 H8
VGL GL2	2 A5
Abbey St *CIND* GL14	151 F6
Abbey Vw *VGL* GL2	320 D1
Abbey Wy *CIR* GL7	249 H4
Abbots Av *KGWD/HNM* BS15	375 H2
Abbots Cl *CHELT* GL50	134 B1
Abbots Cl *CIR* GL7	33 H1
Abbots Leys Rd *COTS* GL54	85 H1
Abbots Ms *CHELTE/BC* GL52	82 E4
Abbots Rd *CIR* GL7	250 A6 🔟
GLE GL4	131 G8
KGWD/HNM BS15	375 H4
TEWK GL20	57 H2
Abbots Vw *CIND* GL14	179 F1
Abbots Wk *CIR* GL7	285 H2

Abbots Wy	
HNLZ/SM/SNYPK/WT BS9	354 B8
STNHO GL10	212 E8
Abbotswood *KGWD/HNM* BS15	366 D7 🔟
YATE/CS BS37	347 F7 🔟
Abbotswood Cl *GLE* GL4	157 K3
Abbotswood Rd *BWTH/CHD* GL3	160 C1
Abbott Rd *THNB/SVB* BS35	340 C1
Abingdon Court La *HGHW* SN6	310 E6
Abingdon Rd *MANG/FISH* BS16	366 A3
Ableton La *HNBRY/STHM* BS10	340 B6
THNB/SVB BS35	328 C8
Abnash *RSTROUD/NAIL* GL6	244 C3
Abraham Cl *EVILLE/WHL* BS5	365 F6 🔟
Abson Rd *MANG/FISH* BS16	368 D1
OLD/WMLY/WICK BS30	368 D5
Acacia Av *MANG/FISH* BS16	366 C2
Acacia Cl *CHELTE/BC* GL52	107 C1
LYD GL15	205 F6 🔟
MANG/FISH BS16	366 C3 🔟
Acacia Dr *DSLY* GL11	266 E3
Acacia Pk *CHELTE/BC* GL52	82 D1
Acacia Rd *MANG/FISH* BS16	366 D3
Acer Gv *VGL* GL2	156 E4
Acomb Crs *CHELTE/BC* GL52	107 H8 🔟
Acre St *STROUD* GL5	214 E7
Acton Rd *MANG/FISH* BS16	366 A3 🔟
Adams Hay	
BRSG/KWL/STAPK BS4	374 C5 🔟
Adams Wy *CLFD* GL16	175 J1
Adderly Ga *MANG/FISH* BS16	357 H7

Addis Rd *CHELTW* GL51	106 B3 🔟
Addymore *DSLY* GL11	266 D1 🔟
Adelaide Gdns *STNHO* GL10	212 E5 🔟
Adelaide Pl *EVILLE/WHL* BS5	365 F6 🔟
MANG/FISH BS16	365 K2 🔟
Adelaide St *GL* GL1	3 E6
Adey's La *WUE* GL12	297 F5
Admiral Cl *CHELTW* GL51	105 H4
Admirals Cl *LYD* GL15	205 F5 🔟
Aesops Orch *CHELTE/BC* GL52	83 J3
Aggs Hi *CHELTE/BC* GL52	107 K5
Aggs La *CHELTE/BC* GL52	60 B6
Aiken St *EVILLE/WHL* BS5	365 F8
Aintree Dr *MANG/FISH* BS16	357 F5
Air Balloon Rd *EVILLE/WHL* BS5	366 A7
Aisne Rd *LYD* GL15	206 D5
Akeman Rd *CIR* GL7	250 A6 🔟
Akermans Orch *NWNT* GL18	73 H6
Albany Rd *STNHO* GL10	212 E5
Albany Ga *BRSTK/PCHW* BS34	355 J1
Albany Rd *CHELT* GL50	106 B7
RDLND/MONT BS6	364 D5 🔟
Albany St *GL* GL1	3 D6
KGWD/HNM BS15	366 C6
Albany Wy *OLD/WMLY/WICK* BS30	376 D1
Albemarle Ga *CHELT* GL50	4 B1
Albemarle Rd *BWTH/CHD* GL3	132 B1
Albert Dr *CHELTE/BC* GL52	4 C1
Albert Gv *EVILLE/WHL* BS5	365 K6 🔟
Alberton Rd *MANG/FISH* BS16	355 K8
Albert Pde *EVILLE/WHL* BS5	365 G6

Albert Pk *RDLND/MONT* BS6 .... 364 D5
Albert Park Pl *RDLND/MONT* BS6 ...... 364 C5
Albert Pl *CHELTE/BC* GL52 .... 4 C3
  HNLZ/SM/SNYPK/WT BS9 .... 353 J7
Albert Rd *CBRISNE* BS2 .... 374 A2
  CHELTE/BC GL52 .... 4 C1
  CIND GL14 .... 150 E7
  CLFD GL16 .... 175 J4
  KGWD/HNM BS15 .... 175 J1
  MANG/FISH BS16 .... 366 E2
  STROUD GL5 .... 243 H5
  THNB/SVB BS35 .... 328 C8
Albert St *CHELT* GL50 .... 4 B2
  GL GL1 .... 3 D4
  LYD GL15 .... 234 A2
Albert Ter *MANG/FISH* BS16 .... 365 K2
Albion Cl *MANG/FISH* BS16 .... 367 F1
Albion Pl *CHELTE/BC* GL52 .... 4 C3
Albion Rd *GL14* 151 F4
  EVILLE/WHL BS5 .... 365 G5
Albion St *CHELTE/BC* GL52 .... 4 C4
  EVILLE/WHL BS5 .... 365 G5
  CIR GL7 .... 249 H3
  GL GL1 .... 2 B4
Albright La *LED* HR8 .... 29 J6
Alcotts Gn *VCL* GL2 .... 102 A3
Alcove Rd *MANG/FISH* BS16 .... 365 J3
Alder Cl *VCL* GL2 .... 130 E2
Aldercombe Rd
  HNLZ/SM/SNYPK/WT BS9 .... 352 E6
Alderdale *LYD* GL15 .... 234 B2
Alderdown Cl *AVONM* BS11 .... 352 C6
Alder Dr *EVILLE/WHL* BS5 .... 365 J5
Aldergate St *STNHO* GL10 .... 213 F7
Alderley Rd *WUE* GL12 .... 321 H5
Aldermoor Wy
  OLD/WMLY/WICK BS30 .... 375 K2
Aldernay Av
  BRSG/KWL/STAPK BS4 .... 374 E2
Alders Gn *VCL* GL2 .... 130 D1
The Alders *CHELTS* GL53 .... 134 E2
Alderton Cl *GLE* GL4 .... 159 G2
  HORF/LLZ BS7 .... 354 C6
Alderton Rd *CHELTW* GL51 .... 105 J6
Alder Wy *STROUD/NAIL* GL6 .... 244 C2
Aldridge Cl *CHELT* GL50 .... 4 A2
Aldsworth Cl *CIR* GL7 .... 255 G7
Alexander Dr *CIR* GL7 .... 249 H8
Alexander Gdns *TET* GL8 .... 302 E6
Alexandra Cl *MANG/FISH* BS16 .... 366 D2
Alexandra Gdns *MANG/FISH* BS16 .. 366 D2
Alexandra Pk *MANG/FISH* BS16 .... 365 K2
  RDLND/MONT BS6 .... 364 A4
Alexandra Pl *MANG/FISH* BS16 .... 366 D2
Alexandra Rd *CHEP* NP16 .... 288 B8
  FRCTL/WBN BS36 .... 345 K7
  GL GL1 .... 3 D3
  HNBRY/STHM BS10 .... 354 A6
  KGWD/HNM BS15 .... 375 J1
Alexandra St *CHELT* GL50 .... 106 B7
Alexandra Wy *TEWK* GL20 .... 34 C7
  THNB/SVB BS35 .... 316 B3
Alford Rd *BRSG/KWL/STAPK* BS4 ..... 374 B4
Alfred Hl *CBRISNE* BS2 .... 364 B5
Alfred Pde *CBRISNE* BS2 .... 364 B6
Alfred Pl *CBRISNE* BS2 .... 364 A6
Alfred St *CBRISNE* BS2 .... 364 E8
  EVILLE/WHL BS5 .... 365 G6
  GL GL1 .... 3 E5
Alice Crs *CHEP* NP16 .... 312 C2
Alington Cl *GL* GL1 .... 3 E4
Alkerton Rd *STNHO* GL10 .... 211 K7
All Alone *COTS* GL54 .... 169 F5
Allanmead Rd *HGRV/WHIT* BS14 ..... 374 A6
Allaston Rd *LYD* GL15 .... 206 B8
Allendale Cl *VCL* GL2 .... 130 E2
Allen Dr *STROUD* GL5 .... 214 B4
Allenfield Rd *CHELTS* GL53 .... 134 C1
Allengrove La
  CHPMW/MSHF SN14 .... 351 J3
Allfoxton Rd *HORF/LLZ* BS7 .... 364 E3
All Hallows Rd *EVILLE/WHL* BS5 ...... 365 F6
Allington Dr
  OLD/WMLY/WICK BS30 .... 376 A2
Allison Av *BRSG/KWL/STAPK* BS4 .... 374 D2
Allison Rd *BRSG/KWL/STAPK* BS4 ... 374 D3
Allotment La *CIR* GL7 .... 251 J5
Allsopp Cl *CIND* GL14 .... 180 B2
Alma Cl *CHELTW* GL51 .... 105 K7
  KGWD/HNM BS15 .... 366 E6
Alma Pl *GL* GL1 .... 2 B6
Alma Rd *CHELTW* GL51 .... 105 K8
  KGWD/HNM BS15 .... 366 E6
Alma Ter *GL* GL1 .... 2 B6
Almeda Rd *EVILLE/WHL* BS5 .... 366 A4
Almond Cl *GLE* GL4 .... 159 F3

Almond Wk *LYD* GL15 .... 234 B2
Almond Wy *MANG/FISH* BS16 .... 367 F1
Almshouses Rd *CLFD* GL16 .... 174 E7
Alney Ter *GL* GL1 .... 2 A2
Alpha Cl *TEWK* GL20 .... 34 B7
Alpine Cl *GLE* GL4 .... 130 D8
Alpine Rd *EVILLE/WHL* BS5 .... 365 G5
Alsop Rd *KGWD/HNM* BS15 .... 366 D6
Alstone Av *CHELTW* GL51 .... 106 B4
Alstone Ct *CHELTW* GL51 .... 106 A4
Alstone La *CHELTW* GL51 .... 106 A4
Althorp Cl *GL* GL1 .... 157 H4
Alton Rd *HORF/LLZ* BS7 .... 354 B4
Altringham Rd *EVILLE/WHL* BS5 ...... 365 H6
Alverton Dr *CHELTE/BC* GL52 .... 82 E4
Alveston Gra *CHCAM* GL55 .... 9 F3
Alveston Hl *THNB/SVB* BS35 .... 316 A8
Alveston Rd *ALMDB* BS32 .... 331 G3
Alveston Wk
  HNLZ/SM/SNYPK/WT BS9 .... 352 D7
Alvin St *GL* GL1 .... 2 C3
Alwins Ct
  OLD/WMLY/WICK BS30 .... 376 A2
Amaranth Wy *CHELTW* GL51 .... 133 K1
Amberley Cl *MANG/FISH* BS16 .... 356 D7
Amberley Pk *BRSTK/PCHW* BS34 ..... 343 F5
  CHELT GL51 .... 105 J4
  GLE GL4 .... 158 D1
  MANG/FISH BS16 .... 356 D7
Amberley Wy *WUE* GL12 .... 335 K1
Amble Cl *KGWD/HNM* BS15 .... 367 F7
Ambleside Av *HNBRY/STHM* BS10 .. 353 K5
Ambrose La *CLFD* GL16 .... 176 B3
Ambrose Pl *CHELT* GL50 .... 4 B3
Ambrose St *CHELT* GL50 .... 4 B3
Amercombe Wk *HGRV/WHIT* BS14 .. 374 C7
America Gdns *NWNT* GL18 .... 73 J6
Ampney La *CIND* GL14 .... 125 H8
Anbrook Crs *GLE* GL4 .... 131 G7
Anchor Rd *CBRIS/FH* BS1 .... 364 A8
  KGWD/HNM BS15 .... 367 G5
Ancient Rd *CLFD* GL16 .... 147 H4
Andereach Cl *HGRV/WHIT* BS14 ...... 374 A6
Anderson Cl *CHELTE/BC* GL52 .... 83 H3
Anderson Dr *STNHO* GL10 .... 213 F7
Andorra Wy *BWTH/CHD* GL3 .... 103 K8
Andover Rd *CHELT* GL50 .... 4 A6
  CHELT GL50 .... 106 B6
Andoversford Link *COTS* GL54 .... 137 J3
Andover St *CHELT* GL50 .... 4 A6
Andover Wk *CHELT* GL50 .... 4 A6
Andrew's Cl *GLE* GL4 .... 86 B1
Angel Fld *CLFD* GL16 .... 175 J4
Angelica Wy *GLE* GL4 .... 159 H1
Angels Gnd
  BRSG/KWL/STAPK BS4 .... 365 K8
Anne Hathaway Dr
  BWTH/CHD GL3 .... 132 C1
Anns Wk *MTCHDN* GL17 .... 123 G6
Ann Wicks Rd *VCL* GL2 .... 210 E1
Ansdell Dr *BWTH/CHD* GL3 .... 132 C8
Ansell Cl *CHELTW* GL51 .... 105 K8
Anstey's Rd *KGWD/HNM* BS15 .... 375 G1
Anstey St *EVILLE/WHL* BS5 .... 365 F5
Antelope Paddock *COTS* GL54 .... 169 G4
Anthea Rd *EVILLE/WHL* BS5 .... 365 J4
Anthony's Cross *NWNT* GL18 .... 97 J2
Antrim Rd
  HNLZ/SM/SNYPK/WT BS9 .... 353 K8
Anvil St *CBRISNE* BS2 .... 364 D8
A P Ellis Rd *COTS* GL54 .... 145 F5
Apperley Cl *YATE/CS* BS37 .... 347 F6
Apperley Dr *VCL* GL2 .... 156 D5
Apperley Pk *RTEWK/TIB* GL19 .... 56 B8
Apple Cl *CHELTE/BC* GL52 .... 107 G1
Appledore Cl *HGRV/WHIT* BS14 .... 374 A6
Applegate *HNBRY/STHM* BS10 .... 353 K5
Apple Orch *CHELTE/BC* GL52 .... 107 G1
The Apple Orch *TEWK* GL20 .... 34 D5
Appleridge La *BRKLY* GL13 .... 293 J2
Appleton Av *CHELTW* GL51 .... 105 F8
Appleton Wy *BWTH/CHD* GL3 .... 103 J7
  CHELTE/BC GL52 .... 83 J4
  GLE GL4 .... 159 G2
April Cl *DSLY* GL11 .... 266 E6
Apseleys Md *ALMDB* BS32 .... 343 G5
Apsley Cl *CIR* GL7 .... 249 H7
Apsley Rd *CIR* GL7 .... 249 H8
Apsley St *EVILLE/WHL* BS5 .... 365 G4
Aragon Wy *BWTH/CHD* GL3 .... 103 H7
Arbour Cl *CHCAM* GL55 .... 9 F3
Arbutus Dr
  HNLZ/SM/SNYPK/WT BS9 .... 352 E7
Archdeacon Ct *GL* GL1 .... 2 B3
Archdeacon St *GL* GL1 .... 2 B3
Archer Cl *OLD/WMLY/WICK* BS30 ..... 376 A3
Archers La *CHELTE/BC* GL52 .... 81 H1
Archer Wk *HGRV/WHIT* BS14 .... 374 D8
Archery Rd *CIR* GL7 .... 250 A5
Archfield Rd *RDLND/MONT* BS6 .... 364 A5
Archibald St *GL* GL1 .... 3 D5
Archway Cl *CIND* GL14 .... 179 F5
Archway Gdns *STROUD* GL5 .... 214 B6
Ardea Cl *VCL* GL2 .... 156 C5

Arden Cl *ALMDB* BS32 .... 343 J8
Arden Rd *CHELTS* GL53 .... 134 C1
Ardenton Wk
  HNBRY/STHM BS10 .... 353 J3
Ardern Cl
  HNLZ/SM/SNYPK/WT BS9 .... 352 D6
Ardmore Cl *GLE* GL4 .... 158 A3
Argyle Dr *YATE/CS* BS37 .... 347 G2
Argyle Rd *CBRISNE* BS2 .... 364 C6
  MANG/FISH BS16 .... 366 B4
Argyle St *EVILLE/WHL* BS5 .... 365 G4
Argyll Pl *VCL* GL2 .... 3 F3
Argyll Rd *CHELTS* GL53 .... 3 F5
  VCL GL2 .... 3 F3
Ariel Lodge Rd *CHELTE/BC* GL52 .... 5 D5
Arkells Ct *WUE* GL12 .... 319 J8
Arkendale Dr *VCL* GL2 .... 156 D6
Arkle Cl *CHELT* GL50 .... 106 C1
Arle Av *CHELTW* GL51 .... 106 B4
Arle Cl *CHELTW* GL51 .... 106 A4
Arle Dr *CHELTW* GL51 .... 106 A4
Arle Gdns *CHELTW* GL51 .... 106 A4
Arle Rd *CHELTW* GL51 .... 106 A3
Arley Cottages
  RDLND/MONT BS6 .... 364 B5
Arley Hl *RDLND/MONT* BS6 .... 364 B5
Arley Pk *RDLND/MONT* BS6 .... 364 B5
Arley Ter *EVILLE/WHL* BS5 .... 365 J5
Arlingham *CHELTW* GL51 .... 133 J1
Arlingham Rd *GL* GL1 .... 157 K2
Arlingham Wy *BRSTK/PCHW* BS34 .. 342 C6
Arlington Ct *CHEP* NP16 .... 288 D2
Arlington Rd
  BRSG/KWL/STAPK BS4 .... 365 H8
Armada Cl *BWTH/CHD* GL3 .... 103 H7
Armada Pl *CBRIS/FH* BS1 .... 364 C6
Armidale Av *RDLND/MONT* BS6 .... 364 C6
Armoury Sq *EVILLE/WHL* BS5 .... 364 E6
Armscote Rd *SHPSTR* CV36 .... 11 F2
Armscroft Cl *VCL* GL2 .... 130 E5
Armscroft Crs *VCL* GL2 .... 3 F4
Armscroft Gdns *VCL* GL2 .... 3 F4
Armscroft Pl *VCL* GL2 .... 3 F4
Armscroft Rd *VCL* GL2 .... 130 E5
Armscroft Wy *VCL* GL2 .... 3 F3
Armstrong Cl *THNB/SVB* BS35 .... 316 D7
Armstrong Dr
  OLD/WMLY/WICK BS30 .... 376 C1
Armstrong Wy *YATE/CS* BS37 .... 346 E3
Arnall Dr *HNBRY/STHM* BS10 .... 353 H5
Arneside Rd *HNBRY/STHM* BS10 ...... 354 A5
Arnold's La *RSTROUD/NAIL* GL6 ...... 270 D3
Arnolds Wy *CIR* GL7 .... 250 A5
Arreton Av *GLE* GL4 .... 130 E8
Arrowhead Cl *GLE* GL4 .... 158 D2
Arrowsmith Dr *STNHO* GL10 .... 213 F5
Arthur Skemp Cl
  EVILLE/WHL BS5 .... 365 F7
Arthur St *EVILLE/WHL* BS5 .... 365 G6
  GL GL1 .... 2 C4
Arundel Cl *GL* GL1 .... 157 J5
Arundel Dr *STROUD* GL5 .... 214 D8
Arundell Mill La *STROUD* GL5 .... 215 F8
Arundel Rd *HORF/LLZ* BS7 .... 364 B3
  TEWK GL20 .... 33 K6
Ascot Cl *MANG/FISH* BS16 .... 357 F5
Ascot Rd *HNBRY/STHM* BS10 .... 353 K5
Ashbourne Cl
  OLD/WMLY/WICK BS30 .... 367 J8
Ashbrook La *CIR* GL7 .... 252 E7
Ashburton Rd *HNBRY/STHM* BS10 .. 354 A5
Ashchurch Rd *TEWK* GL20 .... 33 J8
Ash Cl *BRSTK/PCHW* BS34 .... 33 H7
  CHELTS GL53 .... 135 H2
  CHEP NP16 .... 312 A1
  DSLY GL11 .... 266 E2
  LYD GL15 .... 234 B2
  YATE/CS BS37 .... 347 F3
Ashcombe Cl
  OLD/WMLY/WICK BS30 .... 367 J8
Ashcombe Crs
  OLD/WMLY/WICK BS30 .... 367 K8
Ashcot Ms *CHELTW* GL51 .... 133 J1
Ashcroft Cl *GLE* GL4 .... 159 F4
Ashcroft Gdns *CIR* GL7 .... 249 J6
Ashcroft Rd *CIR* GL7 .... 249 J6
  HNLZ/SM/SNYPK/WT BS9 .... 352 E7
  WUE GL12 .... 298 C4
Ashdale Cl *COTS* GL54 .... 199 F5
Ashdene Av *EVILLE/WHL* BS5 .... 365 H3
Ash Dene Rd *MTCHDN* GL17 .... 149 H1
Asher La *CBRISNE* BS2 .... 364 D7
Ashfield *HGHW* SN6 .... 308 E5
Ashfield Cl *CHELTE/BC* GL52 .... 83 G3
Ashfield Pl *RDLND/MONT* BS6 .... 364 D5
Ashfield Rd *MTCHDN* GL17 .... 122 B8
Ashford Rd *BRSTK/PCHW* BS34 .... 342 E7
  CHELT GL50 .... 4 A6
Ash Gv *GLE* GL4 .... 159 G3
  MANG/FISH BS16 .... 366 C3
  MTCHDN GL17 .... 123 G3
Ashgrove *CHELTS* GL53 .... 135 H2
  SHPSTR CV36 .... 25 F2
  THNB/SVB BS35 .... 316 C5
Ashgrove Av *GLE* GL4 .... 130 E8

HORF/LLZ BS7 .... **364** D2
Ashgrove Cl *VCL* GL2 .... **156** E7
Ashgrove Rd *HORF/LLZ* BS7 .... **364** D2
Ashgrove Wy *GLE* GL4 .... **130** E8 ◩
Ashlands Cl *CHELTW* GL51 .... **105** J3
Ashlands Rd *CHELTW* GL51 .... **105** J3
Ash La *ALMDB* BS32 .... **342** B3
   STNHO GL10 .... **213** J4
   VCL GL2 .... **102** E4
Ashlea Mdw *CHELTE/BC* GL52 .... **82** D2 ◩
Ashleigh La *CHELTE/BC* GL52 .... **83** K5
Ashletts Rd *RSTROUD/NAIL* GL6 .... **218** C5
Ashleworth Gdns *VCL* GL2 .... **156** E6 ◩
Ashley Cl *CHELTW* GL51 .... **367** F6
Ashley Cl *CHELTE/BC* GL52 .... **5** F6
   HORF/LLZ BS7 .... **364** D2
Ashley Court Rd
   RDLND/MONT BS6 .... **364** D4 ◩
Ashley Down Rd *HORF/LLZ* BS7 .... **364** C1
Ashley Dr *RSTROUD/NAIL* GL6 .... **244** A3
Ashley Grove Rd *CBRISNE* BS2 .... **364** D4 ◩
   CBRISNE BS2 .... **364** E5 ◩
Ashley Hl *RDLND/MONT* BS6 .... **364** D3
Ashley Pde *CBRISNE* BS2 .... **364** D4 ◩
Ashley Pk *RDLND/MONT* BS6 .... **364** D3
Ashley Rd *CHELTE/BC* GL52 .... **5** F6
   RDLND/MONT BS6 .... **364** C5
Ashley St *CBRISNE* BS2 .... **364** E5 ◩
Ashman Cl *EVILLE/WHL* BS5 .... **364** E6 ◩
Ashmead *VCL* GL2 .... **150** D1 ◩
Ashmead Dr *CHELTE/BC* GL52 .... **60** B6
Ashmead Rd *CIND* GL14 .... **151** F7
Ashmore Cl *GLE* GL4 .... **158** B2
The Ash Pth *GLE* GL4 .... **159** G3
Ash Ridge Rd *ALMDB* BS32 .... **343** F3
   STROUD GL5 .... **242** C2
   TEWK GL20 .... **34** D6
Ashton Cl *GLE* GL4 .... **159** G3
Ashton Rd *CIR* GL7 .... **278** A3
   MALM SN16 .... **308** D8
   TEWK GL20 .... **36** E1
Ashton Wy *KEYN* BS31 .... **375** K8
Ashville Rd *VCL* GL2 .... **157** H1
Ash Wk *HNBRY/STHM* BS10 .... **353** H1
Ashway *COTS* GL54 .... **169** H4
   LYD GL15 .... **260** D5
Ashwell Cl *HGRV/WHIT* SN14 .... **374** D8
Ashwell Hyett Cl
   RSTROUD/NAIL GL6 .... **187** H6 ◩
Ashwicke Rd *CHPMW/MSHF* SN14 ...... **380** E1
Ashwood Wy *BWTH/CHD* GL3 .... **131** H8
Askwith Rd *GLE* GL4 .... **130** D8
Aspen Dr *VCL* GL2 .... **156** E4
Asquith Rd *CHELTS* GL53 .... **106** E8
Assembly Rooms La
   CBRIS/FH BS1 .... **364** B8 ◩
Aston Bank *RWYE* HR9 .... **96** A2
Aston Bridge Rd *MTCHDN* GL17 .... **149** H1
Aston Cl *CLFD* GL16 .... **175** J3
   COTS GL54 .... **141** K2
Aston Gv *CHELTW* GL51 .... **105** H4 ◩
Aston Rd *CHCAM* GL55 .... **8** C8
   CHCAM GL55 .... **20** C2
Aston Vw *RSTROUD/NAIL* GL6 .... **244** D3
Astor Cl *BWTH/CHD* GL3 .... **132** B8
Astridge Rd *BWTH/CHD* GL3 .... **160** E2
Astry Cl *AVONM* BS11 .... **352** C5
Atchley St *EVILLE/WHL* BS5 .... **365** F7 ◩
Atcombe Rd *STROUD* GL5 .... **242** B6
Athelney Wy *CHELTE/BC* GL52 .... **5** D5
Atherstone *OLD/WMLY/WICK* BS30 .... **376** D1
Atherstone Cl *CHELTW* GL51 .... **105** C3
Atherton Cl *CHELTW* GL51 .... **133** H4 ◩
Atkins Cl *HGRV/WHIT* SN14 .... **374** D8
Atkinson St *BDWAY* WR12 .... **17** J4
Atlas Cl *EVILLE/WHL* BS5 .... **366** A4
Atlas St *CBRISNE* BS2 .... **374** A1
Attwood Cl *CHELTW* GL51 .... **105** K1 ◩
Atwell St *ALMDB* BS32 .... **343** F5
Atwood Dr *AVONM* BS11 .... **352** D4
Aubrey Meads
   OLD/WMLY/WICK BS30 .... **377** F6
Auburn Av
   OLD/WMLY/WICK BS30 .... **376** C3
Audrey Wk
   HNLZ/SM/SNYPK/WT BS9 .... **354** B8
Augustine Wy *BWTH/CHD* GL3 .... **131** H8 ◩
Augustus Wy *LYD* GL15 .... **234** D1
Aust Crs *CHEP* NP16 .... **312** A1
Austen Gv *HORF/LLZ* BS7 .... **354** E6 ◩
Austin Dr *VCL* GL2 .... **102** D3
Austin Rd *CIR* GL7 .... **250** A6 ◩
   TEWK GL20 .... **35** F6
Aust Rd *THNB/SVB* BS35 .... **329** F3
   THNB/SVB BS35 .... **330** C1
Avalon Rd *EVILLE/WHL* BS5 .... **366** B8
Avebury Cl *GL* GL1 .... **157** H4
Avenall Pde *CHELTS* GL53 .... **5** D5
Avening Cl *CHELTS* GL53 .... **158** B1
   KGWD/HNM BS15 .... **366** A6
   RSTROUD/NAIL GL6 .... **271** F3
The Avenue *BRSTK/PCHW* BS34 .... **343** G8

BWTH/CHD GL3 .... **132** A1
Chelts GL53 .... **134** E1
Cir GL7 .... **249** K6
DSLY GL11 .... **266** B3
EVILLE/WHL BS5 .... **365** K7
KEYN BS31 .... **375** K7
MANG/FISH BS16 .... **355** J5
RDLND/MONT BS6 .... **364** C3
RSTROUD/NAIL GL6 .... **244** A3
VCL GL2 .... **130** D2
YATE/CS BS37 .... **347** F5
Averay Rd *MANG/FISH* BS16 .... **365** J4
Averill Cl *BDWAY* WR12 .... **18** D6
Avon Cl *BRSG/KWL/STAPK* BS4 .... **365** K8
   KEYN BS31 .... **376** A8
Avon Crs *BWTH/CHD* GL3 .... **160** D1
   WUE GL12 .... **319** K8
Avondown Cl
   HNBRY/STHM BS10 .... **354** B4 ◩
Avonlea Rd *KGWD/HNM* BS15 .... **375** H1 ◩
Avon Mill La *KEYN* BS31 .... **376** A8
Avon Pk *EVILLE/WHL* BS5 .... **365** H7
Avon Rd *CHELTE/BC* GL52 .... **5** E3
   WUE GL12 .... **319** J2
Avonside Rd *CBRISNE* BS2 .... **365** G8
Avonside Wy
   BRSG/KWL/STAPK BS4 .... **365** K8 ◩
Avon St *CBRISNE* BS2 .... **364** D8
Avonvale Rd *EVILLE/WHL* BS5 .... **365** G7
Avon Vw *KGWD/HNM* BS15 .... **375** G3
   TEWK GL20 .... **33** K6
Avon Walkway
   OLD/WMLY/WICK BS30 .... **376** D8
Avon Wy *HNBRY/STHM* BS10 .... **354** B6
   THNB/SVB BS35 .... **316** C6
Avonwood Cl *AVONM* BS11 .... **352** A8
Avro Rd *COTS* GL54 .... **145** F1
Awdelett Cl *AVONM* BS11 .... **352** D5
Awdry Wy *GLE* GL4 .... **157** K4
Awebridge Wy *GLE* GL4 .... **158** E2
Awkley La *THNB/SVB* BS35 .... **330** C5
Awkward Hl *CIR* GL7 .... **225** G4
Awre Rd *LYD* GL15 .... **207** J4
Aycote Cl *GLE* GL4 .... **158** D1
Ayford La *CHPMW/MSHF* SN14 .... **380** E1
Ayland Cl *NWNT* GL18 .... **73** K6 ◩
Ayland Gdns *GL* GL1 .... **3** E5
Aylmer Crs *HGRV/WHIT* SN14 .... **374** A8
Aylminton Wk *AVONM* BS11 .... **352** D4
Aylton Cl *CHELTW* GL51 .... **105** H8 ◩
Aysgarth Av *CHELTW* GL51 .... **133** J1 ◩
Azalea Dr *CHELTW* GL51 .... **133** K1
Azalea Gdns *VCL* GL2 .... **156** E4

B

Back Albert Pl *CHELTE/BC* GL52 .... **4** C3 ◩
Back Edge La *RSTROUD/NAIL* GL6 ...... **186** E6
Back Ends *CHCAM* GL55 .... **20** D3
Backfields *CBRISNE* BS2 .... **364** C8 ◩
Backfields La *CBRISNE* BS2 .... **364** C6 ◩
Back La *BDWAY* WR12 .... **18** C6
   CHCAM GL55 .... **9** F2
   CHPMW/MSHF SN14 .... **371** K6
   CIR GL7 .... **191** G6
   CIR GL7 .... **254** E8
   COTS GL54 .... **85** H1
   EVE WR11 .... **6** B2
   KEYN BS31 .... **375** K8
   MANG/FISH BS16 .... **368** C3
   MIM GL56 .... **93** J6
   MTCHDN GL17 .... **122** C6
   RSTROUD/NAIL GL6 .... **216** E6
   TET GL8 .... **323** J3
   TEWK GL20 .... **13** J7
   TEWK GL20 .... **36** D5
   WUE GL12 .... **319** J8
Back Montpellier Ter *CHELT* GL50 .... **4** A5
Back of Avon *TEWK* GL20 .... **33** H8
Back of Kingsdown Pde
   RDLND/MONT BS6 .... **364** B6
Back of Mount Pleasant
   TEWK GL20 .... **33** J8 ◩
Back Rw *MIM* GL56 .... **94** C3
Back Stoke La
   HNLZ/SM/SNYPK/WT BS9 .... **353** H8
Back St *BAD* GL9 .... **338** A3
   CIND GL14 .... **180** C2
   HGHW SN6 .... **308** D5
   SHPSTR CV36 .... **11** F2
The Back *CHEP* NP16 .... **288** B5
Back Walls *COTS* GL54 .... **92** C6
Badenham Gv *AVONM* BS11 .... **352** B6
Baden Hill Rd *WUE* GL12 .... **333** J1
Baden Rd *EVILLE/WHL* BS5 .... **365** G7
   KGWD/HNM BS15 .... **367** G7
Bader Av *BWTH/CHD* GL3 .... **132** A1 ◩
Bader Cl *YATE/CS* BS37 .... **347** F3
Badger Cl *GLE* GL4 .... **159** F3
Badgers Cl *ALMDB* BS32 .... **343** H3 ◩
Badger's La *ALMDB* BS32 .... **342** A4

Badgers Wk
   BRSG/KWL/STAPK BS4 .... **374** C4 ◩
Badgers Wy *LYD* GL15 .... **205** F5 ◩
Badger Vale Ct *GL* GL1 .... **157** J1 ◩
Badgeworth *YATE/CS* BS37 .... **347** F8
Badgeworth La *CHELTW* GL51 .... **133** G5
Badgeworth Rd *CHELTW* GL51 .... **132** E1
Badminton Cl *CHELTS* GL53 .... **106** D8 ◩
Badminton Rd *CBRISNE* BS2 .... **364** D5
   FRCTL/WBN BS36 .... **357** C3
   GLE GL4 .... **158** D1
   MANG/FISH BS16 .... **356** E7
   YATE/CS BS37 .... **346** D4
   YATE/CS BS37 .... **348** C6
Badsey La *EVE* WR11 .... **6** C7
Bafford Ap *CHELTS* GL53 .... **135** F2
Bafford Gv *CHELTS* GL53 .... **135** F2
Bafford La *CHELTS* GL53 .... **135** G1
Baglyn Av *KGWD/HNM* BS15 .... **367** F3
Bagpath La *STROUD* GL5 .... **243** F4
Bagstone Rd *WUE* GL12 .... **334** C1
Bagworth Dr
   OLD/WMLY/WICK BS30 .... **376** A3 ◩
Bailey Hl *LYD* GL15 .... **206** B4
Bailey La *LYD* GL15 .... **230** D6
Baileys Court Rd *ALMDB* BS32 .... **343** J8
Baileys Mead Rd
   MANG/FISH BS16 .... **365** G1 ◩
Bailiffe Piece *HGHW* SN6 .... **310** D5
Baines Cl *COTS* GL54 .... **143** H1 ◩
Bakehouse La *CHELT* GL50 .... **106** B7 ◩
Bakersfield
   OLD/WMLY/WICK BS30 .... **376** B3 ◩
Bakers Gnd *BRSTK/PCHW* BS34 .... **355** K1 ◩
Baker's Hl *CHCAM* GL55 .... **9** G3
   CLFD GL16 .... **176** A3
Baker's La *EVE* WR11 .... **14** D5
   RTEWK/TIB GL19 .... **76** D8
Bakers Piece Rd *MTCHDN* GL17 .... **121** K8
Baker St *CHELTW* GL51 .... **4** A2
   GL GL1 .... **2** B5
Balaclava Rd *MANG/FISH* BS16 .... **365** K5 ◩
Bala Rd *CHELTW* GL51 .... **105** K8
Balcarras *CHELTS* GL53 .... **135** J1
Balcarras Gdns *CHELTS* GL53 .... **135** J1
Balcarras Retreat *CHELTS* GL53 ...... **135** J1 ◩
Balcarras Rd *CHELTS* GL53 .... **135** J1
Baldwin St *CBRIS/FH* BS1 .... **364** B8
Balfour Rd *GL* GL1 .... **2** B6
Ballards Cl *CHCAM* GL55 .... **9** F3
Ballards La *SHPSTR* CV36 .... **11** C2
Ballinode Cl *CHELTW* GL51 .... **106** B1
Ballinska Ms *VCL* GL2 .... **131** F1 ◩
Balmoral Cl *BRSTK/PCHW* BS34 .... **355** H2 ◩
Balmoral Ct *MANG/FISH* BS16 .... **367** G1 ◩
Balmoral Rd
   OLD/WMLY/WICK BS30 .... **376** A4
   RDLND/MONT BS6 .... **364** D4
Bamfurlong La *CHELTW* GL51 .... **104** C5
Bampton Dr *MANG/FISH* BS16 .... **356** D5 ◩
Banady La *CHELTE/BC* GL52 .... **81** J1
Baneberry Rd *GLE* GL4 .... **158** C1
Banfield Cl *AVONM* BS11 .... **352** C6
Bangor Gv *BRSG/KWL/STAPK* BS4 .... **374** E1
Bangrove Wk *AVONM* BS11 .... **352** A6 ◩
Bangup La *COTS* GL54 .... **141** K3
Banister Wy *SHPSTR* CV36 .... **25** F2
Bank Rd *KGWD/HNM* BS15 .... **366** D6 ◩
   THNB/SVB BS35 .... **329** F7
Banks Fee La *MIM* GL56 .... **68** E7
Bankside *MANG/FISH* BS16 .... **367** F2 ◩
Bankside Rd
   BRSG/KWL/STAPK BS4 .... **374** C3 ◩
Bank Sq *CHEP* NP16 .... **288** A6 ◩
Bank St *CHEP* NP16 .... **288** A6
   CLFD GL16 .... **175** J4
The Bank *CHELTE/BC* GL52 .... **107** J2 ◩
Bannerman Rd *EVILLE/WHL* BS5 ...... **365** F6 ◩
Banner Rd *RDLND/MONT* BS6 .... **364** C5
Bannetts Tree Crs
   THNB/SVB BS35 .... **332** A1
Baptist Cl *GLE* GL4 .... **131** H8
Baptist St *EVILLE/WHL* BS5 .... **364** C5 ◩
Baptist Wy *MTCHDN* GL17 .... **122** B8
Barbican Rd *GL* GL1 .... **2** B3 ◩
Barbican Wy *GL* GL1 .... **2** B3 ◩
Barbridge Rd *CHELTW* GL51 .... **105** J3
Barcroft Cl *KGWD/HNM* BS15 .... **366** C6 ◩
Barker Pl *CIR* GL7 .... **255** F7 ◩
Barker's Leys *CHELTE/BC* GL52 .... **83** C2
Barkers Md *YATE/CS* BS37 .... **347** H2 ◩
Barker Wk *EVILLE/WHL* BS5 .... **364** E5 ◩
Barkleys Hl *MANG/FISH* BS16 .... **365** G1
Barksdale *COTS* GL54 .... **85** H1
The Barlands *CHELTE/BC* GL52 .... **136** A2
Barley Cl *CHELTW* GL51 .... **105** H1
   FRCTL/WBN BS36 .... **345** H6 ◩
   MANG/FISH BS16 .... **357** C8
   VCL GL2 .... **156** E8
Barleycroft Cl *GLE* GL4 .... **159** F4
Barlow Cl *STNHO* GL10 .... **212** H1 ◩
Barlow Rd *CHELTW* GL51 .... **105** K2 ◩
Barnabas St *CBRISNE* BS2 .... **364** C5 ◩
Barnaby Cl *GL* GL1 .... **3** D6

Barnacre Dr *GLE* GL4.................... 131 H5
Barnage La *LYD* GL15.................... 231 J6
Barn Cl *COTS* GL54...................... 62 A5
  GLE GL4................................ 159 G2
  RSTROUD/NAIL GL6.................. 270 D3
Barn End *CHPMW/MSHF* SN14 ...... 372 A6
Barnes St *EVILLE/WHL* BS5............ 365 H7 ▣
Barnes Wallis Wy
  BWTH/CHD CL3........................ 132 A1 ▣
Barnett Cl *CHELTW* GL51............... 105 J1
Barnett Wy *COTS* GL54................. 169 C4 ▣
  GLE GL4................................ 131 G5
Barn Field Rd *RSTROUD/NAIL* GL6 .. 270 C2
Barnhay *BWTH/CHD* CL3............... 132 A2 ▣
Barn Hill *CLFD* GL16.................... 176 B3
Barnhill Rd *YATE/CS* BS37............ 347 K5
Barn La *EVE* WR11...................... 15 H5
  MTCHDN GL17......................... 121 J8
Barnmeadow Rd *COTS* GL54.......... 62 D8
Barn Owl Wy *BRSTK/PCHW* BS34 ... 355 K1
Barn Wy *CIR* GL7........................ 249 G3
Barnwood Av *GLE* GL4.................. 131 F6
Barnwood Rd *GLE* GL4.................. 131 G6
  VGL GL2................................. 3 F3
  YATE/CS BS37........................ 346 E7
Barrack Sq *GL* GL1..................... 2 B3 ▣
Barratt's Mill La *CHELTS* GL53........ 4 C4 ▣
Barrington Av *CHELTW* GL51.......... 105 F7
Barrington Cl *KGWD/HNM* BS15...... 367 F4
Barrington Cl *KGWD/HNM* BS15...... 366 E5
Barrington Dr *GLE* GL4................. 131 H6
Barrow Cl *GL* GL2....................... 157 F6
Barrowell La *LYD* GL15................. 231 F1 ▣
Barrowfield Rd *STROUD* GL5.......... 214 C5
Barrow Hl *BWTH/CHD* CL3............. 132 B3
  OLD/WMLY/WICK BS30.............. 368 D8
Barrowmead Dr *AVONM* BS11 .... 352 B6
Barrow Rd *CBRISNE* BS2.............. 364 E7
  EVILLE/WHL BS5...................... 365 F7
Barrs Court Av
  OLD/WMLY/WICK BS30.............. 376 B1
Barrs Court Rd
  OLD/WMLY/WICK BS30.............. 376 B1
Barrs La *DSLY* GL11.................... 296 C2
Barry Cl *OLD/WMLY/WICK* BS30 .... 376 D5 ▣
Barry Rd *OLD/WMLY/WICK* BS30..... 376 D4
Bartletts Pk *COTS* GL54............... 92 C7
Bartley Cft *TET* GL8.................... 302 C6
Barton Cl *BRSG/KWL/STAPK* BS4 .. 365 K8 ▣
  CHELTS GL53.......................... 135 G2
  FRCTL/WBN BS36..................... 356 E1
  THNB/SVB BS35...................... 332 A1
Barton Ct *EVILLE/WHL* BS5............ 365 G8 ▣
Bartonend La *RSTROUD/NAIL* GL6 .. 270 C2
Barton Hl *MTCHDN* GL17............... 123 H4
Barton Hill Rd *EVILLE/WHL* BS5...... 365 F6 ▣
Bartonia Gv
  BRSG/KWL/STAPK BS4.............. 374 C5 ▣
Barton La *CIR* GL7...................... 249 H5
Barton Mnr *CBRISNE* BS2.............. 364 E8
Barton Ms *TEWK* GL20................. 33 J8 ▣
Barton Rd *CBRISNE* BS2............... 364 D8
  TEWK GL20............................ 33 H8
Barton St *CBRIS/FH* BS1............... 364 B6 ▣
  GL GL1................................. 3 D5
The Barton *KGWD/HNM* BS15........ 375 G2
Barton V *CBRISNE* BS2................. 364 E8 ▣
Barton Wy *CHELTW* GL51.............. 105 J9
Barwick Rd *CHELTW* GL51............. 133 K1 ▣
Barwood *KGWD/HNM* BS15............ 367 F4
Base La *VGL* GL2........................ 101 K6
Basil Cl *GLE* GL4........................ 159 F2
Bassett Cl *COTS* GL54.................. 62 D8
Bassett Rd *COTS* GL54................. 169 H5
The Bassetts *STROUD* GL5............ 213 K6
Batchfield La *YATE/CS* BS37........... 358 E6
Bateman *GLE* GL4....................... 157 K5 ▣
Bates Cl *EVILLE/WHL* BS5............. 364 E6 ▣
Bathams Cl *MTCHDN* GL17............ 124 B4
Bath Buildings
  RDLND/MONT BS6..................... 364 C5 ▣
Bath Crs *LYD* GL15..................... 205 J3
Bathleaze *STNHO* GL10................. 241 G2 ▣
Bath Pde *CHELTS* GL53................. 4 C5
Bath Pl *CLFD* GL16...................... 147 K8 ▣
  LYD GL15.............................. 234 B3
Bath Rd *BAD* GL9........................ 361 C4
  BRSG/KWL/STAPK BS4.............. 374 C5 ▣
  CHELT GL50........................... 4 B5
  CHELTS GL53.......................... 4 B6
  CHPMW/MSHF SN14.................. 381 K4
  HGHW SN6............................. 310 D6
  KEYN BS31............................. 375 G6
  OLD/WMLY/WICK BS30.............. 367 K8
  OLD/WMLY/WICK BS30.............. 376 E6
  OLD/WMLY/WICK BS30.............. 378 B3
  RSTROUD/NAIL GL6.................. 270 D7
  STNHO GL10........................... 211 K8
  STNHO GL10........................... 213 F7
  STNHO GL10........................... 240 D3
  STNHO GL10........................... 241 F2
  STROUD GL5........................... 214 C8
  STROUD GL5........................... 242 C3

Bath Road Brislington Hl
  BRSG/KWL/STAPK BS4.............. 374 D4
Bath St *CBRIS/FH* BS1................. 364 C8 ▣
  CHELT GL50........................... 4 C4
  MANG/FISH BS16..................... 366 E2
Bath Ter *CHELT* GL50.................. 4 B6 ▣
Bathurst Park Rd *LYD* GL15........... 234 A3
Bathurst Rd *CIR* GL7................... 249 H7 ▣
  GLE GL4................................ 130 B8
Bath Ville Ms *CHELTS* GL53........... 4 B5 ▣
Batley Ct
  OLD/WMLY/WICK BS30.............. 376 E2 ▣
Battenburg Rd *EVILLE/WHL* BS5...... 366 A6
Batten Cl *YATE/CS* BS37............... 348 A5
Batten's La *EVILLE/WHL* BS5.......... 366 A8
Battens Rd *EVILLE/WHL* BS5.......... 366 B7 ▣
Battersby Wy *HNBRY/STHM* BS10 ... 353 C4
Battersea Rd *EVILLE/WHL* BS5........ 365 G6
Battledown Ap *CHELTE/BC* GL52 ..... 5 E5
Battledown Cl *CHELTE/BC* GL52...... 5 E5
Battledown Dr *CHELTE/BC* GL52...... 5 E5
Battledown Md *CHELTE/BC* GL52..... 5 E4
Battle Rd *TEWK* GL20.................. 57 G2
Baugh Gdns *MANG/FISH* BS16....... 356 E5
Baunton La *CIR* GL7.................... 249 G1
Baxter Cl *KGWD/HNM* BS15........... 367 F6 ▣
Bay Gdns *EVILLE/WHL* BS5............ 365 G4 ▣
Baylands *BRKLY* GL13.................. 235 K6
Bayleys Dr *KGWD/HNM* BS15......... 366 C8
Baynham Rd *MTCHDN* GL17........... 123 C5
Baynham's Wk *CLFD* GL16............ 176 B2
Baynham Wy *CHELT* GL50............. 4 B3 ▣
Bays Hl *BRKLY* GL13.................... 235 K6
Bayshill La *CHELT* GL50............... 4 A4
Bayshill Rd *CHELT* GL50............... 4 A4
Bayswater Rd *HORF/LLZ* BS7......... 354 D7
Bay Tree Cl *BRSTK/PCHW* BS34 ..... 342 D7
Bay Tree Rd *GLE* GL4.................. 159 H1
Bazeley Rd *GLE* GL4.................... 158 D4
Beach Av *THNB/SVB* BS35............ 328 C7
Beachgrove Gdns
  MANG/FISH BS16..................... 366 C2
Beachgrove Rd *MANG/FISH* BS16.... 366 B2
Beach Hl *OLD/WMLY/WICK* BS30.... 377 C5
Beach La *OLD/WMLY/WICK* BS30 .... 377 K4
Beachley Rd *CHEP* NP16............... 288 C6
  CHEP NP16............................ 312 D1
Beach Rd *THNB/SVB* BS35............ 328 B7
Beacon Cl *RSTROUD/NAIL* GL6....... 187 J1
Beacon La *MANG/FISH* BS16.......... 356 B1
Beaconlea *KGWD/HNM* BS15.......... 366 D8
Beacon Rd *GLE* GL4.................... 158 D3
Beaconsfield Rd
  BRSG/KWL/STAPK BS4.............. 374 A3
  EVILLE/WHL BS5...................... 365 J6
Beaconsfield St
  EVILLE/WHL BS5...................... 365 F8 ▣
Beacons View Rd *CIND* GL14.......... 151 G5 ▣
The Beagles *STROUD* GL5.............. 213 K7
Beale Cl *HGRV/WHIT* BS14............ 374 D8 ▣
  RSTROUD/NAIL GL6.................. 244 B2
Beale Rd *CHELTW* GL51................ 105 H3 ▣
Beam St *EVILLE/WHL* BS5.............. 365 G7 ▣
Bean Hl *MIM* GL56..................... 69 F6
Beanhill Crs *THNB/SVB* BS35......... 332 A1 ▣
Bean St *EVILLE/WHL* BS5.............. 364 E5 ▣
Bearcroft Gdn *CHCAM* GL55.......... 9 F2
Beard's La *STROUD* GL5............... 214 C7
Bear Hl *STROUD* GL5................... 242 C4
Bearland *GL* GL1........................ 2 B3 ▣
Bearlands *WUE* GL12................... 321 C1
Bear St *WUE* GL12...................... 297 F7
Beauchamp Cl *CIR* GL7................ 255 F7 ▣
Beauchamp Meadow *LYD* GL15....... 234 C2
Beauchamp Rd *HORF/LLZ* BS7........ 354 B2
Beaufort Cl *EVILLE/WHL* BS5.......... 365 H7 ▣
Beaufort Ct *CIR* GL7.................... 249 J7 ▣
Beaufort Crs *BRSTK/PCHW* BS34 .... 355 J2
Beaufort Dr *LYD* GL15................. 234 B4
Beaufort End *EVE* WR11............... 7 H1 ▣
Beaufort Pl *CHEP* NP16................ 288 A6 ▣
  MANG/FISH BS16..................... 356 D5 ▣
  TEWK GL20............................ 57 H2
Beaufort Rd *CHELTE/BC* GL52........ 5 E6
  EVILLE/WHL BS5...................... 365 H7
  FRCTL/WBN BS36..................... 345 G6
  GLE GL4................................ 158 B1
  HORF/LLZ BS7......................... 354 D8
  KGWD/HNM BS15..................... 366 B5 ▣
  MANG/FISH BS16..................... 357 G7
  MANG/FISH BS16..................... 366 E2
  YATE/CS BS37........................ 347 F4
Beaufort St *EVILLE/WHL* BS5......... 364 E6 ▣
Beaufort Wy *HNBRY/STHM* BS10 .... 354 B6
Beaumont Cl
  OLD/WMLY/WICK BS30.............. 376 B3 ▣
Beaumont Dr *CHELTW* GL51.......... 105 H2
Beaumont Pl *LYD* GL15................ 234 A3
Beaumont Rd *CHELTW* GL51.......... 105 H2
  VGL GL2................................ 130 E1

Beaumont St *EVILLE/WHL* BS5 ...... 364 E6 ▣
Beaumont Ter *EVILLE/WHL* BS5 ..... 364 E6 ▣
Beaumoor Pl *CIR* GL7.................. 255 F8 ▣
Beaver Cl *FRCTL/WBN* BS36.......... 345 F7
Beaverstone Cl *CIR* GL7............... 278 D8
Beazer Cl *MANG/FISH* BS16.......... 366 D3 ▣
Becket Cl *MIM* GL56.................... 47 H1
Becket Ct *MANG/FISH* BS16.......... 368 D1
Becketts La *COTS* GL54................ 62 E6
Beckfordcl *TEWK* GL20................. 36 D3
Beckford Rd *EVE* WR11................ 14 D7
  GLE GL4................................ 159 G2
  TEWK GL20............................ 37 J7
Beckspool Rd *MANG/FISH* BS16 ..... 356 C6 ▣
Becky Hl *COTS* GL54................... 115 F4
Bedford Av *CHELTW* GL51............ 105 K4
Bedford Crs *HORF/LLZ* BS7........... 366 A1
Bedford St *GL* GL1...................... 3 D4 ▣
  STROUD GL5........................... 214 E7 ▣
Beech Av *CLFD* GL16................... 176 A1
Beech Cl *CHELTE/BC* GL52............ 107 J2
  OLD/WMLY/WICK BS30.............. 376 B1
  THNB/SVB BS35...................... 332 A1
  VGL GL2................................ 128 D2
  VGL GL2................................ 156 E7
Beechcroft Rd *VGL* GL2................ 130 C1
Beechcroft Wk *HORF/LLZ* BS7....... 354 E6
Beechen Dr *MANG/FISH* BS16........ 366 B4
Beeches Cl *STNHO* GL10.............. 241 G2
Beeches Gn *STROUD* GL5............. 214 D6
Beeches Gv
  BRSG/KWL/STAPK BS4.............. 374 C5 ▣
Beeches Rd *CHELTS* GL53............. 135 H2
  CIND GL14............................. 180 C2 ▣
  CIR GL7................................ 249 K6
The Beeches *ALMDB* BS32............ 343 H6
  BRSG/KWL/STAPK BS4.............. 374 D1 ▣
  OLD/WMLY/WICK BS30.............. 376 D4
Beech Gv *CIR* GL7...................... 250 A5
  STROUD GL5........................... 242 C4
Beech La *RSTROUD/NAIL* GL6........ 187 K6
Beech Lea *CIR* GL7...................... 281 J1
Beech Leaze *THNB/SVB* BS35........ 332 A1
Beechmore Dr *CHELTW* GL51......... 133 J1 ▣
Beechmount Gv *HGRV/WHIT* BS14.. 374 A6
Beech Rd *HORF/LLZ* BS7............... 364 C1
  LYD GL15.............................. 206 A3
Beechurst Av *CHELTE/BC* GL52 ...... 5 D4
Beechurst Wy *CHELTE/BC* GL52 ..... 82 D2 ▣
Beech Wy *CIND* GL14.................. 151 H6
  LYD GL15.............................. 204 E6
Beech Well La *CLFD* GL16............. 148 C7
Beechwood Av *KGWD/HNM* BS15 ... 375 J1
Beechwood Cl *CHELTE/BC* GL52 ..... 5 F5
  HGRV/WHIT BS14..................... 374 B6
Beechwood Dr
  RSTROUD/NAIL GL6.................. 244 B3
Beechwood Gv *GLE* GL4............... 158 A3 ▣
  WUE GL12.............................. 297 H6 ▣
Beechwood Ri *DSLY* GL11............. 266 C3
Beechwood Rd *MANG/FISH* BS16.... 366 A2
Beek's La *CBATH/BATHN* BA1........ 380 B3
  CHPMW/MSHF SN14.................. 371 H8
Beesmoor Rd *FRCTL/WBN* BS36..... 345 H1
Begbrook Dr *MANG/FISH* BS16....... 355 H8
Begbrook La *MANG/FISH* BS16....... 355 K8
Begbrook Pk *MANG/FISH* BS16....... 356 A7
Beggarswell Cl *CBRISNE* BS2......... 364 D6 ▣
Bekdale Cl *VGL* GL2.................... 156 D6 ▣
Belcony *MIM* GL56...................... 23 J5
Belfry Cl *GLE* GL4...................... 131 G6
Belgrave Rd *GL* GL1.................... 2 C4
Bellamy Cl *KGWD/HNM* BS15......... 375 F1
Belland Dr *CHELTS* GL53.............. 135 G2
Bella Vis *CHELTE/BC* GL52............ 83 H3
Bell Bank *MIM* GL56................... 44 B4
Bell Barn Rd
  HNLZ/SM/SNYPK/WT BS9.......... 353 F8
Bell Cl *HNBRY/STHM* BS10............ 354 C7
Bellevue Cl *KGWD/HNM* BS15........ 366 E7 ▣
Belle Vue Cl *STROUD* GL5............ 214 E7
Bellevue Pk
  BRSG/KWL/STAPK BS4.............. 374 C4 ▣
Belle Vue Rd *CIND* GL14.............. 151 F6
  EVILLE/WHL BS5...................... 365 G5
  MTCHDN GL17......................... 121 J6 ▣
  STROUD GL5........................... 215 F7
Bellevue Rd *EVILLE/WHL* BS5........ 366 A6
  KGWD/HNM BS15..................... 367 F7
Bellevue Ter
  BRSG/KWL/STAPK BS4.............. 374 C4 ▣
Bell Hl *MANG/FISH* BS16.............. 365 G2
Bell Hill Rd *EVILLE/WHL* BS5......... 365 K6
Bellhouse Wk *AVONM* BS11.......... 352 D5 ▣
Bell La *CBRIS/FH* BS1.................. 364 B7 ▣
  CIR GL7................................ 252 E7
  CIR GL7................................ 285 C3
  GL GL1................................. 2 C4 ▣
  LED HR8................................ 29 G7
  RSTROUD/NAIL GL6.................. 243 J8 ▣
  STROUD GL5........................... 242 A2
Bell Orch *VGL* GL2..................... 181 F3
Bell Pitch *RSTROUD/NAIL* GL6 .... 214 B3 ▣
Bell Rd *FRCTL/WBN* BS36............. 345 J8
Bells Pl *CIND* GL14..................... 178 E2

CLFD GL16 .... 175 K4
Belmont Cl BWTH/CHD GL3 ...... 131 K8
Belmont Dr BRSTK/PCHW BS34 ...... 355 J1
Belmont La CLFD GL16 ...... 147 K8
Belmont Rd
  BRSG/KWL/STAPK BS4 ...... 374 D3 ⬛
  CHELTE/BC GL52 ...... 4 C3
  LYD GL15 ...... 230 D5
  RDLND/MONT BS6 ...... 364 C4
  STROUD GL5 ...... 215 G8 ⬛
Belmont St CHELT GL50 ...... 365 F5
Belmore Pl CHELT GL50 ...... 4 B5 ⬛
Beloe Rd HORF/LLZ BS7 ...... 364 B1
Belroyal Av BRSG/KWL/STAPK BS4 ...... 374 E3
Belsher Dr KGWD/HNM BS15 ...... 367 G8
Belton Rd EVILLE/WHL BS5 ...... 365 F5
Belvedere Ms RSTROUD/NAIL GL6 ... 244 B5
Belvoir Rd RDLND/MONT BS6 ...... 364 C4
Belworth Dr CHELTW GL51 ...... 105 K7
Bence Ct KGWD/HNM BS15 ...... 375 G1 ⬛
Bendy Bow MALM SN16 ...... 306 B6
Benford Cl MANG/FISH BS16 ...... 356 C6
Benhall Av CHELTW GL51 ...... 105 J6
Bennett Pl SHPSRT CV36 ...... 11 G2
Bennett Rd EVILLE/WHL BS5 ...... 365 J7 ⬛
Bennett's Ct YATE/CS BS37 ...... 347 J5
Bennington St CHELT GL50 ...... 4 B3
Bensaunt Gv HNBRY/STHM BS10 ... 354 D1
Benson Cl GLE GL4 ...... 131 G8 ⬛
Bentley Cl VGL GL2 ...... 157 F4
Bentley La CHELTE/BC GL52 ...... 83 K7
Benton Cl STNHO GL10 ...... 240 E8
Benville Av
  HNLZ/SM/SNYPK/WT BS9 ...... 352 E6
Berenda Dr
  OLD/WMLY/WICK BS30 ...... 376 C3
Berkeley Av CFTN/FAIL BS8 ...... 364 A7 ⬛
  CHELTE/BC GL52 ...... 4 C3 ⬛
  HORF/LLZ BS7 ...... 364 B3
Berkeley Cl BWTH/CHD GL3 ...... 132 A8
  CIR GL7 ...... 278 D8
  MANG/FISH BS16 ...... 357 F6
  STROUD GL5 ...... 213 K7
  WUE GL12 ...... 319 J2
Berkeley Ct CHELTE/BC GL52 ...... 4 C4 ⬛
  VGL GL2 ...... 238 B3
Berkeley Crs LYD GL15 ...... 234 B1
  MANG/FISH BS16 ...... 356 B5 ⬛
Berkeley Gn EVILLE/WHL BS5 ...... 365 G4 ⬛
  MANG/FISH BS16 ...... 356 B5 ⬛
Berkeley Gv EVILLE/WHL BS5 ...... 365 H4 ⬛
Berkeley Md ALMDB BS32 ...... 343 J8
Berkeley Pl CHELTE/BC GL52 ...... 4 C4 ⬛
Berkeley Rd CIR GL7 ...... 277 J1
  HORF/LLZ BS7 ...... 364 B3
  KGWD/HNM BS15 ...... 366 C7 ⬛
  MANG/FISH BS16 ...... 366 A4
  MANG/FISH BS16 ...... 366 D2
Berkeley Sq CFTN/FAIL BS8 ...... 364 A7 ⬛
Berkeley St CHELTE/BC GL52 ...... 4 C4
  EVILLE/WHL BS5 ...... 365 G4
  GL GL1 ...... 2 B3 ⬛
Berkeley Wy MANG/FISH BS16 ...... 357 H7
  TET GL8 ...... 302 C5
Berkshire Rd HORF/LLZ BS7 ...... 364 B3
Berrells Rd TET GL8 ...... 302 B8
The Berrells TET GL8 ...... 302 B8
Berrington Rd CHCAM GL55 ...... 21 G3
Berrycroft BRKLY GL13 ...... 264 A2 ⬛
Berryfield Gld BWTH/CHD GL3 ...... 103 J8 ⬛
Berry Cl RSTROUD/NAIL GL6 ...... 187 H6 ⬛
Berry Hill Crs CIR GL7 ...... 249 J3
Berry Hill Rd CIR GL7 ...... 249 J3
Berry La HORF/LLZ BS7 ...... 354 E8
Berry Lawn GLE GL4 ...... 159 F3
Berrymore Rd STROUD GL5 ...... 242 B4 ⬛
Bertha's Fld BAD GL9 ...... 339 H2
Berwick La HNBRY/STHM BS10 ...... 352 E1
Berwick Rd CHELTE/BC GL52 ...... 83 F1 ⬛
  EVILLE/WHL BS5 ...... 365 F4
Beryl Gv HGRV/WHIT BS14 ...... 374 B6
Besbury Pk RSTROUD/NAIL GL6 ... 243 K7
Besford Rd CHELTE/BC GL52 ...... 84 A3
Besom La YATE/CS BS37 ...... 358 C5
Bessemer Cl CLFD GL16 ...... 175 K5 ⬛
Beta Cl TEWK GL20 ...... 34 B6
Bethel Rd EVILLE/WHL BS5 ...... 365 K6
Bethesda St CHELT GL50 ...... 4 B6 ⬛
Betjeman Cl VGL GL2 ...... 157 J2
Betjeman St
  OLD/WMLY/WICK BS30 ...... 376 B1 ⬛
Bettenson Ri COTS GL54 ...... 169 F4 ⬛
Bettertons Cl CIR GL7 ...... 254 D7
Bevan Ct BRSTK/PCHW BS34 ...... 354 D4
Bevan Gdns TEWK GL20 ...... 34 D5 ⬛
Bevens La EVE WR11 ...... 15 J1
Beverley Av MANG/FISH BS16 ...... 357 F5
Beverley Cl EVILLE/WHL BS5 ...... 366 B8 ⬛
Beverley Cft CHELTW GL51 ...... 105 J4
Beverley Gdns
  HNLZ/SM/SNYPK/WT BS9 ...... 353 J1
Beverstone KGWD/HNM BS15 ...... 366 C6 ⬛
Beverstone Rd CIR GL7 ...... 308 D1
Beverston Gdns AVONM BS11 ...... 352 D4 ⬛
Bevington Cl BRSTK/PCHW BS34 ... 342 C5
Bevington La BRKLY GL13 ...... 263 F8

Bevington Wk BRSTK/PCHW BS34 ... 342 C5
Bewley Wy BWTH/CHD GL3 ...... 103 J8
Bexley Rd MANG/FISH BS16 ...... 366 B3
Beyon Dr DSLY GL11 ...... 238 D8 ⬛
Bibstone KGWD/HNM BS15 ...... 367 G8
Bibsworth Av MANG/FISH BS16 ...... 18 E6
Bibsworth La BDWAY WR12 ...... 18 D4 ⬛
Bibury Av BRSTK/PCHW BS34 ...... 343 F6
Bibury Cl
  HNLZ/SM/SNYPK/WT BS9 ...... 354 B7
Bibury Crs
  HNLZ/SM/SNYPK/WT BS9 ...... 354 B7
  KGWD/HNM BS15 ...... 375 H1
Bibury Rd CHELTW GL51 ...... 105 J6
  GLE GL4 ...... 130 B8
Bickerton Cl HNBRY/STHM BS10 ... 353 H3
Bickford Cl OLD/WMLY/WICK BS30 ... 367 G8
Bickley Cl KGWD/HNM BS15 ...... 375 H4 ⬛
Bicknor St CLFD GL16 ...... 147 K7
Biddestone Rd HORF/LLZ BS7 ...... 354 C6
Bidwell Cl HNBRY/STHM BS10 ...... 353 K3
Bigstone Gv CHEP NP16 ...... 288 C3
Bigwood La CBRIS/FH BS1 ...... 364 A8 ⬛
Bilberry Cl GL4 ...... 159 H7 ⬛
  HNLZ/SM/SNYPK/WT BS9 ...... 352 E6 ⬛
Bilbie Cl HNBRY/STHM BS10 ...... 354 B8
Billbrook Rd BWTH/CHD GL3 ...... 131 J7
Billingham Cl GLE GL4 ...... 130 D8
Billings Wy CHELT GL50 ...... 106 B8
Bilsham La THNB/SVB BS35 ...... 329 G4
Bindon Dr HNBRY/STHM BS10 ...... 354 B2
Binyon Rd COTS GL54 ...... 85 H1
Birchall Av GLE GL4 ...... 158 E4
Birchall Rd RDLND/MONT BS6 ...... 364 A2
Birch Av GLE GL4 ...... 130 D8
Birch Cl BRSTK/PCHW BS34 ...... 342 C7
  CHELTS GL53 ...... 135 J2 ⬛
Birch Dr MANG/FISH BS16 ...... 368 C1
  THNB/SVB BS35 ...... 331 K2
Birches Cl STROUD GL5 ...... 214 E6 ⬛
Birches Dr STROUD GL5 ...... 214 E7
Birches La NWNT GL18 ...... 73 H1
Birchfield Rd CHELTE/BC GL52 ...... 83 G1 ⬛
Birch Gld HGHW SN6 ...... 308 D6
Birchley Rd CHELTE/BC GL52 ...... 5 E5
Birchmore Rd GL GL1 ...... 3 E5
Birch Pk CLFD GL16 ...... 176 B5
Birch Rd CLFD GL16 ...... 176 B2
  DSLY GL11 ...... 266 E2
  KGWD/HNM BS15 ...... 366 E3
  STROUD GL5 ...... 242 C3
  YATE/CS BS37 ...... 347 F4
Birchwood Cl CIND GL14 ...... 150 D5
Birchwood Flds GLE GL4 ...... 157 K3
Birchwood Rd
  BRSG/KWL/STAPK BS4 ...... 374 D2
  LYD GL15 ...... 232 C8
Birdale Cl HNBRY/STHM BS10 ...... 353 C5
Bird Rd BWTH/CHD GL3 ...... 131 K8
Birds Bush La RSTROUD/NAIL GL6 ... 218 B1
Birdwood KGWD/HNM BS15 ...... 366 D8
Birdwood Cl GLE GL4 ...... 159 G2 ⬛
Birgage Rd BAD GL9 ...... 337 K4
Birkdale Cl OLD/WMLY/WICK BS30 ... 367 H4
  YATE/CS BS37 ...... 347 G6
Birkin St CBRISNE BS2 ...... 364 C4
Bishop Manor Rd
  HNBRY/STHM BS10 ...... 354 B7
Bishop Rd CHELTW GL51 ...... 133 J4
  HORF/LLZ BS7 ...... 364 A1
Bishops Cl CHELTE/BC GL52 ...... 83 G3 ⬛
  CHEP NP16 ...... 312 B2 ⬛
Bishops Dr CHELTE/BC GL52 ...... 83 F3
Bishopsfield HGHW SN6 ...... 310 C7 ⬛
Bishops Meadow
  CHELTE/BC GL52 ...... 82 E2 ⬛
Bishops Rd GLE GL4 ...... 131 G8
Bishopstone Rd CHELTW GL51 ...... 105 G5 ⬛
Bishopstone Rd GL GL1 ...... 3 E5
Bishop St CBRISNE BS2 ...... 364 C4
Bishop's Wy ALMDB BS32 ...... 331 G8
Bishopthorpe Rd
  HNBRY/STHM BS10 ...... 354 B7
Bishton La CHEP NP16 ...... 288 C3
Bisley Cl YATE/CS BS37 ...... 346 E7
Bisley Old Rd STROUD GL5 ...... 215 F7
Bisley Rd CHELTW GL51 ...... 105 J6
  GLE GL4 ...... 158 A5
  RSTROUD/NAIL GL6 ...... 216 D4
  STROUD GL5 ...... 215 F8
Bisley St RSTROUD/NAIL GL6 ...... 187 H6 ⬛
Bissex Md MANG/FISH BS16 ...... 357 H1
Bittern Av GLE GL4 ...... 131 F8
Bitterwell Cl FRCTL/WBN BS36 ... 357 K3
Bixhead Wk CLFD GL16 ...... 176 B3
Blaby Cl GLE GL4 ...... 159 H1 ⬛
Blackberry Av MANG/FISH BS16 ... 365 J1 ⬛
Blackberry Cl GLE GL4 ...... 159 G2 ⬛
Black Berry Fld CHELTE/BC GL52 ... 107 J3
Blackberry Gv CHELTE/BC GL52 ... 82 E2 ⬛
Blackberry Hl MANG/FISH BS16 ... 365 J1
Blackbird Av VGL GL2 ...... 103 F8
Blackbird La STNHO GL10 ...... 213 F6 ⬛
Blackboys DSLY GL11 ...... 266 E3

Black Dog Wy GL GL1 ...... 2 C3
Blackfriars CBRIS/FH BS1 ...... 364 B7 ⬛
Blackhorse Hl THNB/SVB BS35 ...... 341 K6
Blackhorse La MANG/FISH BS16 ... 357 G6
Blackhorse Pl MANG/FISH BS16 .. 357 G8 ⬛
Blackhorse Rd KGWD/HNM BS15 ... 366 D6
  MANG/FISH BS16 ...... 357 G8
Black Jack St CIR GL7 ...... 249 J5 ⬛
Blacklow St STROUD GL5 ...... 242 B4
Blackquarries Hl WUE GL12 ...... 297 H7
Blacksmith Hl WUE GL12 ...... 298 C7
Blacksmith La BWTH/CHD GL3 ...... 132 B2 ⬛
  CBATH/BATHN BA1 ...... 380 A8
  RTEWK/TIB GL19 ...... 79 K5
Blacksmiths Cl EVE WR11 ...... 15 J5
Blacksmiths Gnd VGL GL2 ...... 128 D1 ⬛
Blacksmiths La BDWAY WR12 ...... 17 J4 ⬛
  CHELTE/BC GL52 ...... 5 F1
  EVE WR11 ...... 38 C1
  TEWK GL20 ...... 36 E4
  VGL GL2 ...... 101 F7
Blacksmiths Rd TEWK GL20 ...... 37 K7
Blackswarth Rd EVILLE/WHL BS5 ... 365 H7
Blackthorn Dr ALMDB BS32 ...... 343 H7 ⬛
Blackthorn Gdns VGL GL2 ...... 156 E5 ⬛
Blackthorn Wk
  KGWD/HNM BS15 ...... 366 E4 ⬛
Blackwater Wy VGL GL2 ...... 131 G1
Black Wls DSLY GL11 ...... 267 F7 ⬛
Bladon Ms CHELTW GL51 ...... 105 F7 ⬛
Blaisdon Cl YATE/CS BS37 ...... 347 G7
Blaisdon Cl GLE GL4 ...... 159 G2
  HNBRY/STHM BS10 ...... 353 H5
Blaisdon La MTCHDN GL17 ...... 125 F5
Blaisdon Wy CHELTW GL51 ...... 105 J1
Blaise Wk
  HNLZ/SM/SNYPK/WT BS9 ...... 352 E8
Blake Cft CHELTW GL51 ...... 105 J2 ⬛
Blake Hill Wy GLE GL4 ...... 131 F7 ⬛
Blakeney Cl GLE GL4 ...... 157 K3 ⬛
Blakeney Hill Rd LYD GL15 ...... 207 G3 ⬛
Blakeney Mills YATE/CS BS37 ...... 347 F5 ⬛
Blakeney Rd BRSTK/PCHW BS34 ... 342 C5
  HORF/LLZ BS7 ...... 354 E7
Blake Rd CIR GL7 ...... 249 J5
  HORF/LLZ BS7 ...... 355 F8
Blakes Rd THNB/SVB BS35 ...... 316 B5
Blakewell Md RSTROUD/NAIL GL6 ... 187 G6
Blanchards YATE/CS BS37 ...... 348 A6
Blandford Cl
  HNLZ/SM/SNYPK/WT BS9 ...... 353 K8 ⬛
Blenheim Cl COTS GL54 ...... 144 E2 ⬛
  TEWK GL20 ...... 37 J7
Blenheim Ct COTS GL54 ...... 62 C8
Blenheim Dr BRSTK/PCHW BS34... 355 F2
  NWNT GL18 ...... 73 K6 ⬛
  TEWK GL20 ...... 13 K8
  YATE/CS BS37 ...... 346 E2
Blenheim Orch CHELTW GL51 ...... 133 J4
Blenheim Rd GL GL1 ...... 3 D5
Blenheim Sq CHELTW GL51 ...... 105 J3 ⬛
Blenheim St EVILLE/WHL BS5 ...... 364 C5 ⬛
Blenman Cl MANG/FISH BS16 ...... 356 A7 ⬛
Bleriot St COTS GL54 ...... 144 E2
Blethwin Cl HNBRY/STHM BS10 ... 353 H5
Blimeshire LYD GL15 ...... 205 K5
Blind La CHCAM GL55 ...... 20 D4
Blinkhorns Bridge La VGL GL2 ...... 3 F4
Bloomfield Rd
  BRSG/KWL/STAPK BS4 ...... 374 B2
  GL GL1 ...... 2 B6
Bloomfield Road Link
  BRSG/KWL/STAPK BS4 ...... 374 B2
Bloomfield Ter GL GL1 ...... 129 K8
Bloomsbury St CHELTW GL51 ...... 4 A3
Bloxham Rd BDWAY WR12 ...... 17 D5
Bloxhams Orch RTEWK/TIB GL19 ... 77 G6
Bloy St EVILLE/WHL BS5 ...... 365 G5 ⬛
Bluebell Cha
  RSTROUD/NAIL GL6 ...... 244 C2 ⬛
Bluebell Cl GLE GL4 ...... 159 F1 ⬛
  THNB/SVB BS35 ...... 316 D4
Bluebell Dr CHEP NP16 ...... 312 B1 ⬛
Bluebell Gv CHELTW GL51 ...... 133 K1
Bluebell Ri RSTROUD/NAIL GL6 ... 244 C2 ⬛
The Bluebells ALMDB BS32 ...... 343 J7 ⬛
  ALMDB BS32 ...... 343 K7 ⬛
Blue Boys' Pk
  RSTROUD/NAIL GL6 ...... 243 J7 ⬛
Blue La NWNT GL18 ...... 72 D6
Blue Quarry Rd CIR GL7 ...... 250 A5 ⬛
Blue Rock Crs LYD GL15 ...... 205 F5
Blunts Hay CIR GL7 ...... 228 D7
Boakes Dr STNHO GL10 ...... 212 E7
Bockenem Cl THNB/SVB BS35 ...... 316 D7 ⬛
Bodey Cl OLD/WMLY/WICK BS30 ... 376 B1
Bodham Rd CHELTW GL50 ...... 105 J2
Bodiam Av GL GL1 ...... 157 H5
Bodyce Rd THNB/SVB BS35 ...... 332 A1 ⬛
Boleyn Cl BWTH/CHD GL3 ...... 103 H7 ⬛
Bolton Rd HORF/LLZ BS7 ...... 364 C3
Bondend Rd GLE GL4 ...... 159 G4
Bond's La CHPMW/MSHF SN14 ... 371 H5 ⬛
Bond St CBRIS/FH BS1 ...... 364 C6
Bonnington Wk HORF/LLZ BS7 ... 355 F7

Bonville Rd *BRSG/KWL/STAPK* BS4 .... **374** D5
Bootenhay Rd *CHELTE/BC* GL52 ... **83** G2 ②
Borage Cl *BWTH/CHD* GL3 .... **159** H1
Borough Cl *STNHO* GL10 .... **241** G3
Boscombe Crs *MANG/FISH* BS16 ... **357** F7 ①
Boscombe La *RSTROUD/NAIL* GL6 ... **270** A6
Bosley Cl *SHPSTR* CV36 .... **24** E2
Bospin La *STROUD* GL5 .... **242** B5
Boswell St *EVILLE/WHL* BS5 .... **365** G4 ①
Botham Dr
    BRSG/KWL/STAPK BS4 .... **374** D5 ①
Boucher Rd *CBRISNE* BS2 .... **364** E4 ①
Boulton La *DSLY* GL11 .... **267** F6
Boulton Rd *CHELT* GL50 .... **106** D1
Boulton's Rd *KGWD/HNM* BS15 ...... **366** D6
Bouncer's La *CHELTE/BC* GL52 .... **5** F2
Boundary Pl *RTEWK/TIB* GL19 .... **53** G8
Boundary Rd *FRCTL/WBN* BS36 ..... **345** K7
Bourne Cl *FRCTL/WBN* BS36 .... **344** E7
    KGWD/HNM BS15 .... **366** B6
Bourne Lake Pk *HGHW* SN6 .... **309** J8
Bourne La *STROUD* GL5 .... **243** J5
Bourne Rd *KGWD/HNM* BS15 .... **366** A6
    UUSV WR8 .... **12** E1
Bourneville Rd *EVILLE/WHL* BS5 .. **365** H6 ②
Bournside Cl *CHELTW* GL51 .... **106** A7
Bournside Dr *CHELTW* GL51 .... **106** A7
Bournside Rd *CHELTW* GL51 .... **106** A7
Boursland Cl *ALMDB* BS32 .... **343** H4 ①
Bourton Av *BWTH/CHD* GL3 .... **132** B8
Bourton Cl *BRSTK/PCHW* BS34 ..... **343** G6
Bourton Dr *BRSTK/PCHW* BS34 ..... **355** F3
Bourton Rd *GLE* GL4 .... **158** A4
    MIM GL56 .... **69** K1
Boverton Av *BWTH/CHD* GL3 .... **132** B8
Boverton Dr *BWTH/CHD* GL3 .... **132** B8
Boverton Rd *BRSTK/PCHW* BS34 ... **355** F3
Bovone La *VGL* GL2 .... **99** H3
Bowbridge La *CHELTE/BC* GL52 ..... **107** H1
    STROUD GL5 .... **215** F8
Bowbridge Lock *STROUD* GL5 ...... **243** F1
Bowden Cl
    HNLZ/SM/SNYPK/WT BS9 .... **352** E6
Bowden Pl *MANG/FISH* BS16 .... **357** F7 ②
Bowden Rd *EVILLE/WHL* BS5 .... **365** J5 ②
Bowen Cl *CHELTE/BC* GL52 .... **5** E1
Bowen's Hl *CLFD* GL16 .... **175** J4
Bowen's Hill Rd *CLFD* GL16 .... **175** J4
Bowes Lyon Cl *MIM* GL56 .... **69** K2 ①
Bow La *COTS* GL54 .... **115** H8
Bowldown Rd *TET* GL8 .... **300** A6
    TET GL8 .... **324** E3
Bowler Rd *TEWK* GL20 .... **34** D5
Bowl Hl *STROUD* GL5 .... **242** C3
Bowling Green Av *CIR* GL7 .... **249** J4
Bowling Green Ct *MIM* GL56 .... **45** K8 ①
Bowling Green Crs *CIR* GL7 .... **249** J4
Bowling Green La *CIR* GL7 .... **249** J4
Bowling Green Rd *CIR* GL7 .... **249** J4
Bowling Hl *YATE/CS* BS37 .... **347** J5
Bowling Rd *YATE/CS* BS37 .... **347** K6
Bowly Crs *CIR* GL7 .... **278** A2
Bowly Rd *CIR* GL7 .... **249** H8
    GL GL1 .... **129** K8
Bownham Md *STROUD* GL5 .... **242** E4
Bownham Pk *STROUD* GL5 .... **243** F5
Bowsland Av *ALMDB* BS32 .... **343** H4
Bowson Rd *LYD* GL15 .... **205** F4
Bowstreet La *THNB/SVB* BS35 ...... **341** J6
Bow Wow *CIR* GL7 .... **278** E7
Boxbush Cl *CIR* GL7 .... **278** E7 ②
Boxbush Rd *CIR* GL7 .... **278** E7 ①
    CLFD GL16 .... **175** J4
Box La *RSTROUD/NAIL* GL6 .... **243** H8
Boxhedge Farm La
    FRCTL/WBN BS36 .... **358** A3
Box La *RSTROUD/NAIL* GL6 .... **271** C1
Box Rd *DSLY* GL11 .... **238** E6
Box Road Av *DSLY* GL11 .... **238** D6
Boxtree Rd *MTCHDN* GL17 .... **121** J6 ②
Boxwell Rd *TET* GL8 .... **323** J3
Boyce Dr *CBRISNE* BS2 .... **364** E4 ②
Boyd Cl *OLD/WMLY/WICK* BS30 .... **368** D7
Brabazon Rd *BRSTK/PCHW* BS34 ... **355** F4
Bracelands *RSTROUD/NAIL* GL6 .... **244** B1
Bracelands Dr *CLFD* GL16 .... **147** J8 ①
Bracewell Gdns
    HNBRY/STHM BS10 .... **354** A2
Bracey Dr *MANG/FISH* BS16 .... **356** C8 ①
Brackenbury Dr
    BRSTK/PCHW BS34 .... **355** J1
Bracken Cl *LYD* GL15 .... **234** C3
Brackendene *ALMDB* BS32 .... **343** G5 ①
Bracken Dr *LYD* GL15 .... **234** B3
Bradeston Gv *MANG/FISH* BS16 .... **356** A7 ①
Bradford Rd *VGL* GL2 .... **3** F3 ③
Bradfords Cl *NWNT* GL18 .... **73** G6
Bradfords Ct *NWNT* GL18 .... **73** G6 ①
Bradfords La *NWNT* GL18 .... **73** G6
Bradhurst St *EVILLE/WHL* BS5 ..... **365** F8 ②
Bradley Av *AVONM* BS11 .... **352** A8
    FRCTL/WBN BS36 .... **356** E1
Bradley Cl *VGL* GL2 .... **130** E2
Bradley Court Rd *MTCHDN* GL17 .. **123** G4
Bradley Crs *AVONM* BS11 .... **352** A8
Bradley Rd *BRSTK/PCHW* BS34 ..... **342** D6

CHELTS GL53 .... **135** G2
WUE GL12 .... **296** E6
Bradley Stoke Wy *ALMDB* BS32 .... **343** G4 ⑤
    ALMDB BS32 .... **344** A8
Bradley St *WUE* GL12 .... **296** E7
Bradshaw Cl *VGL* GL2 .... **131** G1 ①
Bradstone Rd *FRCTL/WBN* BS36 ... **356** D1 ①
Bradwell Gv *HNBRY/STHM* BS10 ... **354** A6
Braemar Av *HORF/LLZ* BS7 .... **354** D5
Braemar Crs *HORF/LLZ* BS7 .... **354** D5
Brae Wk *GLE* GL4 .... **159** F2
Bragg's La *CBRISNE* BS2 .... **364** D7
Braikenridge Rd
    BRSG/KWL/STAPK BS4 .... **374** C2
Brainsfield
    HNLZ/SM/SNYPK/WT BS9 .... **353** H8
Brake Cl *ALMDB* BS32 .... **343** J8
    KGWD/HNM BS15 .... **367** F7 ③
The Brake *FRCTL/WBN* BS36 .... **357** J1
    YATE/CS BS37 .... **347** G1
Bramble Cha *CHELTE/BC* GL52 ..... **82** E1
Bramble La *STNHO* GL10 .... **213** F6
Bramble Lawn *GLE* GL4 .... **159** F3
Bramble Ri *CHELTE/BC* GL52 .... **107** J3
Bramble Rd *CLFD* GL16 .... **176** A7
The Brambles *BRKLY* GL13 .... **264** A2 ③
Brambling Wk *MANG/FISH* BS16 ... **355** H8
Bramley Cl *THNB/SVB* BS35 .... **330** E3
    WUE GL12 .... **320** D2
Bramley Ct
    OLD/WMLY/WICK BS30 .... **376** A2 ③
Bramley Dr *RTEWK/TIB* GL19 ...... **125** K2
Bramley Ms *BWTH/CHD* GL3 .... **131** J8 ②
Bramley Rd *CHELTW* GL51 .... **105** J3
    TEWK GL20 .... **33** J7
The Bramleys *MTCHDN* GL17 ...... **124** B4 ②
Branch Hill Ri *CHELTS* GL53 .... **135** G2
Branch Rd *CHELTW* GL51 .... **105** F7
The Branch *CIND* GL14 .... **150** D1
Brandash Rd *YATE/CS* BS37 .... **348** A5
Branders *HGHW* SN6 .... **310** D6
Brandon Cl *BWTH/CHD* GL3 .... **103** J8
Brandon Pl *CHELT* GL50 .... **4** A6 ①
Brandon Steep *CBRIS/FH* BS1 ..... **364** A8 ③
Brangwyn Gv *HORF/LLZ* BS7 ...... **355** F8
Branksome Crs
    BRSTK/PCHW BS34 .... **355** F3 ①
Branksome Dr *BRSTK/PCHW* BS34 . **355** F3 ②
    FRCTL/WBN BS36 .... **344** E8
Brans La *MIM* GL56 .... **93** J6
Brantwood Rd
    RSTROUD/NAIL GL6 .... **244** D3
Braunton Rd *HORF/LLZ* BS7 .... **355** F7 ①
Bsenose Rd *TEWK* GL20 .... **13** J8
Brassington Gdns *COTS* GL54 ...... **166** B2 ①
The Bratches *CHCAM* GL55 .... **20** E1
Braydon Av *BRSTK/PCHW* BS34 .... **343** H6
Brayne Ct *OLD/WMLY/WICK* BS30 . **376** A3 ①
Breaches La *ALMDB* BS32 .... **343** H8
Bream Av *CLFD* GL16 .... **204** B5
Bream Cl *LYD* GL15 .... **205** C8
    LYD GL15 .... **231** J1
Brecon Cl *VGL* GL2 .... **156** C3
Brecon Rd
    HNLZ/SM/SNYPK/WT BS9 .... **353** J8
Brecon Wy *CLFD* GL16 .... **148** C7
Bredon *YATE/CS* BS37 .... **347** F7
Bredon Cl *KGWD/HNM* BS15 .... **367** F7 ③
Bredon Nook Rd
    HNBRY/STHM BS10 .... **354** A7 ①
Bredon Rd *TEWK* GL20 .... **33** J7
Bredon Vw *BDWAY* WR12 .... **18** E6 ①
Bregawn Cl *CHELTE/BC* GL52 ...... **82** E4
Brendon Wy *VGL* GL2 .... **131** F1
Brendon Ct
    OLD/WMLY/WICK BS30 .... **376** D2 ①
Brenner St *EVILLE/WHL* BS5 .... **365** F4
Brensham Rd *TEWK* GL20 .... **34** A7 ①
Brent Rd *HORF/LLZ* BS7 .... **364** D1
Brentry Av *EVILLE/WHL* BS5 .... **365** F1
Brentry La *HNBRY/STHM* BS10 .... **353** J4
Brentry Rd *MANG/FISH* BS16 ...... **365** D2
Brereton Wy
    OLD/WMLY/WICK BS30 .... **376** C2
Bretforton Rd *EVE* WR11 .... **6** E1
Brewerton Cl *HNBRY/STHM* BS10 . **354** A1
Brewery Hl
    OLD/WMLY/WICK BS30 .... **377** G6
Brewery La *RSTROUD/NAIL* GL6 ... **270** D3
    STROUD GL5 .... **243** G4
Briarbank Ri *CHELTE/BC* GL52 .... **107** J7
Briar Cl *STROUD* GL5 .... **215** F5
Briarfield Av *KGWD/HNM* BS15 ... **375** H1 ⑦
Briar Lawn *GLE* GL4 .... **159** F3
Briarleaze *THNB/SVB* BS35 .... **331** K4
Briars Cl *BWTH/CHD* GL3 .... **103** J8
Briarside Rd *HNBRY/STHM* BS10 .. **354** A3
Briar Wk *CHELTE/BC* GL52 .... **107** J3
    MANG/FISH BS16 .... **366** C3
Briar Wy *MANG/FISH* BS16 .... **366** B2
Briarwood
    HNLZ/SM/SNYPK/WT BS9 .... **353** H8
Briary Rd *CIR* GL7 .... **257** H8
Briavels Gv *RDLND/MONT* BS6 .... **364** D4

Bricknell Av *TEWK* GL20 .... **13** K8 ①
Brickrow *STROUD* GL5 .... **214** E7
Brick St *CBRISNE* BS2 .... **364** D7
Brick Wk *EVE* WR11 .... **7** G2
Bridewell Dr *EVE* WR11 .... **15** H5
Bridewell St *CBRIS/FH* BS1 .... **364** B7 ③
Bridge Cl *CIR* GL7 .... **249** K8 ①
    VGL GL2 .... **129** H8
Bridge End *CIR* GL7 .... **249** K7 ①
Bridge Farm *VGL* GL2 .... **101** H7
Bridgeleap Rd *MANG/FISH* BS16 .. **357** F6
Bridgemans Cl *BDWAY* WR12 ..... **18** E5 ①
Bridge Meadow Cl *EVE* WR11 ..... **15** J4
Bridgend Ct *STNHO* GL10 .... **212** E8 ①
Bridgend Rd *CHELTW* GL51 .... **105** G7 ①
Bridge Rd *BRKLY* GL13 .... **235** J4
    CIR GL7 .... **249** K8
    EVILLE/WHL BS5 .... **365** F5 ①
    KGWD/HNM BS15 .... **367** F3
    MANG/FISH BS16 .... **367** J2
    MTCHDN GL17 .... **122** D8
    STROUD GL5 .... **213** K8
    VGL GL2 .... **210** D1
    YATE/CS BS37 .... **346** C4
Bridges Ct *MANG/FISH* BS16 ...... **366** B2 ①
Bridges Rd *MANG/FISH* BS16 ...... **356** C8 ③
Bridge-side *STROUD* GL5 .... **214** B8 ③
Bridge St *CBRIS/FH* BS1 .... **364** B8 ①
    CHELTW GL51 .... **106** B2
    CHEP NP16 .... **288** A5
    CIR GL7 .... **254** E7
    EVE WR11 .... **6** C2
    EVILLE/WHL BS5 .... **365** H4 ①
    LYD GL15 .... **207** H4
    NWNT GL18 .... **73** J5
    RSTROUD/NAIL GL6 .... **270** E2 ①
    STROUD GL5 .... **214** B8 ②
Bridget Dr *CHEP* NP16 .... **288** C7
Bridge Wk *HORF/LLZ* BS7 .... **354** E6
Bridge Wy *FRCTL/WBN* BS36 ...... **345** H6
Bridgman Gv *BRSTK/PCHW* BS34 . **355** F3
The Bridle *STROUD* GL5 .... **213** K7
Bridle Wy *THNB/SVB* BS35 .... **331** K2
Briercliffe Rd
    HNLZ/SM/SNYPK/WT BS9 .... **353** F7
Brierley Banks *MTCHDN* GL17 .... **149** K3
Brierley Cl *GLE* GL4 .... **159** J3 ①
Brierley Rd *MTCHDN* GL17 .... **149** K1
Brierly Wy *LYD* GL15 .... **206** D5
Brierly Furlong
    BRSTK/PCHW BS34 .... **355** H3
Brightlands *CIND* GL14 .... **180** C2 ③
Brighton Pk *EVILLE/WHL* BS5 ..... **365** F6 ③
Brighton Pl *KGWD/HNM* BS15 ..... **366** D5 ①
Brighton Rd *BRSTK/PCHW* BS34 .. **342** D6
    CHELTE/BC GL52 .... **5** D4 ②
    RDLND/MONT BS6 .... **364** A5
Brighton St *CBRISNE* BS2 .... **364** C5
Bright St *EVILLE/WHL* BS5 .... **365** F7 ②
    KGWD/HNM BS15 .... **366** D6
Brigstocke Rd *CBRISNE* BS2 .... **364** C5
Brimbles *HORF/LLZ* BS7 .... **355** F4
Brimley *STNHO* GL10 .... **241** F2
Brimscombe Hl *STROUD* GL5 ...... **243** G6
Brimscombe La *STROUD* GL5 ...... **243** H4 ④
Brimsome Meadow *VGL* GL2 ...... **128** D3
Brindle Cl *GLE* GL4 .... **158** E2 ③
Brinkmarsh La *WUE* GL12 .... **317** K3
Brinkworthy Rd *MANG/FISH* BS16 . **355** H8
Brins Ct *BRSTK/PCHW* BS34 .... **355** K2
Brisbane La *YATE/CS* BS37 .... **335** J8
Brionne Wy *VGL* GL2 .... **130** D1
Brisbane St *STNHO* GL10 .... **212** E5
Bristol Br *CBRIS/FH* BS1 .... **364** C8
Bristol Hl *BRSG/KWL/STAPK* BS4 . **374** C4
Bristol Rd *CIR* GL7 .... **249** K7
    COTS GL54 .... **145** F2
    FRCTL/WBN BS36 .... **345** F6
    GL GL1 .... **2** B6
    KEYN BS31 .... **375** J8
    MANG/FISH BS16 .... **356** B6
    STNHO GL10 .... **212** D7
    THNB/SVB BS35 .... **316** B7
    VGL GL2 .... **157** F6
    VGL GL2 .... **238** D3
    WUE GL12 .... **318** C8
Britannia Crs *BRSTK/PCHW* BS34 . **355** H1
Britannia Rd *BRSTK/PCHW* BS34 .. **342** B7
    EVILLE/WHL BS5 .... **365** F5
    KGWD/HNM BS15 .... **366** C6
Britannia Wy *CHELTE/BC* GL52 ... **83** H3
Britten Ct
    OLD/WMLY/WICK BS30 .... **376** A2 ③
Brixton Rd *EVILLE/WHL* BS5 ...... **365** F6
Brizen La *CHELTS* GL53 .... **134** A2
Broadclose Rd *VGL* GL2 .... **103** F3
Broad Cft *ALMDB* BS32 .... **343** G4 ①
Broadfield Av *KGWD/HNM* BS15 .. **366** C6
Broadfield Rd
    BRSG/KWL/STAPK BS4 .... **374** A5
    STNHO GL10 .... **211** K7
Broadlands Av *KEYN* BS31 .... **375** J8
Broadlands Ct *COTS* GL54 .... **143** H1 ③
Broadlands Dr *AVONM* BS11 ...... **352** C5
Broad La *FRCTL/WBN* BS36 .... **357** K1

Broadleaze *AVONM* BS11 .... **352** A7 🄻
   CIR GL7 .... **280** C6 🄻
Broadleys Av
   HNLZ/SM/SNYPK/WT BS9 ...... **353** K7
Broad Leys Rd *GLE* GL4 .... **131** F7
Broadmead *CBRIS/FH* BS1 .... **364** C7
Broadmere Cl *DSLY* GL11 .... **266** C3
Broadmoor Pk *CIND* GL14 .... **150** D3
Broadmoor Rd *CIND* GL14 .... **150** D3
Broadoak Wk *MANG/FISH* BS16 .. **366** B2
Broad Oak Wy *CHELTW* GL51 ...... **105** J8
Broad Pln *CBRISNE* BS2 .... **364** D8 🄻
Broad Quay *CBRIS/FH* BS1 .... **364** B8 🄻
Broad Rd *KGWD/HNM* BS15 .... **366** C5
Broadstone Cl *GLE* GL4 .... **131** D1
Broad St *CBRIS/FH* BS1 .... **364** B7
   CIND GL14 .... **151** H6
   MANG/FISH BS16 .... **366** E2
   NWNT GL18 .... **73** J6
   RTEWK/TIB GL19 .... **76** E8
   STNHO GL10 .... **241** E4
   STROUD GL5 .... **241** K3
   YATE/CS BS37 .... **347** K5
Broadway *YATE/CS* BS37 .... **347** H4 🄻
Broadway Av
   HNLZ/SM/SNYPK/WT BS9 ...... **354** D8
Broadway Cl *CIND* GL14 .... **154** E4
   CIR GL7 .... **283** F7
Broadway La *CIND* GL14 .... **154** E4
   CIR GL7 .... **278** D8
Broadway Rd *BDWAY* WR12 .... **16** D5
   BDWAY WR12 .... **17** J4
   BDWAY WR12 .... **18** E3
   CHCAM GL55 .... **8** E3
   COTS GL54 .... **39** K6
   COTS GL54 .... **63** J1
   HORF/LLZ BS7 .... **364** B1
Broadways Dr *MANG/FISH* BS16 .. **355** K7 🄻
The Broadway *DSLY* GL11 .... **266** C3
   RSTROUD/NAIL GL6 .... **245** C2
Broad Weir *CBRIS/FH* BS1 .... **364** C7
Broadwell Br *CLFD* GL16 .... **176** B3 🄻
Broadwell Cl *GLE* GL4 .... **159** G1 🄻
Broadwell Rd *MIM* GL56 .... **93** K5
Brock Cl *CHELTW* GL51 .... **105** J8
Brockeridge Cl *VCL* GL2 .... **156** E4 🄻
Brockeridge Rd *TEWK* GL20 .... **12** E4
Brockhollands Rd *LYD* GL15 ...... **205** F6
Brockhurst Gdns
   KGWD/HNM BS15 .... **366** A6
Brockhurst Rd *KGWD/HNM* BS15 .. **366** A6
Brockley Acres
   RSTROUD/NAIL GL6 .... **244** C1
Brockley Cl *BRSTK/PCHW* BS34 .. **343** G7 🄻
Brockley Rd *STNHO* GL10 .... **241** F2
Brockmoor La *NWNT* GL18 .... **72** B6
Brockridge La *FRCTL/WBN* BS36 .. **345** J7
Brockworth *YATE/CS* BS37 .... **346** E8
Brockworth Crs *MANG/FISH* BS16 .. **355** K8
Brockworth Rd *BWTH/CHD* GL3 .. **132** B3
Brome Rd *GLE* GL4 .... **159** H1
Bromfield Wk *MANG/FISH* BS16 .. **357** H7 🄻
Bromley Dr *MANG/FISH* BS16 ..... **356** D6
Bromley Heath Av
   MANG/FISH BS16 .... **356** D6
Bromley Heath Rd
   MANG/FISH BS16 .... **356** D6 🄻
Bromley Rd *CLFD* GL16 .... **204** C1
   HORF/LLZ BS7 .... **364** C1
Brompton Cl *KGWD/HNM* BS15 ... **367** G6 🄻
Bronclesea Rd *HORF/LLZ* BS7 ... **354** D5
Bronte Cl *CHELTW* GL51 .... **105** K7 🄻
Brook Cl *COTS* GL54 .... **85** H2
   COTS GL54 .... **169** H5
Brookcote Dr *BRSTK/PCHW* BS34 .. **343** F6
Brook Ct *CHELT* GL50 .... **106** B8
Brooke Rd *CIR* GL7 .... **249** G5
Brookfield Av *HORF/LLZ* BS7 ..... **364** B3 🄻
Brookfield Cl *YATE/CS* BS37 .... **348** A5
Brookfield La *BWTH/CHD* GL3 .... **132** C1
   RDLND/MONT BS6 .... **364** B4 🄻
Brookfield Rd *BRSTK/PCHW* BS34 .. **343** F6
   BWTH/CHD GL3 .... **132** C1
   GLE GL4 .... **131** H7
   RDLND/MONT BS6 .... **364** B4 🄻
Brookfield Wk
   OLD/WMLY/WICK BS30 .... **376** D3 🄻
Brook Hl *RDLND/MONT* BS6 .... **364** C5
Brookland Dr
   RDLND/MONT BS6 .... **364** B1 🄻
Brooklands Pk *VGL* GL2 .... **130** E1
Brook La *MANG/FISH* BS16 .... **355** J8
   MIM GL56 .... **44** B4
   RDLND/MONT BS6 .... **364** D5 🄻
   VGL GL2 .... **102** E5
Brooklea *OLD/WMLY/WICK* BS30 .. **376** C2
Brook Lintons
   BRSG/KWL/STAPK BS4 .... **374** C3 🄻
Brooklyn Cl *CHELTW* GL51 .... **105** K3 🄻
Brooklyn Gdns *CHELTW* GL51 .... **106** A3
Brooklyn Rd *CHELTW* GL51 .... **105** K4
Brookmead *THNB/SVB* BS35 ...... **316** D7 🄻
Brook Rd *CHELTW* GL51 .... **106** A2

Brooksdale La *CHELTS* GL53 ...... **106** C8 🄻
Brookside *MALM* SN16 .... **304** E8 🄻
   MIM GL56 .... **22** A7
   NWNT GL18 .... **73** J5
   TEWK GL20 .... **33** K6
   TEWK GL20 .... **37** K7
Brookside Dr *FRCTL/WBN* BS36 .. **345** H6
Brookside Rd
   BRSG/KWL/STAPK BS4 .... **374** D4
   CIND GL14 .... **150** D5
Brook St *EVILLE/WHL* BS5 .... **365** C7 🄻
   GL GL1 .... **2** C5
   MTCHDN GL17 .... **123** C4
   YATE/CS BS37 .... **347** J5
Brookthorpe *YATE/CS* BS37 .... **347** F6
Brookthorpe Av *AVONM* BS11 .... **352** C6
Brookthorpe Cl *GL1* **157** K3
Brook V *CHELTE/BC* GL52 .... **5** E6
Brook Wy *ALMDB* BS32 .... **343** G5
Brookway Dr *CHELTS* GL53 .... **107** G8
Brookway Rd *CHELTS* GL53 .... **107** G8
Broom Bungalows *GLE* GL4 .... **158** C1 🄻
Broom Hl *CLFD* GL16 .... **147** H8
   MANG/FISH BS16 .... **365** J1
Broomhill Rd
   BRSG/KWL/STAPK BS4 .... **374** D4
The Brooms *MANG/FISH* BS16 .... **357** C4
Brown Cl *CHELTW* GL51 .... **105** J3 🄻
Browning Ct *HORF/LLZ* BS7 .... **355** F6 🄻
Browning Ms *CHELTW* GL51 .... **105** K7 🄻
Browns Hl *RSTROUD/NAIL* GL6 .. **244** A4
Brownshill Rd *RSTROUD/NAIL* GL6 .. **243** H5
Brown's La *STNHO* GL10 .... **213** G8
Brown's Piece *WUE* GL12 .... **297** F8
Broxholme Wk *AVONM* BS11 ...... **352** B6 🄻
Bruce Av *EVILLE/WHL* BS5 .... **365** G5
Bruce Rd *EVILLE/WHL* BS5 .... **365** G5
Brummels Dr *CLFD* GL16 .... **147** J8
Brunel Cl *OLD/WMLY/WICK* BS30 .. **367** J7
Brunel Rd *CHEP* NP16 .... **288** A4
Brunel Wy *STNHO* GL10 .... **212** C6
   THNB/SVB BS35 .... **316** B7
Brunswick Rd *GL* GL1 .... **2** C3 🄻
Brunswick Sq *CBRISNE* BS2 .... **364** C6 🄻
   GL GL1 .... **2** C4 🄻
Brunswick St *CBRISNE* BS2 .... **364** C6
   GL GL50 .... **4** B2
   EVILLE/WHL BS5 .... **365** C7 🄻
The Brush *STROUD* GL5 .... **213** K7 🄻
Bruton Cl *EVILLE/WHL* BS5 .... **365** K6 🄻
Bruton Wy *GL1* **3** D4
Bryansons Cl *MANG/FISH* BS16 .. **355** H8 🄻
Bryants Cl *MANG/FISH* BS16 ...... **356** C5 🄻
Bryant's Hl *EVILLE/WHL* BS5 ..... **366** B8
Bryaston Cl *CHELTW* GL51 .... **106** A4
Bryerland Rd *CHELTW* GL51 .... **160** E2
Brymore Av *CHELTE/BC* GL52 .... **107** G1 🄻
Brymore Cl *CHELTE/BC* GL52 ..... **107** G1
Brynland Av *HORF/LLZ* BS7 .... **364** C2
Bryony Bank *CHELTS* GL53 .... **134** B2 🄻
Bryworth La *CIR* GL7 .... **256** E8
   CIR GL7 .... **284** D2
Buchanan Av *CLFD* GL16 .... **175** J3
Buchanan Cl *CLFD* GL16 .... **175** J3 🄻
Buckholt La *GLE* GL4 .... **160** B7
Buckholt Wy *BWTH/CHD* GL3 .... **160** C1 🄻
Buckingham Av *CHELTW* GL51 ... **105** K4
Buckingham Cl *STNHO* GL10 ..... **211** J6
Buckingham Dr
   BRSTK/PCHW BS34 .... **355** H2
   BWTH/CHD GL3 .... **103** J7 🄻
Buckingham Gdns
   MANG/FISH BS16 .... **356** E8
Buckingham Pl
   MANG/FISH BS16 .... **356** E8 🄻
Buckingham Rd
   BRSG/KWL/STAPK BS4 .... **374** C1 🄻
Buckland Cl *CHELTE/BC* GL52 .... **83** F2 🄻
Buckles Cl *CHELTS* GL53 .... **135** H1
Buckle St *BDWAY* WR12 .... **42** B3
   CHCAM GL55 .... **7** J7
Buckshaft Rd *CIND* GL14 .... **178** C2
Buckstone Cl *CLFD* GL16 .... **176** B1
Budding Rd *STNHO* GL10 .... **211** J6
The Budding *STROUD* GL5 .... **215** G5
Buddleia Cl *GLE* GL4 .... **159** H2 🄻
Bude Av *EVILLE/WHL* BS5 .... **366** A6
Bude Rd *BRSTK/PCHW* BS34 ...... **355** F3
Buller Rd *BRSG/KWL/STAPK* BS4 .. **374** D4
Bulley La *GGL* GL2 .... **126** C3
   VGL GL2 .... **127** G3
Bullfinch Rd *GLE* GL4 .... **130** E1
Bullfinch Wy *VGL* GL2 .... **103** F7 🄻
Bullingham Ct *CHELTW* GL51 ..... **4** A2 🄻
Bull La *COTS* GL54 .... **85** K1
   EVILLE/WHL BS5 .... **365** K6 🄻
   GL GL1 .... **2** C3 🄻
Bull Pitch *DSLY* GL11 .... **267** F5
Bully La *YATE/CS* BS37 .... **335** H2
Bulwark Av *CHEP* NP16 .... **288** B8

Bulwark Rd *CHEP* NP16 .... **288** A7
The Bulwarks *RSTROUD/NAIL* GL6 .. **243** K8
Bunting Hl *RSTROUD/NAIL* GL6 .. **270** C2 🄻
Bunting Wy *RSTROUD/NAIL* GL6 .. **270** B2
Burbank Cl *OLD/WMLY/WICK* BS30 .. **376** B3
Burchells Green Cl
   KGWD/HNM BS15 .... **366** B6
Burchells Green Rd
   KGWD/HNM BS15 .... **366** B5
Burcombe Cl *FRCTL/WBN* BS36 .. **345** K7
Burcombe La *CIR* GL7 .... **192** E7
   CIR GL7 .... **220** B1
Burcombe Wy *RSTROUD/NAIL* GL6 .. **244** D3 🄻
Burden Cl *ALMDB* BS32 .... **343** J8
Burdett Cl *STNHO* GL10 .... **213** F7 🄻
Burdett Rd *STNHO* GL10 .... **213** F7
Burford Dr *STROUD* GL5 .... **214** C7
Burford Ms *GL* GL1 .... **3** E5
Burford Rd *CIR* GL7 .... **250** A5
Burford St *CIR* GL7 .... **285** G2
Burgage Cl *YATE/CS* BS37 .... **347** K6 🄻
The Burgage *CHELTE/BC* GL52 ... **107** H1
Burgess Green Cl
   BRSG/KWL/STAPK BS4 .... **365** J7 🄻
Burghill Rd *HNBRY/STHM* BS10 .. **353** J5
Burghley Ct *FRCTL/WBN* BS36 ... **356** F1 🄻
Burghley Rd *RDLND/MONT* BS6 .. **364** C4
Burgis Rd *HGRV/WHIT* BS14 ...... **374** C8 🄻
Burleigh Cft *GLE* GL4 .... **131** H6
Burleigh La *STROUD* GL5 .... **243** G6
Burleigh Tor *STROUD* GL5 .... **243** H7 🄻
Burleigh Vw *RSTROUD/NAIL* GL6 .. **244** B2
Burleigh Wy *WUE* GL12 .... **335** K1
Burley Av *MANG/FISH* BS16 .... **357** F1
Burley Crest *MANG/FISH* BS16 .. **357** F8
Burley Gv *MANG/FISH* BS16 .... **357** F8
The Buritons *WUE* GL12 .... **318** D4
Burma Av *CHELTE/BC* GL52 .... **5** F3
Burma Rd *RSTROUD/NAIL* GL6 ... **270** C2
Burnbush Cl *HGRV/WHIT* BS14 .. **374** D8
Burnell Dr *CBRISNE* BS2 .... **364** D6
Burneside Cl
   HNBRY/STHM BS10 .... **354** A4 🄻
Burnet Cl *GLE* GL4 .... **158** C1 🄻
Burney Wy *OLD/WMLY/WICK* BS30.. **376** B3 🄻
Burnham Cl *KGWD/HNM* BS15 ... **367** F5 🄻
Burnham Dr *KGWD/HNM* BS15 ... **367** F5
Burns Av *VGL* GL2 .... **157** J2
Burnt Barn Rd *CHEP* NP16 .... **312** A1
Burnt Oak *DSLY* GL11 .... **266** E5
Burrough Wy *FRCTL/WBN* BS36 .. **356** E1
Burton Rd *RAD* GL3 .... **351** F8
Burton St *CHELT* GL50 .... **4** A3
Bury Bar La *NWNT* GL18 .... **73** J6
Burycourt Cl *AVONM* BS11 .... **352** C5 🄻
Bury Court Rd *CIND* GL14 .... **182** C3
Bury Hl *MANG/FISH* BS16 .... **356** C3
Bury Hill La *YATE/CS* BS37 .... **335** J6
Bury La *OLD/WMLY/WICK* BS30 .. **369** H6
   VGL GL2 .... **127** J7
Buscombe Gdns *BWTH/CHD* GL3 .. **131** K3
Bush Av *BRSTK/PCHW* BS34 ...... **355** C1
Bush Cl *STNHO* GL10 .... **211** K6
Bushcombe Cl *CHELTE/BC* GL52 .. **83** J3
Bushcombe La *CHELTE/BC* GL52 .. **83** J3
Bushes La *YATE/CS* BS37 .... **336** E8
Bush Hay *BWTH/CHD* GL3 .... **131** K1
Bushy Wy *CHELTW* GL51 .... **105** H1
Bussage Hl *RSTROUD/NAIL* GL6.. **244** A2
Butcher Hill's La
   RSTROUD/NAIL GL6 .... **270** D3 🄻
Butlers Cl *EVILLE/WHL* BS5........ **365** K7
Butler's Fld *CIR* GL7 .... **285** C1
Butlers Md *LYD* GL15 .... **207** J4
Buttercross La *CHELTE/BC* GL52 .. **107** K3
Buttercup Lawn *GLE* GL4 .... **159** F4
Butterfield Cl *HNBRY/STHM* BS10 .. **354** C7
Butterfield Rd *HNBRY/STHM* BS10.. **354** C7
Buttermere Cl *CHELTW* GL51 ..... **105** J8
Buttermilk La *BWTH/CHD* GL3 ... **103** J8
Butterow West *STROUD* GL5 ...... **242** D1
Butterrow Hl *STROUD* GL5 .... **242** D1
Butterrow La *STROUD* GL5 .... **243** F2
Buttersend La *RTEWK/TIB* GL19 .. **76** A8
Butt Gn *RSTROUD/NAIL* GL6 ...... **187** G5
Buttington Cl *GLE* GL4 .... **159** H1
Buttington Hl *CHEP* NP16 .... **288** D7
Buttington Rd *CHEP* NP16 .... **288** C6 🄻
Buttington Ter *CHEP* NP16 .... **288** D8
Butt La *THNB/SVB* BS35 .... **316** C3
Butt's La *CHELTE/BC* GL52 .... **83** J1
   CHPMW/MSHF SN14 .... **371** F2
   LYD GL15 .... **207** J3
The Butts *GLE* GL4 .... **158** C2
   MALM SN16 .... **304** E8
   NWNT GL18 .... **73** K6
Butt Rd *RSTROUD/NAIL* GL6 ...... **243** J7
Buxton Wk *HORF/LLZ* BS7 .... **354** C6
Byard Rd *VGL* GL2 .... **157** H1
Bybrook Gdns *GLE* GL4 .... **157** K5
Bybrook La *RAD* GL3 .... **157** K5
Bye Md *MANG/FISH* BS16 .... **357** C6
Byfield Cl *CHELTE/BC* GL52 .... **83** J4
Byfords Cl *RTEWK/TIB* GL19 .... **125** J2 🄻

Byfords Rd *RTEWK/TIB* BL19 .... 125 J2
Byron Av *VGL* GL2 .... 157 J2
Byron Pl *MANG/FISH* BS16 .... 366 E2 🔢
Byron Rd *CHELTW* GL51 .... 105 K5
　DSLY GL11 .... 267 C7
　STROUD GL5 .... 214 B6
Byron St *CBRISNE* BS2 .... 364 E5 🔢
　EVILLE/WHL BS5 .... 365 G7 🔢

C

Cabot Cl *YATE/CS* BS37 .... 347 H5
Cadbury Heath Rd
　OLD/WMLY/WICK BS30 .... 376 C1
Caddick Cl *KGWD/HNM* BS15 .... 367 F4
Cade Cl *BRSTK/PCHW* BS34 .... 355 J1
　KGWD/HNM BS15 .... 367 F8
Caernarvon Cl *CHELTW* GL51 ...... 105 J8 🔢
Caernarvon Rd *CHELTW* GL51 ...... 105 J8
Caerwent La *CHEP* NP16 .... 312 B3
Caesar Rd *VGL* GL2 .... 157 J1
Caesars Cl *LYD* GL15 .... 234 C2 🔢
Caine Rd *HORF/LLZ* BS7 .... 354 D7 🔢
Cains Cl *KGWD/HNM* BS15 .... 366 E8
Cainscross Rd *STROUD* GL5 .... 214 B7
Caird St *CHEP* NP16 .... 288 A7
Cairn Gdns *FRCTL/WBN* BS36 ...... 356 E2 🔢
Cairns' Crs *CBRISNE* BS2 .... 364 D5 🔢
Cakebridge Pl *CHELTE/BC* GL52 ..... 5 D2
Cakebridge Rd *CHELTE/BC* GL52 .... 5 D1
Calcutt St *HGHW* SN6 .... 310 E6
Caldbeck Cl *HNBRY/STHM* BS10 .. 354 B4 🔢
Calderdale *GLE* GL4 .... 159 H1
Calderwood Ct *CHELT* GL50 .... 4 B5 🔢
Caldicot Cl *AVONM* BS11 .... 352 E4 🔢
　OLD/WMLY/WICK BS30 .... 376 C4
Caledonian Rd *GLE* GL4 .... 158 D4
California Rd
　OLD/WMLY/WICK BS30 .... 376 C2 🔢
Callaways Rd *SHPSTR* CV36 .... 25 F2
Callicroft Rd *BRSTK/PCHW* BS34... 342 C7 🔢
Callington Rd
　BRSG/KWL/STAPK BS4 .... 374 C5
　HGRV/WRIT BS14 .... 374 B5
Callowhill Ct *CBRIS/FH* BS1 .... 364 C7 🔢
Calspick Wy *VGL* GL2 .... 131 F1 🔢
Calton Rd *GL* GL1 .... 130 A8
Calverley Ms *CHELTW* GL51 .... 133 J1 🔢
Camberley Av *BWTH/CHD* GL3 .... 131 H4 🔢
Camberley Dr *FRCTL/WBN* BS36... 345 F6
Camberwell Rd *CHELTW* GL51 ..... 105 H4
Camborne Rd *HORF/LLZ* BS7 .... 354 E7
Cambourne Pl *LYD* GL15 .... 234 B4
Cambray Pl *CHELT* GL50 .... 4 B4
Cambrian Dr *YATE/CS* BS37 .... 347 G3
Cambrian Rd *TEWK* GL20 .... 57 K2
Cambridge Av *CHELTW* GL51 .... 105 K5
　DSLY GL11 .... 267 C7
Cambridge Crs
　HNLZ/SM/SNYPK/WT BS9 .... 353 J7
Cambridge Rd *HORF/LLZ* BS7 ...... 364 B2
Cambridge St *EVILLE/WHL* BS5 ... 365 G7 🔢
　GL GL1 .... 3 D4 🔢
Cambridge Wy
　RSTROUD/NAIL GL6 .... 243 H8
Camelford Rd *EVILLE/WHL* BS5 ... 365 H5 🔢
Camellia Cl *CHELTW* GL51 .... 134 A1 🔢
Camellia Wk *VGL* GL2 .... 156 E5 🔢
Cameron Wk *HORF/LLZ* BS7 .... 355 G8 🔢
Camerton Rd *EVILLE/WHL* BS5 .... 365 H5 🔢
Cam Gn *DSLY* GL11 .... 267 C1
Camomile Cl *GLE* GL4 .... 159 H1 🔢
Campbell Cl *BWTH/CHD* GL3 ...... 103 G7 🔢
Campbell Farm Dr *AVONM* BS11... 352 B5
Campbell Rd *CLFD* GL16 .... 176 B3
Campbell St *CBRISNE* BS2 .... 364 C5
Camp Gdns *COTS* GL54 .... 92 C6
Campden Av *SHPSTR* CV36 .... 10 C5
Campden La *BDWAY* WR12 .... 19 G3
　COTS GL54 .... 87 F8
Campden Pitch *SHPSTR* CV36 ...... 10 D4
Campden Rd *CHCAM* GL55 .... 21 K1
　CHELTW GL51 .... 105 J6
　GLE GL4 .... 158 A3
　SHPSTR CV36 .... 24 E1
Campden St *SHPSTR* CV36 .... 11 F3
Camp Gdns *COTS* GL54 .... 92 C6
Camp La *CHPMW/MSHF* SN14 ...... 371 G2
Camp Rd *CHELTE/BC* GL52 .... 5 F4
　CHEP NP16 .... 288 B8
　THNB/SVB BS35 .... 291 F8
Camp Vw *FRCTL/WBN* BS36 .... 356 E2
Cam Rd *CHELTE/BC* GL52 .... 5 F2
Cams Gnd *VGL* GL2 .... 100 D8 🔢
The Cam *CHCAM* GL55 .... 21 H3

Canberra *STNHO* GL10 .... 212 E5
Canberra Gv *BRSTK/PCHW* BS34.... 355 F2
Canford La
　HNLZ/SM/SNYPK/WT BS9 .... 353 H6
Canford Rd
　HNLZ/SM/SNYPK/WT BS9 .... 353 H7
Cannans Cl *FRCTL/WBN* BS36 ...... 344 E7
Canning Cl *VGL* GL2 .... 131 G1 🔢
Cann La *OLD/WMLY/WICK* BS30 ... 368 A8
Cannon St *CBRIS/FH* BS1 .... 364 B7 🔢
Cannop Rd *LYD* GL15 .... 177 G8
Canonbury St *BRKLY* GL13 .... 264 B3
Canon Pk *BRKLY* GL13 .... 264 A2
Canon's Wk *KGWD/HNM* BS15 ..... 366 E4
Canterbury Cl *YATE/CS* BS37 .... 347 G3
Canterbury Leys *TEWK* GL20 .... 33 K7
Canterbury St *EVILLE/WHL* BS5 ... 365 F8 🔢
Canterbury Wk *CHELTW* GL51 .... 106 A8
Canters Leaze *WUE* GL12 .... 335 K2
Canton Acre *RSTROUD/NAIL* GL6 .. 187 H5
Cantors Ct *CHELTE/BC* GL52 .... 83 F4 🔢
Cantors Dr *CHELTE/BC* GL52 .... 82 E4
Canvey Cl *HNBRY/STHM* BS10 ..... 354 C7 🔢
Canynge St *CBRIS/FH* BS1 .... 364 C9
Capel Cl *KGWD/HNM* BS15 .... 367 H6
Capel Ct *AVONM* BS11 .... 352 D5
　GLE GL4 .... 158 A7
Capgrave Cl
　BRSG/KWL/STAPK BS4 .... 375 F3
Capgrave Crs
　BRSG/KWL/STAPK BS4 .... 375 F3
Captain Barton Cl *STROUD* GL5 ... 215 G6
Captains Green Rd *LYD* GL15 .... 206 A3
Caraway Gdns *EVILLE/WHL* BS5 .. 365 G4 🔢
Cardigan Cl
　HNLZ/SM/SNYPK/WT BS9 .... 353 K8
Cares Cl *CHELTE/BC* GL52 .... 83 G2 🔢
Carisbrooke Dr *CHELTE/BC* GL52 .. 107 J7 🔢
Carisbrooke Rd *BWTH/CHD* GL3 .. 131 J8
Carisbrook Rd *MTCHDN* GL17 ..... 123 G3
Carlton Gdns *STROUD* GL5 .... 214 E8 🔢
Carlton Pk *EVILLE/WHL* BS5 .... 365 G6
Carlton Pl *CHELTW* GL51 .... 4 A2 🔢
Carlton St *CHELTE/BC* GL52 .... 5 D4
Carlyle Gv *CHELTW* GL51 .... 105 H2 🔢
Carlyle Rd *EVILLE/WHL* BS5 .... 365 G6
Carmarthen Cl *YATE/CS* BS37 ...... 347 H2 🔢
Carmarthen Gv
　OLD/WMLY/WICK BS30 .... 376 C5 🔢
Carmarthen Rd *CHELTW* GL51 .... 105 H8
Carmarthen St *GL* GL1 .... 3 D6 🔢
Carnarvon Rd *RDLND/MONT* BS6 .. 364 A4
Carne Pl *GLE* GL4 .... 130 C5
Caroline La *YATE/CS* BS37 .... 347 K4 🔢
Carpenters La *CIR* GL7 .... 249 K6 🔢
Carrant Rd *TEWK* GL20 .... 33 J7
Carroll Gv *CHELTW* GL51 .... 105 H2
Carsons Cl *MANG/FISH* BS16 .... 367 H3
Carsons Rd *MANG/FISH* BS16 ...... 367 H3
Carter Rd *CHELTW* GL51 .... 105 H2
Carters Orch *VGL* GL2 .... 157 F4
Carters Wy *RSTROUD/NAIL* GL6 ... 270 B1 🔢
Carter Wk *ALMDB* BS32 .... 343 H6 🔢
Cartledge Rd *EVILLE/WHL* BS5 ... 365 C5 🔢
Cartway *CIND* GL14 .... 150 E3
Casey Cl *VGL* GL2 .... 3 E3
Cashes Green Rd *STROUD* GL5 ... 213 K6
Cash Hl *MTCHDN* GL17 .... 121 H6
Casino Pl *CHELT* GL50 .... 4 A6
Cassell Rd *MANG/FISH* BS16........ 366 C1
Cassey Bottom La
　EVILLE/WHL BS5 .... 366 A7 🔢
Castle Cl *HNBRY/STHM* BS10 ...... 353 C4
　RSTROUD/NAIL GL6 .... 187 H7 🔢
Castle Coombe *THNB/SVB* BS35 ... 316 C4
Castle Ct *BRSG/KWL/STAPK* BS4 .. 374 B2
　THNB/SVB BS35 .... 316 A4
Castle Crs *LYD* GL15 .... 231 F1
Castle End *RSTROUD/NAIL* GL6 ... 187 G1
Castle Farm Rd *KGWD/HNM* BS15 .. 375 H4
Castlefields Av *CHELTE/BC* GL52 .. 107 J8
Castlefields Dr *CHELTE/BC* GL52 .. 107 J8
Castlefields Rd *CHELTE/BC* GL52 .. 107 J9
Castleford Gdns *CHEP* NP16 .... 288 B4 🔢
Castleford Hl *CHEP* NP16 .... 288 A4
Castle Gdns *CHCAM* GL55 .... 21 G3
Castle Hill Dr *BWTH/CHD* GL3 .... 160 D2
Castle La *CHPMW/MSHF* SN14 ..... 371 J5
　VGL GL2 .... 183 H4
Castlemaine Dr *CHELTW* GL51 .... 105 G6
Castle Md *STNHO* GL10 .... 241 F3
Castlemead Rd *STROUD* GL5 ...... 214 D8
Castle Ri *STROUD* GL5 .... 214 E8
Castle Rd *KGWD/HNM* BS15 .... 366 C4
　MANG/FISH BS16 .... 358 E8
　OLD/WMLY/WICK BS30 .... 376 D3
Castle St *CBRISNE* BS2 .... 364 C7
　CIR GL7 .... 249 J6
　COTS GL54 .... 85 K1
　STNHO GL10 .... 241 G3
　STROUD GL5 .... 214 E8 🔢
　THNB/SVB BS35 .... 316 A4
Castleton Rd *GLE* GL4 .... 131 F7
Castlett St *COTS* GL54 .... 88 C7

Castle Vw *CHEP* NP16 .... 288 C5 🔢
Catbrain Hl *HNBRY/STHM* BS10 .. 341 K8
Catbrain La *HNBRY/STHM* BS10 .. 341 K8
Catbrook Cl *CHCAM* GL55 .... 20 E5
Catchpot La *YATE/CS* BS37 .... 348 E8
Catherine Hl *THNB/SVB* BS35 ..... 330 D4
Catkin Cl *VGL* GL2 .... 156 F7 🔢
Catswood Ct *STROUD* GL5 .... 215 C5
Catswood La *RSTROUD/NAIL* GL6 .. 215 K3
Cattistock Dr *EVILLE/WHL* BS5 ... 366 A8
Cattybrook Rd *MANG/FISH* BS16 .. 357 K8
　MANG/FISH BS16 .... 367 K1
Cattybrook St *EVILLE/WHL* BS5 .. 365 F6 🔢
Caudle Cl *MTCHDN* GL17 .... 121 H6 🔢
Caudle La *MTCHDN* GL17 .... 121 H7
Causeway Rd *CIND* GL14 .... 151 F4
The Causeway *FRCTL/WBN* BS36 .. 345 J7
　VGL GL2 .... 156 D5
Causley Dr *OLD/WMLY/WICK* BS30.. 376 A1
Cave Dr *MANG/FISH* BS16 .... 356 D8
Cave Gv *MANG/FISH* BS16 .... 357 H7
Cavendish Av *BWTH/CHD* GL3 ..... 132 B7
Cavendish Rd *BRSTK/PCHW* BS34.. 342 D6
Cave St *CBRISNE* BS2 .... 364 C6
Cecil Av *EVILLE/WHL* BS5 .... 365 K5
Cecil Rd *GL* GL1 .... 2 B6
　KGWD/HNM BS15 .... 366 D6
Cecily Hl *CIR* GL7 .... 249 H5
Cedar Cl *BRSTK/PCHW* BS34 .... 342 D7
　CHELTS GL53 .... 135 H1 🔢
　OLD/WMLY/WICK BS30 .... 376 C2 🔢
　STROUD GL5 .... 213 K8
Cedar Court Rd *CHELT* GL50 .... 4 B5 🔢
Cedar Dr *DSLY* GL11 .... 266 E5
Cedar Gdns *STNHO* GL10 .... 213 F6 🔢
Cedar Gv *COTS* GL54 .... 62 D8
Cedar Rd *BWTH/CHD* GL3 .... 132 B7
　CHCAM GL55 .... 9 G2
　TEWK GL20 .... 34 D6
Cedar Wy *CLFD* GL16 .... 176 B2
　FRCTL/WBN BS36 .... 356 D1
　MANG/FISH BS16 .... 368 D1
Cedarwood Dr *GLE* GL4 .... 158 A3
Celandine Bank *CHELTE/BC* GL52 .. 83 H2 🔢
Celandine Cl *THNB/SVB* BS35 ..... 316 D4
Celestine Rd *YATE/CS* BS37 .... 346 E3
Celia Ter *BRSG/KWL/STAPK* BS4 .. 365 K8 🔢
Cemetery La *CIR* GL7 .... 225 H4
　COTS GL54 .... 115 J8
Cemetery Rd *GLE* GL4 .... 130 C8
Cennick Av *KGWD/HNM* BS15 ..... 366 E5
Centaurus Rd *BRSTK/PCHW* BS34.. 342 A7
Centenary Wy *SHPSTR* CV36 .... 10 E2
Central Av *HNBRY/STHM* BS10 .... 340 C3
　KGWD/HNM BS15 .... 375 H1
Central Cross Dr *CHELTE/BC* GL52 .. 4 C2
Central Rd *GL* GL1 .... 2 C6
　STROUD GL5 .... 214 B7
Central Wy *CHELTW* GL51 .... 106 B4
Centurion Cl *GLE* GL4 .... 131 G8 🔢
Centurion Rd *LYD* GL15 .... 234 C2
Centurions Wk *CLFD* GL16 .... 175 K5 🔢
Ceres Cl *OLD/WMLY/WICK* BS30 ... 376 A4
Cerimon Ga *BRSTK/PCHW* BS34 .. 355 J1 🔢
Cerney Wick La *CIR* GL7 .... 309 H1
Cesson Cl *YATE/CS* BS37 .... 348 A5
Chaceley Cl *GLE* GL4 .... 159 G1 🔢
　VGL GL2 .... 156 E6
Chadbournes *BWTH/CHD* GL3 .... 103 K8 🔢
Chad Rd *CHELTW* GL51 .... 105 K5
Chadwick Cl *GLE* GL4 .... 157 K4
Chaffinch Cl *VGL* GL2 .... 103 F7 🔢
Chaffinch Ct *STNHO* GL10 .... 213 F6 🔢
Chaingate La *YATE/CS* BS37 .... 334 B8
Chakehill Cl *HNBRY/STHM* BS10 .. 354 A3
Chakeshill Dr *HNBRY/STHM* BS10 .. 354 A3
Chalcombe Cl *BRSTK/PCHW* BS34.. 343 C6
Chalford Av *CHELTW* GL51 .... 105 F7
Chalford Cl *YATE/CS* BS37 .... 347 F6
Chalford Rd *GLE* GL4 .... 158 A5
Chalks Rd *EVILLE/WHL* BS5 .... 365 H6
Challender Av *HNBRY/STHM* BS10 .. 353 H4
Chamberlayne Cl *COTS* GL54 .... 92 C7
Champion Rd *KGWD/HNM* BS15 .. 367 G4
Champneys Av
　HNBRY/STHM BS10 .... 353 H3 🔢
Chamwells Av *VGL* GL2 .... 3 F1
Chamwells Wk *VGL* GL2 .... 3 F1
Chancel Cl *GLE* GL4 .... 3 F4
Chancel Pk *CHELTS* GL53 .... 107 F8
Chancel Wy *CHELTS* GL53 .... 107 G8
　CIR GL7 .... 285 G2 🔢
Chancery St *EVILLE/WHL* BS5 ..... 365 F7 🔢
Chance St *TEWK* GL20 .... 33 J8 🔢
Chandler Rd *CHELTE/BC* GL52 .... 83 F4
Chandos Dr *BWTH/CHD* GL3 ...... 160 C1
Chandos Rd *KEYN* BS31 .... 375 K7
　STROUD GL5 .... 242 C2
Chandos St *COTS* GL54 .... 85 J1
Channell's Hl
　HNLZ/SM/SNYPK/WT BS9 .... 353 J6
Channel Vw *CHEP* NP16 .... 288 A8
Channon's Hl *MANG/FISH* BS16 .. 365 K2
Chantry Cl *LYD* GL15 .... 234 A5 🔢
Chantry Ct *TET* GL8 .... 302 C7 🔢

Chantry Gdns *MIM* GL56 .... **68** D1 🔲
Chantry Ga *CHELTE/BC* GL52 ...... **82** E4 🔲
Chantry Gv *AVONM* BS11 .... **352** E4 🔲
Chantry La *MANG/FISH* BS16 ..... **357** F5 🔲
Chapel Cl *CIR* GL7 .... **275** F3
  CIR GL7 .... **283** F5 🔲
Chapel Gdns *HNBRY/STHM* BS10 . **353** J5
  MIM GL56 .... **23** J5
  VCL GL2 .... **157** F7
Chapel Hay Cl *BWTH/CHD* GL3 .. **132** A2 🔲
Chapel Hay La *BWTH/CHD* GL3 ... **132** B2
Chapel HI *BRKLY* GL13 .... **264** D7
  CLFD GL16 .... **147** K4
  LYD GL15 .... **233** F5
Chapel La *AVONM* BS11 .... **352** D4
  BAD GL9 .... **351** G8
  BDWAY WR12 .... **17** K4
  CHCAM GL55 .... **7** J8
  CHCAM GL55 .... **9** F4
  CHELT GL50 .... **4** B6 🔲
  CHELTE/BC GL52 .... **83** H3
  CHNTN OX7 .... **119** C1
  CHPMW/MSHF SN14 .... **370** A1
  CIR GL7 .... **221** J1
  COTS GL54 .... **145** J2
  EVILLE/WHL BS5 .... **365** J4
  KGWD/HNM BS15 .... **367** H6
  MALM SN16 .... **306** A6
  MANG/FISH BS16 .... **356** C7
  MIM GL56 .... **44** B4
  MTCHDN OL17 .... **124** E5
  RSTROUD/NAIL GL6 .... **271** J1
  RTEWK/TIB GL19 .... **51** K5
  STROUD GL5 .... **213** K8
  TEWK GL20 .... **35** F2
  VCL GL2 .... **126** C5
  WUE GL12 .... **317** C5
  WUE GL12 .... **321** H6
  YATE/CS BS37 .... **348** E8
Chapel Pitch *NWNT* GL18 .... **96** D3
Chapel St *CIR* GL7 .... **283** F8
  CLFD GL16 .... **175** K1
  EVILLE/WHL BS5 .... **365** F5 🔲
  KGWD/HNM BS15 .... **375** H1
  LYD GL15 .... **207** F4
  THNB/SVB BS35 .... **316** B6
Chapel St *CHELT* GL50 .... **4** B3
  CHNTN OX7 .... **118** C4
  COTS GL54 .... **92** C6
  DSLY GL11 .... **266** D1
  MIM GL56 .... **93** F3
  STROUD GL5 .... **215** F7
  THNB/SVB BS35 .... **316** B6
Chapel Wk *BAD* GL9 .... **339** H3
  CLFD GL16 .... **148** C7 🔲
Chapel Wy *BRSG/KWL/STAPK* BS4 . **374** J8
Chaplin Rd *EVILLE/WHL* BS5 ..... **365** F5
Chapman Wy *CHELTW* GL51 ..... **105** K7 🔲
Chapter St *CBRISNE* BS2 .... **364** C6 🔲
Charbon Ga *BRSTK/PCHW* BS34 . **355** J1 🔲
Charborough Rd
  BRSTK/PCHW BS34 .... **354** D4
Chardstock Av
  HNLZ/SM/SNYPK/WT BS9 .... **352** E6
Chardwar Gdns *COTS* GL54 .... **143** H1 🔲
Charfield Rd *KGWD/HNM* BS15 .. **367** C6 🔲
Charfield Rd *HNBRY/STHM* BS10 . **354** A5
  WUE GL12 .... **296** B8
Chargrove
  OLD/WMLY/WICK BS30 .... **367** J8 🔲
  YATE/CS BS37 .... **347** F7
Chargrove La *CHELTW* GL51 ..... **105** H8
Charis Av *HNBRY/STHM* BS10 ... **354** A7
Charlecombe Rd
  HNLZ/SM/SNYPK/WT BS9 .... **353** H8
Charlecote Av *GL* GL1 .... **157** J6
Charlecote Cnr *CHELTE/BC* GL52 . **82** E3 🔲
Charles Av *BRSTK/PCHW* BS34 .. **355** J2 🔲
Charles Cl *THNB/SVB* BS35 .... **316** E5
Charles Rd *BRSTK/PCHW* BS34 .. **355** F3
Charles St *CBRIS/FH* BS1 .... **364** B6
  CHELTW GL51 .... **4** A2
  GL GL1 .... **3** D4
Charlesway *MIM* GL56 .... **69** F6
Charleswood Rd *LYD* GL15 .... **205** J4
Charlham La *CIR* GL7 .... **280** D7
Charlock Cl *GLE* GL4 .... **158** C2 🔲
Charlotte St *CBRIS/FH* BS1 .... **364** A8
  CBRISNE BS2 .... **364** D6 🔲
Charlotte St South
  CBRIS/FH BS1 .... **364** A8 🔲
Charlton Av *BRSTK/PCHW* BS34 . **354** D4
Charlton Cl *CHELTS* GL53 .... **135** G1
Charlton Court Rd *CHELTE/BC* GL52 . **5** E6
Charlton Dr *CHELTS* GL53 .... **5** D6
Charlton Gdns *HNBRY/STHM* BS10 . **353** J4
Charlton La *CHELTS* GL53 .... **134** D1
  HNBRY/STHM BS10 .... **353** J3
Charlton Mead Dr
  HNBRY/STHM BS10 .... **354** B2
Charlton Park Dr *CHELTS* GL53 .. **4** C6
Charlton Park Ga *CHELTS* GL53 . **106** E8
Charlton Pl *HNBRY/STHM* BS10 . **354** B2 🔲
Charlton Rd *HNBRY/STHM* BS10 . **353** K5

KGWD/HNM BS15 .... **366** B5
TET GL8 .... **302** A7
Charlton St *EVILLE/WHL* BS5 .... **365** F7 🔲
Charlton Wy *VCL* GL2 .... **130** E1
Charminster Rd *MANG/FISH* BS16 . **366** B3
Charnell Rd *MANG/FISH* BS16 ... **366** E2
Charnhill Brow *MANG/FISH* BS16 . **367** G2
Charnhill Crs *MANG/FISH* BS16 .. **367** G2
Charnhill Dr *MANG/FISH* BS16 ... **367** F2
Charnhill Rdg *MANG/FISH* BS16 . **367** G2
Charnhill V *MANG/FISH* BS16 .... **367** G2
Charnwood Cl *CHELTS* GL53 ..... **134** D1 🔲
Charnwood Ct *LYD* GL15 .... **234** B1 🔲
Charnwood Rd *CHELTS* GL53 .... **134** D1 🔲
Charterhouse Rd
  EVILLE/WHL BS5 .... **365** H6 🔲
Chartist La *RTEWK/TIB* GL19 .... **52** D2
Chartist Piece *RTEWK/TIB* GL19 . **53** H7
Chartists Wy *CHEP* NP16 .... **312** A1
Chartist Wy *RTEWK/TIB* GL19 ... **53** C7
Chartwell Cl *VCL* GL2 .... **129** G8
Chase Av *CHELTE/BC* GL52 .... **107** J8
Chasefield La *MANG/FISH* BS16 . **366** B2 🔲
Chase La *GLE* GL4 .... **3** F6
  WUE GL12 .... **320** A8
Chasely Crs *CHELTW* GL51 .... **133** J1 🔲
Chase Rd *KGWD/HNM* BS15 ...... **366** D4
The Chase *BWTH/CHD* GL3 .... **132** B2
  GLE GL4 .... **159** F1
  MANG/FISH BS16 .... **366** C3 🔲
  STROUD GL5 .... **213** K7
Chasewood Cnr
  RSTROUD/NAIL GL6 .... **244** B2 🔲
Chatcombe La *YATE/CS* BS37 .... **347** C2 🔲
Chatcombe Cl *CHELTS* GL53 ...... **135** H2 🔲
Chatcombe Rd *GLE* GL4 .... **158** D1 🔲
Chatsworth Av *GL* GL1 .... **157** J5
Chatsworth Dr *CHELTS* GL53 .... **134** C1
Chatsworth Pk *THNB/SVB* BS35 . **316** C4
Chatsworth Rd
  BRSG/KWL/STAPK BS4 .... **374** B2
  MANG/FISH BS16 .... **366** D3
Chatterton Rd *YATE/CS* BS37 .... **347** F5
Chaucer Cl *GL* GL1 .... **157** K1
Chaucer Rd *DSLY* GL11 .... **267** G7
Chavenage La *TET* GL8 .... **302** A6
Cheapside *CBRISNE* BS2 .... **364** D6 🔲
  STROUD GL5 .... **214** D7
Cheap St *COTS* GL54 .... **194** E2
Chedworth *KGWD/HNM* BS15 .... **366** C3 🔲
  YATE/CS BS37 .... **346** D7
Chedworth Rd *GLE* GL4 .... **157** K3
  HORF/LLZ BS7 .... **354** E8
Chedworth Wy *CHELTW* GL51 ... **105** J6 🔲
Cheese La *CBRISNE* BS2 .... **364** C8
Chelford Gv *BRSTK/PCHW* BS34 . **343** F6 🔲
Chelmsford Av *CHELTW* GL51 ... **134** A1
Chelmsford Wk
  BRSG/KWL/STAPK BS4 .... **374** E1 🔲
Chelsea Cl *CHELTS* GL53 .... **5** D6 🔲
Chelsea Pk *EVILLE/WHL* BS5 .... **365** G6
Chelsea Rd *EVILLE/WHL* BS5 .... **365** F5
Cheltenham La
  RDLND/MONT BS6 .... **364** C4 🔲
Cheltenham Rd *BDWAY* WR12 ... **18** A7
  CHELTE/BC GL52 .... **83** F5
  CIR GL7 .... **249** H3
  COTS GL54 .... **85** C5
  EVE WR11 .... **15** K4
  EVE WR11 .... **16** A1
  RDLND/MONT BS6 .... **364** B5
  RSTROUD/NAIL GL6 .... **187** H6
  RSTROUD/NAIL GL6 .... **216** E5
  TEWK GL20 .... **35** F1
  TEWK GL20 .... **36** E3
  VCL GL2 .... **130** E3
Cheltenham Rd East
  BWTH/CHD GL3 .... **131** H1
Chelt Rd *CHELTE/BC* GL52 .... **5** F2
Chelworth Rd *HCHW* SN6 .... **310** B8
Chepstow Pk *MANG/FISH* BS16 . **357** F5 🔲
Chequers Cl
  OLD/WMLY/WICK BS30 .... **376** D3 🔲
Chequers Rd *GLE* GL4 .... **3** E6
Cherington Rd *KGWD/HNM* BS15 . **375** C1
  YATE/CS BS37 .... **347** F8
Cherington Rd
  HNBRY/STHM BS10 .... **354** A7
Cheriton Cl *CHELTW* GL51 .... **133** K1 🔲
Cheriton Pl
  HNLZ/SM/SNYPK/WT BS9 .... **353** K7
  OLD/WMLY/WICK BS30 .... **367** J8
Cherrington Dr *GLE* GL4 .... **159** G1
Cherry Av *CHELTS* GL53 .... **135** J2
Cherry Bank *NWNT* GL18 .... **73** J7 🔲
Cherry Cl *VCL* GL2 .... **156** E7
Cherry Garden La
  OLD/WMLY/WICK BS30 .... **376** C4
Cherry Garden Rd
  OLD/WMLY/WICK BS30 .... **376** D5
Cherry Gdns
  OLD/WMLY/WICK BS30 .... **376** D5
Cherry Gv *MANG/FISH* BS16 ..... **357** G8
Cherry La *CBRIS/FH* BS1 .... **364** B6 🔲

Cherry Orch *TEWK* GL20 .... **13** J8
  WUE GL12 .... **297** G7
Cherry Orchard Cl *CHCAM* GL55 . **20** E4
Cherry Orchard La
  CHPMW/MSHF SN14 .... **351** H1
  TEWK GL20 .... **12** B8
Cherry Orchard Rd *TET* GL8 ...... **302** C6 🔲
The Cherry Orch *CHELTW* GL51 . **104** C2
Cherry Rd *YATE/CS* BS37 .... **347** J5 🔲
Cherry Tree Cl
  RSTROUD/NAIL GL6 .... **270** C2
Cherrytree Ct *MANG/FISH* BS16 . **368** E1 🔲
Cherrytree Crs *MANG/FISH* BS16 . **366** C4
Cherrytree La *CIR* GL7 .... **250** E4
Cherry Tree La *CLFD* GL16 .... **176** C2 🔲
Cherry Tree Rd *HCHW* SN6 .... **310** C6
Cherrytree Rd *KGWD/HNM* BS15 . **366** C4
Cherry Wk *LYD* GL15 .... **234** A2
Cherry Wd *OLD/WMLY/WICK* BS30 . **368** B7
Cherrywood Gdns *GLE* GL4 .... **158** A3 🔲
Cherston Ct *GLE* GL4 .... **131** G6
Chervil Cl *GLE* GL4 .... **158** D2 🔲
Cherwell Cl *THNB/SVB* BS35 ..... **316** C7 🔲
Chesham Wy *KGWD/HNM* BS15 . **366** D5 🔲
Cheshire Cl *YATE/CS* BS37 .... **347** G3
Cheshire Rd *BWTH/CHD* GL3 .... **103** G8
The Chesils *COTS* GL54 .... **62** E6 🔲
Chesley Hl *OLD/WMLY/WICK* BS30 . **368** B7
Chessel Cl *ALMDB* BS32 .... **343** G4
Chessell Av *THNB/SVB* BS35 ..... **328** E7 🔲
Chessgrove La *MTCHDN* OL17 ... **124** A3
Chestal *DSLY* GL11 .... **267** F5
Chester Cl *RTEWK/TIB* GL19 ..... **79** C1 🔲
Chester Crs *CIR* GL7 .... **249** K6
Chesterfield Av
  RDLND/MONT BS6 .... **364** C4 🔲
Chesterfield Rd *MANG/FISH* BS16 . **366** E1
  RDLND/MONT BS6 .... **364** C4
Chestermaster Cl *ALMDB* BS32 .. **342** E1 🔲
Chester Park Rd *MANG/FISH* BS16 . **366** B1
Chester Rd *EVILLE/WHL* BS5 ..... **365** J5 🔲
  GLE GL4 .... **130** E6
Chesters *OLD/WMLY/WICK* BS30 . **376** B3 🔲
Chester St *CIR* GL7 .... **249** K6
  EVILLE/WHL BS5 .... **365** H1 🔲
Chesterton Gv *CIR* GL7 .... **249** J8
Chesterton La *CIR* GL7 .... **249** G7
Chester Wk *CHELT* GL50 .... **4** B3 🔲
Chestnut Av *STNHO* GL10 .... **213** F6
Chestnut Cl *CIR* GL7 .... **280** D7
  CLFD GL16 .... **176** B2
  RSTROUD/NAIL GL6 .... **270** D2
  TET GL8 .... **302** B6 🔲
  VCL GL2 .... **156** E7 🔲
Chestnut Ct *MANG/FISH* BS16 ... **367** C1
Chestnut Dr *THNB/SVB* BS35 .... **316** C5 🔲
  YATE/CS BS37 .... **347** J5 🔲
Chestnut HI *RSTROUD/NAIL* GL6 . **270** D2
Chestnut La *STROUD* GL5 .... **214** C8
Chestnut Pl *CHELTS* GL53 .... **134** B2 🔲
Chestnut Rd *GLE* GL4 .... **159** G1
  KGWD/HNM BS15 .... **367** F3 🔲
  MANG/FISH BS16 .... **356** D8 🔲
The Chestnuts *GL* GL1 .... **2** B5 🔲
Chestnut Wy *KGWD/HNM* BS15 . **367** F3
Chetwode Cl *HNBRY/STHM* BS10 . **354** B3
Chevening Cl
  BRSTK/PCHW BS34 .... **355** H2 🔲
Cheviot Cl *VCL* GL2 .... **156** E6 🔲
Cheviot Dr *THNB/SVB* BS35 ...... **316** E6
Cheviot Rd *CHELTE/BC* GL52 .... **5** F1 🔲
Cheviot Wy
  OLD/WMLY/WICK BS30 .... **376** D1
Chewton Cl *MANG/FISH* BS16 ... **366** B3
Cheyne Rd
  HNLZ/SM/SNYPK/WT BS9 .... **353** F8
Cheyney Cl *GLE* GL4 .... **130** D8
Chichester Wy *YATE/CS* BS37 ... **347** F3 🔲
Chickadee *LYD* GL15 .... **230** E2
Chicknalls La *LYD* GL15 .... **207** K1
Childswickham Rd *BDWAY* WR12 . **18** B6
Chillington Ct *BRSTK/PCHW* BS34 . **342** C5
Chillwood Cl *YATE/CS* BS37 ...... **346** A3
Chiltern Av *CHELTE/BC* GL52 .... **82** C2
Chiltern Cl *OLD/WMLY/WICK* BS30 . **376** D1
Chiltern Pk *THNB/SVB* BS35 ..... **316** E6
Chiltern Rd *CHELTE/BC* GL52 .... **5** F2
  VCL GL2 .... **156** E6
China Cnr *EVE* WR11 .... **7** C7
The Chine *MANG/FISH* BS16 ..... **355** H1
Chine Vw *MANG/FISH* BS16 ...... **357** F6
Chiphouse Rd *KGWD/HNM* BS15 . **366** E4
Chippenham Rd
  CHPMW/MSHF SN14 .... **372** A6
Chipperfield Dr *KGWD/HNM* BS15 . **367** F5
Chipping Cl *WUE* GL12 .... **297** F2 🔲
Chipping Gdns *WUE* GL12 .... **296** E7 🔲
The Chippings *MANG/FISH* BS16 . **365** H1
Chipping St *TET* GL8 .... **302** C7
Chisbury Cl *EVILLE/WHL* BS5 .... **365** G3 🔲
Chislet Wy *GLE* GL4 .... **157** K5
Chittening Rd *AVONM* BS11 ...... **340** A7
Chock La
  HNLZ/SM/SNYPK/WT BS9 .... **353** J7
Choirs Cl *GLE* GL4 .... **131** G8

Chosen Dr BWTH/CHD GL3........... **131** K1
Chosen View Rd CHELTW GL51... **106** B2
Chosen Wy GLE GL4 .... **131** H6
Christchurch Av
MANG/FISH BS16 .... **366** D1 🔢
Christchurch La
MANG/FISH BS16 .... **366** D1 🔢
Christ Church Rd CHELT GL50 ...... **106** B6
Christmas St CBRIS/FH BS1 .... **364** B7 🔢
Christowe La CHELTS GL53 .... **4** C6
Chubb Cl OLD/WMLY/WICK BS30... **376** A1
Church Av CIR GL7 .... **278** A1
EVILLE/WHL BS5 .... **365** F5 🔢
OLD/WMLY/WICK BS30 .... **367** J7
WUE GL12 .... **294** A7
Church Cl BDWAY WR12 .... **18** C7
FRCTL/WBN BS36 .... **345** H6
Churchdown La BWTH/CHD GL3... **131** K7
VGL GL2 .... **157** F5
Churchend VCL GL2 .... **238** D2
Churchend La WUE GL12 .... **319** H2
Churchfarm Cl YATE/CS BS37 ...... **347** H3
Church Farm La MIM SL56 .... **45** K2 🔢
Church Farm Rd MANG/FISH BS16... **357** J8
Churchfield Rd GLE GL4 .... **159** G4
STROUD GL5 .... **215** F8 🔢
Churchfields CHELTE/BC GL52 ...... **83** G2
Church Gdns LYD GL15 .... **234** A4
Church HI BRSG/KWL/STAPK BS4 ... **374** D4
MTCHDN GL17 .... **148** E2
RSTROUD/NAIL GL6 .... **216** E1 🔢
THNB/SVB BS35 .... **330** D3
Churchhill Rd RSTROUD/NAIL GL6... **243** K5
Churchill Cl
OLD/WMLY/WICK BS30 .... **376** B1 🔢
RSTROUD/NAIL GL6 .... **270** D2 🔢
Churchill Dr
HNLZ/SM/SNYPK/WT BS9 .... **353** F7
Churchill Gv TEWK GL20 .... **34** A8
Churchill PI CIR GL7 .... **255** F7
Churchill Rd
BRSG/KWL/STAPK BS4 .... **374** D2
CHELTS GL53 .... **134** D1
CHNTN OX7 .... **119** C1
CIR GL7 .... **250** A5 🔢
EVE WR11 .... **15** H5
GL GL1 .... **2** C6
RSTROUD/NAIL GL6 .... **270** D2
Churchill Wy MTCHDN GL17 .... **123** G4
RSTROUD/NAIL GL6 .... **187** G6
Church La BAD GL9 .... **350** E1
BDWAY WR12 .... **40** C5
BRKLY GL13 .... **236** A5
BRKLY GL13 .... **264** A3 🔢
BUR/CRTN OX18 .... **172** C3
CBRIS/FH BS1 .... **364** C8
CHELTW GL51 .... **133** J4
CHNTN OX7 .... **118** D4
CHPMW/MSHF SN14 .... **339** K5
CHPMW/MSHF SN14 .... **572** A6
CIND GL14 .... **153** H2
CIR GL7 .... **246** D3
CIR GL7 .... **278** D7
CIR GL7 .... **279** H1
COTS GL54 .... **39** C8
COTS GL54 .... **110** A6
EVILLE/WHL BS5 .... **365** F5
EVILLE/WHL BS5 .... **365** F7 🔢
GL GL1 .... **2** B4 🔢
LYD GL15 .... **203** F8
MIM SL56 .... **69** K1
NWNT GL18 .... **73** J6
RSTROUD/NAIL GL6 .... **270** E2
STNHO GL10 .... **241** C2
STNHO GL10 .... **268** E1
STROUD GL5 .... **214** E7
TET GL8 .... **272** A5 🔢
TET GL8 .... **302** B8
TEWK GL20 .... **57** H1
WUE GL12 .... **297** F7
Church Pde
BRSG/KWL/STAPK BS4 .... **374** D4 🔢
Church Piece CHELTS GL53 .... **135** H1 🔢
Church PI MIM SL56 .... **94** A6
Church Ri VGL GL2 .... **101** G7
Church Rd ALMDB BS32 .... **342** E1
BDWAY WR12 .... **16** D5
BRSTK/PCHW BS34 .... **354** A4
BRSTK/PCHW BS34 .... **355** J3
BWTH/CHD GL3 .... **132** D1
CHELTE/BC GL52 .... **83** F2
CHELTS GL53 .... **134** C2
CHELTW GL51 .... **82** A8
CHELTW GL51 .... **105** K6 🔢
CHEP NP16 .... **288** B6
CIND GL14 .... **150** E7

CIND GL14 .... **179** F5
CIND GL14 .... **180** C2
CIR GL7 .... **225** H4
CIR GL7 .... **254** D1
CIR GL7 .... **276** B7
COTS GL54 .... **88** C8
DSLY GL11 .... **267** F3
EVILLE/WHL BS5 .... **365** H6
FRCTL/WBN BS36 .... **345** C5
FRCTL/WBN BS36 .... **356** E2
HNLZ/SM/SNYPK/WT BS9 .... **353** J7
HORF/LLZ BS7 .... **354** C8
KGWD/HNM BS15 .... **366** E6
KGWD/HNM BS15 .... **375** G1
LYD GL15 .... **231** C5
LYD GL15 .... **233** C5
LYD GL15 .... **234** A5
MANG/FISH BS16 .... **356** B7
MANG/FISH BS16 .... **366** D4
MIM SL56 .... **94** A6
MTCHDN GL17 .... **148** E2
OLD/WMLY/WICK BS30 .... **368** E8 🔢
OLD/WMLY/WICK BS30 .... **369** J5
OLD/WMLY/WICK BS30 .... **377** F6
RSTROUD/NAIL GL6 .... **242** C8 🔢
STNHO GL10 .... **240** E3
STROUD GL5 .... **214** A8
STROUD GL5 .... **242** B4
TEWK GL20 .... **37** K7
THNB/SVB BS35 .... **315** F2
THNB/SVB BS35 .... **316** B4
THNB/SVB BS35 .... **328** C8
THNB/SVB BS35 .... **332** A4
THNB/SVB BS35 .... **341** J5
VGL GL2 .... **101** G7
VGL GL2 .... **130** E2
VGL GL2 .... **181** F5
YATE/CS BS37 .... **347** G3
Churchside MANG/FISH BS16 ...... **356** B7 🔢
Church St TEWK GL20 .... **13** J8
BDWAY WR12 .... **18** D6
BDWAY WR12 .... **19** F2 🔢
CBATH/BATHN BA1 .... **379** J8
CBRIS/FH BS1 .... **364** C8 🔢
CHCAM GL55 .... **20** E3
CHELT GL50 .... **4** B3 🔢
CHELTS GL53 .... **135** G1
CHNTN OX7 .... **118** C4
CHNTN OX7 .... **119** G2
CIND GL14 .... **151** J7
CIR GL7 .... **249** K7
CIR GL7 .... **281** H2
CLFD GL16 .... **203** J2
COTS GL54 .... **92** C6 🔢
EVILLE/WHL BS5 .... **365** F5
GL GL1 .... **2** B4 🔢
LYD GL15 .... **203** F8
MIM SL56 .... **69** K1
NWNT GL18 .... **73** J6
RSTROUD/NAIL GL6 .... **270** E2
STNHO GL10 .... **241** C2
STROUD GL5 .... **243** G2
TET GL8 .... **302** B8
TEWK GL20 .... **57** H1
WUE GL12 .... **297** F7
Church Vw ALMDB BS32 .... **342** D2
BRKLY GL13 .... **264** E6
COTS GL54 .... **90** E1
MIM SL56 .... **45** J2
Churchview Dr GLE GL4 .... **131** F6
Church Wk HGHW SN6 .... **308** C5
LYD GL15 .... **205** H2
LYD GL15 .... **206** E5
Churchward Cl
KGWD/HNM BS15 .... **375** G1 🔢
Churchward Rd YATE/CS BS37 .... **346** D3 🔢
Church Wy GLE GL4 .... **130** E8 🔢
LYD GL15 .... **207** J3
NWNT GL18 .... **73** J6
Churchways Av HORF/LLZ BS7 .... **354** C8
Churchways Crs HORF/LLZ BS7 .... **354** C8
Churn Av CHELTE/BC GL52 .... **5** E3 🔢
Churn Cl CIR GL7 .... **278** D7
Churn HI CIR GL7 .... **221** J1
Cicely Wy GLE GL4 .... **159** H1
Cidermill Cl CHEP NP16 .... **312** B2 🔢
Cidermill La CHCAM GL55 .... **20** E3
Cidermill Orch CHCAM GL55.......... **7** K7
Cinderford Rd LYD GL15.............. **207** H3
Cinder HI CLFD GL16 .... **175** K4
LYD GL15 .... **203** F8
Cinderhill MTCHDN GL17 .... **121** H6
Cinder La CIR GL7 .... **255** C8
The Circle MANG/FISH BS16 ...... **214** E6 🔢
Cirencester Rd BWTH/CHD GL3... **160** E2
CHELTS GL53 .... **106** D3 🔢
CHELTS GL53 .... **107** C8 🔢
CIR GL7 .... **254** D9
CIR GL7 .... **278** E2
CIR GL7 .... **279** C4
CIR GL7 .... **279** J7 🔢

RSTROUD/NAIL GL6 .... **244** E7
STROUD GL5 .... **243** C7
TET GL8 .... **302** C7
City Bank Rd CIR GL7 .... **249** K7
City Rd CBRISNE BS2 .... **364** C6
Claire's Cl STROUD GL5 .... **243** J5 🔢
The Clamp
OLD/WMLY/WICK BS30 .... **376** D3 🔢
Clanna La LYD GL15 .... **232** D7
Clapton Rw COTS GL54 .... **143** H1
Clare Av HORF/LLZ BS7 .... **364** A3
Clare Ct STROUD GL5.................. **215** G7
Claremont Av HORF/LLZ BS7 ...... **364** A3
Claremont Rd GL GL1 .... **3** D3 🔢
HORF/LLZ BS7 .... **364** B3
Claremont St EVILLE/WHL BS5 .... **364** E5
Clarence Av MANG/FISH BS16 .... **366** E1
Clarence Gdns MANG/FISH BS16 ... **366** E1 🔢
Clarence Pde CHELT GL50 .... **4** B4 🔢
Clarence PI CBRISNE BS2 .... **364** A6 🔢
Clarence Rd CBRISNE BS2 .... **364** E7
CHELT GL50 .... **4** C3
CHELTE/BC GL52 .... **4** C5 🔢
KGWD/HNM BS15 .... **366** B5
MANG/FISH BS16 .... **366** D1
TEWK GL20 .... **57** H2
WUE GL12 .... **297** F7
Clarence Sq CHELT GL50 .... **4** C3
Clarence St CHELT GL50 .... **4** B4 🔢
GL GL1 .... **2** C4
Clarendon Rd COTS GL54 .... **62** C7
RDLND/MONT BS6 .... **364** A4
Clare PI CHELTS GL53...................... **4** B6
Clare Rd EVILLE/WHL BS5 .... **365** F4
KGWD/HNM BS15 .... **366** C4
RDLND/MONT BS6 .... **364** B5
Clare St CBRIS/FH BS1 .... **364** B8
CHELTS GL53 .... **4** B6
EVILLE/WHL BS5 .... **365** G6 🔢
GL GL1 .... **2** B3
Clare Wk THNB/SVB BS35............ **316** B4
Claridge Cl GLE GL4 .... **159** F2
Clark Cl SHPSTR CV36 .... **25** F1
Clark Dr MANG/FISH BS16 .... **355** K8
Clarkia Cl BWTH/CHD GL3............ **103** H7
Clark's La CIR GL7 .... **277** K3
LYD GL15 .... **207** H4
Clark St EVILLE/WHL BS5 .... **364** E6
Clarrie Rd TET GL8 .... **302** C7
Claudians Cl GLE GL4 .... **131** C7 🔢
Claudius Wy LYD GL15 .... **234** B2
Clavell Rd HNBRY/STHM BS10...... **353** H4
Claverham Rd MANG/FISH BS16 .. **366** A1 🔢
Clay Bottom EVILLE/WHL BS5 ...... **365** H4
Clayburn Cl VGL GL2 .... **128** E1 🔢
Clayfield YATE/CS BS37................ **347** G7
Clayfield Rd
BRSG/KWL/STAPK BS4 .... **374** D3
Clayfurlong Gv CIR GL7 .... **276** B6
Clay HI EVILLE/WHL BS5 .... **365** J4
Clay La BRSTK/PCHW BS34.......... **343** G7
OLD/WMLY/WICK BS30 .... **376** E6
THNB/SVB BS35 .... **316** E5
Claymore Cresent
KGWD/HNM BS15 .... **366** B5 🔢
Claypit HI YATE/CS BS37 .... **347** K7
Claypits HI STNHO GL10 .... **211** H5
Claypits La STROUD GL5 .... **243** G2
Claypool Rd KGWD/HNM BS15 .... **366** D2
Clay Rd CLFD GL16 .... **148** A7
Clays Rd CLFD GL16 .... **204** A2
Clayton St EVILLE/WHL BS5 .... **365** F6
Clearwater Dr VGL GL2 .... **156** E5
Cleave Av MANG/FISH BS16 .... **356** E2
Cleave Cloud La
CHELTE/BC GL52 .... **107** K3 🔢
Cleave Ct CHELTE/BC GL52.......... **83** F3
Cleevecroft Av CHELTE/BC GL52 ... **83** C2
Cleeve Gdns MANG/FISH BS16 .... **356** E2
Cleeve HI MANG/FISH BS16 .... **356** D2
Cleeve Hill Extension
MANG/FISH BS16 .... **356** E8
Cleevelands Av CHELT GL50.......... **4** B3
CHELT GL50 .... **106** D3
Cleevelands Cl CHELT GL50 .... **106** E1 🔢
Cleevelands Dr CHELT GL50 .... **106** E3
Cleeveland St CHELTW GL51 .... **4** A2
Cleeve La OLD/WMLY/WICK BS30 .. **369** H7
Cleeve Lawns MANG/FISH BS16 .. **356** D2
Cleeve Lodge Rd
MANG/FISH BS16 .... **356** E2
Cleeve Mill La NWNT GL18 .... **73** K6
Cleevemount Cl CHELTE/BC GL52 .. **5** D2
Cleevemount Rd CHELTE/BC GL52 .. **5** D2
Cleeve Park Rd MANG/FISH BS16 .. **356** D2
Cleeve Ri NWNT GL18 .... **73** K6 🔢
Cleeve Rd BRSG/KWL/STAPK BS4 .. **374** A1
CHELTE/BC GL52 .... **60** B8
GLE GL4 .... **158** D2
MANG/FISH BS16 .... **356** E8
MANG/FISH BS16 .... **356** C4
YATE/CS BS37 .... **347** C2
Cleeve View Rd CHELTE/BC GL52 .... **5** E

Cleeve Wood Rd
MANG/FISH BS16 .... **356** D7 🔢

Clegram Rd *GL* GL1 .... **2** B6
Clematis Ct *CHELTE/BC* GL52 .... **82** E3 🔢
Clements End Rd *CLFD* GL16 .... **204** A2
Clement St *CBRISNE* BS2 .... **364** D6
  GL GL1 .... **3** E5
Clencher's Mill La *LED* HR8 .... **29** F1
Clevedale *MANG/FISH* BS16 .... **356** D7
Clevedon Rd *GL* GL1 .... **130** B8
  HORF/LLZ BS7 .... **364** B2
Clevedon Sq *CHELTW* GL51 .... **106** A4 🔢
Clevedon Ter *RDLND/MONT* BS6 .. **364** B6 🔢
Cleveland Cl *THNB/SVB* BS35 .... **316** E5 🔢
Cleve Rd *BRSTK/PCHW* BS34 ...... **354** E2
Cliff Court Dr *MANG/FISH* BS16 .... **356** D6🔢
Clifford Gdns *AVONM* BS11 .... **352** A8
Clifford Rd *MANG/FISH* BS16 ...... **366** C2
Cliffords *HCHW* SN6 .... **310** C6 🔢
Cliff Vw *CHEP* NP16 .... **288** C7
Clifton Pl *EVILLE/WHL* BS5 .... **364** E6
Clingre Down *DSLY* GL11 .... **266** A3
Clingre La *DSLY* GL11 .... **265** K2
Clive Rd *HGRV/WHIT* BS14 .... **374** D7
Cloisters Rd *FRCTL/WBN* BS36 .... **344** E8 🔢
The Cloisters *CHELTE/BC* GL52 .... **82** E2 🔢
Clomoney Wy *VGL* GL2 .... **131** F1 🔢
Close Gdns *COTS* GL54 .... **90** E1 🔢
  TET GL8 .... **302** B7
The Close *BRSTK/PCHW* BS34 ...... **343** C5
  CHELTE/BC GL52 .... **83** J6
  CHELTS GL53 .... **134** D2
  CIR GL7 .... **278** E7
  CIR GL7 .... **285** C1🔢
  CLFD GL16 .... **176** B2
  DSLY GL11 .... **239** J7
  DSLY GL11 .... **266** C2
  FRCTL/WBN BS36 .... **345** J8
  HNBRY/STHM BS10 .... **353** H1
  MANG/FISH BS16 .... **366** D3
  VGL GL2 .... **211** K1
  VGL GL2 .... **238** C3
Clothier Rd
  BRSG/KWL/STAPK BS4 ...... **374** E4 🔢
Clouds Hill Av *EVILLE/WHL* BS5 .... **365** J6
Clouds Hill Rd *EVILLE/WHL* BS5 .... **365** K6
The Cloud *WUE* GL12 .... **297** F7
Clovelly Cl *EVILLE/WHL* BS5 .... **365** K6
Clovelly Rd *EVILLE/WHL* BS5 ...... **365** K6
Clover Cl *CLFD* GL16 .... **176** A7
Cloverdale Dr
  OLD/WMLY/WICK BS30 .... **376** B3
Clover Dr *VGL* GL2 .... **156** E8
Clover Grnd
  HNLZ/SM/SNYPK/WT BS9 ...... **353** K6
Cloverlea Rd
  OLD/WMLY/WICK BS30 .... **376** D1
Clover Leaze *BRSTK/PCHW* BS34 .. **343** H8
Clyde Crs *CHELTE/BC* GL52 .... **5** E2
Clyde Gdns *EVILLE/WHL* BS5 ...... **366** B8 🔢
Clyde Gv *BRSTK/PCHW* BS34 ...... **354** D4
Clyde Rd *BWTH/CHD* GL3 .... **160** D1
  FRCTL/WBN BS36 .... **345** H8
Coach Cl *BRKLY* GL13 .... **264** A3 🔢
Coalsack La *FRCTL/WBN* BS36 .... **357** H1🔢
Coalville Rd *FRCTL/WBN* BS36 .... **345** K7
Coalway Rd *CLFD* GL16 .... **176** A4
Coates Gdns *STNHO* GL10 .... **213** F6 🔢
The Cobbler's Cl *CHELTE/BC* GL52 .. **60** B7 🔢
Cobden St *EVILLE/WHL* BS5 .... **365** G7
Coberley Rd *KGWD/HNM* BS15 ...... **366** C8
Coberley Rd *CHELTW* GL51 .... **105** H6
  GLE GL4 .... **158** A3🔢
Cobham Ct *CHELTW* GL51 .... **106** B3 🔢
Cobham Rd *CHELTW* GL51 .... **106** B3
Cobourg Rd *RDLND/MONT* BS6.... **364** D5
Cochran Cl *BWTH/CHD* GL3 ...... **132** A1 🔢
Cock La *CHPMW/MSHF* SN14........ **370** B1
Cock Rd *KGWD/HNM* BS15.......... **366** E8
Codrington Rd *HORF/LLZ* BS7 ...... **364** B3
Cogan Rd *MANG/FISH* BS16 ...... **366** E8
Cogsall Rd *HGRV/WHIT* BS14 ...... **374** E8 🔢
Colchester Cl *CIND* GL14.......... **153** C5 🔢
  MTCHDN GL17.......... **123** C5
Coldharbour La
  BRSTK/PCHW BS34........ **355** J5
  MANG/FISH BS16 .... **355** J6
  NWNT GL14 .... **73** C3
Coldharbour Rd *LYD* GL15 .... **230** E2
Coldicotts Cl *CHCAM* GL55 .... **20** E4
  EVE WR11 .... **6** B1
Coldicotts La *EVE* WR11 .... **6** B1
Cold Pool La *CHELTW* GL51 ...... **105** G8
Coldray Cl *VGL* GL2 .... **3** F4
Coldwell St *STNHO* GL10 .... **241** H3
Coldwell La *STNHO* GL10 .... **241** H3
Coldwell La *STNHO* GL10 .... **241** H3
Cole Av *VGL* GL2 .... **157** J3
Colebridge Av *VGL* GL2 .... **130** E3
Colebrook Rd *KGWD/HNM* BS15.... **366** C6
Coleford Rd *CHEP* NP16 .... **288** C3
  HNBRY/STHM BS10 .... **354** B6
  LYD GL15 .... **205** J4
Coleridge Rd *EVILLE/WHL* BS5 .... **365** G3 🔢
Colerne Dr *BWTH/CHD* GL3 .... **131** K7

Cole Rd *CBRISNE* BS2 .... **365** F8
Colesborne Cl *YATE/CS* BS37 .... **347** C6 🔢
Colesbourne Rd *CHELTW* GL51 .... **105** H7
Colin Cl *THNB/SVB* BS35 .... **316** B5
Colin Rd *GLE* GL4 .... **131** F5
College Av *MANG/FISH* BS16 .... **366** A1 🔢
College Baths Rd *CHELTS* GL53 ...... **4** C5
College Ct *MANG/FISH* BS16 ...... **366** A1
College Flds *VGL* GL2 .... **131** F2
College Ga *CHELTS* GL53 .... **4** C5
College Gn *CBRIS/FH* BS1 .... **364** A8
College Lawn *CHELTS* GL53 .... **4** C6
College Park Dr
  HNBRY/STHM BS10 .... **353** H5
College Pl *CHELT* GL50 .... **4** B4 🔢
College Rd *CHELTS* GL53 .... **4** C5
  CIND GL14 .... **150** E5
  HNLZ/SM/SNYPK/WT BS9 ...... **353** J7
  MANG/FISH BS16 .... **366** A1
  STROUD GL5 .... **214** C6
  TEWK GL20 .... **13** H8
College Sq *CBRIS* BS1 .... **364** A8 🔢
College St *GL* GL1 .... **2** C3
College Vw *CIR* GL7 .... **277** F3
Collett Cl *KGWD/HNM* BS15 ...... **375** C1 🔢
Colletts Dr *CHELTW* GL51 .... **106** B3
Colletts Flds *BDWAY* WR12 .... **18** E6
Colletts Gdns *BDWAY* WR12 .... **18** E6
Collett Wy *YATE/CS* BS37 .... **346** E3
Colliers Break *MANG/FISH* BS16 .... **367** H1
Colliers Pitch *LYD* GL15 .... **232** C5
Colliers Wd *RSTROUD/NAIL* GL6.... **270** B1
Collin Cl *BDWAY* WR12 .... **18** E2
Collingbourne Rd *GLE* GL4 .... **3** E6 🔢
Collingwood Av
  KGWD/HNM BS15 .... **366** E5 🔢
Collin La *BDWAY* WR12 .... **18** D3
Collin Rd *BRSG/KWL/STAPK* BS4 .... **374** C2
Collins Av *BRSTK/PCHW* BS34 ...... **343** C8
Collins Cl *RTEWK/TIB* GL19 .... **53** C7
Collum End Ri *CHELTS* GL53 ...... **134** D3
Colne Av *CHELTE/BC* GL52 .... **5** E2
Colston Cl *FRCTL/WBN* BS36 ...... **356** E2
  MANG/FISH BS16 .... **366** D3🔢
Colston Hl *MANG/FISH* BS16 ...... **365** J2
Colston Hl *MANG/FISH* BS16 ...... **365** H2
Colston Rd *EVILLE/WHL* BS5 ...... **365** C5
Colston St *CBRIS/FH* BS1 .... **364** B8
  MANG/FISH BS16 .... **366** D3
Coltham Flds *CHELTE/BC* GL52 ...... **5** D5
Coltham Rd *CHELTE/BC* GL52 ...... **5** D6
Colthurst Dr *KGWD/HNM* BS15 .... **375** J1
Coltman Cl *VGL* GL2 .... **3** F4
Colts Cn *YATE/CS* BS37 .... **348** C6
Columbia Cl *GL* GL1 .... **3** D3
Columbia St *CHELTE/BC* GL52 ...... **4** C5 🔢
Colwell Av *BWTH/CHD* GL3 .... **131** J5
Colwyn Dr *CHELTW* GL51 .... **105** J8🔢
Colwyn Rd *EVILLE/WHL* BS5 ...... **365** C5🔢
Combermere *THNB/SVB* BS35........ **316** D6
Combfactory La
  EVILLE/WHL BS5 .... **365** F6🔢
Comb Paddock
  HNLZ/SM/SNYPK/WT BS9 ...... **353** K7
Combrook Cl *GLE* GL4 .... **159** C2🔢
Commercial Rd *GL* GL1 .... **2** B4
  RSTROUD/NAIL GL6 .... **244** C4
Commercial St *CHELT* GL50 .... **4** B6
  CIND GL14 .... **151** F6
The Common East *ALMDB* BS32 .... **343** C5
Commonfield Rd *AVONM* BS11 ...... **352** D5
Common Hl *HCHW* SN6 .... **310** C6
Common Mead La
  MANG/FISH BS16 .... **356** A5
Commonmead La *YATE/CS* BS37 .... **348** D5
Common Rd *FRCTL/WBN* BS36 .... **345** F7🔢
  KGWD/HNM BS15 .... **375** C3
  RSTROUD/NAIL GL6 .... **243** F8
The Common *BRKLY* GL13 .... **264** E3
  BRSTK/PCHW BS34........ **343** F5
  CIR GL7 .... **278** B2
  MANG/FISH BS16 .... **356** B7
Compton Cl *BWTH/CHD* GL3 ...... **103** J6 🔢
  RTEWK/TIB GL19 .... **53** C8
Compton Rd *CHELTW* GL51 ...... **106** B2 🔢
Compton's Aly *TEWK* GL20 ...... **33** H8 🔢
Compton St *EVILLE/WHL* BS5 ...... **365** C7
Comyn Wk *MANG/FISH* BS16 ...... **366** A1
Concorde Dr
  HNBRY/STHM BS10 .... **353** K4🔢
Concorde Wy *GLE* GL4 .... **3** F6
Condicote La *COTS* GL54 .... **90** E1
  COTS GL54 .... **91** F7
Condover Rd
  BRSG/KWL/STAPK BS4 .... **374** E3
Conduit Hl *CHCAM* GL55 .... **20** D5
Conduit Pl *CBRISNE* BS2 .... **364** E5🔢
Conduit Rd *CBRISNE* BS2 .... **364** E5
Conduit St *GL* GL1 .... **2** C6
Coneygar Rd *CIR* GL7 .... **254** C1
Coneygree La *BDWAY* WR12 .... **41** J1
Coney Hill Pde *GLE* GL4 .... **130** E7 🔢
Coney Hill Rd *GLE* GL4 .... **131** F7
Congleton Rd *EVILLE/WHL* BS5 .... **365** H6🔢

Conham Hl *KGWD/HNM* BS15 ...... **375** F1
Conham Rd *KGWD/HNM* BS15 .... **374** E1
Conham V *KGWD/HNM* BS15 ...... **374** E1
  KGWD/HNM BS15 .... **375** C1
Conifer Cl *FRCTL/WBN* BS36 ...... **345** C5
  MANG/FISH BS16 .... **356** D8 🔢
The Conifers *GL* GL1 .... **3** E6 🔢
Conigree La *TEWK* GL20 .... **57** H2
Coniston Av
  HNLZ/SM/SNYPK/WT BS9 ...... **353** C8
Coniston Cl
  OLD/WMLY/WICK BS30 ...... **367** K8🔢
Coniston Rd *BRSTK/PCHW* BS34 .... **342** C6
  CHELTW GL51 .... **105** J7
  VGL GL2 .... **130** C2
Connemara Cl *NWNT* GL18 .... **73** H7🔢
Constable Cl *KEYN* BS31 .... **376** A8🔢
Constable Rd *HORF/LLZ* BS7 ...... **354** E8
Constance Cl *STROUD* GL5 .... **242** B1
Constantine Av *BRSTK/PCHW* BS34.. **355** J1
Convent Cl *HNBRY/STHM* BS10...... **353** F3
Convent La *STROUD* GL5 .... **242** B7
Conway Rd *BRSG/KWL/STAPK* BS4 .. **374** B2
  BWTH/CHD GL3 .... **131** J6
Conygar Rd *TET* GL8 .... **302** C6
Conygre Gv *BRSTK/PCHW* BS34 ... **355** C3🔢
Conygre Rd *BRSTK/PCHW* BS34 .... **355** F3
Cook Cl *OLD/WMLY/WICK* BS30 ...... **376** D2
Cooke's Dr *THNB/SVB* BS35 .... **341** J5
Cooks Cl *ALMDB* BS32 .... **343** C3
Cooks La *FRCTL/WBN* BS36 .... **357** K3
  RTEWK/TIB GL19 .... **30** C7
Cooksley Rd *EVILLE/WHL* BS5 ...... **365** C6
Cooks Orch *GL* GL1 .... **3** E2
Cookspool *TET* GL8 .... **302** C6 🔢
Cookworthy Cl *EVILLE/WHL* BS5 .. **365** F8🔢
Coomb Dr *CIND* GL14 .... **178** C1 🔢
Coombe Av *THNB/SVB* BS35 ...... **316** B4🔢
Coombe Bridge Av
  HNLZ/SM/SNYPK/WT BS9 ...... **353** F8
Coombe Cl *HNBRY/STHM* BS10 .... **353** F3🔢
Coombe Dl
  HNLZ/SM/SNYPK/WT BS9 ...... **352** E8
Coombe Gdns
  HNLZ/SM/SNYPK/WT BS9 ...... **353** C8
Coombe Glen La *CHELTW* GL51 .... **105** H8
Coombe La
  HNLZ/SM/SNYPK/WT BS9 ...... **353** F8
  STNHO GL10 .... **241** H4
  WUE GL12 .... **297** H6
Coombe Meade *CHELTE/BC* GL52 .. **83** H3🔢
Coombe Rd *EVILLE/WHL* BS5 ...... **365** C4🔢
  WUE GL12 .... **297** C6
Coombes Wy
  OLD/WMLY/WICK BS30 .... **376** E2
Coombe Wy *HNBRY/STHM* BS10.... **353** H5
Coombs Rd *CLFD* GL16 .... **175** K3
Cooperage Rd *EVILLE/WHL* BS5 .... **365** C5
Co-operation Rd *EVILLE/WHL* BS5 .. **365** C5
Cooper Rd
  HNLZ/SM/SNYPK/WT BS9 ...... **353** H7
  THNB/SVB BS35 .... **316** B7
Coopers Dr *YATE/CS* BS37 .... **347** H1
Coopers Elm *VGL* GL2 .... **157** F4
Coopers Rd *CLFD* GL16 .... **147** J7
Cooper's Vw *BWTH/CHD* GL3 ...... **160** C1🔢
Coopers Wy *NWNT* GL18 .... **73** K6
The Coots *HGRV/WHIT* BS14 ...... **374** D8
Cope Pk *ALMDB* BS32 .... **343** C1
Copley Ct *KGWD/HNM* BS15 ...... **375** K1🔢
Copley Dr *CLFD* GL16 .... **175** K5🔢
Copley Gdns *HORF/LLZ* BS7 ...... **355** F8🔢
Copper Beech Vw *VGL* GL2 .... **156** E5
Coppice Daw Pitch
  RTEWK/TIB GL19 .... **125** J4
Coppice Ga *CHELTW* GL51 .... **105** K1
Coppice Hl *RSTROUD/NAIL* GL6 .... **244** E4
Coppice Rd *MTCHDN* GL17 .... **120** E8
The Coppice *ALMDB* BS32 .... **343** J7
Copsehill Rd *COTS* GL54 .... **115** C4
Copse Rd *BRSG/KWL/STAPK* BS4.... **374** A3
The Copse *GLE* GL4 .... **131** C7 🔢
Copt Elm Cl *CHELTS* GL53 .... **107** C8
Copt Elm Rd *CHELTS* GL53 .... **107** C8
Coral Cl *GL* GL1 .... **157** H3
Corbet Cl *AVONM* BS11 .... **352** D4
Corder's La *MIM* GL56 .... **69** K1
Cordingley Cl *BWTH/CHD* GL3 ...... **132** A2
Cordwell Wk
  HNBRY/STHM BS10 .... **354** B7🔢
Corey Cl *CBRISNE* BS2 .... **364** D5🔢
Corfe Cl *CHELTE/BC* GL52 .... **107** J3🔢
Corfe Pl *OLD/WMLY/WICK* BS30 ...... **376** C5
Coriander Dr *ALMDB* BS32 .... **344** A7
  BWTH/CHD GL3 .... **103** H8
Coriander Wk *EVILLE/WHL* BS5 .... **365** C4🔢
Corinium Ga *CIR* GL7 .... **249** K5
Cormorant Av *TEWK* GL20 .... **57** K2🔢
Corncroft La *GLE* GL4 .... **158** E4
Corndean La *COTS* GL54 .... **85** J5
Corner Farm Dr *EVE* WR11 .... **7** C2🔢
Corner Rd *LYD* GL15 .... **205** K5
Cornfield Cl *ALMDB* BS32 .... **343** C5
Cornfield Dr *CHELTE/BC* GL52 ...... **82** E2🔢
  VGL GL2 .... **156** E7

The Cornfields *CHELTE/BC* GL52 ...... **82** E2
Cornfield Wy *CIR* GL7 .... **14** D4
Cornflower Rd *GLE* GL4 .... **159** G1
Cornhill *STROUD* GL5 .... **214** E7
Cornish Cl *HGRV/WHIT* BS14 ...... **374** D8 ⓲
Cornish Rd *HGRV/WHIT* BS14 ...... **374** D8
Cornish Wk *HGRV/WHIT* BS14 ...... **374** D8
Cornmeadow Dr *CHELTW* GL51 ...... **105** H1 ⓲
Corn St *CBRIS* BS1 .... **364** B8
Cornwall Av *CHELTW* GL51 .... **106** A4
Cornwall Crs *YATE/CS* BS37 .... **347** H3
Cornwall Rd *HORF/LLZ* BS7 .... **364** B2
Corolin Rd *VGL* GL2 .... **157** H2
Coronation Av *MANG/FISH* BS16 .... **366** A2
Coronation Cl *CHCAM* GL55 .... **20** D3 ⓲
  OLD/WMLY/WICK BS30 .... **376** B1 ⓲
Coronation Gv *VGL* GL2 .... **3** F3
Coronation Pl *CBRIS/FH* BS1 .... **364** B8 ⓲
Coronation Rd *CHELTE/BC* GL52 ..... **5** E1
  CIND GL14 .... **151** F7
  KCWD/HNM BS15 .... **367** G7
  MANG/FISH BS16 .... **366** E1
  OLD/WMLY/WICK BS30 .... **376** C1
  STROUD GL5 .... **214** D8
  TET GL8 .... **302** B5
Coronation St *CIR* GL7 .... **254** D7
Corpus St *CHELTS* GL53 .... **4** C5 ⓲
The Corriett *DSLY* GL11 .... **266** E1 ⓲
Corsend Rd *RTEWK/TIB* GL19 .... **76** C7
Cossham Cl *THNB/SVB* BS35 .... **316** C4 ⓲
Cossham Rd *EVILLE/WHL* BS5 .... **365** H6
  MANG/FISH BS16 .... **368** C3
Cossham St *MANG/FISH* BS16 .... **367** H1
Cossham Wk *EVILLE/WHL* BS5 ...... **366** A5
Costard Av *SHPSTR* CV36 .... **24** E1 ⓲
Costers Cl *THNB/SVB* BS35 .... **316** A8
Cote La Pk
  HNLZ/SM/SNYPK/WT BS9 .... **353** J7 ⓲
Cote Pk *HNLZ/SM/SNYPK/WT* BS9 .. **353** C8
Cotham Brow
  RDLND/MONT BS6 .... **364** B4 ⓲
Cotham Gdns *RDLND/MONT* BS6 .... **364** B5
Cotham Lawn Rd
  RDLND/MONT BS6 .... **364** A6
Cotham Pk *RDLND/MONT* BS6 .... **364** A5
Cotham Pk North
  RDLND/MONT BS6 .... **364** A5
Cotham Rd *RDLND/MONT* BS6 .... **364** A6
Cotham Rd South
  RDLND/MONT BS6 .... **364** B6
Cotham Side *RDLND/MONT* BS6 ..... **364** B5
Cotham V *RDLND/MONT* BS6 .... **364** A5
Cotman Wk *HORF/LLZ* BS7 .... **355** F8
Cotrith Gv *HNBRY/STHM* BS10 ..... **353** C3
Cotsmore Cl *MIM* GL56 .... **70** B1
Cotswold Av *CIR* GL7 .... **249** H7
  STNHO GL10 .... **211** K7 ⓲
Cotswold Cl *CIR* GL7 .... **249** H7
  RSTROUD/NAIL GL6 .... **243** K5 ⓲
  TET GL8 .... **302** C6 ⓲
  TEWK GL20 .... **13** K8
Cotswold Edge *CHCAM* GL55 .... **9** F2
Cotswold Gdns *MIM* GL56 .... **70** A1
  TEWK GL20 .... **33** J7
  VGL GL2 .... **131** F1 ⓲
  WUE GL12 .... **297** G2
Cotswold Gn *STNHO* GL10 .... **213** G6
Cotswold La *YATE/CS* BS37 .... **348** E6
Cotswold Md *RSTROUD/NAIL* GL6 ... **187** F3 ⓲
Cotswold Rd *CHELTE/BC* GL52 ...... **5** E2
  STROUD GL5 .... **214** A6
  YATE/CS BS37 .... **347** K6
Cotswold Vw *CHELTE/BC* GL52 ...... **83** H3
  KCWD/HNM BS15 .... **366** D4
  RTEWK/TIB GL19 .... **55** C8 ⓲
  WUE GL12 .... **319** K8 ⓲
  WUE GL12 .... **319** K1 ⓲
Cotswold Wy *BDWAY* WR12 .... **18** E7
  BDWAY WR12 .... **40** E6
  BATH/BATHN BA1 .... **378** C6 ⓲
  CHCAM GL55 .... **20** C2
  CHELTE/BC GL52 .... **108** C3
  CHELTW GL51 .... **161** K1
  COTS GL54 .... **64** A6
  COTS GL54 .... **85** H7
  COTS GL54 .... **108** C6
  DSLY GL11 .... **266** C8
  DSLY GL11 .... **268** C1
  RSTROUD/NAIL GL6 .... **187** H3
  STNHO GL10 .... **240** E6
  WUE GL12 .... **297** G7 ⓲
  YATE/CS BS37 .... **349** F5
  YATE/CS BS37 .... **360** E1
Cottage Fld *VGL* GL2 .... **128** D1 ⓲
Cottage Pitch *NWNT* GL18 .... **73** J4
Cottage Pl *CBRISNE* BS2 .... **364** B6 ⓲
Cottage Rake Av *CHELTW* GL51 ..... **106** C1
Cotswold Ri *STROUD* GL5 .... **215** F7
Cotswold Rd *GLE* GL4 .... **130** C8
  TEWK GL20 .... **33** J7
Cottington Ct *RDLND/MONT* BS6 .... **375** K1 ⓲
Cottisford Rd *EVILLE/WHL* BS5 ..... **365** F2
Cottle Gdns *HGRV/WHIT* BS14 ...... **374** E8
Cottle Rd *HGRV/WHIT* BS14 .... **374** E8
Cotton Cl *GLE* GL4 .... **159** H1

Cotton's La *EVE* WR11 .... **14** C5
  TET GL8 .... **302** B8
Cottonwood Dr
  OLD/WMLY/WICK BS30 .... **376** B3
Cottrell Av *KCWD/HNM* BS15 .... **366** B4
Cottrell Rd *EVILLE/WHL* BS5 .... **365** C3
Coulson Wk *KCWD/HNM* BS15 ...... **366** C4 ⓲
Counterpool Rd *KCWD/HNM* BS15 .. **366** C7
Counterslip *CBRIS/FH* BS1 .... **364** C8
Counterslip Gdns
  HGRV/WHIT BS14 .... **374** B8
Countess Lilias Rd *CIR* GL7 .... **249** J8 ⓲
Countess Wk *MANG/FISH* BS16 ...... **355** H8 ⓲
County Court Rd *CHELT* GL50 .... **4** B4 ⓲
Court Av *BRSTK/PCHW* BS34 .... **355** K1 ⓲
Court Cl *HORF/LLZ* BS7 .... **254** E8
Court Dr *RTEWK/TIB* GL19 .... **79** F2
Courtenay St *CHELT* GL50 .... **4** B2
Court Farm *MALM* SN16 .... **306** C6
  RTEWK/TIB GL19 .... **99** F6
Court Farm La *MTCHDN* GL17 .... **123** C4
Court Farm Rd
  OLD/WMLY/WICK BS30 .... **375** J7 ⓲
Courtfield Dr *CHELTE/BC* GL52 ..... **107** H8 ⓲
Courtfield Gv *MANG/FISH* BS16..... **366** A4
Courtfield Rd *VGL* GL2 .... **156** E6
Court Gdn *DSLY* GL11 .... **268** B8
Court Gdns *VGL* GL2 .... **129** H8
Court Pl *GLE* GL4 .... **131** F8
Court Rd *BWTH/CHD* GL3 .... **132** B5
  CHELTE/BC GL52 .... **107** J2
  FRCTL/WBN BS36 .... **345** F6
  HORF/LLZ BS7 .... **354** D8
  KCWD/HNM BS15 .... **366** D7
  LYD GL15 .... **206** B8
  STNHO GL10 .... **240** B3
  UUSV WR8 .... **12** E3
  WUE GL12 .... **318** D2
Court Meadow *BRKLY* GL13 .... **294** A3
  BRKLY GL13 .... **294** A5
  WUE GL12 .... **297** G7
Courtney Cl *TEWK* GL20 .... **57** H3
Courtney Rd *KCWD/HNM* BS15 ..... **366** E7
Courtney Wy *KCWD/HNM* BS15 .... **367** C7
Court Orch *WUE* GL12 .... **297** G7
Court Rd *GLE* GL4 .... **131** F8
Courtside Ms
  RDLND/MONT BS6 .... **364** A5 ⓲
Court View Cl *ALMDB* BS32 .... **342** E1
Court Wy *STROUD* GL5 .... **242** C1
Courville Ct *THNB/SVB* BS35 .... **332** A2
Cousins Cl *HNBRY/STHM* BS10 .... **353** F3 ⓲
Cousins Ms
  BRSG/KWL/STAPK BS4 .... **365** K8 ⓲
Cousins Wy *MANG/FISH* BS16 ...... **357** C6
Cousley Cl *BWTH/CHD* GL3 .... **131** J7
Couzens Cl *YATE/CS* BS37 .... **347** K4
Couzens Pl *BRSTK/PCHW* BS34 .... **355** K1 ⓲
Coventry Cl *TEWK* GL20 .... **57** J2 ⓲
Coventry Wk
  BRSG/KWL/STAPK BS4 .... **365** K8 ⓲
Coverham Cl *CLFD* GL16 .... **147** K8 ⓲
Coverham Rd *CLFD* GL16 .... **175** J1
Cowcombe Hl *RSTROUD/NAIL* GL6 .. **244** B7
Cowhorn Hl
  OLD/WMLY/WICK BS30 .... **376** D2
Cowley Cl *CHELTW* GL51 .... **105** H7
Cowley Rd *GLE* GL4 .... **158** A3
Cowl La *COTS* GL54 .... **85** J1
Cowismead Cl *CHELTW* GL51 .... **133** H4
Cowper Rd *CHELTW* GL51 .... **105** J5 ⓲
Cowper St *EVILLE/WHL* BS5 .... **365** G7 ⓲
Cowship La *WUE* GL12 .... **318** D7
Cowslip Meadow *CHELTE/BC* GL52 .. **83** H3
Cowswell La *RSTROUD/NAIL* GL6 ... **244** B3
Coxbury & Wyegate La *CLFD* GL16... **202** C3
Cox Ct *OLD/WMLY/WICK* BS30 .... **376** A2
Coxmoor Cl *CHNTN* OX7 .... **119** F2
Cox's Hl *HGHW* SN6 .... **308** H1
Cox's Wy *BWTH/CHD* GL3 .... **131** J8
  LYD GL15 .... **205** F5
Coxwell St *CIR* GL7 .... **249** J5
Cozens La *CHNTN* OX7 .... **119** F2
Crabtree La *CIR* GL7 .... **250** B7 ⓲
  CIR GL7 .... **250** B7 ⓲
Crabtree Pk *CIR* GL7 .... **255** F6
Crab Tree Pl *CHELT* GL50 .... **4** A2
Crabtree Wk *EVILLE/WHL* BS5 ...... **365** H4 ⓲
Craddock Rd *NWNT* GL18 .... **73** H7
Cradock Cl
  OLD/WMLY/WICK BS30 .... **376** C2 ⓲
Crail Vw *COTS* GL54 .... **169** H5
Cranberry Wk
  HNLZ/SM/SNYPK/WT BS9 .... **352** E6 ⓲

Cranbourne Rd
  BRSTK/PCHW BS34 .... **342** D7
Cranbrook Rd *RDLND/MONT* BS6 ... **364** A3
Crandell Cl *HNBRY/STHM* BS10 ..... **353** H2
Crane Cl *KCWD/HNM* BS15 .... **367** H6 ⓲
Cranford Cl *CHELTE/BC* GL52 .... **83** J3
Cranham *YATE/CS* BS37 .... **346** E7 ⓲
Cranham Cl *GLE* GL4 .... **159** C1 ⓲
  KCWD/HNM BS15 .... **367** F4 ⓲
Cranham Dr *BRSTK/PCHW* BS34 .... **343** C5
Cranham La *BWTH/CHD* GL3 .... **132** B3
Cranham Rd *CHELTE/BC* GL52 ...... **5** D5
  HNBRY/STHM BS10 .... **354** A6
Cranhams La *CIR* GL7 .... **249** H8
Cranleigh Court Rd
  YATE/CS BS37 .... **347** F4 ⓲
Cranmoor Gn *THNB/SVB* BS35 ..... **329** F7
Cranmore Av *KEYN* BS31 .... **375** K8 ⓲
Cranmore Crs *HNBRY/STHM* BS10 .. **354** B5
Cranside Av *RDLND/MONT* BS6 .... **364** A3 ⓲
Cransley Crs
  HNLZ/SM/SNYPK/WT BS9 .... **354** A7
Crantock Dr *ALMDB* BS32 .... **343** G1
Crantock Rd *YATE/CS* BS37 .... **347** F5
Cranwell Cl *GLE* GL4 .... **158** C2
The Crapen *DSLY* GL11 .... **266** C2
Crashmore La *TEWK* GL20 .... **36** A1
Craven Cl *OLD/WMLY/WICK* BS30 .. **376** A1
Craven Dr *BWTH/CHD* GL3 .... **103** J8
Craven Wy *OLD/WMLY/WICK* BS30.. **376** A1
Crawley Hl *DSLY* GL11 .... **268** B3
Crawley La *DSLY* GL11 .... **268** B3
Crawshay Pl *CIND* GL14 .... **150** E6
The Crease *NWNT* GL18 .... **73** K6 ⓲
Credon Rd *GLE* GL4 .... **131** G5
Crescent Cl *CLFD* GL16 .... **175** J3
  STNHO GL10 .... **212** E6
Crescentdale *VGL* GL2 .... **102** C8
Crescent Pl *CHELT* GL50 .... **4** B4 ⓲
Crescent Rd *MANG/FISH* BS16 ...... **356** C8
  STNHO GL10 .... **212** E6
The Crescent *BRKLY* GL13 .... **235** K6
  BWTH/CHD GL3 .... **132** B8
  CLFD GL16 .... **175** K4 ⓲
  CLFD GL16 .... **175** J3
  DSLY GL11 .... **266** D2
  HNLZ/SM/SNYPK/WT BS9 .... **352** E8
  HNLZ/SM/SNYPK/WT BS9 .... **354** A8
  MANG/FISH BS16 .... **355** K5
  MANG/FISH BS16 .... **366** D3
  MTCHDN GL17 .... **123** C4
  OLD/WMLY/WICK BS30 .... **368** D7
The Crest *BRSG/KWL/STAPK* BS4... **374** B4
Crest Wy *GLE* GL4 .... **131** H5
Creswicke Av *KCWD/HNM* BS15 ... **375** H1 ⓲
Crew's Hole Rd *EVILLE/WHL* BS5 ... **365** K8 ⓲
Cribbs Cswy *HNBRY/STHM* BS10.... **341** K2 ⓲
  HNBRY/STHM BS10 .... **353** J7
Cricklade Rd *CIR* GL7 .... **250** A8
  HORF/LLZ BS7 .... **364** C2
Cricklade St *CIR* GL7 .... **249** J5 ⓲
  CIR GL7 .... **252** D6
Criftycraft La *BWTH/CHD* GL3 ..... **132** A3
Cripps Rd *CIR* GL7 .... **249** J6 ⓲
Crispin Cl *COTS* GL54 .... **62** D1
  VGL GL2 .... **130** E1
Crispin La *THNB/SVB* BS35 .... **316** B5 ⓲
Crispin Rd *COTS* GL54 .... **62** D1
Crispin Wy *KCWD/HNM* BS15 ...... **367** F4
Critchford La *COTS* GL54 .... **88** D7
Croft Av *CHELTS* GL53 .... **135** C1
  MANG/FISH BS16 .... **365** G2 ⓲
Croft Cl *BWTH/CHD* GL3 .... **132** B5
  NWNT GL18 .... **73** K5
  OLD/WMLY/WICK BS30 .... **376** E1
Crofters Wk *ALMDB* BS32 .... **343** H4
Croft Gdns *CHELTS* GL53 .... **135** H1
Croft Holm *MIM* GL56 .... **70** D1
The Croftlands *TEWK* GL20 .... **13** K8 ⓲
Croft La *CIR* GL7 .... **191** C1
  HGHW SN6 .... **310** D1
Crofton Av *HORF/LLZ* BS7 .... **354** D8 ⓲
Croft Rd *CHELTS* GL53 .... **135** C1
  NWNT GL18 .... **73** K1
Crofts End Rd *EVILLE/WHL* BS5..... **365** J1
Crofts Fld *TEWK* GL20 .... **32** D5 ⓲
Croft St *CHELTS* GL53 .... **106** C1
The Croft *CIR* GL7 .... **254** E1
  DSLY GL11 .... **266** E1
  MANG/FISH BS16 .... **365** G2
  OLD/WMLY/WICK BS30 .... **376** D3 ⓲
  RSTROUD/NAIL GL6 .... **187** H1
Croft Thorne Cl *CHELTW* GL51 ..... **133** K1 ⓲
Croft Vw
  HNLZ/SM/SNYPK/WT BS9 .... **354** A8 ⓲
Crokeswood Wk *AVONM* BS11 ...... **352** C5 ⓲
Crome Rd *HORF/LLZ* BS7 .... **355** F7
Cromer Rd *EVILLE/WHL* BS5 .... **365** C1
Cromers Cl *TEWK* GL20 .... **34** D5 ⓲
Cromhall La *WUE* GL12 .... **318** A3
Cromwell Ct *KCWD/HNM* BS15 .... **375** K1 ⓲
Cromwell Rd *CHELTE/BC* GL52 ..... **5** E
  CHEP NP16 .... **312** A5
  EVILLE/WHL BS5 .... **366** A4
  RDLND/MONT BS6 .... **364** B8

Cromwells Hide
MANG/FISH BS16 .... 365 J1 🔢
Cromwell St *GL* GL1 .... 2 C4
Crooked Rd CI MTCHDN GL17 .. 121 K6 🔢
Croomes HI MANG/FISH BS16 ...... 356 D6
Cropthorne Rd HORF/LLZ BS7 .... 354 E5 🔢
Cropthorne Rd South
HORF/LLZ BS7 .... 354 E6 🔢
Cross Farm CI LYD GL15 .... 233 H6
Crossfield Rd MANG/FISH BS16.... 366 E3
Crossfields COTS GL54 .... 137 J3 🔢
Cross Hands Rd THNB/SVB BS35 .. 329 F7
Cross Keys La *GL* GL1 .... 2 C5
Crossleaze Rd KGWD/HNM BS15 .. 375 H3 🔢
Crossley CI FRCTL/WBN BS36 ...... 345 F7 🔢
Cross Leys SHPSTR CV36 .... 11 H2 🔢
Crossman Av FRCTL/WBN BS36 .... 376 A7
Cross St KEYN BS31 .... 376 A7
KGWD/HNM BS15 .... 366 C5
Cross Tree La ALMDB BS32 .... 343 H6
Crossways Rd THNB/SVB BS35 .... 316 D5
Crow Ash CLFD GL16 .... 175 K1
Crow Ash Rd CLFD GL16 .... 175 J1
Crowfield La NWNT GL18 .... 50 A4
Crowgate La CIND GL14 .... 154 C6
Crow La CBRIS/FH BS1 .... 364 B8 🔢
HNBRY/STHM BS10 .... 353 H4
Crow Meadow WUE GL12 .... 320 D2
Crown CI CHELTE/BC GL52 .... 83 F3
Crown Dr CHELTE/BC GL52 .... 83 F4
Crown Gdns
OLD/WMLY/WICK BS30 .... 367 H7
Crown Hill EVILLE/WHL BS5 .... 365 K6
Crown Hill Wk EVILLE/WHL BS5 .. 365 K6
Crown La LYD GL15 .... 205 G2
Crownleaze MANG/FISH BS16 ...... 366 D3
Crown Meadow CLFD GL16 .... 176 D5 🔢
Crown Rd KGWD/HNM BS15 .... 366 D4
OLD/WMLY/WICK BS30 .... 367 J8
Crows Gv ALMDB BS32 .... 343 H3
Crowther Pk HORF/LLZ BS7 .... 364 E2
Crowther Rd HORF/LLZ BS7 .... 364 E2
Crowthers Av YATE/CS BS37 .... 347 C3
Croydon St EVILLE/WHL BS5 ...... 365 F6
Crucible CI CLFD GL16 .... 175 K5
Crudwell La TET GL8 .... 303 H8
The Crunnis ALMDB BS32 .... 343 J8
Crypt Ct *GL* GL1 .... 157 J3
Crythan Wk CHELTW GL51 .... 133 K1 🔢
Cuckoo La CLFD GL16 .... 357 F3
Cuckoo Rw RSTROUD/NAIL GL6 .. 243 H6
Cud La RSTROUD/NAIL GL6.......... 186 D6
Cudnall St CHELTS GL53 .... 5 E6
Cuffington Av
BRSG/KWL/STAPK BS4 .... 374 C2
Culleysgate La
OLD/WMLY/WICK BS30 .... 369 H8
Cullimore Vw CIND GL14 .... 178 E1
Cullingham La RTEWK/TIB GL19.... 53 C7
Culross CI CHELT GL50.................... 4 C1
Culverhay WUE GL12 .... 297 F7
Culver HI STROUD GL5 .... 242 C6
Culverhill Rd YATE/CS BS37 .... 347 J5
Culvers Rd KEYN BS31 .... 375 H3
Culver St CBRIS/FH BS1 .... 364 A8 🔢
NWNT GL18 .... 73 J7
The Culvert ALMDB BS32 .... 343 H6 🔢
Cumberland Crs CHELTW GL51 .. 106 A5
Cumberland Gv
RDLND/MONT BS6 .... 364 D4 🔢
Cumberland St CBRISNE BS2 ...... 364 C6 🔢
Cumbria CI THNB/SVB BS35 .... 316 E5
Cunningham Gdns
MANG/FISH BS16 .... 366 B1 🔢
Cupola CI CLFD GL16 .... 175 K5
Curlew CI MANG/FISH BS16 .... 355 K8 🔢
TEWK GL20 .... 34 C5 🔢
Curlew Rd *GLE* GL4 .... 130 E8
Cursey La CHELTW GL51 .... 81 F1
RTEWK/TIB GL19 .... 80 C1
The Cursus CIR GL7 .... 285 G1
Curtis Hayward Dr VGL GL2........ 156 E5
Curtis La BRSTK/PCHW BS34 ...... 356 A3
Cut And Fry Rd LYD GL15 .... 206 C4
Cutham La CIR GL7 .... 221 H3
Cuthwine PI CIR GL7 .... 285 C1
Cutler Rd STROUD GL5 .... 215 F6
Cutsdean CI CHELTE/BC GL52 ...... 82 D2
Cuttsheath Rd WUE GL12 .... 317 J6
Cutwell TET GL8 .... 302 B8
Cynder Wy MANG/FISH BS16 ...... 357 O5
Cypress Gv
HNLZ/SM/SNYPK/WT BS9 ...... 354 A8
Cypress Rd TEWK GL20 .... 57 K2
Cypress Wk CHPMW/MSHF SN14 .... 373 F2 🔢
Cyrus St MANG/FISH BS16 .... 357 H7 🔢

D

Daffodil CI *GLE* GL4 .... 159 G1
Daffodil Leaze STNHO GL10 .... 241 H3
Daffodil Wy NWNT GL18 .... 48 B6

Daglingworth Pth CIR GL7 .... 247 J6
Dagmar Rd CHELT GL50 .... 4 A6
Dainty St *GL* GL1 .... 3 D6 🔢
Dairy Farm HGHW SN6 .... 308 C6
Dairy La EVE WR11 .... 38 C2
Daisy Bank STROUD GL5 .... 215 G8
Daisybank Rd CHELTS GL53 .... 134 E4 🔢
Daisy Green La WUE GL12 .... 296 B4
Daisy Rd EVILLE/WHL BS5 .... 365 G4
Daldry Gdns THNB/SVB BS35 ...... 330 E3 🔢
Dale CI *GLE* GL4 .... 158 B1
Dale St CBRISNE BS2 .... 364 D6
COTS GL54 .... 113 G3
EVILLE/WHL BS5 .... 365 K6
Dale Wk CHELTE/BC GL52 .... 83 C3
Dalkeith Av KGWD/HNM BS15 .... 366 C5 🔢
Dallaway STROUD GL5 .... 243 G4
Dalrymple Rd CBRISNE BS2 .... 364 C5 🔢
Dalton Sq CBRISNE BS2 .... 364 C6 🔢
Damery La BRKLY GL13.................. 294 E3
WUE GL12 .... 294 E3
The Damsels TET GL8 .... 302 C7
Damson CI *GLE* GL4 .... 159 G2
Danbury Crs HNBRY/STHM BS10 .. 354 A5
Danbury Wk
HNBRY/STHM BS10 .... 354 A5 🔢
Danby CI CIND GL14 .... 151 G6
Danby Rd LYD GL15 .... 206 C3
Dancey Rd BWTH/CHD GL3 .... 103 H8
Dane CI VGL GL2 .... 130 E1 🔢
Dane La CIR GL7 .... 246 C2
Danes HI CHEP NP16 .... 288 D7
Danford La RTEWK/TIB GL19 ...... 76 D8
Daniels Rd STROUD GL5 .... 215 H8
Darell CI VGL GL2 .... 157 F7
Dark La CHELTW GL51 .... 82 A7
CIR GL7 .... 221 J2
RSTROUD/NAIL GL6 .... 244 C4
RSTROUD/NAIL GL6 .... 270 C2
STROUD GL5 .... 242 D1
Darks Rd NWNT GL18 .... 72 A8
Darley CI HNBRY/STHM BS10...... 353 F3
Darnley Av HORF/LLZ BS7 .... 354 D8
Darren Rd CLFD GL16 .... 175 K1
Dart CI THNB/SVB BS35 .... 316 B8 🔢
VGL GL2 .... 157 F4
Darters CI LYD GL15 .... 234 A4 🔢
Dart Rd CHELTE/BC GL52 .... 5 F2
Darwin CI CHELTW GL51 .... 105 G5
Darwin Rd *GLE* GL4 .... 158 B1
Daston CI BDWAY WR12 .... 18 E6 🔢
Daubeny CI MANG/FISH BS16 ...... 366 B1
Davallia Dr CHELTW GL51 .... 133 K1 🔢
Daventry Ter *GL* GL1 .... 3 D5 🔢
Davey St CBRISNE BS2 .... 364 D5
David French Ct CHELTW GL51 .. 134 A1 🔢
Davids CI THNB/SVB BS35 .... 332 A2
David's La THNB/SVB BS35 .... 332 A2
David's Rd HGRV/WHIT BS14 ...... 374 B3
David St CBRISNE BS2 .... 364 D7 🔢
Davies Dr BRSG/KWL/STAPK BS4 .. 374 E1 🔢
Davies Rd MIM GL56 .... 46 B8
Davis CI OLD/WMLY/WICK BS30 .. 376 A1 🔢
Davis St THNB/SVB BS35 .... 316 A4
Dawes CI CIR GL7 .... 256 D3
The Dawes VGL GL2 .... 157 F6
Dawley CI FRCTL/WBN BS36 ...... 344 F7 🔢
The Dawneys MALM SN16 .... 304 E8
Dawn Ri KGWD/HNM BS15.......... 367 G5
Daws CI MANG/FISH BS16 .... 366 B2 🔢
Day House La WUE GL12 .... 321 G6
Daylesford CI CHELTW GL51 ...... 105 H6
Days Ct MALM SN16 .... 304 E8
Day's La MIM GL56 .... 44 B4
Day's Rd CBRISNE BS2 .... 364 E8
Deacon CI CHELTW GL51 .... 105 K7 🔢
FRCTL/WBN BS36 .... 356 E1
Deacons PI CHELTE/BC GL52 ...... 82 E4 🔢
Deakin CI CHELTW GL51 .... 82 B7
Dean Av THNB/SVB BS35 .... 316 C4
Dean CI KGWD/HNM BS15 .... 375 F2
Dean Ct LYD GL15 .... 234 B1
Dean Crs CIND GL14 .... 151 J7
Deanery Rd CBRIS/FH BS1 .... 364 A8 🔢
KGWD/HNM BS15 .... 367 H6
Dean La CHELTE/BC GL52 .... 81 J1
YATE/CS BS37 .... 346 E7
Deans Ct CHELTW GL51 .... 105 K7 🔢
Dean's Dr EVILLE/WHL BS5 .... 366 A4 🔢
Deansfield HGHW SN6 .... 310 D7
Deans Md AVONM BS11 .... 352 C6
Dean's Quarry STROUD GL5........ 243 H6
Dean's Ter *GL* GL1 .... 2 C2 🔢
Dean St CBRISNE BS2 .... 364 C6
Dean's Wk *GL* GL1 .... 2 C2
MTCHDN GL17 .... 122 D7
Deans Wy CHELTE/BC GL52 .... 83 F3
GL GL1 .... 2 C2
Deansway Rd MTCHDN GL17 ...... 123 G8
Dean Vw CIND GL14 .... 178 E1
De Clifford Rd AVONM BS11 ...... 352 E4
Deep Pit Rd EVILLE/WHL BS5 .... 365 K5

Deep St CHELTE/BC GL52 .... 5 F1
Deerhurst Rd KGWD/HNM BS15 .. 366 E4 🔢
YATE/CS BS37 .... 346 E6
Deerhurst CI *GLE* GL4 .... 159 C2 🔢
Deerhurst PI VGL GL2 .... 156 E5
Deering CI AVONM BS11 .... 352 D5
Deer Pk LYD GL15 .... 206 A4
Deer Park Rd BWTH/CHD GL3 .. 131 J5 🔢
De Havilland Rd COTS GL54 ...... 145 F1
Deerswood KGWD/HNM BS15 .... 367 G4
Delabere Av MANG/FISH BS16 .... 366 B1
Delabere Rd CHELTE/BC GL52 .... 83 C4
Delavale Rd COTS GL54 .... 62 D8
Delkin Rd DSLY GL11 .... 266 D2
The Dell ALMDB BS32 .... 343 J7
GL GL1 .... 131 C7
MIM GL56 .... 44 C3 🔢
OLD/WMLY/WICK BS30 .... 376 D1 🔢
TEWK GL20 .... 13 J7
Dell Vw CHEP NP16 .... 288 C6
Delmont Gv STROUD GL5 .... 214 E6
Delphinium Dr CHELTE/BC GL52 .. 82 E3 🔢
Delta Dr TEWK GL20 .... 34 B6
Delvin Rd HNBRY/STHM BS10 .... 354 A6
Denbigh Dr CHEP NP16 .... 312 C1
Denbigh Rd CHELTW GL51 .... 105 J8
Denbigh St CBRISNE BS2 .... 364 C5
Denehurst MTCHDN GL17 .... 149 K1
Denham CI CHELTE/BC GL52 ...... 83 J3
GL GL1 .... 157 J5
Denley CI CHELTE/BC GL52 .... 83 F4
Denmark Av CBRIS/FH BS1 ...... 364 A8 🔢
Denmark Dr CHEP NP16 .... 288 D7
Denmark PI HORF/LLZ BS7 .... 364 C3 🔢
Denmark Rd *GL* GL1 .... 3 D2
Denmark St CBRIS/FH BS1 .... 364 A8
Dennisworth MANG/FISH BS16 .. 368 D1 🔢
Dennor Pk HGRV/WHIT BS14 ...... 374 A7
Denny Isle Dr THNB/SVB BS35 .... 340 C1
Denton Patch MANG/FISH BS16 .. 357 H7 🔢
Dent's La RTEWK/TIB GL19........ 100 C3
Dentwood Gv
HNLZ/SM/SNYPK/WT BS9 ...... 352 D7
Denys Ct THNB/SVB BS35............ 330 D3
Derby Rd *GL* GL1 .... 3 E5
HORF/LLZ BS7 .... 364 C3
Derby St EVILLE/WHL BS5 .... 365 H4
Dermot St CBRISNE BS2 .... 364 E5 🔢
Derricke Rd HGRV/WHIT BS14 .... 374 E8
Derrick Rd KGWD/HNM BS15...... 366 D6
The Derry HGHW SN6 .... 308 C6
Derwent CI BRSTK/PCHW BS34 .. 342 E6
BWTH/CHD GL3 .... 160 C1
Derwent Dr TEWK GL20 .... 33 K6
Derwent Rd EVILLE/WHL BS5 .... 365 K5
Desford CI *GLE* GL4 .... 159 H1 🔢
Despenser Rd TEWK GL20 .... 57 H2
Detmore CI CHELTE/BC GL52 ...... 135 J1
Devereaux Crs STROUD GL5 .... 213 J7
Devereaux Rd STROUD GL5.......... 213 J8
De Verose Ct KGWD/HNM BS15 .. 375 K2
The Devil's Elbow
RSTROUD/NAIL GL6 .... 271 C2
Devil's La WUE GL12 .... 319 H4
Devon Av CHELTW GL51 .... 105 K5
Devon Gv EVILLE/WHL BS5 .... 365 G5
Devon Rd EVILLE/WHL BS5 .... 365 G5
Devonshire PI TEWK GL20 .... 57 J2 🔢
Devonshire St CHELT GL50 .... 4 A3 🔢
Dewey CI CHELTE/BC GL52 .... 83 H3
Dewfalls Dr ALMDB BS32 .... 343 H5
Dial La MANG/FISH BS16.............. 356 D8
Diamond Rd EVILLE/WHL BS5 .... 365 K7
Diana Gdns ALMDB BS32 .... 343 J6
Dianas CI BWTH/CHD GL3 .... 131 H8 🔢
Dibden CI MANG/FISH BS16 ...... 357 G6
Dibden La MANG/FISH BS16........ 357 G7
TEWK GL20 .... 38 A7
Dibden Rd MANG/FISH BS16 ...... 357 G6
Dickens CI *GLE* GL4 .... 158 B1
HORF/LLZ BS7 .... 354 E6
Dickens Ms *GLE* GL4 .... 158 B1 🔢
Didsbury CI HNBRY/STHM BS10 .. 353 H5
Digbeth St COTS GL54 .... 92 C6 🔢
Digby Ct TEWK GL20 .... 33 J6
Dighton Ga BRSTK/PCHW BS34 .. 355 J1 🔢
Dighton St CBRISNE BS2 .... 364 B6
Dikler CI COTS GL54 .... 143 K2
Dill Av CHELTW GL51 .... 105 J2
Dimore CI VGL GL2 .... 156 E7
Dinas Rd CHELTW GL51 .... 105 K8
Dinely St *GL* GL1 .... 3 D5
Dingle CI
HNLZ/SM/SNYPK/WT BS9 ...... 352 E8
Dingle Rd
HNLZ/SM/SNYPK/WT BS9 ...... 352 E9
The Dingle FRCTL/WBN BS36...... 356 E3
HNLZ/SM/SNYPK/WT BS9 ...... 352 E7
YATE/CS BS37 .... 347 H2
Dingle Vw
HNLZ/SM/SNYPK/WT BS9 ...... 352 E7
Dinglewell *GLE* GL4 .... 131 H7
Dinglewood CI
HNLZ/SM/SNYPK/WT BS9 ...... 353 F7 🔢
Dings Wk CBRISNE BS2 .... 364 E8 🔢

Discovery Rd *BWTH/CHD* GL3 .... 131 H8
Distel Cl *CHELTW* GL51 .... 106 C1
Ditch La *CIR* GL7 .... 196 C8
Dixon Rd *BRSG/KWL/STAPK* BS4 .... 374 E4
Dockham Rd *CIND* GL14 .... 151 G6
Dockins Hill Wy *MTCHDN* GL17 ...... 123 G7
Dock La *TEWK* GL20 .... 13 J7
Dock Rd *BRKLY* GL13 .... 235 H5
Dodd Dr *COTS* GL54 .... 145 F2
Dodington Cl *GLE* GL4 .... 131 F7
Dodington Cl *GLE* GL4 .... 347 K8
Dodington Rd *YATE/CS* BS37 ...... 347 K8
Dodington Rd *YATE/CS* BS37 ...... 347 K7
Dodisham Wk *MANG/FISH* BS16 ...... 356 B8
Dog La *CHELTW* GL51 .... 133 H8
Dollar St *CIR* GL7 .... 249 J5
Dolman Cl *HNBRY/STHM* BS10 .... 353 H8
Domby Cl *CLFD* GL16 .... 175 K5
Dominion Rd *MANG/FISH* BS16 ...... 365 K3
Doncaster Rd *HNBRY/STHM* BS10 .. 353 K5
Doncombe HI
CHPMW/MSHF SN14 .... 372 E7
Doncombe La
CHPMW/MSHF SN14 .... 373 F7
Dongola Av *HORF/LLZ* BS7 ...... 364 C2
Dongola Rd *HORF/LLZ* BS7 ...... 364 C2
The Donkey Fld *CIR* GL7 .... 251 J5
Donkey La *MIM* GL56 .... 44 B5
Donside *CIR* GL7 .... 249 G3
Doone Rd *HORF/LLZ* BS7 .... 354 D6
Dora Wk *GL* GL1 .... 3 D6
Dorcas Av *BRSTK/PCHW* BS34 ...... 355 K1
Dorchester Rd *HORF/LLZ* BS7 ...... 354 D7
Dorester Cl *HNBRY/STHM* BS10 ...... 354 A2
Dorian Cl *HORF/LLZ* BS7 .... 354 C7
Dorian Rd *HORF/LLZ* BS7 .... 354 C7
Dorian Wy *HNBRY/STHM* BS10 ...... 354 C6
Dorington Ct
RSTROUD/NAIL GL6 .... 244 B2
Dormer Cl *FRCTL/WBN* BS36 ...... 345 K8
Dormer Rd *CHELTW* GL51 .... 105 K2
Dorney La *GL* GL1 .... 2 C6
Dorrit Cl *GL* GL4 .... 130 B8
Dorset Av *CHELTW* GL51 .... 106 A4
Dorset Gv *CBRISNE* BS2 .... 364 E4
Dorset Rd
HNLZ/SM/SNYPK/WT BS9 ...... 353 K8
KGWD/HNM BS15 .... 366 D5
Dorset Wy *YATE/CS* BS37 .... 347 J3
Doubledays *HGHW* SN6 .... 310 F6
Double Vw *CIND* GL14 .... 151 F7
Douglas Rd *HORF/LLZ* BS7 ...... 354 D7
KGWD/HNM BS15 .... 366 D7
Douro Rd *CHELT* GL50 .... 106 B5
Dovecote *YATE/CS* BS37 .... 347 G2
Dovedale *THNB/SVB* BS35 .... 316 D7
Dove La *CBRISNE* BS2 .... 364 D6
Dovercourt Rd *HORF/LLZ* BS7 ...... 364 E1
Doverdale Dr *VGL* GL2 .... 131 F2
Dover Hay *CHELTW* GL51 ...... 105 K8
Dover's Vw *CHCAM* GL55 .... 7 K7
Dove St *CHELT* GL50 .... 364 B6
Dove St South *CBRISNE* BS2 ...... 364 B6
Dovey Ct *OLD/WMLY/WICK* BS30 .... 376 D1
Dowdeswell Cl
HNBRY/STHM BS10 .... 353 H3
Dowding Cl *YATE/CS* BS37 ...... 348 A4
Dowding Wy *BWTH/CHD* GL3 .... 132 A1
Dowers' La *CIR* GL7 .... 220 C7
Down Ampney Rd *CIR* GL7 ...... 280 A8
Downend Pk *HORF/LLZ* BS7 ...... 354 D8
Downend Park Rd
MANG/FISH BS16 .... 366 D1
Downend Rd *HORF/LLZ* BS7 ...... 364 D1
KGWD/HNM BS15 .... 366 D5
MANG/FISH BS16 .... 366 C1
Downfield *STROUD* GL5 .... 214 B6
Downfield Cl *THNB/SVB* BS35 ...... 316 C5
Downfield Dr *FRCTL/WBN* BS36 .. 345 H6
Downfield La *TEWK* GL20 .... 13 F7
Downfield Rd *STROUD* GL5 ...... 214 B7
Down Hatherley La *VGL* GL2 ...... 103 G4
Downleaze *MANG/FISH* BS16 ...... 356 D6
Down Leaze *THNB/SVB* BS35 ...... 332 A1
Downman Rd *HORF/LLZ* BS7 ...... 364 E1
Down Rd *CHPMW/MSHF* SN14 ...... 372 D2
FRCTL/WBN BS36 .... 356 E2
THNB/SVB BS35 .... 332 A1
Downs Cl *THNB/SVB* BS35 .... 332 A1
Downs Cote Av
HNLZ/SM/SNYPK/WT BS9 ...... 353 H8
Downs Cote Dr
HNLZ/SM/SNYPK/WT BS9 ...... 353 H8
Downs Cote Gdns
HNLZ/SM/SNYPK/WT BS9 ...... 353 H8
Downs Cote Pk
HNLZ/SM/SNYPK/WT BS9 ...... 353 H8
Downs Cote Vw
HNLZ/SM/SNYPK/WT BS9 ...... 353 H8
Downside Close
OLD/WMLY/WICK BS30 ...... 376 A1
Downs Rd
HNLZ/SM/SNYPK/WT BS9 ...... 353 J8
The Downs *WUE* GL12 .... 319 H7
Downs Wy *CIR* GL7 .... 221 J8

The Down *ALMDB* BS32 .... 331 H3
THNB/SVB BS35 .... 331 K1
Downton Rd *STNHO* GL10 .... 212 E8
Down Vw *RSTROUD/NAIL* GL6 ...... 244 D2
Downy Cl *VGL* GL2 .... 156 E4
Dowty Rd *CHELTW* GL51 .... 105 J4
Doynton La *CHPMW/MSHF* SN14 .. 369 K3
Dozule Cl *STNHO* GL10 .... 241 F3
Dragon Rd *FRCTL/WBN* BS36 ...... 356 D2
Dragonswell Rd
HNBRY/STHM BS10 .... 353 J4
Dragon Wk *EVILLE/WHL* BS5 ...... 365 K5
Drag Rd *RWYE* HR9 .... 146 E1
Drake Cl *BWTH/CHD* GL3 .... 103 H7
Drake La *DSLY* GL11 .... 267 C5
Drakes Pl *CHELT* GL50 .... 106 B5
Drapers Ct *CHELTE/BC* GL52 ...... 83 H3
Draper's La *RTEWK/TIB* GL19 ...... 77 H2
Draycott *DSLY* GL11 .... 238 D7
Draycott Crs *DSLY* GL11 .... 238 D9
Draycott Rd *HORF/LLZ* BS7 ...... 364 D1
Drayton Cl *CHELTW* GL51 .... 106 B1
GLE GL4 .... 158 E2
HGRV/WHIT BS14 .... 374 A6
Drayton Rd *CHELTW* GL51 ...... 105 J6
HNLZ/SM/SNYPK/WT BS9 ...... 353 E6
Drayton Wy *GLE* GL4 .... 158 E1
Dr Brown's Cl *RSTROUD/NAIL* GL6 .. 243 H8
Dr Browns Rd *RSTROUD/NAIL* GL6 .. 243 H7
Dr Crawfords Wy
RSTROUD/NAIL GL6 .... 243 H8
Dr Crouch's Rd
RSTROUD/NAIL GL6 .... 244 B1
Drews Cl *BWTH/CHD* GL3 .... 132 A2
Drews Ct *BWTH/CHD* GL3 .... 132 A2
Driffield Rd *LYD* GL15 .... 234 C1
Drifton HI *CHPMW/MSHF* SN14 ...... 362 F7
Drift Wy *CIR* GL7 .... 249 G8
Drinkwater La *EVE* WR11 .... 6 B2
Drivemoor *GLE* GL4 .... 159 F3
The Drive *DSLY* GL11 .... 266 D2
Dr Newton's Wy *STROUD* GL5 ...... 214 D8
Druetts Cl *HNBRY/STHM* BS10 ...... 354 C8
Druids Cl *GLE* GL4 .... 130 E7
Druids Oak *VGL* GL2 .... 157 F6
Drummond Ct
OLD/WMLY/WICK BS30 ...... 376 A2
Drummond Rd *CBRISNE* BS2 ...... 364 C5
MANG/FISH BS16 .... 365 K3
Drury La *RTEWK/TIB* GL19 ...... 52 A2
Drybrook Rd *MTCHDN* GL17 ...... 122 C8
Dryleaze *KEYN* BS31 .... 375 K7
WUE GL12 .... 296 F3
YATE/CS BS37 .... 347 G1
Dryleaze Rd *MANG/FISH* BS16 .... 355 K8
Dry Meadow La *VGL* GL2 .... 102 E7
Dubbers La *EVILLE/WHL* BS5 ...... 365 J4
Dublin Crs
HNLZ/SM/SNYPK/WT BS9 ...... 353 K8
Duchess Wy *MANG/FISH* BS16 ...... 365 H1
Ducie Rd *EVILLE/WHL* BS5 ...... 365 F7
MANG/FISH BS16 .... 366 E2
Ducie St *GL* GL1 .... 3 D6
Duck St *WUE* GL12 .... 333 H1
Duckworth Cl *CHELTS* GL53 ...... 134 D1
Dudbridge HI *STROUD* GL5 ...... 214 B8
Dudbridge Meadow
STROUD GL5 .... 242 B1
Dudbridge Rd *STROUD* GL5 ...... 214 B8
STROUD GL5 .... 242 B1
Duderstadt Cl *STROUD* GL5 ...... 214 B6
Dudley Cl
OLD/WMLY/WICK BS30 ...... 376 A2
Dudley Gv *HORF/LLZ* BS7 .... 354 D6
Dudley Rd *EVE* WR11 .... 7 H1
Duffield's La *MONM* NP25 ...... 174 B4
Dugar Wk *RDLND/MONT* BS6 ...... 364 A3
Dugdale Rd *CIR* GL7 .... 249 J5
Duglynch La *COTS* GL54 .... 62 A5
Duke of York Rd *CLFD* GL16 ...... 146 A8
Duke St *CHELTE/BC* GL52 .... 5 D4
Dukes Wy *TEWK* GL20 .... 57 J3
Dulverton Pl *MIM* GL56 .... 46 B8
Dulverton Rd *HORF/LLZ* BS7 ...... 364 B2
Dumaine Av *BRSTK/PCHW* BS34 .. 355 J1
Dumbleton Gv *CHELTW* GL51 .... 105 F8
Dunalley Pde *CHELT* GL50 .... 4 B2
Dunalley St *CHELT* GL50 .... 4 B3
Dunbar Cl *CHELTW* GL51 .... 105 H2
Duncombe La *KGWD/HNM* BS15 .. 366 A4
Duncombe Rd
KGWD/HNM BS15 .... 366 B5
Duncroft Rd *GLE* GL4 .... 131 H5
Dundas Cl *HNBRY/STHM* BS10 .. 353 C4
Dundridge Gdns
EVILLE/WHL BS5 .... 366 A8
Dundridge La *EVILLE/WHL* BS5 ...... 365 K8
Dundry Cl *KGWD/HNM* BS15 ...... 366 D8
Dunkeld Av *BRSTK/PCHW* BS34 .. 354 D4
Dunkirk Rd *MANG/FISH* BS16 ...... 365 K3
Dunlin Cl *VGL* GL2 .... 156 D4
Dunmail Rd *HNBRY/STHM* BS10 .. 354 A4
Dunsdown La
CHPMW/MSHF SN14 .... 370 E1
Dunsmore Gn *RTEWK/TIB* GL19 .. 55 K1

Dunstan Gln *BWTH/CHD* GL3 ...... 132 B2
Dunster Cl *CHELTW* GL51 .... 105 H3
GL GL1 .... 157 H5
Dunster Gdns *CHELTW* GL51 ...... 105 H3
OLD/WMLY/WICK BS30 ...... 376 C4
Dunster Gv *CHELTW* GL51 .... 105 H3
Dunster Rd *CHELTW* GL51 .... 105 H3
Durand Cl *VGL* GL2 .... 102 E8
Durban Rd *BRSTK/PCHW* BS34 .... 342 D6
Durbin Wk *EVILLE/WHL* BS5 ...... 364 E6
Durbridge Rd *RTEWK/TIB* GL19 .... 51 H5
Durham Cl *CHELTW* GL51 .... 134 A1
Durham Rd *CBRISNE* BS2 .... 364 E4
GLE GL4 .... 130 E6
WUE GL12 .... 319 H1
Durley HI *KEYN* BS31 .... 375 G6
Durley La *KEYN* BS31 .... 375 J7
Durn's Rd *WUE* GL12 .... 297 C7
Dursley Cl *YATE/CS* BS37 .... 347 G5
Dursley Rd *GLE* GL4 .... 66 C5
VGL GL2 .... 258 D4
Durweston Wk *HGRV/WHIT* BS14 .... 374 B6
Dutton Cl *HGRV/WHIT* BS14 ...... 374 C8
Dutton Leys *COTS* GL54 .... 169 H5
Duttons La *MTCHDN* GL17 ...... 121 K8
Dutton Wk *HGRV/WHIT* BS14 ...... 374 C8
Dye House Rd *WUE* GL12 .... 320 D1
Dyersbrook *WUE* GL12 .... 297 F7
Dyer's La *CHCAM* GL55 .... 20 B3
YATE/CS BS37 .... 334 C8
YATE/CS BS37 .... 346 C3
Dyer St *CIR* GL7 .... 249 K6
Dyke House La *LED* HR8 .... 29 F7
Dylan Thomas Ct
OLD/WMLY/WICK BS30 ...... 376 B1
Dynevor St *GL* GL1 .... 3 D6
Dyrham Cl
HNLZ/SM/SNYPK/WT BS9 ...... 354 B8
KGWD/HNM BS15 .... 367 F6
THNB/SVB BS35 .... 316 C3
Dyrham Pde *BRSTK/PCHW* BS34 .. 343 G6
Dyrham Rd *KGWD/HNM* BS15 ...... 367 F6

E

Eagle Crs *MANG/FISH* BS16 ...... 368 E2
Eagle Dr *BRSTK/PCHW* BS34 ...... 342 C6
Eagle Mill Cl *STROUD* GL5 .... 243 F1
Eagle Rd *BRSG/KWL/STAPK* BS4 .. 374 C4
Eagle Wy *GLE* GL4 .... 158 E1
Eardisland Rd *GLE* GL4 .... 158 A4
Earl Russell Wy
EVILLE/WHL BS5 .... 365 F7
Earls Cnr *MALM* SN16 .... 306 A6
Earlsmead *MANG/FISH* BS16 ...... 365 H2
Earlstone Cl
OLD/WMLY/WICK BS30 ...... 376 B2
Earlstone Crs
OLD/WMLY/WICK BS30 ...... 376 B1
Earl St *CBRIS/FH* BS1 .... 364 B6
Early Wy *HNBRY/STHM* BS10 ...... 354 C6
Earthcott Rd *THNB/SVB* BS35 .... 332 E6
Easedale Cl *HNBRY/STHM* BS10 .. 354 B4
East Approach Dr *CHELTE/BC* GL52 .. 4 C1
Eastbourne Rd *EVILLE/WHL* BS5 .. 365 F6
Eastbrook Rd *GLE* GL4 .... 130 E6
Eastbury Cl *THNB/SVB* BS35 ...... 316 C5
Eastbury Rd *MANG/FISH* BS16 .... 366 A2
Eastcott Wy *BWTH/CHD* GL3 ...... 103 J8
East Cft *HNLZ/SM/SNYPK/WT* BS9 .. 354 A7
East Dr *STROUD* GL5 .... 213 J7
East End *COTS* GL54 .... 169 H6
East End Rd *CHELTS* GL53 ...... 135 J1
Eastern Av *GLE* GL4 .... 3 F6
GLE GL4 .... 130 E6
MTCHDN GL17 .... 123 G5
Eastern Wy *CIND* GL14 .... 178 E2
Eastfield *HGHW* SN6 .... 308 D5
HNLZ/SM/SNYPK/WT BS9 ...... 353 K7
Eastfield Dr *YATE/CS* BS37 .... 347 G2
Eastfield Rd
HNLZ/SM/SNYPK/WT BS9 ...... 353 J7
RDLND/MONT BS6 .... 364 B4
RSTROUD/NAIL GL6 .... 243 K8
Eastfield Ter
HNLZ/SM/SNYPK/WT BS9 ...... 353 K7
East Gable *CHELTE/BC* GL52 ...... 83 H3
Eastgate St *GL* GL1 .... 3 D4
Eastgate Rd *RDLND/MONT* BS6 .... 364 D5
East Hill Eastfield Rd
HNLZ/SM/SNYPK/WT BS9 ...... 353 J7
Eastington Rd *COTS* GL54 .... 169 H5
Eastlake St *HORF/LLZ* BS7 .... 355 F7
Eastland Av *THNB/SVB* BS35 ...... 316 C4
Eastland Rd *THNB/SVB* BS35 ...... 316 C4
Eastleigh Cl *MANG/FISH* BS16 .... 366 E2
Eastleigh Rd *HNBRY/STHM* BS10 .. 354 B5
MANG/FISH BS16 .... 366 E2
Eastley Cl *WUE* GL12 .... 294 A7
Easton Hill Rd *THNB/SVB* BS35 .. 316 D4
Easton Rd *CBRISNE* BS2 .... 364 E7
EVILLE/WHL BS5 .... 365 F6

Easton Wy *EVILLE/WHL* BS5 .... 364 E5
Eastover CI
  HNLZ/SM/SNYPK/WT BS9 .... 353 J6
East Pde
  HNLZ/SM/SNYPK/WT BS9 .... 352 E8
East Pk *EVILLE/WHL* BS5 .... 365 G4
East Park Dr *EVILLE/WHL* BS5 .... 365 G4 ◘
East Priory CI
  HNLZ/SM/SNYPK/WT BS9 .... 353 J7
East St *CBRISNE* BS2 .... 364 D6 ◘
  LYD GL15 .... 203 F8
  MIM GL56 .... 70 A1
  TEWK GL20 .... 33 H8 ◘
East Vw *MANG/FISH* BS16 .... 357 G5
Eastville CI *GLE* GL4 .... 3 F5
Eastwood Crs
  BRSG/KWL/STAPK BS4 .... 374 E2
Eastwood Rd
  BRSG/KWL/STAPK BS4 .... 374 E2
  MTCHDN GL17 .... 122 D8 ◘
Eaton CI *MANG/FISH* BS16 .... 366 B2
Eaton PI *CHELT* GL50 .... 4 B5 ◘
Ebenezer La
  HNLZ/SM/SNYPK/WT BS9 .... 353 F8 ◘
Ebenezer St *EVILLE/WHL* BS5 .... 365 H7 ◘
Ebley Rd *STNHO* BS10 .... 213 H8
Ebor Rd *VGL* GL2 .... 130 E5
Ebrington CI *GLE* GL4 .... 131 F6 ◘
Eddys La *MTCHDN* GL17 .... 121 G8
Edendale Approach Rd
  CHELTW GL51 .... 105 G6
Eden Gv *HORF/LLZ* BS7 .... 354 E5
Eden's HI *NWNT* GL18 .... 74 E3
Edenwall Rd *CLFD* GL16 .... 176 A7
Edgecorner La
  CHPMW/MSHF SN14 .... 363 G3
Edgecumbe Rd
  RDLND/MONT BS6 .... 364 B4 ◘
Edge End Rd *CLFD* GL16 .... 176 B4
Edge Hills CI *CIND* GL14 .... 151 F5 ◘
Edge Hills Rd *CIND* GL14 .... 151 F5
Edge La *RSTROUD/NAIL* GL6 .... 186 E6
Edge Rd *RSTROUD/NAIL* GL6 .... 187 E6
Edgeware Rd *MANG/FISH* BS16 .... 366 C2 ◘
Edgewood CI *HGRV/WHIT* BS14 .... 374 A6 ◘
  OLD/WMLY/WICK BS30 .... 376 B3
Edgeworth *YATE/CS* BS37 .... 346 E8
Edgeworth CI *GLE* GL4 .... 159 G1 ◘
  CLFD GL16 .... 176 B4
Edington Gv *HNBRY/STHM* BS10 .... 353 J4
Edmond Rd *CHEP* NP16 .... 288 D6 ◘
Edmund CI *MANG/FISH* BS16 .... 356 D8 ◘
Edmund Ct *MANG/FISH* BS16 .... 358 D8
Edna Av *BRSG/KWL/STAPK* BS4 .... 374 D3
Edward Av *BRSG/KWL/STAPK* BS4 .... 374 D3
Edward Rd
  BRSG/KWL/STAPK BS4 .... 374 A2 ◘
  KGWD/HNM BS15 .... 366 C6
Edwards CI *CIR* GL7 .... 252 B5
  MTCHDN GL17 .... 148 C1
Edward St *CHELT* GL50 .... 4 A6
  EVILLE/WHL BS5 .... 365 H4 ◘
  EVILLE/WHL BS5 .... 365 G5 ◘
Edwin Short CI
  OLD/WMLY/WICK BS30 .... 377 F6
Edwy Pde *GL* GL1 .... 2 C2
Effingham Rd *RDLND/MONT* BS6 .... 364 C4
Egerton Brow *HORF/LLZ* BS7 .... 364 B2 ◘
Egerton Rd *HORF/LLZ* BS7 .... 364 B2
Eggshill La *YATE/CS* BS37 .... 347 F5
Eighth Av *HORF/LLZ* BS7 .... 355 F6
Elberton Rd *KGWD/HNM* BS15 .... 367 G6 ◘
Elberton Rd
  HNLZ/SM/SNYPK/WT BS9 .... 352 D7
  THNB/SVB BS35 .... 314 D8
  THNB/SVB BS35 .... 330 E3
Elbury Rd *KGWD/HNM* BS15 .... 366 C4
Elderberry Wk
  HNBRY/STHM BS10 .... 354 A4
Eldersfield CI *COTS* GL54 .... 62 D7 ◘
  VGL GL2 .... 156 E4
Elderwood Dr
  OLD/WMLY/WICK BS30 .... 376 B3
Elderwood Rd
  HGRV/WHIT BS14 .... 374 A7 ◘
Elderwood Wy *GL* GL1 .... 157 J3
Eldon Av *CHELTE/BC* GL52 .... 5 E4 ◘
Eldon Rd *CHELTE/BC* GL52 .... 5 D4
Eldon Wy *BRSG/KWL/STAPK* BS4 .... 365 J2
Eldorado Crs *CHELT* GL50 .... 106 B5
Eldorado Rd *CHELT* GL50 .... 106 A5
Eleventh Av *HORF/LLZ* BS7 .... 355 F5 ◘
Elfin Rd *MANG/FISH* BS16 .... 366 A1
Elf Meadow *CIR* GL7 .... 252 E7
Elgin Av *HORF/LLZ* BS7 .... 354 C5
Elgin Rd *MANG/FISH* BS16 .... 366 B4
Eliot CI *HORF/LLZ* BS7 .... 354 E6
  VGL GL2 .... 157 J2
Elizabeth CI *THNB/SVB* BS35 .... 316 D6
Elizabeth Crs *BRSTK/PCHW* BS34 .... 355 J2
Elizabeth Gdns *CIR* GL7 .... 281 J1
  TET GL8 .... 302 B6 ◘
Elizabeths Ms
  BRSG/KWL/STAPK BS4 .... 365 K8 ◘

Elizabeth Wy *CIR* GL7 .... 278 A2
Ellacombe Rd
  OLD/WMLY/WICK BS30 .... 375 H4 ◘
Ellan Hay Rd *ALMDB* BS32 .... 344 A8
Ellenborough Rd *CHELTE/BC* GL52 .. 83 G5 ◘
Ellendene Dr *TEWK* GL20 .... 35 H7
Ellenor Dr *TEWK* GL20 .... 37 K7
Ellerncroft Rd *WUE* GL12 .... 296 D6
Ellesmere CI *GLE* GL4 .... 131 H6 ◘
Ellesmere Gv *CHELT* GL50 .... 106 B8 ◘
Ellesmere Rd
  BRSG/KWL/STAPK BS4 .... 374 C5 ◘
  KGWD/HNM BS15 .... 366 D6 ◘
Ellicks CI *ALMDB* BS32 .... 343 J4
Ellicott Rd *HORF/LLZ* BS7 .... 354 D8
Ellinghurst CI
  HNBRY/STHM BS10 .... 353 J4 ◘
Elliott Av *MANG/FISH* BS16 .... 356 C5
Elliott PI *CHELTW* GL51 .... 105 H7
Elliott Rd *CIR* GL7 .... 249 K8
Ellison Rd *BWTH/CHD* GL3 .... 131 J8 ◘
Ellison Rd *CHELTW* GL51 .... 105 J4
Elliston La *RDLND/MONT* BS6 .... 364 A4
Elliston Rd *RDLND/MONT* BS6 .... 364 A4
Ellsworth Rd *HNBRY/STHM* BS10 .... 353 H4
Ellwood Rd *CLFD* GL16 .... 176 A8
Elmbridge Rd *VGL* GL2 .... 130 E4
Elmbury Dr *TEWK* GL20 .... 34 A8
Elm CI *BRSTK/PCHW* BS34 .... 343 H7
  CHELTE/BC GL52 .... 107 G1
  CHELTW GL51 .... 106 B3
  CHEP NP16 .... 288 C3
  SHPSTR CV36 .... 11 G2
  STNHO GL10 .... 241 G2
  YATE/CS BS37 .... 347 G5
Elm Ct *LYD* GL15 .... 232 C8
Elmcroft Crs *HORF/LLZ* BS7 .... 364 E2
Elmdale *CHEP* NP16 .... 288 A5
Elmdale Crs *THNB/SVB* BS35 .... 316 C5
Elm Dr *BWTH/CHD* GL3 .... 132 B8
Elmfield *KGWD/HNM* BS15 .... 366 E8
Elmfield Av *CHELTW* GL51 .... 4 A1
Elmfield CI *KGWD/HNM* BS15 .... 366 E8 ◘
Elmfield Rd *CHELTW* GL51 .... 4 A1 ◘
  HNLZ/SM/SNYPK/WT BS9 .... 353 J6 ◘
Elm Garden Dr *CHELTW* GL51 .... 104 E7
Elm Gv *CHCAM* GL5 .... 22 B1
  RTEWK/TIB GL19 .... 125 J2
Elmgrove Av *EVILLE/WHL* BS5 .... 365 F6 ◘
Elmgrove Dr *YATE/CS* BS37 .... 347 H4 ◘
Elmgrove Pk *RDLND/MONT* BS6 .... 364 B5 ◘
Elmgrove Rd *BWTH/CHD* GL3 .... 131 H7
  MANG/FISH BS16 .... 365 J1
  RDLND/MONT BS6 .... 364 B5
Elmgrove Rd East *VGL* GL2 .... 156 E7
Elmgrove Rd West *VGL* GL2 .... 156 D7
Elmhirst Gdns *YATE/CS* BS37 .... 347 J4
Elmhurst Av *EVILLE/WHL* BS5 .... 365 H3
Elming Down CI *ALMDB* BS32 .... 343 H8 ◘
Elmira Rd *GLE* GL4 .... 158 B2 ◘
Elmlea Rd *STNHO* GL10 .... 241 G2
Elmleaze *VGL* GL2 .... 131 F3
Elmleigh Av *MANG/FISH* BS16 .... 367 C1 ◘
Elmleigh CI *MANG/FISH* BS16 .... 367 C1 ◘
Elmleigh Rd *MANG/FISH* BS16 .... 367 G1
Elmley CI *EVE* WR11 .... 14 D5
Elmore Gv *BRSTK/PCHW* BS34 .... 354 E4
  YATE/CS BS37 .... 347 H6 ◘
Elmore La *VGL* GL2 .... 156 C4
Elmore Rd *BRSTK/PCHW* BS34 .... 354 E8
  HORF/LLZ BS7 .... 354 E4
Elm Pk *BRSTK/PCHW* BS34 .... 354 E4
  CHEP NP16 .... 288 C4
  HORF/LLZ BS7 .... 364 C1
  KGWD/HNM BS15 .... 366 E8
  SHPSTR CV36 .... 25 F2
  STROUD GL5 .... 214 A6
  TEWK GL20 .... 34 D6
Elms Gv *BRSTK/PCHW* BS34 .... 343 F5
Elm Side *VGL* GL2 .... 103 F1
Elms Rd *STNHO* GL10 .... 212 E6
Elm St *CHELTW* GL51 .... 106 B2
Elm Tree Av *MANG/FISH* BS16 .... 357 G7
Elmtree CI *KGWD/HNM* BS15 .... 366 D5
Elm Vw *CIR* GL7 .... 307 H2
Elmvil Rd *TEWK* GL20 .... 34 A7
Elm Wd *YATE/CS* BS37 .... 347 G6
Elphick Rd *CIR* GL7 .... 249 H2 ◘
Elstree Rd *EVILLE/WHL* BS5 .... 365 J5
Elstub La *DSLY* GL11 .... 266 C1
Elton La *HORF/LLZ* BS7 .... 364 B4
Elton Rd *CIND* GL14 .... 151 K6
  CIND GL14 .... 152 A6
  HORF/LLZ BS7 .... 364 B3
  KGWD/HNM BS15 .... 366 B5
Elton St *CBRISNE* BS2 .... 364 D6 ◘
Ely Gv *HNLZ/SM/SNYPK/WT* BS9 .... 352 D7
Embassy Rd *EVILLE/WHL* BS5 .... 365 J5
Embassy Wk *EVILLE/WHL* BS5 .... 365 J5
Embleton Rd *HNBRY/STHM* BS10 .... 353 K4
Embrook Rd *MIM* GL56 .... 93 J6 ◘
Emerald CI *GL* GL1 .... 157 J3
Emersons Green La
  MANG/FISH BS16 .... 357 H8

Emerson Sq *HORF/LLZ* BS7 .... 354 E6
Emersons Wy *MANG/FISH* BS16 .. 357 J7 ◘
Emery Rd
  BRSG/KWL/STAPK BS4 .... 374 E5 ◘
Emet Gv *MANG/FISH* BS16 .... 357 H8
Emet La *MANG/FISH* BS16 .... 357 H8
Emlyn Rd *EVILLE/WHL* BS5 .... 365 G4
Emma-chris Wy
  BRSTK/PCHW BS34 .... 355 G4
Emmerson La *CIR* GL7 .... 245 K8
Emperor CI *CHELTW* GL51 .... 105 H4 ◘
Empire Wy *VGL* GL2 .... 157 H1
Emra CI *EVILLE/WHL* BS5 .... 365 K5 ◘
Enborne CI *GLE* GL4 .... 157 K5 ◘
Enfield Rd *MANG/FISH* BS16 .... 366 A3
Engine Common La *YATE/CS* BS37 .... 334 E3
England's Crs *FRCTL/WBN* BS36 .... 344 E7
Ennerdale Av *VGL* GL2 .... 130 C1
Ennerdale Rd *HNBRY/STHM* BS10 .. 354 B4
Enterprise Wy *CHELTW* GL51 .... 106 B3
Epney CI *BRSTK/PCHW* BS34 .... 342 D5
Epney Rd *GL* GL1 .... 157 J3
Epsom CI *MANG/FISH* BS16 .... 357 F5
Epworth Rd *HNBRY/STHM* BS10 .... 353 J4
Erin Pk *STROUD* GL5 .... 242 C1
Erinn Pk *BWTH/CHD* GL3 .... 132 B8
Ermin CI *CIR* GL7 .... 250 A8
Erminster Dr *BWTH/CHD* GL3 .... 131 J7
Ermin St *BWTH/CHD* GL3 .... 132 B8
Ermin Wy *BWTH/CHD* GL3 .... 161 F2
Ernleet Rd *RDLND/MONT* BS6 .... 364 A4 ◘
Ernest Barker CI
  EVILLE/WHL BS5 .... 365 F7 ◘
Ernestville Rd *MANG/FISH* BS16 .... 365 K3
Eros CI *STROUD* GL5 .... 242 C1
Errington CI *MIM* GL56 .... 70 B1
Ervine Ter *CBRISNE* BS2 .... 364 D6
Eskdale *THNB/SVB* BS35 .... 316 D7
Esland PI *CIR* GL7 .... 249 K8
Essery Rd *EVILLE/WHL* BS5 .... 365 G4
Essex Av *CHELTW* GL51 .... 106 A4
Essex CI *BWTH/CHD* GL3 .... 103 J6 ◘
Essex PI *COTS* GL54 .... 115 G2
Esson Rd *KGWD/HNM* BS15 .... 366 B5
Estate Rd *CIND* GL14 .... 150 D4
Estcote Rd *CIR* GL7 .... 249 J5
Estcourt CI *GL* GL1 .... 3 E1
Estcourt Rd *GL* GL1 .... 3 D1
Estoril *YATE/CS* BS37 .... 347 H5
Etheldene Rd *STROUD* GL5 .... 213 K6
Etheridge PI *VGL* GL2 .... 3 F4 ◘
Eton Rd *BRSG/KWL/STAPK* BS4 .... 374 C3
Ettington CI *CHELTW* GL51 .... 105 G3 ◘
Ettrick Dr *MANG/FISH* BS16 .... 356 B8
Eugene St *CBRISNE* BS2 .... 364 B6
  EVILLE/WHL BS5 .... 364 D6 ◘
Evans CI *BRSG/KWL/STAPK* BS4 .... 374 E1
Evans Wk *GLE* GL4 .... 158 D2 ◘
Evelyn CI *CHELTS* GL53 .... 134 E1
Evelyn Rd *HNBRY/STHM* BS10 .... 354 A7 ◘
Evenlode Av *CHELTE/BC* GL52 .... 5 E3 ◘
Evenlode Gdns *MIM* GL56 .... 70 B1
Evenlode Rd *GLE* GL4 .... 157 K5
  MIM GL56 .... 70 B1
Everest Av *MANG/FISH* BS16 .... 365 J2
Everest CI *RSTROUD/NAIL* GL6 .... 243 G8
Everest Rd *CHELTS* GL53 .... 134 E2
  MANG/FISH BS16 .... 365 J2
Everlands *DSLY* GL11 .... 266 E1
Eve Rd *EVILLE/WHL* BS5 .... 365 F6
Everside CI *DSLY* GL11 .... 238 D8 ◘
Everside La *DSLY* GL11 .... 238 D8
Evesham Rd *BDWAY* WR12 .... 17 K2
  CHELT GL50 .... 82 E7
  CHELTE/BC GL52 .... 4 C2 ◘
  CHELTE/BC GL52 .... 83 F2
  COTS GL54 .... 62 D5
  COTS GL54 .... 92 B5
Evington Rd *CHELTW* GL51 .... 105 J4
Ewelme CI *DSLY* GL11 .... 267 G6
Ewens Rd *CHELTE/BC* GL52 .... 5 E5
Ewlyn Rd *CHELTS* GL53 .... 106 D8
Exley CI *OLD/WMLY/WICK* BS30.... 376 D1
Exmouth Ct *CHELTS* GL53 .... 4 B6 ◘
Exmouth St *CHELTS* GL53 .... 4 B6
Eyer's La *CBRISNE* BS2 .... 364 D7 ◘
Eynon CI *CHELTS* GL53 .... 134 C1

F

Fabian Dr *BRSTK/PCHW* BS34 .... 355 J1
Factory Rd *FRCTL/WBN* BS36 .... 345 F7
Failand Wk
  HNLZ/SM/SNYPK/WT BS9 .... 352 E8 ◘
Faircare CI *HORF/LLZ* BS7 .... 365 F1
Fairfax CI *CIR* GL7 .... 249 K7
Fairfax Rd *CIR* GL7 .... 249 K7
Fairfax St *CBRIS/FH* BS1 .... 364 C7
Fairfield *HGHW* SN6 .... 310 D6
Fairfield Av *CHELTS* GL53 .... 106 D8
Fairfield CI *CHPMW/MSHF* SN14.... 371 K6
  CLFD GL16 .... 175 K5 ◘

Fairfield Pde *CHELTS* GL53.............. 106 D8
Fairfield Park Rd *CHELTS* GL53 ... 106 D8 🖫
Fairfield Rd *CHELTS* GL53.............. 106 D8
  CHEP NP16 .... 288 A8
  LYD GL15 .... 234 A3
  RDLND/MONT BS6 .... 364 D4
Fairfields *CIND* GL14 .... 150 E6 🖫
Fairfield St *CHELTS* GL53 .... 106 D8 🖫
Fairfield Wk *CHELTS* GL53 .... 106 D8
Fairford Cl *KGWD/HNM* BS15...... 367 F4 🖫
Fairford Crs *BRSTK/PCHW* BS34 ... 343 F6
Fairford Rd *CIR* GL7 .... 254 C2
Fairford Wy *GLE* GL4 .... 3 F6 🖫
Fairhaven *YATE/CS* BS37 .... 347 H5 🖫
Fairhaven Av *BWTH/CHD* GL3 ...... 132 C8
Fairhaven Cl *CHELTS* GL53 .... 106 D8 🖫
  RDLND/MONT BS6 .... 364 A2 🖫
Fairhaven St *CHELTS* GL53 .... 106 D8
Fair Lawn *OLD/WMLY/WICK* BS30.... 376 D2
Fairlyn Dr *KGWD/HNM* BS15........ 367 F3
Fairmile Gdns *VGL* GL2 .... 130 D1
Fairmount Rd *CHELTW* GL51 .... 105 K5 🖫
Fairview *CHPMW/MSHF* SN14..... 373 J8
Fairview Cl *CHELTE/BC* GL52 .... 5 D3 🖫
Fair View Cl *RSTROUD/NAIL* GL6... 270 D1 🖫
Fairview Rd *CHELTE/BC* GL52 .... 5 D4 🖫
  KGWD/HNM BS15........................ 367 F6
Fairview St *CHELTE/BC* GL52 .... 4 C3
Fairwater Pk *GLE* GL4 .... 131 F5
Fairway *BRSG/KWL/STAPK* BS4 ... 374 C5
  TEWK GL20 .... 34 D6
Fairway Cl *OLD/WMLY/WICK* BS30 ... 376 C2
Fairways Av *CLFD* GL16 .... 175 K5 🖫
Falcon Cl *BRSTK/PCHW* BS34....... 342 C6
  HNLZ/SM/SNYPK/WT BS9 .... 353 H6
  VGL GL2 .... 102 E8 🖫
Falconbere Rd
  HNLZ/SM/SNYPK/WT BS9 .... 353 J6
Falcondale Wk
  HNLZ/SM/SNYPK/WT BS9 .... 353 J6
Falcon Dr *BRSTK/PCHW* BS34 ...... 342 C6
Falcon Wk *BRSTK/PCHW* BS34 ..... 342 C6
Falcon Wy *THNB/SVB* BS35 .... 316 D4
Faldo Cl *GLE* GL4 .... 159 H1
Falfield Rd
  BRSG/KWL/STAPK BS4 .... 374 B3 🖫
  GL GL1 .... 157 J3
Falfield Wk *HNBRY/STHM* BS10 ... 354 A6 🖫
Falkland Pl *CHELTW* GL51 .... 105 H3
Falkland Rd *RDLND/MONT* BS6 ... 364 D4 🖫
Falkner St *GL* GL1 .... 2 C5
Fallowfield
  OLD/WMLY/WICK BS30 .... 376 D2
Fallows Rd *COTS* GL54 .... 169 H5
Falmouth Rd *HORF/LLZ* BS7 .... 364 C1
Fancy Rd *LYD* GL15 .... 177 J8
Fane Cl *HNBRY/STHM* BS10 .... 353 J2 🖫
Faraday Cl *GL* GL1 .... 3 D6 🖫
Far Handstones
  OLD/WMLY/WICK BS30 .... 376 D2
Faringdon Rd *CHELTW* GL51 .... 105 H7 🖫
Farington Rd
  HNLZ/SM/SNYPK/WT BS9 .... 354 B7
Farleigh Cl *CHELTE/BC* GL52 .... 107 J8 🖫
Farley Cl *BRSTK/PCHW* BS34 .... 343 G7
Farman Cl *COTS* GL54 .... 144 E2
Farm Cl *MANG/FISH* BS16 .... 357 H8 🖫
Farmcote *VGL* GL12 .... 318 C4
Farmcote Cl *RSTROUD/NAIL* GL6.. 244 B2
Farmcote Gdns *COTS* GL54 .... 85 H1
Farm Ct *MANG/FISH* BS16 .... 356 F2 🖫
Farmers La *BDWAY* WR12 .... 17 J4
Farmfield Rd *CHELTW* GL51 .... 133 K1
Farm Hill *TET* GL8 .... 271 K6
Farmhill Crs *STROUD* GL5 .... 214 D6
Farmhill La *STROUD* GL5 .... 214 B6
Farmington Ri *COTS* GL54 .... 169 H4 🖫
Farmington Rd *CHELTW* GL51 ...... 105 J6
  COTS GL54 .... 169 H4 🖫
Farm La *CHELTS* GL53 .... 134 B2
  CHELTW GL51 .... 133 H5
  TET GL8 .... 323 J8
  TEWK GL20 .... 13 J8
  THNB/SVB BS35 .... 341 F8
Farm Lees *WUE* GL12 .... 295 J8
Farm Rd *MANG/FISH* BS16 .... 356 F2 🖫
  MTCHDN GL17 .... 121 H8
  RSTROUD/NAIL GL6 .... 218 C5
Farm St *GL* GL1 .... 2 C5 🖫
Farndale *EVILLE/WHL* BS5 .... 366 A8 🖫
Farrant Av *BWTH/CHD* GL3 .... 103 J8
Farriers Cft *RSTROUD/NAIL* GL6.. 244 B2 🖫
Farriers End *VGL* GL2 .... 157 F4
Farriers Reach *CHELTE/BC* GL52 .. 82 D2 🖫
The Farriers *CIR* GL7 .... 256 D2
Farr's La *STROUD* GL5 .... 214 E7
Far Sandfield *BWTH/CHD* GL3 ...... 132 A1
Farthing Cft *VGL* GL2 .... 128 D2
The Farthings *COTS* GL54 .... 166 B3
Far Wells Rd *RSTROUD/NAIL* GL6... 216 E6
Far Westrip *STNHO* GL10 .... 213 H6

Fauconberg Rd *CHELT* GL50 .... 4 A4 🖫
Faulkner's Cl *CIR* GL7 .... 282 E1
Fawkes Cl *KGWD/HNM* BS15........ 367 H6
Fawkes Pl *STROUD* GL5 .... 214 E7 🖫
Fawley Dr *CHELTE/BC* GL52 .... 107 J2
Featherbed La *THNB/SVB* BS35 ... 291 F8
Featherstone Rd
  MANG/FISH BS16 .... 365 K2 🖫
Feeder Rd *CBRISNE* BS2 .... 365 G8
Felix Rd *EVILLE/WHL* BS5 .... 365 F6
Felstead Rd *HNBRY/STHM* BS10 ... 354 C5
Feltham Rd *MANG/FISH* BS16 ...... 368 E1
Fenhill Cl *MIM* GL56 .... 68 C1
Fennel Cl *GLE* GL4 .... 158 E2
Fennel Dr *ALMDB* BS32 .... 344 A7
Fennell Gv *HNBRY/STHM* BS10 ... 353 J4 🖫
Fennell's Vw *STROUD* GL5 .... 215 G5
Fenton Rd *HORF/LLZ* BS7 .... 364 B2
Fermaine Av
  BRSG/KWL/STAPK BS4 .... 374 C3
Fernbank Rd *RDLND/MONT* BS6.. 364 A4
Fernbrook Cl *MANG/FISH* BS16.... 356 D5
Fern Cl *HNBRY/STHM* BS10 .... 353 K3
Ferndale Av
  OLD/WMLY/WICK BS30 .... 376 A3
Ferndale Cl *CIND* GL14 .... 151 F5 🖫
  VGL GL2 .... 130 D1 🖫
Ferndale Rd *HORF/LLZ* BS7 .... 354 E4
  RSTROUD/NAIL GL6 .... 214 C3 🖫
Ferndales Cl *CHELTW* GL51 .... 133 K1 🖫
Ferndene *ALMDB* BS32................... 343 G4
Ferndown *AVONM* BS11 .... 352 C7 🖫
Ferney *DSLY* GL11 .... 267 G6
Fern Gv *BRSTK/PCHW* BS34 .... 343 H7
Fernhill *ALMDB* BS32 .... 331 F6
Fernhill La *AVONM* BS11.............. 352 D5
Fernhurst Rd *EVILLE/WHL* BS5 .... 365 K5 🖫
Fernihough Av *EVE* WR11 .... 7 H1
Fern Lawn *GLE* GL4 .... 159 F4
Fernleaze *FRCTL/WBN* BS36 .... 345 J8
Fernleigh Crs *CHELTW* GL51 .... 105 J8
Fern Rd *CLFD* GL16 .... 204 C1
  MANG/FISH BS16 .... 366 D1
The Ferns *TET* GL8 .... 302 B7
Fern St *CBRISNE* BS2 .... 364 D5
Ferris Court Vw
  RSTROUD/NAIL GL6 .... 244 B2
Ferry Gdns *VGL* GL2 .... 156 D5 🖫
Ferry St *CBRIS/FH* BS1 .... 364 C8 🖫
Ferry Wy *CHEP* NP16 .... 312 D2 🖫
Festival Rd *STNHO* GL10 .... 212 E7
Fewster Rd *RSTROUD/NAIL* GL6... 270 D2
Fewster Sq *RSTROUD/NAIL* GL6... 270 D2 🖫
Fiddes Rd *RDLND/MONT* BS6 .... 364 A2
Fiddler's Green La *CHELTW* GL51 ... 105 G5
The Fiddle *HGHW* SN6 .... 310 C7
Fidges La *RSTROUD/NAIL* GL6 ..... 216 C8
Field Badgers *CHCAM* GL55 .... 20 E4
Field Cl *CIR* GL7 .... 278 E7
  COTS GL54 .... 62 A5
Fieldcote Dr *BWTH/CHD* GL3 ...... 131 H7
Field Ct *TET* GL8 .... 302 B6
Field Court Dr *VGL* GL2 .... 156 E6
Field Court Gdns *VGL* GL2 .... 156 E6
Fielden *GLE* GL4 .... 159 F3
Field End *BWTH/CHD* GL3 .... 103 J7
Fieldfare *GLE* GL4 .... 159 F1
Field Farm Cl *BRSTK/PCHW* BS34 ... 355 K2
Fieldgate Rd *CHELTE/BC* GL52 .... 83 G2
Field La *CHPMW/MSHF* SN14....... 360 D8
  DSLY GL11 .... 238 B8
  DSLY GL11 .... 239 H7
  DSLY GL11 .... 266 B2
  OLD/WMLY/WICK BS30 .... 375 K3
  THNB/SVB BS35 .... 314 D6
  THNB/SVB BS35 .... 332 E3
Field View Dr *MANG/FISH* BS16 ... 356 C8
Fields La *BDWAY* WR12 .... 18 E3
Fields Rd *COTS* GL54 .... 195 F3
Field View Dr *MANG/FISH* BS16 ... 356 C8
Fieldways *RSTROUD/NAIL* GL6 .... 270 C2
Fiennes Cl *MANG/FISH* BS16 .... 366 E2 🖫
Fiennes Ct *CBRIS/FH* BS1 .... 364 B7 🖫
Fiery La *DSLY* GL11 .... 268 C4
Filbert Cl *GLE* GL4 .... 159 F3 🖫
Filby Dr *BRSTK/PCHW* BS34 .... 343 G6 🖫
Filton Av *BRSTK/PCHW* BS34 .... 355 F3
  HORF/LLZ BS7 .... 354 C8
Filton Gv *HORF/LLZ* BS7 .... 354 C8
Filton La *BRSTK/PCHW* BS34 .... 355 H4
Filton Rd *BRSTK/PCHW* BS34 ...... 355 H4
  HORF/LLZ BS7 .... 354 D7
  MANG/FISH BS16 .... 355 K5
Filton Wy *GLE* GL4 .... 3 F1
Filwood Cl *MANG/FISH* BS16 .... 366 B3 🖫
Filwood Dr *KGWD/HNM* BS15 ...... 367 H5
Filwood Rd *MANG/FISH* BS16 ...... 366 A3

Finch Cl *THNB/SVB* BS35 .... 316 C4
Finchcroft La *CHELTE/BC* GL52 ... 107 J3
Finch Rd *VGL* GL2 .... 103 F8
  YATE/CS BS37 .... 347 H6
Finlay Pl *GLE* GL4 .... 158 B1 🖫
Finlay Rd *GLE* GL4 .... 158 B1
Finstock Cl *CHELTW* GL51 .... 105 K6 🖫
Fircroft Cl *GLE* GL4 .... 131 H6
Fircroft Rd *VGL* GL2 .... 130 B1 🖫
Fire Engine La
  FRCTL/WBN BS36 .... 345 K7 🖫
Firethorne Cl *VGL* GL2 .... 130 D1 🖫
Firework Cl *KGWD/HNM* BS15...... 367 H6
Firgrove Crs *YATE/CS* BS37 .... 347 J4
Fir Rd *CHPMW/MSHF* SN14 .... 373 F8
Firs Cl *CHNTN* OX7 .... 118 D4
Firs Rd *RSTROUD/NAIL* GL6 .... 270 E1
First Av *BRSG/KWL/STAPK* BS4 ... 374 D1
  DSLY GL11 .... 267 G6
The Firs *CHELTW* GL51 .... 82 B7
Fir Tree Cl *BRSTK/PCHW* BS34 .... 342 C7
  CHELTE/BC GL52 .... 5 E1
Fir Tree La *EVILLE/WHL* BS5 .... 366 A8
Fir View Rd *CIND* GL14 .... 178 C2
Firwood Dr *GLE* GL4 .... 158 A3
Fisher Av *KGWD/HNM* BS15......... 367 G5
Fisher Cl *COTS* GL54 .... 92 C7 🖫
Fisherman's Wk *CHEP* NP16 .... 312 B1 🖫
Fisher Rd *KGWD/HNM* BS15......... 367 G5
Fishers *BRKLY* GL13 .... 264 C5
Fishers Wy *STROUD* GL5 .... 242 C2
Fish Hl *BDWAY* WR12....................... 19 G7
Fishponds Rd *EVILLE/WHL* BS5 ... 365 G4
Fishpool Hl *HNBRY/STHM* BS10 ... 353 K2
Fitchett Wk *HNBRY/STHM* BS10 ... 353 H5 🖫
Fitzhamon Pk *TEWK* GL20 .... 34 E7
Fitzhardinge Wy *BRKLY* GL13 ...... 264 A2
Fitzroy Rd *MANG/FISH* BS16 .... 366 B4
Five Acre Rd *MANG/FISH* BS16 .... 355 K7
Five Acres *DSLY* GL11 .... 266 E6
Five Mile Dr *MIM* GL56 .... 43 G3
Five Trees Ct *TET* GL8 .... 302 B6 🖫
Flaxley Rd *GLE* GL4 .... 157 K3
Flaxley St *CIND* GL14.................... 151 F6
Flaxman Cl *HORF/LLZ* BS7 .... 355 F8
Flaxpits La *FRCTL/WBN* BS36 ...... 344 D8
Flecker's Dr *CHELTW* GL51 .... 105 K7
Fleece Rd *BDWAY* WR12 .... 18 D5
Fleet La *TEWK* GL20 .... 12 E8
  TEWK GL20 .... 34 A1
Fleet Rd *TEWK* GL20 .... 12 E8
Fleming Cl *VGL* GL2 .... 102 E8
Flint Rd *CHELTW* GL51 .... 105 J8
Florence Pk *ALMDB* BS32 .... 343 F1
Florence Rd *MANG/FISH* BS16 ..... 366 E3
Florida Bvd *CIR* GL7 .... 283 F1
Florida Dr *CHELTE/BC* GL52 .... 107 J2
Flowers Hl *BRSG/KWL/STAPK* BS4 ... 374 D5
Flowers Hill Cl
  BRSG/KWL/STAPK BS4 .... 374 D5 🖫
Flower Wy *VGL* GL2 .... 3 F1
The Folders *LYD* GL15 .... 234 B3 🖫
Foley Cl *GLE* GL4 .... 157 K3 🖫
Foley Ri *RTEWK/TIB* GL19.............. 76 E8
Foley Rd *NWNT* GL18 .... 73 J6
Folland Av *BWTH/CHD* GL3 .... 131 K8
Folland Dr *COTS* GL54 .... 144 E1
Folliot Cl *MANG/FISH* BS16.......... 356 A6
Folly Bridge Cl *YATE/CS* BS37 ..... 347 F4 🖫
Folly Brook Rd *MANG/FISH* BS16... 357 G4
Folly Fld *COTS* GL54 .... 115 J7 🖫
Folly La *CBRISNE* BS2 .... 364 E8
  CHELT GL50 .... 4 B2
  CLFD GL16 .... 147 J5
  STROUD GL5 .... 214 E6
Folly Ri *STROUD* GL5 .... 215 F5
Folly Rd *YATE/CS* BS37 .... 345 F2
The Folly *MANG/FISH* BS16 .... 357 F7
Fontana Cl *OLD/WMLY/WICK* BS30... 376 C5
Fonthill Rd *HNBRY/STHM* BS10... 354 B4
Fontmell Cl *HGRV/WHIT* BS14 ..... 374 C7 🖫
Fontwell Dr *MANG/FISH* BS16 ..... 357 F5
Footes La *FRCTL/WBN* BS36 .... 345 H7
Footshill Cl *KGWD/HNM* BS15 ..... 366 C7
Footshill Dr *KGWD/HNM* BS15..... 366 C7
Footshill Rd *KGWD/HNM* BS15 .... 366 C8
Fop St *DSLY* GL11 .... 268 A5
Forbes Cl *GLE* GL4 .... 131 H8
Forde Cl *OLD/WMLY/WICK* BS30 .. 376 A1 🖫
Ford St *EVILLE/WHL* BS5 .... 365 G8 🖫
Forest Av *MANG/FISH* BS16 .... 366 B3
Forest Cl *CLFD* GL16 .... 146 E8
Forest Dr *HNBRY/STHM* BS10 ...... 354 A5
Forest Edge *KGWD/HNM* BS15 .... 375 H2
Foresters Rd *TEWK* GL20 .... 57 H2
Forest Hills *ALMDB* BS32 .... 343 F4
Forest Patch *CLFD* GL16............... 175 J1
Fore St *HGHW* SN6 .... 308 D5
Forest Ri *CIND* GL14 .... 151 G5
  MTCHDN GL17 .... 148 E2
Forest Rd *CIND* GL14.................... 151 F6

CLFD GL16 ..... 176 A7
CLFD GL16 ..... 176 B1
KGWD/HNM BS15 ..... 366 D7
LYD GL15 ..... 205 F5
LYD GL15 ..... 234 A1
MANG/FISH BS16 ..... 366 B3
MTCHDN GL17 ..... 121 K8
WUE GL2 ..... 318 D2
Forest Vale Rd CIND GL14 ..... 150 D3
Forest Vw CIND GL14 ..... 178 E1
Forest View Rd BRKLY GL13 ..... 264 C3
GLE GL4 ..... 158 A5
Forest Wk KGWD/HNM BS15 ..... 366 C7
MANG/FISH BS16 ..... 366 B4
The Forty HGHW SN6 ..... 310 D7
Forge HI MTCHDN GL17 ..... 120 D8
MTCHDN GL17 ..... 148 E1
Forge La NWNT GL18 ..... 75 C3
Forsdene Wk CLFD GL16 ..... 176 B4
Forsythe Wy GLE GL4 ..... 3 F6
Forsythia CI BWTH/CHD GL3 ..... 103 J8 [2]
Fortey Rd COTS GL54 ..... 169 G4
Fortfields DSLY GL11 ..... 267 F6 [1]
Fortina CI CHELT GL50 ..... 106 C1 [1]
Fort La DSLY GL11 ..... 267 F6
The Fortress DSLY GL11 ..... 267 F6
Fort View Ter STROUD GL5 ..... 214 A8
Forty Acre La STROUD GL5 ..... 215 J7
THNB/SVB BS35 ..... 332 A3
The Forty HGHW SN6 ..... 310 D7
Foscombe La RTEWK/TIB GL19 ..... 77 F5
Fosscross La COTS GL54 ..... 195 J8
Fosse CI CIR GL7 ..... 250 A5
GLE GL4 ..... 131 C8
Fossedale Av HGRV/WHIT BS14 ..... 374 C8
Fosse Folly COTS GL54 ..... 92 C5 [1]
Fosse La COTS GL54 ..... 92 C5 [1]
Fosseway Av MIM GL56 ..... 69 K2
Fosseway CI MIM GL56 ..... 70 A2
Fosseway Dr MIM GL56 ..... 70 A2
Foss Fld CIR GL7 ..... 191 G6
Foss La THNB/SVB BS35 ..... 291 J7
Foster CI CHELTE/BC GL52 ..... 83 C1
Foster St EVILLE/WHL BS5 ..... 365 F4
Foundry La EVILLE/WHL BS5 ..... 365 K4
Foundry Rd CIND GL14 ..... 150 D5
Fountain Crs WUE GL12 ..... 297 G8
Fountaine CI EVILLE/WHL BS5 .. 365 G4 [10]
Fountains Dr
OLD/WMLY/WICK BS30 ..... 367 F9
Fountain St RSTROUD/NAIL GL6 ..... 270 D3
Fountain Wy CHEP NP16 ..... 312 B2 [3]
Four Acre Av MANG/FISH BS16 ..... 356 C6
Four Acre CI HGHW SN6 ..... 308 D6
Four Acre Crs MANG/FISH BS16 ..... 356 E5
Four Acre Rd MANG/FISH BS16 ..... 356 C6
Fourth Av GLE GL4 ..... 267 C6
HORF/LLZ BS7 ..... 354 E4
Fowler's HI CIR GL7 ..... 226 D8
Fowler's Rd CHNTN OX7 ..... 119 G2
Fox Av YATE/CS BS37 ..... 347 F4
Foxborough Gdns ALMDB BS32 .. 343 H4 [3]
Fox CI BWTH/CHD GL3 ..... 159 H1
STROUD GL5 ..... 213 J7
Foxcote KGWD/HNM BS15 ..... 367 F7
VGL GL2 ..... 130 D1 [3]
Foxcote HI SHPSTR CV36 ..... 11 F3
Foxcott HGHW SN6 ..... 310 C2
Fox Ct OLD/WMLY/WICK BS30 ..... 376 A3
Foxcroft CI ALMDB BS32 ..... 343 H3
Foxcroft Rd EVILLE/WHL BS5 ..... 365 H6
Fox Den Rd BRSTK/PCHW BS34 ..... 355 H3
Fox Elms Rd GLE GL4 ..... 158 A4
Foxe Rd FRCTL/WBN BS36 ..... 345 G6
Foxes Bank Dr CIR GL7 ..... 249 H8 [1]
RSTROUD/NAIL GL6 ..... 244 C2
Foxes Bridge Rd CIND GL14 ..... 150 D5
Foxes CI COTS GL54 ..... 115 H8 [1]
RSTROUD/NAIL GL6 ..... 244 C2
Foxes Dell RSTROUD/NAIL GL6 ..... 270 C1
Foxfield Av ALMDB BS32 ..... 343 H3
Foxglove CI GLE GL4 ..... 159 C1
MANG/FISH BS16 ..... 365 J2 [1]
THNB/SVB BS35 ..... 316 D4 [3]
Foxglove Wk CLFD GL16 ..... 176 A7
Foxgrove Dr CHELTE/BC GL52 ..... 5 E4
Fox HI TET GL8 ..... 302 C7
Foxholes La ALMDB BS32 ..... 331 C3
Foxleaze HGHW SN6 ..... 310 D5
Foxleigh Crs VGL GL2 ..... 131 C1 [3]
Foxmoor CHELTE/BC GL52 ..... 82 E2 [1]
Foxmoor La STROUD GL5 ..... 213 J6
Fox's La CLFD GL16 ..... 176 B4
Foxtail CI GLE GL4 ..... 158 C2
Foxwell Dr BWTH/CHD GL3 ..... 131 J6
Fraley Rd
HNLZ/SM/SNYPK/WT BS9 ..... 353 J7
Frampton Ct
OLD/WMLY/WICK BS30 ..... 376 A2 [1]
Frampton Crs MANG/FISH BS16 ..... 366 C2
Frampton Dr BDWAY WR12 ..... 18 E2 [1]
Frampton End Rd
FRCTL/WBN BS36 ..... 345 J5
Frampton Ms CHELTW GL51 ..... 105 F7 [2]
Frampton Rd GL GL1 ..... 2 B6
France La BAD GL9 ..... 338 A4

Francis PI OLD/WMLY/WICK BS30.... 376 A2
Francis Rd HNBRY/STHM BS10 .... 354 A6 [1]
Francis St CHELTS GL53 ..... 4 B6
Francis Wy OLD/WMLY/WICK BS30.. 367 K8
Francombe Gv
HNBRY/STHM BS10 ..... 354 C8
Frank Brookes Rd
CHELTW GL51 ..... 106 A2 [1]
Franklin La CBRISNE BS2 ..... 364 D5 [7]
Franklin St CBRISNE BS2 ..... 364 D5
Frazier's Folly CIR GL7 ..... 278 D2
Freame CI RSTROUD/NAIL GL6 ..... 244 B2
Frederick Thomas Rd DSLY GL11 .. 266 C2
Freeland Buildings
EVILLE/WHL BS5 ..... 365 G4 [11]
Freemans CI TEWK GL20 ..... 12 D7 [1]
Freemantle Gdns
EVILLE/WHL BS5 ..... 365 G3 [1]
Freemantle Rd EVILLE/WHL BS5 . 365 G3 [2]
Freestone Rd CBRISNE BS2 ..... 364 E8 [1]
Free Tank CBRISNE BS2 ..... 364 D8
Freezinghill La
OLD/WMLY/WICK BS30 ..... 378 D3
Fremantle La
RDLND/MONT BS6 ..... 364 B5 [1]
Fremantle Rd
RDLND/MONT BS6 ..... 364 B5 [3]
Frenchay HI MANG/FISH BS16 ..... 356 B7
Frenchay Park Rd
MANG/FISH BS16 ..... 355 K8
Frenchay Rd MANG/FISH BS16 ..... 356 C7
French La CLFD GL16 ..... 174 E7
MONM NP25 ..... 174 B6
Freshland Wy KGWD/HNM BS15... 366 D6
Fretherne Rd GL GL1 ..... 157 K3
Frewin CI CHELTW GL51 ..... 105 H4
Frewins La CIND GL14 ..... 125 K8
Friars CI CHELT GL50 ..... 134 B1 [1]
Friar's Wk NWNT GL18 ..... 73 J5
Friary Grange Pk
FRCTL/WBN BS36 ..... 344 E8
Friary Rd GLE GL4 ..... 131 G8
HORF/LLZ BS7 ..... 364 B5
Fridays Ham La HGHW SN6 ..... 309 F3
Friday St RSTROUD/NAIL GL6 ..... 187 H6 [1]
RSTROUD/NAIL GL6 ..... 243 J8
VGL GL2 ..... 181 G3
Fripp CI EVILLE/WHL BS5 ..... 365 F8 [3]
Frith La WUE GL12 ..... 335 J3
The Frith RSTROUD/NAIL GL6 ..... 244 B3
Frithwood CI
RSTROUD/NAIL GL6 ..... 244 B3 [1]
Frithwood Pk
RSTROUD/NAIL GL6 ..... 244 B3 [2]
Frocester HI STNHO GL10 ..... 240 C5
Frog Furlong La VGL GL2 ..... 103 F5
Frog La CBRIS/FH BS1 ..... 364 A8 [5]
DSLY GL11 ..... 296 A1
FRCTL/WBN BS36 ..... 346 A6
RTEWK/TIB GL19 ..... 125 J2
SHPSTR CV36 ..... 11 F3
STNHO GL10 ..... 240 A4
Frogmarsh La STROUD GL5 ..... 242 B6
Frogmore La RTEWK/TIB GL19 ..... 125 J2 [1]
Frogmore St CBRIS/FH BS1 ..... 364 A8 [3]
Frome Av STROUD GL5 ..... 214 C8
Frome Ct THNB/SVB BS35 ..... 316 C6
Frome Gdns STROUD GL5 ..... 214 A8
Frome Gln FRCTL/WBN BS36 ..... 356 E2
Frome Park Rd STROUD GL5 ..... 214 C8
Frome PI MANG/FISH BS16 ..... 365 J1 [1]
Frome Rd YATE/CS BS37 ..... 348 A5
Fromeside STROUD GL5 ..... 214 D8
Frome St CBRISNE BS2 ..... 364 D6 [7]
Frome Valley Wy MANG/FISH BS16.. 356 A7
Frome Valley Walkway
FRCTL/WBN BS36 ..... 346 A4
FRCTL/WBN BS36 ..... 356 E3
MANG/FISH BS16 ..... 356 C7
YATE/CS BS37 ..... 346 E3
Frome Valley Wy YATE/CS BS37 ..... 348 C6
Frome Vw FRCTL/WBN BS36 ..... 345 H7
Frome Wy FRCTL/WBN BS36 ..... 356 E1
Front St SHPSTR CV36 ..... 11 G2
STNHO GL10 ..... 240 E8
Froomshaw Rd MANG/FISH BS16... 356 A7
Fry's CI MANG/FISH BS16 ..... 365 H2 [1]
Frys Rd KGWD/HNM BS15 ..... 366 A4 [3]
KGWD/HNM BS15 ..... 366 E5 [3]
Fulbrook CI CHELTW GL51 ..... 105 H1 [2]
Fullers Av HGHW SN6 ..... 310 D6
Fuller's La RTEWK/TIB GL19 ..... 76 D6
Fulmar CI THNB/SVB BS35 ..... 316 D4 [3]
Fulton Rd COTS GL54 ..... 145 F2
Furber CI EVILLE/WHL BS5.... ..... 366 B8
Furber Rdg EVILLE/WHL BS5 ..... 366 B8
Furber Rd EVILLE/WHL BS5 ..... 366 B8
Furber V EVILLE/WHL BS5 ..... 366 B8
Furlong La CHELTE/BC GL52 ..... 83 F5
Furlong Meadow SHPSTR CV36 ..... 25 F2
Furlong Rd GL GL1 ..... 2 C6
The Furlong
HNLZ/SM/SNYPK/WT BS9 ..... 366 A1
Furnace CI CIND GL14 ..... 150 E6 [1]
Furnace La NWNT GL18 ..... 73 H4

Furnace Va LYD GL15 ..... 207 G4
Furnwood EVILLE/WHL BS5.... ..... 366 A8
Furze Cft VGL GL2 ..... 157 F7
Furze Hill Rd SHPSTR CV36 ..... 25 F2
Furze La CHCAM GL55 ..... 9 H7
Furze Rd MANG/FISH BS16 ..... 366 C3
The Furze GLE GL4 ..... 158 C2
Furzewood KGWD/HNM BS15.... 367 F6

G

Gabb La RTEWK/TIB GL19 ..... 56 A8
Gable CI THNB/SVB BS35 ..... 341 J4
Gable Point CHELTE/BC GL52.... 83 H3
Gable Rd EVILLE/WHL BS5 ..... 364 E5 [1]
Gadshill Dr BRSTK/PCHW BS34 ..... 355 J1
EVILLE/WHL BS5 ..... 365 G3
Gadshill Rd CHELTS GL53 ..... 135 H3
EVILLE/WHL BS5 ..... 365 G3
Gadwell Rd TEWK GL20 ..... 57 K1
Gages CI KGWD/HNM BS15 ..... 367 F7
Gages Rd KGWD/HNM BS15 ..... 367 F7
Gainsborough Dr GL GL1 ..... 157 J4
Gallivan CI BRSTK/PCHW BS34.... 343 F7
Gallops La CHELTE/BC GL52 ..... 107 K5
Gambier Parry Gdns VGL GL2 ..... 3 D1
Gambles La CHELTE/BC GL52 ..... 83 J4
Gambril La WUE GL12 ..... 318 A1
Ganborough Rd MIM GL56 ..... 68 D6
Gander La TEWK GL20 ..... 36 B7
TEWK GL20 ..... 57 H1
Gannaway La TEWK GL20 ..... 34 A7
Gannet CI BWTH/CHD GL3 ..... 160 E1 [3]
Gannicox Rd STROUD GL5 ..... 214 C7
Ganzell La DSLY GL11 ..... 267 C3
Garden City Wy CHEP NP16 ..... 288 A6 [3]
Garden CI CHCAM GL55 ..... 9 F3
CIR GL7 ..... 249 J7 [3]
EVE WR11 ..... 38 C1
Gardeners Wy NWNT GL18 ..... 73 H6 [1]
STNHO GL10 ..... 241 G2
Gardenia Gv CHELTW GL51 ..... 133 K1
Garden Rd CHELTS GL53 ..... 135 G2
The Gardens CHELTE/BC GL52 ..... 4 C1 [1]
MANG/FISH BS16 ..... 355 K5
The Garden STROUD GL5 ..... 242 C8
Garden Wy VGL GL2 ..... 3 F1
Gardiner CI RSTROUD/NAIL GL6.... 244 C2
Gardiners CI BWTH/CHD GL3 ..... 103 J8 [1]
Gardner's La CHELTW GL51 ..... 4 A1
Garfield Rd EVILLE/WHL BS5 ..... 366 A6
Garlands Rd LYD GL15 ..... 232 F2 [1]
Garnalls Rd GLE GL4 ..... 158 E2
Garnett PI MANG/FISH BS16 ..... 357 F7
Garrett Dr ALMDB BS32 ..... 343 H7 [2]
Garvey CI CHEP NP16 ..... 312 B2
The Gaskins HORF/LLZ BS7 ..... 364 E1 [1]
Gas La CBRISNE BS2 ..... 364 E8
Gassons Rd CIR GL7 ..... 285 C1
The Gastons AVONM BS11 ..... 352 C6
Gasworks La COTS GL54 ..... 143 H1
Gatcombe CI CHELTE/BC GL52 ..... 82 E3 [1]
Gatcombe Dr BRSTK/PCHW BS34.... 355 J2
Gatesby Md BRSTK/PCHW BS34 ..... 355 J1
Gatmeres Rd GLE GL4 ..... 158 E3 [1]
Gatton Rd CBRISNE BS2 ..... 364 E5
Gatton Wy GLE GL4 ..... 131 H5
Gaunt's Earthcott La ALMDB BS32.. 344 B1
Gaunt's La CBRIS/FH BS1 ..... 364 A8 [2]
Gaunts Rd YATE/CS BS37 ..... 347 K6
Gayner Rd HORF/LLZ BS7 ..... 354 E5
Gays Rd KGWD/HNM BS15 ..... 375 C2
Gaythorne Crs YATE/CS BS37 ..... 347 F4
Gazelle CI GLE GL4 ..... 157 F4
Gazzard CI FRCTL/WBN BS36 ..... 344 E7
Gee Moors KGWD/HNM BS15 ..... 367 F7 [3]
Genista Wy CHELTW GL51 ..... 133 K1 [7]
George CI RSTROUD/NAIL GL6 ..... 187 H6 [3]
George Dowty Dr TEWK GL20 ..... 34 D5 [1]
George La CHCAM GL55 ..... 20 E4
CHPMW/MSHF SN14 ..... 371 J5
CIND GL14 ..... 151 J4
George Readings Wy
CHELTW GL51 ..... 105 K2
George Rd LYD GL15 ..... 206 A3
George St EVILLE/WHL BS5 ..... 365 G6 [3]
GL GL1 ..... 3 D3 [3]
RSTROUD/NAIL GL6 ..... 216 E5
RSTROUD/NAIL GL6 ..... 270 E2
STROUD GL5 ..... 214 E7
George Whitefield CI GLE GL4 ..... 158 E2 [3]
George Whitefield Ct
CBRIS/FH BS1 ..... 364 C7 [3]
Georgian CI GLE GL4 ..... 159 C3
Geralds Wy RSTROUD/NAIL GL6 ..... 244 C3
Gere CI GLE GL4 ..... 157 K5
Gerrard CI COTS GL54 ..... 145 F3
Gerrards Rd SHPSTR CV36 ..... 25 F1
Gerrish Av EVILLE/WHL BS5 ..... 365 G6
MANG/FISH BS16 ..... 367 F1
Gervase Rd COTS GL54 ..... 62 D7
Gibraltar Wy CHEP NP16 ..... 312 D2

Gibson Cl *STROUD* GL5 .... 215 H7
Gibson Rd *BWTH/CHD* GL3 .... 103 C7
   RDLND/MONT BS6 .... 364 B5
Giddynap La *STROUD* GL5 .... 242 C7
Giffard Wy *CHELTS* GL53 .... 134 C2
Gifford Cl *VGL* GL2 .... 130 E1
   YATE/CS BS37 .... 334 C6
Gifford Rd *HNBRY/STHM* BS10 .... 353 H2
Gilbert Hl *BRKLY* GL13 .... 264 A2
Gilbert Rd *EVILLE/WHL* BS5 .... 365 G6
   KGWD/HNM BS15 .... 366 D5
   VGL GL2 .... 130 E1
Gilberts La *GLE* GL4 .... 158 B7
Gilda Crs *HGRV/WHIT* BS14 .... 374 A8
Gilder Rd *CHELTE/BC* GL52 .... 83 F4
Gilders Paddock
   CHELTE GL52 .... 83 F2
Giles Av *HGHW* SN6 .... 310 D7
Giles Cox *VGL* GL2 .... 157 F6
Gillard Cl *KGWD/HNM* BS15 .... 366 B6
Gillard Rd *KGWD/HNM* BS15 .... 366 B6
Gill Av *MANG/FISH* BS16 .... 356 B8
Gillett Cl *COTS* GL54 .... 85 J1
Gillingham Hl *EVILLE/WHL* BS5 .... 375 G1
Gillingstool *THNB/SVB* BS35 .... 316 C6
Gillray Cl *HORF/LLZ* BS7 .... 355 F8
Gilpin Av *GLE* GL4 .... 131 H5
Gilpin Cl *KGWD/HNM* BS15 .... 367 F5
Gilroy Cl *OLD/WMLY/WICK* BS30 ... 376 C3
Gilslake Av *HNBRY/STHM* BS10 .... 353 K3
Gimson Cl *GLE* GL4 .... 157 K4
Gipsy La *RSTROUD/NAIL* GL6 .... 245 F5
   STNHO GL10 .... 240 E5
Gipsy Patch La *BRSTK/PCHW* BS34 .. 343 G8
The Glades *EVILLE/WHL* BS5 .... 365 J4
Gladiator Cl *BWTH/CHD* GL3 .... 160 C1
Gladstone Dr *MANG/FISH* BS16 ...... 366 E3
Gladstone La *FRCTL/WBN* BS36 ...... 345 J7
Gladstone Rd *CHELTS* GL53 .... 135 C1
   GL GL1 .... 129 J8
   HGRV/WHIT BS14 .... 374 A8
   KGWD/HNM BS15 .... 366 D5
Gladstone St *EVILLE/WHL* BS5 .... 365 H7
   MANG/FISH BS16 .... 366 D3
Glaisdale Rd *MANG/FISH* BS16........ 366 A1
Glamorgan Rd *CHELTW* GL51 .... 105 J8
Glanville Gdns *KGWD/HNM* BS15 ... 366 E7
Glass House La *CBRISNE* BS2 .... 374 A1
Glastonbury Cl
   OLD/WMLY/WICK BS30 .... 376 A1
Glebe Cl *CIR* GL7 .... 249 H2
   COTS GL54 .... 92 C6
   MTCHDN GL17 .... 123 G3
   NWNT GL18 .... 73 H5
   VGL GL2 .... 210 D3
Glebe Ct *NWNT* GL18 .... 73 H5
Glebe Farm Ct *CHELTW* GL51 .... 133 K1
Glebe Fld *ALMDB* BS32 .... 342 E1
Glebeland Dr *TEWK* GL20 .... 13 K8
Glebelands Rd
   BRSTK/PCHW BS34 .... 354 E3
Glebe La *CIR* GL7 .... 276 B7
Glebe Orch *LED* HR8 .... 26 B8
Glebe Rd *BDWAY* WR12 .... 16 D5
   CHELTE/BC GL52 .... 5 F1
   EVILLE/WHL BS5 .... 365 J6
   NWNT GL18 .... 73 H6
   RSTROUD/NAIL GL6 .... 243 K8
The Glebe *CIR* GL7 .... 246 D3
   THNB/SVB BS35 .... 328 E2
Glebe Wy *NWNT* GL18 .... 73 H5
Gledemoor Dr *FRCTL/WBN* BS36 .... 345 K7
Glena Av *BRSG/KWL/STAPK* BS4 .... 374 A4
Glenarm Rd
   BRSG/KWL/STAPK BS4 .... 374 C4
Glenarm Wk
   BRSG/KWL/STAPK BS4 .... 374 D4
Glenburn Rd *KGWD/HNM* BS15 ...... 366 B5
Glencairn Av *GL* GL1 .... 157 J5
Glencairn Ct *CHELTW* GL51 .... 106 A6
Glencairn Park Rd *CHELTW* GL51 .... 106 A6
Glencoe La *MTCHDN* GL17 .... 123 C7
Glen Ct *STNHO* GL10 .... 213 F6
Glencoyne Sq *HNBRY/STHM* BS10 .. 344 A4
Glendale *MANG/FISH* BS16 .... 356 E6
   MANG/FISH BS16 .... 366 C3
Glendare St *EVILLE/WHL* BS5.......... 365 G8
Glendower Cl *BWTH/CHD* GL3 .... 103 H6
Gleneagles *YATE/CS* BS37 .... 347 F5
Gleneagles Dr
   HNBRY/STHM BS10 .... 353 F3
Gleneagles Rd
   OLD/WMLY/WICK BS30 .... 367 H8
Glenfall *YATE/CS* BS37 .... 347 F7
Glenfall St *CHELTE/BC* GL52 .... 5 D3
Glenfall Wy *CHELTE/BC* GL52 .... 107 H8
Glenfrome Rd *CBRISNE* BS2............ 364 E4
   EVILLE/WHL BS5 .... 365 F3
Glen La *BRSG/KWL/STAPK* BS4....... 374 C4
Glenlea Cv *CHELTW* GL51 .... 133 K1
Glen Pk *EVILLE/WHL* BS5 .... 365 G4
Glen Park Crs *STROUD* GL5 .... 242 C3
Glen Park Gdns *EVILLE/WHL* BS5 .... 366 A6
Glenroy Av *KGWD/HNM* BS15 .... 366 B5
Glensanda Ct *CHELT* GL50 .... 4 B5

Glenside Cl *MANG/FISH* BS16......... 356 C7
Glenside Pk *MANG/FISH* BS16 .... 365 J1
The Glen *KGWD/HNM* BS15 .... 375 G2
   YATE/CS BS37 .... 347 G4
Glenthorne Cl *STNHO* GL10 .... 213 F5
Glentworth Rd
   RDLND/MONT BS6 .... 364 A4
Glenwood *MANG/FISH* BS16 .... 366 C3
Glenwood Dr
   OLD/WMLY/WICK BS30 .... 376 C2
Glenwood Rd *HNBRY/STHM* BS10 .. 354 A7
Glevum Cl *VGL* GL2 .... 3 F1
Glevum Wy *GLE* GL4 .... 159 G2
Gloster Ades Rd *EVE* WR11 .... 7 F2
Gloster Av *EVILLE/WHL* BS5 .... 365 H3
Gloucester Cl *BRSTK/PCHW* BS34 ... 355 H1
   CHCAM GL55 .... 9 F3
Gloucester La *CBRISNE* BS2 .... 364 D7
Gloucester Pl *CHELTE/BC* GL52 .... 4 C3
Gloucester Rd *ALMDB* BS32 .... 343 G1
   BRKLY GL13 .... 235 J6
   BRSTK/PCHW BS34 .... 343 F5
   CBATH/BATHN BA1 .... 379 K6
   CHELTW GL51 .... 104 E7
   CHEP NP16 .... 288 C4
   CIR GL7 .... 249 G2
   CLFD GL16 .... 175 K4
   COTS GL54 .... 137 H3
   HORF/LLZ BS7 .... 364 B4
   MANG/FISH BS16 .... 366 E3
   MTCHDN GL17 .... 123 H5
   NWNT GL18 .... 74 E4
   RSTROUD/NAIL GL6 .... 187 H4
   RTEWK/TIB GL19 .... 53 H8
   RTEWK/TIB GL19 .... 57 H7
   STNHO GL10 .... 213 F6
   TEWK GL20 .... 57 H2
   THNB/SVB BS35 .... 316 C4
   THNB/SVB BS35 .... 331 K4
Gloucester Rd North
   BRSTK/PCHW BS34 .... 354 C4
   HORF/LLZ BS7 .... 354 D5
Gloucestershire Wy
   BWTH/CHD GL3 .... 132 D2
   CHELTE/BC GL52 .... 61 H6
   CHEP NP16 .... 288 A6
   CLFD GL16 .... 177 F5
   COTS GL54 .... 66 A5
   COTS GL54 .... 87 F1
   COTS GL54 .... 91 K4
   COTS GL54 .... 114 D7
   COTS GL54 .... 136 C8
   COTS GL54 .... 141 G2
   COTS GL54 .... 164 A1
   LYD GL15 .... 204 E5
   LYD GL15 .... 259 J1
   MTCHDN GL17 .... 96 B8
   RTEWK/TIB GL19 .... 125 G2
Gloucester St *CBRISNE* BS2 .... 364 C6
   CIR GL7 .... 249 H4
   COTS GL54 .... 85 H2
   EVILLE/WHL BS5 .... 365 H3
   NWNT GL18 .... 73 K6
   STROUD GL5 .... 214 E7
   WUE GL12 .... 296 E6
Glynbridge Gdns *CHELTW* GL51...... 105 K1
Glyndthorpe Gv *CHELTW* GL51 ...... 133 J1
Glynfield Ri *STROUD* GL5 .... 213 J7
Glynrosa Rd *CHELTS* GL53 .... 135 H1
Goddard Wy *GLE* GL4 .... 157 K4
Godfrey Cl *CHELTW* GL51 .... 106 A7
Godfrey Ct
   OLD/WMLY/WICK BS30 .... 376 A2
Godwin Rd *COTS* GL54 .... 62 D7
Goffenton Dr *MANG/FISH* BS16 ..... 356 B8
Goldcrest Ct *STNHO* GL10 .... 213 F6
Goldcrest Rd *YATE/CS* BS37 .... 347 H1
Golden Cl *GL* GL1 .... 157 J4
Golden Farm Rd *CIR* GL7 .... 250 A6
Golden La *WUE* GL12 .... 320 D2
Golden Miller Rd *CHELT* GL50 .... 106 C1
Golden V *BWTH/CHD* GL3 .... 103 K8
Golden Vw *STROUD* GL5 .... 243 J5
Golden Valley La
   OLD/WMLY/WICK BS30 .... 377 C5
Goldfinch Wy *MANG/FISH* BS16 ..... 368 E2
Goldney Av
   OLD/WMLY/WICK BS30 .... 367 J7
Goldsborough Cl *GLE* GL4 .... 3 F6
Goldsbury Wk *AVONM* BS11 .... 352 C5
Goldsmith Rd *CHELTW* GL51 .... 105 J4
Golf Club La *BWTH/CHD* GL3 .... 160 A2
Golf Course La *BRSTK/PCHW* BS34 . 354 D5
Golf Course Rd
   RSTROUD/NAIL GL6 .... 187 H5
Gooch St *OLD/WMLY/WICK* BS30 .. 376 D3
Goodhind St *EVILLE/WHL* BS5 .... 364 E6
Goodier's La *TEWK* GL20 .... 12 E8
Goodmoor Crs *BWTH/CHD* GL3...... 103 J8
Goodneston Rd *MANG/FISH* BS16 .. 366 A5
Goodrich Hl *RTEWK/TIB* GL19 .... 77 G6
Goodridge Av *VGL* GL2 .... 157 G3
Goodring Hd *AVONM* BS11 .... 352 C5
Good Shepherd Cl
   HORF/LLZ BS7 .... 364 A2

Goodwin Ct *GL* GL1 .... 2 C6
Goodwood Gdns
   MANG/FISH BS16 .... 357 F5
Goodyere St *GL* GL1 .... 2 C5
Goose Acre *ALMDB* BS32 .... 343 K8
   ALMDB BS32 .... 344 A8
Gooseacre La *CIR* GL7 .... 249 J4
Goosegreen *FRCTL/WBN* BS36 ...... 345 H6
Goose Gn *OLD/WMLY/WICK* BS30 . 367 J5
   YATE/CS BS37 .... 347 G3
Goose Green Wy *YATE/CS* BS37 ..... 346 E2
Goose La *CIND* GL14 .... 154 D6
Gopshill La *COTS* GL54 .... 62 A5
Gordon Av *EVILLE/WHL* BS5........... 365 J5
Gordon Cl *EVILLE/WHL* BS5 .... 365 J5
   VGL GL2 .... 128 E1
Gordon Rd *CBRISNE* BS2 .... 364 D5
   CHELTS GL53 .... 134 C1
   EVILLE/WHL BS5 .... 365 H4
Gorham Cl *AVONM* BS11 .... 352 E4
Gorlands Rd *YATE/CS* BS37 .... 348 A5
Gorse Cl *COTS* GL54 .... 143 K1
   GLE GL4 .... 159 H2
Gorse Cover Rd *THNB/SVB* BS35 .... 328 C5
Gorse Hl *EVE* WR11 .... 14 D4
   MANG/FISH BS16 .... 366 C3
Gorse La *CHPMW/MSHF* SN14 ...... 370 C6
   CLFD GL16 .... 204 A1
Gorse Meadow *COTS* GL54 .... 143 K2
The Gorse *COTS* GL54 .... 143 J1
Gosditch *HGHW* SN6 .... 308 C6
   HGHW SN6 .... 310 C2
Gosditch St *CIR* GL7 .... 249 J5
Gosforth Rd *HNBRY/STHM* BS10 .... 353 K5
Goshawk Rd *VGL* GL2 .... 157 F3
Gossington Br *VGL* GL2 .... 238 C6
Goss Wood Cnr *VGL* GL2 .... 156 E6
Gotherington Flds
   CHELTE/BC GL52 .... 59 K6
Gotherington La *CHELTE/BC* GL52 ... 83 G1
Gotley Rd *BRSG/KWL/STAPK* BS4 ... 374 C4
Gott Dr *BRSG/KWL/STAPK* BS4 ...... 374 C1
Gouda Wy *GL* GL1 .... 2 C2
Gould Dr *TEWK* GL20 .... 34 D5
Goulter St *EVILLE/WHL* BS5 .... 365 F8
Gourney Cl *AVONM* BS11 .... 352 D4
Gover Rd *KGWD/HNM* BS15 .... 375 H3
Gowle Rd *STROUD* GL5 .... 215 F8
Grace Cl *YATE/CS* BS37 .... 348 A5
Grace Ct *MANG/FISH* BS16 .... 356 D8
Grace Dr *COTS* GL54 .... 169 G4
   KGWD/HNM BS15 .... 367 G5
Grace Park Rd
   BRSG/KWL/STAPK BS4 .... 374 C5
Grace Rd *MANG/FISH* BS16 .... 366 C1
Graces Pitch *NWNT* GL18 .... 73 J6
Graeme Cl *MANG/FISH* BS16 .... 366 A1
Grafton La *RTEWK/TIB* GL19 .... 31 G8
Grafton Rd *CHELT* GL50 .... 4 A6
   VGL GL2 .... 3 F2
Graham Pl *CHELTW* GL51 .... 105 H5
Graham Rd *EVILLE/WHL* BS5 .... 365 F5
   MANG/FISH BS16 .... 357 F7
Grahamstown Gv *CHEP* NP16 .... 288 D6
Grahamstown Rd *CHEP* NP16......... 288 C7
Grainger Ct *AVONM* BS11 .... 352 A7
Grampian Cl
   OLD/WMLY/WICK BS30 .... 376 D2
Granbrook La *CHCAM* GL55 .... 9 G2
Grandmother's Rock La
   OLD/WMLY/WICK BS30 .... 378 A4
Grange Av *BRSTK/PCHW* BS34 .... 343 G8
   KGWD/HNM BS15 .... 375 J1
Grange Cl *ALMDB* BS32 .... 343 G4
   RSTROUD/NAIL GL6 .... 243 H8
Grange Cl North
   HNLZ/SM/SNYPK/WT BS9 .... 353 K8
Grange Ct *CIR* GL7 .... 249 H2
   KGWD/HNM BS15 .... 375 J1
   TEWK GL20 .... 34 E5
Grange Court La *RTEWK/TIB* GL19 .. 125 J3
Grange Court Rd *CIND* GL14 .... 153 K2
   HNLZ/SM/SNYPK/WT BS9 .... 353 J8
Grange Dr *CHELTE/BC* GL52 .... 83 F3
   MANG/FISH BS16 .... 356 C8
Grange Pk
   HNLZ/SM/SNYPK/WT BS9 .... 353 K8
   MANG/FISH BS16 .... 356 C6
Grange Rd *EVE* WR11 .... 6 B1
   GL GL1 .... 157 J4
   GLE GL4 .... 157 K5
   TEWK GL20 .... 34 E5
The Grange *CHNTN* OX7 .... 119 F2
   HNLZ/SM/SNYPK/WT BS9 .... 353 F7
Grange Vw *STROUD* GL5................. 214 E6
Grangeville Cl
   OLD/WMLY/WICK BS30 .... 376 C3
Grange Wk *CHELTS* GL53 .... 135 H1
Grangewood Cl
   MANG/FISH BS16 .... 356 C8
Granley Cl *CHELTW* GL51 .... 105 K6
Granley Dr *CHELTW* GL51 .... 105 K6
Granley Gdns *CHELTW* GL51 .... 105 K6
Granley Rd *CHELTW* GL51 .... 105 K6
Granna La *CHELTE/BC* GL52 .... 60 E5

Granny's La *KGWD/HNM* BS15 ...... 366 E8 ⊠
Gransmoor Gra *BWTH/CHD* GL3 ..... 131 K7
Grantham La *KGWD/HNM* BS15 ..... 366 C6 ⊠
Grantham St *CHELT* GL50 .... 366 C5
Grantley Crs *CIR* GL7 .... 249 J7 ⊠
Grantson Cl *BRSG/KWL/STAPK* BS4.. 374 D4
Granville Cl *KGWD/HNM* BS15 ...... 375 D3
Granville St *CHELT* GL50 .... 4 A3
   EVILLE/WHL BS5 .... 365 C8
   GL GL1 .... 129 J8
Grasby Cl *GLE* GL4 .... 131 C7 ⊠
Grasington Dr *YATE/CS* BS37 .... 347 J5
Grasmere Cl *HNBRY/STHM* BS10 ... 353 J6
Grasmere Rd *CHELTW* GL51 .... 105 K7 ⊠
   VGL GL2 .... 130 E2
Grassmere Gdns
   OLD/WMLY/WICK BS30 .... 367 K8
Gratitude Rd *EVILLE/WHL* BS5........ 365 H5
Gratton Cl *CHELT* GL50 .... 106 C8
Gratton St *CHELT* GL50 .... 4 B6 ⊠
Gravel Hill Rd *YATE/CS* BS37 .... 347 H2
Gravel Pit La *CHELTW* GL51 .... 105 H1
Gravel Pit Cl *TEWK* GL20 .... 13 K8 ⊠
Gravel Wk *CHELTE/BC* GL52 .... 83 J6
Graveney Cl
   BRSG/KWL/STAPK BS4 .... 374 C5 ⊠
Graveney Rd *COTS* GL54............... 169 C4
Gravney Ct *CHELTW* GL51 .... 105 J2
Gray Cl *VGL* GL2 .... 103 F7
Grayle Rd *HNBRY/STHM* BS10 ...... 353 H3
Grayling Cl *GLE* GL4 .... 159 G2 ⊠
Gray Rd *CIR* GL7 .... 278 D2 ⊠
Gray's Cl *HNBRY/STHM* BS10 .... 353 C4 ⊠
Gray's La *MALM* GL56 .... 70 A1
Grayston Cl *TEWK* GL20 .... 33 K6
Great Ann St *CBRISNE* BS2........... 364 C4
Great Brockeridge
   HNLZ/SM/SNYPK/WT BS9 .... 353 H8
Great Dowles
   OLD/WMLY/WICK BS30 .... 376 B2
Greatfield Dr *CHELTS* GL53........... 135 F1
Greatfield La *CHELTW* GL51 .... 133 K1 ⊞
Great George St *CBRISNE* BS2....... 364 C4
Great Gv *GLE* GL4 .... 131 F7
Great Leaze
   OLD/WMLY/WICK BS30 .... 376 B2
Great Meadow Rd *ALMDB* BS32 .... 343 K7
Great Norwood St *CHELT* GL50 ...... 4 A6
Great Park Rd *ALMDB* BS32 .... 343 C3
Great Stoke Wy
   BRSTK/PCHW BS34..................... 355 H4
Great Western La *CL* GL1 .... 3 E4 ⊠
Great Western Rd *BRKLY* GL13 ..... 235 H5 ⊠
   CHELT GL50 .... 4 A3
   GL GL1 .... 3 D3
Great Western Ter *CHELT* GL50 ...... 4 A3
Grebe Cl *GLE* GL4 .... 158 E1
Grebe Sq *COTS* GL54 .... 144 E2
Green Acre *BWTH/CHD* GL3 .... 160 C1
   LYD GL15 .... 205 F7
Greenacres *TEWK* GL20 .... 12 D7
Greenaways *NWNT* GL18 .... 73 H5 ⊠
Green Bank *BWTH/CHD* GL3 .... 160 C2
Greenbank Av *EVILLE/WHL* BS5 ..... 365 C5
Greenbank Av West
   EVILLE/WHL BS5 .... 365 F5 ⊠
Greenbank Cl *MTCHDN* GL17 .... 122 D8
Greenbank Rd *EVILLE/WHL* BS5 .... 365 J5
   KGWD/HNM BS15 .... 375 J1
Greenbank Vw *EVILLE/WHL* BS5 ... 365 C4
Green Cl *BDWY* WR12 .... 17 J4
   BWTH/CHD GL3 .... 160 C2
   DSLY GL11 .... 268 C4
   EVE WR11 .... 7 C2
Green Colley Cl *RWYE* HR9 .... 120 B2 ⊠
Green Cft *EVILLE/WHL* BS5 .... 366 A5
Green Dell Cl
   HNBRY/STHM BS10 .... 353 F3 ⊠
Greenditch St *THNB/SVB* BS35 ..... 330 A5
Greendown *EVILLE/WHL* BS5 .... 366 A7
Green Dragon Rd
   FRCTL/WBN BS36 .... 356 D1
Greenfield Av
   HNBRY/STHM BS10 .... 354 B6 ⊠
Greenfield Rd *CLFD* GL16 .... 175 K3
   HNBRY/STHM BS10 .... 354 B5 ⊠
   MTCHDN GL17 .... 148 E1
Greenfields Cl *SHPSTR* CV36 .... 25 F1
Green Gdns *BWTH/CHD* GL3 .... 160 C2
Green Hayes *YATE/CS* BS37 .... 348 A6
Greenhill *THNB/SVB* BS35 .... 332 A2
Greenhill Cl *CIND* GL14 .... 151 C5
Greenhill Ct *GL* GL1 .... 157 C4
Greenhill Down *THNB/SVB* BS35... 332 A2
Greenhill Gdns *THNB/SVB* BS35 ... 332 A2
Greenhill La *AVONM* BS11 .... 352 E5 ⊠
   THNB/SVB BS35 .... 331 K3
Greenhill Rd *THNB/SVB* BS35........ 332 A2
Greenhills Cl *CHELTS* GL53 .... 134 E1
Greenhills Rd *CHELTS* GL53 .... 134 E1
Greenhouse La
   RSTROUD/NAIL GL6 .... 187 J7
The Greenings *CHELTW* GL51 ...... 133 K1 ⊞

Greenlands Wy
   HNBRY/STHM BS10 .... 353 C2
Green La *BWTH/CHD* GL3 .... 131 J8
   BWTH/CHD GL3 .... 132 A3
   BWTH/CHD GL3 .... 161 C3
   CHPM/MSHF SN14 .... 371 J6
   COTS GL54 .... 195 C2
   FRCTL/WBN BS36 .... 344 C7
   HNBRY/STHM BS10 .... 340 E5
   MALM SN16 .... 70 D7
   SHPSTR CV36 .... 25 F1
   TEWK GL20 .... 34 B7
   THNB/SVB BS35 .... 328 D6
   VGL GL2 .... 156 E8
   VGL GL2 .... 184 A7
   WUE GL12 .... 317 H5
Green Lane Cl *COTS* GL54 .... 115 C7
   SHPSTR CV36 .... 25 F1 ⊠
Greenleaze *BRSG/KWL/STAPK* BS4.. 374 A5
Greenleaze Av *MANG/FISH* BS16 .. 356 D5
Green Meadow Bank
   CHELTE/BC GL52 .... 82 E2
Greenmore Rd
   BRSG/KWL/STAPK BS4 .... 374 A4
Greenore *KGWD/HNM* BS15 .... 366 C7
Greenpark Rd
   HNBRY/STHM BS10 .... 354 C5 ⊠
Green's Cl *COTS* GL54 .... 144 D7
Green Side *BRSG/KWL/STAPK* BS16 .. 357 C8
Greenside Cl
   HNBRY/STHM BS10 .... 353 F3 ⊠
Green St *BWTH/CHD* GL3 .... 160 C2
   CHEP NP16 .... 288 A7
   DSLY GL11 .... 267 C5
Greenstreet *STNHO* GL10 .... 213 F6 ⊠
Green St *TEWK* GL20 .... 32 A6
The Green *BRSTK/PCHW* BS34..... 355 J2
   CHCAM GL55 .... 20 E4
   CHNTN OX7 .... 119 C1
   CIND GL14 .... 180 B2
   CIR GL7 .... 250 A6
   CIR GL7 .... 254 D7
   DSLY GL11 .... 268 C4 ⊠
   KGWD/HNM BS15 .... 366 C4
   MALM SN16 .... 306 A6
   MIM GL56 .... 46 A8 ⊠
   SHPSTR CV36 .... 47 J4
   TET GL8 .... 302 C7
   THNB/SVB BS35 .... 330 E4
   WUE GL12 .... 318 D6
Greenview
   OLD/WMLY/WICK BS30 .... 376 B4 ⊠
Green Wy *BWTH/CHD* GL3 .... 160 C1
Greenway *CHELTE/BC* GL52 .... 83 H3
Greenway Cl *CHELTW* GL51 .... 133 H5 ⊠
Greenway Dr
   HNBRY/STHM BS10 .... 354 B6 ⊠
Greenway La *CHELTE/BC* GL52 .... 5 F6
   CHELTS GL53 .... 134 B7
   CHELTW GL51 .... 133 H5
   CHPM/MSHF SN14 .... 379 C2
   COTS GL54 .... 62 B5
Greenway Pk
   HNBRY/STHM BS10 .... 354 B6 ⊠
Greenway Rd *CIND* GL14 .... 150 E7
   MIM GL56 .... 44 B3
Greenways *COTS* GL54 .... 62 E7 ⊠
   KGWD/HNM BS15 .... 367 C5 ⊠
   LYD GL15 .... 233 K3
Greenways Dr *CLFD* GL16.............. 176 A6
Greenways Rd *YATE/CS* BS37 .... 347 H2
The Greenway
   MANG/FISH BS16 .... 366 C3
Greenwood Cl *BWTH/CHD* GL3 .... 131 K8
   HORF/LLZ BS7 .... 354 C7
Greenwood Dr *THNB/SVB* BS35 ... 331 K2
Greet Rd *COTS* GL54 .... 62 B8
Gregory Ct
   OLD/WMLY/WICK BS30 .... 367 C8 ⊠
Grenadier Cl *BWTH/CHD* GL3 .... 131 H8
Grenadier Rd *CHELTW* GL51 .... 105 J2 ⊠
Grenville Cl *BWTH/CHD* GL3 .... 103 H6
   EVILLE/WHL BS5 .... 365 K6
Grenville Rd *RDLND/MONT* BS6 .... 364 C3
Gretton Rd *CHELTE/BC* GL52 .... 60 D6
   COTS GL54 .... 62 D7
Greve Ct *OLD/WMLY/WICK* BS30 .. 376 A2 ⊠
Grevel La *CHCAM* GL55 .... 20 E2
Greville Cl *GL* GL1.......................... 2 C1
Greville Ct *CHELTW* GL51 .... 105 K6 ⊠
Grevil Rd *CHELTW* GL51................ 105 K2
Greyfriars Wk *CIR* GL7 .... 249 H8 ⊠
Greyhound Gdns *VGL* GL2 .... 131 F1
Greylag Crs *TEWK* GL20 .... 57 K1
Greys Cl *RSTROUD/NAIL* GL6 .... 244 B2 ⊠
Greystoke Av *HNBRY/STHM* BS10.. 353 J6
Greystoke Gdns
   HNLZ/SM/SNYPK/WT BS9 .... 353 J6 ⊠
Greystones *MANG/FISH* BS16 .... 356 E5 ⊠
Greystones La *COTS* GL54 .... 115 J8
Grierson Cl *BWTH/CHD* GL3 .... 131 K8 ⊠
Griffin Cl *COTS* GL54 .... 92 C6
Griffiths Av *CHELTW* GL51 .... 105 K6
Griffon Cl *VGL* GL2 .... 157 F3
Griggs Cl *CHCAM* GL55 .... 20 E3

Grimsbury Rd *KGWD/HNM* BS15..... 367 C6
Grimwade Cl *CHELTW* GL51 .... 105 K5
Grindell Rd *EVILLE/WHL* BS5 .... 365 H7
Grisedale Cl *VGL* GL2 .... 130 E1
Grist Mill Cl *CHELTW* GL51 .... 105 H1
Grittleton Rd *HORF/LLZ* BS7 .... 354 C6
Grosvenor Pl South
   CHELTE/BC GL52 .... 4 C4 ⊠
Grosvenor Rd *CBRISNE* BS2.......... 364 C6
   STNHO GL10 .... 213 F5
   VGL GL2 .... 3 F3
Grosvenor St *CHELTE/BC* GL52 .... 4 C4 ⊠
Grosvenor Ter *CHELTE/BC* GL52 ..... 4 C4 ⊠
Grove Av *EVE* WR11 .... 7 H1
   HNLZ/SM/SNYPK/WT BS9 .... 352 E7
Grove Bank *MANG/FISH* BS16 ...... 356 C5
Grove Crs *CLFD* GL16.................... 175 K3
   GLE GL4 .... 131 F5
Grovefield *RTEWK/TIB* GL19 .... 31 C7
Grovefield Wy *CHELTW* GL51 .... 105 F7
Grove Gdns *TET* GL8 .... 302 B5
Grovelands *GLE* GL4 .... 131 C5
Grovelands Cl *CHELTS* GL53 .... 107 C8 ⊠
Grove La *CHPM/MSHF* SN14......... 360 A7
   CIR GL7 .... 249 K5
   LYD GL15 .... 206 B8
   VGL GL2 .... 211 K2
Grove Pk *BRSG/KWL/STAPK* BS4 .. 374 C3 ⊠
   RDLND/MONT BS6 .... 364 A4
Grove Park Av
   BRSG/KWL/STAPK BS4 .... 374 C4
Grove Park Rd
   BRSG/KWL/STAPK BS4 .... 374 C4
   STROUD GL5 .... 214 E6
Grove Rd *BWTH/CHD* GL3 .... 103 H8
   CLFD GL16 .... 147 J8
   HNLZ/SM/SNYPK/WT BS9 .... 353 F6
   LYD GL15 .... 205 J5
   LYD GL15 .... 233 K3
   MANG/FISH BS16 .... 365 J2
Grovesend Rd *THNB/SVB* BS35 .... 316 E2
Grove St *CHELT* GL50 .... 4 A3
   GL GL1 .... 3 D5
The Grove *CHELT* GL50 .... 106 B6
   CHELTE/BC GL52 .... 5 E4
   MALM SN16 .... 305 J5
   MIM GL56 .... 70 B1 ⊠
   OLD/WMLY/WICK BS30 .... 376 B2
   STROUD GL5 .... 241 K2
   TET GL8 .... 272 A6
   YATE/CS BS37 .... 334 C6
Grove Vw *MANG/FISH* BS16 .... 355 J8 ⊠
Grump St *SHPSTR* CV36 .... 11 F3
Guernsey Av
   BRSG/KWL/STAPK BS4 .... 374 C2
Guest Av *MANG/FISH* BS16............ 357 H8
Guggle La *COTS* GL54 .... 169 C4
Guildford Rd
   BRSG/KWL/STAPK BS4 .... 374 D1
Guildings Wy *STNHO* GL10 .... 241 C1
Guinea La *MANG/FISH* BS16 .... 366 A1 ⊠
Guinea St *GL* GL1 .... 3 D2
Guise Av *BWTH/CHD* GL3 .... 160 D2
Guise Cl *VGL* GL2 .... 157 F6
Gullivers Pl *YATE/CS* BS37 .... 347 J6
Gully La *BRKLY* GL13 .... 292 E7
The Gully *FRCTL/WBN* BS36 .... 345 F7
Gumstool Hl *TET* GL8 .... 302 C7 ⊠
Gunhouse La *STROUD* GL5 .... 243 F1
Gunning Cl *KGWD/HNM* BS15 ...... 366 D8
Gunter's Hl *EVILLE/WHL* BS5 .... 366 A8 ⊠
Gupshill Cl *TEWK* GL20 .... 57 H3 ⊠
Gurney Av *GLE* GL4 .... 157 K4
Gwentlands Cl *CHEP* NP16 .... 288 A7
Gwernant Rd *CHELTW* GL51 .... 105 K8
Gwinnette Cl *CHELTW* GL51 .... 133 J4
Gwy Ct *CHEP* NP16 .... 288 B5 ⊠
Gwyn St *CBRISNE* BS2................... 364 C5
Gyde Rd *RSTROUD/NAIL* GL6 .... 187 H5
Gypsy La *NWNT* GL18 .... 72 A8

H

Hacket Hl *THNB/SVB* BS35 .... 317 F6
Hacket La *THNB/SVB* BS35............ 316 E6
Hadfield Cl *RTEWK/TIB* GL19 .... 53 C7
Hadley Ct
   OLD/WMLY/WICK BS30 .... 367 H8 ⊠
Hadley Rd *DSLY* GL11 .... 266 C2 ⊠
Hadow Wy *VGL* GL2....................... 157 F6
Hadrian Cl *LYD* GL15 .... 234 B2
Hadrians Wy *GLE* GL4 .... 131 H7
Hague Av *DSLY* GL11 .... 266 D2 ⊠
Hailes Rd *GLE* GL4 .... 131 F7
Hailes St *COTS* GL54...................... 85 K1
Hakeburn Rd *CIR* GL7 .... 249 J5 ⊠
Halbrow Crs *MANG/FISH* BS16 ..... 366 C1
Hale Cl *KGWD/HNM* BS15 .... 375 J2 ⊠
Hale La *RSTROUD/NAIL* GL6 .... 187 H6
Hales Cl *CHELTE/BC* GL52 .... 5 E4
Hales Horn Cl *ALMDB* BS32 .... 343 H8
Hale's Rd *CHELTE/BC* GL52........... 5 D5

Halfway Br *VGL* GL2 .... 126 E4
Halfway Pitch *RSTROUD/NAIL* GL6 ... 214 D2
Halifax Rd *YATE/CS* BS37 .... 347 F2
Halland Rd *CHELTS* GL53 .... 134 D1
Hallards Cl *AVONM* BS11 .... 352 B6
Hallen Cl *HNBRY/STHM* BS10 .... 353 F3
Hall End La *YATE/CS* BS37 .... 334 E4
Hallen Dr
  HNLZ/SM/SNYPK/WT BS9 .... 352 E7
Hallen Rd *HNBRY/STHM* BS10 .... 352 E2
  HNBRY/STHM BS10 .... 353 C3
Hall La *CBATH/BATHN* BA1 .... 378 E4
  CBATH/BATHN BA1 .... 379 H4
  CHPMW/MSHF SN14 .... 379 H3
  YATE/CS BS37 .... 349 H1
Hallmead Cl *CHELTW* GL51 ..... 105 H1 ▣
Hall Rd *CHELTS* GL53 .... 134 D2
Hallsfield *HGHW* SN6 .... 310 D6
Halls Rd *KGWD/HNM* BS15 .... 366 D6 ▣
Halmore La *BRKLY* GL13 .... 236 C5
Halsbury Rd *RDLND/MONT* BS6 .... 364 A2
Halstock Av *MANG/FISH* BS16 .... 365 K3 ▣
Halston Dr *CBRISNE* BS2 .... 364 D6
Hamble Cl *THNB/SVB* BS35 .... 316 C6
Hambledon Cl *CIR* GL7 .... 278 C3 ▣
Hambridge La *CIR* GL7 .... 285 G1
Hambrook La *BRSTK/PCHW* BS34 ... 355 K2
Hambrook St *CHELTE/BC* GL52 .... 5 F6
Hambutts Dr *RSTROUD/NAIL* GL6 ... 187 G6
Hambutts Md *RSTROUD/NAIL* GL6 .. 187 G6
Ham Cl *CHELTE/BC* GL52 .... 107 J7
Hamelin Cl *RTEWK/TIB* GL19 .... 125 J2
Hamer St *VGL* GL2 .... 3 E4
Ham Farm La *MANG/FISH* BS16 ..... 357 H8
Hamfield La *BRKLY* GL13 .... 263 J3
Hamilton Cft *CIR* GL7 .... 281 J2
Hamilton Rd *EVILLE/WHL* BS5 .... 364 E6 ▣
Hamilton St *CHELTS* GL53 .... S E6 ▣
Ham La *CIR* GL7 .... 278 D8
  CIR GL7 .... 283 E7
  MANG/FISH BS16 .... 355 J8
  OLD/WMLY/WICK BS30 .... 369 C5
  THNB/SVB BS35 .... 291 G8
Hamlen Cl *RTEWK/TIB* GL19 .... 125 J2
Hamlet Cl *CHELTW* GL51 .... 105 J4
Hammersmith Bottom *CIR* GL7 ...... 256 A1
Hammersmith Rd
  EVILLE/WHL BS5 .... 365 H6 ▣
Ham Mill La *STROUD* GL5 .... 243 F3
Hammond Cl
  BRSG/KWL/STAPK BS4 .... 374 C5 ▣
Hammond Dr *COTS* GL54 .... 169 G4 ▣
Hammond Gdns
  HNLZ/SM/SNYPK/WT BS9 .... 353 G7 ▣
Hammonds *HGHW* SN6 .... 310 E6 ▣
Hammond Wy *CIR* GL7 .... 249 H6 ▣
  GLE GL4 .... 131 F5 ▣
Hampden Cl *YATE/CS* BS37 .... 347 F2
Hampden Rd
  BRSG/KWL/STAPK BS4 .... 374 A3 ▣
Hampden Wy *GL* GL1 .... 2 C4 ▣
Hampshire Gdns *CLFD* GL16 .... 175 J2
Hampshire Wy *YATE/CS* BS37 .... 347 H2 ▣
Hampstead Rd
  BRSG/KWL/STAPK BS4 .... 374 B3
Hampton Cl *BWTH/CHD* GL3 ... 131 K7 ▣
  CHELT GL50 .... 134 A1 ▣
  OLD/WMLY/WICK BS30 .... 376 B1
Hampton Gv *CIR* GL7 .... 281 H1
Hampton Hl *TET* GL8 .... 272 A4
Hampton Pl *BWTH/CHD* GL3 .... 103 J6
Hampton St *KGWD/HNM* BS15 ...... 366 D5 ▣
  TET GL8 .... 302 B6
Ham Rd *CHELTE/BC* GL52 .... 107 J7
  RTEWK/TIB GL19 .... 77 H5
Hams Rd *KEYN* BS31 .... 376 A7
  LYD GL15 .... 234 B3
The Ham *DSLY* GL11 .... 266 A1
Hanbury Cl *KGWD/HNM* BS15 .... 375 J1
Handel Av *EVILLE/WHL* BS5 .... 365 H7 ▣
Handford Wy
  OLD/WMLY/WICK BS30 .... 376 C3 ▣
Hanford Cl *HGRV/WHIT* BS14 .... 374 C7 ▣
Hang Hill Rd *LYD* GL15 .... 204 E5
Hanham Rd *KGWD/HNM* BS15 .... 366 B8
Hanley La *CHEP* NP16 .... 259 J7 ▣
Hanman Rd *GL* GL1 .... 2 C6
Hannah Crs *CIR* GL7 .... 278 D3
Hannah Pl *VGL* GL2 .... 103 G7
Hannam Cl *CHELTS* GL53 .... 134 D1
Hanover Ct *CBRIS/FH* BS1 .... 364 C7 ▣
Hanover St *CHELT* GL50 .... 4 B2
  EVILLE/WHL BS5 .... 365 G7 ▣
Hanover Wy *BWTH/CHD* GL3 .... 103 H7
Hanson Av *SHPSTR* CV36 .... 24 E1 ▣
Hanstone Cl *CIR* GL7 .... 249 H8
Harbour Rd *LYD* GL15 .... 234 B6
Harbourside *TEWK* GL20 .... 33 J7
Harbour Vw *TEWK* GL20 .... 33 J7 ▣
Harbury Ms *GL* GL1 .... 3 E5
Harbury Rd
  HNLZ/SM/SNYPK/WT BS9 .... 354 A7
Harcombe Hl *FRCTL/WBN* BS36 ..... 356 E2
Harcombe Rd *FRCTL/WBN* BS36 ..... 356 D1
Harcourt Av *EVILLE/WHL* BS5 .... 366 A8 ▣
Harcourt Hl *RDLND/MONT* BS6 ...... 364 A3

Hardenhuish Rd
  BRSG/KWL/STAPK BS4 .... 374 C1
Harding's Dr *DSLY* GL11 .... 266 E3
Hardwick Av *CHEP* NP16 .... 288 A6 ▣
Hardwick Bank Rd *TEWK* GL20 ...... 34 B3
Hardwick Cl
  BRSG/KWL/STAPK BS4 .... 374 D3
  OLD/WMLY/WICK BS30 .... 376 E1 ▣
Hardwicke *YATE/CS* BS37 .... 346 E7
Hardy Ct *OLD/WMLY/WICK* BS30 ... 376 A1
Hardy La *ALMDB* BS32 .... 330 D6
Hardy Rd *CHELTE/BC* GL52 .... 83 G2
Harebell Pl *GLE* GL4 .... 159 F1
Harefield Cl *KGWD/HNM* BS15 ...... 375 H4 ▣
Hare La *GL* GL1 .... 2 C3 ▣
Harescombe *YATE/CS* BS37 .... 347 G2
Haresdown Hl *CIR* GL7 .... 275 F7
Haresfield La *VGL* GL2 .... 185 F1
Harewood Cl *GL* GL1 .... 157 J5
Harewood Rd *EVILLE/WHL* BS5 ..... 366 A5
Harford Br *COTS* GL54 .... 113 K4
Harford Cl
  HNLZ/SM/SNYPK/WT BS9 .... 352 E7 ▣
Harford Dr *MANG/FISH* BS16 .... 356 C5
Harlech Wy
  OLD/WMLY/WICK BS30 .... 376 C4 ▣
Harleston St *EVILLE/WHL* BS5 .... 364 E6 ▣
Harleys Fld *GLE* GL4 .... 131 F7
Harmer Cl *HNBRY/STHM* BS10 .... 353 H3
Harnham La *COTS* GL54 .... 166 B2
Harold Rd *LYD* GL15 .... 206 C3
Harolds Wy *KGWD/HNM* BS15 ...... 366 C8 ▣
Harper Rd *STROUD* GL5 .... 214 A6 ▣
Harpfield Rd *CHELTE/BC* GL52 ...... 83 F4
Harp Hl *CHELTE/BC* GL52 .... 5 F4
Harptree Ct
  OLD/WMLY/WICK BS30 .... 376 B2 ▣
Harrington Av *HGRV/WHIT* BS14 ... 374 D8
Harrington Cl
  OLD/WMLY/WICK BS30 .... 377 F6
Harrington Dr *CHELTW* GL51 .... 105 J7 ▣
Harrington Gv
  HGRV/WHIT BS14 .... 374 D8 ▣
Harrington Rd *HGRV/WHIT* BS14 ... 374 D8 ▣
Harrington Wk *HGRV/WHIT* BS14 .. 374 D8 ▣
Harris Barton *FRCTL/WBN* BS36 ... 345 G7
Harris Cl *BWTH/CHD* GL3 .... 132 A1
Harris Ct *OLD/WMLY/WICK* BS30 ... 376 A2 ▣
Harris Gdns *COTS* GL54 .... 144 E2 ▣
Harrison Cl *CIND* GL14 .... 180 B2 ▣
  MANG/FISH BS16 .... 357 H8 ▣
Harrison Rd *CHELTW* GL51 .... 133 H4
Harrison Wy *LYD* GL15 .... 234 C4
Harris Rd *HGHW* SN6 .... 308 E5
Harrowdene Rd
  BRSG/KWL/STAPK BS4 .... 374 A3
Harrow Rd *BRSG/KWL/STAPK* BS4 . 374 C3
Harry Stoke Rd
  BRSTK/PCHW BS34 .... 355 J3
Harry Yates Wy *CHELTW* GL51 ..... 105 H2
Hartbury Cl *CHELTW* GL51 .... 105 J3
Hart Gn *CIND* GL14 .... 150 E8
Hartington Rd *GL* GL1 .... 129 J3
Hartland Rd *GLE* GL4 .... 130 B8
Hart La *MTCHDN* GL17 .... 121 J6
Hartlebury Wy *CHELTE/BC* GL52 ... 107 J8
Hartley Bridge Hl
  RSTROUD/NAIL GL6 .... 270 B6
Hartley Cl *CHELTS* GL53 .... 135 F2
  YATE/CS BS37 .... 348 A5
Harts Cft *YATE/CS* BS37 .... 347 H2 ▣
Harvest Av *ALMDB* BS32 .... 343 H5
Harvesters Vw *CHELTE/BC* GL52 ... 82 D2 ▣
Harvest Gv *CHELTW* GL51 ..... 105 H1 ▣
Harvest Wy *VGL* GL2 .... 157 F7
Harvey Cl *VGL* GL2 .... 157 J1
Harvey's La *COTS* GL54 .... 85 H1
Harwell Cl *GLE* GL4 .... 157 K5 ▣
Hasfield Cl *VGL* GL2 .... 156 E5
Hasfield Rd *RTEWK/TIB* GL19 .... 77 F2
Haskins Ct
  OLD/WMLY/WICK BS30 .... 376 B2 ▣
Haslette Wy *CHELTW* GL51 .... 133 J1
Hassell Dr *CBRISNE* BS2 .... 364 E7
Hastings Pl *TEWK* GL20 .... 57 H2 ▣
Hastings Rd *CIND* GL14 .... 150 E6
Hatchet La *BRSTK/PCHW* BS34 ...... 355 J2
Hatchet Rd *BRSTK/PCHW* BS34 ...... 355 J2
Hatchmere *THNB/SVB* BS35 .... 316 D6
Hatfield Rd *GL* GL1 .... 3 E6
Hathaway Cl *VGL* GL2 .... 157 H2
Hatherley *YATE/CS* BS37 .... 347 G2
Hatherley Brake *CHELTW* GL51 ..... 105 J2 ▣
Hatherley Court Rd *CHELTW* GL51 .. 106 B7
Hatherley Ga *CHELTW* GL51 .... 106 B6
Hatherley La *CHELTW* GL51 .... 105 G6
Hatherley Rd *CHELTW* GL51 .... 105 H7
  GL GL1 .... 3 E6
  HORF/LLZ BS7 .... 364 C2
Hatherop St *CHELT* GL50 .... 106 B7
Hatherop Rd *CIR* GL7 .... 255 F7
Hathway Wk *EVILLE/WHL* BS5 .... 364 E6
Hatters' La *YATE/CS* BS37 .... 348 A5

Hatton Cl *MTCHDN* GL17 .... 148 E4
Havelock Rd *BWTH/CHD* GL3 .... 131 J6
Haven Av *STNHO* GL20 .... 212 E8
The Haven *KGWD/HNM* BS15 .... 366 E5
Haw Br *RTEWK/TIB* GL19 .... 78 D2
Hawburn Cl
  BRSG/KWL/STAPK BS4 .... 374 C4
Hawcombe Ms *CHELTW* GL51 ... 133 K1 ▣
Haweswater Cl
  OLD/WMLY/WICK BS30 .... 367 K8 ▣
Haweswater Rd *CHELTW* GL51 ...... 105 J8 ▣
Hawk Cl *GLE* GL4 .... 159 F1
Hawker Sq *COTS* GL54 .... 145 F2
Hawkesbury Rd *BAD* GL9 .... 337 H1
Hawkesbury Dr *BRSTK/PCHW* BS34 .. 343 H8 ▣
  MANG/FISH BS16 .... 365 J2
Hawkins Cl
  OLD/WMLY/WICK BS30 .... 376 D2 ▣
Hawkins Crs *ALMDB* BS32 .... 343 H6
Hawkins St *CBRISNE* BS2 .... 364 D7 ▣
Hawkley Dr *ALMDB* BS32 .... 343 H5
Hawkridge Dr *MANG/FISH* BS16 .... 368 E1 ▣
Hawkswood Rd *CHELT* GL50 .... 134 B1 ▣
Hawksworth Dr *KGWD/HNM* BS15 .. 375 G2 ▣
Haw La *THNB/SVB* BS35 .... 330 E4 ▣
Haw Rd *CLFD* GL16 .... 148 C2
Haw St *DSLY* GL11 .... 239 K2 ▣
  WUE GL12 .... 296 E2
Hawthorn Av *KGWD/HNM* BS15 .... 375 G1 ▣
Hawthorn Cl *BRSTK/PCHW* BS34 ... 342 C1
  CHEP NP16 .... 312 A2 ▣
  WUE GL12 .... 319 J2 ▣
Hawthorn Crs *THNB/SVB* BS35 ...... 316 C4 ▣
Hawthorn Dr *BWTH/CHD* GL3 .... 131 H1 ▣
  CHELTE/BC GL52 .... 83 H3 ▣
  CLFD GL16 .... 204 A2
Hawthorne Av *GLE* GL4 .... 130 E8
Hawthorne Cl *MANG/FISH* BS16 .... 368 E8 ▣
Hawthorne Hl *NWNT* GL18 .... 72 D4 ▣
The Hawthornes *CHELTW* GL51 .... 105 H8 ▣
  MANG/FISH BS16 .... 367 F2
Hawthorn Ri *STROUD* GL5 .... 213 K6 ▣
Hawthorn Rd *CHELTW* GL51 .... 105 J3 ▣
Hawthorns Rd *MTCHDN* GL17 .... 122 C5
The Hawthorns *DSLY* GL11 .... 266 C1
  LYD GL15 .... 234 B3 ▣
  RSTROUD/NAIL GL6 .... 244 A2
Hawthorn Wy *BRSTK/PCHW* BS34 .. 355 J1 ▣
  SHPSTR CV36 .... 25 F2
Haycroft Cl *CHELTE/BC* GL52 .... 82 E2 ▣
Haycroft Dr *GLE* GL4 .... 159 F4
Hayden La *CHELTW* GL51 .... 104 E4
Hayden Rd *CHELTW* GL51 .... 105 J7
Haydock Cl *MANG/FISH* BS16 .... 357 F5 ▣
Haydon Gdns *HORF/LLZ* BS7 .... 365 F1 ▣
Haydons Cl *CHCAM* GL55 .... 21 F2 ▣
Hayeley Dr *BRSTK/PCHW* BS34 ..... 343 J8
Hayes Cl *CBRISNE* BS2 .... 364 E3
Hayes Ct *VGL* GL2 .... 102 B8 ▣
Haye's La *BAD* GL9 .... 350 E4
  CIR GL7 .... 192 E7
Hayes Rd *CHELTE/BC* GL52 .... 5 D3 ▣
  RSTROUD/NAIL GL6 .... 270 C7 ▣
Hayfield *CHPMW/MSHF* SN14 .... 372 A6
Hayfield Wy *CHELTE/BC* GL52 .... 82 D3 ▣
Hayhedge La *RSTROUD/NAIL* GL6 .. 217 H5 ▣
Hay La *CIR* GL7 .... 224 D4 ▣
  RSTROUD/NAIL GL6 .... 270 C7
Hay Leaze *YATE/CS* BS37 .... 347 F2 ▣
The Haymarket *CBRIS/FH* BS1 .... 364 B7 ▣
Haymead La *TET* GL8 .... 323 K4
Haymes Dr *CHELTE/BC* GL52 .... 83 J1 ▣
Haymes Rd *CHELTE/BC* GL52 .... 83 J1 ▣
Haynes La *MANG/FISH* BS16 .... 366 D7 ▣
Hay St *BDWAY* WR12 .... 18 E3 ▣
Hay St *CHPMW/MSHF* SN14 .... 372 A6
Hayssum's Cl *CHCAM* GL55 .... 20 E4 ▣
Haythorn Cl *MANG/FISH* BS16 ...... 367 F2 ▣
Haytor Pk
  HNLZ/SM/SNYPK/WT BS9 .... 353 F5
Hayward Cl *GLE* GL4 .... 131 F7
Hayward Rd *EVILLE/WHL* BS5 .... 365 G4 ▣
  MANG/FISH BS16 .... 366 D3 ▣
Haywards La *CHELTE/BC* GL52 ...... 5 E5 ▣
Hayward's Rd *CHELTE/BC* GL52 ..... 5 E6 ▣
Haywood Pitch *RWYE* HR9 .... 72 A4
Hazebrouck Cl *CHELTW* GL51 .... 105 J3 ▣
Hazelbury Dr
  OLD/WMLY/WICK BS30 .... 367 J3 ▣
Hazelbury Rd *HGRV/WHIT* BS14 .... 374 B6 ▣
Hazel Cl *VGL* GL2 .... 130 D7
Hazel Cresent *THNB/SVB* BS35 ...... 316 D5 ▣
Hazelcroft *BWTH/CHD* GL3 .... 103 K8 ▣
Hazeldene Rd *BRSTK/PCHW* BS34 .. 342 E7 ▣
Hazel Gdns *THNB/SVB* BS35 .... 331 K2 ▣
Hazelgrove *FRCTL/WBN* BS36 .... 356 D1 ▣
Hazel Gv *HORF/LLZ* BS7 .... 354 E6 ▣
Hazel La *ALMDB* BS32 .... 331 J3 ▣
Hazel Rd *MTCHDN* GL17 .... 122 D6
The Hazels *GL* GL1 .... 131 G2
Hazelton Rd *HORF/LLZ* BS7 .... 364 B3 ▣
Hazlecote La *TET* GL8 .... 270 B6
Hazledean Rd *CHELTW* GL51 .... 105 H2 ▣
Hazlewood Cl *CHELT* GL50 .... 134 B1

Hazlitt Cft *CHELTW* GL51 .... 105 H2
Headford Av *EVILLE/WHL* BS5... 366 B7
Headington Cl
 KGWD/HNM BS15 .... 375 J2 ⊞
Headlam Cl *GLE* GL4 .... 157 K5 ⊞
The Headlands *STROUD* GL5 .... 242 B4
The Headland *CHEP* NP16 .... 312 C2
Healey Dr *CHPMW/MSHF* SN14 ... 360 A8 ⊞
Heapey Cl *CHELTW* GL51 .... 105 H4 ⊞
Hearne Cl *CHELTS* GL53.............. 107 H8
Hearne Rd *CHELTS* GL53.............. 107 H8
Heart of England Wy *CHCAM* GL55 ... 9 C5
Heath Cl *FRCTL/WBN* BS36............ 344 E8
Heathcote Dr *FRCTL/WBN* BS36 ... 345 K7
Heathcote Rd *MANG/FISH* BS16 ... 366 E1 ⊞
 MANG/FISH BS16 .... 366 E1 ⊞
Heathcote Wk *KGWD/HNM* BS15 ... 366 C4
Heath Ct *MANG/FISH* BS16 .... 356 D7 ⊞
Heathdean Rd *BWTH/CHD* GL3 ... 103 H8 ⊞
Heather Av *FRCTL/WBN* BS36......... 345 H8
 GLE GL4 .... 159 H2
Heather Cl *KGWD/HNM* BS15..... 366 B6
 STROUD GL5 .... 242 C2
Heathfield Rd *STROUD* GL5 .... 214 B5
Heathfields *MANG/FISH* BS16 ...... 356 D6
Heath Gdns *FRCTL/WBN* BS36...... 345 J8
 MANG/FISH BS16 .... 356 D6
Heath House La
 MANG/FISH BS16 .... 365 G1 ⊞
Heath Ri *OLD/WMLY/WICK* BS30 ... 376 C1 ⊞
Heath Rd *EVILLE/WHL* BS5........... 365 F3
 KGWD/HNM BS15 .... 375 G2
 MANG/FISH BS16 .... 356 D7
Heath St *EVILLE/WHL* BS5 .... 365 G4
Heathville Rd *GL* GL1 .... 3 D2
Heath Wk *MANG/FISH* BS16......... 356 D7
Heazle Pl *STROUD* GL5 .... 214 E6
Hebden Cl *BWTH/CHD* GL3.......... 160 D1
Heber St *EVILLE/WHL* BS5 .... 365 G1
Hedgeditch La *TET* GL8 .... 326 B7
Hedgemead Vw *MANG/FISH* BS16 ... 365 H1
The Hedgerow *VGL* GL2 .... 3 F1 ⊞
Hedwick St *EVILLE/WHL* BS5 ...... 365 J7
Helens Cl *CHELTW* GL51 .... 105 H3
Hembury Cl *VGL* GL2 .... 156 D3
Hemmingsdale Rd *VGL* GL2 .... 2 A4 ⊞
Hemming Wy *CHELTE/BC* GL52..... 83 F3
The Hempelands *COTS* GL54........ 195 H4
Hemplow Cl *HGRV/WHIT* BS14 ...... 374 C7
Hempsted La *ALMDB* BS32 .... 342 E4
Hempton La *AVONM* BS11 .... 352 B6
Henacre Rd *AVONM* BS11 .... 352 B6
Henbury Rd *HNBRY/STHM* BS10 ... 353 C4 ⊞
 HNLZ/SM/SNYPK/WT BS9 ...... 353 J6
 KGWD/HNM BS15 .... 375 C1 ⊞
Henbury Road Henbury HI
 HNLZ/SM/SNYPK/WT BS9 ...... 353 H6
Hencliffe Rd *HGRV/WHIT* BS14 ...... 374 C8
Hencliffe Wy *KGWD/HNM* BS15 ... 375 G3
Henderson Rd *KGWD/HNM* BS15 ... 375 G1
Hendingham Cl *GL* GL1................ 157 H4
Hendrick Dr *CHEP* NP16 .... 288 C6 ⊞
Heneage La *WUE* GL12 .... 294 B6
Henfield Crs
 OLD/WMLY/WICK BS30 .... 376 C2
Henfield Rd *FRCTL/WBN* BS36...... 357 J2
Hengrove Av *HGRV/WHIT* BS14..... 374 A6
Hengrove La *HGRV/WHIT* BS14 .... 374 A6
Henleaze Pk
 HNLZ/SM/SNYPK/WT BS9 ...... 364 A1
Henleaze Park Dr
 HNLZ/SM/SNYPK/WT BS9 ...... 354 A8
Henleaze Ter
 HNLZ/SM/SNYPK/WT BS9 ...... 353 K7
Henlow Dr *CHELTW* GL51 .... 105 G5
Henley Pl *GL* GL1 .... 129 K8
Henley Rd *CHELTW* GL51 .... 105 G3
 LYD GL15 .... 205 F5
Henlow Dr *CHPMW/MSHF* GL11 ... 267 F6
Henrietta St *CBRISNE* BS2 .... 364 B6 ⊞
 CHELT GL50 .... 4 B3
 EVILLE/WHL BS5 .... 365 F5 ⊞
Henry Rd *GL* GL1 .... 3 D3
Henry Ryder St *GLE* GL4 .... 131 H8 ⊞
Henry St *GL* GL1 .... 3 D3
Henry Williamson Ct
 OLD/WMLY/WICK BS30 .... 376 B1 ⊞
Henshaw Cl *KGWD/HNM* BS15 ... 366 C4 ⊞
Henshaw Rd *KGWD/HNM* BS15.... 366 C4
Henshaw Wk *KGWD/HNM* BS15 ... 366 C4
Hentley Tor *WUE* GL12 .... 297 G8
Hepburn Rd *CBRIS/FH* BS1 .... 364 C6
Herapath St *EVILLE/WHL* BS5 ..... 365 G8
Herbert Crs *EVILLE/WHL* BS5 ..... 365 H3 ⊞
Herbert Howells Cl *LYD* GL15 ...... 234 A4 ⊞
Herbert St *EVILLE/WHL* BS5........ 365 G6
 GL GL1 .... 3 E5 ⊞
Herberts Wy *LYD* GL15 .... 206 C5
Hercules Cl *BRSTK/PCHW* BS34 ... 343 H8
Herd La *TET* GL8 .... 302 C7
Hereford Pl *CHELT* GL50 .... 4 A3 ⊞
Hereford Rd *CBRISNE* BS2 .... 364 E4 ⊞
Hereward Rd *CIR* GL7 .... 249 J5
Herkomer Cl *HORF/LLZ* BS7 .... 355 F7
Hermitage Dr *DSLY* GL11 .... 267 F6
Hermitage Rd *MANG/FISH* BS16 ... 366 D1
Hermitage St *CHELTS* GL53 .... 4 B6
Heron Cl *CHELTW* GL51 .... 105 H3
Heron Rd *EVILLE/WHL* BS5 .... 365 F5
Heron Wy *GLE* GL4 .... 158 E1
 YATE/CS BS37 .... 347 H7
Hersta Cl *CIR* GL7 .... 250 A6 ⊞
Hertford Rd *CHELTE/BC* GL52 .... 83 F2
Hesding Cl *KGWD/HNM* BS15 ...... 375 H5 ⊞
Hester's Way La *CHELTW* GL51 ... 105 H2
Hester's Way Rd *CHELTW* GL51 ... 105 H3
Hethersett Rd *GL* GL1 .... 3 E5 ⊞
Hetton Gdns *CHELTS* GL53 .... 107 G1
Hewelsfield La *LYD* GL15 .... 231 F1
Hewland Ct *AVONM* BS11 .... 352 E4
Hewlett Pl *CHELTE/BC* GL52 .... 4 C4 ⊞
Hewlett Rd *CHELTE/BC* GL52 .... 4 C4
Hewlett Wy *CIND* GL14 .... 178 E2
Heyford Av *EVILLE/WHL* BS5 ...... 365 F3
Heywood Rd *CIND* GL14 .... 151 F5
Hiam's La *VGL* GL2 .... 100 E3
Hiatt Rd *RSTROUD/NAIL* GL6 ...... 243 F1
Hibbs Cl *CHPMW/MSHF* SN14 ..... 371 K6
Hickley Gdns *BWTH/CHD* GL3 ...... 132 C1
Hicks Av *DSLY* GL11 .... 266 D2
 MANG/FISH BS16 .... 357 H6
Hicks Beach Rd *CHELTW* GL51 ... 105 H3
Hicks Common Rd
 FRCTL/WBN BS36 .... 344 E8
Hicks Ct
 OLD/WMLY/WICK BS30 .... 376 A2 ⑩
Hidcote Av *CHELTW* GL51 .... 134 A1 ⊞
Hidcote Cl *RSTROUD/NAIL* GL6 ... 244 B2 ⊞
Hidcote Rd *CHCAM* GL55 .... 9 K7
Highbank Pk *VGL* GL2 .... 130 B1
High Beech Av *CLFD* GL16 .... 176 B1
Highbeech Rd *LYD* GL15 .... 204 E6
 MTCHDN GL17 .... 149 G1
Highbury La *CHELTE/BC* GL52 .... 4 C4 ⊞
Highbury Rd *HORF/LLZ* BS7 .... 354 D7
 LYD GL15 .... 204 E6
 MONM NP25 .... 174 B6
Highbury Vls *CBRISNE* BS2 .... 364 A6 ⊞
Highclere Rd *VGL* GL2 .... 156 E4
Highcroft
 OLD/WMLY/WICK BS30 .... 367 J8 ⊞
High Delf Wy *LYD* GL15 .... 205 J5
High Elm *KGWD/HNM* BS15 .... 366 E8 ⊞
Higher Newmarket Rd
 RSTROUD/NAIL GL6 .... 270 B2
Highett Dr *EVILLE/WHL* BS5 .... 364 E5 ⊞
Highfield *GL* GL1 .... 207 H4
Highfield Av *KGWD/HNM* BS15 ... 375 J1
Highfield Cl *LYD* GL15 .... 204 E5
Highfield Gdns
 OLD/WMLY/WICK BS30 .... 376 D4
Highfield Gv *HORF/LLZ* BS7 .... 364 B1
Highfield La *LYD* GL15 .... 234 E1
 YATE/CS BS37 .... 349 H1
Highfield Pl *GLE* GL4 .... 3 F6
Highfield Rd *GLE* GL4 .... 3 F6
 LYD GL15 .... 204 E5
 LYD GL15 .... 234 C1
 MTCHDN GL17 .... 121 J6
 RSTROUD/NAIL GL6 .... 214 C3
 STROUD GL5 .... 215 G8
 TET GL8 .... 302 B5
 YATE/CS BS37 .... 347 J5
Highfields *BAD* GL9 .... 337 K4
Highfields Ap *DSLY* GL11 .... 267 G6 ⊞
Highfields Cl *BRSTK/PCHW* BS34 ... 355 K3
Highfield Wy *RSTROUD/NAIL* GL6 ... 244 A2
High Furlong *DSLY* GL11 .... 266 D1 ⊞
High Gv *HNLZ/SM/SNYPK/WT* BS9 ... 352 E7
Highgrove Wy *BWTH/CHD* GL3 ... 103 H7
Highland Rd *CHELTS* GL53 .... 134 C2
Highlands Dr *DSLY* GL11 .... 296 C2
Highleaze Rd
 OLD/WMLY/WICK BS30 .... 376 D2
Highlife Dr *VGL* GL2 .... 157 G5
Highmore Gdns *HORF/LLZ* BS7 ... 355 J7
Highnam Ct *BRSTK/PCHW* BS34 ... 343 F5
High Nash *CLFD* GL16 .... 175 K5
High Orchard St *GL* GL1 .... 2 B4 ⊞
High Pk *HGRV/WHIT* BS14 .... 374 A5
High Rd *HGHW* SN6 .... 308 D5
High St *BAD* GL9 .... 337 H2
 BAD GL9 .... 350 E4
 BDWAY WR12 .... 18 E6 ⊞
 BDWAY WR12 .... 40 C5
 BRKLY GL13 .... 264 A4
 CBRIS/FH BS1 .... 364 B7 ⊞
 CBRIS/FH BS1 .... 364 B7 ⊞
 CHCAM GL55 .... 9 G2
 CHCAM GL55 .... 20 E3
 CHELT GL50 .... 4 B4 ⊞
 CHELTE/BC GL52 .... 4 C4
 CHELTE/BC GL52 .... 107 J2
 CHELTW GL51 .... 4 A3
 CHEP NP16 .... 288 A6
 CHPMW/MSHF SN14 .... 370 B2
 CHPMW/MSHF SN14 .... 371 J6
 CIND GL14 .... 149 J3
 CIND GL14 .... 151 H6
 CIND GL14 .... 151 F5
CIND GL14 .... 153 H5
CIND GL14 .... 180 C2
CIR GL7 .... 254 E7
CIR GL7 .... 278 D8
CIR GL7 .... 281 J1
CIR GL7 .... 281 H2
CIR GL7 .... 283 F8
CIR GL7 .... 285 G3
CLFD GL16 .... 175 K4
CLFD GL16 .... 203 J1
COTS GL54 .... 92 C6
COTS GL54 .... 115 H8
COTS GL54 .... 165 K3
COTS GL54 .... 169 G4
DSLY GL11 .... 238 D8
EVE WR11 .... 7 G2
EVILLE/WHL BS5 .... 365 F5
FRCTL/WBN BS36 .... 344 D8
GL GL1 .... 3 D6
GLE GL4 .... 159 C4
HGHW SN6 .... 310 D7
HNLZ/SM/SNYPK/WT BS9 .... 353 J6
KEYN BS31 .... 375 K8
KGWD/HNM BS15 .... 366 E6
KGWD/HNM BS15 .... 367 H6
KGWD/HNM BS15 .... 375 H1
LYD GL15 .... 204 E6
LYD GL15 .... 207 H4
LYD GL15 .... 231 F1
LYD GL15 .... 233 K4
LYD GL15 .... 233 K4
MANG/FISH BS16 .... 366 C2
MIM GL56 .... 44 B4
MIM GL56 .... 45 K8 ⊞
MIM GL56 .... 68 E2
MTCHDN GL17 .... 121 H6
MTCHDN GL17 .... 122 D6
MTCHDN GL17 .... 123 C4
MTCHDN GL17 .... 149 H1
NWNT GL18 .... 73 J5
OLD/WMLY/WICK BS30 .... 367 K4
OLD/WMLY/WICK BS30 .... 368 D8
OLD/WMLY/WICK BS30 .... 369 H5
OLD/WMLY/WICK BS30 .... 376 E2
OLD/WMLY/WICK BS30 .... 377 F8
RSTROUD/NAIL GL6 .... 216 E6
RSTROUD/NAIL GL6 .... 243 J8 ⊞
RSTROUD/NAIL GL6 .... 244 D4
STNHO GL10 .... 213 F7
STNHO GL10 .... 241 G3
STROUD GL5 .... 214 E7
STROUD GL5 .... 242 B5
TET GL8 .... 271 K5
TEWK GL20 .... 13 J8
TEWK GL20 .... 33 H7
THNB/SVB BS35 .... 316 B5
VGL GL2 .... 181 F3
VGL GL2 .... 182 D2
WUE GL12 .... 297 F7 ⊞
WUE GL12 .... 319 J8
WUE GL12 .... 320 D2
WUE GL12 .... 321 H1
YATE/CS BS37 .... 345 K2
YATE/CS BS37 .... 347 K5
High Vw *CHEP* NP16 .... 288 A6 ⊞
 VGL GL2 .... 129 C3
Highview Rd *CIND* GL14 .... 151 G6 ⊞
 KGWD/HNM BS15 .... 366 E6
 LYD GL15 .... 206 B3
 MTCHDN GL17 .... 122 B8
Highview Wy *LYD* GL15 .... 205 H6
Highway *YATE/CS* BS37 .... 347 H4
Highwood Av *CHELTS* GL53 .... 106 C3
Highwood La *BRSTK/PCHW* BS34 ... 342 C7
 HNBRY/STHM BS10 .... 342 B7
Highwood Rd *BRSTK/PCHW* BS34 ... 342 C7
 HNBRY/STHM BS10 .... 342 B7
Highworth Crs *YATE/CS* BS37 ..... 347 K6
Highworth Rd
 BRSG/KWL/STAPK BS4 .... 374 C1
 GL GL1 .... 130 B8
Hiilrise *LYD* GL15 .... 205 F5
Hilcote Dr *COTS* GL54 .... 143 J2
Hildyard Cl *VGL* GL2 .... 156 E7
Hilands Dr *CHELTS* GL53 .... 134 D2
Hillary Rd *CHELTS* GL53 .... 134 E2
Hillborough Rd *GLE* GL4 .... 158 A3
Hillbrook Rd *THNB/SVB* BS35 ..... 316 D6 ⊞
Hill Burn *HNLZ/SM/SNYPK/WT* BS9 ... 354 A6
Hillburn Rd *EVILLE/WHL* BS5 ..... 366 A6
Hill Cl *DSLY* GL11 .... 266 D2 ⊞
Hilcot Cl *VGL* GL2 .... 156 E5
Hill Court Rd *CHELTE/BC* GL52 .... 4 C1
Hill Crest *BRSG/KWL/STAPK* BS4 ... 374 A5
 VGL GL2 .... 100 E8
Hillcrest *BRKLY* GL13 .... 264 B3
 CHPMW/MSHF SN14 .... 373 J8
 THNB/SVB BS35 .... 316 B5
Hillcrest La *CLFD* GL16 .... 176 B3
Hillcrest Rd *CLFD* GL16 .... 175 K1
 STROUD GL5 .... 214 A6
Hill End Dr *HNBRY/STHM* BS10 ... 353 F3
Hill End Rd *TEWK* GL20 .... 12 D8 ⊞
 TEWK GL20 .... 12 E6
Hillersland La *CLFD* GL16 .... 147 J3
Hillesley Rd *WUE* GL12 .... 320 D2

Hillfield CHELTW GL51 .... **105** K5
  STROUD GL5 .... **214** B7 4
Hillfield Court Rd GL GL1 .... 3 E3
Hillfields du MANG/FISH BS16 .... **366** C3
Hill Gv HNLZ/SM/SNYPK/WT BS9 .... **354** A8
Hillgrove St CBRISNE BS2 .... **364** C6 8
Hillgrove St North CBRISNE BS2 .. **364** B6 7
Hill Hay Rd GLE GL4 .... **158** E3
Hill House Rd MANG/FISH BS16 .... **367** F1
Hillier Cl STROUD GL5 .... **215** F5 5
Hillier Dr CHELTW GL51 .... **133** K1
Hill La THNB/SVB BS35 .... **291** J6
  YATE/CS BS37 .... **349** F7
Hill Lawn BRSG/KWL/STAPK BS4 ..... **374** C3
Hillmill La WUE GL12 .... **321** H2
Hill Rd DSLY GL11 .... **266** E5
  GLE GL4 .... **158** B2
  WUE GL12 .... **297** G8
Hillsborough Rd
  BRSG/KWL/STAPK BS4 .... **374** B2
Hillsdon Rd
  HNLZ/SM/SNYPK/WT BS9 .... **353** H6
Hillside EVE WR11 .... **14** D5
  MANG/FISH BS16 .... **367** F1
  RSTROUD/NAIL GL6 .... **245** F2
Hillside Av KGWD/HNM BS15 .... **366** C5
Hillside Cl CHELTE/BC GL52 .... **83** J3 5
  CHELTW GL51 .... **106** A7
  FRCTL/WBN BS36 .... **345** J7
  LYD GL15 .... **205** F5
Hillside Gdns CHELTE/BC GL52.... **83** J3
Hillside La FRCTL/WBN BS36 .... **345** J7 2
Hillside Rd EVILLE/WHL BS5 .... **366** A7
  MTCHDN GL17 .... **122** D5
Hillside Ter MTCHDN GL17 .... **120** E8 1
Hill St CBRIS/FH BS1 .... **364** A7
  EVILLE/WHL BS5 .... **365** K6
  STROUD GL5 .... **234** A3
The Hill ALMDB BS32 .... **343** F2
  STROUD GL5 .... **214** D7
Hilltop LYD GL15 .... **206** E6
Hill Top Cl STROUD GL5 .... **215** G7
Hilltop Gdns EVILLE/WHL BS5 .... **366** A7
Hill Top La NWNT GL18 .... **73** K4
Hilltop Rd CHELT GL50 .... **106** D1
Hilltop Rd MANG/FISH BS16 .... **366** D4
Hilltop Vw DSLY GL11 .... **266** C2
  EVILLE/WHL BS5 .... **366** A7
Hill Top Vw RSTROUD/NAIL GL6 ... **244** B2 3
Hill Vw HNLZ/SM/SNYPK/WT BS9 .. **354** A8
  LYD GL15 .... **234** A3
  MANG/FISH BS16 .... **366** D4
Hillview Av BWTH/CHD GL3 .... **132** B3
Hill View Cl OLD/WMLY/WICK BS30.. **376** C2
Hillview Dr BWTH/CHD GL3 .... **131** H6
Hillview La TEWK GL20 .... **12** D7
Hillview Ri CLFD GL16 .... **147** J8
Hillview Rd BWTH/CHD GL3 .... **131** H6
Hill View Rd CHELTE/BC GL52 ...... **5** F3 5
  MANG/FISH BS16 .... **368** E1
  UUSV WR8 .... 2 C6
Hilton Cl VGL GL2 .... **129** H8
Hinders La RTEWK/TIB GL19 .... **125** F4
Hinton Dr OLD/WMLY/WICK BS30 ... **367** J8
Hinton Rd BDWAY WR12 .... **17** G3
  EVILLE/WHL BS5 .... **365** G5
  GL GL1 .... 3 D2
  MANG/FISH BS16 .... **366** A2 1
Hisnams Fld CHELTE/BC GL52 ...... **83** F3 3
Hitchen Cl CHPMW/MSHF SN14 ..... **371** K6
Hitchen Hollow CHEP NP16 .... **312** D2
Hitchings LYD GL15 .... **207** H3
The Hithe STROUD GL5 .... **242** D3
The Hobbins SHPSTR CV36 .... **24** E1
Hobb's La CBRIS/FH BS1 .... **364** A8 8
  CIR GL7 .... **192** E7
  KGWD/HNM BS15 .... **367** H5
  MTCHDN GL17 .... **124** C3
Hobby Cl CHELTS GL53 .... **134** C1
Hockey's La MANG/FISH BS16 .... **366** A2 3
Hoddon La MANG/FISH BS16 .... **368** E1
Hodges Wy CIND GL14 .... **150** E7 8
Hogarth Wk HORF/LLZ BS7 .... **355** F7
Holbrook La
  OLD/WMLY/WICK BS30 .... **368** C7
Holcot Cl CLFD GL16 .... **176** B4
Holcot Rd CLFD GL16 .... **176** B5
Holdenhurst Rd KGWD/HNM BS15.. **366** C5
Holder Cl TET GL8 .... **302** B7
Holder Rd CHELTE/BC GL52 .... **83** F4 1
Holders La NWNT GL18 .... **73** F2
Holford Crs CIR GL7 .... **283** G8
Hollams Rd TEWK GL20 .... **33** J7
Holland Ct GL GL1 .... 3 E2
Hollies Hl RSTROUD/NAIL GL6 .... **270** C2
Hollies La CBATH/BATHN BA1 .... **381** F4
Hollingham La RSTROUD/NAIL GL6.. **270** A5
Hollins Cl CHEP NP16 .... **288** B5 2
Hollis Gdns CHELTW GL51 .... **105** H8
Hollis Rd CHELTW GL51 .... **105** H8
Holloway HI CHPMW/MSHF SN14.... **362** E6
Holloway Rd RSTROUD/NAIL GL6 .... **216** E6
Hollow La STROUD GL5 .... **215** F7
Hollow Rd ALMDB BS32 .... **342** E2

KGWD/HNM BS15 .... **366** E6
The Hollows EVE WR11 .... **15** K4
  FRCTL/WBN BS36 .... **357** J4
The Hollow MTCHDN GL17 .... **122** B7
Hollybush Cl BAD GL9 .... **351** G8
Holly Cl CHEP NP16 .... **312** A1 3
  EVILLE/WHL BS5 .... **366** A4
  MANG/FISH BS16 .... **368** C1
  THNB/SVB BS35 .... **331** K2
Holly Crs KGWD/HNM BS15 .... **366** E5 3
Holly Dr CHPMW/MSHF SN14 ...... **373** F8 1
Holly End VGL GL2 .... **157** F6
Holly Gn KGWD/HNM BS15............. **367** G5
Holly Gv MANG/FISH BS16 .... **366** C3
The Holly Gv VGL GL2 .... **157** F6
Hollyguest Rd KGWD/HNM BS15 ... **366** E8
Hollyhill Rd CIND GL14 .... **150** D5
Holly Hill Rd KGWD/HNM BS15 ...... **367** F6
Hollyheck La
  RSTROUD/NAIL GL6 .... **187** H6 3
Holly La CLFD GL16 .... **204** C1
Hollyleigh Av BRSTK/PCHW BS34 .. **354** D4
Holly Lodge Rd EVILLE/WHL BS5 ... **365** K4
Hollyridge HGRV/WHIT BS14 .... **374** B8
Holly Rd SHPSTR CV36 .... **25** F2
Holly Tree Gdn STROUD GL5 .... **213** K8 8
Holly Tree Pl LYD GL15 .... **206** D5
Hollywell Rd MTCHDN GL17 .... **123** G3
Hollywood La THNB/SVB BS35 .... **341** J7
Hollywood Rd
  BRSG/KWL/STAPK BS4 .... **374** C3
Holmdale Rd BRSTK/PCHW BS34 ... **355** F3
Holmes Hill Rd EVILLE/WHL BS5 .... **365** K6
Holmes St EVILLE/WHL BS5 .... **365** F8 3
Holm La THNB/SVB BS35 .... **329** J4
Holmleigh Rd GL GL1 .... **157** J3
Holmwood KGWD/HNM BS15 .... **375** H1
Holmwood Cl FRCTL/WBN BS36 .. **344** D8 3
  GL GL1 .... **157** K4 3
Holmwood Dr GL GL1 .... **157** K4 3
Holmwood Gdns
  HNLZ/SM/SNYPK/WT BS9 .... **353** J6
Holsom Cl HGRV/WHIT BS14 .... **374** D8
Holsom Rd HGRV/WHIT BS14 ...... **374** E8 2
Holst Wy GL GL4 .... **157** K4
Holtham Av BWTH/CHD GL3 .... **103** K7
Holton Rd HORF/LLZ BS7 .... **354** E8
Holtsdown La CBATH/BATHN BA1 .. **380** C6
Holts Rd NWNT GL18 .... **73** H6
The Holt GLE GL4 .... **131** C7
Holyrood Cl BRSTK/PCHW BS34 ... **355** H2 3
Holy Well Cl
  BRSG/KWL/STAPK BS4 .... **365** J8 3
Holywell Rd DSLY GL11 .... **266** E2
  WUE GL12 .... **297** C6
Homeapple Hl
  OLD/WMLY/WICK BS30 .... **368** A7
Home Ct HNBRY/STHM BS10 .... **354** C4
  MIM GL56 .... **93** K5
Homecroft Dr CHELTW GL51 .... **105** J1
Home Farm Wy THNB/SVB BS35 ..... **341** J5
Homefield RSTROUD/NAIL GL6 ...... **270** B3
  THNB/SVB BS35 .... **316** D6 3
  YATE/CS BS37 .... **347** C3
Home Field Cl MANG/FISH BS16 ..... **357** H8
Homefield Rd MANG/FISH BS16 ..... **368** D1
Home Gnd HGHW SN6 .... **310** C6
  HNLZ/SM/SNYPK/WT BS9 .... **353** K7
Homeground La CIR GL7 .... **255** C7
Homeleaze Rd
  HNBRY/STHM BS10 .... **354** B3
Home Md OLD/WMLY/WICK BS30 ... **376** B2
Homemead Dr
  BRSG/KWL/STAPK BS4 .... **374** C5 8
Home Orch YATE/CS BS37 .... **347** F4
Homestead Cl TEWK GL20 .... **13** K8 3
Homestead Gdns
  MANG/FISH BS16 .... **356** B5
Homestead Rd
  BRSTK/PCHW BS34 .... **354** D3
Honeyborne Wy WUE GL12 .... **335** K1 8
Honeybourne Rd EVE WR11 .... 7 J6
Honey Hill Rd KGWD/HNM BS15 ..... **367** F6
Honeymead HGRV/WHIT BS14 .... **374** B8 3
Honeysuckle La ALMDB BS32 ..... **343** J4 8
  CHELTE/BC GL52 .... **107** J3 8
Honeysuckle Dr GLE GL4 .... **159** C1
Honey Suckle La
  MANG/FISH BS16 .... **365** J2 8
Honeysuckle Wy CHELTE/BC GL52.. **82** E3 2
Honeythorn Cl VGL GL2 .... **129** H7
Honiton Rd MANG/FISH BS16 .... **366** A3
Honyatt Rd GL GL1 .... 3 D2
Hookshouse La TET GL8 .... **301** J8
  TET GL8 .... **325** F3
Hook's La NWNT GL18 .... **74** D3
Hoo La CHCAM GL55 .... **20** D3
  RTEWK/TIB GL19 .... **57** C6
Hope Mill La STROUD GL5 .... **243** C4
Hope Orch CHELTW GL51 .... **105** H2
Hope Rd YATE/CS BS37 .... **346** C4
Hopes Cl LYD GL15 .... **234** C4

Hope St CHELTW GL51 .... **106** B3
Hopewell Rd CBRISNE BS2 .... **364** D3 8
Hopewell Gdns AVONM BS11 .... **352** B7
Hopewell St GL GL1 .... 3 D5
Hopkin Cl THNB/SVB BS35 .... **316** D7
Hopland Cl OLD/WMLY/WICK BS30 .. **376** C3
Hopp's Rd KGWD/HNM BS15 .... **366** D7
Hopton Rd DSLY GL11 .... **266** E1
Hopyard La NWNT GL18 .... **73** J4
The Hopyard TEWK GL20 .... **34** C5
Horcott Rd CIR GL7 .... **254** D8
Horfield Rd CBRISNE BS2 .... **364** B7
Horley Rd CBRISNE BS2 .... **364** E5
Hornbeam Ms VGL GL2 .... **130** D1 3
Horn La MIM GL56 .... **70** E8
Horns Rd STROUD GL5 .... **215** F8
Horsbere Rd BWTH/CHD GL3 .... **131** J6
Horsecroft Gdns
  OLD/WMLY/WICK BS30 .... **367** C8 3
Horse Fair La CHELTS GL53 .... **135** C1 8
Horsefair La NWNT GL18 .... **73** G5
Horsefair St CHELTS GL53 .... **107** C8
The Horsefair CBRIS/FH BS1 .... **364** C7
Horse La THNB/SVB BS35 .... **316** D1
Horsepool La LYD GL15 .... **230** E2
  OLD/WMLY/WICK BS30 .... **369** H6
Horse Pool La RWYE HR9 .... **146** E1 8
The Horsepool CLFD GL16 .... **147** J8 8
Horseshoe La YATE/CS BS37 .... **347** K5
Horse St YATE/CS BS37 .... **348** A6
Horsford Rd WUE GL12 .... **319** K1
Horslea MTCHDN GL17 .... **149** F1
Horsley Cl GLE GL4 .... **159** C1
Horsley Hl RSTROUD/NAIL GL6 ...... **270** C5
Horsley Rd RSTROUD/NAIL GL6 ..... **270** C4
Hortham La ALMDB BS32 .... **331** C8
Horton Hl YATE/CS BS37 .... **349** F1
Horton Rd GL GL1 .... 3 E3
  YATE/CS BS37 .... **348** A4
Horton St CBRISNE BS2 .... **364** D8
Horwood Cl
  OLD/WMLY/WICK BS30 .... **376** B2 3
Horwood La WUE GL12 .... **335** K2
Hospital Rd MIM GL56 .... **45** K8
Host St CBRIS/FH BS1 .... **364** B7 3
Hottom Gdns HORF/LLZ BS7 .... **354** E7
Hot Water La KGWD/HNM BS15 ..... **367** F3
Houlton St CBRISNE BS2 .... **364** D6
Hounds Rd YATE/CS BS37 .... **347** K6
Howard Av EVILLE/WHL BS5 .... **365** J6
Howard Cl TEWK GL20 .... **34** D6
Howard Cl CLFD GL16 .... **176** B3
  MANG/FISH BS16 .... **366** D2
  TEWK GL20 .... **34** D6
  THNB/SVB BS35 .... **316** C4 3
Howard St EVILLE/WHL BS5 .... **365** J5
  .... 2 C6
Howcroft BWTH/CHD GL3 .... **132** A2
Howell Rd CHELTW GL51 .... **105** K2
Howell's La CLFD GL15 .... **179** J8
Howells Md MANG/FISH BS16 .... **357** H7 3
Howells Rd TEWK GL20 .... **33** J8
Howes Cl OLD/WMLY/WICK BS30 .. **367** C8
Howett Rd EVILLE/WHL BS5 .... **365** C7 3
Howgate Cl GLE GL4 .... **131** H8
Howmead BRKLY GL13 .... **264** A2
Howsmoor La MANG/FISH BS16 ..... **357** H6
Hoylake Dr OLD/WMLY/WICK BS30.. **367** H8
Hucclecote La BWTH/CHD GL3 ..... **132** B4
Hucclecote Rd BWTH/CHD GL3 ... **131** H6
Huckford La FRCTL/WBN BS36 ..... **357** C2
Huckford Rd FRCTL/WBN BS36 ..... **356** E1
Huckley Wy ALMDB BS32 .... **343** K8
Huddleston Rd COTS GL54 .... **62** D7 3
Hudd's Hill Rd EVILLE/WHL BS5..... **365** K6
Hudd's Vale Rd EVILLE/WHL BS5 .. **365** J6 8
Hudman's Cl TEWK GL20 .... **12** E8 3
Hudson Cl EVE WR11 .... 7 H1
  YATE/CS BS37 .... **347** H6
Hudson La CIND GL14 .... **178** C1
Hudson St CHELT GL50 .... 4 B2
Hudsons Vw CIND GL14 .... **178** E1
Hughenden Rd HORF/LLZ BS7 ..... **354** C1
Hughes Crs CHEP NP16 .... **288** A7
Hughes Ter LYD GL15 .... **205** C1
Hulbert Cl
  BRSG/KWL/STAPK BS4 .... **375** F4 3
  CHELTW GL51 .... **82** A7
Hulbert Crs CHELTW GL51 .... **133** K1
Hulse Rd BRSG/KWL/STAPK BS4 .. **374** C5
Humber Pl BWTH/CHD GL3 .... **160** D1
Humber Rd CHELTE/BC GL52 .... 5 E3
Humberstan Wk AVONM BS11 ..... **352** A6 3
Humphreys Rd RSTROUD/NAIL GL6.. **214** A5
Humphreys Barton
  BRSG/KWL/STAPK BS4 .... **374** E1
Hungerford Cl
  BRSG/KWL/STAPK BS4 .... **374** D6
Hungerford Crs
  BRSG/KWL/STAPK BS4 .... **374** D6
Hungerford Gdns
  BRSG/KWL/STAPK BS4 .... **374** D6
Hungerford Rd
  BRSG/KWL/STAPK BS4 .... **374** D6

Hungerford St CHELT GL50 .... 4 B2 🔲
Hungerford Wk
    BRSG/KWL/STAPK BS4 .... 374 D5
Hunger Hl DSLY GL11 .... 266 E6
Hung Rd AVONM BS11 .... 352 A8
Hunters CI KGWD/HNM BS15 ..... 375 H1 🔲
Hunters Dr KGWD/HNM BS15 .... 367 F5
Hunters Ga GLE GL4 .... 159 F2
Hunters Md BAD GL9 .... 338 A4
Hunters Rd CHELTE/BC GL52 .... 82 E2
    KGWD/HNM BS15 .... 375 H1
Hunters Rd East
    KGWD/HNM BS15 .... 375 H1
Hunter's Wy BRSTK/PCHW BS34 .... 355 F3
    COTS GL54 .... 137 J2
    STROUD GL5 .... 213 K7
Hunthill CIND GL14 .... 154 A4
Huntingdon CI STROUD GL5 .... 213 K8 🔲
Huntley CI GLE GL4 .... 159 G1
Huntscote Rd CHELTW GL51 .... 106 A1
Huntsfield CI CHELT GL50 .... 4 C1 🔲
Hunts Grove Vw VGL GL2 .... 157 H7
Huntsmans CI CHELTE/BC GL52 ..... 83 G2 🔲
Huntsmans Meet COTS GL54 .... 137 J2 🔲
Hurcombe Wy BWTH/CHD GL3 .... 132 C3
Hurlingham Rd RDLND/MONT BS6 .. 364 D4
Hurst CI VGL GL2 .... 131 F1
Hurstwood Rd MANG/FISH BS16 ... 366 D1
Hutton CI
    HNLZ/SM/SNYPK/WT BS9 .... 353 C7
Huxley CI CIR GL7 .... 278 E7
Huxley Rd GL GL1 .... 3 D6
Huxley Wy CHELTE/BC GL52 .... 82 D2
Huyton Rd EVILLE/WHL BS5 .... 365 J3 🔲
Hyatts Wy CHELTE/BC GL52 .... 83 G3
Hyde Av THNB/SVB BS35 .... 316 B8 🔲
Hyde CI GL GL1 .... 3 E3
Hyde La CHELT GL50 .... 82 D7
    CIND GL14 .... 180 E1
    GL GL1 .... 3 E3
    VGL GL2 .... 211 J1
Hyde Park Cnr RTEWK/TIB GL19 .... 51 K3
Hyde's La CHPMW/MSHF SN14 .... 370 D3
The Hyde COTS GL54 .... 85 H1
Hyett Rd STROUD GL5 .... 214 A7
Hygrove La VGL GL2 .... 128 B5
Hyland Gv
    HNLZ/SM/SNYPK/WT BS9 .... 353 H6

I

Icehouse La MIM GL56 .... 68 D4
Icombe CI CHELTE/BC GL52 .... 83 F3 🔲
Ida Rd EVILLE/WHL BS5 .... 365 G6 🔲
Idsall Dr CHELTE/BC GL52 .... 107 J2
Idstone Rd MANG/FISH BS16 .... 366 B2 🔲
Iles CI KGWD/HNM BS15 .... 375 J2
ilmington Rd SHPSTR CV36 .... 11 K1
Ilsyn Gv HGRV/WHIT BS14 .... 374 C7
Imber Court CI HGRV/WHIT BS14 .. 374 A6
Imjin Rd CHELTE/BC GL52 .... 5 F3
Imperial Circ CHELT GL50 .... 4 B4 🔲
Imperial La CHELT GL50 .... 4 B4 🔲
Imperial Rd HGRV/WHIT BS14 ...... 374 B6
Imperial Sq CHELT GL50 .... 4 B4 🔲
Inchbrook Rd RSTROUD/NAIL GL6 .. 242 C8
India Rd GL GL1 .... 3 E5
Ingleside Rd KGWD/HNM BS15 ..... 366 C5
Inglestone Rd WUE GL12 .... 335 K1
Ingmire Rd EVILLE/WHL BS5 .... 365 F3
Ingst Rd THNB/SVB BS35 .... 330 A2
Inkerman CI HORF/LLZ BS7 .... 354 C7
The Inner Down ALMDB BS32 .... 331 H3
Inner Loop Rd CHEP NP16 .... 288 C8
Innerstone La RTEWK/TIB GL19 .... 52 A6
Innsworth La BWTH/CHD GL3 ...... 103 H1
    VGL GL2 .... 130 E1
Insley Gdns GLE GL4 .... 131 H6
Inverlea Ct CHCAM GL55 .... 9 F2
Ipswich Dr BRSG/KWL/STAPK BS4 . 365 J8
Irena Rd MANG/FISH BS16 .... 365 K4 🔲
Iron Acton CI YATE/CS BS37 .... 346 C3
Iron Hogg La WUE GL12 .... 317 J3
Ironmonger's La BRKLY GL13 .... 264 C3
Ironmould La
    BRSG/KWL/STAPK BS4 .... 375 F4
Ironstone CI LYD GL15 .... 204 E6 🔲
Irving CI MANG/FISH BS16 .... 366 E2 🔲
Isbourne Rd CHELTE/BC GL52 .... 5 F3 🔲
Isbourne Wy COTS GL54 .... 62 E6
Isleys Ct OLD/WMLY/WICK BS30 .. 376 A3 🔲
Ismay Rd CHELT GL51 .... 105 J2
Ison Hill Rd HNBRY/STHM BS10 .... 353 F5 🔲
Itchington Rd THNB GL13 .... 316 B4
    THNB/SVB BS35 .... 333 G2
Ivor Rd EVILLE/WHL BS5 .... 365 G6
Ivory CI GL GL1 .... 157 J4
Ivy Bank CHELTE/BC GL52 .... 107 J3 🔲
Ivy La EVE WR11 .... 6 B1
    MANG/FISH BS16 .... 366 A3 🔲
Izod's CI CHCAM GL55 .... 20 D4 🔲

J

Jackbarrow Rd CIR GL7 .... 191 G6
Jackson Cl THNB/SVB BS35 .... 329 F7 🔲
Jackson Crs VGL GL2 .... 103 G8
Jackson Rd CHNTN OX7 .... 118 D4
    CIR GL7 .... 278 D3
Jacobs CI TET GL8 .... 302 C5 🔲
Jacob St CBRISNE BS2 .... 364 C7
Jamaica St CBRISNE BS2 .... 364 B6
James CI MANG/FISH BS16 .... 366 E2 🔲
James Grieve Rd BWTH/CHD GL3 .. 159 H1
Jameson Ct MIM GL56 .... 69 K1 🔲
James Orch BRKLY GL13 .... 263 K3
James Rd MANG/FISH BS16 .... 366 E3
James St CBRISNE BS2 .... 364 E4
    EVILLE/WHL BS5 .... 364 D6
James Wk LYD GL15 .... 205 K5
James Wy BWTH/CHD GL3 .... 132 A8
Jane St EVILLE/WHL BS5 .... 365 F7
Japonica CI BWTH/CHD GL3 .... 103 J7 🔲
Japonica Dr CHELTW GL51 .... 134 A1
Jardine Dr CHELTE/BC GL52 .... 82 E2
Jarvis St EVILLE/WHL BS5 .... 365 F8
Jasmin CI GLE GL4 .... 159 F2
Jasmine Gv AVONM BS11 .... 352 E4 🔲
Jasmin Wy CHELTW GL51 .... 133 K1
Javelin Wy BWTH/CHD GL3 .... 160 D1
Jay's Md WUE GL12 .... 297 G3
Jaythorpe GLE GL4 .... 159 F3
Jean Rd BRSG/KWL/STAPK BS4 ..... 374 D2
Jefferies CI CIR GL7 .... 255 F7
Jefferies Hill Bottom
    KGWD/HNM BS15 .... 375 G1
Jeffery Ct OLD/WMLY/WICK BS30 . 367 H8
Jenkin's La RSTROUD/NAIL GL6 .... 186 E7
Jenner CI GLE GL4 .... 131 H6
    YATE/CS BS37 .... 348 B6
Jenner Ct BRKLY GL13 .... 264 A3 🔲
Jenner Wk CHELT GL50 .... 4 B5 🔲
Jersey Av BRSG/KWL/STAPK BS4 ... 374 E2
    CHELTE/BC GL52 .... 5 D4
Jersey Rd GL GL1 .... 3 D5
Jersey St CHELTE/BC GL52 .... 4 C5 🔲
Jesson Rd CHELTE/BC GL52 .... 83 G3
Jessop Av CHELT GL50 .... 4 A4
Jessop Dr COTS GL54 .... 169 G3
Jewson CI GLE GL4 .... 157 K4 🔲
Jeynes Rw TEWK GL20 .... 33 J7
Jocelyn Rd HORF/LLZ BS7 .... 354 D7
Jockey La EVILLE/WHL BS5 .... 366 A7
John Bevan CI STROUD GL5 .... 215 F6 🔲
John Daniels Wy BWTH/CHD GL3 .. 131 J2 🔲
John of Gaunt Rd CIR GL7 .... 283 F8
Johnson Dr
    OLD/WMLY/WICK BS30 .... 376 A1
Johnsons La EVILLE/WHL BS5 .... 365 H5
Johnsons Rd EVILLE/WHL BS5 ...... 365 H5
Johnsons Wy LYD GL15 .... 206 C4
Johnstone CI RTEWK/TIB GL19 ..... 53 G8 🔲
Johnstone Rd NWNT GL18 .... 73 H6
John St CBRIS/FH BS1 .... 364 E3 🔲
    CBRISNE BS2 .... 364 E4 🔲
    KGWD/HNM BS15 .... 366 C6
    STROUD GL5 .... 214 E7 🔲
John Tame CI CIR GL7 .... 255 F6
John Wesley Rd EVILLE/WHL BS5 .. 366 B8
John Woolfe Ct MIM GL56 .... 21 H8
Jordans CI BDWAY WR12 .... 18 C3
Jordans Wy VGL GL2 .... 130 B1
Jordan Wk ALMDB BS32 .... 343 H6
Josend Crs RTEWK/TIB GL19 .... 55 F8
Joyford Hl CLFD GL16 .... 147 K8
Joyner Rd CHELTW GL51 .... 106 A2
Joys Green Rd MTCHDN GL17 .... 148 E1
Jubilee CI DSLY GL11 .... 238 C8
Jubilee Crs MANG/FISH BS16 .... 357 C8
Jubilee Dr TEWK GL20 .... 13 K8
    THNB/SVB BS35 .... 316 C6
Jubilee Gdns CIR GL7 .... 278 D8
    YATE/CS BS37 .... 347 J4 🔲
Jubilee La WUE GL12 .... 318 C7
Jubilee PI RTEWK/TIB GL19 .... 53 G8
Jubilee Rd BRSG/KWL/STAPK BS4 . 374 B5
    CBRISNE BS2 .... 364 E5
    DSLY GL11 .... 266 E4
    EVILLE/WHL BS5 .... 365 K7
    KGWD/HNM BS15 .... 366 C6
    LYD GL15 .... 234 C3
    MTCHDN GL17 .... 123 G6
    RSTROUD/NAIL GL6 .... 270 C1
Jubilee St CBRISNE BS2 .... 364 D5
Jubilee Wy BRKLY GL13 .... 235 K6
    THNB/SVB BS35 .... 314 C6
    YATE/CS BS37 .... 334 E4
    YATE/CS BS37 .... 347 H1
Judge's La NWNT GL18 .... 96 E5
Julian CI GLE GL4 .... 131 F6 🔲
Julius Rd HORF/LLZ BS7 .... 364 B3
Julius Wy LYD GL15 .... 234 B2
Jumpers La BRKLY GL13 .... 264 A3
Junction Rd
    BRSG/KWL/STAPK BS4 .... 374 B2

Juniper Av GLE GL4 .... 158 D2
Juniper Ct EVILLE/WHL BS5 .... 365 G4 🔲
    STNHO GL10 .... 213 F6
Juniper Wy ALMDB BS32 .... 343 K7
Jupiter Rd BRSTK/PCHW BS34 ...... 342 B7
Jupiter Wy GLE GL4 .... 131 H8
Justice Rd MANG/FISH BS16 .... 366 A3 🔲
Justicia Wy CHELTW GL51 .... 133 K1

K

Kansas Dr CIR GL7 .... 283 F1
Kathdene Gdns HORF/LLZ BS7 ...... 364 D3
Katherine Dr WUE GL12 .... 319 H1 🔲
Katherine's Wk CIR GL7 .... 285 H2
Kaybourne Crs BWTH/CHD GL3 .... 132 B1
Kayte CI CHELTE/BC GL52 .... 83 F4
Kayte La CHELTE/BC GL52 .... 83 G5
Keats Av VGL GL2 .... 157 J2
Keats Gdns STROUD GL5 .... 214 C5 🔲
Keble CI CIR GL7 .... 277 H1
    CIR GL7 .... 285 H1 🔲
Keble Lawns CIR GL7 .... 255 F7 🔲
Keble Rd MIM GL56 .... 70 A2
    RSTROUD/NAIL GL6 .... 244 E3
The Keelings CIND GL14 .... 150 E5
Keels HGHW SN6 .... 310 C5
Keen's Gv THNB/SVB BS35 .... 328 E3
Keepers MI CHELTE/BC GL52 .... 83 H3
The Keep OLD/WMLY/WICK BS30 .. 376 E1
Keetley CI SHPSTR CV36 .... 25 F2
Keinton Wk HNBRY/STHM BS10 ... 353 J4
Kelbra Crs FRCTL/WBN BS36 .... 345 H8
Kellaway Av
    HNBRY/STHM BS10 .... 354 C8 🔲
    RDLND/MONT BS6 .... 364 B1
Kellaway Crs HORF/LLZ BS7 .... 354 B1
Kells Meend CLFD GL16 .... 147 J8
Kells Rd CLFD GL16 .... 147 J8
Kellys La CHEP NP16 .... 259 G4
Kelston Gdns
    HNBRY/STHM BS10 .... 354 B6 🔲
Kelston Gv KGWD/HNM BS15 ...... 366 E6
Kelston Rd HNBRY/STHM BS10 ..... 354 A6
Kelston Wk MANG/FISH BS16 .... 366 C2
Kemble CI KGWD/HNM BS15 .... 366 E8 🔲
Kemble Dr CIR GL7 .... 249 H8
Kemble Gv CHELTW GL51 .... 105 F7
Kemble Rd GLE GL4 .... 157 K4
Kemerton Rd CHELT GL50 .... 106 B8
    TEWK GL20 .... 13 J8
Kemperleye Wy ALMDB BS32 .... 343 H7 🔲
Kempsford Acre
    CHELTE/BC GL52 .... 83 H3 🔲
Kemps La RSTROUD/NAIL GL6 ...... 187 H7
Kempton CI THNB/SVB BS35 .... 316 B3 🔲
Kempton Gv CHELTW GL51 .... 105 H4
Kencourt CI VGL GL2 .... 3 F3 🔲
Kendall Gdns MANG/FISH BS16 .... 366 D2
Kendall Rd MANG/FISH BS16 .... 366 D2
Kendal Rd HORF/LLZ BS7 .... 354 E7
    VGL GL2 .... 130 E3
Kendon Dr HNBRY/STHM BS10 .... 354 B7
Kendon Wy HNBRY/STHM BS10 ... 354 B6
Kendrick St STROUD GL5 .... 214 E7 🔲
Kenelm Dr CHELTS GL53 .... 106 C8 🔲
Kenelm Gdns CHELT GL50 .... 106 B8 🔲
Kenelm Ri COTS GL54 .... 62 D7
Kenilworth Av YATE/CS BS37 .... 347 H6
Kenilworth Av GL GL1 .... 3 E3
Kenilworth Dr
    OLD/WMLY/WICK BS30 .... 376 C5 🔲
Kenilworth Rd
    RDLND/MONT BS6 .... 364 A5 🔲
Kenmore Crs HORF/LLZ BS7 .... 354 C5
Kenmore Dr HORF/LLZ BS7 .... 354 C5
Kenmore Gv HORF/LLZ BS7 .... 354 C5 🔲
Kennard Ri EVILLE/WHL BS5 .... 366 C7
Kennard Rd KGWD/HNM BS15 ..... 366 C6
Kennedy CI GLE GL4 .... 131 H5
Kennedy Wy YATE/CS BS37 .... 347 G5
Kennel Dr BAD GL9 .... 350 E4
Kennel La BWTH/CHD GL3 .... 160 C1
    MIM GL56 .... 92 E2
Kenneth Ct CHELTS GL53 .... 134 E2
Kenneth Rd
    BRSG/KWL/STAPK BS4 .... 374 C4
Kennett Gdns GLE GL4 .... 159 G2
Kennet Wy THNB/SVB BS35 .... 316 C6
Kennington Av HORF/LLZ BS7 ...... 364 C2
    KGWD/HNM BS15 .... 366 D5 🔲
Kennion Rd EVILLE/WHL BS5 .... 366 A7 🔲
Kennmoor CI
    OLD/WMLY/WICK BS30 .... 367 G8
Kenn Rd EVILLE/WHL BS5 .... 366 A7
Kensington CI THNB/SVB BS35 ..... 316 B4 🔲
Kensington Pk
    EVILLE/WHL BS5 .... 364 E5 🔲🔲
Kensington Park Rd
    BRSG/KWL/STAPK BS4 .... 374 B4
Kensington Rd EVILLE/WHL BS5 ... 366 A6 🔲

MANG/FISH BS16 .... 366 D2
RDLND/MONT BS6 .... 364 A5
Kent Av YATE/CS BS37 .... 347 H3
Kent Cl BRSTK/PCHW BS34 ..... 355 H2
BWTH/CHD GL3 .... 132 E2
Kent End HGHW SN6 .... 308 C5
Kentmere Cl CHELTW GL51 .... 105 J7
Kenton Dr VGL GL2 .... 130 E1
Kenton Ms
HNLZ/SM/SNYPK/WT BS9 ...... 364 A1
Kent Rd HORF/LLZ BS7 .... 364 C3
Kents Gn KGWD/HNM BS15 ...... 366 E4
Keriston Av BWTH/CHD GL3 ...... 131 J1
Kerrin La LYD GL15 .... 260 D2
Kersterman Rd
RDLND/MONT BS6 .... 364 B3
Kerstin Cl CHELT GL50 .... 106 C1
Kestrel Cl BRSTK/PCHW BS34 ... 342 C6
CHELTS GL53 .... 134 C1
THNB/SVB BS35 .... 316 D4
YATE/CS BS37 .... 347 H6
Kestrel Ct STNHO GL10 .... 213 F7
Kestrel Dr MANG/FISH BS16 ..... 368 E2
Kestrel Gdns VGL GL2 .... 157 F3
Kestrel Wy TEWK GL20 .... 34 C5
Keswick Cl VGL GL2 .... 3 F2
Keswick Rd CHELTW GL51 .... 105 J7
Keswick Wk HNBRY/STHM BS10 .. 354 A4
Kevin Cl GLE GL4 .... 131 F6
Kew Pl CHELTS GL53 .... 4 B6
Kews La NWNT GL18 .... 72 D6
Kew Wk BRSG/KWL/STAPK BS4 .. 374 D6
Keynsham Bank CHELTE/BC GL52 .. 5 D5
Keynsham By-pass KEYN BS31 .. 375 K7
Keynsham La LYD GL15 .... 260 A2
Keynsham Rd CHELTS GL53 .... 4 C5
OLD/WMLY/WICK BS30 .... 376 A7
Keynsham St CHELTE/BC GL52 .. 5 D5
Keys Av HORF/LLZ BS7 .... 354 D7
Keyte Rd SHPSTR CV36 .... 11 H2
Kibble's La CIND GL14 .... 178 E1
Kidnalls Rd LYD GL15 .... 205 K5
Kidnams Wk VGL GL2 .... 211 J1
Kidnappers La CHELTS GL53 ..... 134 B2
CHELTS GL53 .... 134 B1
Kilham La COTS GL54 .... 138 B5
Kilkenny St CBRISNE BS2 .... 364 D8
Killcott Rd WUE GL12 .... 321 H6
Kilminster Ct BWTH/CHD GL3 ... 103 J8
Kilmore La TEWK GL20 .... 12 D8
Kiln Cl KGWD/HNM BS15 .... 366 B5
Kilnhurst Cl
OLD/WMLY/WICK BS30 .... 376 A4
Kilwert Cl BRSG/KWL/STAPK BS4 .. 374 C1
Kimberley Av MANG/FISH BS16 .. 366 C1
Kimberley Cl VGL GL2 .... 234 B3
MANG/FISH BS16 .... 357 F7
VGL GL2 .... 131 F2
Kimberley Crs MANG/FISH BS16 .. 366 C1
Kimberley Dr VGL GL2 .... 234 B3
Kimberley Rd KGWD/HNM BS15 .. 366 D5
MANG/FISH BS16 .... 366 C1
Kimberley Wk CHELTE/BC GL52 .. 107 J4
Kimmins Rd STNHO GL10 .... 213 G6
King Alfreds Rd CHEP NP16 ...... 288 C7
King Alfred Wy CHELTE/BC GL52 .. 5 D5
Kingcomb La CHCAM GL55 .... 20 B2
King Edward's Av GL GL1 .... 130 A8
Kingfisher Cl ALMDB BS32 .... 343 J4
THNB/SVB BS35 .... 316 D4
Kingfisher Dr MANG/FISH BS16 .. 355 J8
Kingfisher Ri VGL GL2 .... 156 D5
Kingfisher Rd YATE/CS BS37 ..... 347 J6
King George Cl CHELTS GL53 ..... 107 F8
King Georges Fld COTS GL54 .... 92 D6
Kingham Rd CHNTN OX7 .... 119 K1
King Henry Cl CHELTS GL53 ...... 107 F8
King Johns Ct TEWK GL20 .... 33 H7
King John's Rd KGWD/HNM BS15 .. 366 B4
King La YATE/CS BS37 .... 337 F8
Kingley St STROUD GL5 .... 214 A7
King Rd BRSG/KWL/STAPK BS4 .. 374 A5
Kingrove Crs YATE/CS BS37 ...... 348 A6
Kingrove La YATE/CS BS37 .... 348 A7
Kings Av KGWD/HNM BS15 .... 375 G2
RDLND/MONT BS6 .... 364 A2
King's Barton St GL GL1 .... 3 D4
Kingsclere Dr CHELTE/BC GL52 .. 82 E3
Kingscote Av YATE/CS BS37 ...... 347 H8
Kingscote Cl BWTH/CHD GL3 .... 132 B2
CHELTW GL51 .... 105 H7
Kingscote Dr GLE GL4 .... 159 G1
Kingscote Gv CHELTW GL51 ...... 105 H7
Kingscote Pk EVILLE/WHL BS5 .. 366 B8
Kingscote Rd East CHELTW GL51 .. 105 H7
Kingscote Rd West CHELTW GL51 .. 105 H8
Kingscourt La STROUD GL5 .... 242 C2
Kingscroft Rd BWTH/CHD GL3 ... 131 J7
Kingsdale Cl BDWAY WR12 .... 18 E6
Kingsditch La CHELTW GL51 ..... 106 A2
Kingsdown DSLY GL11 .... 266 E4

Kingsdown Pde
RDLND/MONT BS6 .... 364 B6
Kings Dr DSLY GL11 .... 266 E4
HORF/LLZ BS7 .... 364 A1
KGWD/HNM BS15 .... 375 G2
Kings Elm VGL GL2 .... 103 F1
Kingsfield La KGWD/HNM BS15 .. 366 E8
KGWD/HNM BS15 .... 375 K1
OLD/WMLY/WICK BS30 .... 375 K2
Kings Ga TEWK GL20 .... 34 A8
Kings Head La COTS GL54 .... 166 B3
Kingshill Cir GL7 .... 250 B6
Kingshill Rd CIR GL7 .... 250 B8
DSLY GL11 .... 266 E4
Kingshill Rd
BRSG/KWL/STAPK BS4 .... 374 A5
DSLY GL11 .... 266 E4
Kingsholm Ct GL GL1 .... 2 C1
Kingsholme Rd KGWD/HNM BS15 .. 366 D5
Kingsholm Rd GL GL1 .... 2 C2
HNBRY/STHM BS10 .... 354 B6
Kingsholm Sq GL GL1 .... 2 C1
Kingsland Rd CBRISNE BS2 .... 364 E8
Kingsland Road Br CBRISNE BS2 .. 364 E8
Kingsleigh Ct KGWD/HNM BS15 .. 367 F7
Kingsleigh Gdns
KGWD/HNM BS15 .... 367 F7
Kingsley Gdns CHELTW GL51 .... 105 J5
Kingsley Rd EVILLE/WHL BS5 .... 365 G5
GLE GL4 .... 158 C1
RDLND/MONT BS6 .... 364 B4
Kings Md CIND GL14 .... 180 B2
Kingsmead CIR GL7 .... 250 A8
CIR GL7 .... 285 C1
GLE GL4 .... 159 G2
RSTROUD/NAIL GL6 .... 243 K6
Kingsmead Av CHELTW GL51 .... 105 K2
Kingsmead Cl CHELTW GL51 .... 105 K2
Kings Meade CLFD GL16 .... 175 K4
Kings Meadow COTS GL54 .... 115 H6
Kingsmead Rd CHELTW GL51 .... 105 K2
EVILLE/WHL BS5 .... 366 A5
Kingsmead Wk EVILLE/WHL BS5 .. 366 A5
King's Mill La RSTROUD/NAIL GL6 .. 187 G8
Kings Park Av CBRISNE BS2 ...... 365 G8
King Sq CBRISNE BS2 .... 364 B6
King Square Av CBRISNE BS2 .... 364 B6
King's Rd BRSG/KWL/STAPK BS4 .. 374 B5
CHELTE/BC GL52 .... 5 D4
STNHO GL10 .... 213 F5
STROUD GL5 .... 214 D8
Kings Sq OLD/WMLY/WICK BS30 .. 376 C6
Kings St RSTROUD/NAIL GL6 ..... 243 J8
Kingston Cl MANG/FISH BS16 ... 357 G7
Kingston Dr CHELTW GL51 .... 105 G5
MANG/FISH BS16 .... 357 G7
Kingstone Av GLE GL4 .... 131 H5
Kingston Rd TEWK GL20 .... 34 C6
VGL GL2 .... 238 A1
King St CBRIS/FH BS1 .... 364 B8
CHELT GL50 .... 4 B3
CIR GL7 .... 249 K7
EVILLE/WHL BS5 .... 365 G5
KGWD/HNM BS15 .... 366 B6
STROUD GL5 .... 214 E7
Kingsville Rd CHELTW GL51 ...... 106 A1
Kings Wk GL GL1 .... 2 C3
Kingsway BRSTK/PCHW BS34 ... 343 G8
CIR GL7 .... 250 C8
CLFD GL16 .... 176 B3
DSLY GL11 .... 266 E3
EVILLE/WHL BS5 .... 366 B7
Kingsway Av KGWD/HNM BS15 .. 366 B6
Kingsway Crs KGWD/HNM BS15 .. 366 B6
Kingsway La MTCHDN GL17 ...... 121 J7
Kings Well La COTS GL54 .... 145 J5
Kings Weston La AVONM BS11 .. 352 B6
Kings Weston Rd AVONM BS11 .. 352 D6
AVONM BS11 .... 353 F4
Kingswood Cl CHELTE/BC GL52 .. 83 F3
Kingswood Rd WUE GL12 .... 321 H6
Kington La THNB/SVB BS35 ...... 315 K5
Kington Rd THNB/SVB BS35 ...... 315 H1
King William Av CBRIS/FH BS1 .. 364 B8
King William Dr CHELTS GL53 ... 107 F8
Kinmoor GLE GL4 .... 159 F3
Kinsale Rd HGRV/WHIT BS14 .... 374 B7
Kinsham La TEWK GL20 .... 35 G2
Kipling Cl VGL GL2 .... 157 J2
Kipling Rd CHELTW GL51 .... 105 J5
DSLY GL11 .... 267 G7
HORF/LLZ BS7 .... 355 F5
Kirby Rd COTS GL54 .... 145 F3
Kirkby Rd AVONM BS11 .... 352 C5
Kirtlington Rd EVILLE/WHL BS5 .. 365 F3
Kitchener Av GL GL1 .... 158 A1
Kitefield CHELTW GL51 .... 105 J5
Kite Hay Cl MANG/FISH BS16 ... 365 J1
Kites CI ALMDB BS32 .... 343 G4
Kitesnest La STROUD GL5 .... 242 C2
Klondyke Av LYD GL15 .... 234 B3
Knap La RSTROUD/NAIL GL6 ..... 187 H1
WUE GL12 .... 318 D3
Knapp La CHELT GL50 .... 4 A3

DSLY GL11 .... 266 D1
GL11 .... 268 A1
LYD GL15 .... 232 E8
RSTROUD/NAIL GL6 .... 215 K4
RSTROUD/NAIL GL6 .... 243 K6
Knapp Rd CHELT GL50 .... 4 A3
THNB/SVB BS35 .... 316 D5
WUE GL12 .... 297 C7
Knapps La EVILLE/WHL BS5 ...... 365 J4
The Knapp DSLY GL11 .... 266 E4
YATE/CS BS37 .... 347 H1
Knighton Rd HNBRY/STHM BS10 .. 354 C5
Knightsbridge Crs CHELTS GL53 .. 5 D6
Knights Crs NWNT GL18 .... 73 C6
Knights Wy NWNT GL18 .... 73 C6
TEWK GL20 .... 33 K8
Knightwood Rd
BRSTK/PCHW BS34 .... 355 K1
Knockley Patch LYD GL15 .... 205 F4
Knole Cl ALMDB BS32 .... 342 D2
Knole La HNBRY/STHM BS10 ..... 353 J3
Knole Pk ALMDB BS32 .... 342 D3
The Knoll CIR GL7 .... 283 F7
STROUD GL5 .... 215 F7
Knollys End VGL GL2 .... 157 F6
Knovill Cl AVONM BS11 .... 352 D5
Knowles Rd GL GL1 .... 3 D6
Knowsley Rd MANG/FISH BS16 .. 365 J5
Knox Rd LYD GL15 .... 205 H7
Kyderminster Rd COTS GL54 ..... 62 D7
Kyght Cl KGWD/HNM BS15 .... 367 C6
Kynges Mill Cl MANG/FISH BS16 .. 356 A7

L

Laburnum Ct CHELTW GL51 ...... 105 G4
Laburnum Gdns VGL GL2 .... 157 F5
Laburnum Gv MANG/FISH BS16 .. 366 B2
Laburnum Rd GL GL1 .... 157 K1
KGWD/HNM BS15 .... 375 H1
STNHO GL10 .... 212 E7
Laburnum Wk STNHO GL10 ...... 213 F7
Lacca Cl VGL GL2 .... 131 F1
Lacey Cl HGRV/WHIT BS14 .... 374 D8
Lacock Dr OLD/WMLY/WICK BS30 .. 376 A1
Lacy Cl VGL GL2 .... 102 E8
Ladd Cl KGWD/HNM BS15 .... 367 F7
Ladden Ct THNB/SVB BS35 .... 316 C6
The Ladder RSTROUD/NAIL GL6 .. 270 E2
Ladman Gv HGRV/WHIT BS14 ... 374 D8
Ladybellegate St GL GL1 .... 2 B4
Lady Chapel Rd GLE GL4 .... 131 C8
Lady Margaret Cl CHEP NP16 ... 312 B2
Lady Md HGHW SN6 .... 310 D6
Ladysmith Rd CHELTE/BC GL52 .. 5 F5
GL GL1 .... 130 A8
Ladywell Cl VGL GL2 .... 129 H7
Laggar La STROUD GL5 .... 242 B5
Lake La VGL GL2 .... 127 F3
VGL GL2 .... 182 E8
VGL GL2 .... 210 D1
Lake Rd HNBRY/STHM BS10 ..... 354 A7
Lakers GL CLFD GL16 .... 147 K8
Lakeside CIR GL7 .... 254 D8
CIR GL7 .... 279 F7
MANG/FISH BS16 .... 365 J3
Lake Side NWNT GL18 .... 73 C3
Lakeside Av LYD GL15 .... 234 C4
Lakeside Dr LYD GL15 .... 234 C4
Lake St CHELTE/BC GL52 .... 107 H1
VGL GL2 .... 155 H1
Lake View Rd EVILLE/WHL BS5 .. 365 H6
Lakewood Crs HNBRY/STHM BS10 .. 353 K6
Lakewood Rd HNBRY/STHM BS10 .. 353 K6
Lambert Av CHELTW GL51 .... 133 H5
Lambert Cl CHELTW GL51 .... 133 H5
Lambert Dr CHELTW GL51 .... 133 H5
Lambert Gdns CHELTW GL51 .... 133 H5
Lamberts Fld COTS GL54 .... 143 J1
Lamb La CIND GL14 .... 151 F6
Lambley Rd EVILLE/WHL BS5 .... 365 J6
Lambourn Cl VGL GL2 .... 131 C3
Lambourne Av RTEWK/TIB GL19 .. 125 K3
Lambrook Rd MANG/FISH BS16 .. 366 A2
Lambs Barn Pitch NWNT GL18 .. 73 H3
Lambsdowne DSLY GL11 .... 266 D3
Lambsquay Rd CLFD GL16 .... 176 A8
CLFD GL16 .... 203 K1
Lamb St CBRISNE BS2 .... 364 D7
Lamord Ga BRSTK/PCHW BS34 .. 355 J1
Lampern Vw DSLY GL11 .... 268 B5
Lampeter Rd
HNLZ/SM/SNYPK/WT BS9 ...... 353 H7
The Lampreys GLE GL4 .... 130 D8
Lanaway Rd MANG/FISH BS16 .. 356 B8
Lancashire Rd HORF/LLZ BS7 ... 364 C3
Lancaster Cl BRSTK/PCHW BS34 .. 355 H2
Lancaster Cl LYD GL15 .... 234 B1
Lancaster Dr LYD GL15 .... 234 B1
Lancaster Rd CBRISNE BS2 .... 364 E4
CIR GL7 .... 283 C8
TEWK GL20 .... 57 J2

YATE/CS BS37 .... 347 G3
Lancaster St EVILLE/WHL BS5 .... 365 G7 🔲
Lancaut La CHEP NP16 .... 258 B8
Lancelot Ct VGL GL2 .... 238 B2
Landseer Av HORF/LLZ BS7 .... 355 F7
The Land FRCTL/WBN BS36 .... 345 J7
Lanercost Rd HNBRY/STHM BS10 ... 354 A4
Lanesborough Ri
   HGRV/WHIT BS14 .... 374 C7
Lanescourt TEWK GL20 .... 33 H8
The Lanes CHELTS GL53 .... 134 A2
The Lane BDWAY WR12 .... 40 E1
   MIM GL56 .... 71 J7
   RSTROUD/NAIL GL6 .... 213 K4
   SHPSTR CV36 .... 25 G6
   THNB BS35 .... 341 H4
Langdale Gdns VGL GL2 .... 130 E1 🔲
Langdale Rd CHELTW GL51 .... 105 K7
   MANG/FISH BS16 .... 365 K2 🔲
Langdon Rd CHELTS GL53 .... 106 D8
Langet CIR GL7 .... 278 C7
Langetts Rd CLFD GL16 .... 175 K4
Langfield CI HNBRY/STHM BS10 ... 353 H3 🔲
Langford Wy KGWD/HNM BS15 ...... 366 D7
Langham Rd
   BRSG/KWL/STAPK BS4 .... 374 A4 🔲
Langley La BUR/CRTN OX18 .... 287 K1
Langley Mow MANG/FISH BS16 ... 357 H7 🔲
Langley Rd COTS GL54 .... 84 D1
   GLE GL4 .... 158 D1
Langridge La CBATH/BATHN BA1 ... 378 E7
Langthorn CI FRCTL/WBN BS36 ...... 345 H4
Langtoft Rd STROUD GL5 .... 215 G2
Langton CI GLE GL4 .... 131 G5
Langton Court Rd
   BRSG/KWL/STAPK BS4 .... 374 C1
Langton Grove Rd CHELTS GL53 ... 5 E6 🔲
Langton PI CHELTS GL53 .... 5 E6 🔲
Langton Rd
   BRSG/KWL/STAPK BS4 .... 374 C1
Langton Wy
   BRSG/KWL/STAPK BS4 .... 365 J8
Lanham Gdns VGL GL2 .... 157 F7
Lannett Rd GL GL1 .... 130 A8
Lansdown STROUD GL5 .... 214 E7
   YATE/CS BS37 .... 347 G6 🔲
Lansdown Castle Dr
   CHELTW GL51 .... 105 K6 🔲
Lansdown CI CHELTW GL51 .... 106 A6 🔲
   KGWD/HNM BS15 .... 366 D4
Lansdown Crs CHELT GL50 .... 106 B6
Lansdown Crescent La
   CHELT GL50 .... 106 B6
Lansdown La
   OLD/WMLY/WICK BS30 .... 377 J6
Lansdown Lodge Dr
   CHELTW GL51 .... 106 A6 🔲
Lansdown Pde CHELT GL50 .... 106 B6
Lansdown Place La CHELT GL50 .... 4 A5
   CHELT GL50 .... 4 A5
Lansdown Rd CBATH/BATHN BA1 ... 378 D7
   CHELT GL50 .... 4 A5
   CHELTW GL51 .... 106 A6
   GL GL1 .... 3 D2
   KGWD/HNM BS15 .... 366 D4
   MANG/FISH BS16 .... 358 E8
   RDLND/MONT BS6 .... 364 A5
Lansdown Ter
   RDLND/MONT BS6 .... 364 B1 🔲
Lansdown Terrace La CHELT GL50 ...... 4 A4
Lansdown Wk KGWD/HNM BS15 ... 366 E6
   LYD GL15 .... 205 F2
Lantern CI BRKLY GL13 .... 264 A3 🔲
   CIND GL14 .... 150 A6
Lapdown La BAD GL9 .... 361 H5
Laphams Ct
   OLD/WMLY/WICK BS30 .... 376 A2 🔲🔲
Lapwing Al ALMDB BS32 .... 343 H4
   TEWK GL20 .... 34 C5 🔲
Lapwing Gdns MANG/FISH BS16 ... 355 K8 🔲
Larch CI CHELTS GL53 .... 135 H1
The Larches GLE GL4 .... 131 G7
Larchmere Gv CHELTW GL51 .... 133 J1 🔲
Larch Ri CHELTS GL53 .... 134 B2
Larch Rd CHPMW/MSHF SN14 .... 373 F8
   KGWD/HNM BS15 .... 366 E3
Larch Wy BRSTK/PCHW BS34 .... 342 C7
Larchwood Dr GLE GL4 .... 158 A3
Larkfield FRCTL/WBN BS36 .... 345 K7 🔲
Larkham CI GLE GL4 .... 158 D3
Larkhay Rd BWTH/CHD GL3 .... 131 J5
Larkhill CI CHEP NP16 .... 288 A7 🔲
Lark Ri CLFD GL16 .... 175 J3
Larkrise DSLY GL11 .... 266 D1
Lark's Fld MANG/FISH BS16 .... 365 J1 🔲
Larksfield GL5 .... 242 D2
Lark's La YATE/CS BS37 .... 333 H3
Larksleaze Rd
   OLD/WMLY/WICK BS30 .... 375 K4
Larkspear CI GLE GL4 .... 158 A1
Larkspur CI THNB/SVB BS35 .... 316 D4
Larput PI CHELT GL50 .... 4 B2
Lasne Crs BWTH/CHD GL3 .... 160 D2

Lassington Gv VGL GL2 .... 128 C1
Lassington La VGL GL2 .... 128 C1
Latchen MTCHDN GL17 .... 124 B4
Latchen Orch MTCHDN GL17 ...... 124 B4 🔲
Latimer CI BRSG/KWL/STAPK BS4 ... 374 D2
Latimer Rd CIND GL14 .... 151 G5
Latteridge La THNB/SVB BS35 .... 333 G6
Latteridge Rd YATE/CS BS37 .... 345 K2
Latton Rd HORF/LLZ BS7 .... 354 D6
Launceston Av KGWD/HNM BS15 ... 375 G1
Launceston Rd
   KGWD/HNM BS15 .... 366 B5 🔲
Laundry Rd CLFD GL16 .... 174 E7
Laura CI VGL GL2 .... 3 F1
Laurel Av TEWK GL20 .... 57 K2
Laureldene CLFD GL16 .... 204 A3
Laurel Dr CHELTE/BC GL52 .... 5 F1
   CHPMW/MSHF SN14 .... 373 F8
Laurel Ga GLE GL4 .... 159 H2
The Laurels GL GL1 .... 3 D6 🔲
   HNBRY/STHM BS10 .... 341 J8
   MANG/FISH BS16 .... 357 G8
Laurel St KGWD/HNM BS15 .... 366 D6
Laurence CI CHELTW GL51 .... 133 H4
Laurie Crs
   HNLZ/SM/SNYPK/WT BS9 .... 354 B8
Laurie Lee Ct
   OLD/WMLY/WICK BS30 .... 376 B1 🔲
Lavender CI THNB/SVB BS35 .... 316 D5
Lavender La GL GL4 .... 249 J7
Lavender Ms CHELTE/BC GL52 ... 82 E3 🔲
Lavender Rd CHELTW GL51 .... 133 K1
Lavender Vw GLE GL4 .... 159 H2
Lavender Wy ALMDB BS32 .... 343 K7
Lavenham Rd YATE/CS BS37 .... 346 D4
Lavers CI KGWD/HNM BS15 .... 366 D6
Lavington Dr VGL GL2 .... 131 G2
Lavington Rd EVILLE/WHL BS5 .... 366 B8
Lawford Av BRSTK/PCHW BS34 .... 343 G4
Lawfords Ga CBRISNE BS2 .... 364 D7
Lawn Av MANG/FISH BS16 .... 366 B1
Lawn Crs CHELTW GL51 .... 133 J4
Lawn Rd MANG/FISH BS16 .... 366 B1
   RTEWK/TIB GL19 .... 77 G6
Lawnside RSTROUD/NAIL GL6 .... 270 D3
Lawns Pk STROUD GL5 .... 242 B4
Lawns Rd YATE/CS BS37 .... 347 G4
The Lawns CHELTE/BC GL52 .... 60 C7
   GLE GL4 .... 159 F3
   STNHO GL10 .... 212 E6
Lawrence Av EVILLE/WHL BS5 .... 365 F5 🔲
Lawrence CI CHELTE/BC GL52 ...... 107 H8 🔲
   KGWD/HNM BS15 .... 367 G4
Lawrence Dr YATE/CS BS37 .... 346 D4
Lawrence Gv DSLY GL11 .... 266 D4
Lawrence HI EVILLE/WHL BS5 .... 365 F7
Lawrence Rd CIR GL7 .... 249 H7
   TET GL8 .... 272 B5
Lawrence's Meadow
   CHELTE/BC GL52 .... 60 B6 🔲
Lawrence Wy GL GL1 .... 2 C2
Lawrence Wy North GL GL1 .... 2 B1
Lawrence Weston Rd
   AVONM BS11 .... 352 C3
   AVONM BS11 .... 352 E5 🔲
Lawson Gld CHELTS GL53 .... 135 G2 🔲
Laxey Rd HORF/LLZ BS7 .... 354 D7
Laxton CI THNB/SVB BS35 .... 330 E3
Laxton Dr WUE GL12 .... 320 D2
Laxton Rd BWTH/CHD GL3 .... 131 J8
   CHELTW GL51 .... 105 J4
Laymore Rd CIND GL14 .... 150 D5
Laynes Rd BWTH/CHD GL3 .... 131 J6
Leacey Ct BWTH/CHD GL3 .... 103 J7 🔲
Lea Crs VGL GL2 .... 130 E1 🔲
Leacy Ms BWTH/CHD GL3 .... 103 J7
Leadon CI BWTH/CHD GL3 .... 160 C1
Leafield Rd CIR GL7 .... 255 F7
Leaman Cl YATE/CS BS37 .... 347 K5 🔲
Leamington Rd BDWAY WR12 .... 18 D4
Leaping Stocks Rd RWYE HR9 .... 146 D5
Leap V MANG/FISH BS16 .... 357 G6
Leap Valley Crs MANG/FISH BS16 ... 357 F6
Lea Rd BWTH/CHD GL3 .... 160 D1
Lears Dr CHELTE/BC GL52 .... 83 G3
Leaside CI DSLY GL11 .... 266 E2
Leasow La COTS GL54 .... 144 A2
The Leasows CHAM GL55 .... 20 D4
Leaze CI BRKLY GL13 .... 264 A3
The Leazes STROUD GL5 .... 215 F7
The Leaze CIR GL7 .... 278 D8
   HGHW SN6 .... 308 D5
   YATE/CS BS37 .... 347 F4
Lechlade Rd CIR GL7 .... 256 D3
   FGDN SN7 .... 285 J5
   HGHW SN6 .... 284 E8
Lechmere Rd CHELTW GL51 .... 105 J3 🔲
Leckhampton Farm Ct
   CHELTS GL53 .... 134 B3 🔲
Leckhampton Ga CHELTW GL51 ... 134 A2 🔲
Leckhampton HI CHELTS GL53 .... 134 C7
Leckhampton La CHELTW GL51 ...... 134 A4
Leckhampton Rd CHELTS GL53 ...... 134 D2
Ledbury Rd MANG/FISH BS16 .... 366 C2
Ledbury Road Crs RTEWK/TIB GL19 ... 53 F7

Ledmore Rd CHELTS GL53 .... 107 H8
Leechpool Wy YATE/CS BS37 .... 347 G1
Lee CI BRSTK/PCHW BS34 .... 342 D6
   CHELTW GL51 .... 105 K3
Lee Rd TEWK GL20 .... 34 D6
Lees HI KGWD/HNM BS15 .... 366 E4
Lees La OLD/WMLY/WICK BS30 ...... 376 E1
Leicester Sq MANG/FISH BS16 ... 366 D3 🔲
Leicester Wk
   BRSG/KWL/STAPK BS4 .... 374 C1
Leigh La CBATH/BATHN BA1 .... 379 K3
   YATE/CS BS37 .... 358 D5
Leighton Rd
   BRSG/KWL/STAPK BS4 .... 374 A4
   CHELTE/BC GL52 .... 5 D4
Leinster CI CHELTW GL51 .... 105 G3
Lemon La CBRISNE BS2 .... 364 C6
Lena Av EVILLE/WHL BS5 .... 365 G5
Lena St EVILLE/WHL BS5 .... 365 F5
The Lennards CIR GL7 .... 278 E5
Lensbrook LYD GL15 .... 207 G7
Leonard La CBRIS/FH BS1 .... 364 C7
Leonard Rd EVILLE/WHL BS5 .... 365 G7
   GL GL1 .... 130 B8
Leonards Av EVILLE/WHL BS5 .... 365 G5 🔲
Leopold Rd RDLND/MONT BS6 ...... 364 C4
Letch Hill Dr COTS GL54 .... 143 H1
Letch La COTS GL54 .... 143 H1
Leven CI VGL GL2 .... 131 F2
Lever's HI DSLY GL11 .... 240 C8
Lewington Rd MANG/FISH BS16 ... 366 C2
Lewins Md CBRIS/FH BS1 .... 364 B7 🔲🔲
Lewin St EVILLE/WHL BS5 .... 365 H7 🔲
Lewis Av VGL GL2 .... 102 B8
Lewis CI OLD/WMLY/WICK BS30 ... 376 E1
Lewisham Rd GL GL1 .... 158 A1
Lewis La CIR GL7 .... 249 K6
Lewis Rd CHELTW GL51 .... 105 H4
Lewis St CBRISNE BS2 .... 374 A1
Lewiston Rd STROUD GL5 .... 243 J5
Lewis Wy CHEP NP16 .... 312 B2 🔲
Lewton La FRCTL/WBN BS36 .... 344 E7
Ley La THNB/SVB BS35 .... 330 D3
Ley Orch BDWAY WR12 .... 19 F2
Ley Rd CIND GL14 .... 126 D3
Leysbourne CHAM GL55 .... 20 E3 🔲
Leys CI EVE WR11 .... 15 J1
Leyson Rd CHELTW GL51 .... 105 G8
The Leys BRKLY GL13 .... 264 A2
Libby's Dr STROUD GL5 .... 215 F6
Libertus Ct CHELTW GL51 .... 106 A5 🔲
Libertus Rd CHELTW GL51 .... 105 K5
Lichfield Dr CHELT GL50 .... 134 A1
Lichfield Rd
   BRSG/KWL/STAPK BS4 .... 365 J8
   GLE GL4 .... 130 E6
Lidderdale Rd COTS GL54 .... 145 F3
Liddington CI CHELTS GL53 .... 134 D1
Liddington Rd VGL GL2 .... 131 G3
Lifford Gdns BDWAY WR12 .... 18 C6
Lightenbrook La VGL GL2 .... 238 A3
Lightwood La RSTROUD/NAIL GL6 ... 214 A3
Lilac CI CHELTW GL51 .... 134 A1
   HNBRY/STHM BS10 .... 354 A5
Lilac Wy GL GL1 .... 157 J3
   VGL GL2 .... 156 E5
Lillian St EVILLE/WHL BS5 .... 365 G6 🔲
Lilliesfield Av GLE GL4 .... 131 G6
Lilliput Av YATE/CS BS37 .... 347 J6
Lilliput Ct YATE/CS BS37 .... 347 J6
Lilly Hall La LED HR8 .... 27 G1
Lilstock Av HORF/LLZ BS7 .... 364 D2
Limber HI CHELTW GL51 .... 106 C1
Lime Av BAD GL9 .... 350 C5
Lime CI CHELTE/BC GL52 .... 107 G4
   HNBRY/STHM BS10 .... 353 K3
Lime Cft YATE/CS BS37 .... 347 J2
Lime Gv STROUD GL5 .... 214 E7 🔲
   THNB/SVB BS35 .... 331 K1
Lime Kiln CI BRSTK/PCHW BS34 ... 355 H4
Lime Kiln Gdns ALMDB BS32 ...... 343 H3 🔲
Limekiln Gv VGL GL2 .... 128 D1
Limekiln La RSTROUD/NAIL GL6 .... 217 G3
Limekiln Rd WUE GL12 .... 334 E4
Limerick CI RDLND/MONT BS6 ...... 364 C4
Lime Rd KGWD/HNM BS15 .... 375 F1
   TEWK GL20 .... 57 K3
Limes CI CIR GL7 .... 249 J7 🔲
Limes PI HGHW SN6 .... 307 J2
Limes Rd CIR GL7 .... 276 B7
The Limes BAD GL9 .... 350 E4
   VGL GL2 .... 130 A1 🔲
Limestone Link
   CBATH/BATHN BA1 .... 381 F8
   CHPMW/MSHF SN14 .... 379 K1
Lime St RTEWK/TIB GL19 .... 54 B6
Lime Tree Av BDWAY WR12 .... 18 D5
Lime Wy LYD GL15 .... 234 B2
Linacre Crs CIR GL7 .... 249 H8 🔲
Lincoln Av CHELTW GL51 .... 134 A1
Lincoln CI TEWK GL20 .... 57 G2
Lincoln Green La TEWK GL20 .... 57 G3
Lincoln St EVILLE/WHL BS5 .... 365 F7
Lincombe Av MANG/FISH BS16 ...... 356 D8
Lincombe Rd MANG/FISH BS16 ...... 366 C1

Linden Av *CHELTE/BC* GL52 .... 107 G1
Linden Cl *CHELTE/BC* GL52 .... 107 G1
  CHEP NP16 .... 312 A1 🔟
  CHPMW/MSHF SN14 .... 373 F8
  FRCTL/WBN BS36 .... 344 E8
  KGWD/HNM BS15 .... 366 B4
Linden Dr *ALMDB* BS32 .... 343 H6
Linden Rd *GL* GL1 .... 2 B6
Lindsay Rd *HORF/LLZ* BS7 .... 364 E2
Linegar Wood Rd *CIND* GL14 ..... 178 E1
Linfoot Rd *TET* GL8 .... 302 B7
Lingfield Pk *FRCTL/WBN* BS36.... 357 F5
Linkend Rd *RTEWK/TIB* GL19 .... 55 F3
Link Rd *BRSTK/PCHW* BS34 .... 354 D3
  LYD GL15 .... 205 K4
  TEWK GL20 .... 33 J8 🔟
  YATE/CS BS37 .... 347 H5
The Links *CLFD* GL16 .... 175 J5 🔟
Links Vw *CIR* GL7 .... 249 H1
Linnell Cl *HORF/LLZ* BS7 .... 355 F8 🔟
Linnet Cl *BRSTK/PCHW* BS34 .... 342 C6
  GLE GL4 .... 158 E1
Linsley Wy *GLE* GL4 .... 157 K5 🔟
Lintern Crs *OLD/WMLY/WICK* BS30.. 367 G8
Lintham Dr *KGWD/HNM* BS15 ..... 367 F8
Linwell Cl *CHELTE/BC* GL52 .... 106 B1
Linworth Rd *CHELTE/BC* GL52 ..... 83 G3
Lion Cl *VGL* GL2 .... 157 F4 🔟
Lipson Rd *CHELTW* GL51 .... 105 J2
Lisle Pl *WUE* GL12 .... 296 E7
Lithgow Rd *COTS* GL54 .... 145 F3
Little Acorns *CHELTE/BC* GL52 ..... 82 E1
Little Ann St *CBRISNE* BS2 .... 364 D7
Little Bishop St *CBRISNE* BS2 ..... 364 C6 🔟
Little Bristol La *WUE* GL12 .... 319 J1
Little Cleevemount *CHELTE/BC* GL52.. 5 D2
Littlecote Cl *CHELTE/BC* GL52 ..... 82 E3 🔟
Littledean *YATE/CS* BS37 .... 347 G8
Littledean Hill Rd *CIND* GL14 ..... 151 G6
Little Dowles
  OLD/WMLY/WICK BS30 .... 376 B2 🔟
Littledown Rd *CHELTS* GL53 .... 134 E2
Little Elmbridge *VGL* GL2 .... 131 F2
Little Fld *GLE* GL4 .... 131 F7 🔟
Littlefield *VGL* GL2 .... 156 E4
Little George St *CBRISNE* BS2 ..... 364 D6
Little Green La *THNB/SVB* BS35 ... 328 C7
Little Hayes *MANG/FISH* BS16 ..... 356 D8 🔟
Little Herbert's Cl *CHELTS* GL53 .. 135 H1 🔟
Little Herbert's Rd *CHELTS* GL53... 135 H1
Little Holbury *VGL* GL2 .... 211 J1
Little Horcott La *CIR* GL7 .... 254 E8 🔟
Little King St *CBRIS/FH* BS1 .... 364 B8
Little Lancaridge *VGL* GL2 .... 128 D2
Little Md *AVONM* BS11 .... 352 D5
Little Meadow *ALMDB* BS32 .... 343 K6
Little Normans *VGL* GL2 .... 130 E1
Little Orch *CHELTE/BC* GL52 .... 82 E2 🔟
Little Parr Cl *MANG/FISH* BS16 ... 365 G1 🔟
Little Paul St *CBRISNE* BS2 .... 364 A6
Little Stoke La *BRSTK/PCHW* BS34.. 343 C7
Little Withey Md
  HNLZ/SM/SNYPK/WT BS9 .... 353 H8
Littleworth *CHCAM* GL55 .... 20 D3
Livia Wy *LYD* GL15 .... 234 D2
Llandilo St *GL* GL1 .... 3 D6 🔟
Llanthony Rd *VGL* GL2 .... 2 A5
Lime Tree Ct *GL* GL1 .... 158 A1 🔟
Lobleys Dr *GLE* GL4 .... 159 H1
Locking Hl *STROUD* GL5 .... 214 E7 🔟
Lockleaze Rd *HORF/LLZ* BS7 .... 354 E8
Locombe Hl *CIR* GL7 .... 229 F6
Locombe Rd *WUE* GL12 .... 297 G8
Lodersfield *CIR* GL7 .... 285 G2
Lodge Cswy *MANG/FISH* BS16...... 365 K3
Lodge Dr
  OLD/WMLY/WICK BS30 .... 376 D4 🔟
Lodge Gdns *LYD* GL15 .... 203 F8 🔟
Lodge Hl *KGWD/HNM* BS15 .... 366 C4
Lodge La *KGWD/HNM* BS15 .... 232 E3
Lodgemore Cl *STROUD* GL5 .... 214 C7
Lodgemore La *STROUD* GL5.......... 214 C7
Lodge Pl *CBRIS/FH* BS1 .... 364 A7 🔟
Lodge Rd *KGWD/HNM* BS15 .... 366 C4
  OLD/WMLY/WICK BS30 .... 368 C6
  YATE/CS BS37 .... 346 C4
Lodgeside Av *KGWD/HNM* BS15 ... 366 C5 🔟
Lodgeside Gdns *KGWD/HNM* BS15... 366 C5
Lodge St *CBRIS/FH* BS1 .... 364 A7 🔟
Lodge Wk *MANG/FISH* BS16......... 356 D8
Lodore Rd *MANG/FISH* BS16 .... 365 K3 🔟
Lodway Rd *BRSG/KWL/STAPK* BS4.. 374 D2
Logan Rd *HORF/LLZ* BS7 .... 364 B3
Logus Ct
  OLD/WMLY/WICK BS30 .... 376 A2 🔟
Loiterpin *LYD* GL15 .... 207 H2
Lomond Rd *HORF/LLZ* BS7 .... 354 D5
London La *CBRISNE* BS2 .... 364 D5 🔟
  CHELTE/BC GL52 .... 4 C5
  CHELTE/BC GL52 .... 136 A2
  CHELTS GL53 .... 5 E6
  CIR GL7 .... 249 K6
  GL GL1 .... 3 D3
  MIM GL56 .... 46 A8

OLD/WMLY/WICK* BS30 .... 367 J7
OLD/WMLY/WICK* BS30 .... 369 G8
SHPSTR* CV36 .... 25 F2
STROUD* GL5 .... 214 E8
STROUD* GL5 .... 243 F1
TET* GL8 .... 302 D5
TET* GL8 .... 302 B6 🔟
London St *KGWD/HNM* BS15 .... 366 D6
Lone La *MONM* NP25 .... 174 A7
Long Acres Cl
  HNLZ/SM/SNYPK/WT BS9 .... 353 F7
Longaston Cl *VGL* GL2 .... 238 B2
Longaston La *VGL* GL2 .... 238 B1
Long Beach Rd
  OLD/WMLY/WICK BS30 .... 376 B4
Longborough Dr *GLE* GL4 .... 159 G1
Long Cl *ALMDB* BS32 .... 343 J8
  MANG/FISH BS16 .... 356 C8
Long Cft *YATE/CS* BS37 .... 347 F1
Long Cross *AVONM* BS11 .... 352 A6
Longden Rd *MANG/FISH* BS16...... 357 F8
Long Eaton Dr *HGRV/WHIT* BS14.. 374 A6
Long Eights *TEWK* GL20 .... 34 C5
Long Fld *VGL* GL2 .... 100 D8
Longfield *VGL* GL2 .... 156 E4 🔟
Longfield Rd *HORF/LLZ* BS7......... 364 C3
Longford *YATE/CS* BS37 .... 346 E6
Longford Av *HNBRY/STHM* BS10 .. 354 B6
Longford La *VGL* GL2 .... 102 C8
Longford Ms *VGL* GL2 .... 102 B8 🔟
Long Furlong *CHELTE/BC* GL52 ..... 60 A7
Long Furlong La *TET* GL8 .... 326 A1
Long Handstones
  OLD/WMLY/WICK BS30 .... 376 B2
Longhill Rd *CIR* GL7 .... 219 H5
Longhope Cl *GLE* GL4 .... 159 G1 🔟
Longhope Rd *RTEWK/TIB* GL19 ... 125 H3
Longland Ct *VGL* GL2 .... 3 F1 🔟
  VGL GL2 .... 130 D1 🔟
Longland Gdns *VGL* GL2 .... 3 F1
Longlands Cl *CHELTE/BC* GL52 ..... 83 H2 🔟
Longlands Rd *CHELTE/BC* GL52 ..... 83 H3
Longleat Av *VGL* GL2 .... 157 J5
Longleat Cl
  HNLZ/SM/SNYPK/WT BS9 .... 364 A1 🔟
Longlength La *RSTROUD/NAIL* GL6.. 270 E6
Longmead Av *HORF/LLZ* BS7........ 364 B1
Long Meadow *MANG/FISH* BS16... 365 H1
Longmore Av *COTS* GL54 .... 145 F2
Long Mynd Av *CHELTW* GL51 ...... 105 J8
Longney Pl *BRSTK/PCHW* BS34..... 342 D5
Longney Rd *GL* GL1 .... 157 J3
Longreach Gv *HGRV/WHIT* BS14 .. 374 C7
Longridge La *RTEWK/TIB* GL19 .... 77 F8
Long Rd *MANG/FISH* BS16 .... 367 G1
Long Rw *CBRIS/FH* BS1 .... 364 C8 🔟
Longs Dr *YATE/CS* BS37 .... 346 E3 🔟
  YATE/CS BS37 .... 347 H4 🔟
Longsmith St *GL* GL1 .... 2 B3 🔟
Long St *DSLY* GL11 .... 267 J5
  TET GL8 .... 302 C7 🔟
  WUE GL12 .... 297 F7
Longs Vw *WUE* GL12 .... 295 J8
Longtree Cl *TET* GL8 .... 302 B5
Longville Cl *GLE* GL4 .... 159 H1
Longway Av *CHELTS* GL53 .... 135 F2
Longwood *BRSG/KWL/STAPK* BS4 .. 375 F4
The Lonk *CLFD* GL16 .... 147 K8
Lonsdale Rd *VGL* GL2 .... 130 E4
Loop Rd *CHEP* NP16 .... 288 D8
Lorain Wk *HNBRY/STHM* BS10 ..... 353 H4
Lord Eldon Dr *CHEP* NP16 .... 312 B2 🔟
Lords Gn *CHELTE/BC* GL52 .... 83 J3
Lord's Hl *CLFD* GL16 .... 175 K4
Loriners Cl *VGL* GL2 .... 157 F4
Lorton Rd *HNBRY/STHM* BS10 ..... 353 K5
The Lotts *HCHW* SN6 .... 308 D6
Louisa St *CBRISNE* BS2 .... 364 D7 🔟
Louise Av *MANG/FISH* BS16 .... 367 G1 🔟
Lovedays Md *STROUD* GL5 .... 214 E6
Love La *CIR* GL7 .... 249 K8
  YATE/CS BS37 .... 347 J6
Lovell Av *OLD/WMLY/WICK* BS30.. 376 E2 🔟
Lovell's Hl *KGWD/HNM* BS15 .... 375 H5 🔟
Loveringe Cl *HNBRY/STHM* BS10 ... 353 H2
Lovett Cl *RTEWK/TIB* GL19 .... 53 G7
Lowdilow La *CHELTW* GL51 .... 81 H5
Lower Ashley Rd
  EVILLE/WHL BS5 .... 364 E5 🔟
  RDLND/MONT BS6 .... 364 D5 🔟
Lower Berrycroft *BRKLY* GL13 ..... 264 A3
Lower Chapel La
  FRCTL/WBN BS36 .... 345 J7
Lower Chapel Rd
  KGWD/HNM BS15 .... 375 H1 🔟
Lower Cheltenham Pl
  RDLND/MONT BS6 .... 364 D5
Lower Churchfield Rd
  STROUD GL5 .... 215 F8 🔟
Lower Church La *CBRISNE* BS2 ..... 364 A7
Lower Church St *CHEP* NP16 .... 288 D5
Lower Cock Rd *KGWD/HNM* BS15 .. 377 F7
Lower College St
  CBRIS/FH BS1 .... 364 A8 🔟

Lower Common *LYD* GL15 .... 232 E5
Lower Court Rd *ALMDB* BS32 ...... 342 E1
Lower Cft *CIR* GL7 .... 255 F7
Lower Gay St *CBRISNE* BS2 .... 364 B6 🔟
Lower Grove Rd
  MANG/FISH BS16 .... 365 J2 🔟
Lower Hanham Rd
  KGWD/HNM BS15 .... 375 H1
Lower High St *CHCAM* GL55 .... 20 D3
Lower House Crs
  BRSTK/PCHW BS34 .... 355 F2
Lower Kitesnest La
  RSTROUD/NAIL GL6 .... 214 B3
Lower Knole La
  HNBRY/STHM BS10 .... 353 J3
Lower Lamb St *CBRIS/FH* BS1 ..... 364 A8 🔟
Lower Lode La *TEWK* GL20 .... 57 F2
Lower Maudlin St *CBRISNE* BS2 ... 364 B7
Lower Meadow *VGL* GL2 .... 157 F7
Lower Mill St *CHELTW* GL51 .... 106 B4
Lower Moor Rd *YATE/CS* BS37 ..... 347 G2
Lower Newmarket Rd
  RSTROUD/NAIL GL6 .... 270 B2
Lower Park St *COTS* GL54 .... 92 C6
Lower Poole Rd *DSLY* GL11 .... 267 F6
Lower Quay St *GL* GL1 .... 2 B3 🔟
Lower Rd *CIND* GL14 .... 179 F5
  CLFD GL16 .... 175 K1
  LYD GL15 .... 206 A3
  LYD GL15 .... 231 F1
Lower Station Rd
  MANG/FISH BS16 .... 365 K2
Lower Stone Cl *FRCTL/WBN* BS36.. 345 J6
Lower St *MIM* GL56 .... 44 C4
  RSTROUD/NAIL GL6 .... 214 B3
  STROUD GL5 .... 214 E8
Lower Tockington Rd
  ALMDB BS32 .... 331 F6
Lower Tuffley La *VGL* GL2 .... 157 H2
Lower Washwell La
  RSTROUD/NAIL GL6 .... 187 H1
Loweswater Cl *CHELTW* GL51 ...... 105 K7
Loweswater Rd *CHELTW* GL51 ..... 105 K7
Lowfield Rd *TET* GL8 .... 302 B6
Lowlis Cl *HNBRY/STHM* BS10 ...... 353 H3 🔟
Lowther Rd *HNBRY/STHM* BS10 ... 354 A4 🔟
Lucas Cl *BRSG/KWL/STAPK* BS4 ... 374 C6
Luckington Rd *HORF/LLZ* BS7 ..... 354 C6
Ludgate Hl *WUE* GL12 .... 297 G7 🔟
Ludlow Cl *CBRISNE* BS2 .... 364 D5
  OLD/WMLY/WICK BS30 .... 376 C4
Ludlow Rd *HORF/LLZ* BS7 .... 354 E7
Ludwell Cl *FRCTL/WBN* BS36 ...... 356 D1 🔟
The Luggs *STNHO* GL10 .... 241 G3 🔟
Luke La *BWTH/CHD* GL3 .... 103 G8
Lullington Rd
  BRSG/KWL/STAPK BS4 .... 374 A4
Lulworth Crs *MANG/FISH* BS16 .... 357 F6
Lurks La *RSTROUD/NAIL* GL6 .... 214 D2
Lux Furlong
  HNLZ/SM/SNYPK/WT BS9 .... 352 D7
Luxton St *EVILLE/WHL* BS5 .... 365 F6 🔟
Lych Gate Ms *LYD* GL15 .... 234 A4
Lydbrook Cl *YATE/CS* BS37 .... 347 F6 🔟
Lyddington Rd *HORF/LLZ* BS7 ..... 354 C5
Lydfield Rd *LYD* GL15 .... 234 A3
Lydiard Cft *KGWD/HNM* BS15 ..... 375 H2
Lydney Rd *HNBRY/STHM* BS10 ..... 354 B6
  LYD GL15 .... 204 E7
  MANG/FISH BS16 .... 366 E2
Lyefield Rd East *CHELTS* GL53 ..... 107 G8
Lyefield Rd West *CHELTS* GL53 .... 107 G8
Lye La *CHELTE/BC* GL52 .... 83 K5
Lygon Ct *CIR* GL7 .... 255 F8
Lynch Cr
  OLD/WMLY/WICK BS30 .... 376 A2 🔟
Lynch Rd *BRKLY* GL13 .... 263 K3
  RSTROUD/NAIL GL6 .... 242 A4
Lyncombe Wk *MANG/FISH* BS16 .. 366 B4 🔟
Lyncroft *VGL* GL2 .... 127 K7
Lyndale Rd *EVILLE/WHL* BS5 .... 365 H6
  YATE/CS BS37 .... 347 F5
Lyndhurst Cl *CHELTE/BC* GL52 ..... 83 H3 🔟
Lyndhurst Rd
  HNLZ/SM/SNYPK/WT BS9 .... 353 H7
Lyndley Cha *CHELTE/BC* GL52 ..... 82 D2
Lyng Cl *GLE* GL4 .... 131 G6
Lynmouth Rd *BWTH/CHD* GL3 ..... 131 H8
  CBRISNE BS2 .... 364 E4 🔟
Lynn Rd *MANG/FISH* BS16 .... 365 H1 🔟
Lynton Pl *EVILLE/WHL* BS5........... 365 G6
Lynton Rd *GLE* GL4 .... 131 H7
Lynton Wy *MANG/FISH* BS16 ...... 356 B5
Lynwood Rd *LYD* GL15 .... 234 A1
Lynworth La *TEWK* GL20 .... 12 D8
Lynworth Pl *CHELTE/BC* GL52 ...... 5 E2
Lyons Court Rd *HGRV/WHIT* BS14.. 374 C7
Lypiatt Dr *CHELT* GL50 .... 4 A5
Lypiatt La *CHELT* GL50 .... 4 A5
Lypiatt Rd *CHELT* GL50 .... 4 A5
Lypiatt St *CHELT* GL50 .... 4 A6
Lypiatt Vw *RSTROUD/NAIL* GL6 ... 244 A2
Lyppiatt Rd *EVILLE/WHL* BS5........ 365 H6
Lyppincourt Rd
  HNBRY/STHM BS10 .... 353 J3

Lysander Ct *BWTH/CHD* GL3 .... **132** A1 🖸
Lysander Rd *BRSTK/PCHW* BS34.... **342** A8
   HNBRY/STHM BS10 .... **341** K8
Lysander Wk *BRSTK/PCHW* BS34 ... **355** J1 🖸
Lysons Av *GL* GL1................................. 2 B6
Lytchet Dr *MANG/FISH* BS16 ..... **357** F6 🖸
Lytton Gv *HORF/LLZ* BS7 .... **354** E6

M

Macarthur Rd *COTS* GL54........... **169** C4
Macauley Rd *HORF/LLZ* BS7 .... **354** E6
Machen Rd *CLFD* GL16 .... **176** B3
Machin Gdns
   HNBRY/STHM BS10 .... **353** J3 🖸
Machin Rd *HNBRY/STHM* BS10 .... **353** H3
Mackenzie Wy *CHELTW* GL51...... **106** A1
Mackie Av *BRSTK/PCHW* BS34.... **355** F4 🖸
Mackie Gv *BRSTK/PCHW* BS34.... **355** F4 🖸
Mackie Rd *BRSTK/PCHW* BS34.... **355** F4 🖸
Macmillan Wy *CIR* GL7 .... **193** F7 🖸
   CIR GL7... **220** B5
   CIR GL7... **274** C1
   COTS GL54 .... **115** F5
   COTS GL54 .... **141** K3
   COTS GL54 .... **168** B4
   MIM GL56 .... 94 B4
   TET GL8 .... **273** H5
   TET GL8 .... **301** C8
   TET GL8 .... **324** C6
Macmillian Wy *TET* GL8 .... **301** H6
Macrae Ct *KGWD/HNM* BS15 ..... **366** E6 🖸
Madeline Ct *MANG/FISH* BS16 .. **365** K4 🖸
Madison Cl *YATE/CS* BS37 .... **347** F4
Madleaze Rd *GL* GL1 .... 2 A5
Madocke Rd *CHEP* NP16 .... **288** C7 🖸
Maesbury *KGWD/HNM* BS15 ..... **366** E8
Magdala Rd *GL* GL1 .... 3 E4 🖸
Magdalene Pl *CBRISNE* BS2 ...... **364** D5
Magdalen Rd *TET* GL8................ **302** B6
Maggs Cl *HNBRY/STHM* BS10 ... **354** A3
Maggs La *EVILLE/WHL* BS5 .... **365** J4
Magnolia Cl *CHEP* NP16 .... **312** B1 🖸
Magnolia Wk *VGL* GL2 .... **156** E5 🖸
Magpie Bottom La
   KGWD/HNM BS15 .... **366** C8 🖸
Magpie Ct *STNHO* GL10 .... **215** F6 🖸
Maida Vale Rd *CHELTS* GL53 ..... **106** D8 🖸
Maidenhall *VGL* GL2 .... **128** D1
Main Rd *CLFD* GL16 .... **176** B2
   LYD GL15 .... **205** K4
   LYD GL15 .... **232** E8
   LYD GL15 .... **260** D2
   MANG/FISH BS16 .... **367** J3
   RSTROUD/NAIL GL6 .... **214** B2
Main St *BDWAY* WR12 .... 18 E2
   CHNTN OX7 .... **118** D4
   EVE WR11 .... 6 C2
   EVE WR11 .... 15 J5
   MIM GL56 .... 94 C3
   SHPSTR CV36 .... 25 G6
   TEWK GL20 .... 36 E1
Main Vw *FRCTL/WBN* BS36 ...... **345** K7
Maisemore Av *YATE/CS* BS37 ... **347** G8
Maisemore Rd *BRSTK/PCHW* BS34 .. **343** F5
Maitlands *GLE* GL4....................... **186** B1
Makin Cl *OLD/WMLY/WICK* BS30 ... **376** D1 🖸
Malden Rd *CHELTE/BC* GL52 .... 4 C3
The Maldens *SHPSTR* CV36 .... 24 E1
Maldon Gdns *GL* GL1 .... 3 D6
Maidowers La *EVILLE/WHL* BS5 ... **366** A5
Malet Cl *VGL* GL2 .... **130** E1 🖸
Mallard Cl *ALMDB* BS32 .... **343** H4
   EVILLE/WHL BS5 .... **365** K5
   VGL GL2.. **156** D5
   YATE/CS BS37 .... **347** J6
Malleson Rd *CHELTE/BC* GL52 ...... 60 A6
Mallow Cl *MANG/FISH* BS16 ..... **316** D4
Malmains Dr *MANG/FISH* BS16 .. **356** B5
Malmesbury Cl
   OLD/WMLY/WICK BS30 .... **376** A1 🖸
   RDLND/MONT BS6 .... **364** A2 🖸
Malmesbury Rd *CHELTW* GL51 ... **106** A1
   GLE GL4 .... 3 F6
Malmsey Cl *TEWK* GL20.............. 57 J3
Malthouse La *CHELT* GL50 .... 4 B2 🖸
   COTS GL54 .... 85 J1 🖸
   COTS GL54 .... **115** G4 🖸
Malthouse Wk *TET* GL8 .... **302** B6 🖸
Malvern Ct *EVILLE/WHL* BS5 .... **365** K7
Malvern Dr *OLD/WMLY/WICK* BS30.. **376** D1
   THNB/SVB BS35 .... **316** D6
Malvern Pl *CHELT* GL50.............. **106** B6
Malvern Rd *BRSG/KWL/STAPK* BS4.. **374** C3
   CHELT GL50 .... **106** B5
   EVILLE/WHL BS5 .... **365** K7
   GL GL1 .... 3 D1
   RTEWK/TIB GL19 .... 53 H7
The Malverns *GLE* GL4 .... **131** F8
Malvern St *CHELTW* GL51 .... **106** B2
Malvern Wy *CLFD* GL16............. **148** C7

Mancroft Av *AVONM* BS11 .... **352** B7
Mandalay Dr *VGL* GL2 .... **103** F1
Mandara Gv *VGL* GL4.................. **159** F2
Mandarin Wy *CHELTW* GL51...... **106** B1
Mangotsfield Rd *MANG/FISH* BS16.. **367** F2
Mankley Rd *STNHO* GL10 .... **241** F2
Manley Gdns *VGL* GL2 .... **130** E1 🖸
Mannings Rd *MTCHDN* GL17 ..... **122** D5
Manor Av *DSLY* GL11 .... **266** D1
Manor Cl *ALMDB* BS32 .... **331** F5
   CIR GL7... **249** H1
   CIR GL7... **255** F7 🖸
   DSLY GL11 .... **238** C8
   EVE WR11 .... 7 G2 🖸
   FRCTL/WBN BS36 .... **345** J8
   TEWK GL20 .... **243** H8
   TEWK GL20 .... 36 B8
Manor Ct *CHELTW* GL51 .... 82 A8
Manor Court Dr *HORF/LLZ* BS7 ... **354** C7
Manor Farm *COTS* GL54............ **144** C2 🖸
Manor Farm *CHNTN* OX7 .... **119** F1
Manor Farm Crs *ALMDB* BS32 ... **343** H5
Manor Gdns *STROUD* GL5 .... **242** C4
Manor Gv *ALMDB* BS32 .... **343** F6 🖸
   MANG/FISH BS16 .... **367** G2
Manor La *CHELTE/BC* GL52 .... 60 C6
   EVE WR11 .... 6 C2
   FRCTL/WBN BS36 .... **345** F7
   WUE GL12 .... **297** C7 🖸
   WUE GL12 .... **319** J2
Manor Orch *HGHW* SN6 .... **310** C6
Manor Pk *ALMDB* BS32................ **331** G4
   CHELTW GL51 .... **133** H1
   TEWK GL20 .... 33 K6
   VGL GL2.. **131** G2
Manor Pl *MANG/FISH* BS16 ...... **356** C5
   TEWK GL20 .... 57 J3 🖸
Manor Rd *CHELTW* GL51 .... 82 A8
   HORF/LLZ BS7 .... **364** C2
   LYD GL15 .... **234** C3
   MANG/FISH BS16 .... **365** K1
   MANG/FISH BS16 .... **367** G2
   OLD/WMLY/WICK BS30 .... **377** K1
   YATE/CS BS37 .... **334** C7
Manor St *RSTROUD/NAIL* GL6 ... **216** E5
Manor Wk *THNB/SVB* BS35 .... **316** B3
Manor Wy *YATE/CS* BS37 .... **348** A4
Manse Gdns *CHELTW* GL51 ...... **105** K7 🖸
Mansell Cl *VGL* GL2 .... **157** J1
Manse Rd *MTCHDN* GL17 .... **122** D6
Manser Cl *CHELT* GL50.................... 4 B2 🖸
Mansfield Ms *VGL* GL2............... **157** F7 🖸
Manston Cl *HGRV/WHIT* BS14 ... **374** B7
Manworthy Rd
   BRSG/KWL/STAPK BS4 .... **374** C5
Manx Rd *HORF/LLZ* BS7 .... **354** D7
Maple Av *CHEP* NP16 .... **312** A2
   MANG/FISH BS16 .... **366** C3
   THNB/SVB BS35 .... **316** C5
Maple Cl *BRSTK/PCHW* BS34 .... **343** G7
   DSLY GL11 .... **266** E3
   OLD/WMLY/WICK BS30 .... **376** D3
   VGL GL2.. **156** E6
Maple Ct *VGL* GL2 .... **131** G2 🖸
Maple Dr *BWTH/CHD* GL3 .... **132** B7
   CHELTS GL53 .... **135** H1
   STROUD GL5 .... **214** C5
Mapleleaze *BRSG/KWL/STAPK* BS4 .. **374** C3
Maplemeade *HORF/LLZ* BS7 .... **364** A2 🖸
Mapleridge La *YATE/CS* BS37..... **336** A7
Maple Rd *BRSG/KWL/STAPK* BS4 ... **374** C1
   HORF/LLZ BS7 .... **364** B2
The Maples *CIR* GL7 .... **277** H1
   GLE GL4 .... **131** G8 🖸
Maple Wk *MANG/FISH* BS16...... **366** B4 🖸
Marbeck Rd *HNBRY/STHM* BS10... **353** K5
Marchant Cl *CHELTW* GL51 .... **105** K3
Mardale Cl *HNBRY/STHM* BS10 ... **354** A4 🖸
Mardon Rd *BRSG/KWL/STAPK* BS4.. **365** H8
Marefield Cl *GLE* GL4.................. **131** G7 🖸
Margaret Rd *TEWK* GL20 .... 57 J2
Margery La *CLFD* GL16 .... **203** G2
Margrett Rd *CHELT* GL50 .... 4 B2
Marians Wk *CLFD* GL16 .... **147** J8
Marina Gdns *MANG/FISH* BS16 .. **365** J3
Marion Rd *KGWD/HNM* BS15 ... **375** G3
Marion Wk *EVILLE/WHL* BS5 .... **366** A7
Marissal Cl *HNBRY/STHM* BS10.. **353** G3
Marissal Rd *HNBRY/STHM* BS10 .. **353** G3
Mariston Wy
   OLD/WMLY/WICK BS30 .... **367** J8
Marjoram Cl *GLE* GL4 .... **159** H1 🖸
Marjoram Pl *ALMDB* BS32 .... **343** K7
Market La *COTS* GL54 .... 62 E5
Market Pde *GL* GL1...................... 2 C5 🖸
Market Pl *CHPMW/MSHF* SN14... **572** A6
   CIR GL7... **249** J5
   CIR GL7... **254** E7 🖸
   CLFD GL16 .... **175** K4 🖸
   TET GL8 .... **302** C7 🖸
Market Sq *COTS* GL54 .... 92 C6 🖸
   MANG/FISH BS16 .... **366** C3 🖸
Market St *CHELTW* GL51 .... 4 A3
   CIND GL14 .... **151** F5 🖸
   RSTROUD/NAIL GL6 .... **270** D3 🖸

WUE GL12 .... **297** F7
Mark La *CBRIS/FH* BS1 .... **364** A8
Marlborough Av
   EVILLE/WHL BS5 .... **365** J3 🖸
Marlborough Cl *CHELTE/BC* GL52 ... 82 E3 🖸
   CHELTS GL53 .... **107** F8 🖸
Marlborough Crs *GLE* GL4 .... **130** C8
Marlborough Dr *MANG/FISH* BS16 .. **356** B5
Marlborough Hl
   RDLND/MONT BS6 .... **364** B6
Marlborough Hill Pl
   CBRISNE BS2 .... **364** B6 🖸
Marlborough Rd *GLE* GL4............... 3 E6
Marlborough St
   EVILLE/WHL BS5 .... **365** J3 🖸
Marle HI *RSTROUD/NAIL* GL6 ... **244** D4
Marle HI Pde *CHELT* GL50 .... 4 B2
Marle Hill Rd *CHELT* GL50............... 4 B2
Marleyfield Cl *BWTH/CHD* GL3 .. **103** J7 🖸
Marleyfield Wy *BWTH/CHD* GL3 .. **103** J7
Marley La *RSTROUD/NAIL* GL6 .. **245** F5
Marling Cl *STROUD* GL5 .... **242** D6
Marling Crs *STROUD* GL5 .... **214** A7
Marling Rd *EVILLE/WHL* BS5 .... **366** A7 🖸
Marlstone Rd *DSLY* GL11 .... **266** D2
Marlwood Dr *HNBRY/STHM* BS10.. **353** J3
Marment Rd *DSLY* GL11 .... **266** C2
Marmion Crs *HNBRY/STHM* BS10 .. **353** H3
Marram Cl *GLE* GL4 .... **159** H1
Marshacre La *THNB/SVB* BS35 .. **314** D8
Marshall Av *SHPSTR* CV36 .... 24 E1
Marshall's La *CIND* GL14 .... **151** F5 🖸
Marsham Wy
   OLD/WMLY/WICK BS30 .... **375** K1
Marsh Cl *CHELTW* GL51................... 4 A2 🖸
   FRCTL/WBN BS36 .... **356** C2
Marsh Common *THNB/SVB* BS35 .. **329** F8
Marsh Dr *CHELTW* GL51 .... 4 A2
Marshfield La
   OLD/WMLY/WICK BS30 .... **377** H5
Marshfield Rd *BAD* GL9 .... **361** J5
   MANG/FISH BS16 .... **366** B2
Marsh Gdns *CHELTW* GL51 .... 4 A2
Marsh La *CHELTW* GL51 .... 4 A2
   CHPMW/MSHF SN14 .... **363** H2
   EVILLE/WHL BS5 .... **365** G7
   STNHO GL10 .... **241** F3
Marshmouth La *COTS* GL54 ...... **143** J1 🖸
Marsh Rd *CHEP* NP16 .... **312** B1 🖸
   STNHO GL10 .... **240** E2
Marsh St *CBRIS/FH* BS1 .... **364** B8 🔟
Marsh Ter *CHELTW* GL51 .... **133** H4
Marshwall La *ALMDB* BS32 .... **330** D8
Marsh Wy *CLFD* GL16 .... **204** A2
Marsland Rd *CHELTW* GL51 ...... **105** H4
Marston Rd
   BRSG/KWL/STAPK BS4 .... **374** A4 🖸
   CHELTE/BC GL52........................... 5 D1
Marten Cl *BWTH/CHD* GL3 .... **159** J1
Marten Rd *CHEP* NP16 .... **288** A8
Martin Cl *BRSTK/PCHW* BS34.... **342** C6
   CIR GL7... **249** J7 🖸
Martindale Rd *BWTH/CHD* GL3 .. **103** K8
Martingale Rd
   BRSG/KWL/STAPK BS4 .... **374** C2
Martins Cl *KGWD/HNM* BS15 ... **375** H1 🖸
Martin's Rd *KGWD/HNM* BS15 ... **375** H1
The Martins *CHEP* NP16 .... **288** C5 🖸
   STROUD GL5 .... **213** K6
Marybush La *CBRISNE* BS2 .... **364** C7 🖸
Marygold Leaze
   OLD/WMLY/WICK BS30 .... **376** B2 🖸
Mary Gv *VGL* GL2 .... **128** D1
Mary Rose Av *BWTH/CHD* GL3... **103** H1
Mary St *EVILLE/WHL* BS5 .... **365** H6 🖸
Masefield Av *VGL* GL2................. **157** J2
Masefield Rd *CIR* GL7................. **249** H8 🖸
Masefield Wy *HORF/LLZ* BS7 ... **354** E7 🖸
Maskelyne Av *HNBRY/STHM* BS10.. **354** B7
Mason Rd *STROUD* GL5 .... **215** H7
Masons Vw *FRCTL/WBN* BS36 .. **344** E7
Massey Pde *GL* GL1 .... 3 D6 🖸
Massey Rd *GLE* GL4....................... 3 E6
Matford Cl *FRCTL/WBN* BS36..... **356** C1
   HNBRY/STHM BS10 .... **354** B2
Matford La *BRKLY* GL13 .... **294** B2
Mathern Wy *CHEP* NP16 .... **312** A1 🖸
Mathews Wy *STROUD* GL5 .... **214** B6
Matson Av *GLE* GL4 .... **158** E3 🖸
Matson La *GLE* GL4...................... **158** D4
Matson Pl *GL* GL1.......................... 3 E6
Matthews Cl *HGRV/WHIT* BS14 .. **374** E8
Matthew's Rd
   EVILLE/WHL BS5 .... **365** G7 🔟
Maugersbury Pk *COTS* GL54 ...... 92 C7
Maules La *MANG/FISH* BS16....... **355** K4
Maunsell Rd *AVONM* BS11 .... **352** D4
Maurice Rd *RDLND/MONT* BS6 .. **364** C4
Mautravers Cl *ALMDB* BS32 ...... **343** H7
Mawley Rd *CIR* GL7 .... **254** D1
Maxse Rd *BRSG/KWL/STAPK* BS4.. **374** A3
Mayalls Ct *RTEWK/TIB* GL19 ...... 55 G8
The Mayalls *TEWK* GL20 .... 12 E8
Maybec Gdns *EVILLE/WHL* BS5 ... **366** A8 🖸

Maybourne
BRSG/KWL/STAPK BS4 .... **375** F4 2
Maybrook St *BRKLY* GL13 .... **264** A3
May Bush La *RWYE* HR9 .... **146** E1
Maycliffe Pk *RDLND/MONT* BS6 .... **364** D4
Maycroft La *BRKLY* GL13 .... **264** D8
DSLY GL11 .... **295** F1
May Evans Cl *DSLY* GL11 .... **266** D1 3
Mayfair Cl *VGL* GL2 .... **129** H6
Mayfield Av *MANG/FISH* BS16 .... **366** A4
Mayfield Cl *CHELTE/BC* GL52 .... **83** F4 3
Mayfield Dr *BWTH/CHD* GL3 .... **131** H5
GLE GL4 .... **131** H6
Mayfield Pk *MANG/FISH* BS16 .... **366** A4
Mayfield Pk North
MANG/FISH BS16 .... **366** A4
Mayfield Pk South
MANG/FISH BS16 .... **366** A4
May La *CHCAM* GL55 .... **22** A2
DSLY GL11 .... **266** E5
May Meadow La *MTCHDN* GL17 .... **123** G5
Maypole Gn *LYD* GL15 .... **204** E6
Maypole Rd *LYD* GL15 .... **204** E6
May's Crs *COTS* GL54 .... **169** G4
Mays La *TET* GL8 .... **272** B6
Maythorn Dr *CHELTW* GL51 .... **105** H2 3
May Tree Cl *CIR* GL7 .... **247** K8
May Tree Sq *GLE* GL4 .... **130** E7
Mayville Av *BRSTK/PCHW* BS34 .... **354** E3
Maywood Crs *MANG/FISH* BS16 .... **366** B2
Maywood Rd *MANG/FISH* BS16 .... **366** C2
Maze St *EVILLE/WHL* BS5 .... **365** F8 3
Maze Wk *CLFD* GL16 .... **147** J8
Mead Cl *AVONM* BS11 .... **352** A4 3
CHELTS GL51 .... **134** E1
Meade-king Cl *CHELTE/BC* GL52 .... **83** H3
Meadgate *MANG/FISH* BS16 .... **357** H6
Mead La *LYD* GL15 .... **233** K5
THNB/SVB BS35 .... **330** D4
Meadoway *CHELTE/BC* GL52 .... **82** E4
Meadowbank *LYD* GL15 .... **234** C3
Meadow Cl *CHELTW* GL51 .... **105** C5 3
CIR GL7 .... **249** J7
LYD GL15 .... **207** F5
MANG/FISH BS16 .... **357** F7
TEWK GL20 .... **34** A6
Meadow Court Dr
OLD/WMLY/WICK BS30 .... **376** D3
Meadowcroft *GLE* GL4 .... **159** C1
MANG/FISH BS16 .... **357** G6 3
Meadowland Rd
HNBRY/STHM BS10 .... **353** G2
Meadow La *CHELTW* GL51 .... **133** J1 3
Meadow La (West) *STROUD* GL5 .... **214** A8
Meadowleaze *VGL* GL2 .... **131** F3
Meadow Md *FRCTL/WBN* BS36 .... **345** H6
YATE/CS BS37 .... **347** G1
Meadow Rd *CIND* GL14 .... **151** G6
CIR GL7 .... **249** J7
STNHO GL10 .... **213** F6
WUE GL12 .... **318** D2
YATE/CS BS37 .... **347** J5 3
Meadows Dean *MTCHDN* GL17 .... **123** H5
Meadowside *THNB/SVB* BS35 .... **316** D6 3
The Meadows *KGWD/HNM* BS15 .... **375** J7 3
Meadow St *CBRISNE* BS2 .... **364** C7 3
Meadowsweet Av
BRSTK/PCHW BS34 .... **355** F3
EVILLE/WHL BS5 .... **366** A5
Meadow V *DSLY* GL11 .... **266** D2 3
Meadow Vw *FRCTL/WBN* BS36 .... **345** H6
Meadow Wk *ALMDB* BS32 .... **343** J5
BWTH/CHD GL3 .... **103** K7 3
CHNTN OX7 .... **119** F2
CIR GL7 .... **278** C7
STROUD GL5 .... **214** A8 3
Mead Rd *BRSTK/PCHW* BS34 .... **343** K8
CHELTS GL51 .... **134** E1
GLE GL4 .... **131** G8
YATE/CS BS37 .... **348** A6
Meads Cl *CHELTE/BC* GL52 .... **83** G3
CLFD GL16 .... **175** J3
The Meads *CHPMW/MSHF* SN14 .... **363** H3
MANG/FISH BS16 .... **357** F7
TET GL8 .... **323** J3
The Mead *BRSTK/PCHW* BS34 .... **355** F2 3
CIR GL7 .... **249** H5
HGHW SN6 .... **308** D6
THNB/SVB BS35 .... **332** A1
Meadvale *CI VGL* GL2 .... **102** B8 3
Meadway
HNLZ/SM/SNYPK/WT BS9 .... **352** E3
Mead Wy *THNB/SVB* BS35 .... **316** B7
Meadway Rd *STNHO* GL10 .... **212** E8 3
Meardon Rd *HGRV/WHIT* BS14 .... **374** D8 3
Medina Cl *THNB/SVB* BS35 .... **316** C7 3
Medoc Cl *CHELTW* GL51 .... **106** B1
Medway Ct *THNB/SVB* BS35 .... **316** D6
Medway Crs *BWTH/CHD* GL3 .... **160** D1
Medway Dr *FRCTL/WBN* BS36 .... **345** H7
Meendhurst Rd *CIND* GL14 .... **150** E7
Meend La *MTCHDN* GL17 .... **121** J7
Meerbrook Wy *VGL* GL2 .... **157** F7 3

Meere Bank *AVONM* BS11 .... **352** D5
Meerstone Wy *GLE* GL4 .... **159** F3
Meg Thatchers Cl
EVILLE/WHL BS5 .... **366** B7 3
Melbourne Cl *CHELTS* GL53 .... **106** C8
STNHO GL10 .... **212** E5
Melbourne Dr *STNHO* GL10 .... **212** E6
YATE/CS BS37 .... **347** K5
Melbourne Rd *HORF/LLZ* BS7 .... **364** B2
Melbourne St *GL* GL1 .... **3** E6
Melbourne St East *GL* GL1 .... **3** D6
Melbourne St West *GL* GL1 .... **3** D6
Melick Cl *GLE* GL4 .... **158** C1 3
Melita Rd *RDLND/MONT* BS6 .... **364** C3
Melmore Gdns *CIR* GL7 .... **250** A8
Melody Wy *VGL* GL2 .... **131** G1 3
Melrose Av *YATE/CS* BS37 .... **347** H4
Melrose Cl *YATE/CS* BS37 .... **347** J4
Melton Crs *HORF/LLZ* BS7 .... **354** E7
Melville *COTS* GL54 .... **115** H6
Melville Rd *BWTH/CHD* GL3 .... **131** H1
Memorial Cl *KCWD/HNM* BS15 .... **375** G2
Memorial Rd *KGWD/HNM* BS15 .... **375** G1
Mendip Cl *CHELTE/BC* GL52 .... **5** E2
VGL GL2 .... **156** E6 3
Mendip Crs *MANG/FISH* BS16 .... **357** C7
Mendip Rd *CHELTE/BC* GL52 .... **5** E2 3
Mendip Vw
OLD/WMLY/WICK BS30 .... **368** C7
Mendip View Av *MANG/FISH* BS16 .... **366** A3
Meon Rd *CHCAM* GL55 .... **9** C1
Merchants Md *VGL* GL2 .... **156** D5 3
Merchants' Rd *GL* GL1 .... **2** B4 3
Merchant St *CBRIS/FH* BS1 .... **364** C7 3
Mercia Dr *CBRISNE* BS2 .... **364** E4
Mercia Rd *COTS* GL54 .... **62** D8 3
Mercian Cl *CIR* GL7 .... **2** C2
Mercian Wy *CHPMW/MSHF* NP16 .... **288** C7
Mercia Rd *COTS* GL54 .... **62** D8 3
Mercier Cl *YATE/CS* BS37 .... **347** H4
Mercury Wy *GLE* GL4 .... **131** H8
Merestones Cl *CHELT* GL50 .... **106** B8
Merestones Dr *CHELT* GL50 .... **106** B8 3
Merestones Rd *CHELT* GL50 .... **106** B8 3
Merevale Rd *VGL* GL2 .... **3** F2
Merfield Rd
BRSG/KWL/STAPK BS4 .... **374** A4 3
Meridian Rd *RDLND/MONT* BS6 .... **364** A5
Meriton St *CBRISNE* BS2 .... **374** A1
Merlin Cl *CHELTS* GL53 .... **134** C1
HNLZ/SM/SNYPK/WT BS9 .... **353** H5
Merlin Dr *VGL* GL2 .... **156** E4
Merlin Hvn *WUE* GL12 .... **296** E7
Merlin Rdg *MANG/FISH* BS16 .... **368** E2 3
Merlin Rd *BRSTK/PCHW* BS34 .... **342** A8
Merlin Wy *CHELTS* GL53 .... **134** C1
YATE/CS BS37 .... **347** H1
Merrett's Orch *VGL* GL2 .... **238** B3
Merriville Gdns *CHELTW* GL51 .... **106** A3 3
Merriville Rd *CHELTW* GL51 .... **106** A3
Merrywalks *STROUD* GL5 .... **214** D7
Merryweather Cl *ALMDB* BS32 .... **343** G6
Mersey Rd *CHELTE/BC* GL52 .... **5** E5
Merstham Rd *CBRISNE* BS2 .... **364** E4 10
Merton Rd *HORF/LLZ* BS7 .... **364** C1
The Mertons *CIND* GL14 .... **180** B2 2
Mervyn Rd *HORF/LLZ* BS7 .... **364** C2
Meteor Wy *BWTH/CHD* GL3 .... **160** C1 3
Metford Pl *RDLND/MONT* BS6 .... **364** A3 3
Metz Wy *GL* GL1 .... **3** E4
GLE GL4 .... **130** E6
Meysey Cl *CIR* GL7 .... **281** J1
Michaelmas Ct *GL* GL1 .... **3** E2
Michaels Md *CIR* GL7 .... **249** H8 3
Michaels Wy *CLFD* GL16 .... **204** A2 3
Mickle Md *VGL* GL2 .... **128** D1 3
Mickleton Rd *EVE* WR11 .... **7** J1
SHPSTR CV36 .... **11** F1
Middle Av *CBRIS/FH* BS1 .... **364** B8 10
Middle Cft *GLE* GL4 .... **131** F7
Middlecroft *STNHO* GL10 .... **211** K7
Middledown Rd
CHPMW/MSHF SN14 .... **370** A5
Middle Gnd *HGHW* SN6 .... **310** C6
Middlehay Ct *CHELTE/BC* GL52 .... **82** E3 3
STROUD GL5 .... **215** F7
Middle Hill Crs *RSTROUD/NAIL* GL6 .... **244** D3
Middle Leazes *STROUD* GL5 .... **215** F7
Middle Rd *BUR/CRTN* OX18 .... **173** F8
KGWD/HNM BS15 .... **366** E3
STROUD GL5 .... **243** C3
Middle Spillman's *STROUD* GL5 .... **214** C8
Middle St *CHEP* NP16 .... **288** A6 3
SHPSTR CV36 .... **11** C3
STROUD GL5 .... **214** E7
Middleton Lawn *VGL* GL2 .... **103** C7 3
Middleton Rd *AVONM* BS11 .... **352** B6
Middle Tynings
RSTROUD/NAIL GL6 .... **270** C2 3
Middle Wy *CHEP* NP16 .... **312** B1
Midland Rd *CBRISNE* BS2 .... **364** D7
CIR GL7 .... **249** K8
GL GL1 .... **2** C5
MANG/FISH BS16 .... **366** D2

STNHO GL10 .... **212** E6
Midland St *CBRISNE* BS2 .... **364** D8 3
Midland Ter *MANG/FISH* BS16 .... **365** K3 3
Midland Wy *THNB/SVB* BS35 .... **316** B6
Midway *RSTROUD/NAIL* GL6 .... **244** D3
Midwinter Av *CHELTW* GL51 .... **4** A2 3
Midwinter Gdns *CHELTW* GL51 .... **4** A1
Midland Rd *COTS* GL54 .... **169** G4
Mildred St *EVILLE/WHL* BS5 .... **365** C7
Mile End Rd *CLFD* GL16 .... **176** A3
Miles Ct
OLD/WMLY/WICK BS30 .... **376** A2 10
Milestone Wk *CLFD* GL16 .... **204** A2
Milford Av *OLD/WMLY/WICK* BS30 .... **368** D7
Milford Cl *VGL* GL2 .... **130** D1
Millard Cl *HNBRY/STHM* BS10 .... **354** A4 3
Mill Av *BDWAY* WR12 .... **18** B7
CBRIS/FH BS1 .... **364** B8
Millbank *DSLY* GL11 .... **266** E1
Millbank Cl *BRSG/KWL/STAPK* BS4 .... **374** D3
Millbridge Rd *BWTH/CHD* GL3 .... **131** J7
Millbrook Av
BRSG/KWL/STAPK BS4 .... **374** E3 3
Millbrook Cl *GL* GL1 .... **3** E4 3
OLD/WMLY/WICK BS30 .... **367** J8
Millbrook Gdns *CHELTW* GL51 .... **106** B4 3
Millbrook Gn *LYD* GL15 .... **233** H5
Millbrook Ley *MIM* GL56 .... **92** E2
Millbrook Rd *YATE/CS* BS37 .... **346** D4
Millbrook St *CHELTW* GL51 .... **106** B4
GL GL1 .... **3** D5
Mill Cl *CIR* GL7 .... **278** E7
FRCTL/WBN BS36 .... **345** J7
WUE GL12 .... **297** G8
Mill Crs *YATE/CS* BS37 .... **358** D2
Millend *LYD* GL15 .... **207** J4
Millend La *STNHO* GL10 .... **211** K7
Miller Cl *RTEWK/TIB* GL19 .... **77** G6
Miller's Court *VGL* GL2 .... **131** F1 3
Miller's Court Rd *RCTMLV* WR13 .... **31** K1
Millers Dr *OLD/WMLY/WICK* BS30 .... **376** D1
Millers Dyke *VGL* GL2 .... **156** D5 3
Millers Gn *MTCHDN* GL17 .... **122** B7
Mill Farm Dr *STROUD* GL5 .... **214** A6
Millfield *EVE* WR11 .... **15** K4 3
THNB/SVB BS35 .... **316** C4
Millfield Dr *OLD/WMLY/WICK* BS30 .... **367** J8
Millfields *BWTH/CHD* GL3 .... **131** J6
Mill Gv *VGL* GL2 .... **156** D5
Millham Rd *CHELTE/BC* GL52 .... **83** C2
Mill HI *CHEP* NP16 .... **230** B7
LYD GL15 .... **230** D6
Millhill La *CLFD* GL16 .... **175** H8
Millhouse Dr *CHELT* GL50 .... **106** C1
Millin Av *GLE* GL4 .... **157** K3
Milling Cl *HGHW* SN6 .... **308** D5 3
Milling Crs *LYD* GL15 .... **233** H6
Mill La *ALMDB* BS32 .... **330** E5
BWTH/CHD GL3 .... **132** D8
CHCAM GL55 .... **9** F2
CHELTE/BC GL52 .... **81** J2
CHELTE/BC GL52 .... **107** J2
CIR GL7 .... **254** D7
CIR GL7 .... **285** J3
COTS GL54 .... **85** J1 3
COTS GL54 .... **91** J7
COTS GL54 .... **115** G4
FRCTL/WBN BS36 .... **345** H6
MTCHDN GL17 .... **124** C5
NWNT GL18 .... **72** B8
OLD/WMLY/WICK BS30 .... **369** H5
OLD/WMLY/WICK BS30 .... **376** D1
OLD/WMLY/WICK BS30 .... **377** C5
RSTROUD/NAIL GL6 .... **160** A8
RTEWK/TIB GL19 .... **52** D6
RTEWK/TIB GL19 .... **52** D2
RTEWK/TIB GL19 .... **52** E5
TET GL8 .... **272** A5
UUSV WR8 .... **13** F3
WUE GL12 .... **294** A7
YATE/CS BS37 .... **348** D8
Mill Pitt Gdns *BWTH/CHD* GL3 .... **131** J6
Millpond End *STROUD* GL5 .... **242** C4 3
Mill Rd *FRCTL/WBN* BS36 .... **356** D2
Mills Cl *BDWAY* WR12 .... **18** D2
Mill St *CHELTE/BC* GL52 .... **107** H1
GL GL1 .... **3** E4
TEWK GL20 .... **33** C8 3
Mill Vw *COTS* GL54 .... **169** G4
Millview *MIM* GL56 .... **44** C4
Millward Gv *MANG/FISH* BS16 .... **366** C2
Mill Wy *DSLY* GL11 .... **266** D2
Milne Pastures *TEWK* GL20 .... **34** B7 3
Milner Gn *OLD/WMLY/WICK* BS30 .... **376** D1
Milner Rd *HORF/LLZ* BS7 .... **364** D1
Milo Pl *GL* GL1 .... **130** A8
Milsom St *CHELT* GL50 .... **4** A3
EVILLE/WHL BS5 .... **364** E6
Milton Av *CHELTW* GL51 .... **105** J5 3
VGL GL2 .... **157** J1
Milton Cl *YATE/CS* BS37 .... **347** F4
Milton Gv *STROUD* GL5 .... **215** G7
Milton Pk *EVILLE/WHL* BS5 .... **365** C7 10
Milton Rd *CHELTW* GL51 .... **254** D8
Milton Rd *CHELTW* GL51 .... **105** K5

HORF/LLZ BS7 .... 354 C8
YATE/CS BS37 .... 347 F4
Milton St CIR GL7 .... 254 D8
Milverton Gdns
RDLND/MONT BS6 .... 364 D4
Milward Rd KEYN BS31 .... 375 K8
Mimosa Av CHELTW GL51 .... 134 A2
Mina Rd CBRISNE BS2 .... 364 D3
Mine Pitts La RWYE HR9 .... 146 E2
Minerva Cl GLE GL4 .... 131 H8
Minerva Wk CIND GL15 .... 234 B1
Minetts Av CHELTE/BC GL52 .... 83 G3
Minety La MALM SN16 .... 306 D8
Minnow La BUR/CRTN OX18 .... 173 F8
Minor's La HNBRY/STHM BS10 .... 340 C6
Minster Cl CHELTE/BC GL52 .... 82 E2
Minster Gdns GLE GL4 .... 131 H8
Minstrel Wy BWTH/CHD GL3 .... 103 H6
Minto Rd CBRISNE BS2 .... 364 E4
Miserden Rd CHELTW GL51 .... 105 H6
Miss Grace's La CHEP NP16 .... 258 E3
Mission Rd YATE/CS BS37 .... 346 C2
Mitchell La CBRIS/FH BS1 .... 364 C8
Mitchell Wk
OLD/WMLY/WICK BS30 .... 367 K8
Mitford Br SHPSTR CV36 .... 25 C7
Mitre Pitch WUE GL12 .... 297 C7
Mitre St CHELTS GL53 .... 4 C5
Mitton Wy TEWK GL20 .... 33 K6
Mivart St EVILLE/WHL BS5 .... 365 F4
Moat La CHELTU GL51 .... 81 C8
RTEWK/TIB GL19 .... 53 C6
RTEWK/TIB GL19 .... 97 K7
RTEWK/TIB GL19 .... 98 A1
The Moat CHNTN OX7 .... 119 F1
VGL GL2 .... 157 F5
Modecombe Gv
HNBRY/STHM BS10 .... 353 H3
Moffat Rd RSTROUD/NAIL GL6 .... 270 C1
Mogg St CBRISNE BS2 .... 364 E4
Mogridge Cl BWTH/CHD GL3 .... 131 J7
Monarch Cl GLE GL4 .... 159 C2
Monarch's Wy BAD GL9 .... 337 J3
CHCAM GL55 .... 20 D7
CHCAM GL55 .... 21 F1
CIR GL7 .... 248 D8
CIR GL7 .... 275 H1
COTS GL54 .... 115 J2
COTS GL54 .... 143 H1
COTS GL54 .... 167 K8
COTS GL54 .... 169 F3
COTS GL54 .... 194 D4
EVILLE/WHL BS5 .... 365 H4
KCWD/HNM BS15 .... 375 C4
MIM GL56 .... 69 C8
MIM GL56 .... 92 D5
OLD/WMLY/WICK BS30 .... 368 E8
OLD/WMLY/WICK BS30 .... 376 A7
TET GL8 .... 299 C8
TET GL8 .... 302 B7
TET GL8 .... 303 F7
WUE GL12 .... 321 K6
YATE/CS BS37 .... 348 A7
Monica Dr CHELT GL50 .... 4 C1
Monkey Meadow TEWK GL20 .... 34 D5
Monkey Puzzle Cl STROUD GL5 .... 214 A8
Monk Rd HORF/LLZ BS7 .... 364 B2
Monks Av KCWD/HNM BS15 .... 366 B1
Monks Cft CBRISNE BS2 .... 105 J5
Monks La TEWK GL20 .... 58 D3
Monks Meadow LED HR8 .... 26 A8
Monk's Park Av HORF/LLZ BS7 .... 354 C5
Monks Park Wy HNBRY/STHM BS10 .... 354 C6
Monkton Rd KCWD/HNM BS15 .... 375 C2
Monmouth Hl ALMDB BS32 .... 342 B2
Monmouth Rd CLFD GL16 .... 148 B8
HORF/LLZ BS7 .... 364 B2
Monsdale Cl HNBRY/STHM BS10 .... 353 J4
Monsdale Dr HNBRY/STHM BS10 .... 353 J3
Monson Av CHELT GL50 .... 4 B3
Montague Cl BRSTK/PCHW BS34 .... 355 J1
Montague Hl CBRISNE BS2 .... 364 B6
Montague Hl South
CBRISNE BS2 .... 364 B6
Montague St CBRISNE BS2 .... 364 B6
Monterey Cl CHELTW GL20 .... 57 K3
Montfort Rd VGL GL2 .... 130 D1
Montgomery Cl BWTH/CHD GL3 .... 131 K8
Montgomery Rd CHELTW GL51 .... 105 H8
Montpellier Cl GL1 .... 2 C4
Montpellier Dr CHELT GL50 .... 4 B5
Montpellier Gv CHELT GL50 .... 4 B6
Montpellier Pde CHELT GL50 .... 4 B5
Montpellier Retreat CHELT GL50 .... 4 B5
Montpellier Rd LYD GL15 .... 205 C5
Montpellier Spa Rd CHELT GL50 .... 4 B5
Montpellier St CHELT GL50 .... 4 A5
Montpellier Ter CHELT GL50 .... 4 A5
Montpellier Vls CHELT GL50 .... 4 B6
Montpellier Wk CHELT GL50 .... 4 A5
Montreal Av HORF/LLZ BS7 .... 354 D6
Montrose Av RDLND/MONT BS6 .... 364 A5
Montrose Dr
OLD/WMLY/WICK BS30 .... 367 H8

Montrose Pk
BRSG/KWL/STAPK BS4 .... 374 C4
Montroy Cl
HNLZ/SM/SNYPK/WT BS9 .... 354 A8
Montserrat STROUD GL5 .... 243 F3
Moon's La RSTROUD/NAIL GL6 .... 245 F1
Moon St CBRISNE BS2 .... 364 C6
Moor Court Dr CHELTE/BC GL52 .... 5 D3
Moor Croft Dr
OLD/WMLY/WICK BS30 .... 376 A2
Moordell Cl YATE/CS BS37 .... 347 F5
Moorend Cr CHELTS GL53 .... 106 C8
Moorend Gdns AVONM BS11 .... 352 B7
Moorend Gld CHELTS GL53 .... 107 F8
Moorend Gv CHELTS GL53 .... 134 C1
Moorend La VGL GL2 .... 238 B3
Moorend Park Rd CHELTS GL53 .... 106 C8
Moorend Rd CHELTS GL53 .... 107 F8
CHELTS GL53 .... 134 D1
MANG/FISH BS16 .... 356 D3
RTEWK/TIB GL19 .... 54 A5
Moorend St CHELTS GL53 .... 106 C8
Moore Rd COTS GL54 .... 115 H8
Moorfield Rd BWTH/CHD GL3 .... 160 D1
Moorgate CIR GL7 .... 285 F2
Moor Gv AVONM BS11 .... 352 B6
Moor Hall Pl STROUD GL5 .... 214 A6
Moorhen Ct VGL GL2 .... 156 D4
Moorhill St EVILLE/WHL BS5 .... 365 F5
Moorhouse La AVONM BS11 .... 352 B1
HNBRY/STHM BS10 .... 352 D2
Moorland Cl CIND GL14 .... 151 F5
Moorland Rd YATE/CS BS37 .... 347 F5
Moorlands Rd MANG/FISH BS16 .... 366 A4
Moor La ALMDB BS32 .... 330 D7
CIR GL7 .... 255 F8
COTS GL54 .... 115 J7
Moorpark Av YATE/CS BS37 .... 346 E5
Moors Av CHELTW GL51 .... 106 A5
Moorslade La WUE GL12 .... 294 A6
Moor St CHEP NP16 .... 288 A6
GL GL1 .... 3 D6
VGL GL2 .... 182 D5
Mop Hale MIM GL56 .... 44 C3
Mopla Rd CHEP NP16 .... 288 B4
Moravian Rd KCWD/HNM BS15 .... 366 D6
Morcroft Pl LYD GL15 .... 205 J5
Morden Wk HGRV/WHIT BS14 .... 374 C7
Morestall Dr CIR GL7 .... 249 H8
Moreton Cl CHELTE/BC GL52 .... 83 G4
Moreton La TEWK GL20 .... 13 K7
Morgans La MTCHDN GL17 .... 122 B8
Morgan St CBRISNE BS2 .... 364 D5
Mork La LYD GL15 .... 203 F7
Mork Rd LYD GL15 .... 202 E7
Morlands Dr CHELTS GL53 .... 135 H2
Morley Av BWTH/CHD GL3 .... 103 J8
MANG/FISH BS16 .... 367 G2
Morley Cl BRSTK/PCHW BS34 .... 343 F7
MANG/FISH BS16 .... 366 D3
Morley Rd MANG/FISH BS16 .... 366 D3
Morley Sq HORF/LLZ BS7 .... 364 C2
Morley St CBRISNE BS2 .... 364 D5
EVILLE/WHL BS5 .... 365 F5
Morley Ter KCWD/HNM BS15 .... 366 D5
Morman Cl MTCHDN GL17 .... 122 A6
Morningside Cl CHELTE/BC GL52 .... 107 J2
Mornington Dr CHELTS GL53 .... 106 D8
Morpeth St GL GL1 .... 3 D6
Morris Cl LYD GL15 .... 206 C3
Morris Hill Cl CHELTW GL51 .... 82 B8
Morris Orch DSLY GL11 .... 238 D8
Morris Rd BDWAY WR12 .... 18 D6
HORF/LLZ BS7 .... 364 E1
Morse La MTCHDN GL17 .... 122 A6
Morse Rd EVILLE/WHL BS5 .... 365 G7
MTCHDN GL17 .... 122 A7
Mortimer Rd BRSTK/PCHW BS34 .... 355 F5
VGL GL2 .... 130 E1
Morton St EVILLE/WHL BS5 .... 365 F7
GL GL1 .... 3 D6
THNB/SVB BS35 .... 316 C2
Morton Wy THNB/SVB BS35 .... 316 E6
Morwent Cl GLE GL4 .... 131 G8
Mosedale MIM GL56 .... 70 B1
Moselle Dr BWTH/CHD GL3 .... 103 J8
Mosley Crs STROUD GL5 .... 214 A7
Mosley Rd STROUD GL5 .... 214 A6
Mottershead Dr VGL GL2 .... 103 G7
Mottershead Rd CIR GL7 .... 278 D3
Moulder Rd TEWK GL20 .... 33 K8
Mountbatten Cl YATE/CS BS37 .... 347 F3
Mount Cl FRCTL/WBN BS36 .... 345 F6
MTCHDN GL17 .... 122 D8
Mount Crs FRCTL/WBN BS36 .... 356 E1
Mounteney's La WUE GL12 .... 320 B8
Mount Gdns KCWD/HNM BS15 .... 366 D8
Mount Hill Rd KCWD/HNM BS15 .... 366 C8
Mountjoy's La CIND GL14 .... 151 F5
Mountjoy's Lane End
CIND GL14 .... 151 F5
Mount Pleasant CHEP NP16 .... 288 A6
CIR GL7 .... 285 G2
LYD GL15 .... 234 C4
WUE GL12 .... 297 G7

Mount Pleasant Cl COTS GL54 .... 92 D6
Mount Pleasant Rd CIND GL14 .... 151 F7
Mount St CIR GL7 .... 249 J7
GL GL1 .... 2 B3
Mousell La CIND GL14 .... 151 F6
Mousetrap La COTS GL54 .... 115 G8
Mow Barton YATE/CS BS37 .... 347 F4
Mowberry Cl VGL GL2 .... 130 E1
Mowbray Av TEWK GL20 .... 57 J3
Mowbray Rd HGRV/WHIT BS14 .... 374 B7
Moyle Old School La
CHEP NP16 .... 288 C2
Muirfield OLD/WMLY/WICK BS30 .... 367 G8
Mulberry Cl KCWD/HNM BS15 .... 366 E6
VGL GL2 .... 156 E6
Mulberry Dr KCWD/HNM BS15 .... 367 F5
Mulberry Wk
HNLZ/SM/SNYPK/WT BS9 .... 352 E6
Muller Av HORF/LLZ BS7 .... 364 D2
Muller Rd EVILLE/WHL BS5 .... 365 G3
HORF/LLZ BS7 .... 354 D8
HORF/LLZ BS7 .... 364 E2
Mulready Cl HORF/LLZ BS7 .... 355 G8
Mumbleys La THNB/SVB BS35 .... 315 J7
Munday Cl RSTROUD/NAIL GL6 .... 244 B2
Munsley Gv GLE GL4 .... 158 E3
Murcot Rd EVE WR11 .... 17 H2
Murray Cl CHELTE/BC GL52 .... 83 F1
Murrells Rd CLFD GL16 .... 147 K3
Murvagh Cl CHELTS GL53 .... 4 C6
Muscroft Rd CHELTE/BC GL52 .... 107 K2
Musgrove Cl AVONM BS11 .... 352 E4
Mushet Pl CLFD GL16 .... 175 J5
Mutsilver Ms VGL GL2 .... 131 G1
Muzzle Patch VGL GL2 .... 99 H6
Myers Rd VGL GL2 .... 3 F4
Myrtle Cl GLE GL4 .... 158 C1
Myrtle Pl CHEP NP16 .... 288 B5
Myrtle Rd CBRISNE BS2 .... 364 A6
The Myrtles CHEP NP16 .... 288 C4
Mythe Rd TEWK GL20 .... 33 H6

N

Naas La LYD GL15 .... 234 D7
VGL GL2 .... 157 G7
Nags Head Hl EVILLE/WHL BS5 .... 366 A8
Nailsworth Av YATE/CS BS37 .... 347 G5
Naishcombe Hl
OLD/WMLY/WICK BS30 .... 368 C7
The Naite THNB/SVB BS35 .... 291 H8
Napier Miles Rd AVONM BS11 .... 352 C6
Napier Rd EVILLE/WHL BS5 .... 365 F4
Napier St EVILLE/WHL BS5 .... 365 F8
GL GL1 .... 3 D4
Napping La MTCHDN GL17 .... 124 B4
The Napping MTCHDN GL17 .... 124 B3
Narles Rd VGL GL2 .... 238 E5
Narroways Rd CBRISNE BS2 .... 364 E3
Narrowcut La RSTROUD/NAIL GL6 .... 270 B5
Narrow La MANG/FISH BS16 .... 366 E2
Narrow Pln CBRISNE BS2 .... 364 C8
The Narrows CHCAM GL55 .... 20 A4
Naseby Wk EVILLE/WHL BS5 .... 365 K5
Nash Dr HORF/LLZ BS7 .... 355 G7
Nash's La CHCAM GL55 .... 10 B8
CHCAM GL55 .... 22 B1
Nash Wy CLFD GL16 .... 175 K5
Nasse Ct DSLY GL11 .... 266 D1
Nastend La STNHO GL10 .... 212 B6
Nature Cl BWTH/CHD GL3 .... 160 B1
Naunton Crs CHELTS GL53 .... 106 D1
Naunton La CHELTS GL53 .... 106 E8
Naunton Pde CHELTS GL53 .... 4 B6
Naunton Park Cl CHELTS GL53 .... 106 E8
Naunton Park Rd CHELTS GL53 .... 106 E8
Naunton Rd GLE GL4 .... 130 E7
Naunton Ter CHELTS GL53 .... 4 B6
Naunton Wy CHELTS GL53 .... 106 D8
Neads Dr
OLD/WMLY/WICK BS30 .... 376 D1
Neath Rd EVILLE/WHL BS5 .... 365 H6
Nebsworth La SHPSTR CV36 .... 10 B5
Needham Av VGL GL2 .... 157 H8
Nellands Cl SHPSTR CV36 .... 11 G3
Nelson Rd MANG/FISH BS16 .... 366 D1
MANG/FISH BS16 .... 366 D2
Nelson St CBRIS/FH BS1 .... 364 B7
CHEP NP16 .... 288 B6
GL GL1 .... 130 B8
STROUD GL5 .... 214 E7
TEWK GL20 .... 33 H8
Nene Cl VGL GL2 .... 156 E4
Neptune Cl GLE GL4 .... 131 H8
Netham Rd EVILLE/WHL BS5 .... 365 H8
Nethercote Dr COTS GL54 .... 143 J1
Nethercote Farm Dr COTS GL54 .... 143 J2
Netherend Crs LYD GL15 .... 260 D1
Netherhope La CHEP NP16 .... 288 D1
Netheridge Cl VGL GL2 .... 157 G2
Netherley La RTEWK/TIB GL19 .... 31 G6
Netherwood Gdns CHELTW GL51 .... 106 A3

Nettlestone Cl
  HNBRY/STHM BS10 .... 353 G2 [1]
Nettleton Rd CHELTW GL51 .. 105 F7
  CHPMW/MSHF SN14 .... 363 H3
  GL GL1 .... 3 D4 [3]
Nevalan Dr EVILLE/WHL BS5 .. 366 A8
Neville Rd KGWD/HNM BS15 .. 366 E4
  TEWK GL20 .... 57 J1
Nevil Rd HORF/LLZ BS7 .... 364 C2
Newark Rd GL GL1 .... 129 J8
New Barn Av CHELTE/BC GL52 .. 5 E1
New Barn Cl CHELTE/BC GL52 .. 5 E1
New Barn La CHELTE/BC GL52 .. 106 E1
Newbrick Rd BRSTK/PCHW BS34 .. 356 A1
Newbridge Cl
  BRSG/KWL/STAPK BS4 .... 365 H8
Newbridge Rd
  BRSG/KWL/STAPK BS4 .... 365 H8
New Brunswick Av
  EVILLE/WHL BS5 .... 366 B7
New Buildings MANG/FISH BS16 .. 365 K2
Newbury Rd HORF/LLZ BS7 .... 354 E7
New Cheltenham Rd
  KGWD/HNM BS15 .... 366 D5
New Church St TET GL8 .... 302 B7
Newcombe Pl
  HNLZ/SM/SNYPK/WT BS9 .. 353 H7
Newcourt Pk CHELTS GL53 .... 107 H3
Newcourt Rd CHELTS GL53 .... 135 C1
New Cut DSLY GL11 .... 268 B5
Newent Av KGWD/HNM BS15 .. 366 B7
Newent La RTEWK/TIB GL19 .. 125 H3
Newerne St LYD GL15 .... 234 A3
New Fosseway Rd
  HGRV/WHIT BS14 .... 374 A8
Newfoundland Rd
  CBRISNE BS2 .... 364 E5 [13]
Newfoundland St CBRISNE BS2 .. 364 C6
Newfoundland Wy CBRISNE BS2 .. 364 D6
Newgate CBRIS/FH BS1 .... 364 C7
Newgrounds La VGL GL2 ...... 209 J8
New Inn La GL GL1 .... 2 C3 [8]
  TET GL8 .... 272 A6
New Kingsley Rd CBRISNE BS2 .. 364 D8 [3]
Newlands Av FRCTL/WBN BS36 .. 345 J7
The Newlands MANG/FISH BS16 .. 356 B7
Newland St CLFD GL16 .... 175 H5
  GL GL1 .... 3 D3 [8]
New La THNB/SVB BS35 .... 332 C1
New Leaze ALMDB BS32 .... 343 G3
Newleaze Gdns TET GL8 ...... 302 A6 [1]
Newlyn Wk
  BRSG/KWL/STAPK BS4 .... 374 A5 [1]
Newlyn Wy YATE/CS BS37 ..... 347 H4
Newman Cl YATE/CS BS37 ..... 358 D2
Newmarket Av CBRIS/FH BS1 .. 364 B7 [13]
Newmarket Rd
  RSTROUD/NAIL GL6 .... 270 C2
New Mills La WUE GL12 .... 321 J3
Newnham Cl HGRV/WHIT BS14 .. 374 C7
Newnham Pl
  BRSTK/PCHW BS34 .... 342 D5 [1]
Newnton Hl TET GL8 .... 303 F4
Newnton Rd TET GL8 .... 302 D2
Newpit La OLD/WMLY/WICK BS30 .. 377 C3
New Queen St KGWD/HNM BS15 .. 366 D5
New Rd BRSTK/PCHW BS34 .... 354 D3
  BRSTK/PCHW BS34 .... 355 G4
  CHCAM GL55 .... 22 B1
  CHELTE/BC GL52 .... 83 J5
  CHNTN OX7 .... 118 D4
  CIND GL14 .... 149 G5
  CLFD GL16 .... 149 G6
  CLFD GL16 .... 176 B5
  CLFD GL16 .... 177 F4
  DSLY GL11 .... 266 C2
  DSLY GL11 .... 296 C2
  LYD GL15 .... 204 D6
  LYD GL15 .... 205 H3
  LYD GL15 .... 205 K8
  LYD GL15 .... 206 A4
  LYD GL15 .... 207 G4
  LYD GL15 .... 232 E4
  MIM GL56 .... 46 A8
  MTCHDN GL17 .... 123 G5
  MTCHDN GL17 .... 148 E4
  RSTROUD/NAIL GL6 .... 271 H1
  STROUD GL5 .... 242 A2
  THNB/SVB BS35 .... 330 E4
  WUE GL12 .... 296 D8
  WUE GL12 .... 317 J8
  YATE/CS BS37 .... 334 C6
  YATE/CS BS37 .... 334 E5
New Rutland Ct CHELT GL50 .. 4 B2 [3]
New Stadium Rd EVILLE/WHL BS5 .. 365 F4
New Station Rd MANG/FISH BS16 .. 366 A2
Newstead Rd GLE GL4 .... 131 G6
New St BDWAY WR12 .... 17 J4
  BRKLY GL13 .... 235 J6
  CBRISNE BS2 .... 364 D7
  CHELT GL50 .... 4 A3
  CHELTS GL53 .... 135 H1 [3]
  EVE WR11 .... 6 C1
  GL GL1 .... 2 C5
  MTCHDN GL17 .... 123 G5

  RSTROUD/NAIL GL6 .... 187 H6
  STNHO GL10 .... 241 G3
  WUE GL12 .... 295 J8
New Thomas St CBRISNE BS2 .. 364 D8 [3]
Newton Av GLE GL4 .... 130 E7
Newton Cl CHELTW GL51 ...... 105 J4
  KGWD/HNM BS15 .... 367 G5
  RTEWK/TIB GL19 .... 125 J3
Newton Rd CHELTW GL51 ..... 105 J4
  OLD/WMLY/WICK BS30 .... 376 E1
Newton St EVILLE/WHL BS5 .... 364 E6
Newtown WUE GL12 .... 319 J1
Newtown Rd CIND GL14 .... 150 D3
New Tyning La YATE/CS BS37 .. 349 G3
New Wk KGWD/HNM BS15 .... 375 G1
Niblett's HI EVILLE/WHL BS5 .. 366 A8
Niblett's HI EVILLE/WHL BS5 .. 366 A8
Nibley La YATE/CS BS37 .... 346 B3
Nicholas La EVILLE/WHL BS5 .. 366 A8
Nicholas Rd EVILLE/WHL BS5 .. 365 F5
Nicholettes
  OLD/WMLY/WICK BS30 .... 376 A1
Nicholls La FRCTL/WBN BS36 .. 344 E7
Nicolson Cl BWTH/CHD GL3 ... 103 C8
Nigel Pk AVONM BS11 .... 352 A7
Nightingale Cl FRCTL/WBN BS36 .. 345 G8
  THNB/SVB BS35 .... 316 A4 [8]
Nightingale La
  FRCTL/WBN BS36 .... 345 G7 [1]
Nind La WUE GL12 .... 321 F2
Nine Elms Rd VGL GL2 .... 131 C2
Nine Tree HI CBRISNE BS2 .... 364 B5
Nine Wells Rd CLFD GL16 ..... 147 K8
Ninth Av HORF/LLZ BS7 .... 355 F5
Noake Rd BWTH/CHD GL3 .... 131 J6
Noble Av OLD/WMLY/WICK BS30 .. 376 D2
Nodens Wy LYD GL15 .... 234 C2
Norbury Av GLE GL4 .... 158 D2
Nordown Cl DSLY GL11 .... 266 D2
Nordown Rd DSLY GL11 .... 266 D2
Norfolk Av CBRISNE BS2 ...... 364 C6 [16]
  CHELTW GL51 .... 105 F7
  RDLND/MONT BS6 .... 364 C4 [3]
Norfolk St GL GL1 .... 2 B4
Norley Rd HORF/LLZ BS7 ..... 354 D7
Normal Ter CHELT GL50 .... 4 B3
Norman Ball Wy VGL GL2 .... 3 F4
Normanby Rd EVILLE/WHL BS5 .. 365 F5 [3]
Norman Gv KGWD/HNM BS15 .. 366 D1 [3]
Norman HI DSLY GL11 .... 266 D2 [1]
Norman Rd CBRISNE BS2 ..... 364 E4 [11]
  OLD/WMLY/WICK BS30 .... 367 H6
Norman Wy MTCHDN GL17 .... 121 J6
Norrisville Rd
  RDLND/MONT BS6 .... 364 C5 [3]
Norse Wy CHEP NP16 .... 288 D7
Nortenham Cl CHELTE/BC GL52 .. 82 D2 [3]
North Av MTCHDN GL17 .... 122 D6
  TEWK GL20 .... 35 F6
Northbank Cl CHELTW GL51 ... 105 F7 [5]
Northbrook Rd GLE GL4 ...... 130 E5
Northcote Rd EVILLE/WHL BS5 .. 365 J6
  MANG/FISH BS16 .... 357 F8
Northcote St EVILLE/WHL BS5 .. 365 F5 [3]
Northcot La MIM GL56 .... 44 E2 [3]
North Cft
  OLD/WMLY/WICK BS30 .... 376 E2 [3]
North Devon Rd MANG/FISH BS16 .. 366 A1
North East Rd THNB/SVB BS35 .. 316 C4 [8]
Northen Cl CIR GL7 .... 283 C8
Northend Av KGWD/HNM BS15 .. 366 D4
Northend Rd KGWD/HNM BS15 .. 366 E4
Northfield YATE/CS BS37 ...... 347 F6
Northfield Av KGWD/HNM BS15 .. 375 J1
Northfield Rd EVILLE/WHL BS5 .. 366 B7
  GLE GL4 .... 158 B1
  TET GL8 .... 302 C6
Northfield Sq GLE GL4 .... 158 B1 [8]
Northfields Rd
  RSTROUD/NAIL GL6 .... 270 D2
Northfield Ter CHELT GL50 .... 4 B3
Northgate St GL GL1 .... 2 C3
North Hall Ms CHELTE/BC GL52 .. 5 D3
North Hill Rd CIR GL7 .... 250 A8 [3]
North Home Rd CIR GL7 ...... 250 A7
Northland La CIND GL14 ...... 180 E8
Northlands Wy TET GL8 .... 302 C6
Northleaze TET GL8 .... 302 C6
Northleaze La YATE/CS BS37 .. 333 K8
North Meadow Rd HGHW SN6 .. 310 C6
Northmoor La CIR GL7 .... 278 E5
Northover Rd
  HNLZ/SM/SNYPK/WT BS9 .. 353 H5
North Pk KGWD/HNM BS15 ... 366 E5
North Pl CHELT GL50 .... 4 C3 [3]
North Rd BRSTK/PCHW BS34 .. 355 J2
  CLFD GL16 .... 176 B3
  FRCTL/WBN BS36 .... 345 F7
  GL GL1 .... 3 D1
  RDLND/MONT BS6 .... 364 B4
  RTEWK/TIB GL19 .... 125 J3
  THNB/SVB BS35 .... 316 C4
  YATE/CS BS37 .... 334 D8
  YATE/CS BS37 .... 346 E4
North Rd East CHELTW GL51 .. 105 F7

North Rd West CHELTW GL51 .. 105 F7
North Stoke La
  OLD/WMLY/WICK BS30 .... 377 H6
North St CHELTE/BC GL52 ..... 4 B3
  COTS GL54 .... 62 D8
  MANG/FISH BS16 .... 366 D1
  OLD/WMLY/WICK BS30 .... 376 D2
  WUE GL12 .... 319 J8
Northumberland Rd
  RDLND/MONT BS6 .... 364 A4
North Upton La GLE GL4 ...... 131 G7
North Vw MANG/FISH BS16 ... 366 D2 [2]
Northville Rd HORF/LLZ BS7 .. 354 E5
North Wall HGHW SN6 .... 310 D6
Northway BRSTK/PCHW BS34 .. 355 F2
North Wy CIR GL7 .... 249 J6 [8]
Northway La TEWK GL20 ...... 33 K7
  TEWK GL20 .... 34 D5
Northwaylane TEWK GL20 .... 34 C6
Northwick Rd HORF/LLZ BS7 .. 354 D6
  THNB/SVB BS35 .... 329 F6
Northwood Cl CIND GL14 ..... 151 F5
Northwoods Wk
  HNBRY/STHM BS10 .... 354 B3 [1]
Norton Cl COTS GL54 .... 62 D7
  KGWD/HNM BS15 .... 367 F7 [7]
Norton Rdg RSTROUD/NAIL GL6 .. 270 B3 [3]
Norton Vw CHCAM GL55 ...... 9 F3
Nortonwood RSTROUD/NAIL GL6 .. 270 B1
Norwich Dr BRSG/KWL/STAPK BS4 .. 365 J3
  CHELTW GL51 .... 106 A8
Norwood Rd CHELT GL50 ..... 4 A6
Nostle Rd COTS GL54 .... 169 H5
Notch Rd CIR GL7 .... 191 C6
Notgrove Cl CHELTW GL51 .... 105 J6 [3]
  GL GL1 .... 157 J4
Notley Pl BWTH/CHD GL3 ..... 131 J7
Nottingham Rd CHELTE/BC GL52 .. 83 F1
  HORF/LLZ BS7 .... 364 C3
Nourse Cl CHELTS GL53 .... 134 B2
Noverton Av CHELTE/BC GL52 .. 107 K2
Noverton La CHELTE/BC GL52 .. 107 J2
Nugent HI RDLND/MONT BS6 .. 364 B5
Nunnery La DSLY GL11 .... 266 E7
Nunny Cl CHELTW GL51 .... 105 G5
Nupdown Rd THNB/SVB BS35 .. 291 J1
Nup End RTEWK/TIB GL19 .... 77 G6
Nupend Gdns MTCHDN GL17 .. 124 B4 [3]
Nupend La MTCHDN GL17 .... 124 A4
Nup End La RTEWK/TIB GL19 .. 77 G6
The Nurseries CHELTE/BC GL52 .. 82 E4 [3]
  WUE GL12 .... 333 H1
Nursery Cl CHCAM GL55 ...... 9 H1
  CIR GL7 .... 249 K8
  MIM GL56 .... 46 A7
  STROUD GL5 .... 215 F8 [8]
Nursery Gdns HNBRY/STHM BS10 .. 353 J3 [3]
Nursery Rd CIR GL7 .... 250 A8 [3]
The Nursery STNHO GL10 ..... 241 G2
Nursery Vw CIR GL7 .... 278 A3
Nut Cft GLE GL4 .... 3 F6
Nutfield Gv BRSTK/PCHW BS34 .. 355 F4
Nuthatch Dr MANG/FISH BS16 .. 355 K8
Nuthatch Gdns MANG/FISH BS16 .. 356 A8
Nuthill GLE GL4 .... 159 H3
Nutley Av GL GL1 .... 157 J4
Nutmeg Cl GLE GL4 .... 159 F2 [3]
Nut Orchard La TEWK GL20 .. 12 D8 [3]
Nympsfield KGWD/HNM BS15 .. 366 A8
Nympsfield Rd GL GL1 .... 157 J3
  RSTROUD/NAIL GL6 .... 269 K1
  RSTROUD/NAIL GL6 .... 270 C2

O

Oak Av CHELTE/BC GL52 ...... 5 E6
Oakbank GLE GL4 .... 158 A2
Oakbrook Dr CHELTW GL51 ... 105 G2
Oak Cl BRSTK/PCHW BS34 .... 343 H7
  CHEP NP16 .... 312 A1
  YATE/CS BS37 .... 347 F3
Oak Crs LYD GL15 .... 232 C8
Oakcroft Cl GLE GL4 .... 159 F3 [8]
Oakdale Av MANG/FISH BS16 .. 356 D6
Oakdale Cl MANG/FISH BS16 .. 356 E6
Oakdale Ct MANG/FISH BS16 .. 356 E7 [3]
Oakdale Rd MANG/FISH BS16 .. 356 E6
Oakdene Av EVILLE/WHL BS5 .. 365 H3
Oak Dr BWTH/CHD GL3 .... 132 B8
  DSLY GL11 .... 266 E3
  STROUD GL5 .... 214 D8
  TEWK GL20 .... 34 C6
Oakenhill Rd
  BRSG/KWL/STAPK BS4 .... 374 D4
Oakenhill Wk
  BRSG/KWL/STAPK BS4 .... 374 D4
Oakes La BAD GL9 .... 350 B8
Oakfield Rd CHELTE/BC GL52 .. 83 C3
  KGWD/HNM BS15 .... 366 D7
Oakfields CLFD GL16 .... 175 J4
Oakfield St CHELT GL50 .... 106 B7
The Oak Fld CIND GL14 .... 151 C6

Oakfield Wy *BRKLY* GL13 .... **235** K5
Oakford La *CBATH/BATHN* BA1 ...... **381** F6
  CHPMW/MSHF SN14 .... **381** G4
Oakhanger Dr *AVONM* BS11 .... **352** D5
Oakhill Av *OLD/WMLY/WICK* BS30.... **376** D4
Oakhill Pitch *LYD* GL15 .... **231** G8
Oakhill Rd *MTCHDN* GL17 .... **123** G4 🎵
Oakhunger La *BRKLY* GL13............ **263** J2
Oakhurst Cl *BWTH/CHD* GL3 .... **131** H1
Oakhurst Ri *CHELTE/BC* GL52 .... **5** E5
Oakland Av *EVILLE/WHL* BS5 .... **365** J6 🎵
  MTCHDN GL17........................ **122** D8 🎵
Oaklands *CIR* GL7 .... **249** J8
  CLFD GL16 .... **204** A2
Oaklands Cl *MANG/FISH* BS16 ...... **367** H1 🎵
Oaklands Dr *ALMDB* BS32 .... **342** E2
  MANG/FISH BS16 .... **356** A6
  OLD/WMLY/WICK BS30 .... **376** D4 🎵
Oaklands Pk *CIR* GL7................ **205** H5
Oaklands Rd *MANG/FISH* BS16 ...... **367** G1 🎵
Oakland St *CHELTS* GL53 .... **5** E6 🎵
Oak La *EVILLE/WHL* BS5 .... **365** K4
  TEWK GL20 .... **13** J8
Oaklea Rd *LYD* GL15 .... **206** C3
Oakleaze *FRCTL/WBN* BS36 .... **345** K7 🎵
Oakleaze Rd *THNB/SVB* BS35 .... **316** C5
Oakleigh Av *EVILLE/WHL* BS5 ...... **365** H6 🎵
Oakleigh Gdns
  OLD/WMLY/WICK BS30 .... **376** D4
Oakley Flats *CIR* GL7................ **283** F8
Oakley Rd *CHELTE/BC* GL52 .... **5** F4
  CIR GL7 .... **249** H8
  HORF/LLZ BS7 .... **354** D7
Oakley Wy *LYD* GL15 .... **204** E7
Oak Manor Dr *CHELTE/BC* GL52 ...... **5** E4
Oakmeade Pk
  BRSG/KWL/STAPK BS4 ...... **374** A4 🎵
Oak Meadow *LYD* GL15.............. **206** B8
Oakridge *VGL* GL2.................... **100** D8
Oakridge Cl *GLE* GL4 .... **159** G1 🎵
  KGWD/HNM BS15 .... **367** G7
Oak Rd *CIR* GL7 .... **280** E7
  HGHW SN6............................ **311** G2
  HORF/LLZ BS7 .... **364** C1
Oaks La *RWYE* HR9 .... **96** C3
The Oaks *CHELTW* GL51 .... **105** H6
  CIR GL7 .... **276** D7 🎵
  GLE GL4 .... **131** G8
Oak St *CIR* GL7 .... **285** G2
Oak Tree Av *MANG/FISH* BS16 ...... **368** D2
Oak Tree Cl *KGWD/HNM* BS15 ...... **375** H3 🎵
  VGL GL2 .... **156** E7
Oaktree Cl *AVONM* BS11 .... **352** A7
Oaktree Crs *ALMDB* BS32 .... **343** F4
Oaktree Gdn *GLE* GL4 .... **158** E3 🎵
Oak Wy *CIND* GL14.................... **151** J6
  CIR GL7 .... **278** D8
  RTEWK/TIB GL19.................... **125** J3
  STNHO GL10 .... **213** F7
Oakwood Av
  HNLZ/SM/SNYPK/WT BS9 ...... **353** K8
Oakwood Cl *CIND* GL14 .... **151** F5 🎵
  LYD GL15 .... **204** E5
Oakwood Dr *BWTH/CHD* GL3 ...... **131** H8
Oakwood Rd *CLFD* GL16 .... **204** A1
  HNLZ/SM/SNYPK/WT BS9 ...... **353** K8
  LYD GL15 .... **204** E5
Oatfield *VGL* GL2 .... **156** E4
Oatfield Rd *VGL* GL2 .... **182** E8
Oathill La *CIR* GL7 .... **274** A6
Oberon Av *EVILLE/WHL* BS5........ **365** J4
O'brien Rd *CHELTW* GL51 .... **106** A2 🎵
Ocker Hl *RSTROUD/NAIL* GL6 ...... **214** A4
Octavia Pl *LYD* GL15 .... **234** B2
Oddington Rd *COTS* GL54.......... **92** D6
Offas Cl *CHEP* NP16 .... **288** C7
Offa's Dyke Pth *CHEP* NP16 .... **258** C5 🎵
  LYD GL15 .... **230** A4
Office Rd *CIND* GL14 .... **150** E7
Ogbourne Cl *VGL* GL2................ **131** G3
Okebourne Cl *HNBRY/STHM* BS10 .. **353** K2
Okebourne Rd
  HNBRY/STHM BS10 .... **353** K3
Okus Rd *CHELTS* GL53 .... **135** G1
Oldacre Dr *CHELTE/BC* GL52 .... **83** G1
Old Ashley Hl
  RDLND/MONT BS6 .... **364** D4 🎵
Old Aust Rd *ALMDB* BS32 .... **331** G8
Old Bath Rd *CHELTS* GL53.......... **134** E1
Old Bread St *CBRISNE* BS2 .... **364** D4
Old Brewery La *TET* GL8 .... **302** B7 🎵
Old Bristol Rd *RSTROUD/NAIL* GL6 .. **270** D3
Old Bulwark Rd *CHEP* NP16 .... **288** A7
Old Burford Rd *CHNTN* OX7........ **118** D4
Oldbury Cha
  OLD/WMLY/WICK BS30 .... **376** B4
Oldbury Cl *CHELTW* GL51 .... **105** H3 🎵
Oldbury Court Dr
  MANG/FISH BS16 .... **356** B8 🎵
Oldbury Court Rd
  MANG/FISH BS16 .... **366** A1
Oldbury La *OLD/WMLY/WICK* BS30.. **378** A1
  THNB/SVB BS35 .... **316** B2

Oldbury Orch *BWTH/CHD* GL3...... **132** B2
Oldbury Rd *CHELTW* GL51 .... **105** H3
  TEWK GL20 .... **33** H8
Oldbutt Rd *SHPSTR* CV36 .... **24** E1
Old Cheltenham Rd *VGL* GL2 ...... **131** F2
Old Coach Rd *CHEP* NP16 .... **312** E3
  CHPMW/MSHF SN14 .... **373** J4
Old Common *STROUD/NAIL* GL6 .... **243** K7
The Old Common
  RSTROUD/NAIL GL6 .... **244** B3
Old Court Dr *RTEWK/TIB* GL19...... **99** F5
Old Dam Rd *LYD* GL15 .... **206** D7
Old Dean Rd *MTCHDN* GL17 .... **123** G3
Old Down Hl *ALMDB* BS32 .... **331** H3
Old Down Rd *BAD* GL9 .... **350** C6
Oldends La *STNHO* GL10 .... **212** D6
Old Farm La *EVILLE/WHL* BS5 ...... **366** B8 🎵
Oldfield *TEWK* GL20 .... **33** J8
Oldfield Crs *CHELTW* GL51 .... **105** K6
Oldfields La *THNB/SVB* BS35 ...... **332** C1
Old Forge Cl *CHNTN* OX7 .... **118** D4
Old Gloucester Rd *CHELTW* GL51 .. **104** C4
  COTS GL54 .... **114** E8
  FRCTL/WBN BS36 .... **344** B7
  MANG/FISH BS16 .... **356** B6
  THNB/SVB BS35 .... **332** B1
  WUE GL12 .... **317** H4
Old Hall Cl *BDWAY* WR12 .... **16** C5 🎵
Old Hl *MTCHDN* GL17................ **124** C4
  TET GL8 .... **272** B5
Old Horsley Rd
  RSTROUD/NAIL GL6 .... **270** D3
Old Hospital La *TEWK* GL20 .... **33** J7 🎵
Old King Street Ct
  CBRIS/FH BS1 .... **364** C7 🎵
Oldlands Av *FRCTL/WBN* BS36...... **345** J8
Old La (Simmonds La) *RWYE* HR9.... **72** A6
Old London Rd *WUE* GL12 .... **296** E6
Old Manor Cl *WUE* GL12 .... **319** J1
Old Manor Gdns *CHCAM* GL55 ...... **9** G2
Old Manor La *TEWK* GL20 .... **33** K6
Old Market *RSTROUD/NAIL* GL6 .... **270** D2
Old Market St *CBRISNE* BS2 .... **364** D7
Old Millbrook Ter *CHELTW* GL51 .. **106** B4 🎵
Old Mill Cl *YATE/CS* BS37 .... **358** D2
The Old Ml *BDWAY* WR12 .... **18** C6 🎵
Oldminster Rd *BRKLY* GL13 .... **235** J5
Old Moat *VGL* GL2.................... **102** A4
Old Monmouth Rd *MTCHDN* GL17 .. **124** B4
Old Neighbourhood
  RSTROUD/NAIL GL6 .... **244** C4
Old Orchard Ct *CIR* GL7 .... **254** C5
Old Painswick Rd *GLE* GL4 .... **130** D8 🎵
Old Park Hl *CBRISNE* BS2 .... **364** A7 🎵
Old Quarry Ri *AVONM* BS11 .... **352** A7
Old Rectory Cl *STROUD* GL5 .... **242** C1
Old Rectory Gdns *MIM* CL56........ **68** E7 🎵
Old Rectory Rd *WUE* GL12 .... **320** D1
Old Reddings Cl *CHELTW* GL51 ...... **105** G7 🎵
Old Reddings Rd *CHELTW* GL51 .... **105** G7
Old Rd *CHELTE/BC* GL52 .... **83** J6
  CLFD GL16 .... **176** B5
  SHPSTR CV36 .... **25** F1
  VGL GL2 .... **101** G6
Old Rw *GL* GL1 .... **3** D5 🎵
Old Station Dr *CHELTS* GL53 .... **106** D8
Old Station Rd *NWNT* GL18 .... **73** H5
Old Station Wy *CLFD* GL16 .... **175** K5
Old Town *WUE* GL12 .... **297** F7
Old Town Ms *LYD* GL15.............. **233** K4
Old Tram Rd *GL* GL1.................. **2** B4
Old Vicarage La *CIR* GL7 .... **276** B7
Oldwood La *YATE/CS* BS37 .... **334** D6
Olio La *CHELTS* GL53 .... **4** C5 🎵
Olive Gdns *THNB/SVB* BS35 .... **331** K2 🎵
Olive Gv *DSLY* GL11 .... **266** E4
Olney Rd *RSTROUD/NAIL* GL6 ...... **243** H7
Olveston Rd *HORF/LLZ* BS7 .... **364** C1
Olympus Cl *BRSTK/PCHW* BS34...... **343** H8 🎵
Olympus Pk *VGL* GL2 .... **157** G4
Olympus Rd *BRSTK/PCHW* BS34 .... **342** B7
Onslow Rd *NWNT* GL18.............. **73** K6
Oram Ct *OLD/WMLY/WICK* BS30 .... **376** A3
The Orangery *GLE* GL4 .... **131** G7 🎵
Orange St *CBRISNE* BS2 .... **364** D6
Orchard Av *BDWAY* WR12 .... **18** E8
  CBRIS/FH BS1 .... **364** A8 🎵
  CHELTW GL51 .... **105** K4
  CHEP NP16 .... **312** A1
  THNB/SVB BS35 .... **316** C5
Orchard Bank *COTS* GL54 .... **144** D7 🎵
Orchard Bvd
  OLD/WMLY/WICK BS30 .... **376** C2
Orchard Cl *CHCAM* GL55 .... **9** G1 🎵
  CIR GL7 .... **285** F2 🎵
  CLFD GL16 .... **147** K8
  CLFD GL16 .... **203** H1
  DSLY GL11 .... **266** D1
  EVE WR11 .... **6** C2
  FRCTL/WBN BS36 .... **344** D3
  KEYN BS31 .... **375** J8 🎵
  KGWD/HNM BS15.................... **366** D5
  LYD GL15 .... **233** H6
  MTCHDN GL17...................... **123** D4
  SHPSTR CV36 .... **25** F1 🎵

STNHO GL10 .... **241** H3 🎵
TEWK GL20 .... **13** K8
VGL GL2 .... **130** A1
VGL GL2 .... **156** D7
WUE GL12 .... **319** J1
YATE/CS BS37 .... **347** H4
Orchard Ct *COTS* GL54 .... **62** A4
  RSTROUD/NAIL GL6 .... **187** H6
  STNHO GL10 .... **212** E7 🎵
  TEWK GL20 .... **33** J8 🎵
Orchard Dr *BWTH/CHD* GL3 .... **132** B2
  TEWK GL20 .... **12** D7
  THNB/SVB BS35 .... **313** J7 🎵
Orchard End *RTEWK/TIB* GL19 ...... **79** G1 🎵
Orchard Farm Cl *CHEP* NP16 ...... **288** D7 🎵
Orchard Fld *TET* GL8................ **272** A6 🎵
Orchard Gdns *KGWD/HNM* BS15.... **367** F6
Orchard Ga *LYD* GL15 .... **207** H4 🎵
Orchard Gra *THNB/SVB* BS35 ...... **316** B4 🎵
The Orchard Gv *CHELTW* GL51 ...... **133** H5 🎵
Orchard La *CBRIS/FH* BS1 .... **364** A8 🎵🎵
Orchard Lea *THNB/SVB* BS35 ...... **332** A1 🎵
Orchard Leaze *DSLY* GL11 .... **266** B2
Orchard Md *RSTROUD/NAIL* GL6 .... **187** H7
  RSTROUD/NAIL GL6 .... **270** D2 🎵
Orchard Ri *CIND* GL14................ **180** B2
  DSLY GL11 .... **266** D5 🎵
  MIM CL56 .... **68** E6 🎵
  RTEWK/TIB GL19.................... **99** C5
  THNB/SVB BS35 .... **330** E4
Orchard Rd *CHELTE/BC* GL52 .... **83** F3
  CLFD GL16 .... **175** K4
  COTS GL54 .... **85** H1
  EVILLE/WHL BS5 .... **365** K6 🎵
  FRCTL/WBN BS36 .... **345** K7 🎵
  HORF/LLZ BS7 .... **364** C2
  KGWD/HNM BS15 .... **366** E6
  LYD GL15 .... **234** B4
  MANG/FISH BS16 .... **368** D1
  MTCHDN GL17...................... **148** E1
  NWNT GL18 .... **73** H1
  STROUD GL5 .... **213** J8
  TEWK GL20 .... **37** K7
  VGL GL2 .... **131** G2
Orchard Sq *EVILLE/WHL* BS5 .... **365** H7 🎵
The Orchards *KGWD/HNM* BS15 .... **367** F6
  LYD GL15 .... **234** A3
Orchard St *CBRIS/FH* BS1 .... **364** A8 🎵🎵
  WUE GL12 .... **297** F7
The Orchard *BRSTK/PCHW* BS34 .... **355** K1
  CIR GL7 .... **254** E7 🎵
  DSLY GL11 .... **268** B5
  LYD GL15 .... **260** D1
  WUE GL12 .... **333** H1
Orchard V *KGWD/HNM* BS15 ...... **367** F7
Orchard Vw *STROUD* GL5............ **242** C1
Orchard Wk *WUE* GL12 .... **320** D2 🎵
Orchard Wy *BWTH/CHD* GL3 ...... **103** K7
  CHELTW GL51 .... **105** K3
  CHNTN OX7 .... **119** F2
  CLFD GL16 .... **147** K8
  RTEWK/TIB GL19.................... **125** K2
Oridge St *RTEWK/TIB* GL19 .... **76** A3
Oriel Gv *MIM* CL56.................... **70** A2
Oriel Rd *CHELT* GL50 .... **4** B4 🎵
Oriole Wy *GLE* GL4.................... **130** E8
Orion Dr *BRSTK/PCHW* BS34 .... **343** H8
Orland Wy *OLD/WMLY/WICK* BS30 .. **376** B3
Orlebar Gdns *AVONM* BS11 .... **352** D4
Orlham La *LED* HR8.................... **27** J1
Ormerod Rd *CHEP* NP16 .... **288** D7
Ormond Pl *CHELT* GL50 .... **4** B4 🎵
Ormonds Cl *ALMDB* BS32 .... **343** J4
Ormsley Cl *BRSTK/PCHW* BS34 ...... **343** G6
Orpen Gdns *HORF/LLZ* BS7 .... **365** F1
Orpheus Av *BRSTK/PCHW* BS34 .... **343** H8
Orrisdale Ter *CHELTS* GL53 .... **4** C5 🎵
Osborne Av *HORF/LLZ* BS7 .... **364** D3 🎵
Osborne Cl *BRSTK/PCHW* BS34 ...... **355** H2 🎵
Osborne Rd *THNB/SVB* BS35 .... **328** B7
Osborne Vls *CBRISNE* BS2 .... **364** A8 🎵
Osbourne Av *GL* GL1 .... **157** J5
Osier Cl *GLE* GL4 .... **158** C2
Osprey Cl *GLE* GL4 .... **159** F1
Osprey Dr *STNHO* GL10.............. **213** F6
Osprey Pk *THNB/SVB* BS35 .... **316** D3
Osprey Rd *CHELTS* GL53 .... **134** C1
  EVILLE/WHL BS5 .... **365** G7 🎵
Osric Rd *GL* GL1...................... **130** B8
Othello Cl *CHELTW* GL51 .... **105** J4
Otter Rd *BWTH/CHD* GL3 .... **159** H1
Otters Fld *COTS* GL54 .... **62** B6
Ottery Cl *AVONM* BS11 .... **352** C5
Ottrells Md *ALMDB* BS32 .... **343** H3
Oval Ap *VGL* GL2...................... **210** D1
The Oval *GL* GL1 .... **129** K8
  VGL GL2 .... **210** D1
Overbrook Cl *GLE* GL4................ **130** E5
Overbrook Dr *CHELTE/BC* GL52...... **5** D2
Overbrook Rd *VGL* GL2 .... **156** E6
Overbury Rd *GL* GL1 .... **3** E5 🎵
Overbury St *CHELTS* GL53 .... **5** E6 🎵
Over Cswy *GL* GL1.................... **129** H3
Overhill Rd *CIR* GL7 .... **249** H2
Over La *ALMDB* BS32.................. **342** A5

ALMDB BS32 .... 342 E2
Overley Rd *CIR* GL7 .... 247 H1
Overdale Rd *MANG/FISH* BS16 .... 366 C4
Overnhill Ct *MANG/FISH* BS16 .... 366 C1
Overnhill Rd *MANG/FISH* BS16 .... 366 C1
Over Old Rd *GL2* 100 E1
Overton La *VGL* GL2 .... 182 A4
Overton Park Rd *CHELT* GL50 .... 4 A4 🔢
Overton Rd *CHELT* GL50 .... 4 A4
   HORF/LLZ BS7 .... 364 B4
Owen St *EVILLE/WHL* BS5 .... 365 F6 🔢
Owl Cl *GL4* 159 F1
Owls End Rd *CHELTE/BC* GL52 .... 83 G2 🔢
Owls Eye Cl *CLFD* GL16 .... 176 B2 🔢
Owls Head Rd *KGWD/HNM* BS15 .... 366 E8
Oxbarton *BRSTK/PCHW* BS34 .... 355 K1
The Oxebode *GL* GL1 .... 2 C3
Oxen Leaze *ALMDB* BS32 .... 343 J4 🔢
Oxford Cl *CHELTE/BC* GL52 .... 5 D5 🔢
Oxford Pas *CHELT* GL50 .... 4 B3 🔢
Oxford Pl *EVILLE/WHL* BS5 .... 364 E5 🔢
Oxford Rd *GL* GL1 .... 3 D2
Oxfordshire Wy *COTS* GL54 .... 115 J7
   COTS GL54 .... 116 E3
Oxford St *CBRISNE* BS2 .... 364 E8
   CHELTE/BC GL52 .... 5 D5
   CHEP NP16 .... 288 A6 🔢
   EVILLE/WHL BS5 .... 365 C7 🔢
   GL GL1 .... 3 D3
   LYD GL15 .... 234 A4
   MIM GL56 .... 70 A1 🔢
   RDLND/MONT BS6 .... 364 A6
Oxford Wy *CHELTW* GL51 .... 134 A1
Oxleaze Cl *TET* GL8 .... 302 B6
Oxleaze La *VGL* GL2 .... 3 F2
Oxleaze Rd *TET* GL8 .... 303 J1
Oxmead Cl *CHELTE/BC* GL52 .... 83 H2
Oxmoor *GLE* GL4 .... 159 F5
Oxstalls Dr *VGL* GL2 .... 3 F1 🔢
Oxstalls La *VGL* GL2 .... 3 F2
Oxstalls Wy *VGL* GL2 .... 3 F1
   VGL GL2 .... 130 D1 🔢
Ozleworth *KGWD/HNM* BS15 .... 367 G6 🔢

P

Packer's Rd *CIND* GL14 .... 151 F6
Packhorse La *CIR* GL7 .... 225 H4
Paddock Cl *ALMDB* BS32 .... 343 H4
   MANG/FISH BS16 .... 357 J8 🔢
Paddock Gdns *THNB/SVB* BS35 .... 332 A1
   VGL GL2 .... 131 F1
Paddock Ri *STNHO* GL10 .... 213 F7
The Paddocks *CIR* GL7 .... 249 J1
   THNB/SVB BS35 .... 316 D5
Padin Cl *RSTROUD/NAIL* GL6 .... 244 C2
Paganhill La *STROUD* GL5 .... 214 B6
Paganhill La *STROUD* GL5 .... 214 B7
Page Rd *MANG/FISH* BS16 .... 366 D2
Page's La *TEWK* GL20 .... 33 G1
Pagets Cl *CHELTE/BC* GL52 .... 83 G4
Painswick Av *BRSTK/PCHW* BS34 .... 343 F6
Painswick Dr *YATE/CS* BS37 .... 347 G5 🔢
Painswick Old Rd *STROUD* GL5 .... 214 E4
Painswick Rd *BWTH/CHD* GL3 .... 160 B3
   CHELT GL50 .... 4 A6
   GLE GL4 .... 3 E6
   GLE GL4 .... 158 E2
   GLE GL4 .... 160 A7
   RSTROUD/NAIL GL6 .... 214 D4
   STROUD GL5 .... 214 D4
Palmdale Cl
   OLD/WMLY/WICK BS30 .... 376 B4 🔢
Palmer Av *GLE* GL4 .... 159 H1
Palmers Cl *OLD/WMLY/WICK* BS30 .... 367 G8
Palmers Leaze *ALMDB* BS32 .... 344 A7
Palm Rd *TEWK* GL20 .... 57 K2
Pancake La *RTEWK/TIB* GL19 .... 80 A5
Parabola Cl *CHELT* GL50 .... 4 A4
Parabola La *CHELT* GL50 .... 4 A4
Parabola Rd *CHELT* GL50 .... 4 A5 🔢
The Parade *AVONM* BS11 .... 352 A8 🔢
   YATE/CS BS37 .... 347 J5 🔢
Paragon Ter *CHELTS* GL53 .... 4 B5 🔢
Parawell La *LYD* GL15 .... 204 C7
Park Av *ALMDB* BS32 .... 342 E4
   EVILLE/WHL BS5 .... 365 J6
   FRCTL/WBN BS36 .... 345 H7
   FRCTL/WBN BS36 .... 345 H7
   VGL GL2 .... 130 E1
Park Brake *VGL* GL2 .... 128 D2
Parkbury Cl *CHELTW* GL51 .... 106 A4
Park Cl *CIR* GL7 .... 255 F7
   KGWD/HNM BS15 .... 366 E7
   LYD GL15 .... 231 G1
   OLD/WMLY/WICK BS30 .... 376 C1 🔢
   TET GL8 .... 302 C7
Park Crs *EVILLE/WHL* BS5 .... 365 H6
   MANG/FISH BS16 .... 356 C5
   OLD/WMLY/WICK BS30 .... 376 C1
Park Dr *VGL* GL2 .... 157 F5
Park End *HGHW* SN6 .... 308 D5 🔢

Parkend Br *VGL* GL2 .... 183 K4
Parkend Rd *CLFD* GL16 .... 176 B5
Park End Rd *GL* GL1 .... 2 C1
Parkend Rd *LYD* GL15 .... 205 F5
   LYD GL15 .... 206 B3
Parkend Wk *CLFD* GL16 .... 176 B5
   CLFD GL16 .... 204 A2
Parker Pl *BDWAY* WR12 .... 18 D6
Parkers Av *OLD/WMLY/WICK* BS30 .... 368 E7
Parkers Barton
   EVILLE/WHL BS5 .... 365 F8 🔢
Parkers Cl *HNBRY/STHM* BS10 .... 354 C2
Parkers La *MIM* GL56 .... 69 K1
Park Farm *COTS* GL54 .... 115 H7
Park Farm Ct
   OLD/WMLY/WICK BS30 .... 376 A2 🔢
Parkfield Av *EVILLE/WHL* BS5 .... 365 H7 🔢
Parkfield Rd *MANG/FISH* BS16 .... 358 C7
Park Gv *LYD* GL15 .... 205 H5
   RDLND/MONT BS6 .... 364 A1
Park Hill *AVONM* BS11 .... 352 A8
Park Hill La *LYD* GL15 .... 259 J2
Park Hill Common *LYD* GL15 .... 259 J2
Park Hill La *LYD* GL15 .... 259 F2
Park Hill La *LYD* GL15 .... 259 J2
Parkhurst Av *MANG/FISH* BS16 .... 366 B2 🔢
Parkland Cl *CHELTS* GL53 .... 135 F2
Park Farm *COTS* GL54 .... 115 H7
   DSLY GL11 .... 266 D2
Parklands *KGWD/HNM* BS15 .... 366 D6 🔢
   VGL GL2 .... 156 E5
   WUE GL12 .... 297 F6
Parkland Sq *CIR* GL7 .... 249 H8
Parkland Wy *THNB/SVB* BS35 .... 316 B3
Park La *CBRISNE* BS2 .... 364 A7 🔢
   CHELTE/BC GL52 .... 83 H8
   CIR GL7 .... 249 J2
   COTS GL54 .... 109 K5
   DSLY GL11 .... 266 D2
   FRCTL/WBN BS36 .... 345 H7
   FRCTL/WBN BS36 .... 357 C2
   SHPSTR CV36 .... 10 D1
   STROUD GL5 .... 242 B8
   WUE GL12 .... 298 A6
Park Ms *CHELT* GL50 .... 106 C8
Park Pl *CBRISNE* BS2 .... 364 A7
   CHELT GL50 .... 4 A6
   EVILLE/WHL BS5 .... 365 J3
   HGHW SN6 .... 308 D6
Park Rd *AVONM* BS11 .... 352 A8
   CHCAM GL55 .... 20 D4
   CLFD GL16 .... 147 J8
   CLFD GL16 .... 175 K3
   GL GL1 .... 2 C4
   HORF/LLZ BS7 .... 354 D5
   KGWD/HNM BS15 .... 366 D5
   MANG/FISH BS16 .... 365 H1
   MANG/FISH BS16 .... 366 E1
   MIM GL56 .... 44 B3
   NWNT GL18 .... 99 J2
   OLD/WMLY/WICK BS30 .... 376 C1
   RSTROUD/NAIL GL6 .... 270 E3
   STNHO GL10 .... 212 E6
   STROUD GL5 .... 215 F8
   THNB/SVB BS35 .... 316 B4
   WUE GL12 .... 318 D2
Park Road Crs
   RSTROUD/NAIL GL6 .... 270 E3 🔢
Park Rw *CBRIS/FH* BS1 .... 364 A7
   FRCTL/WBN BS36 .... 345 G6
Parkside *CLFD* GL16 .... 175 K4
   FRCTL/WBN BS36 .... 344 E8
Parkside Dr *BWTH/CHD* GL3 .... 103 K3
Parkside Gdns *EVILLE/WHL* BS5 .... 365 F2
Parks Rd *MTCHDN* GL17 .... 123 H5
Parkstone Av *HORF/LLZ* BS7 .... 354 D8
Park St *BAD* GL9 .... 338 C4
   CBRIS/FH BS1 .... 364 A7
   CHELT GL50 .... 4 A3
   CIR GL7 .... 249 J5 🔢
   CIR GL7 .... 254 E7
   COTS GL54 .... 92 C6
   EVILLE/WHL BS5 .... 365 K6 🔢
   GL GL1 .... 2 C3
   YATE/CS BS37 .... 345 K2
Park Street Av *CBRIS/FH* BS1 .... 364 A7 🔢
The Park *ALMDB* BS32 .... 343 G3
   CHELT GL50 .... 106 C8
   COTS GL54 .... 92 C7
   KEYN BS31 .... 375 K8
   KGWD/HNM BS15 .... 366 E6
   MANG/FISH BS16 .... 356 B5
   OLD/WMLY/WICK BS30 .... 376 C5
   TEWK GL20 .... 34 C5
Park Vw *CHEP* NP16 .... 288 D6
   CIR GL7 .... 249 H2
   KGWD/HNM BS15 .... 366 E7
   MTCHDN GL17 .... 121 J6
   VGL GL2 .... 182 D7
Park View Dr *THNB/SVB* BS35 .... 316 C4
Park View Rd *BRKLY* GL13 .... 263 K3
Parkwall Crs
   OLD/WMLY/WICK BS30 .... 376 A2
Parkwall Rd
   OLD/WMLY/WICK BS30 .... 376 B2

Parkway *BRSTK/PCHW* BS34 .... 356 A2
Park Wy *CIR* GL7 .... 277 K2
   OLD/WMLY/WICK BS30 .... 376 C1
Parkwood Crs *BWTH/CHD* GL3 .... 131 H8
Parkwood Gv *CHELTS* GL52 .... 135 C2
Parliament St *GL* GL1 .... 2 C4 🔢
   STROUD GL5 .... 214 E7
Parliment Ct *STROUD* GL5 .... 214 E7 🔢
Parnall Crs *YATE/CS* BS37 .... 346 E4
Parnall Rd *MANG/FISH* BS16 .... 366 A3
Parragate Rd *CIND* GL14 .... 150 E5
Parr Cl *BWTH/CHD* GL3 .... 103 H7 🔢
Parry Rd *GL* GL1 .... 130 B8
Parslow Barton
   EVILLE/WHL BS5 .... 366 A7 🔢
Parsonage Farm *HGHW* SN6 .... 310 D7 🔢
Parsonage St *DSLY* GL11 .... 266 E5 🔢
Parsons Av *BRSTK/PCHW* BS34 .... 355 K1
Parsons Cl *SHPSTR* CV36 .... 35 F1
Parsons Ct *RSTROUD/NAIL* GL6 .... 243 J8 🔢
Parsons La *CHCAM* GL55 .... 7 K8
   RTEWK/TIB GL19 .... 52 D3
Parsons Wk
   OLD/WMLY/WICK BS30 .... 367 K7
Partition St *CBRIS/FH* BS1 .... 364 A8 🔢
Parton Dr *BWTH/CHD* GL3 .... 132 A1
Parton Rd *BWTH/CHD* GL3 .... 103 K8
Partridge Cl *STNHO* GL10 .... 213 F6 🔢
   VGL GL2 .... 157 J1
Partridge Rd *MANG/FISH* BS16 .... 368 C3
Partridge Wy *CIR* GL7 .... 250 A5
Passage Rd *HNBRY/STHM* BS10 .... 353 H2
   HNBRY/STHM BS10 .... 353 J3 🔢
   HNBRY/STHM BS10 .... 353 J1
   HNLZ/SM/SNYPK/WT BS9 .... 353 J6
   VGL GL2 .... 180 E3
   VGL GL2 .... 182 C6
Passage Road Brentry Hl
   HNBRY/STHM BS10 .... 353 J3
Passage St *CBRIS/FH* BS1 .... 364 C8
Pastor's Hl *LYD* GL15 .... 205 F6
Pasture La *MIM* GL56 .... 44 C4
Patch Elm La *YATE/CS* BS37 .... 334 A3
The Patches *MTCHDN* GL17 .... 121 K8
Patch La *YATE/CS* BS37 .... 334 C6
Paterson Rd *CIR* GL7 .... 250 A6
Pates Av *CHELTW* GL51 .... 106 B4
Patseamur Ms *VGL* GL2 .... 131 C1 🔢
Patterdale Cl *CHELTW* GL51 .... 105 K1 🔢
Paul Md *RSTROUD/NAIL* GL6 .... 186 D5
Pauls Cft *HGHW* SN6 .... 310 E7
Paul's Ri *STROUD* GL5 .... 242 C4
Paul St *CBRISNE* BS2 .... 364 A6
   GL GL1 .... 3 D6 🔢
Paulton Dr *HORF/LLZ* BS7 .... 364 A2
Pauntley Court Dr
   RTEWK/TIB GL19 .... 51 H7
Pavilion Rd *CHEP* NP16 .... 312 D4
Paxhill La *TEWK* GL20 .... 12 D7
Payford Br *RTEWK/TIB* GL19 .... 51 J6
Paygrove La *VGL* GL2 .... 131 F2
Payne Dr *EVILLE/WHL* BS5 .... 365 F7 🔢
Paynes Meadow *VGL* GL2 .... 211 K1
Paynes Pitch *BWTH/CHD* GL3 .... 132 B3
Peach Cl *TEWK* GL20 .... 57 K2
Peache Rd *MANG/FISH* BS16 .... 356 B5
Peacock Cl *CHELTW* GL51 .... 105 H4 🔢
   GLE GL4 .... 159 J5
   NWNT GL18 .... 73 J6 🔢
Peacock Gdns *NWNT* GL18 .... 73 J6 🔢
Peacock La *CIND* GL14 .... 178 E1
Peacocks La *KGWD/HNM* BS15 .... 366 C6
Peak La *DSLY* GL11 .... 240 A8
Peakstile Piece *CHELTE/BC* GL52 .... 83 H3 🔢
Pearces Hl *MANG/FISH* BS16 .... 356 B7
Pearce Wy *MANG/FISH* BS16 .... 157 H2
Pearcroft Rd *STNHO* GL10 .... 213 F8
The Pear Orch *TEWK* GL20 .... 34 D5 🔢
Pearsall Rd
   OLD/WMLY/WICK BS30 .... 375 K4
Peart Cl *VGL* GL2 .... 3 E4
Pear Tree Cl *CHCAM* GL55 .... 20 E4 🔢
   CHELTE/BC GL52 .... 83 J3 🔢
   VGL GL2 .... 156 E7
Pear Tree Hey *YATE/CS* BS37 .... 347 G1 🔢
Peartree La *EVILLE/WHL* BS5 .... 366 B8
   KGWD/HNM BS15 .... 367 F4 🔢
Pear Tree Rd *ALMDB* BS32 .... 343 G4
Pearwood Wy *GL* GL1 .... 157 J4 🔢
Pecked La *CHELTE/BC* GL52 .... 83 C2
Peel Cl *CHELTS* GL53 .... 135 J1 🔢
Peel St *CBRISNE* BS2 .... 364 D6
Pegasus Gdns *VGL* GL2 .... 157 F4
Pegasus Rd *BRSTK/PCHW* BS34 .... 342 B7
Peghouse Cl *STROUD* GL5 .... 215 F6
Peghouse Ri *STROUD* GL5 .... 215 F6
Pelham Crs *BWTH/CHD* GL3 .... 103 J8
Pemberton Ct *MANG/FISH* BS16 .... 366 C1 🔢
Pembridge Cl *CHELTE/BC* GL52 .... 107 J8
Pembroke Av *AVONM* BS11 .... 352 A8 🔢
Pembroke Rd *AVONM* BS11 .... 352 A8 🔢
   CHELTW GL51 .... 105 J3
   CHEP NP16 .... 312 A1
   KGWD/HNM BS15 .... 366 E4 🔢
Pembroke St *CBRISNE* BS2 .... 364 C6 🔢

CIND GL14 .... 151 F6
GL1 .... 3 D5
Pembury Rd GLE GL4 .... 158 A2
Penard Wy KGWD/HNM BS15 ...... 367 F7 ⓲
Penda Pl CHEP NP16 .... 288 C6
Pendennis Av MANG/FISH BS16 .. 366 D2 ⓲
Pendennis Pk
BRSG/KWL/STAPK BS4 .... 374 C4
Pendennis Rd MANG/FISH BS16 ... 366 D1
Pendil Cl CHELTW GL51 .... 82 B8
Pendock Cl
OLD/WMLY/WICK BS30 .... 376 D5 ⓲
VGL GL2 .... 156 E5 ⓲
Pendock Ct MANG/FISH BS16 ...... 357 H7 ⓲
Pendock Rd FRCTL/WBN BS36 .... 356 E1
MANG/FISH BS16 .... 356 B8
Penfield Rd CBRISNE BS2............. 364 E4
Penharva Cl CHELTW GL51 .... 105 K3
Penhill Rd GLE GL4 .... 158 D1
Penmoel La CHEP NP16 .... 288 C3
Penmoyle Gdns CHEP NP16 .... 288 C2 ⓲
Penn Dr MANG/FISH BS16 .... 356 C5
Penngrove
OLD/WMLY/WICK BS30 .... 376 B3 ⓲
Pennine Cl VGL GL2 .... 156 E6
Pennine Rd CHELTE/BC GL52...... 5 F1
OLD/WMLY/WICK BS30 .... 376 D2
Penn La STNHO GL10................... 241 H3
Penn St CBRIS/FH BS1 .... 364 C7
Pennsylvania Av CHELTW GL51 .. 105 K3
Penny Cl VGL GL2 .... 131 F2
Pennylands Bank BDWAY WR12 . 18 A4
Penny La GLE GL4 .... 237 J4
Pennyroyal Gv
MANG/FISH BS16 .... 365 J1 ⓲
Pennywell Rd EVILLE/WHL BS5 .. 364 D7
EVILLE/WHL BS5 .... 364 E6
EVILLE/WHL BS5 .... 364 E5 ⓲
Pen Park Rd HNBRY/STHM BS10 .. 354 A3
Penpole Av AVONM BS11 .... 352 A8
Penpole La AVONM BS11 .... 352 A7
Penpole Pk AVONM BS11 .... 352 A7 ⓲
Penpole Pl AVONM BS11 .... 352 A8
Penrith Rd CHELTW GL51 .... 105 K8
Penrose Cl RSTROUD/NAIL GL6 .. 214 A3
Penrose Dr BRSTK/PCHW BS34 .. 343 H7 ⓲
Penrose Rd BRSTK/PCHW BS34 .. 103 F3
Pensfield Pk HNBRY/STHM BS10 . 344 B3
Pensile Rd RSTROUD/NAIL GL6 ... 271 F2
Pentathlon Wy CHELTW GL51 ..... 106 D1 ⓲
Pentland Av THNB/SVB BS35 ...... 316 A6
Perch Cl CLFD GL16 .... 176 C2
Perch Dr CLFD GL16 .... 176 C2
Percy St GL GL1 .... 3 D6 ⓲⓲
Peregrine Cl VGL GL2 .... 157 F3
Peregrine Rd CHELTS GL53 .... 134 C1
Perricks Cl CIND GL14 .... 153 J3
Perrinpit Rd FRCTL/WBN BS36 ... 344 D3
Perrinsfield CIR GL7 .... 257 H8
Perrott Rd KGWD/HNM BS15 ...... 367 C5 ⓲
Perry Cl FRCTL/WBN BS36 .... 356 D2
NWNT GL18 .... 73 K6
Perrygrove Rd CLFD GL16 .... 175 K6
CLFD GL16 .... 204 A2
Perrymans La MANG/FISH BS16 .. 356 A8
Perry Orch GLE GL4 .... 159 G4
STROUD GL5 .... 213 K6 ⓲
Perrys Lea ALMDB BS32 .... 343 H4 ⓲
Perry St EVILLE/WHL BS5 .... 364 E6 ⓲⓲
Perry Wy VGL GL2 .... 211 F2
Persh La VGL GL2 .... 101 F7
Perth STNHO GL10 .... 212 E5
Perwell Ct TEWK GL20 .... 13 J7
Peter Pennell Cl CHELTW GL51 ... 105 J2
Peters Fld VGL GL2 .... 128 E1 ⓲
Peter's St STNHO GL10 .... 239 K3
Peter's Ter EVILLE/WHL BS5 .... 365 F7
Petersway Gdns
EVILLE/WHL BS5 .... 366 A8 ⓲
Petherton Cl KGWD/HNM BS15 ... 366 A7
Petherton Gdns HGRV/WHIT BS14 . 374 A7
Petherton Rd HGRV/WHIT BS14 . 374 A6
Pettigrove Gdns
KGWD/HNM BS15 .... 366 E7
Pettigrove Rd KGWD/HNM BS15 . 366 E8
Pettycroft MTCHDN GL17 .... 121 J7
Petty La CHELTE/BC GL52............. 84 B3
Petty Marsh LYD GL15 .... 231 F2
Petworth Cl GL GL1 .... 157 J6
Pevelands DSLY GL11 .... 266 D1
Peverell Cl HNBRY/STHM BS10 ... 353 H3
Peverell Dr HNBRY/STHM BS10 .. 353 H3
Pheasant La CHELTW GL51 .... 104 E5
Pheasant Md STNHO GL10 .... 213 F6 ⓲⓲
The Pheasantry CIR GL7.............. 280 E7
Pheasant Wy CIR GL7 .... 250 B5
Phelps Wy RTEWK/TIB GL19 ...... 99 G6
Philadelphia Ct CBRIS/FH BS1 .... 364 C7 ⓲
Philip's Cl LYD GL15 .... 206 D5
Philip St STROUD GL5 .... 374 A1
GL GL1 .... 2 B6 ⓲
Phillimore Gdns VGL GL2 .... 210 E1
Phillimore Rd DSLY GL11 .... 266 C2
Phillips La RTEWK/TIB GL19 .... 52 E2
Phillips Rd BDWAY WR12 .... 18 D5

Phoenix Dr CHEP NP16 .... 312 C2 ⓲
Phoenix Gv RDLND/MONT BS6 .. 364 A1
Phoenix Wy CIR GL7 .... 249 J6 ⓲
Piccadilly COTS GL54 .... 88 C8
STROUD GL5 .... 215 F7
Piccadilly Wy CHELTE/BC GL52 .. 107 K2 ⓲
Pickedmoor La THNB/SVB BS35 .. 315 H1
Pickering Cl CHELTS GL53 .... 106 C8 ⓲
Pickering Rd CHELTS GL53 .... 106 C8 ⓲
Picton La RDLND/MONT BS6 ...... 364 C5
Picton St RDLND/MONT BS6 .... 364 C5
The Piece BWTH/CHD GL3 .... 132 A2
Pike Cnr BDWAY WR12 .... 18 E2
Pike House Cl HCHW SN6............ 310 C6
Pike La RSTROUD/NAIL GL6 .... 270 D3
Pike Rd CIR GL7 .... 191 G6
CLFD GL16 .... 175 K3
Pile Marsh EVILLE/WHL BS5 .... 365 H7
Pilford Av CHELTS GL53 .... 134 E1
Pilford Cl CHELTS GL53 .... 134 E1
Pilford Ct CHELTS GL53 .... 134 E3
Pilford Rd CHELTS GL53 .... 134 E3
Pilgrim Cl GLE GL4 .... 131 G8 ⓲
Pilgrims Wy MANG/FISH BS16 ... 356 D6 ⓲
Pilgrims Whf
BRSG/KWL/STAPK BS4 .... 365 J7 ⓲
Pilgrove Cl CHELTW GL51 .... 105 H1
Pilgrove Wy CHELTW GL51 .... 105 H1
Pilkington Ct BRSTK/PCHW BS34 . 355 G4
Pillcroft Cl CHELTW GL51 .... 160 E1
Pillcroft Rd CHELTW GL51 .... 160 E1
Pilley Crs CHELTS GL53 .... 134 D2
Pilley La CHELTS GL53 .... 134 D2
Pillingers Rd KGWD/HNM BS15 .. 366 C7
Pillowell Rd LYD GL15 .... 205 J5
Pillows Green Rd RTEWK/TIB GL19 . 53 H6
Pilning St THNB/SVB BS35 .... 330 A6
Pimpernel Md ALMDB BS32 .... 343 J7 ⓲
Pincoate VGL GL2 .... 100 D8
Pincot La RSTROUD/NAIL GL6 ..... 215 F1
Pincots La WUE GL12 .... 335 K3
Pine Bank CHELTE/BC GL52 .... 83 H3
Pine Cl CHELTE/BC GL52 .... 5 E5
THNB/SVB BS35 .... 316 C5
Pine Crest Wy LYD GL15 .... 204 E6 ⓲
Pinedale LYD GL15........................ 232 B8
Pine Gv HORF/LLZ BS7 .... 354 D5
Pine Grove Pl HORF/LLZ BS7 ...... 364 B3 ⓲
Pinemount Rd BWTH/CHD GL3 ... 131 J7
Pine Rd HNBRY/STHM BS10 .... 353 K3
Pinery Rd GLE GL4 .... 131 G7 ⓲
Pines Rd OLD/WMLY/WICK BS30 . 376 D5
The Pines COTS GL54 .... 62 E6 ⓲
Pine Tree Dr GLE GL4 .... 131 G6
Pinetrees CHELTS GL53 .... 135 F1
Pine Tree Wy LYD GL15 .... 207 F4
Pinetum Dr VGL GL2 .... 127 K2
Pineway GLE GL4 .... 130 D8
Pinewood KGWD/HNM BS15 ...... 367 F5 ⓲
Pinewood Cl CIND GL14 .... 151 G5
HNLZ/SM/SNYPK/WT BS9 ...... 353 K7
Pinewood Rd VGL GL2 .... 156 E6
Pinewood Wy
CHPMW/MSHF SN14 .... 372 E7
Pingry La CLFD GL16 .... 175 H8
Pinkers Md MANG/FISH BS16 ..... 357 J8
Pinlocks GLE GL4 .... 159 G3
Pinnells End La DSLY GL11 .... 239 H6
Pintail Cl VGL GL2 .... 156 D5
Pioneer Pk BRSG/KWL/STAPK BS4 . 374 B1
Pipe La CBRIS/FH BS1 .... 364 A8
Piper Rd YATE/CS BS37 .... 347 G3 ⓲
Pipers Gv VGL GL2 .... 128 D1 ⓲
Pippin Cl BWTH/CHD GL3 .... 131 J8 ⓲
NWNT GL18 .... 73 K6
Pippin Ct
OLD/WMLY/WICK BS30 .... 376 A2 ⓲⓲
Pippins Rd TEWK GL20 .... 13 K8
Pirton Crs BWTH/CHD GL3 .... 131 K1
Pirton La BWTH/CHD GL3 .... 103 J8
Pitchcombe YATE/CS BS37 .... 346 E7 ⓲
Pitchcombe Gdns
HNLZ/SM/SNYPK/WT BS9 ...... 353 F7
Pitch La RDLND/MONT BS6 .... 364 B5
The Pitch RSTROUD/NAIL GL6 .... 244 A4
Pithay CBRIS/FH BS1 .... 364 B7 ⓲⓲
Pithay Ct CBRIS/FH BS1 .... 364 B7 ⓲⓲
Pitman Pl WUE GL12 .... 297 G8
Pitman Rd CHELTW GL51 .... 105 J5
Pitt Rd HORF/LLZ BS7 .... 364 C1
Pittsfield HCHW SN6.................... 310 D7
Pitt St GL GL1 .... 2 C3
Pittville Circ CHELTE/BC GL52 .... 5 D3 ⓲
Pittville Circus Rd
CHELTE/BC GL52 .... 5 D3 ⓲
Pittville Cl THNB/SVB BS35 .... 316 C3 ⓲
Pittville Crs CHELTE/BC GL52 .... 5 D2 ⓲
Pittville Crescent La
CHELTE/BC GL52 .... 5 D2
Pittville Lawn CHELTE/BC GL52.... 4 C3
Pittville Ms CHELTE/BC GL52 .... 4 C3
Place HI NWNT GL18 .... 72 B6
The Plain NWNT GL18 .... 214 C4
Plantation Crs TEWK GL20 .... 13 K8 ⓲
Players Cl MANG/FISH BS16 .... 356 B2

Playford Gdns AVONM BS11 .... 352 A6
Pleasant Rd MANG/FISH BS16 .... 366 D1
Pleasant Stile CIND GL14 .... 151 J8
Pleydells HCHW SN6 .... 310 D6 ⓲
The Pleydells CLG7 .... 251 H5 ⓲
The Plies CIR GL7 .... 254 E8
Plock Ct VGL GL2 .... 130 B3
Ploughmans Wy VGL GL2 .... 156 E8 ⓲
Plover Cl YATE/CS BS37 .... 346 E4
Plummer's HI EVILLE/WHL BS5 ... 365 J6
Plumpton Ct MANG/FISH BS16 ... 357 F5 ⓲
Plum Tree Cl GLE GL4 .... 159 G2 ⓲
Pochard Cl VGL GL2 .... 156 D4
Pockhill La COTS GL54 .... 115 G8
Poden La CHCAM GL55 .... 7 K3
Podsmead Pl GL GL1 .... 157 K1
Podsmead Rd GL GL1 .... 157 K2
Poets' Cl EVILLE/WHL BS5 .... 365 H6 ⓲
Poets Pth LED HR8 .... 27 F4
NWNT GL18 .... 49 J2
Poets' Path No 1 NWNT GL18 ..... 49 K2
NWNT GL18 .... 51 F4
Poets' Path No 2 NWNT GL18 ..... 50 B1
Point Rd TET GL8 .... 272 A6
Polefield Gdns CHELTW GL51 ..... 106 B6
Pollards La LYD GL15 .... 207 G5
Polly Barnes Cl
KGWD/HNM BS15 .... 375 G1 ⓲
Polly Barnes HI KGWD/HNM BS15 . 375 G1
Pomphrey HI MANG/FISH BS16... 367 J2
Ponsford Rd
BRSG/KWL/STAPK BS4 .... 374 A5
Ponting Cl EVILLE/WHL BS5 .... 366 A5 ⓲
Pool Cnr ALMDB BS32.................. 331 F4
Poole Court Dr YATE/CS BS37 ..... 347 C4
Poole Gnd VGL GL2 .... 128 D3 ⓲
Pooles La STROUD GL5 .... 242 A2 ⓲
Poole Wy CHELT GL50.................... 4 A3
Poolhay Cl RTEWK/TIB GL19 ...... 54 E4 ⓲
Pool Rd KGWD/HNM BS15 .... 366 E3
Poolway Ct CLFD GL16 .... 175 K4 ⓲
Poolway Pl CLFD GL16 .... 175 K4
Poolway Ri CLFD GL16 .... 175 K3
Poolway Rd CLFD GL16 .... 176 A3 ⓲
Popes Cl CHELT GL50..................... 4 B2
Pope's Ct CIR GL7 .... 249 G2
Popes Meade VGL GL2 .... 128 E1 ⓲
Poplar Av
HNLZ/SM/SNYPK/WT BS9 ...... 353 F8 ⓲
Poplar Cl GL GL1 .... 157 K2
OLD/WMLY/WICK BS30 .... 367 J8 ⓲
Poplar Rd MANG/FISH BS16 .... 368 D1
Poplar La WUE GL12 .... 335 K2
Poplar Pl MANG/FISH BS16 .... 366 A3 ⓲
Poplar Rd EVILLE/WHL BS5 .... 365 K5
KGWD/HNM BS15 .... 375 F1
OLD/WMLY/WICK BS30 .... 367 K8
Poplars Cl CHCAM GL55 .... 20 D4
The Poplars CHELTW GL51 .... 133 J1
Poplar Ter KGWD/HNM BS15 ..... 367 F6 ⓲
Poplar Wy VGL GL2 .... 156 E7
Poppy Fld VGL GL2 .... 100 E8 ⓲
Poppy Md ALMDB BS32 .... 343 J7
Porchester Rd BWTH/CHD GL3 ... 131 H7
Portland Pl CHELTE/BC GL52 .... 4 C3 ⓲⓲
MANG/FISH BS16 .... 366 D3 ⓲
Portland Sq CBRISNE BS2 .... 364 C6 ⓲⓲
CHELTE/BC GL52 .... 4 C3 ⓲⓲
Portland St CBRISNE BS2 .... 364 A6
CHELTE/BC GL52 .... 4 C3
MANG/FISH BS16 .... 366 D3 ⓲
Port La STROUD GL5 .... 243 H5
Porturet Wy CHELTS GL53 .... 107 H8 ⓲
Portwall Rd CHEP NP16 .... 288 C6
Portway GLE GL4........................... 159 H5
Portway La YATE/CS BS37 .... 348 A4
Portwell HGHW SN6 .... 310 D7 ⓲
Postlip Wy CHELTW GL51 .... 105 H6 ⓲
Post Office La CHELT GL50 .... 84 A1 ⓲
CHELTE/BC GL52 .... 84 A3
MIM GL56 .... 44 E2
TEWK GL20 .... 33 H8 ⓲
Post Office Sq CIR GL7 .... 278 C2
The Post Paddocks LYD GL15 ..... 260 C1
Potlicker's La CIR GL7 .... 224 E2
Potters Croft CHEP NP16 .... 312 D2
Potters Field Rd CHELTE/BC GL52 . 83 J3
Potters Pond WUE GL12 .... 297 F7
Pound Cl BWTH/CHD GL3 .... 160 C2
CIR GL7 .... 278 A2
TEWK GL20 .... 12 D8
Pound Dr MANG/FISH BS16 .... 365 K1
Pound HI TET GL8 .... 272 A6 ⓲
Pound La CHCAM GL55 .... 9 F3
COTS GL54 .... 144 C2
MANG/FISH BS16 .... 365 K2
VGL GL2 .... 181 F4
VGL GL2 .... 184 C1
Pound Rd KGWD/HNM BS15 ...... 367 F4
The Pound ALMDB BS32 .... 342 E1
COTS GL54 .... 144 C2
Pountney Dr EVILLE/WHL BS5 .. 365 F6 ⓲⓲
Powells Wy TET GL8 .... 327 F2
Powis La TET GL8......................... 272 B5
Pow's Rd KGWD/HNM BS15 .... 366 D7

Poyntz Ct
 OLD/WMLY/WICK BS30 .... **376** A3 🔢
Preddy's La *EVILLE/WHL* BS5 .... **366** A8
Prescott Cl *YATE/CS* BS37 .... **347** F6 🔢
Prescott Av *GLE* GL4 .... **158** D2
Prescott Wk *CHELTE/BC* GL52 .... **5** F1
Press Moor Dr
 OLD/WMLY/WICK BS30 .... **376** A3 🔢
Prestbury *YATE/CS* BS37 .... **347** F6
Prestbury Rd *CHELTE/BC* GL52 .... **4** C3
Preston Cl *CHEP* NP16 .... **312** B2 🔢
Prestwick Cl
 BRSG/KWL/STAPK BS4 .... **374** C5 🔢
Pretoria Rd *BRSTK/PCHW* BS34 ...... **342** D6
Price St *GL* GL1 .... **2** B6
Priestwood Cl
 HNBRY/STHM BS10 .... **353** J3 🔢
Primrose Cl *ALMDB* BS32 .... **343** H4 🔢
 GLE GL4 .... **158** C2 🔢
 KGWD/HNM BS15 .... **366** B5
Primrose Ct *MIM* GL56 .... **70** A1
Primrose Dr *CLFD* GL16 .... **176** A7
 THNB/SVB BS35 .... **316** D4
Primrose Hill Rd *LYD* GL15 .... **234** A2
Primrose La *KGWD/HNM* BS15 ...... **366** C6
Primrose Wy *LYD* GL15 .... **234** A1
Prince Albert Ct *BWTH/CHD* CL3 ... **132** A8
Prince Charles Rd *CIR* GL7 .... **255** F7
Prince Crs *RTEWK/TIB* GL19 .... **53** C8
Princes Ct *OLD/WMLY/WICK* BS30 . **376** A2 🔢
Princes' Pl *HORF/LLZ* BS7 .... **364** C3 🔢
Prince's St *CBRISNE* BS2 .... **5** D4
Prince St *GL* GL1 .... **3** D4 🔢
Prinknash Cl *GLE* GL4 .... **158** E2 🔢
Prinknash Rd *GLE* GL4 .... **158** E2 🔢
Priors Lea *YATE/CS* BS37 .... **347** G5
Priors Rd *CHELTE/BC* GL52 .... **5** F5
Priory Av
 HNLZ/SM/SNYPK/WT BS9 .... **353** J7
Priory Court Rd
 HNLZ/SM/SNYPK/WT BS9 .... **353** J7
Priory Dene
 HNLZ/SM/SNYPK/WT BS9 .... **353** J7 🔢
Priory Flds *RSTROUD/NAIL* GL6 ...... **270** B6
Priory Gdns *HORF/LLZ* BS7 .... **354** D6
Priory La *CHELTE/BC* GL52 .... **83** G2
Priory Pl *CHELTS* GL53 .... **4** C5
Priory Rd *BRSG/KWL/STAPK* BS4 .... **374** A4
 GL GL1 .... **2** B3 🔢
 GL GL1 .... **2** C2 🔢
 KEYN BS31 .... **375** K7
Priory St *CBRISNE* BS2 .... **4** C4
Priory Ter *CHELTE/BC* GL52 .... **5** D4
Priory Wy *TET* GL8 .... **302** C6
Pritchard St *CBRISNE* BS2 .... **364** C6
Private Rd *STROUD* GL5 .... **242** D3
Probertsbarn La *CLFD* GL16 .... **120** C8
Probyn Cl *MANG/FISH* BS16 .... **356** A7 🔢
Promenade *CHELT* GL50 .... **4** B4 🔢
Prospect Av *KGWD/HNM* BS15 ...... **366** B5 🔢
Prospect Cl *FRCTL/WBN* BS36 ...... **356** E2 🔢
 THNB/SVB BS35 .... **341** H4
Prospect Crs *KGWD/HNM* BS15 ..... **367** F4
Prospect La *FRCTL/WBN* BS36 ...... **345** F6 🔢
Prospect Pl *CIR* GL7 .... **249** K7
 CLFD GL16 .... **175** K4 🔢
 EVILLE/WHL BS5 .... **365** C6
Prospect Rd *CIND* GL14 .... **150** E6
 THNB/SVB BS35 .... **328** C8
Prosper La *CLFD* GL16 .... **176** B5
Pry La *BDWAY* WR12 .... **18** A6
Puck Pit La *COTS* GL54 .... **62** E8
Puckrup La *TEWK* GL20 .... **33** F1
Pudlicott La *CHCAM* GL55 .... **22** A4
Pullar Cl *CHELTE/BC* GL52 .... **83** F2 🔢
Pullen Ct *CHELTE/BC* GL52 .... **60** B6
Pullens Rd *RSTROUD/NAIL* GL6 ..... **187** H5
Pullin Ct *OLD/WMLY/WICK* BS30 ... **376** E2 🔢
Pumphreys Rd *CHELTS* GL53 .... **135** G1
Pump La *ALMDB* BS32 .... **331** H2
 TET GL8 .... **327** G2
Purbeck Wy *CHELTE/BC* GL52 .... **107** J3
Purcell Rd *BWTH/CHD* CL3 .... **103** H6
Purdown Rd *HORF/LLZ* BS7 .... **364** D1
Purley Av *CIR* GL7 .... **249** K6 🔢
Purley Rd *CIR* GL7 .... **249** K6
Pursey Dr *ALMDB* BS32 .... **343** J8
Purslane Cl *GLE* GL4 .... **158** D2
Purton Cl *KGWD/HNM* BS15 .... **366** E8
Purton Pl *LYD* GL15 .... **234** C4
Purton Rd *HORF/LLZ* BS7 .... **364** B4 🔢
Puxley Cl *HGRV/WHIT* BS14 .... **374** D8 🔢
Puzzle Cl *LYD* GL15 .... **204** E6 🔢
Pye Cft *ALMDB* BS32 .... **343** J3
Pyecroft Av
 HNLZ/SM/SNYPK/WT BS9 .... **353** K7
Pyke Rd *TEWK* GL20 .... **34** A8
Pylers Wy *LYD* GL15 .... **234** B4
Pynne Cl *HGRV/WHIT* BS14 .... **374** D9
Pyrton Ms *CHELTW* GL51 .... **133** J1 🔢
Pystol La *LYD* GL15 .... **231** F1

Q

Quabbs La *MTCHDN* GL17................ **122** C7
The Quadrangle *YATE/CS* BS37 .... **358** E2
Quadrant East
 MANG/FISH BS16 .... **366** C3 🔢
Quadrant West *MANG/FISH* BS16 .... **366** C3
Quail Cl *GLE* GL4 .... **131** G7
Quail Mdw *TET* GL8 .... **302** B6
Quaker La *THNB/SVB* BS35 .... **316** B5 🔢
Quaker's Cl *MANG/FISH* BS16 ...... **356** D6 🔢
Quakers' Friars *CBRIS/FH* BS1 ...... **364** C7 🔢
Quaker's Rd *MANG/FISH* BS16 ...... **356** D6
Quantock Cl
 OLD/WMLY/WICK BS30 .... **376** D1
Quantock Rd *VGL* GL2 .... **156** E6
Quarhouse La *STROUD* GL5 .... **243** J4
The Quarries *ALMDB* BS32 .... **343** F1
Quarrington Rd *HORF/LLZ* BS7 ...... **364** C1
Quarry Barton *MANG/FISH* BS16 ... **356** C2
Quarry Cl *CIR* GL7 .... **249** H2
Quarry Gdns *DSLY* GL11 .... **266** B2
Quarry La *AVONM* BS11 .... **352** E5
 FRCTL/WBN BS36 .... **356** E2
Quarry Md *THNB/SVB* BS35 .... **331** K1
Quarry Rd *KGWD/HNM* BS15 .... **366** D8
 MANG/FISH BS16 .... **356** C7 🔢
 THNB/SVB BS35 .... **331** K1
 YATE/CS BS37 .... **347** J5
The Quarry *CIR* GL7 .... **225** F4
 CIR GL7 .... **255** F7
 DSLY GL11 .... **266** B2
Quarry Vw *CIR* GL7 .... **256** D3
Quarry Wy *MANG/FISH* BS16 .... **357** C5
 MANG/FISH BS16 .... **365** J1
Quat Goose La *CHELTW* GL51....... **82** A7
Quayside *CHEP* NP16 .... **288** A8
Quayside La *EVILLE/WHL* BS5 ...... **365** K8 🔢
Quay St *CBRIS/FH* BS1 .... **364** B7 🔢
 GL GL1 .... **2** B3 🔢
 TEWK GL20 .... **33** H8 🔢
The Quay *GL* GL1 .... **2** B3
Quedgeley *YATE/CS* BS37............. **346** E6
Queen Anne's Rd *CIR* GL7 .... **250** A6 🔢
Queen Ann Rd *EVILLE/WHL* BS5 .... **365** F7
Queen Charlotte St *CBRIS/FH* BS1 . **364** B8 🔢
Queen Elizabeth Dr *CIR* GL7 .... **250** A6
Queens Acre *CIND* GL14 .... **180** B2
Queen's Cl *BWTH/CHD* CL3 .... **131** J5
Queen's Circ *CHELT* GL50 .... **4** B1 🔢
Queens Down Gdns
 BRSG/KWL/STAPK BS4 .... **374** A3
Queen's Dr *HORF/LLZ* BS7 .... **364** C2
 KGWD/HNM BS15 .... **375** G2
 STROUD GL5 .... **214** A7
Queens Fld *CIR* GL7 .... **255** F7
Queensholm Av
 MANG/FISH BS16 .... **356** E5 🔢
Queensholm Cl *MANG/FISH* BS16 .. **356** E5
Queensholm Crs *MANG/FISH* BS16 . **356** D5
Queensholm Dr *MANG/FISH* BS16 .. **356** E6
Queens La *CHELT* GL50 .... **4** A5 🔢
Queensmead *RSTROUD/NAIL* GL6 ... **187** G7
Queen Sq *CBRIS/FH* BS1 .... **364** B8
Queen Square Av
 CBRIS/FH BS1 .... **364** B8 🔢
Queen's Retreat *CHELTW* GL51 ..... **106** B4 🔢
Queens Rd *BRSG/KWL/STAPK* BS4 . **374** B5
 CHELT GL51 .... **106** A6
 CHEP NP16 .... **288** A8
 EVILLE/WHL BS5 .... **365** K7
 HORF/LLZ BS7 .... **364** C2
 MANG/FISH BS16 .... **368** D1
 OLD/WMLY/WICK BS30 .... **376** B2
 STNHO GL10 .... **213** F7
 STROUD GL5 .... **214** D8
 TEWK GL20 .... **57** J2
Queens Sq *COTS* GL54 .... **85** J1
Queen St *CBRISNE* BS2 .... **364** C7
 CHELTW GL51 .... **4** A2
 CIR GL7 .... **249** K7
 COTS GL54 .... **194** E1
 EVILLE/WHL BS5 .... **365** H3 🔢
 KGWD/HNM BS15 .... **366** B7
 LYD GL15 .... **234** B2
Queens Wk *THNB/SVB* BS35 .... **316** B3
Queensway *BRSTK/PCHW* BS34 .... **343** G8
 CLFD GL16 .... **176** B4
Queens Wy *WUE* GL12 .... **297** F8
Queen Victoria St *CBRISNE* BS2 .... **364** E8 🔢
Queenwood Gv *CHELTE/BC* GL52 ... **107** K1
Quenneys Cl *GLE* GL4 .... **158** E3
Querns La *CIR* GL7 .... **249** J6 🔢
Querns Rd *CIR* GL7 .... **249** J6

Quietways *STNHO* GL10 .... **212** E6
Quinton Cl *BWTH/CHD* CL3 .... **103** K8 🔢

R

Rackham Cl *HORF/LLZ* BS7 .... **355** F8
Rackhay *CBRIS/FH* BS1 .... **364** B8 🔢
Radburn Cl *MIM* GL56 .... **70** B1 🔢
Radley Rd *MANG/FISH* BS16 .... **366** B2
Radnor Rd *CHELTW* GL51 .... **105** J8
 HORF/LLZ BS7 .... **364** B1
Raeburn Rd *EVILLE/WHL* BS5 ...... **366** B7
Rag La *WUE* GL12....................... **335** F1
Raglan Pl *HORF/LLZ* BS7 .... **364** B5 🔢
 THNB/SVB BS35 .... **316** B6
Raglan Rd *HORF/LLZ* BS7 .... **364** B5
Raglan St *GL* GL1 .... **3** D4 🔢
Raglan Wy *CHEP* NP16 .... **312** B1
 DSLY GL11 .... **268** B5
Raikes Rd *GL* GL1 .... **129** K8
Railton Jones Cl
 BRSTK/PCHW BS34.................... **355** J3
Railway Dr *CLFD* GL16................. **175** K4
Railway Rd *CIND* GL14 .... **178** E1
Railway Ter *MANG/FISH* BS16 ...... **366** C1
Ralph Rd *HORF/LLZ* BS7 .... **364** D2
Ram Hl *FRCTL/WBN* BS36 .... **357** K2
Ramscombe La
 CBATH/BATHN BA1................... **380** E8
Ramsdale Rd *VGL* GL2 .... **157** H3
Ramsey Rd *HORF/LLZ* BS7 .... **354** D7
Rance Pitch *GLE* GL4 .... **159** G4
Randall Cl *KGWD/HNM* BS15 ...... **367** F4
Randall Rd *COTS* GL54 .... **145** F3
Randalls Fld
 RSTROUD/NAIL GL6 .... **187** H7 🔢
Randalls Gn *RSTROUD/NAIL* GL6 ... **244** D3
Randolph Av *YATE/CS* BS37 .... **347** F2
Randolph Cl *CHELTS* GL53 .... **107** F8 🔢
Randwick Rd *GL* GL1 .... **157** K4
Rangers Av *DSLY* GL11 .... **267** F7
Rangers Wk *KGWD/HNM* BS15 ...... **375** H2
The Range *VGL* GL2 .... **128** D1
Ranmoor *GLE* GL4 .... **159** F3
Rannoch Rd *BRSTK/PCHW* BS34 .... **354** D4
Ratcliffe Dr *BRSTK/PCHW* BS34 .... **355** J1
Ratcliff Lawns *CHELTE/BC* GL52 .... **83** H6
Rathbone Cl *FRCTL/WBN* BS36 ...... **357** J1
Rathmore Cl *COTS* GL54 .... **62** D8
Ravendale Dr
 OLD/WMLY/WICK BS30 .... **376** C3
Ravenglass Crs
 HNBRY/STHM BS10 .... **354** A4
Ravenhead Dr *HGRV/WHIT* BS14 ... **374** A6
Ravensgate Rd *CHELTS* GL53........ **135** H2
Ravenswood Rd
 RDLND/MONT BS6 .... **364** A5
Rawens Wd
 OLD/WMLY/WICK BS30 .... **376** C3 🔢
Rayleigh Rd
 HNLZ/SM/SNYPK/WT BS9 .... **353** F7
Raymill *BRSG/KWL/STAPK* BS4 .... **375** F4 🔢
Reaburn Cl *CHELTE/BC* GL52 ...... **107** H8 🔢
Reades Piece *EVE* WR11.................. **7** G2
Read Wy *CHELTE/BC* GL52 .... **83** F4
Rea La *VGL* GL2 .... **157** F1
Rectory Cl *COTS* GL54 .... **91** J7
 GLE GL4 .... **159** G4
 YATE/CS BS37 .... **347** H3 🔢
Rectory La *BRSTK/PCHW* BS34 .... **354** E3
 HGHW SN6........................... **310** E6
 TET GL8 .... **272** A5
 VGL GL2 .... **129** G8
 WUE GL12 .... **318** C5
Rectory Meadow *MTCHDN* GL17 ... **124** A2
Rectory Rd *FRCTL/WBN* BS36 ...... **345** H6
 GLE GL4 .... **158** E2
Red Admiral Dr *GLE* GL4.............. **159** G2
Redbrook Rd *MONM* NP25 .... **174** B6
Redcar Cft *FRCTL/WBN* BS36 ...... **357** F5 🔢
Redcliff Backs *CBRIS/FH* BS1 ...... **364** B8
Redcliff St *CBRIS/FH* BS1 .... **364** C8
Redcross St *CBRISNE* BS2 .... **364** D7 🔢
Redding Cl *VGL* GL2 .... **156** E5
Reddings Cl *LYD* GL15 .... **232** C8
Reddings Pk *CHELTW* GL51 .... **105** H7 🔢
Reddings Rd *CHELTW* GL51 .... **105** G7
The Reddings *CHELTW* GL51 .... **105** F7
 CHEP NP16 .... **312** B1 🔢
 KGWD/HNM BS15 .... **367** F4
Red Ditch La *RTEWK/TIB* GL19...... **51** K4
Redesdale Pl *MIM* GL56 .... **69** K2
Redfield Hl *OLD/WMLY/WICK* BS30 . **376** E2
Redfield Rd *BRSTK/PCHW* BS34 .... **343** H7
Redford La *MANG/FISH* BS16 ...... **369** F2
Redgrove Pk *CHELTW* GL51 .... **105** H7
Redgrove Rd *CHELTW* GL51 .... **105** K2
Redham La *THNB/SVB* BS35 .... **329** K5
Redhill Cl *MANG/FISH* BS16 .... **365** J3
Redhill Dr *MANG/FISH* BS16......... **365** J3
Redhill La *THNB/SVB* BS35 .... **314** C8

Red House La *ALMDB* BS32 .... **343** F2
HNLZ/SM/SNYPK/WT BS9 ..... **353** C8
Redhouse La *CLFD* GL16 .... **147** K3 🔟
STROUD GL5 .... **213** K6
Redland Cl *VGL* GL2 .... **3** F1
Redland Court Rd
RDLND/MONT BS6 .... **364** A3
Redland Gv *RDLND/MONT* BS6 .... **364** A4
Redland Rd *RDLND/MONT* BS6 .... **364** B4
Red La *TEWK* GL20 .... **33** H7
Red Lion La *HGHW* SN6 .... **310** E6
Rednock Dr *DSLY* GL11 .... **266** E4
Redpoll Wy *GL4* **130** E8
Red Rover Cl *CHELT* GL50 .... **106** C1
Redshelf Wk *HNBRY/STHM* BS10 .. **354** A3
Redstart Wy *GL4* **130** E8
Redthorne Wy *CHELTW* GL51 ...... **133** J1
Red Well Rd *GLE* GL4 .... **158** A4
Redwick Cl *AVONM* BS11 .... **352** E4
Redwick Gdns *THNB/SVB* BS35 .... **328** E7
Redwick Rd *THNB/SVB* BS35 .... **328** D5
Redwind Wy *GL2* **131** J7
Redwing Gdns *MANG/FISH* BS16 .. **355** J8 🔟
Redwood Cl *GL* GL5 .... **157** K2
OLD/WMLY/WICK BS30 ...... **376** B3 🔟
Redwood Dr *TEWK* GL20 .... **34** D5 🔟
Reed Cl *HNBRY/STHM* BS10 .... **354** D7 🔟
Reed Ct *OLD/WMLY/WICK* BS30 .. **376** A3 🔟
Reedling Cl *MANG/FISH* BS16 ...... **355** J8 🔟
Reeds *HGHW* SN6 .... **310** C6
Reevers Rd *NWNT* GL18 .... **73** H5
Reeves Cl *CIR* GL7 .... **249** C8 🔟
Regency Dr
BRSG/KWL/STAPK BS4 .... **375** F4 🔟
Regents Cl *THNB/SVB* BS35 .... **316** B3
Regent St *CHELT* GL50 .... **4** B4 🔟
GL GL1 .... **2** C5
KGWD/HNM BS15 .... **366** C6
LYD GL15 .... **234** A3
STNHO GL10 .... **213** F8
Regent Wy *CHEP* NP16 .... **288** A5 🔟
Regis Cl *CHELTS* GL53 .... **135** G1
Reine Barnes La *DSLY* GL11 .... **267** F6
Remus Cl *GLE* GL4 .... **131** H8 🔟
Rendcomb Cl *GLE* GL4 .... **159** C2 🔟
Rendcomb Dr *CIR* GL7 .... **249** C7
Repton Rd *BRSG/KWL/STAPK* BS4 .. **374** E2
Reservoir Rd *GLE* GL4 .... **158** B2
STROUD GL5 .... **215** F3
Reynold's Wk *HORF/LLZ* BS7 ...... **354** E7
Ribble Cl *BWTH/CHD* GL3 .... **160** D1
Ribblesdale *THNB/SVB* BS35 .... **316** C6
Ricardo Rd *RSTROUD/NAIL* GL6 ... **243** H8
Richard Pl *TEWK* GL20 .... **57** J5
Richards Rd *CHELTW* GL51 .... **106** B2 🔟
Richeson Cl *HNBRY/STHM* BS10 .. **353** H4
Richeson Wk *HNBRY/STHM* BS10 .. **353** H4
Richmond Av *BRSTK/PCHW* BS34 .. **355** J1
GLE GL4 .... **130** E8
RDLND/MONT BS6 .... **364** D4 🔟
Richmond Cl *HGHW* SN6 .... **308** D5
Richmond Dr *CHELTE/BC* GL52 ...... **5** E4 🔟
Richmond Gdns *VGL* GL2 .... **130** E1
Richmond Rd *EVILLE/WHL* BS5 .... **365** J6
MANG/FISH BS16 .... **357** J1
RDLND/MONT BS6 .... **364** D4 🔟
The Richmonds *GLE* GL4 .... **159** F2
Rickyard Wy *VGL* GL2 .... **211** J3
The Ride *KGWD/HNM* BS15 .... **367** G4
Ridgehill
HNLZ/SM/SNYPK/WT BS9 .... **354** A8
HNLZ/SM/SNYPK/WT BS9 .... **364** A1
Ridgemont Rd *STROUD* GL5 .... **215** G2
Ridgemount Cl *BWTH/CHD* GL3 ... **132** B8
Ridge Pl *MTCHDN* GL17 .... **148** E4
The Ridge *AVONM* BS11 .... **352** A7
FRCTL/WBN BS36 .... **345** J7
RSTROUD/NAIL GL6 .... **244** A2
Ridgeway *FRCTL/WBN* BS36 .... **345** J7
LYD GL15 .... **206** C3
YATE/CS BS37 .... **347** J4
Ridgeway Av *HNBRY/STHM* BS10 .. **353** H5
Ridgeway Pde *EVILLE/WHL* BS5 .. **365** J3 🔟
Ridgeway Rd *MANG/FISH* BS16 .. **365** J3
The Ridgeway *HNBRY/STHM* BS10.. **353** J5
MALM SN16 .... **304** E8
RSTROUD/NAIL GL6 .... **244** B1
Riding Barn Hl
OLD/WMLY/WICK BS30 ...... **368** B8
Ridingleaze *AVONM* BS11 .... **352** C5
Ridings Cl *YATE/CS* BS37 .... **347** J4
Ridings Rd *RFCTL/WBN* BS36 ...... **345** J8
The Ridings *FRCTL/WBN* BS36 ..... **345** J8
RSTROUD/NAIL GL6 .... **270** E3
VGL GL2 .... **101** C7
Ridler Rd *LYD* GL15 .... **234** C4
Ringer's Cl *RTEWK/TIB* GL19 .... **79** C1
Ring Fence *LYD* GL15 .... **232** B3
Ringfield Cl *RSTROUD/NAIL* GL6 .. **270** E3 🔟
Ringwood Cs *HNBRY/STHM* BS10.. **354** B5
Ripley Rd *EVILLE/WHL* BS5 .... **366** A5
Ripon Cl *MANG/FISH* BS16 .... **357** F5
Ripon Rd *BRSG/KWL/STAPK* BS4 .. **365** J8
Rippledale Cl *CHELTW* GL51 .... **105** J7
Rising Sun La *CHELTE/BC* GL52 ...... **84** A4

Rissington Cl *CHELTW* GL51 .... **105** J6 🔟
Rissington Rd *COTS* GL54 .... **143** J1 🔟
GLE GL4 .... **158** A4
Rivelands Rd *CHELTW* GL51 .... **82** B7 🔟
River Leys *CHELTW* GL51 .... **105** K1
Rivermead *VGL* GL2 .... **2** C1
VGL GL2 .... **130** A1 🔟
River Rd *YATE/CS* BS37 .... **347** J5 🔟
Riverside Cl *CHELTE/BC* GL52 ..... **107** H8 🔟
Riverside Ct
BRSG/KWL/STAPK BS4 .... **365** K8
Riverside Pk *THNB/SVB* BS35 ...... **328** B8
Riverside Wk *EVILLE/WHL* BS5 .... **365** K8 🔟
Riverside Wy *KGWD/HNM* BS15 ... **375** H3
Riversley Rd *VGL* GL2 .... **130** E4
River St *CBRISNE* BS2 .... **364** D7
River Vw *CHEP* NP16 .... **288** A6 🔟
MANG/FISH BS16 .... **365** J1
Riverview Wy *CHELTW* GL51 .... **106** A1
River Wy *CIR* GL7 .... **278** C7
Riverwood Rd *MANG/FISH* BS16 .. **356** C5
Riviera Crs *MANG/FISH* BS16 ...... **366** E2
Roach's La *BAD* GL9 .... **350** C5
Road Hl *CHPMW/MSHF* SN14 ...... **381** J5
COR/BOX SN14 .... **381** K6
Robbers Rd *STNHO* GL10 .... **213** J4
Robbins Cl *ALMDB* BS32 .... **343** K8
CHPMW/MSHF SN14 .... **371** K6
STROUD GL5 .... **213** J8
Robbins Ct *MANG/FISH* BS16 ...... **357** H8
Robel Av *FRCTL/WBN* BS36 .... **345** C6
Robert Burns Av *CHELTW* GL51 .. **105** H7
Robert Ct *MANG/FISH* BS16 .... **357** H7
Robert Franklin Wy *CIR* GL7 ...... **279** F7
Robert Raikes Av *GLE* GL4 .... **157** K4 🔟
Roberts Cl *CHELTE/BC* GL52 .... **83** F7 🔟
CIR GL7 .... **249** H3
Robertson Dr
BRSG/KWL/STAPK BS4 .... **365** K8
Robertson Rd *CHELTW* GL51 .... **133** H4 🔟
EVILLE/WHL BS5 .... **365** C4
Roberts Rd *BWTH/CHD* GL3 .... **103** H7
CHELTE/BC GL52 .... **107** K2 🔟
Robert St *EVILLE/WHL* BS5 .... **365** F4 🔟
EVILLE/WHL BS5 .... **365** F7 🔟
Robin Cl *HNBRY/STHM* BS10 .... **353** K4
RSTROUD/NAIL GL6 .... **244** C3 🔟
TEWK GL20 .... **34** C5 🔟
Robin Ct *STNHO* GL10 .... **213** F6
Robinhood St *GL* GL1 .... **2** B6
Robins Cl *CHELTE/BC* GL52 .... **5** E3 🔟
Robins End *VGL* GL2 .... **103** F7 🔟
Robinson Dr *EVILLE/WHL* BS5 ..... **364** C6 🔟
Robinson La *CIR* GL7 .... **192** E7
Robinson Rd *GL* GL1 .... **2** B6
Robinswood Gdns *GLE* GL4 .... **158** B1
Robin Wy *YATE/CS* BS37 .... **347** H7
Rochester Rd
BRSG/KWL/STAPK BS4 .... **374** D1
CHELT GL50 .... **134** A1 🔟
Rock & Fountain La *CIND* GL14 ... **154** B5
Rock Cl *BRSG/KWL/STAPK* BS4 ... **374** D4 🔟
Rockingham Gdns *AVONM* BS11 .. **352** C6 🔟
Rockland Gv *MANG/FISH* BS16 .... **365** H1 🔟
Rockland Rd *MANG/FISH* BS16 .... **356** C7
Rock La *BRSTK/PCHW* BS34 .... **355** K2
CIND GL14 .... **154** A5
CLFD GL16 .... **175** K6
Rockness Hl *RSTROUD/NAIL* GL6 .. **270** D4
Rock Rd *DSLY* GL11 .... **266** B2
OLD/WMLY/WICK BS30 ...... **369** H6
Rockside Av *MANG/FISH* BS16 .... **357** F6
Rockside Dr
HNLZ/SM/SNYPK/WT BS9 .... **353** K8
Rockside Gdns *FRCTL/WBN* BS36 .. **345** J6 🔟
MANG/FISH BS16 .... **357** F6 🔟
Rocks Rd *MTCHDN* GL17 .... **120** E8
The Rocks *CLFD* GL16 .... **203** K1
Rockstowes Wy
HNBRY/STHM BS10 .... **354** B3
Rock St *RTEWK/TIB* GL19 .... **56** A4
THNB/SVB BS35 .... **316** B6
The Rock *BRSG/KWL/STAPK* BS4 .. **374** D3
Rock Villa La *CHEP* NP16 .... **288** B5
Rockwell Av *AVONM* BS11 .... **352** D5
Rockwood Rd *CHEP* NP16 .... **288** A7
Rodborough La *YATE/CS* BS37 .... **346** E7
Rodborough Av *STROUD* GL5 ...... **214** D3
Rodborough Hl *STROUD* GL5 .... **214** D8
Rodborough La *STROUD* GL5 ...... **242** E1
Rodbourne Rd
HNBRY/STHM BS10 .... **354** B7
Rodford Wy *YATE/CS* BS37 .... **346** E7
Rodley La *LYD* GL15 .... **234** C3
Rodley Sq *LYD* GL15 .... **234** C3
Rodney Av *KGWD/HNM* BS15 ...... **366** A6
Rodney Cl *VGL* GL2 .... **3** F1
Rodney Crs *BRSTK/PCHW* BS34 ... **354** C2
Rodney Rd *CHELT* GL50 .... **4** B4 🔟
KGWD/HNM BS15 .... **366** A5
Rodney Wk *KGWD/HNM* BS15 ...... **366** A5
Rodway Hl *MANG/FISH* BS16 .... **367** G2
Rodway La *VGL* GL2 .... **77** J8

Rodway Rd *BRSTK/PCHW* BS34 .... **342** D7
MANG/FISH BS16 .... **367** G1
Rodway Vw *KGWD/HNM* BS15 ...... **367** F3
Roebuck Mdw *MTCHDN* GL17 ..... **121** K8 🔟
Roegate Dr
BRSG/KWL/STAPK BS4 .... **365** J8 🔟
Rogers Cl *OLD/WMLY/WICK* BS30 .. **376** D1
Rokeby Av *RDLND/MONT* BS6 ...... **364** A5
The Rollers *RSTROUD/NAIL* GL6 .. **270** D2
Rolleston Wy *CHELTW* GL51 .... **105** K7 🔟
Rolling Stones *CHCAM* GL55 .... **20** E3
Roman Farm Ct *AVONM* BS11 ..... **352** E4 🔟
Roman Hackle Av *CHELT* GL50 ... **106** C1
Roman Rd *CHELTW* GL51 .... **106** A5
GLE GL4 .... **131** C8
Roman Wk *BRSG/KWL/STAPK* BS4 .. **374** B3
BRSTK/PCHW BS34 .... **355** J1 🔟
Roman Wy *CIND* GL14 .... **151** H6
CIR GL7 .... **285** H1
CLFD GL16 .... **175** K5
COTS GL54 .... **115** J7
Romney Av *HORF/LLZ* BS7 .... **365** F1
Romney Cl *GL* GL1 .... **158** A1
Romney Dr *TET* GL8 .... **302** A6 🔟
Ronald Rd *MANG/FISH* BS16 ...... **355** K8 🔟
Ronayne Wk *MANG/FISH* BS16 .... **356** C8
Rookery La *BRKLY* GL13 .... **236** A7
CLFD GL16 .... **203** C2
OLD/WMLY/WICK BS30 ...... **369** H3
THNB/SVB BS35 .... **329** J8
Rookery Rd *VGL* GL2 .... **103** F3
Rooksmoor Hl *STROUD* GL5 .... **242** C3
Roosevelt Av *CHELTE/BC* GL52 ...... **5** E5 🔟
Ropewalk *TEWK* GL20 .... **33** J8
The Rope Wk *STROUD* GL5 .... **243** C3
Rose Acre *HNBRY/STHM* BS10 ..... **353** J3
Rose and Crown Pas *CHELT* GL50 .. **4** B3 🔟
Rosebay Md *MANG/FISH* BS16 ..... **365** J2 🔟
Roseberry Pk *EVILLE/WHL* BS5 .... **365** H6
Roseberry Rd *EVILLE/WHL* BS5 ... **365** C2 🔟
Rosebery Av *CBRISNE* BS2 .... **364** E5 🔟
GL GL1 .... **158** A1
Rosebery Mt *DSLY* GL11 .... **267** G6 🔟
Rosebery Pk *DSLY* GL11 .... **267** G6
Rosebery Rd *DSLY* GL11 .... **267** G6
Rose Cl *FRCTL/WBN* BS36 .... **356** E2
Rosedale Av *STNHO* GL10 .... **213** F7
Rosedale Rd *MANG/FISH* BS16 .... **366** B3
Rosefield Crs *TEWK* GL20 .... **33** K8
Rose Green Rd *EVILLE/WHL* BS5 .. **365** H4
Rosehill Ct *CIR* GL7 .... **249** J5
Rosehill St *CHELTE/BC* GL52 .... **5** D5
Rosehip Wy *CHELTE/BC* GL52 ..... **82** E2 🔟
Rose La *FRCTL/WBN* BS36 .... **345** K7
Roselarge Gdns
HNBRY/STHM BS10 .... **353** J4 🔟
Rosemary Cl *ALMDB* BS32 .... **343** K7
GLE GL4 .... **158** E2
Rosemary La *CHEP* NP16 .... **259** F4
EVILLE/WHL BS5 .... **365** C4
Rosemary Ter *WGE* GL12 .... **297** F8
Rose Md *HORF/LLZ* BS7 .... **354** E7 🔟
Rose Oak Dr *FRCTL/WBN* BS36 .... **345** K7 🔟
Rose Oak Gdns
FRCTL/WBN BS36 .... **345** K7 🔟
Rose Oak La *FRCTL/WBN* BS36 .... **345** K7
Rose Rd *EVILLE/WHL* BS5 .... **365** J7
Rosery Cl
HNLZ/SM/SNYPK/WT BS9 .... **353** J6
The Rosery *MANG/FISH* BS16 ...... **366** C3 🔟
Roseville Av
OLD/WMLY/WICK BS30 ...... **376** B4
Rose Wk *MANG/FISH* BS16 .... **366** C3
Rose Wy *CIR* GL7 .... **250** A8
Rosewood Av *THNB/SVB* BS35 ..... **331** K1
Rosling Rd *HORF/LLZ* BS7 .... **354** C8
Roslyn Rd *RDLND/MONT* BS6 .... **364** A5
Rossall Av *BRSTK/PCHW* BS34 .... **343** C8
Rossall Rd *BRSG/KWL/STAPK* BS4 .. **374** C3
Ross Cl *YATE/CS* BS37 .... **347** K4
Rossiter's La *EVILLE/WHL* BS5 ..... **366** A4
Rosslyn Wy *THNB/SVB* BS35 .... **316** C3
Ross Rd *CLFD* GL16 .... **147** J7
MTCHDN GL17 .... **123** C3
NWNT GL18 .... **73** H5
Rothermere Cl *CHELTW* GL51 ..... **133** K1 🔟
Rothleigh *CHELTW* GL51 .... **133** J1
Rougemont Gv *CHEP* NP16 .... **312** B2 🔟
The Roundabouts *STROUD* GL5 .. **243** H5 🔟
Roundmoor Gdns
HGRV/WHIT BS14 .... **374** C7 🔟
Roundways *FRCTL/WBN* BS36 ...... **345** J2 🔟
Rousham Rd *EVILLE/WHL* BS5 ...... **364** E3
Rowan Av *MANG/FISH* BS16 .... **366** A4
Rowanfield Rd *CHELTW* GL51 ...... **106** A5
Rowan Gdns *BWTH/CHD* GL3 ...... **132** B7
Rowan Gv *DSLY* GL11 .... **266** E3
The Rowans *CHELTE/BC* GL52 .... **83** H3
Rowan Wy *CHELTW* GL51 .... **133** J1 🔟
KGWD/HNM BS15 .... **375** C3 🔟
Rowcroft *STROUD* GL5 .... **214** D7
Rowcroft Retreat *STROUD* GL5 .. **214** D7 🔟
Rowland Av *MANG/FISH* BS16 ..... **365** C2 🔟
Rowlandson Gdns
HORF/LLZ BS7 .... **355** F8 🔟

Rowley *DSLY* GL11 .... 266 E1
The Row *THNB/SVB* BS35 .... 313 J7
Roxton Dr *CHELTW* GL51 .... 105 G7
Royal Cl *HNBRY/STHM* BS10 .... 353 F3
Royal Fort Rd *CFTN/FAIL* BS8 ... 364 A7 ⑧
Royal Oak Ms *CHELT* GL50 .... 4 B3 ⑧
Royal Oak Rd *GL* GL1 .... 2 B2
  MTCHDN GL17 .... 149 H1
Royal Parade Ms *CHELT* GL50 .... 4 A5
Royal Rd *MANG/FISH* BS16 .... 357 G8
Royal Spring *MTCHDN* GL17 .... 124 D5
Royal Well La *CHELT* GL50 .... 4 A4
Royal Well Pl *CHELT* GL50 .... 4 A5
Royal Well Rd *CHELT* GL50 .... 4 B4 ⑩
Royate Hl *EVILLE/WHL* BS5 .... 365 H4
Roycroft Rd *BRSTK/PCHW* BS34 .... 355 F4
Roy King Gdns
  OLD/WMLY/WICK BS30 .... 376 D1
Royston Wk *HNBRY/STHM* BS10 ... 354 B4
Rozel Rd *HORF/LLZ* BS7 .... 354 C8
Ruardean Rd *MTCHDN* GL17 .... 121 J8
Rudford Cl *BRSTK/PCHW* BS34 ..... 345 F5
Rudge Cl *KGWD/HNM* BS15 .... 367 F4
The Rudge *VGL* GL2 .... 101 H6
Rudgeway Pk *THNB/SVB* BS35 ...... 331 J5
Rudhall Gv *HNBRY/STHM* BS10 .... 354 C7
Rudthorpe Rd *HORF/LLZ* BS7 .... 354 C1
Ruffet Cl *CLFD* GL16 .... 175 K6
Ruffet Rd *CLFD* GL16 .... 175 J4
The Ruffitt *CIND* GL14 .... 151 H5
Rugby Rd *BRSG/KWL/STAPK* BS4 .. 374 C3
Rumsey Cl *GLE* GL2 .... 159 G2
Runnings Rd *CHELTW* GL51 .... 106 A1
The Runnings *CHELTW* GL51 .... 82 A8
Runnymead Av
  BRSG/KWL/STAPK BS4 .... 374 C5
Runnymede *CHELTW* GL51 .... 133 J1
  KGWD/HNM BS15 .... 366 E5 ⑩
Runswick Rd
  BRSG/KWL/STAPK BS4 .... 374 B3
Rupert St *CBRIS/FH* BS1 .... 364 B7
  EVILLE/WHL BS5 .... 364 D8
Ruscombe Rd *ALMDB* BS32 .... 343 H4
Rush Cl *ALMDB* BS32 .... 343 H4
Rushley La *COTS* GL54 .... 85 K1
Rushmead La
  CHPMW/MSHF SN14 .... 371 J4
Rushton Dr *FRCTL/WBN* BS36 ..... 345 K7
Rushworth Cl *CHELTW* GL51 .... 105 H4
Rushy *OLD/WMLY/WICK* BS30 ..... 376 B2
Rushyleaze *LYD* GL15 .... 234 B4
Rushy Wy *MANG/FISH* BS16 .... 357 G5
Ruskin Gv *HORF/LLZ* BS7 .... 354 E6
Ruspidge Cl *GLE* GL4 .... 159 G1 ⑨
Ruspidge Rd *CIND* GL14 .... 178 E2
Russell Av *KGWD/HNM* BS15 .... 366 D7
Russell Gv *RDLND/MONT* BS6 ...... 364 A1
Russell Pl *CHELTW* GL51 .... 4 A2 ⑨
Russell St *MANG/FISH* BS16 .... 366 B4
Russell St *CHELTW* GL51 .... 4 A2 ⑨
  GL GL1 .... 3 D4
  STROUD GL5 .... 214 E7 ⑩
Russell Town Av *EVILLE/WHL* BS5 .. 365 F6
Russet Cl *GL* GL1 .... 157 H3
  TEWK GL20 .... 13 K8 ⑦
  THNB/SVB BS35 .... 330 E3
Russet Ct *WUE* GL12 .... 320 D2 ⑨
Russet Rd *CHELTW* GL51 .... 105 K3
Russett Wy *NWNT* GL18 .... 73 K6
Russ St *CBRISNE* BS2 .... 364 D8
Rustic Cl *GLE* GL4 .... 158 E2
Rutherford Cl
  OLD/WMLY/WICK BS30 .... 376 B3 ⑨
Rutherford Wy *CHELTW* GL51 ...... 106 A1
Rutland Av *OLD/WMLY/WICK* BS30 .. 376 B4
Rutland Rd *HORF/LLZ* BS7 .... 364 C3 ⑧
Ryalls La *VGL* GL2 .... 238 C1
Rydal Rd *VGL* GL2 .... 3 F1
Ryder Cl *DSLY* GL11 .... 266 E2
Ryde Rd *BRSG/KWL/STAPK* BS4 ... 374 A4 ⑧
Rye Av *CHELTW* GL51 .... 105 H1 ⑨
Ryeclose *COTS* GL54 .... 143 J1
Rye Crs *COTS* GL54 .... 143 K1 ⑨
Ryecroft Rd *FRCTL/WBN* BS36 ..... 345 J6
Ryecroft St *GL* GL1 .... 3 D5
Ryedown La
  OLD/WMLY/WICK BS30 .... 376 D5
Ryelands Cl *GL* GL1 .... 157 J3
Ryelands Cl *STNHO* GL10 .... 212 E6 ⑨
Ryelands Rd *LYD* GL15 .... 205 F6
  STNHO GL10 .... 212 E6
The Ryelands *RSTROUD/NAIL* GL6 .. 213 K5
Ryeleaze Cl *STROUD* GL5 ...... 214 E7 ⑪
Ryeleaze Rd *STROUD* GL5 ...... 214 E7 ⑫
Ryeworth Dr *CHELTE/BC* GL52 ...... 5 F6
Ryeworth Rd *CHELTE/BC* GL52 ...... 5 F6
Ryland Cl *TET* GL8 .... 302 C5
Ryland Pl *CBRISNE* BS2 .... 364 E4 ⑫
Rylestone Cl *FRCTL/WBN* BS36 .... 345 F6
Rysdale Rd
  HNLZ/SM/SNYPK BS9 .... 353 H8

S

Sabre Cl *VGL* GL2 .... 157 G3
Sabrina Wy *LYD* GL15 .... 234 B2
Saddlers La *CHELT* GL50 .... 4 A6 ⑧
Saddlers Rd *VGL* GL2 .... 157 F4
Sadlier Cl *AVONM* BS11 .... 352 B6
Saffron Cl *GLE* GL4 .... 158 C1
Saffron Rd *TEWK* GL20 .... 33 H8 ⑧
Sages Md *ALMDB* BS32 .... 343 J6 ⑧
St Aidans Cl *CHELTW* GL51 ...... 105 J4 ⑧
  EVILLE/WHL BS5 .... 366 B8 ⑧
St Aidan's Rd *EVILLE/WHL* BS5 ... 366 A8
St Albans Cl *CHELT* GL50 .... 134 A1 ⑧
St Albans Rd *VGL* GL2 .... 157 J1
St Aldams Dr *MANG/FISH* BS16 ... 368 D1
St Aldate St *GL* GL1 .... 2 C3
St Aldwyn Rd *GL* GL1 .... 130 B8
St Aldwyn's Cl *HORF/LLZ* BS7 ... 354 D6 ⑧
St Andrews
  OLD/WMLY/WICK BS30 .... 367 H8
  RTEWK/TIB GL19 .... 77 G6
  YATE/CS BS37 .... 347 H5
St Andrew's Av *CHEP* NP16 ..... 288 A7 ⑧
St Andrews Cl *TEWK* GL20 .... 34 E7
St Andrew's Rd
  RDLND/MONT BS6 .... 364 D4 ⑪
  RDLND/MONT BS6 .... 364 C4 ⑧
St Annal's Rd *CIND* GL14 .... 151 F6
St Anne's Av *KEYN* BS31 .... 375 J8
St Anne's Cl *BWTH/CHD* GL3 ... 132 B8 ⑧
  CHELTE/BC GL52 .... 5 D5 ⑧
  OLD/WMLY/WICK BS30 .... 376 C2
St Anne's Dr *FRCTL/WBN* BS36 ... 345 J7
  OLD/WMLY/WICK BS30 .... 368 D7
  OLD/WMLY/WICK BS30 .... 376 D4
St Anne's Park Rd
  BRSG/KWL/STAPK BS4 .... 374 D1
St Anne's Rd
  BRSG/KWL/STAPK BS4 .... 365 H8
  CHELTE/BC GL52 .... 4 C4 ⑩
  EVILLE/WHL BS5 .... 366 B8
St Anne's Ter
  BRSG/KWL/STAPK BS4 .... 374 D1
  CHELTE/BC GL52 .... 4 C4
St Annes Wy *LYD* GL15 .... 231 F1
St Ann St *CHEP* NP16 .... 288 B5
St Ann Wy *GL* GL1 .... 2 B5
St Arild's Rd *BAD* GL9 .... 339 H2
St Aubin's Av
  BRSG/KWL/STAPK BS4 .... 374 E3
St Augustine's Pde *CBRIS/FH* BS1 . 364 B8
St Barbara's Cl *TEWK* GL20 .... 35 F7
St Barnabas Cl *GLE* GL4 .... 158 A2
  OLD/WMLY/WICK BS30 .... 367 J7 ⑧
St Bartholomews *NWNT* GL18 ... 73 J6 ⑧
St Bartholomews Cl *DSLY* GL11 .. 266 D1 ⑧
St Bartholomew's Rd
  HORF/LLZ BS7 .... 364 D3 ⑧
St Bede's Rd *KGWD/HNM* BS15 ... 366 D3
St Bernard's Rd *AVONM* BS11 ..... 352 A4
St Brelades Gv
  BRSG/KWL/STAPK BS4 .... 374 D1
St Brendan's Rd *STROUD* GL5 ... 215 G7 ⑧
St Briavels Dr *YATE/CS* BS37 ...... 347 F6
St Briavels Rd *LYD* GL15 .... 259 K3
Saintbridge Cl *GLE* GL4 .... 158 E1
Saintbridge Pl *GLE* GL4 .... 158 D1 ⑧
St Bruel's Cl *LYD* GL15 .... 231 G1 ⑧
St Catherine St *GL* GL1 .... 2 C2
St Cloes Pitch *STROUD* GL5 .... 242 C6
St Cyril's Rd *STNHO* GL10 .... 213 F7 ⑧
St David's Av
  OLD/WMLY/WICK BS30 .... 376 C1
St Davids Cl *CHELTW* GL51 .... 106 A8
  CHEP NP16 .... 288 A7 ⑧
  GL GL1 .... 157 J3
St David's Crs
  BRSG/KWL/STAPK BS4 .... 374 D1
  DSLY GL11 .... 266 D4 ⑧
St Davids Rd *TEWK* GL20 .... 34 E7
  THNB/SVB BS35 .... 316 C5
St Edwards Ct *MIM* GL56 .... 69 K2 ⑧
St Edwards Dr *COTS* GL54 .... 92 D6
St Edwards Wk *CHELTS* GL53 .... 107 G8 ⑧
St Edyth's Rd
  HNLZ/SM/SNYPK/WT BS9 .... 352 D8
St Ewens Rd *CHEP* NP16 .... 288 A8
St Fagans Ct
  OLD/WMLY/WICK BS30 ...... 376 C4 ⑧
St Francis Dr *FRCTL/WBN* BS36 ... 345 F8
  OLD/WMLY/WICK BS30 .... 368 D7
St Francis Rd *KEYN* BS31 .... 375 H8
St Gabriel's Rd
  EVILLE/WHL BS5 .... 364 E6 ⑬
St George Rd *CHEP* NP16 .... 288 A7
St Georges Av *EVILLE/WHL* BS5 .. 365 K8 ⑪
  STNHO GL10 .... 241 G2
St George's Cl *CHELTW* GL51 .... 106 B4 ⑧
  DSLY GL11 .... 267 F3
  GL GL1 .... 157 J3
  MIM GL56 .... 70 A1
  STNHO GL10 .... 241 G2 ⑧

St George's Dr *CHELTW* GL51 .... 106 B4
St George's Pl *CHELT* GL50 .... 4 B3 ⑧
St Georges Rd *BWTH/CHD* GL3 ... 160 B1
  CBRIS/FH BS1 .... 364 A8
  TEWK GL20 .... 34 E6
  CHELT GL50 .... 4 A4
  CHELTW GL51 .... 106 B4
  DSLY GL11 .... 266 E3
St George's St *CHELT* GL50 .... 4 B3
St Georges Wy *CHEP* NP16 ...... 312 D2 ⑧
St Giles Barton *WUE* GL12 ..... 321 H6 ⑧
St Gregory's Rd *HORF/LLZ* BS7 ... 354 D6
St Gregory's Wk *HORF/LLZ* BS7 .. 354 E6 ⑧
St Helens Dr
  OLD/WMLY/WICK BS30 .... 368 E7
  OLD/WMLY/WICK BS30 .... 376 D4
St Helen's Wk *EVILLE/WHL* BS5 .. 366 A5
St Helier Av
  BRSG/KWL/STAPK BS4 .... 374 E3 ⑧
St Ivel Wy *OLD/WMLY/WICK* BS30 .. 367 J8
St James' *VGL* GL2 .... 157 F5
St James' Cl *VGL* GL2 .... 157 F5
St James Ct *MIM* GL56 .... 69 K2 ⑧
St James Pk *CLFD* GL16 .... 176 A8
St James' Pl *CHELT* GL50 .... 4 A6 ⑧
St James' Sq *CHELT* GL50 .... 4 B4
St James's St *MANG/FISH* BS16 .. 367 C1
St James St *CHELTE/BC* GL52 ... 4 C4 ⑪
  GL GL1 .... 3 D5
St Johns Av *BWTH/CHD* GL3 ..... 103 J7
  CHELTE/BC GL52 .... 4 C4
St John's Cl *CHELTE/BC* GL52 ... 83 F2 ⑧
  CIR GL7 .... 249 H3
St Johns Ct *KEYN* BS31 .... 375 K8
St Johns La *GL* GL1 .... 2 C3
St John's Rd *CIR* GL7 .... 249 J4
  MTCHDN GL17 .... 121 J6
  VGL GL2 .... 238 C3
St Johns Sq *CIND* GL14 .... 150 E8
St John's St *CIR* GL7 .... 285 H2
  CLFD GL16 .... 175 J4 ⑧
St John St *BAD* GL9 .... 338 A3
  THNB/SVB BS35 .... 316 B5
St Johns Wy *YATE/CS* BS37 .... 348 A4
St Joseph's Rd
  HNBRY/STHM BS10 .... 353 K3
St Judes Cl *CHELTS* GL53 .... 5 D6
St Kilda Pde *GL* GL1 .... 3 D4 ⑪
St Ladoc Rd *KEYN* BS31 .... 375 J4
St Lawrence Cl *CIR* GL7 .... 249 H4
  VGL GL2 .... 102 A3
St Lawrence Rd *CIR* GL7 .... 285 G2
  GLE GL4 .... 131 F7
St Leonards Cl *GLE* GL4 .... 159 C4
St Leonard's Rd
  EVILLE/WHL BS5 .... 365 G4 ⑬
  HORF/LLZ BS7 .... 354 C8
St Lucia Cl *HORF/LLZ* BS7 .... 354 C6
St Lucia Crs *HORF/LLZ* BS7 ...... 354 C7
St Luke's Gdns
  BRSG/KWL/STAPK BS4 .... 374 D4
St Luke's Pl *CHELTS* GL53 .... 4 C5 ⑧
St Luke's Rd *CHELT* GL50 .... 4 B5
St Lukes St *GL* GL1 .... 2 B5 ⑧
St Luke St *EVILLE/WHL* BS5 .... 365 F7 ⑪
St Margaret's Cl *KEYN* BS31 ..... 375 J8 ⑧
St Margaret's Dr
  HNLZ/SM/SNYPK/WT BS9 .... 364 A1 ⑧
  TEWK GL20 .... 37 J7
St Margaret's Rd *CHELT* GL50 ...... 4 B3
  GLE GL4 .... 131 H6 ⑧
  MTCHDN GL17 .... 121 J6
  TEWK GL20 .... 37 K7
St Marks Cl *KEYN* BS31 .... 375 K8 ⑧
St Mark's Rd *EVILLE/WHL* BS5 ... 365 F5
St Mark's Ter *EVILLE/WHL* BS5 .. 365 F5 ⑩
St Mark St *GL* GL1 .... 2 C2
St Martin's Gdns
  BRSG/KWL/STAPK BS4 .... 374 A5 ⑧
St Martin's La
  CHPMW/MSHF SN14 .... 371 K6
St Martin's Pk
  CHPMW/MSHF SN14 .... 371 K6 ⑧
St Martin's Rd
  BRSG/KWL/STAPK BS4 .... 374 A5
St Martin's Wk
  BRSG/KWL/STAPK BS4 .... 374 A5 ⑧
St Mary's Cl *CIR* GL7 .... 283 G8
  COTS GL54 .... 91 J6
St Marys Dr *CIR* GL7 .... 255 F7
St Mary's Fld *CIR* GL7 .... 281 H1
St Mary's Hl *STROUD* GL5 .... 242 C8
St Mary's La *TEWK* GL20 .... 33 H8
St Mary's Rd *CIR* GL7 .... 250 A6 ⑧
  TET GL8 .... 302 B6
  TET GL8 .... 33 G8
St Mary's Sq *GL* GL1 .... 2 C3
  LYD GL15 .... 234 C3
St Mary's St *GL* GL1 .... 2 C3 ⑧
  RSTROUD/NAIL GL6 .... 187 H6 ⑧
St Mary St *CHEP* NP16 .... 288 A6
  THNB/SVB BS35 .... 316 B6 ⑧
St Mary's Wy *YATE/CS* BS37 .... 347 H4
St Matthew's Av
  RDLND/MONT BS6 .... 364 B5 ⑧

St Matthew's Rd
RDLND/MONT BS6 .... 364 B6
St Matthias Pk CBRISNE BS2 .... 364 D7
St Michaels Av CHELTE/BC GL52 ...... 83 G3
St Michael's Cl FRCTL/WBN BS36 ... 344 E7
MTCHDN GL17 .... 123 C4
St Michaels Ct
KCWD/HNM BS15 .... 366 B6
St Michael's HI CBRISNE BS2 ...... 364 A6
St Michael's Pk CFTN/FAIL BS8 .... 364 A6
St Michaels Pl STROUD GL5 ...... 213 K6
St Michaels Pl CHELT GL50 ...... 134 B1
CIR GL7 .... 249 J7
St Michael's Sq GL GL1 .... 2 C4
St Nicholas Cl TEWK GL20 .... 36 B8
St Nicholas Dr CHELT GL50 ...... 106 D1
St Nicholas Pk
EVILLE/WHL BS5 .... 365 F5
St Nicholas St CBRISNE BS2 ..... 364 D5
St Oswald's Rd GL GL1 .... 2 C2
St Patricks Rd TEWK GL20 .... 34 E7
St Pauls Ct MIM GL56 .... 69 K2
St Paul's La CHELT GL50 .... 4 B2
St Paul's Pde CHELT GL50 .... 4 B2
St Paul's Rd CHELT GL50 .... 4 B2
GL GL1 .... 2 C5
St Paul's St North CHELT GL50 ... 4 B2
St Paul's St South CHELT GL50 ... 4 B3
St Paul St CBRISNE BS2 .... 364 C6
St Peters Cl CHELTW GL51 ...... 106 A3
CIND GL14 .... 180 C2
CIR GL7 .... 274 C5
EVE WR11 .... 15 J1
St Peters Ct MIM GL56 .... 69 K2
St Peter's Crs FRCTL/WBN BS36 ... 345 H7
St Peters Rd CIR GL7 .... 249 J6
GLE GL4 .... 158 E3
St Peter's Sq CHELTW GL51 ..... 106 A2
St Peters Wy COTS GL54 .... 62 D8
St Philips Cswy
BRSG/KWL/STAPK BS4 .... 374 B2
CBRISNE BS2 .... 365 F8
St Philip's Cl BWTH/CHD GL3 .... 131 J6
St Philips Pd CBRISNE BS2 ...... 364 E7
St Philips Rd CBRISNE BS2 ...... 364 E7
St Philip's St CHELT GL50 .... 4 A6
St Pierre Dr
OLD/WMLY/WICK BS30 ...... 367 H8
St Ronan's Av RDLND/MONT BS6 .. 364 A5
St Saviours Rd FRCTL/WBN BS36 .. 345 H8
St Stephen's Av CBRIS/FH BS1 ... 364 B8
St Stephens Cl CHELT GL50 ..... 106 B7
KCWD/HNM BS15 .... 366 E3
St Stephen's Rd CHELT GL50 .... 106 B7
MANG/FISH BS16 .... 366 D3
St Stephen's St CBRIS/FH BS1 ... 364 B7
St Swithins Cl LYD GL15 .... 206 B1
St Swithuns Rd VGL GL2 .... 129 G8
St Tecla Rd CHEP NP16 .... 288 A8
St Tewdric Rd CHEP NP16 ...... 288 A7
St Thomas Cl CBRIS/FH BS1 .... 364 C8
St Thomas St East
CBRIS/FH BS1 .... 364 C8
St Vincent Wy RDLND/MONT GL3 .. 103 J6
St Werburgh's Pk CBRISNE BS2 .. 364 E4
St Werburgh's Rd
CBRISNE BS2 .... 364 D4
St Whites Rd CIND GL14 .... 150 E3
Salamanca Rd CHELTE/BC GL52 .. 5 F3
Salem Rd FRCTL/WBN BS36 ..... 345 F7
Salisbury Av CHELTW GL51 ..... 134 A1
KCWD/HNM BS15 .... 366 B6
Salisbury Gdns MANG/FISH BS16 .. 366 E1
Salisbury Rd
BRSG/KWL/STAPK BS4 .... 374 C1
GL GL1 .... 3 E5
MANG/FISH BS16 .... 356 E8
RDLND/MONT BS6 .... 364 B8
Salisbury St EVILLE/WHL BS5 ... 365 F8
Salix Ct CHELTW GL51 .... 133 K2
Sallis Cl TEWK GL20 .... 34 C4
Sallybarn Cl
OLD/WMLY/WICK BS30 ...... 375 K4
Sallys Wy FRCTL/WBN BS36 .... 345 F7
Salmons Wy MANG/FISH BS16 .. 357 G6
Salter's La COTS GL54 .... 65 J8
Salter St BRKLY GL13 .... 264 A3
Salthrop Rd HORF/LLZ BS7 ..... 364 C3
Saltmarsh Dr AVONM BS11 ..... 352 C5
Salt Wy CIR GL7 .... 226 B5
Samian Wy BRSTK/PCHW BS34 .. 355 J1
Samuel St EVILLE/WHL BS5 ..... 365 G6
Samuel White Rd
KCWD/HNM BS15 .... 375 H3
Samuel Wright Cl
OLD/WMLY/WICK BS30 ...... 376 E1
Sanatorium Rd GLE GL4 .... 160 A7
Sandalwood Dr VGL GL2 .... 129 H7
Sandbach Rd
BRSG/KWL/STAPK BS4 .... 374 C2
Sandbed Rd CBRISNE BS2 ...... 364 E4
Sandfield LED HR8 .... 29 G8
Sandfield La EVE WR11 .... 15 G4
Sandfield Rd BWTH/CHD GL3 ... 132 B1

The Sandfield TEWK GL20 .... 34 D5
Sandford Leaze TET GL8 .... 272 A5
Sandford Mill Cl CHELTS GL53 ... 5 D6
Sandford Mill Rd CHELTS GL53 .. 5 D6
Sandford Rd CHELTS GL53 ...... 4 C6
LYD GL15 .... 233 F6
Sandford St CHELT GL50 .... 4 C5
Sandford Wy GL GL1 .... 157 H4
Sandgate Rd
BRSG/KWL/STAPK BS4 .... 374 C3
Sand HI BRSG/KWL/STAPK BS4 .. 374 B2
Sandholme Rd MANG/FISH BS16 .. 356 E6
Sandholme Rd
BRSG/KWL/STAPK BS4 .... 374 B2
Sandhurst Cl BRSTK/PCHW BS34 .. 343 F5
Sandhurst La VGL GL2 .... 101 K8
VGL GL2 .... 102 B3
Sandhurst Rd
BRSG/KWL/STAPK BS4 .... 374 C2
CHELTE/BC GL52 .... 107 H8
GL GL1 .... 2 C1
Sandling Av HORF/LLZ BS7 ..... 354 E7
Sandown Cl MANG/FISH BS16 ... 357 F5
Sandown Rd
BRSG/KWL/STAPK BS4 .... 374 C2
BRSTK/PCHW BS34 .... 355 G3
CHELTE/BC GL52 .... 83 F2
Sandpiper Cl VGL GL2 .... 156 D5
Sandpits La BAD GL9 .... 337 K5
RSTROUD/NAIL GL6 213
Sandpool La CIR GL7 .... 274 E3
Sandringham Av GL GL1 .... 157 J5
MANG/FISH BS16 .... 356 E6
Sandringham Pk
MANG/FISH BS16 .... 356 E6
Sandringham Rd
BRSG/KWL/STAPK BS4 .... 374 C3
BRSTK/PCHW BS34 .... 355 H2
Sands Cl BDWAY WR12 .... 18 D5
Sands Croft Av BDWAY WR12 .. 18 E5
Sands HI CHPMW/MSHF SN14 .. 370 C3
Sandstar Cl VGL GL2 .... 131 F7
The Sands BDWAY WR12 ...... 18 D5
Sandstone Ri FRCTL/WBN BS36 .. 356 D2
Sandtumps LYD GL15 .... 232 A8
Sandwich Rd
BRSG/KWL/STAPK BS4 .... 374 C2
Sandy Cl ALMDB BS32 .... 343 J8
Sandycroft Rd BWTH/CHD GL3 .. 103 J7
Sandy La CHELTS GL53 .... 135 F2
COTS GL54 .... 144 D1
EVILLE/WHL BS5 .... 365 G3
LYD GL15 .... 230 E3
THNB/SVB BS35 .... 313 J7
Sandy Lane Rd CHELTS GL53 ... 135 F1
Sandyleaze
HNLZ/SM/SNYPK/WT BS9 ... 353 J7
VGL GL2 .... 131 F3
Sandy Ldg YATE/CS BS37 ...... 347 G6
Sandy Park Rd
BRSG/KWL/STAPK BS4 .... 374 B2
Sandy Pluck La CHELTW GL51 .. 133 F6
Saniger La BRKLY GL13 .... 235 J7
Sankey Gv MIM GL56 .... 70 A2
Sappercombe La CHELTS GL53 .. 135 H1
Sapperton Rd GLE GL4 .... 158 B1
Sapphire Cl GL GL1 .... 157 H4
Sarah St EVILLE/WHL BS5 ...... 365 F7
Sarnedy Rd CLFD GL16 .... 175 K4
Sarum Crs HNBRY/STHM BS10 .. 354 A5
Sassoon Ct
OLD/WMLY/WICK BS30 ...... 376 A1
Satchfield Cl HNBRY/STHM BS10 .. 353 H4
Satchfield Crs HNBRY/STHM BS10 .. 353 H4
Sates Wy
HNLZ/SM/SNYPK/WT BS9 ... 354 A8
Saturn Cl GLE GL4 .... 131 H8
Saunders Cl MTCHDN GL17 .... 124 D1
Saunders Rd MANG/FISH BS16 .. 366 E2
Savage HI CLFD GL16 .... 174 D2
Savages Wood Rd ALMDB BS32 .. 343 H6
Savernake Rd GLE GL4 .... 3 E6
Saville Cl CHELT GL50 .... 4 C1
Savoy Rd BRSG/KWL/STAPK BS4 .. 374 C2
Saw Mill La THNB/SVB BS35 ... 316 D5
Sawpit La RTEWK/TIB GL19 .... 79 G1
Sawpits La MIM GL56 .... 94 A5
Sawyers Ri RTEWK/TIB GL19 ... 77 G6
Saxon Cl HGHW SN6 .... 310 D7
VGL GL2 .... 130 E1
Saxon Pl CHEP NP16 .... 288 C7
Saxon Rd CBRISNE BS2 .... 364 E4
CIR GL7 .... 250 A5
Saxon Wy ALMDB BS32 .... 343 G5
CHELTE/BC GL52 .... 5 D5
Sayers Crs BWTH/CHD GL3 .... 160 C1
Saylittle Ms VGL GL2 .... 131 G1
Say Wk OLD/WMLY/WICK BS30 .. 367 K7
Scandrett Cl
HNBRY/STHM BS10 .... 353 G3
Scantleberry Cl
MANG/FISH BS16 .... 356 D6
Scar HI RSTROUD/NAIL GL6 .... 271 F1
Scarr Rd NWNT GL18 .... 73 J1

School Cl BRSTK/PCHW BS34 ... 343 G6
CLFD GL16 .... 176 B4
DSLY GL11 .... 266 C2
EVILLE/WHL BS5 .... 365 H4
School Crs LYD GL15 .... 234 B1
RTEWK/TIB GL19 .... 93 H8
Schooler's La MIM GL56 .... 94 C3
School HI CHEP NP16 .... 288 A6
CIR GL7 .... 191 G6
CIR GL7 .... 249 G2
School La BAD GL9 .... 350 E4
CHELTE/BC GL52 .... 83 J6
CHELTW GL51 .... 133 J4
CIR GL7 .... 249 K7
CIR GL7 .... 251 J6
CIR GL7 .... 278 D7
CIR GL7 .... 281 H2
COTS GL54 .... 138 B4
EVE WR11 .... 6 C2
MIM GL56 .... 44 B4
MTCHDN GL17 .... 121 H7
MTCHDN GL17 .... 124 C3
MTCHDN GL17 .... 148 E3
RSTROUD/NAIL GL6 .... 218 D5
VGL GL2 .... 156 D6
VGL GL2 .... 211 J1
School Md CHELTW GL51 ...... 106 A4
School Ms GLE GL4 .... 158 D2
School Rd BDWAY WR12 .... 16 C5
BRSG/KWL/STAPK BS4 .... 374 D4
CHELTE/BC GL52 .... 83 G2
CHELTS GL53 .... 107 H8
CIR GL7 .... 276 B7
DSLY GL11 .... 267 G6
FRCTL/WBN BS36 .... 345 F6
KCWD/HNM BS15 .... 366 C6
LYD GL15 .... 205 K5
MTCHDN GL17 .... 120 E8
MTCHDN GL17 .... 121 J6
MTCHDN GL17 .... 148 E1
OLD/WMLY/WICK BS30 ...... 376 B2
OLD/WMLY/WICK BS30 ...... 376 C3
RSTROUD/NAIL GL6 .... 243 J8
RTEWK/TIB GL19 .... 79 F2
TEWK GL20 .... 37 K7
WUE GL12 .... 297 F7
School St EVE WR11 .... 7 G2
School Wk YATE/CS BS37 ...... 347 H4
School Wy THNB/SVB BS35 .... 328 C8
The Scop ALMDB BS32 .... 342 F1
Scott Av VGL GL2 .... 157 J2
Scott Ct OLD/WMLY/WICK BS30 .. 376 A1
Scott Lawrence Cl
MANG/FISH BS16 .... 356 A7
Scott Wk OLD/WMLY/WICK BS30 .. 367 K7
Scott Wy YATE/CS BS37 .... 347 H6
Scowles Rd CLFD GL16 .... 175 G4
Scrubbett's La TET GL8 .... 299 F5
Seabright Cl CHELTW GL51 .... 105 J1
Seabroke Rd GL GL1 .... 3 D2
Seabrook Rd BWTH/CHD GL3 .. 160 B1
Seacome Rd CHELTW GL51 .... 105 J4
Seagry Cl HNBRY/STHM BS10 .. 354 C5
Searle Court Av
BRSG/KWL/STAPK BS4 .... 374 D1
Seaton Rd EVILLE/WHL BS5 .... 365 G5
Sebert St GL GL1 .... 3 D2
Second Av DSLY GL11 .... 267 G6
Secret La GL GL1 .... 2 C2
Sedbury La CHEP NP16 .... 288 C5
Seddon Rd CBRISNE BS2 ...... 364 E4
Sedgefield Gdns
MANG/FISH BS16 .... 357 F5
Sedgewick Gdns CHELTW GL51 .. 105 H8
Sedgley Cl GL GL1 .... 157 J4
Sedgley Rd CHELTE/BC GL52 ... 83 F2
Sefton Park Rd HORF/LLZ BS7 .. 364 D3
Sefton Wk CHELTW GL51 ...... 105 H8
Selborne Rd CHELTE/BC GL52 .. 83 F2
HORF/LLZ BS7 .... 364 D1
Selbrooke Crs MANG/FISH BS16 .. 356 C8
Selby Rd EVILLE/WHL BS5 ..... 365 K5
Selkirk Cl CHELTE/BC GL52 .... 5 D3
Selkirk Gdns CHELTE/BC GL52 .. 5 D3
Selkirk Rd KCWD/HNM BS15 ... 366 C4
Selkirk St CHELTE/BC GL52 .... 4 C3
Sellars Rd VGL GL2 .... 156 D7
Selsey Rd STROUD GL5 .... 242 A4
Selsley HI STROUD GL5 .... 242 A1
Selworthy CHELTW GL51 ...... 133 J1
KCWD/HNM BS15 .... 366 E7
Selworthy Rd
BRSG/KWL/STAPK BS4 .... 374 A4
Selwyn Cl STNHO GL10 .... 241 G1
Selwyn Rd GLE GL4 .... 3 D5
Seneca Pl EVILLE/WHL BS5 .... 365 H7
Seneca St EVILLE/WHL BS5 .... 365 H7
Seneca Wy CHELTW GL51 ..... 106 B1
Serio Rd GL GL1 .... 2 C2
Sevelm CHELTW GL51 .... 133 J1
Seven Acres GLE GL4 .... 131 F7
Sevenacres
RSTROUD/NAIL GL6 .... 270 C2
Sevenleaze La RSTROUD/NAIL GL6 .. 159 F8
RSTROUD/NAIL GL6 .... 186 D4

Seven Stars Rd *CIND* GL14 .... 150 E4
Seventh Av *GLE* GL4 .... 157 K4
HORF/LLZ BS7 .... 355 F5 2
Seven View Rd *THNB/SVB* BS35 .. 316 C4
Severn Av *CHEP* NP16 .... 288 C5
Severnbank Av *VGL* GL15 .... 234 C3
Severn Br *THNB/SVB* BS35 .... 313 G6
Severn Cl *WUE* GL12 .... 319 J2 8
Severn Crs *CHEP* NP16 .... 288 A7
Severn Dr *BRKLY* GL13 .... 264 A2
THNB/SVB BS35 .... 316 B4
Severn La *BRKLY* GL13 .... 262 E5
Severn Oaks *VGL* GL2 .... 157 F7
Severn Rd *AVONM* BS11 .... 340 B6
BRKLY GL13 .... 235 H6
CHELTE/BC GL52 .... 5 E2
DSLY GL11 .... 266 C2
GL GL1 .... 2 B4
HNBRY/STHM BS10 .... 340 B4
LYD GL15 .... 234 B4
STNHO GL10 .... 212 E6
THNB/SVB BS35 .... 329 F5
Severn St *CIND* GL14 .... 180 C2
Severnvale Dr *VGL* GL2 .... 156 E5
Severn Vw *CIND* GL14 .... 151 C5
Severn View Rd *LYD* GL15 .... 206 C3
LYD GL15 .... 232 B8
Severn Wy *BRKLY* GL13 .... 236 E1
BRKLY GL13 .... 263 G1
BRSTK/PCHW BS34 .... 342 D5
RTEWK/TIB GL19 .... 56 B7
THNB/SVB BS35 .... 313 K5
THNB/SVB BS35 .... 328 D8
VGL GL2 .... 129 F7
VGL GL2 .... 180 D5
Severnwood Gdns
THNB/SVB BS35 .... 340 C1
Sevier St *CBRISNE* BS2 .... 364 E4
Seymour Av *HORF/LLZ* BS7 .... 364 C2 2
Seymour Ga *CHCAM* GL55 .... 20 E3 2
Seymour Pl *COTS* GL54 .... 85 J1
TEWK GL20 .... 57 H1
Seymour Rd *EVILLE/WHL* BS5 .... 364 F5
GL GL1 .... 129 K8
HORF/LLZ BS7 .... 364 C2
KCWD/HNM BS15 .... 366 C5 3
MANG/FISH BS16 .... 366 D2
Seyton Wk *BRSTK/PCHW* BS34 ...... 355 J1
Sezincote Cl *RSTROUD/NAIL* GL6 .. 244 B1 1
Shackel Hendy Ms
MANG/FISH BS16 .... 367 H1 2
Shackleton Av *YATE/CS* BS37 .... 347 H6
Shackleton Cl *BWTH/CHD* GL3 .... 131 K1
Shadwell Rd *HORF/LLZ* BS7 .... 364 B3
Shaftesbury Av
RDLND/MONT BS6 .... 364 C5
Shaft Rd *THNB/SVB* BS35 .... 328 C6
Shakespeare Av *HORF/LLZ* BS7 ...... 354 E6
VGL GL2 .... 157 J2
Shakespeare Ct *TEWK* GL20 .... 33 H8 7
Shakespeare Rd *CHELTE* GL51 .... 105 J5
DSLY GL11 .... 267 G7
Shaldon Rd *HORF/LLZ* BS7 .... 354 C2
Shalford Cl *CIR* GL7 .... 249 H7 2
The Shambles *STROUD* GL5 .... 214 E7 13
Shamrock Cl *BWTH/CHD* GL3 .... 103 H8
Shamrock Rd *EVILLE/WHL* BS5 .... 365 H3 3
Shanklin Dr *BRSTK/PCHW* BS34 ..... 355 F5 2
Shannon Ct *THNB/SVB* BS35 .... 316 D6 4
Shannon Wy *TEWK* GL20 .... 34 B7
Shapcott Cl
BRSG/KWL/STAPK BS4 .... 374 A5 4
Sharps Wy *CHEP* NP16 .... 312 B1 3
Shaw Green La *CHELTE/BC* GL52 ..... 107 H1
Shaymoor La *THNB/SVB* BS35 .... 341 H2
Shearmore Cl *HORF/LLZ* BS7 .... 354 E7 3
Shearwater Gv *VGL* GL2 .... 103 F8
Sheep Fair La
CHPMW/MSHF SN14 .... 371 K7
Sheepscombe Cl *CHELTW* GL51 ...... 105 J6 6
Sheep St *CHCAM* GL55 .... 20 D4
CIR GL7 .... 249 J6
COTS GL54 .... 92 C6
Sheepwood Cl *HNBRY/STHM* BS10.. 353 J3
Sheepwood Rd
HNBRY/STHM BS10 .... 353 J4
Sheevaun Ct *VGL* GL2 .... 131 F1 8
Shelburne Rd *CHELTW* GL51 .... 105 K7
Sheldare Barton
EVILLE/WHL BS5 .... 366 B7 8
Sheldare Dr *MANG/FISH* BS16 .... 355 K8
Shelduck Rd *GL* GL2 .... 156 C5
Shellard Rd *BRSTK/PCHW* BS34 ..... 354 E3
Shellards La *THNB/SVB* BS35 .... 332 C2
THNB/SVB BS35 .... 333 F4
Shellards Rd
OLD/WMLY/WICK BS30 .... 376 A3
Shelley Av *CHELTW* GL51 .... 105 J5
VGL GL2 .... 157 J2
Shelley Cl *EVILLE/WHL* BS5 .... 365 K6
Shelley Rd *CHELTW* GL51 .... 105 J5
Shelley Wy *HORF/LLZ* BS7 .... 354 E6
Shellmor Av *BRSTK/PCHW* BS34 .... 343 H5 1
Shellmor Cl *ALMDB* BS32 .... 343 H5 1
BRSTK/PCHW BS34 .... 343 G5

Shelly Rd *DSLY* GL11 .... 267 G7
Shephard Md *TEWK* GL20 .... 57 G1
Shepherdine Cl *LYD* GL15 .... 234 C3
Shepherd Rd *GL* GL1 .... 157 H3
Shepherd's Cl *CHCAM* GL55 .... 20 D4
MANG/FISH BS16 .... 366 E1
STROUD GL5 .... 215 F6 2
Shepherds Cft *STROUD* GL5............ 215 F6
Shepherd's Leaze *WUE* GL12 .... 297 G8 1
Shepherds Md *TET* GL8 .... 302 C5
Shepherds Wk *WUE* GL12 .... 297 G8 2
Shepherds Wy *BWTH/CHD* GL3 ...... 103 H7
CIR GL7 .... 249 J4
COTS GL54 .... 92 D6
COTS GL54 .... 169 F4
Shepherds Well *STROUD* GL5 .... 243 F5 1
Sheppard Rd *MANG/FISH* BS16 ...... 356 C8
Sheppard Wy *RSTROUD/NAIL* GL6 .. 243 G7
Shepperdine Rd *THNB/SVB* BS35 ... 291 H2
Sherborne Av *ALMDB* BS32 .... 343 J8
Sherbourne Cl *KCWD/HNM* BS15 ... 367 F4
Sherbourne Ct *STNHO* GL10 .... 213 F6 11
Sherbourne St *EVILLE/WHL* BS5 ..... 365 J6
Shergar Cl *GLE* GL4 .... 159 F2
Sheridan Rd *HORF/LLZ* BS7 .... 354 E5
Sheridan Wy
OLD/WMLY/WICK BS30 .... 376 B4
The Sherry *COTS* GL54 .... 88 C1
Sherston Cl *MANG/FISH* BS16 .... 366 B1
Sherston Rd *HORF/LLZ* BS7 .... 354 C6 1
Sherwell Rd
BRSG/KWL/STAPK BS4 .... 374 D3
Sherwood Gn *VGL* GL2 .... 102 B8
Sherwood Rd *KCWD/HNM* BS15 ..... 366 A5
TET GL8 .... 302 B7
Shetland Rd *HNBRY/STHM* BS10.... 354 B5
Shields Av *HORF/LLZ* BS7 .... 354 E4
Shiels Dr *ALMDB* BS32 .... 343 H7 8
Shilton Cl *KCWD/HNM* BS15 .... 367 F7 7
Shimsey Cl *MANG/FISH* BS16 .... 356 C8 1
Shipley Mow *MANG/FISH* BS16 ...... 357 H8
Shipley Rd
HNLZ/SM/SNYPK/WT BS9 .... 353 J6
Shipnran Ct *MANG/FISH* BS16 .... 366 E2 7
Shipton's Grave La
RSTROUD/NAIL GL6 .... 270 E5
Shipway Ct *CHELTE/BC* GL52 .... 83 F2 8
Shirehampton Rd *AVONM* BS11 ...... 352 B7
HNLZ/SM/SNYPK/WT BS9 .... 352 E8 2
Shire Hl *CHPMW/MSHF* SN14 .... 361 K7
Shire Wy *YATE/CS* BS37 .... 346 E8
Shophouse Rd *LYD* GL15 .... 203 K3
Shop La *BAD* GL9 .... 350 E4
EVE WR11 .... 6 C1
Short Hedges Cl *COTS* GL54 .... 169 H5 1
Shorthill Rd *YATE/CS* BS37 .... 358 C2 3
Shortlands Rd *AVONM* BS11 .... 352 C5 8
Short St *CHELTS* GL53 .... 106 C8
Short Wy *THNB/SVB* BS35 .... 316 B7
Shortwood Hl *MANG/FISH* BS16 ..... 367 K1
Shortwood Rd *MANG/FISH* BS16 .... 368 C2
RSTROUD/NAIL GL6 .... 270 B3
Shortwood Vw
KCWD/HNM BS15 .... 367 F6 8
Shotts La *NWNT* GL18 .... 72 A8
Shoulderway La *SHPSTR* CV36 .... 25 F5
Shrubbery Rd *MANG/FISH* BS16 ..... 366 D1
Shrublands *CHELTS* GL53 .... 135 F1
Shurdington Rd *BWTH/CHD* GL3 .... 160 D1
CHELTS GL53 .... 134 B1
CHELTW GL51 .... 133 G6
Shutehay Dr *DSLY* GL11 .... 266 D1
Shute St *STNHO* GL10 .... 241 G3
Shutter La *CHELTE/BC* GL52 .... 60 A6
Sibland *THNB/SVB* BS35 .... 316 D6
Sibland Cl *THNB/SVB* BS35 .... 316 D6 2
Sibland Rd *THNB/SVB* BS35 .... 316 D6
Sibland Wy *THNB/SVB* BS35 .... 316 C6
Sibree Cl *RSTROUD/NAIL* GL6 .... 244 A3
Sidcot *BRSG/KWL/STAPK* BS4 .... 375 F4
Siddington Rd *CIR* GL7 .... 250 A8
Sideland Cl *HGRV/WHIT* BS14 .... 374 D8
Sidelands Rd *MANG/FISH* BS16 ...... 356 C8
Sidings Rd *CHNTN* OX7 .... 119 K1
The Sidings *WUE* GL12 .... 319 K1 2
Sidney St *CHELTE/BC* GL52 .... 4 C4
GL GL1 .... 3 E4
Signal Rd *MANG/FISH* BS16 .... 366 E2
Silcock Cl *BWTH/CHD* GL3 .... 103 H7
Silklands Gv
HNLZ/SM/SNYPK/WT BS9 .... 353 E8 8
Silk Mill La *COTS* GL54 .... 85 K1
Silley's Cl *CHEP* NP16 .... 288 B2 8
Silverbirch Cl *BRSTK/PCHW* BS34 .. 343 H7
Silver Birch Cl *VGL* GL2 .... 156 E5 3
Silver Cl *GL* GL1 .... 157 J3
Silverhill Rd *HNBRY/STHM* BS10.... 353 G3
Silver St *CBRIS/FH* BS1 .... 364 B7 17

CIND GL14 .... 151 J7
CIR GL7 .... 249 J5 3
CIR GL7 .... 278 D6
DSLY GL11 .... 240 A7
DSLY GL11 .... 267 F5 1
MTCHDN GL17 .... 123 C5
TET GL8 .... 302 C7 2
VGL GL2 .... 181 G3
Silverthorn Cl *CHELT* GL50 .... 134 B1 8
Silverthorne La *CBRISNE* BS2 .... 364 E8
Silvertree Gdns *STROUD* GL5 .... 243 G3 1
Silverwood Wy *CHELTW* GL51 .... 133 J1 18
Simmonds Rd *GLE* GL4 .... 131 H7
Simmonds Vw *BRSTK/PCHW* BS34 .. 355 K2
Simon Rd *VGL* GL2 .... 130 E1
Simpson Rd *SHPSTR* CV36 .... 25 F1
Sims La *VGL* GL2 .... 157 F2
Sinclair Rd *CHELTW* GL51 .... 133 H5
Sinderberry Dr *TEWK* GL20 .... 34 D5
Sinope St *GL* GL1 .... 3 D4 12
Sir John's La *EVILLE/WHL* BS5 .... 365 F2
HORF/LLZ BS7 .... 365 F2
Siskin Rd *COTS* GL54 .... 144 E1
Sissinghurst Gv *CHELTW* GL51 .... 134 A1 7
Sisson End *VGL* GL2 .... 131 F4
Sisson Rd *VGL* GL2 .... 130 E4
Siston Cl *KCWD/HNM* BS15 .... 367 G4
Siston La *OLD/WMLY/WICK* BS30 ... 368 A5
Siston Pk *KCWD/HNM* BS15 .... 367 G4
Sivell Cl *VGL* GL2 .... 102 C8
Six Acres *GLE* GL4 .... 159 H5
Sixth Av *HORF/LLZ* BS7 .... 354 E5
Skillicorne Ms *CHELTW* GL51 .... 106 A6 8
Skinner St *GL* GL1 .... 2 C2
Skipton Ct *KCWD/HNM* BS15 .... 375 K1 8
Skylark Wy *GLE* GL4 .... 158 D1
Slade Brook *STROUD* GL5 .... 215 G6
Slade Rd *LYD* GL15 .... 206 B3
The Slade *DSLY* GL11 .... 267 F6 2
Slad La *RSTROUD/NAIL* GL6 .... 215 J4
STROUD GL5 .... 215 H6
Slad Rd *RSTROUD/NAIL* GL6 .... 187 K8
STROUD GL5 .... 215 F6
The Slad *CIND* GL14 .... 151 K6
Slaney St *GL* GL1 .... 3 D6
Slimbridge Cl *YATE/CS* BS37 .... 347 H7
Slimbridge La *BRKLY* GL13 .... 236 D5
Slimbridge Rd *GL* GL1 .... 157 K3
Sloan St *EVILLE/WHL* BS5 .... 365 H6
Slough La *CHPMW/MSHF* SN14 ...... 379 J2
Slymbridge Av
HNBRY/STHM BS10 .... 353 J2
Smallbrook Rd *BDWAY* WR12 .... 18 D4
Small La *MANG/FISH* BS16 .... 365 J1
Small St *CBRIS/FH* BS1 .... 364 B7
Smarts Gn *YATE/CS* BS37 .... 348 A6
Smith Barry Crs *COTS* GL54 .... 145 F2
Smith Barry Rd *COTS* GL54 .... 145 F2
Smiths Ct *TEWK* GL20 .... 33 H8 8
Smiths Hl *CLFD* GL16 .... 176 C8
Smith's La *TEWK* GL20 .... 33 H8 8
Smith St *CHPMW/MSHF* SN14 .... 363 G7
Smithville Cl *LYD* GL15 .... 231 G1
Smithville Pl *LYD* GL15 .... 231 G1
Smithy Cl *CLFD* GL16 .... 147 K3
Smithy La *COTS* GL54 .... 62 D5
Smithyman Ct *CIND* GL14 .... 180 C2 2
The Smithy *CIR* GL7 .... 250 A7 1
LYD GL15 .... 207 J3 1
Smythe Meadow
RSTROUD/NAIL GL6 .... 244 B4 1
Smythe Rd *CHELTW* GL51 .... 82 B8
Snake Dr *CIR* GL7 .... 254 C1
Snead Pk *GLE* GL4 .... 159 H1 5
Sneedhams Rd *GLE* GL4 .... 158 D4
Snipehill Br *CHEP* NP16 .... 288 E4
Snipe Rd *COTS* GL54 .... 144 E2 8
Snowberry Wk *EVILLE/WHL* BS5 ..... 365 J6 8
Snowdon Cl *MANG/FISH* BS16 .... 365 K2
Snowdon Gdns *BWTH/CHD* GL3 ..... 103 J7
Snowdonia Rd *TEWK* GL20 .... 57 K2
Snowdon Rd *MANG/FISH* BS16 ...... 365 K1
Snowdrop Cl *GLE* GL4 .... 159 C1 10
Snowshill Cl *GLE* GL4 .... 131 F7 8
Snowshill Dr *CHELTE/BC* GL52 .... 82 E3
Snowshill Rd *BDWAY* WR12 .... 18 D2
GLE GL4 .... 131 G7
Snowswick La *FGDN* SN7 .... 285 J7
Sodbury Rd *WUE* GL12 .... 335 J3
Solent Wy *THNB/SVB* BS35 .... 316 D7 8
Solway Rd *CHELTW* GL51 .... 105 H3
Somerby Cl *ALMDB* BS32 .... 343 H7 8
Somerdale Rd *KEYN* BS31 .... 376 A7
Somerdale Rd North *KEYN* BS31 .... 376 A7
Somerford Rd *CIR* GL7 .... 249 J7
Somergate Rd *CHELTW* GL51 .... 105 H2
Somerset Av *CHELTW* GL51 .... 106 A4
DSLY GL11 .... 267 F6
YATE/CS BS37 .... 347 K3
Somerset Cl *WUE* GL12 .... 320 C2
Somerset Crs
BRSTK/PCHW BS34 .... 355 K1 8
Somerset Pl *GL* GL1 .... 2 B5 8
TEWK GL20 .... 57 J3 8

Somerset Rd *CIND* GL14 .... 150 E6
Somerset St *CBRISNE* BS2 .... 364 B6
Somerset Wy *CHEP* NP16 .... 312 B1
Somerton Cl *KGWD/HNM* BS15 ... 366 E7
Somerton Rd *HORF/LLZ* BS7 ...... 354 C8 🔟
Somerville Ct *CIR* GL7 .... 249 H8 🔟
Somme Rd *CHELTE/BC* GL52 .... 5 F3
Sommerville Rd
 RDLND/MONT BS6 .... 364 C3
Sommerville Rd South
 RDLND/MONT BS6 .... 364 D4 🔢
Sopwith Rd *COTS* GL54 .... 144 E1
Sorrel Cl *GLE* GL4 .... 158 C2
 THNB/SVB BS35 .... 316 D4
Soundwell Rd
 KGWD/HNM BS15 .... 366 C5 🔟
Southall Ter *NWNT* GL18 .... 96 E4
Southam La *CHELTE/BC* GL52 ...... 83 F6
South Av *TEWK* GL20 .... 35 F7
 YATE/CS BS37 .... 346 D5
Southbank *STROUD* GL5 .... 242 B4
Southbrook Rd *GLE* GL4 .... 130 E5
South Cerney Rd *CIR* GL7 .... 278 B2
South Cl *VGL* GL2 .... 3 F1
Southcourt Cl *CHELTS* GL53 ...... 134 D1
Southcourt Dr *CHELTS* GL53 ...... 134 D1
South Cft
 HNLZ/SM/SNYPK/WT BS9 ...... 354 A7
South Dene
 HNLZ/SM/SNYPK/WT BS9 ...... 353 C8
Southdown Rd
 HNLZ/SM/SNYPK/WT BS9 ...... 353 H6
Southend La *NWNT* GL18 .... 73 J7
Southern Av *GL1* 157 K2
Southernhay *MANG/FISH* BS16 .. 366 C2
Southern Rd *KGWD/HNM* BS15 ... 366 D5
Southey Av *KGWD/HNM* BS15 ..... 366 D5
Southey St *CBRISNE* BS2 .... 364 D5
Southfield Rd *RSTROUD/NAIL* GL6 .. 243 H8 🔟
 TET GL8 .... 302 B8
Southfield Ap *CHELTS* GL53 .... 134 E2
Southfield Av *KGWD/HNM* BS15 .. 366 E5
Southfield Cl *CHELTS* GL53 .... 134 C2
Southfield Ct
 HNLZ/SM/SNYPK/WT BS9 ...... 353 J7 🔟
Southfield Ri *CHELTS* GL53 .... 134 C2
Southfield Rd *CLFD* GL16 .... 175 K3
 GLE GL4 .... 158 B2
 HNLZ/SM/SNYPK/WT BS9 ...... 353 J7
 RDLND/MONT BS6 .... 364 B5 🔟
 STROUD GL5 .... 242 C4
Southgate Crs *STROUD* GL5 ...... 242 C1 🔟
Southgate Dr *CHELTS* GL53 .... 5 D6
Southgate Gdns *STROUD* GL5 .... 242 C1 🔟
Southgate St *GL1* .... 2 C4 🔟
South Gv *RDLND/MONT* BS6 ...... 364 A1
South Hayes *EVILLE/WHL* BS5 ... 365 F2
South Lynn Gdns *SHPSTR* CV36 .. 25 F1 🔟
Southmead *CIR* GL7 .... 250 A8
Southmead La *RSTROUD/NAIL* GL6.. 188 E8
Southmead Rd
 BRSTK/PCHW BS34 .... 342 E7
 HNBRY/STHM BS10 .... 354 A6
 HNLZ/SM/SNYPK/WT BS9 ...... 353 K7
Southmead Wy
 HNBRY/STHM BS10 .... 354 B6
Southover Cl
 HNLZ/SM/SNYPK/WT BS9 ...... 353 J6
South Pde *ALMDB* BS32 .... 331 H8
Southover Av
 HNLZ/SM/SNYPK/WT BS9 ...... 352 E6
Southwood Cl *CIND* GL14 .... 151 F5
Southwood Dr
 HNLZ/SM/SNYPK/WT BS9 ...... 352 D6
Southwood Dr East
 HNLZ/SM/SNYPK/WT BS9 ...... 352 E6
Southwood La *CHELT* GL50 .... 4 A5
Sovereign Cha *RTEWK/TIB* GL19 .. 53 H7
Spa Gdns *TEWK* GL20 .... 34 A7
Spalding Cl *CBRISNE* BS2 .... 364 E3
Spaniorum Vw *THNB/SVB* BS35 .. 341 H4
Spark Hl *DSLY* GL11 .... 238 D8 🔟
Spar Rd *YATE/CS* BS37 .... 347 H4
Sparrow Hl *CLFD* GL16 .... 175 J3
Spartan Cl *GLE* GL4 .... 131 G8 🔟
Speculation Rd *CIND* GL14 .... 150 D3
Speech House Rd *CIND* GL14 ...... 150 C8

 CLFD GL16 .... 176 C3
Speedwell Rd *EVILLE/WHL* BS5 .. 176 B2
Speedwell Av *EVILLE/WHL* BS5 .. 365 H7 🔟
Speedwell Cl *GLE* GL4 .... 159 G1
 THNB/SVB BS35 .... 316 A1
Speedwell Rd *EVILLE/WHL* BS5 .. 365 K5
 KGWD/HNM BS15 .... 366 B1
Spencer Cl *BWTH/CHD* GL3 .... 131 H7
Spencer's Ct *THNB/SVB* BS35 .... 316 B8
Spenser Av *CHELTW* GL51 .... 105 J5
Spenser Rd *CHELTW* GL51 .... 105 J5
Sperringate *CIR* GL7 .... 249 K7 🔟
Spey Cl *THNB/SVB* BS35 .... 316 C5
 VGL GL2 .... 157 F4
Spider La *STROUD* GL5 .... 215 F8
Spillman's Pitch *STROUD* GL5 ... 214 C8 🔟
Spillman's Rd *STROUD* GL5 .... 214 C8
The Spindles *CHELTS* GL53 .... 134 A2
Spine Rd (East) *HGHW* SN6 .... 308 E3
Spine Rd West *CIR* GL7 .... 307 J4
Spinnaker Rd *VGL* GL2 .... 129 H6
Spinney Ct *STROUD* GL5 .... 243 H5 🔟
Spinney Rd *GLE* GL4 .... 131 F7
The Spinney *ALMDB* BS32 .... 343 J7
 CHELTE/BC GL52 .... 4 C1
 CIR GL7 .... 285 C2
 FRCTL/WBN BS36 .... 345 H7 🔟
Spires Vw *MANG/FISH* BS16 ...... 365 J1 🔟
Spire Wy *GLE* GL4 .... 131 F6
Spitalgate La *CIR* GL7 .... 249 J5
Spital La *HGHW* SN6 .... 310 E7
Spittle Leys *COTS* GL54 .... 62 D8
Splatt Br *VGL* GL2 .... 210 C4
Spout Hl *LYD* GL15 .... 232 C7
Spouthouse La *DSLY* GL11 .... 266 D1
Spout La *MTCHDN* GL17 .... 122 B7
Spratsgate La *CIR* GL7 .... 277 J2
 CIR GL7 .... 307 J1
Spread Eagle Rd *GL1* .... 2 C3 🔟
Springbank Cl *CHELTW* GL51 .... 105 H2
Springbank Dr *CHELTW* GL51 .... 105 H2
Springbank Gv *CHELTW* GL51 .... 105 H2
Springbank Rd *CHELTW* GL51 .... 105 H2
Springbank Wy *CHELTW* GL51 ... 105 H2
Spring Dl *RTEWK/TIB* GL19 .... 126 C4
Springdale Cl *VGL* GL2 .... 156 D6
Springfield *COTS* GL54 .... 143 H2
 DSLY GL11 .... 266 C2
 MIM GL56 .... 44 C3
 TEWK GL20 .... 33 J7
 THNB/SVB BS35 .... 316 C6 🔟
 VGL GL2 .... 156 E7
Springfield Av *HORF/LLZ* BS7 ... 364 D1
 MANG/FISH BS16 .... 357 C8
Springfield Cl *CHELTW* GL51 ..... 105 F7
 CLFD GL16 .... 176 C4
 MANG/FISH BS16 .... 357 C7 🔟
 SHPSTR CV36 .... 25 F2
Springfield Dr *CIND* GL14 .... 150 E4
Springfield La *BDWAY* WR12 .... 18 C5
Springfield Rd *CIR* GL7 .... 249 H8
 CIR GL7 .... 254 C1
 LYD GL15 .... 234 A2
 MANG/FISH BS16 .... 357 C8 🔟
 RDLND/MONT BS6 .... 364 B5 🔟
 SHPSTR CV36 .... 25 F2
 STROUD GL5 .... 213 K6 🔟
 STROUD GL5 .... 214 E6
Springfields *BRSTK/PCHW* BS34 .. 354 E4
 TET GL8 .... 302 D6
Springfields Ct *DSLY* GL11 .... 266 C2
Spring Gdns *LYD* GL15 .... 254 C1
 CIR GL7 .... 285 C2
Springhill *DSLY* GL11 .... 267 H2
Spring Hl *CBRISNE* BS2 .... 364 B6 🔟
 KGWD/HNM BS15 .... 366 E4
 RSTROUD/NAIL GL6 .... 270 D2
 STNHO GL10 .... 212 A6
Springhill Cl *RSTROUD/NAIL* GL6 .. 270 D2
Springhill Crs *RSTROUD/NAIL* GL6.. 270 D2
Springhill (Old Court) *DSLY* GL11 .. 267 F3 🔟
Spring La *CHELTE/BC* GL52 .... 84 A4
 CHELTE/BC GL52 .... 107 H1
 STROUD GL5 .... 214 E8
 STROUD GL5 .... 243 E8
Springlease *MANG/FISH* BS16 ... 357 C7
Spring Meadow Rd *LYD* GL15 .... 234 C1
The Springs *LYD* GL15 .... 234 A3 🔟
Springvale *COTS* GL54 .... 115 H6
Springville Cl
 OLD/WMLY/WICK BS30 .... 376 B3 🔟
Springwell Gdns *BWTH/CHD* GL3 .. 103 H7
Springwood Dr
 HNBRY/STHM BS10 .... 353 F3
Spruce Ride *CLFD* GL16 .... 177 J2
Spruce Rd *CLFD* GL16 .... 176 B2
Spruce Wy *BRSTK/PCHW* BS34 .. 342 C7 🔟
The Square *COTS* GL54 .... 88 C8
 LYD GL15 .... 231 F1 🔟
 MTCHDN GL17 .... 121 H6
 STROUD GL5 .... 214 E6 🔟
Squires Cl *RSTROUD/NAIL* GL6 .. 244 E3
Squires Ct
 OLD/WMLY/WICK BS30 .... 376 A3 🔟
Squires Leaze *THNB/SVB* BS35 .. 316 D4

The Squires *BDWAY* WR12 .... 17 K4 🔟
Squirrel Cl *VGL* GL2 .... 156 E7
Stadium Rd *RDLND/MONT* BS6 .. 364 A1
Stafford Cl *CLFD* GL16 .... 176 B3 🔟
Stafford Crs *THNB/SVB* BS35 .... 316 B5
Stafford Rd *CBRISNE* BS2 .... 364 E4 🔟
Staffords Ct
 OLD/WMLY/WICK BS30 .... 367 G8 🔟
Stag Hl *LYD* GL15 .... 206 A3
Staites Orch *GLE* GL4 .... 159 G7
Stamage's La *RSTROUD/NAIL* GL6.. 187 C7
Stambourne La *BRKLY* GL13 ...... 236 A6
Stamp's Meadow *VGL* GL2 .... 130 B1 🔟
Stanborough La *COTS* GL54 .... 112 D7
Stanbridge Cl *MANG/FISH* BS16 .. 357 F8 🔟
Stanbridge Rd *MANG/FISH* BS16 .. 357 F8
Stanbury Av *MANG/FISH* BS16 .. 366 B1
Stanbury Ms *BWTH/CHD* GL3 ..... 131 H8
Stancombe La *COTS* GL54 .... 62 E8
Stancombe Vw *COTS* GL54 .... 62 E8
Standfast Rd *HNBRY/STHM* BS10.. 353 H3
Standish Av *BRSTK/PCHW* BS34 .. 343 F5
Standish Cl *HNBRY/STHM* BS10 .. 353 H5 🔟
Standish La *VGL* GL2 .... 184 C3
Standle La *DSLY* GL11 .... 265 J4
Standon Wy
 HNBRY/STHM BS10 .... 354 A4 🔟
Stanfield Cl *HORF/LLZ* BS7 .... 354 E8 🔟
Stanford Cl *FRCTL/WBN* BS36 ... 345 F6
Stanford Rd *LYD* GL15 .... 233 K3
 TEWK GL20 .... 34 D6
Stanhope Rd
 OLD/WMLY/WICK BS30 .... 376 A4
Stank La *VGL* GL2 .... 156 C8
Stanleigh Ter *VGL* GL2 .... 101 G7
Stanley Av *BRSTK/PCHW* BS34 .. 355 F4
 HORF/LLZ BS7 .... 364 C3
Stanley Cha *EVILLE/WHL* BS5 ... 365 H4
Stanley Crs *BRSTK/PCHW* BS34 .. 355 F4
Stanley Gdns
 OLD/WMLY/WICK BS30 .... 376 C2
Stanley Md *ALMDB* BS32 .... 343 J4 🔟
Stanley Pk *EVILLE/WHL* BS5 .... 365 F5
Stanley Park Rd *MANG/FISH* BS16.. 366 E3
Stanley Pl *CHELTW* GL51 .... 105 H3 🔟
Stanley Rd *CHELTE/BC* GL52 .... 5 F4
 GL GL1 .... 130 A3
 KGWD/HNM BS15 .... 367 H5
 RDLND/MONT BS6 .... 364 A4
Stanley Ter *GL2* .... 2 C6 🔟
The Stanley *GLE* GL4 .... 159 H4
Stanley Vw *STROUD* GL5 .... 242 B1
Stanley Wk *GLE* GL4 .... 159 H5
Stanmoor *GLE* GL4 .... 159 F3
Stansby Crs *BWTH/CHD* GL3 ..... 103 J8
Stanshawe Crs *YATE/CS* BS37 .. 347 G5
Stanshawes Dr *YATE/CS* BS37 .. 347 F5
Stanshaw Rd *MANG/FISH* BS16 .. 356 A7
Stanshaws Cl *BRSTK/PCHW* BS34.. 343 F4
Stanthill Dr *DSLY* GL11 .... 267 F6
Stanton Cl *KGWD/HNM* BS15 .... 367 F5
Stanton Dr *CHELTW* GL51 .... 82 A7
Stanton Rd *HNBRY/STHM* BS10 .. 354 C5
 STROUD GL5 .... 214 A6
 TEWK GL20 .... 33 J7
Stanton Wy *CHELTW* GL51 .... 105 J6 🔟
Stantway La *CIND* GL14 .... 154 A6
Stanway OLD/WMLY/WICK* BS30.. 376 C5
Stanway Rd *BDWAY* WR12 .... 40 B5
 CHELTW GL51 .... 105 H6
 GLE GL4 .... 130 E7
Stanway Wood Dr
 CHELTE/BC GL52 .... 82 E2 🔟
Stanwick Crs *CHELTW* GL51 ..... 106 B1 🔟
Stanwick Dr *CHELTW* GL51 ...... 106 B1
Stanwick Gdns *CHELTW* GL51 .. 106 B2
Staple Grove Crs
 EVILLE/WHL BS5 .... 366 A7 🔟
Staplehill Rd *MANG/FISH* BS16 .. 366 B2
Staples Rd *YATE/CS* BS37 .... 347 H4 🔟
Stapleton Cl *MANG/FISH* BS16 .. 365 H1 🔟
Stapleton Rd *EVILLE/WHL* BS5 .. 365 G3
Star Barn Rd *FRCTL/WBN* BS36 .. 344 E7
Star Hl *RSTROUD/NAIL* GL6 .... 270 C1
Star La *MANG/FISH* BS16 .... 365 K3
 TET GL8 .... 272 B7
Starling Ct *STNHO* GL10 .... 213 G6 🔟
Station Av *MANG/FISH* BS16 ..... 366 A2
Station Cl *BWTH/CHD* GL3 .... 132 B1
 OLD/WMLY/WICK BS30 .... 367 J6
 YATE/CS BS37 .... 348 B6
Station Dr *TEWK* GL20 .... 13 K8
Station La *HORF/LLZ* BS7 .... 364 C2
 MTCHDN GL17 .... 124 B4
 TEWK GL20 .... 33 J7
Station Rd *AVONM* BS11 .... 352 A8
 BAD GL9 .... 351 F6
 BDWAY WR12 .... 18 B5
 BRKLY GL13 .... 236 A8
 BRKLY GL13 .... 364 A2
 BRSG/KWL/STAPK BS4 .... 374 C4
 BRSTK/PCHW BS34 .... 343 G4
 BRSTK/PCHW BS34 .... 354 E3
 BRSTK/PCHW BS34 .... 355 F3
 BWTH/CHD GL3 .... 132 A2

CHCAM GL55 .... 21 G2
CHELTE/BC GL52 .... 83 G2
CHEP NP16 .... 288 A6
CHNTN OX7 .... 118 E5
CHNTN OX7 .... 119 F3
CIND GL14 .... 180 B1
CIR GL7 .... 276 B7
CIR GL7 .... 278 E7
CIR GL7 .... 285 H1
CLFD GL16 .... 176 A7
COTS GL54 .... 115 H7
COTS GL54 .... 137 J2
DSLY GL11 .... 266 E1
EVE WR11 .... 6 B1
EVE WR11 .... 14 E6
EVE WR11 .... 15 H1
FRCTL/WBN BS36 .... 356 E2
FRCTL/WBN BS36 .... 357 J1
GL GL1 .... 2 C3
GL GL1 .... 3 D4
HNBRY/STHM BS10 .... 353 C3
HORF/LLZ BS7 .... 364 D2
KEYN BS31 .... 375 K8
KGWD/HNM BS15 .... 367 F3
LYD GL15 .... 234 A5
LYD GL15 .... 260 D3
MANG/FISH BS16 .... 366 A2
MIM GL56 .... 44 C3
MIM GL56 .... 46 A8
OLD/WMLY/WICK BS30 .... 367 J7
RDLND/MONT BS6 .... 364 B4
RSTROUD/NAIL GL6 .... 270 D2
STROUD GL5 .... 242 C5
TEWK GL20 .... 33 J7
TEWK GL20 .... 36 E2
THNB/SVB BS35 .... 328 B8
THNB/SVB BS35 .... 341 H2
WUE GL12 .... 319 J8
WUE GL12 .... 319 J1
YATE/CS BS37 .... 345 K3
YATE/CS BS37 .... 346 E4
YATE/CS BS37 .... 357 H1
Station St CHELT GL50 .... 4 A3
CIND GL14 .... 150 E5
TEWK GL20 .... 33 H8
Station Ter CIND GL14 .... 150 E5
Station Wy MANG/FISH BS16 .... 366 A2
Staunton CI GLE GL4 .... 159 G2 [11]
Staunton Rd CLFD GL16 .... 174 E1
CLFD GL16 .... 175 G2
Staveley Crs HNBRY/STHM BS10 ... 354 A4
Staverton Connection
CHELTW GL51 .... 104 D5
Stavordale Gv HGRV/WHIT BS14 .... 374 A3
Staynes Crs KGWD/HNM BS15 ...... 366 E6 [2]
Steam Mills Rd CIND GL14 .... 150 D2
Stean Bridge Rd ALMDB BS32 ...... 343 J8
Steel Av LYD GL15 .... 234 B3
Steel Ct OLD/WMLY/WICK BS30 .... 376 A3
Steeple CI GLE GL4 .... 131 F6 [8]
Steeple Vw LYD GL15 .... 234 A4 [8]
Steep La CHEP NP16 .... 288 A6
Stella Wy CHELTE/BC GL52 .... 82 D2
Stenders Rd MTCHDN GL17 .... 123 C5
The Stephens STROUD GL5 .... 123 F5
Stephens Dr
OLD/WMLY/WICK BS30 .... 376 A1
Stephens PI CLFD GL16 .... 176 B3
Stephen St EVILLE/WHL BS5 .... 365 C6
Stepney Rd EVILLE/WHL BS5 .... 365 C5
Stepney Wk EVILLE/WHL BS5 .... 365 C5
Stepping Stone La
RSTROUD/NAIL GL6 .... 187 C8
Steps CI DSLY GL11 .... 238 D8 [4]
Step's La TET GL8 .... 272 A3
Stepstairs La CIR GL7 .... 249 K7
Sterling CI COTS GL54 .... 92 D6
Sterling Ct CHELTW GL51 .... 106 B4 [8]
Sterncourt Rd MANG/FISH BS16 ... 356 A7
Sterrys Rd RWYE HR9 .... 72 A6
Stevans CI VGL GL2 .... 130 C1 [1]
Stevens Wk ALMDB BS32 .... 343 H6
Stevens Wy RSTROUD/NAIL GL6 ... 270 B5
Steward Rd TEWK GL20 .... 34 D6
Stewarts Mill La GLE GL4 .... 159 C2
St Giles's Road TEWK GL20 .... 13 J8
Stibbs Ct
OLD/WMLY/WICK BS30 .... 376 A2 [8]
Stibbs HI EVILLE/WHL BS5 .... 366 A7
Sticky La VGL GL2 .... 156 E8
Stidcote La WUE GL12 .... 334 B3
Stidcot La WUE GL12 .... 333 J1
Stile Acres AVONM BS11 .... 352 C5
Stinchcombe YATE/CS BS37 .... 347 G5 [8]
Stirling Ct YATE/CS BS37 .... 347 F2 [2]
Stirling Rd
BRSG/KWL/STAPK BS4 .... 374 B3 [8]
Stirling Wy GL GL1 .... 157 H4
The Stirrup STROUD GL5 .... 213 K7
Stocken CI RSTROUD/NAIL GL6 ...... 270 A4 [8]
Stock HI THNB/SVB BS35 .... 315 F5
Stock La BRKLY GL13 .... 264 A3
Stockley Wy GLE GL4 .... 159 F8
The Stocks RSTROUD/NAIL GL6 ...... 213 K4

Stockton CI
OLD/WMLY/WICK BS30 .... 376 C3 [8]
Stockwell Av MANG/FISH BS16 ...... 357 G8
Stockwell La MANG/FISH BS16 .... 357 F7
Stockwell Dr MANG/FISH BS16 ...... 357 G8
Stockwell Gn CIND GL14 .... 150 E7
Stockwell La CHELTE/BC GL52 .... 83 K3
LYD GL15 .... 233 H6
Stockwells MIM GL56 .... 70 A1
Stockwood HI KEYN BS31 .... 375 H7
Stockwood Ms
BRSG/KWL/STAPK BS4 .... 374 E1 [8]
Stockwood Rd
BRSG/KWL/STAPK BS4 .... 374 E5
HGRV/WHIT BS14 .... 375 F8
Stoke Bridge Av
BRSTK/PCHW BS34 .... 343 H8
Stokefield CI THNB/SVB BS35 .... 316 B5
Stoke Gv
HNLZ/SM/SNYPK/WT BS9 .... 353 G8
Stoke Hamlet
HNLZ/SM/SNYPK/WT BS9 .... 353 H8 [1]
Stoke La BRSTK/PCHW BS34 .... 343 G6
HNLZ/SM/SNYPK/WT BS9 .... 353 H8 [2]
MANG/FISH BS16 .... 355 J7
Stokemead BRSTK/PCHW BS34 ..... 343 G6 [1]
Stoke Mdw ALMDB BS32 .... 343 H5
Stoke Paddock Rd
HNLZ/SM/SNYPK/WT BS9 .... 353 F8
Stoke Park CI CHELTE/BC GL52 ...... 83 F2 [1]
Stoke Park Ct CHELTE/BC GL52 ...... 82 E2
Stoke Rd CHELTE/BC GL52 .... 81 K1
CHELTE/BC GL52 .... 82 E2
Stokes Ct
OLD/WMLY/WICK BS30 .... 376 B2 [9]
Stokes Cft CBRIS/FH BS1 .... 364 C6
Stokes Rd TEWK GL20 .... 33 H6
Stoke View Rd
MANG/FISH BS16 .... 365 K3 [8]
Stone Br MIM GL56 .... 47 G1
Stonebridge Pk EVILLE/WHL BS5 .... 365 H4
Stonechat Av GLE GL4 .... 158 E1
Stonechat Gdns MANG/FISH BS16 .. 355 J8
Stone CI GLE GL4 .... 131 G7
Stonecote Rdg
RSTROUD/NAIL GL6 .... 244 B2
Stonecroft CI CHELTE/BC GL52 .... 82 E2 [8]
Stoneford La EVE WR11 .... 6 D4
Stonehenge Rd GLE GL4 .... 3 F6 [8]
Stonehill OLD/WMLY/WICK BS30 ... 375 K2
Stonehouse Ct COTS GL54 .... 91 J7 [8]
Stonelea La FRCTL/WBN BS36 .... 356 E2
Stonelea DSLY GL11 .... 266 E4
Stoneleigh CI CHELTS GL53 .... 134 D3 [8]
Stoneleigh Dr
OLD/WMLY/WICK BS30 .... 376 A1
The Stone Rd RTEWK/TIB GL19 .... 53 G8
Stones La HGHW SN6 .... 310 B5
Stoneville St CHELTW GL51 .... 4 A3
Stoney Cft OLD/WMLY/WICK BS30 .. 376 A3
Stoney Pool CIR GL7 .... 252 D8
Stoney Rd RWYE HR9 .... 72 A7
Stoney Stile Rd THNB/SVB BS35 .... 332 A1
Stony Riding RSTROUD/NAIL GL6 .. 244 D4
Stonnington Rd STNHO GL10 .... 713 F7
Stothard Rd HORF/LLZ BS7 .... 355 F7
Stottbury Rd HORF/LLZ BS7 .... 364 E3
Stoulgrove La CHEP NP16 .... 288 C2
Stoulton Gv HNBRY/STHM BS10 ... 353 J3 [8]
Stout Ct SHPSR CV36 .... 25 F1 [8]
Stourden CI MANG/FISH BS16 .... 356 A7 [8]
Stourton Dr
OLD/WMLY/WICK BS30 .... 376 A2
Stover Rd YATE/CS BS37 .... 346 C4
Stow Br COTS GL54 .... 115 K3
Stow Ct CHELTW GL51 .... 106 A5 [8]
Stowe La LYD GL15 .... 202 E4
Stowell Hill Rd WUE GL12 .... 317 H8
Stowell Ms GLE GL4 .... 131 F7
Stowe Rd LYD GL15 .... 202 D7
Stow Hill Rd WUE GL12 .... 317 G8
Stowick Crs AVONM BS11 .... 352 E5
Stow Rd CHNTN OX7 .... 118 C4
CIR GL7 .... 250 B2
MIM GL56 .... 69 K2
Strachans CI STROUD GL5 .... 214 C7
Stradbrook Av EVILLE/WHL BS5 ..... 366 B7
Stradling Rd AVONM BS11 .... 352 E4
Straight La RTEWK/TIB GL19 .... 53 H7
Straight St CBRISNE BS2 .... 364 D8 [7]
Strand La CIND GL14 .... 153 H7
Stratford CI VGL GL2 .... 157 J2 [8]
Stratford St EVE WR11 .... 7 J1
SHPSR CV36 .... 11 G1
STROUD GL5 .... 214 B6
Strathmore Rd HORF/LLZ BS7 .... 354 C8
Stratton Hts CIR GL7 .... 249 H1
Stratton Rd GL GL1 .... 3 D5
Stratton St CBRISNE BS2 .... 364 C6
Strawberry La CIR GL7 .... 281 J2
Strawbridge Rd
EVILLE/WHL BS5 .... 365 F7 [8]
Stream CI HNBRY/STHM BS10 .... 354 B3
Stream La NWNT GL18 .... 74 B4
Streamleaze THNB/SVB BS35 .... 316 C6

Streamside CHELTE/BC GL52 .... 83 F2 [8]
STROUD GL5 .... 214 E7 [8]
Stream Side MANG/FISH BS16 .... 357 F8
Streamside Rd YATE/CS BS37 .... 347 J3 [8]
The Stream MANG/FISH BS16 .... 356 B4
The Street BAD GL9 .... 339 J3
DSLY GL11 .... 239 J6
DSLY GL11 .... 268 B5
DSLY GL11 .... 296 B2
HGHW SN6 .... 281 K8
HGHW SN6 .... 310 B2
MALM SN16 .... 306 B6
RSTROUD/NAIL GL6 .... 270 B5
STNHO GL10 .... 240 E3
STROUD GL5 .... 242 C3
TET GL8 .... 323 J4
TET GL8 .... 326 B6
THNB/SVB BS35 .... 330 E3
THNB/SVB BS35 .... 332 B1
VGL GL2 .... 210 D3
Stretford Av EVILLE/WHL BS5 .... 365 H6 [8]
Stretford Rd EVILLE/WHL BS5 .... 365 H6
Strickland Rd CHELTE/BC GL52 .... 5 D5
Stride CI THNB/SVB BS35 .... 328 C8 [8]
Striguil Rd CHEP NP16 .... 288 A8
Stringer's CI STROUD GL5 .... 242 C2
Stringer's Dr STROUD GL5 .... 242 C1
Strode Common THNB/SVB BS35 ... 331 K1
Strode Gdns THNB/SVB BS35 .... 331 K1
Strongbow Rd CHEP NP16 .... 288 A8
Stroud Rd BRSTK/PCHW BS34 .... 342 C6
CIR GL7 .... 248 C6
GLE GL4 .... 2 C6
GLE GL4 .... 158 A4
RSTROUD/NAIL GL6 .... 187 F8
RSTROUD/NAIL GL6 .... 216 E5
RSTROUD/NAIL GL6 .... 270 D2
Stuart St EVILLE/WHL BS5 .... 365 G7
Studland Dr CHELTE/BC GL52 .... 107 J2
Stump La BWTH/CHD GL3 .... 131 K6
Stumpwell La WUE GL12 .... 296 B4
Sturden La MANG/FISH BS16 .... 356 C3
Sturmer CI YATE/CS BS37 .... 347 G2
Sturminster CI HGRV/WHIT BS14 ... 374 C8
Sturminster Rd HGRV/WHIT BS14 .. 374 C7
Sturmyes Rd RSTROUD/NAIL GL6 .. 244 E3
Sudbrook Wy GLE GL4 .... 158 D1
Sudeley Dr CIR GL7 .... 278 D8
Sudgrove Pk GLE GL4 .... 159 G1 [11]
Sudmeadow Rd VGL GL2 .... 129 H5
Suffolk CI TET GL8 .... 302 C5 [2]
Suffolk Pde CHELT GL50 .... 4 B6
Suffolk PI CIR GL7 .... 280 D7
Suffolk Sq CHELT GL50 .... 4 A5
Sugley La RSTROUD/NAIL GL6 .... 270 A4
Sulgrave CI GL GL1 .... 157 J5
Summer CI STROUD GL5 .... 215 G7
Summer Crs STROUD GL5 .... 215 G7
Summerfield CI CHELTW GL51 .... 105 K1 [8]
MIM GL56 .... 44 C3
Summerhayes
OLD/WMLY/WICK BS30 .... 376 E1 [8]
Summerhill Rd EVILLE/WHL BS5 ..... 365 K6
Summerhill Ter EVILLE/WHL BS5 ... 365 K7 [1]
Summerhouse La CHEP NP16 .... 312 B2 [8]
Summerland Dr BWTH/CHD GL3 .... 132 A1
Summerleaze KEYN BS31 .... 375 K7 [1]
LYD GL15 .... 234 A3
MANG/FISH BS16 .... 366 C3
Summerleaze Rd LYD GL15 .... 234 B4
Summers Dr
OLD/WMLY/WICK BS30 .... 369 J5
Summersfield CI
RSTROUD/NAIL GL6 .... 243 K8
Summersfield Rd
RSTROUD/NAIL GL6 .... 243 K7
Summers Md YATE/CS BS37 .... 347 G2
Summers Rd CBRISNE BS2 .... 364 E5 [17]
COTS GL54 .... 62 D8
Summer St STROUD GL5 .... 215 G7
Sundays HI ALMDB BS32 .... 342 E2
Sundayshill La BRKLY GL13 .... 293 F6
Sunderland Ct BWTH/CHD GL3 ...... 132 A1 [8]
Sundridge Pk YATE/CS BS37 .... 347 G6 [1]
Sun Green CI LYD GL15 .... 204 E5 [8]
Sun Green Rd LYD GL15 .... 204 E5
The Sunground TET GL8 .... 272 A5
Sunningdale YATE/CS BS37 .... 347 G6
Sunningdale Dr
OLD/WMLY/WICK BS30 .... 367 H8
Sunny Bank CLFD GL16 .... 175 J3 [8]
KGWD/HNM BS15 .... 366 B6
Sunnybank Rd CLFD GL16 .... 175 J3 [8]
Sunnycroft CI CHELTE/BC GL52 .... 83 G4
Sunnycroft Ms GLE GL4 .... 158 A1 [8]
Sunnydene BRSG/KWL/STAPK BS4 . 374 C2 [8]
Sunnyfield La CHELTW GL51 .... 133 G1
Sunnyfield Rd VGL GL2 .... 156 D6
Sunny HI
HNLZ/SM/SNYPK/WT BS9 .... 352 E7 [1]
Sunnyhill Dr AVONM BS11 .... 352 A8 [8]
Sunnymead CI MTCHDN GL17 .... 122 D6 [8]
Sunnyside FRCTL/WBN BS36 .... 345 H7 [8]
Sunnyside La MANG/FISH BS16 ...... 356 B4
YATE/CS BS37 .... 346 E3

Sunnyvale Dr
OLD/WMLY/WICK BS30 .... 376 C3
Sunny Wk KGWD/HNM BS15 .... 366 B5
Sunridge MANG/FISH BS16 .... 356 D8
Sunrise Gv BRSG/KWL/STAPK BS4 .... 374 C2
Sun Rise Rd LYD GL15 .... 204 E5
Sunset La CHELTE/BC GL52 .... 83 J6
Sunset Pl RTEWK/TIB GL19 .... 125 J3
Sun St CHELTW 4 A2
  TEWK GL20 .... 33 H7
Sun Tump LYD GL15 .... 204 E6
Surrey Av CHELTW GL51 .... 105 K4
Surrey Rd HORF/LLZ BS7 .... 364 C3
Surrey St CBRISNE BS2 .... 364 C6
Sussex Av CHELTW GL51 .... 106 A4
Sussex Gdns BWTH/CHD GL3 .... 131 K7
Sussex St CBRISNE BS2 .... 364 C6
Sutherland Av MANG/FISH BS16 .... 356 E7
  YATE/CS BS37 .... 347 F2
Sutton Av BRSG/KWL/STAPK BS4 .. 374 C2
Sutton Cl DSLY GL11 .... 267 F6
Sutton Rd CIND GL14 .... 151 H8
  CIND GL14 .... 179 F4
Swaish Dr OLD/WMLY/WICK BS30 .. 376 A3
Swallow Crs VGL GL2 .... 103 F8
Swallow Cft STNHO GL10 .... 211 K7
Swallow Dr BRSTK/PCHW BS34 .... 342 C6
Swallow Pk THNB/SVB BS35 .... 316 C5
Swallows St BRSTK/PCHW BS34 .... 355 J2
Swallowtail Cl CHELTW GL51 .... 105 H4
Swan Cl CIR GL7 .... 285 G2
  MIM GL56 .... 69 K1
Swane Rd HGRV/WHIT BS14 .... 374 E8
Swan La FRCTL/WBN BS36 .... 342 C6
  LYD GL15 .... 207 J3
Swanley La BRKLY GL13 .... 294 E1
Swanmoor Crs
  HNBRY/STHM BS10 .... 353 J2
Swan Rd GL GL1 .... 3 D2
  LYD GL15 .... 234 A3
Swanscombe Pl CHELTW GL51 ...... 133 J1
Swansfield CIR GL7 .... 257 H8
Swan St STROUD GL5 .... 214 E7
Swanswell Dr CHELTW GL51 .... 105 J6
Sweden La TEWK GL20 .... 36 E4
Sweetbriar Cl CHELTE/BC GL52 ...... 82 E2
Sweetbriar St GL GL1 .... 2 C2
Sweets Cl KGWD/HNM BS15 .... 366 E4
Sweets Rd KGWD/HNM BS15 .... 366 D4
Swells Hl STROUD GL5 .... 243 G5
Swift Rd GLE GL4 .... 159 F1
Swifts Hill Vw STROUD GL5 .... 215 G5
Swilgate Rd TEWK GL20 .... 57 H1
Swindon Cl CHELTW GL51 .... 4 A2
Swindon La CHELTW GL51 .... 82 B8
Swindon Rd CHELT GL50 .... 4 B3
  CHELTW GL51 .... 4 A2
  CHELTW GL51 .... 106 B1
  CIR GL7 .... 249 K6
  CIR GL7 .... 250 B8
  HGHW SN6 .... 310 E7
Swindon St CHELT GL50 .... 4 A2
Swinhay La WUE GL12 .... 295 J7
Swish La MTCHDN GL17 .... 122 J7
Swordfish Cl BWTH/CHD GL3 .... 132 K1
Swynford Cl CIR GL7 .... 283 F8
Sybil Rd GLE GL4 .... 130 B8
Sycamore Av CHEP NP16 .... 312 A1
Sycamore Cl EVILLE/WHL BS5 ...... 365 J5
  GL GL1 .... 157 G2
  KGWD/HNM BS15 .... 375 G3
Sycamore Dr BRSTK/PCHW BS34 .. 342 C7
  STROUD GL5 .... 215 F6
  THNB/SVB BS35 .... 316 C5
Sycamore Rd MTCHDN GL17 .... 122 D8
  TEWK GL20 .... 34 D6
Sydenham Hl RDLND/MONT BS6 .... 364 B5
Sydenham La RDLND/MONT BS6 .... 364 B5
Sydenham Rd CHELTE/BC GL52 ...... 5 D4
  RDLND/MONT BS6 .... 364 B5
Sydenham Rd South
  CHELTE/BC GL52 .... 5 D5
Sydenham Ter GL GL1 .... 2 C6
Sydenham Villas Rd
  CHELTE/BC GL52 .... 5 D5
Sydenham Wy KGWD/HNM BS15 .. 375 H3
Sydney STNHO GL10 .... 212 C5
Sylvan Cl CLFD GL16 .... 175 K5
Sylvan Wy
  HNLZ/SM/SNYPK/WT BS9 .... 352 D8
Symington Rd MANG/FISH BS16 .... 366 B5
Symn La WUE GL12 .... 297 F7
Synwell La WUE GL12 .... 297 G7
Syon Rd RSTROUD/NAIL GL6 .... 243 K8
Syston Cl KGWD/HNM BS15 .... 366 D5

T

Tabernacle Pitch WUE GL12 .... 297 F7
Tabernacle Rd KGWD/HNM BS15 .... 366 B5
  WUE GL12 .... 296 E6
Tabernacle Wk STROUD GL5 .... 242 D1

Tabrams Pitch
  RSTROUD/NAIL GL6 .... 270 E2
Tackley Rd EVILLE/WHL BS5 .... 365 F3
Tadwick La CBATH/BATHN BA1 ...... 379 H5
Tainmor Cl VGL GL2 .... 131 G1
Tait's Hl DSLY GL11 .... 266 A2
Tait's Hill Rd DSLY GL11 .... 266 B3
Talbot Av KGWD/HNM BS15 .... 366 B5
Talbot Ms GL GL1 .... 129 K8
Talbot Rd BRSG/KWL/STAPK BS4 .. 374 A4
  CHELTW GL51 .... 106 A6
Talbot Sq COTS GL54 .... 92 B6
Tallows Wk TET GL8 .... 302 C6
Talgarth Rd HORF/LLZ BS7 .... 364 D2
Tallard's Pl CHEP NP16 .... 288 C2
Tall Elms Cl BWTH/CHD GL3 .... 131 K1
Tallis Rd BWTH/CHD GL3 .... 103 H6
Tally Ho La COTS GL54 .... 112 C5
Tamar Cl THNB/SVB BS35 .... 316 D7
Tamarisk Cl CHELTW GL51 .... 134 A3
Tamar Rd BWTH/CHD GL3 .... 132 D8
  CBRISNE BS2 .... 365 G8
  CHELTE/BC GL52 .... 5 E3
Tamesis Dr CIR GL7 .... 276 D7
Tanglewood Wy
  RSTROUD/NAIL GL6 .... 244 B2
Tanhouse La YATE/CS BS37 .... 334 E7
Tankard's Cl CFTN/FAIL BS8 .... 364 A7
Tankards Hl MIM GL56 .... 23 G4
Tanner Cl OLD/WMLY/WICK BS30 .. 376 A1
Tanners Cl BWTH/CHD GL3 .... 132 C8
Tanner's La CHELTW GL51 .... 105 K3
  CHPMW/MSHF SN14 .... 371 J6
Tanner's Rd CHELTW GL51 .... 105 K3
The Tanyard
  OLD/WMLY/WICK BS30 .... 376 C4
Tapscott Cl WUE GL12 .... 296 E7
Tapsters OLD/WMLY/WICK BS30 .. 376 B2
Target Cl STROUD GL5 .... 215 H7
Tarlton Cl GLE GL4 .... 159 G2
Tarragon Pl ALMDB BS32 .... 343 K7
Tarrington Rd GL GL1 .... 3 D6
Tatchley La CHELTE/BC GL52 .... 5 F1
  CHELTE/BC GL52 .... 107 J2
Taunton Wk HORF/LLZ BS7 .... 354 E7
Taurus Cl VGL GL2 .... 130 B1
Tayberry Gv CHELTW GL51 .... 133 K2
Tayler Rd COTS GL54 .... 169 G4
Taylor Cl KGWD/HNM BS15 .... 367 F6
Taylors Gnd VGL GL2 .... 157 F4
Tayman Cl HNBRY/STHM BS10 .... 354 C8
Tayman Rdg
  OLD/WMLY/WICK BS30 .... 376 E6
Taynton Cl OLD/WMLY/WICK BS30 .. 376 C4
Teal Cl ALMDB BS32 .... 343 H4
  VGL GL2 .... 156 D5
Teasel Cl VGL GL2 .... 130 B1
Teasel Md ALMDB BS32 .... 343 J7
Teddington Gdns GLE GL4 .... 130 C8
Ted Preston Cl TEWK GL20 .... 57 J2
Teewell Av MANG/FISH BS16 .... 366 E2
Teewell Cl MANG/FISH BS16 .... 366 E2
Teewell Hl MANG/FISH BS16 .... 366 E2
Telephone Av CBRIS/FH BS1 .... 364 B8
Telford's Br VGL GL2 .... 129 H2
Telford Wk EVILLE/WHL BS5 .... 366 A5
Teme Rd CHELTE/BC GL52 .... 5 E3
Templar Rd YATE/CS BS37 .... 347 G5
Temple Back CBRIS/FH BS1 .... 364 C8
Temple Cir GLE GL4 .... 131 C6
  LYD GL15 .... 233 K3
Templefields COTS GL54 .... 137 H3
Temple Rose St CBRIS/FH BS1 .... 364 C8
Temple St CBRIS/FH BS1 .... 364 C8
Temple Wy CBRIS/FH BS1 .... 364 C8
Templeway LYD GL15 .... 233 K4
Templeway West LYD GL15 .... 233 J3
Tenby St EVILLE/WHL BS5 .... 365 F7
Tennessee Gv
  RDLND/MONT BS6 .... 364 A1
Tenniscourt Rd KGWD/HNM BS15 .. 367 G5
Tennyson Av VGL GL2 .... 157 J2
Tennyson Cl KEYN BS31 .... 376 A8
Tennyson Rd CHELTW GL51 .... 105 K5
  DSLY GL11 .... 267 G3
  HORF/LLZ BS7 .... 364 C1
Tensing Rd CHELTS GL53 .... 134 D2
Tenth Av HORF/LLZ BS7 .... 355 F5
Tereslake Gn HNBRY/STHM BS10 .. 354 B2
Tern Cl GLE GL4 .... 130 E8
Terrell Gdns EVILLE/WHL BS5 ...... 365 H7
Terrell St CBRISNE BS2 .... 364 B6
Terry Ruck Cl CHELTW GL51 .... 105 H4
Tetbury Cl BRSTK/PCHW BS34 ...... 343 G6
Tetbury Hl TET GL8 .... 272 A6
Tetbury La MALM SN16 .... 304 D8
  RSTROUD/NAIL GL6 .... 270 E4
  RSTROUD/NAIL GL6 .... 271 D7
  TET GL8 .... 323 J3
Tetbury Rd CIR GL7 .... 249 F8
  GLE GL4 .... 158 A5
  KGWD/HNM BS15 .... 366 B6
Tetbury St RSTROUD/NAIL GL6 .... 243 J8
  CHELTW GL51 .... 81 H8
Tewkesbury Rd CBRISNE BS2 ...... 364 E1
  CHELTW GL51 .... 106 A2
  COTS GL54 .... 92 A5
  NWNT GL18 .... 73 J5
  TEWK GL20 .... 34 A5
  VGL GL2 .... 3 D1
  VGL GL2 .... 102 B8
  VGL GL2 .... 130 B1
Thackeray Wk HORF/LLZ BS7 ...... 354 E6
Thames Cl WUE GL12 .... 319 J2
Thames La HGHW SN6 .... 310 E6
Thames Pth CIR GL7 .... 276 A3
  CIR GL7 .... 285 F3
  HGHW SN6 .... 311 F6
Thames Rd CHELTE/BC GL52 .... 5 E5
Thames St CIR GL7 .... 285 C3
Thames Vw HGHW SN6 .... 308 D6
Thatchers Cl EVILLE/WHL BS5 ...... 366 B7
Thatchers End CHELTE/BC GL52 .... 83 H3
Theescombe Hl STROUD GL5 .... 242 D8
The High Gv CHELTE/BC GL52 ...... 82 E3
Theocs Cl TEWK GL20 .... 57 G2
There-and-back-again La
  CFTN/FAIL BS8 .... 364 A7
Theresa Av HORF/LLZ BS7 .... 364 C2
Theresa St GL GL1 .... 2 B6
Thessaly Rd CIR GL7 .... 249 G2
Theyer Cl BWTH/CHD GL3 .... 160 C1
Thicket Av MANG/FISH BS16 .... 366 C8
Thicket Rd MANG/FISH BS16 .... 366 C2
Thicket Wk THNB/SVB BS35 .... 316 C5
Thickwood La
  CHPMW/MSHF SN14 .... 373 J8
Thiery Rd BRSG/KWL/STAPK BS4 .. 374 B4
Thingwall Pk MANG/FISH BS16 .... 365 J3
Third Av DSLY GL11 .... 267 G6
  HORF/LLZ BS7 .... 354 E5
Thirlestaine Rd CHELTS GL53 .... 4 B6
Thirlmere Ct
  OLD/WMLY/WICK BS30 .... 367 K8
Thirlmere Rd
  BRSTK/PCHW BS34 .... 342 E6
  CHELTW GL51 .... 105 J7
Thistledown Cl CHELTW GL51 ...... 105 H2
Thistle Downs TEWK GL20 .... 34 C5
Thomas Av MANG/FISH BS16 .... 357 H5
Thomas Moore Cl
  BWTH/CHD GL3 .... 103 J6
Thomas Pring Wk
  EVILLE/WHL BS5 .... 366 A5
Thomas Stock Gdns GLE GL4 .... 131 G8
Thomas St CBRISNE BS2 .... 364 C6
  CHEP NP16 .... 288 A6
  CIR GL7 .... 249 J5
  GL GL1 .... 3 D5
Thomas St North
  RDLND/MONT BS6 .... 364 B5
Thomond Cl CHELTW GL51 .... 4 A1
Thompson Dr CHELTS GL53 .... 134 D2
Thompson Rd CIR GL7 .... 278 D2
  HGRV/WHIT BS14 .... 374 D8
  STROUD GL5 .... 215 F6
Thompson Wy VGL GL2 .... 103 F8
Thomson Rd EVILLE/WHL BS5 ...... 365 F6
Thoresby Cl CHELT GL50 .... 106 E1
Thoresby Av GL GL1 .... 157 J5
Thornbury Cl CHELTW GL51 .... 106 B4
Thornbury Rd THNB/SVB BS35 .... 332 A1
Thorncliffe Dr CHELTW GL51 .... 106 B6
Thorn Cl YATE/CS BS37 .... 347 F5
Thornhaugh Ms CHELTW GL51 .... 133 J1
Thornhayes Cl
  FRCTL/WBN BS36 .... 345 G6
Thornhill Ct GL GL1 .... 157 K1
The Thornhills MANG/FISH BS16 .. 356 B8
Thornleigh Rd HORF/LLZ BS7 ...... 364 C1
Thornmead Gv
  HNBRY/STHM BS10 .... 353 J4
Thorns Farm YATE/CS BS37 .... 347 G5
Thorn Tree Dr CHEP NP16 .... 312 B2
Thornwell Rd CHEP NP16 .... 312 B1
Thornycroft Cl HORF/LLZ BS7 ...... 355 F7
Threadneedle St STROUD GL5 ...... 214 E7
Three Ashes La NWNT GL18 .... 73 J3
Three Queens' La CBRIS/FH BS1 .. 364 C8
Three Sisters La CHELTE/BC GL52 .. 107 K3
Thrissell St EVILLE/WHL BS5 .... 364 E6
Thrupp La STROUD GL5 .... 243 H4
  STROUD GL5 .... 243 F1
Thrush Cl GLE GL4 .... 130 E8
Thurlow Rd EVILLE/WHL BS5 .... 365 G4
Thurstons Barton
  EVILLE/WHL BS5 .... 365 J5
Tibberton KGWD/HNM BS15 .... 367 G6
Tibberton Gv CHELTW GL51 .... 105 F7
Tibberton La RTEWK/TIB GL19 ...... 125 K2
Tibbiwell La RSTROUD/NAIL GL6 .. 187 H6
Tiberius Av LYD GL15 .... 234 B2
Tichborne Rd EVILLE/WHL BS5 .... 365 C2
Tide Gv AVONM BS11 .... 352 C6
Tidenham Wy BRSTK/PCHW BS34 .. 342 D5
Tidswell Cl VGL GL2 .... 157 F6
Tilling Rd HNBRY/STHM BS10 ...... 354 C7
Tilling Wk HNBRY/STHM BS10 ...... 354 C7
Tillis Vw CLFD GL16 .... 174 D1
Tilney Rd CHELT GL50 .... 4 B1

Tilnor Crs *DSLY* GL11 .... 266 D2
Tilsdown *DSLY* GL11 .... 266 D2
Tilsdown Cl *DSLY* GL11 .... 266 C2
Tilting Rd *THNB/SVB* BS35 .... 316 B4
Timbercombe La *CHELTS* GL53 ..... 135 H3
Timber Dene *MANG/FISH* BS16 ...... 365 H2
Timbrells Cl *CIR* GL7 .... 278 D2
Timmis Cl *GLE* GL4 .... 158 E2 ⑨
Timms Gn *BDWAY* WR12 .... 18 E2
Timperley Wy *CHELTW* GL51 .... 133 H1
Tindell Ct
    OLD/WMLY/WICK BS30 .... 376 A2 ⑲
Tinglesfield *CIR* GL7 .... 249 H2
Tinker's Cl *MIM* GL56 .... 70 A1
Tinkley La *STNHO* GL10 .... 240 E8
Tinmans Gn *MONM* NP25 .... 174 B6 ⑪
Tintern Av *EVILLE/WHL* BS5 .... 365 H6 ⑪
Tintern Cl *OLD/WMLY/WICK* BS30 .. 367 F8 ⑫
Tintern Rd *GLE* GL4 .... 157 K3
Tippetts Rd *KGWD/HNM* BS15 ...... 366 D8
Tirle Bank Wy *TEWK* GL20 .... 34 A8
Tirlebrookgra *TEWK* GL20 .... 35 F3
Tirley Cl *VGL* GL2 .... 156 E5
Tirley St *RTEWK/TIB* GL19 .... 55 C8
Tiverton Cl *CHELTW* GL51 .... 105 H3 ⑧
Tiverton Wk *MANG/FISH* BS16 ...... 366 A4
Tivoli La *CHELT* GL50 .... 4 A6
Tivoli Ms *CHELT* GL50 .... 4 A6 ⑧
Tivoli Rd *CHELT* GL50 .... 4 A6
Tivoli St *CHELT* GL50 .... 4 A6
Tivoli Wk *CHELT* GL50 .... 106 B6 ⑧
Toadsmoor Rd
    RSTROUD/NAIL GL6 .... 243 K5
Tobacco Cl *COTS* GL54 .... 85 H2 ⑪
Tobacconist Rd
    RSTROUD/NAIL GL6 .... 243 J8
Tobyfield Cl *CHELTE/BC* GL52 .... 83 G3
Tobyfield La *CHELTE/BC* GL52 .... 83 F3 ⑪
Tobyfield Rd *CHELTE/BC* GL52 .... 83 G3
Tockington La *ALMDB* BS32 .... 330 C8
Tockington Park La
    THNB/SVB BS35 .... 331 J6
Toghill La *OLD/WMLY/WICK* BS30 .. 369 J5
Toll Down Wy
    CHPMW/MSHF SN14 .... 363 G3
Tolsey La *TEWK* GL20 .... 33 H8
Tommy Taylor's La *CHELT* GL50 .... 4 B1
Tom Price Cl *CHELTE/BC* GL52 ...... 4 C4 ⑫
Tone Dr *BWTH/CHD* GL3 .... 160 D1
Tooke Rd *RSTROUD/NAIL* GL6 .... 243 G7
Top Rd *CIND* GL14 .... 179 F5
    CIR GL7 .... 282 E7
Torchacre Ri *DSLY* GL11 .... 266 E5
Tormarton Crs
    HNBRY/STHM BS10 .... 353 H2
Tormarton Rd *BAD* GL9 .... 362 E1
    CHPMW/MSHF SN14 .... 372 A1
Toronto Rd *HORF/LLZ* BS7 .... 354 E6
Torrance Cl
    OLD/WMLY/WICK BS30 .... 367 K8
Tortworth Rd *HORF/LLZ* BS7 .... 364 C1
Totterdown La *CIR* GL7 .... 282 E1
Touching End La
    CHPMW/MSHF SN14 .... 371 K6 ②
Touchstone Av
    BRSTK/PCHW BS34 .... 355 J1
Tower Cl *GLE* GL4 .... 131 F6
Tower Hl *CBRISNE* BS2 .... 364 C7
Tower House Dr *RTEWK/TIB* GL19 .. 52 D3
Tower La *CBRIS/FH* BS1 .... 364 B7
    OLD/WMLY/WICK BS30 .... 367 G8
Tower Rd *KGWD/HNM* BS15 .... 366 C5
    LYD GL15 .... 206 B3
Tower Rd North *KGWD/HNM* BS15 . 367 H6
Tower Rd South
    OLD/WMLY/WICK BS30 .... 367 G8
Tower St *CBRIS/FH* BS1 .... 364 C8 ⑦
    CIR GL7 .... 249 K6
Townsend *ALMDB* BS32 .... 342 D2
    MTCHDN GL17 .... 121 H7
    MTCHDN GL17 .... 123 C4
Townsend Cl *LYD* GL15 .... 231 C1
Townsend St *CHELT* GL51 .... 4 A2
Tozers Hl *BRSC/KWL/STAPK* BS4 .. 374 B4 ⑪
T Parkside Cl *BWTH/CHD* GL3 ...... 103 H8
Trafalgar Dr *BWTH/CHD* GL3 .... 103 H8
Trafalgar Rd *CIR* GL7 .... 249 J4 ②
Trafalgar St *CHELT* GL50 .... 4 B5 ⑩
Trajan Cl *GLE* GL4 .... 131 H8 ⑦
The Tram Rd *CLFD* GL16 .... 175 J4
Tramway Rd
    BRSG/KWL/STAPK BS4 .... 374 B3
    CIND GL14 .... 178 E2
Tranmere Av *HNBRY/STHM* BS10 .. 353 J2
Tranmere Gv *HNBRY/STHM* BS10 .. 353 J3
Tranton La *THNB/SVB* BS35 .... 292 C2
Tratman Wk
    HNBRY/STHM BS10 .... 353 H3 ⑦
Travers Wk *BRSTK/PCHW* BS34 ..... 355 J1
Tredegar Rd *MANG/FISH* BS16 ...... 366 B3
Tredworth Rd *GL* GL1 .... 3 D6
Treefield Pl *CBRISNE* BS2 .... 364 E4 ⑱
Treelands Cl *CHELTS* GL53 .... 134 D1
Treelands Dr *CHELTS* GL53 .... 134 D1
Tree Leaze *YATE/CS* BS37 .... 347 H4

Trelawney Av *EVILLE/WHL* BS5 .. 365 H6 ⑫
Trelawney Pk
    BRSG/KWL/STAPK BS4 .... 374 C3
Trelawney Rd *RDLND/MONT* BS6 ... 364 A5
Trenchard Gdns *CIR* GL7 .... 278 D3
Trenchard St *CBRIS/FH* BS1 .... 364 A8
Trench La *ALMDB* BS32 .... 343 H5
    FRCTL/WBN BS36 .... 343 K4
Trendlewood Pk *MANG/FISH* BS16.. 365 J2
Trenerry Rd *DSLY* GL11 .... 239 K7
Trent Dr *THNB/SVB* BS35 .... 316 D7
Trentham Cl *CBRISNE* BS2 .... 364 E4 ⑰
Trent Rd *BWTH/CHD* GL3 .... 160 D1
Tresham Cl *ALMDB* BS32 .... 343 H4
Tretawn Gdns *TEWK* GL20 .... 34 A8
Trevelyan Wk
    HNBRY/STHM BS10 .... 353 H3 ③
Treverdowe Wk
    HNBRY/STHM BS10 .... 353 F3
Trevethin Cl *KGWD/HNM* BS15 ..... 366 C7 ⑪
Trevisa Crs *BRKLY* GL13 .... 264 A3
Trevisa Gv *HNBRY/STHM* BS10 ..... 354 A2
Trevor Rd *BWTH/CHD* GL3 .... 131 H8
Trewsbury Rd *CIR* GL7 .... 247 K8
The Triangle *VGL* GL2 .... 130 E3
Tribune Pl *GLE* GL4 .... 131 G8
Trident Cl *MANG/FISH* BS16 .... 357 C5
Trier Wy *GL* GL1 .... 2 C5
Trinity Ct *RSTROUD/NAIL* GL6 ...... 243 K8
Trinity La *CHELTE/BC* GL52 .... 4 C3 ⑫
Trinity Rd *CBRISNE* BS2 .... 364 E7
    CIR GL7 .... 249 J7
    GLE GL4 .... 131 H8
    MTCHDN GL17 .... 122 D8
    STROUD GL5 .... 215 F8 ⑧
Trinity St *CBRISNE* BS2 .... 364 E7
    TEWK GL20 .... 33 H8
Trinity Wk *CBRISNE* BS2 .... 364 D7
Trinity Wy *CIND* GL14 .... 151 F5
Troon *YATE/CS* BS37 .... 347 G6
Troon Dr
    OLD/WMLY/WICK BS30 .... 367 H8 ⑤
Troopers' Hill Rd *EVILLE/WHL* BS5 365 K8
Trotman Av *DSLY* GL11 .... 266 D1
Troughton Pl *TEWK* GL20 .... 33 H8
Trowbridge Rd
    HNBRY/STHM BS10 .... 354 A5
Trowbridge Wk
    HNBRY/STHM BS10 .... 354 A5 ②
Trubshaw Ct *BWTH/CHD* GL3 .... 132 A1
Tryes Rd *CHELT* GL50 .... 106 C8
Trygrove *GLE* GL4 .... 131 F8 ⑧
Trym Rd *HNLZ/SM/SNYPK/WT* BS9 . 353 J7
Trymwood Cl *HNBRY/STHM* BS10... 353 H4
Tucker St *CBRISNE* BS2 .... 364 D7 ⑬
Tuckett La *MANG/FISH* BS16 .... 356 C7 ②
Tuckwell Rd *CIR* GL7 .... 283 G8
Tudor Cl *OLD/WMLY/WICK* BS30 .. 376 D3
Tudor Lodge Dr *CHELT* GL50 .... 4 A6
Tudor Pl *TEWK* GL20 .... 57 J2
Tudor Rd *CBRISNE* BS2 .... 364 D5 ⑭
    CIR GL7 .... 250 A5 ②
    EVILLE/WHL BS5 .... 365 C5
    KGWD/HNM BS15 .... 375 H1
Tudor St *GL* GL1 .... 129 J8
Tudor Wk *CLFD* GL16 .... 147 J8 ⑬
Tuffley Av *GL* GL1 .... 129 J8
Tuffley Crs *GL* GL1 .... 157 K1
Tuffley La *GL* GL1 .... 157 J3
Tuffley Rd *HNBRY/STHM* BS10 ..... 354 A6
Tufthorn Av *CLFD* GL16 .... 175 K5 ⑦
Tufthorn Cl *CLFD* GL16 .... 176 A6
Tufthorn Rd *CLFD* GL16 .... 176 A7
Tufton Av *AVONM* BS11 .... 352 C6
Tug Wilson Close *TEWK* GL20 .... 34 D4 ⑪
The Tulworths *VGL* GL2 .... 130 D1 ⑧
Tunacre *VGL* GL2 .... 100 D8
Tuners La *MALM* SN16 .... 304 E8
Tuners Cl *CHELTW* GL51 .... 105 J6
Turley Rd *EVILLE/WHL* BS5 .... 365 H5 ⑧
Turnberry
    OLD/WMLY/WICK BS30 .... 367 H8 ⑫
Turnbridge Rd *HNBRY/STHM* BS10. 354 A2
Turnbury Crs *YATE/CS* BS37 .... 347 G6
Turner Gdns *HORF/LLZ* BS7 .... 355 F8 ⑧
Turner Rd *DSLY* GL11 .... 266 C2
Turners *VGL* GL2 .... 128 D2
Turners Ct
    OLD/WMLY/WICK BS30 .... 376 A2 ⑳
Turnpike Av *WUE* GL12 .... 297 G8 ⑧
Turnpike Cl *YATE/CS* BS37 .... 347 G4 ⑪
Turnpike End *CHEP* NP16 .... 312 D2
Turnpike Ga *WUE* GL12 .... 319 J8
Turnstone Dr *VGL* GL2 .... 156 D5
Turville Dr *HORF/LLZ* BS7 .... 354 E8
Tusculum Wy *MTCHDN* GL17 .... 123 G4
Tutnalls St *LYD* GL15 .... 234 B3
Tweed Cl *THNB/SVB* BS35 .... 316 C6
Tweenbrook Av *GL* GL1 .... 130 A8
Twenty La *OLD/WMLY/WICK* BS30 . 367 K8
The Twenties *CIR* GL7 .... 278 A2
Twenty Acres Rd
    HNBRY/STHM BS10 .... 354 A4 ⑦
Twickenham Rd
    RDLND/MONT BS6 .... 364 A1 ④

Twinberrow La *DSLY* GL11 .... 267 F7
Twixtbears *TEWK* GL20 .... 33 H7 ⑪
Two Hedges Rd *CHELTE/BC* GL52 .... 83 G3
Two Mile Ct *KGWD/HNM* BS15 ..... 366 B6 ⑬
Twomile Hill Rd *KGWD/HNM* BS15 . 366 B6
Two Mile La *VGL* GL2 .... 128 B2
Twyning Rd *UUSV* WR8 .... 12 E3
The Twynings *KGWD/HNM* BS15 ... 366 E4
Twyver Bank *GLE* GL4 .... 159 H3
Twyver Cl *GLE* GL4 .... 159 H3
Tybalt Wy *BRSTK/PCHW* BS34 ...... 355 J1
Tylea Cl *CHELTW* GL51 .... 105 G7
Tyler Cl *KGWD/HNM* BS15 .... 366 E8
Tyler's La *MANG/FISH* BS16 .... 366 D1 ⑳
Tyler St *CBRISNE* BS2 .... 364 D8
Tylers Wy *CHEP* NP16 .... 288 D6
    LYD GL15 .... 206 C3
Tyndale Av *MANG/FISH* BS16 .... 366 A2
    YATE/CS BS37 .... 347 F3
Tyndale Cl *DSLY* GL11 .... 296 C2 ⑧
Tyndale Rd *BWTH/CHD* GL3 .... 131 J6
    DSLY GL11 .... 266 B2
    KGWD/HNM BS15 .... 366 E4 ⑬
    VGL GL2 .... 238 A5
Tyndale Vw *THNB/SVB* BS35 .... 316 B6 ⑧
Tyndall Av *CFTN/FAIL* BS8 .... 364 A7
Tyndalls Rd *EVILLE/WHL* BS5 .... 365 F6 ⑭
Tyndalls Park Ms *CBRISNE* BS2 .... 364 A6 ⑧
Tyndalls Wy *HNBRY/STHM* BS10 ... 354 C6
Tyne Rd *HORF/LLZ* BS7 .... 364 B3
Tyne St *CBRISNE* BS2 .... 364 E4
Tyning Cl *YATE/CS* BS37 .... 347 G4
Tyning Crs *VGL* GL2 .... 238 B3
Tynings Ct *BWTH/CHD* GL3 .... 132 B1 ⑪
Tynings Rd *RSTROUD/NAIL* GL6 .... 270 C2
The Tynings *RSTROUD/NAIL* GL6 .. 243 K7 ⑪
Tyrrel Wy *BRSTK/PCHW* BS34 .... 33 J8
Tythe Ct *DSLY* GL11 .... 266 D1
Tytherington Rd *THNB/SVB* BS35... 317 F8
Tythe Rd *BDWAY* WR12 .... 18 D5
Tythings Crs *NWNT* GL18 .... 73 H6
The Tythings *NWNT* GL18 .... 73 H6

U

Uley Rd *DSLY* GL11 .... 267 G6
Ullenwood Rd *GLE* GL4 .... 131 F7 ⑧
Ullswater Cl
    OLD/WMLY/WICK BS30 .... 367 K8 ⑧
    YATE/CS BS37 .... 347 G3
Ullswater Rd *CHELTW* GL51 .... 105 J7 ⑧
    HNBRY/STHM BS10 .... 353 K5
Undercliff Av *CHELTS* GL53 .... 134 D3
Undercliff Ter *CHELTS* GL53 .... 134 D3
Underhill Rd *GLE* GL4 .... 158 E2
    WUE GL12 .... 319 J1
Underwood Cl *THNB/SVB* BS35 ..... 332 A2
Union Rd *CBRISNE* BS2 .... 364 E8
    CLFD GL16 .... 176 A3
Union St *CBRIS/FH* BS1 .... 364 B7 ⑱
    CHELTE/BC GL52 .... 4 C3
    COTS GL54 .... 92 C6
    DSLY GL11 .... 267 F6
    GL GL1 .... 3 D2
    STROUD GL5 .... 214 E7
Unity St *CBRIS/FH* BS1 .... 364 A8 ⑧
    CBRISNE BS2 .... 364 D7
    KGWD/HNM BS15 .... 366 C6
University Farm *MIM* GL56 .... 69 K1 ⑧
University Rd *CFTN/FAIL* BS8 .... 364 A7
University Wk *CFTN/FAIL* BS8 .... 364 A7
Unlawater La *CIND* GL14 .... 180 C1
Unwin Cl *CHELTW* GL51 .... 105 G7
Unwin Rd *CHELTW* GL51 .... 105 G7
Upcott *HGHW* SN6 .... 310 C2
Up Hatherley Wy *CHELTW* GL51 ... 133 H1
Uphill Rd *HORF/LLZ* BS7 .... 364 D1 ⑧
    MTCHDN GL17 .... 148 E2
Uplands Cl *CIND* GL14 .... 151 G5 ②
Uplands Rd *MANG/FISH* BS16 ...... 366 C3
    STROUD GL5 .... 214 E6
Upper Bath Rd *THNB/SVB* BS35 ... 316 B6 ⑧
Upper Bath St *CHELT* GL50 .... 4 B6
Upper Belmont Rd *HORF/LLZ* BS7 . 364 C3
Upper Bilson Rd *CIND* GL14 .... 150 E5
Upper Chapel La
    FRCTL/WBN BS36 .... 345 J7
Upper Cheltenham Pl
    RDLND/MONT BS6 .... 364 C5
Upper Church Rd *STROUD* GL5 ..... 213 K7
Upper Church St *CHEP* NP16 .... 288 A5
Upper Churnside *CIR* GL7 .... 250 A6
Upper End Ct *EVE* WR11 .... 6 C2
Upperfield Rd *CHELTW* GL51 .... 106 A1 ⑧
Upper Hayes Rd
    RSTROUD/NAIL GL6 .... 270 C1
Upper Kitesnest La
    RSTROUD/NAIL GL6 .... 214 B3
Upper Leazes *STROUD* GL5 .... 215 F7

Upper Lynch Rd
  RSTROUD/NAIL GL6 .... **244** E3
Upper Maudlin St *CBRISNE* BS2 ..... **364** B7
Upper Mill La *CHELTE/BC* GL52 .... **107** K1
Upper Nelson St *CHEP* NP16 .... **288** A6 ⑪
Upper Norwood St
  CHELTS GL53 .... **106** C8 ⑧
Upper Park St *CHELTE/BC* GL6 .... **5** D5
Upper Poole Rd *DSLY* GL11 .... **267** F6
Upper Quay St *GL* GL1 .... **2** B3 ⑫
Upper Queen's Rd *STNHO* GL10 ...... **213** F7 ⑦
Upper Rd *LYD* GL15 .... **205** K5
Upper Rodley Rd *CIND* GL14 .... **154** B6
Upper Sandhurst Rd
  BRSG/KWL/STAPK BS4 .... **374** C2
Upper Springfield Rd
  STROUD GL5 .... **214** E6 ④
Upper Station Rd
  MANG/FISH BS16 .... **366** C2
Upper Stone Cl *FRCTL/WBN* BS36 ... **345** J7
Upper Stowfield Rd
  MTCHDN GL17 .... **120** C7
Upper St *CHPMW/MSHF* SN14 .... **370** B2
Upper Tockington Rd
  THNB/SVB BS35 .... **330** E4
Upper Tynings
  RSTROUD/NAIL GL6 .... **270** C2 ⑤
The Upper Tynings
  RSTROUD/NAIL GL6 .... **213** K6
Upper Washwell
  RSTROUD/NAIL GL6 .... **187** H5
Upper Wells St *CBRIS/FH* BS1 .... **364** A8 ⑰
Upthorpe *DSLY* GL11 .... **267** F1
Upthorpe La *DSLY* GL11 .... **239** F8
Upton Cl *GL4* **131** C7
Upton Gdns *TET* GL8 .... **302** B5
Upton Hl *GLE* GL4 .... **159** H5
Upton La *GLE* GL4 .... **159** H1
  GLE GL4 .... **186** B1
Upton St *GL* GL1 .... **3** D5
Urfords Dr *MANG/FISH* BS16 .... **356** C8 ⑧
Usk Wy *BWTH/CHD* GL3 .... **160** D1

V

Vaisey Fld *VGL* GL2 .... **211** K1
Vaisey Rd *CIR* GL7 .... **249** H2
Valanders La *SHPSTR* CV36 .... **11** G3
Vale Bank *VGL* GL2 .... **181** F3
Valentine Cl *CHEP* NP16 .... **312** B2
Valerian Cl *AVONM* BS11 .... **352** B8
  GLE GL4 .... **131** C7
Vale Rd *CIR* GL7 .... **249** H2
The Vale *MANG/FISH* BS16 .... **358** B7
Vallenders Rd *TEWK* GL20 .... **13** J8
Valley Cl *RSTROUD/NAIL* GL6 .... **243** K5
Valley Gdns *MANG/FISH* BS16 ...... **357** F6
Valley La *GLE* GL4 .... **159** J5
Valley Vw *DSLY* GL11 .... **266** D2
Valley View Rd *STROUD* GL5 .... **215** G8
Valley Wy *CHPMW/MSHF* SN14 .... **373** K8
The Valls *ALMDB* BS32 .... **343** K8
Valma Rocks *EVILLE/WHL* BS5 ...... **366** A8 ⑧
Van Der Breen St
  RSTROUD/NAIL GL6 .... **216** E5
Vandyck Av *KEYN* BS31 .... **376** A8
Varley Av *BWTH/CHD* GL3 .... **131** K8
Varnister La *MTCHDN* GL17 .... **121** K6
Varnister Rd *MTCHDN* GL17 .... **121** J6
Vassall Ct *MANG/FISH* BS16 .... **366** B1
Vassall Rd *MANG/FISH* BS16 .... **366** B1
Vatch La *RSTROUD/NAIL* GL6 .... **244** A2
Vatch Vw *STROUD* GL5 .... **215** C5
Vattingstone La *THNB/SVB* BS35 ... **331** J1
Vaughan La *HNBRY/STHM* BS10 .... **353** H3
Vauxhall *NWNT* GL18 .... **73** G6
Vauxhall Rd *GL* GL1 .... **3** D5
Vauxhall Ter *GL* GL1 .... **3** D5 ⑥
Vayre Cl *YATE/CS* BS37 .... **348** A5
Velhurst Dr *RSTROUD/NAIL* GL6 ... **244** A5
Velthouse La *MTCHDN* GL17 .... **124** C4
The Vennings *DSLY* GL11 .... **238** D8
Venns Acre *WUE* GL12 .... **297** F9
Vensfield Rd *VGL* GL2 .... **156** E4
Vention La *MTCHDN* GL17 .... **120** E8
Ventnor Rd *BRSTK/PCHW* BS34 .... **355** F3
  EVILLE/WHL BS5 .... **365** K5
Vera Rd *MANG/FISH* BS16 .... **365** K4
Verbena Cl *GLE* GL4 .... **159** G5 ①
Vernal Cl *GLE* GL4 .... **159** H1
Vernals La *WUE* GL12 .... **296** A6
Verney Cl *YATE/CS* BS37 .... **106** E8 ③
Verney Rd *STNHO* GL10 .... **213** F7
The Verneys *CHELTS* GL53 .... **106** E8 ③
Vernon Pl *CHELTS* GL53 .... **4** C4 ⑬
Verrier Rd *EVILLE/WHL* BS5 .... **365** G7 ⑬

Vertican Rd *VGL* GL2 .... **103** F8
Vervain Cl *BWTH/CHD* GL3 .... **103** J7
Verwood Dr
  OLD/WMLY/WICK BS30 .... **376** D5
Vetch Cl *GLE* GL4 .... **158** C2
Viburnum Vw *GLE* GL4 .... **159** H1 ⑧
Vicarage Cl *BWTH/CHD* GL3 .... **132** A2
  CHELTW GL51 .... **133** J4
  LYD GL15 .... **234** A5 ②
Vicarage Ct *CLFD* GL16 .... **175** K4 ⑧
  KGWD/HNM BS15 .... **375** G1 ⑪
Vicarage La *BDWAY* WR12 .... **17** J4
  BWTH/CHD GL3 .... **132** C8
  BWTH/CHD GL3 .... **160** C1
  THNB/SVB BS35 .... **328** E7
  VGL GL2 .... **181** F4
  VGL GL2 .... **210** D3
  WUE GL12 .... **321** H6 ②
Vicarage Rd *EVILLE/WHL* BS5 .... **365** G6
  FRCTL/WBN BS36 .... **357** J1
  GL GL1 .... **3** E6
  KGWD/HNM BS15 .... **375** G2 ①
  THNB/SVB BS35 .... **328** E7
Vicarage St *RSTROUD/NAIL* GL6 ... **187** H6
Vicars Cl *MANG/FISH* BS16 .... **366** B2 ⑧
Vickers Rd *COTS* GL54 .... **145** F1
Victoria Av *EVILLE/WHL* BS5 .... **365** G7
Victoria Cl *THNB/SVB* BS35 .... **316** B3
Victoria Crs *THNB/SVB* BS35 .... **328** C3
Victoria Dr *STNHO* GL10 .... **211** K7
Victoria Gdns
  RDLND/MONT BS6 .... **364** B5 ⑥
Victoria Pde *EVILLE/WHL* BS5 .... **365** G6
Victoria Pk *KGWD/HNM* BS15 .... **366** D6
  MANG/FISH BS16 .... **366** A1
Victoria Pl *CHELTE/BC* GL52 .... **5** D4 ⑧
Victoria Retreat *CHELT* GL50 .... **4** B6 ②
Victoria Rd *CHEP* NP16 .... **312** B1
  CIR GL7 .... **249** K6
  CIR GL7 .... **254** D1
  CLFD GL16 .... **175** J4
  KGWD/HNM BS15 .... **375** H1
  LYD GL15 .... **234** H3
  OLD/WMLY/WICK BS30 .... **376** C1
  STROUD GL5 .... **243** H5
  VGL GL2 .... **102** B8
Victoria St *CBRIS/FH* BS1 .... **364** C8
  CHELT GL50 .... **4** B2
  CIND GL14 .... **150** E6
  COTS GL54 .... **143** H1
  GL GL1 .... **3** D5
  MANG/FISH BS16 .... **3** D5
  RSTROUD/NAIL GL6 .... **187** H6 ⑧
Victoria Ter *CBRISNE* BS2 .... **374** A1
  CHELTE/BC GL52 .... **5** D4
Victoria V *CIND* GL14 .... **150** E6
Victoria Wk *RDLND/MONT* BS6 ..... **364** B5
Victor St *EVILLE/WHL* BS5 .... **365** F8 ⑪
Victory Cl *BWTH/CHD* GL3 .... **103** A1 ⑧
Victory Rd *GL* GL1 .... **3** D6
  RSTROUD/NAIL GL6 .... **214** B3
View Ct *OLD/WMLY/WICK* BS30 ... **368** E8
Village Av *COTS* GL54 .... **113** H2
Village Rd *YATE/CS* BS37 .... **347** F5 ②
Village Rd *CHELTW* GL51 .... **105** K2
Villiers Rd *EVILLE/WHL* BS5 .... **365** F5
Vilner La *THNB/SVB* BS35 .... **316** B7
Vilverie Md *CHELTE/BC* GL52 .... **82** D2 ⑧
Vimpany Cl *HNBRY/STHM* BS10 .... **353** H3
Vimpennys La *THNB/SVB* BS35 ..... **341** F5
Vincent Av *GL* GL1 .... **157** J5
Vincent Cl *AVONM* BS11 .... **352** E4
Vine Ct *CHELTW* GL51 .... **4** A2 ②
Vineries Cl *CHELTS* GL53 .... **134** C2
Viner's La *BAD* GL9 .... **351** H8
Vine Ter *GL* GL1 .... **3** D2
Vine Wy *TEWK* GL20 .... **57** J3
Vineyard La *WUE* GL12 .... **320** D1
Vineyards Cl *CHELTS* GL53 .... **135** H2
Vineyard St *COTS* GL54 .... **85** J1
Vining Wk *EVILLE/WHL* BS5 .... **365** H6 ⑪
Vinney La *YATE/CS* BS37 .... **336** C6
Vinny Av *MANG/FISH* BS16 .... **357** G7
Vintery Leys
  HNLZ/SM/SNYPK/WT BS9 .... **353** K7
Virginia Cl *YATE/CS* BS37 .... **347** J5
Virginia Rd *TEWK* GL20 .... **34** D6
Vittoria Wk *CHELT* GL50 .... **4** B5 ⑪
Vizard Cl *DSLY* GL11 .... **267** F6
Voxwell La *CHELTE/BC* GL52 .... **82** E3
Voyce Cl *GLE* GL4 .... **157** K4 ⑧
Vulcan Wy *GLE* GL4 .... **131** H8
Vyners Cl *CIR* GL7 .... **249** J8

W

Wade Rd *YATE/CS* BS37 .... **346** C3
Wades La *RSTROUD/NAIL* GL6 ...... **214** E3
Wades Rd *BRSTK/PCHW* BS34 ...... **355** F3
Wade St *CBRISNE* BS2 .... **364** D6
Wadham Cl *CIR* GL7 .... **256** D3 ⑧
Wadham Dr *MANG/FISH* BS16 ...... **356** B5

Wadham Gv *MANG/FISH* BS16 ...... **367** H1
Wagtail Dr *TEWK* GL20 .... **34** C5 ④
Wainbridge Crs *THNB/SVB* BS35 ... **328** E7
Wainbrook Dr *EVILLE/WHL* BS5 .... **365** H4
Wainlode La *RTEWK/TIB* GL19 .... **78** D4
Wakefield Cl *CIR* GL7 .... **283** F8 ②
Wakeford Rd *MANG/FISH* BS16 ..... **357** G7 ⑨
Waldrist Cl *CHELTW* GL51 .... **105** K1
Walham La *VGL* GL2 .... **2** C1
Walker Cl *EVILLE/WHL* BS5 .... **365** F7
  MANG/FISH BS16 .... **357** G7
Walkers Gdn *COTS* GL54 .... **169** H5
Walker's La *MTCHDN* GL17 .... **121** K7
Walker St *CBRISNE* BS2 .... **364** A6
Walker Wy *THNB/SVB* BS35 .... **316** B7
Walkley Hl *STROUD* GL5 .... **242** C1
Walkley Rd *TEWK* GL20 .... **33** J7 ③
Walk Mill La *WUE* GL12 .... **320** D2
The Walk *WUE* GL12 .... **320** D2
Wallbridge *STROUD* GL5 .... **214** D7 ②
Walliscote Av
  HNLZ/SM/SNYPK/WT BS9 .... **354** A8
Walliscote Rd
  HNLZ/SM/SNYPK/WT BS9 .... **354** A8
Wallscourt Rd *BRSTK/PCHW* BS34 .. **355** F4
Wallscourt Rd South
  BRSTK/PCHW BS34 .... **355** F5
Wallsend La *CHPMW/MSHF* SN14 ... **371** F1
Walnut Av *YATE/CS* BS37 .... **347** J4
Walnut Bank Dr *TEWK* GL20 .... **36** C7
Walnut Cl *BDWAY* WR12 .... **18** C6
  CHELTE/BC GL52 .... **4** C1
  CLFD GL16 .... **176** B5
  GLE GL4 .... **159** F3 ⑧
  THNB/SVB BS35 .... **316** D5
Walnut Crs *KGWD/HNM* BS15 .... **367** F6
Walnut Dr *CHPMW/MSHF* SN14 .... **373** F8
Walnut La *KGWD/HNM* BS15 .... **367** G6 ⑧
Walnut Tree Cl *ALMDB* BS32 .... **342** E1 ②
Walshe Av *YATE/CS* BS37 .... **348** A5
Walsingham Rd
  RDLND/MONT BS6 .... **364** C4
Walton Av *BRSG/KWL/STAPK* BS4 .. **374** C1
Walton Cl *GLE* GL4 .... **159** G3
  OLD/WMLY/WICK BS30 .... **376** D5 ⑨
Walton Heath *YATE/CS* BS37 .... **347** H5
Walton Ri
  HNLZ/SM/SNYPK/WT BS9 .... **353** J6
Walton St *EVILLE/WHL* BS5 .... **365** F5
Walwyn Cl *MTCHDN* GL17 .... **123** G5
Wanscow Wk
  HNLZ/SM/SNYPK/WT BS9 .... **353** K8
Wapley Hl *YATE/CS* BS37 .... **359** G2
Wapley Rd *YATE/CS* BS37 .... **359** J3
Ward Av *VGL* GL2 .... **103** G8
Ward Cl *CHELTE/BC* GL52 .... **83** G2 ⑧
Warden Hill Cl *CHELTW* GL51 .... **105** K8 ②
Warden Hill Rd *CHELTW* GL51 .... **105** K8
Wardens' Wy *COTS* GL54 .... **86** E5
  COTS GL54 .... **113** F3
Ward Rd *COTS* GL54 .... **169** G4
Wards Rd *CHELTM* GL51 .... **105** H8
Warend Hl *DSLY* GL11 .... **266** E8
Warman Cl *HGRV/WHIT* BS14 .... **374** E8
Warman Rd *HGRV/WHIT* BS14 ...... **374** E8
Warmer's Inn La *MALM* SN16 .... **327** H6
Warmington Rd *HGRV/WHIT* BS14 . **374** B6
Warneford Pl *MMI* GL56 .... **70** A1
Warner Cl *KGWD/HNM* BS15 .... **367** F3 ⑧
The Warns
  OLD/WMLY/WICK BS30 .... **376** B2 ⑧
Warren Cl *ALMDB* BS32 .... **343** H3 ⑧
  BWTH/CHD GL3 .... **103** J7
  CHELTW GL51 .... **105** K8
Warren Crs *DSLY* GL11 .... **296** B2
Warren Rd *BRSTK/PCHW* BS34 ..... **355** F3
  TEWK GL20 .... **34** C6
Warren Slade *CHEP* NP16 .... **312** B1 ⑧
Warren Wy *YATE/CS* BS37 .... **347** G3 ②
Warrington Rd
  BRSG/KWL/STAPK BS4 .... **374** C4
Warth La *THNB/SVB* BS35 .... **328** E3
  VGL GL2 .... **181** G2
Warwick Av *EVILLE/WHL* BS5 .... **365** F5 ⑫
  GL GL1 .... **157** J5
Warwick Cl
  OLD/WMLY/WICK BS30 .... **376** C4 ⑧
  STROUD GL5 .... **242** C2
  THNB/SVB BS35 .... **316** A5
Warwick Crs *CHELTE/BC* GL52 ...... **107** H8
Warwick Pl *CHELTE/BC* GL52 .... **4** C3 ⑧
  TEWK GL20 .... **57** J2
Warwick Rd *EVILLE/WHL* BS5 .... **365** F5
Washingpool Hill Rd *ALMDB* BS32 .. **331** G4
Washington Av *EVILLE/WHL* BS5 ... **365** G5
Wasley Rd *CHELTW* GL51 .... **105** J5
Watch Elm Cl *ALMDB* BS32 .... **343** G8
Watercress Rd *CBRISNE* BS2 .... **364** D3
Waterdale Cl *HNBRY/STHM* BS10 ... **354** A7
  VGL GL2 .... **156** D6 ②
Waterdale Gdns
  HNLZ/SM/SNYPK/WT BS9 .... **354** A7
Waterford Cl *THNB/SVB* BS35 .... **316** D6

Waterford Rd
 HNLZ/SM/SNYPK/WT BS9 ...... **353** K8 🛭
Water La *BRSG/KWL/STAPK* BS4 ..... **374** C5
 CBRIS/FH BS1 .... **364** C8
 CHELTE/BC GL52 .... **107** H8 🗗
 KGWD/HNM BS15 .... **375** G4
 STROUD GL5 .... **242** A2
 STROUD GL5 .... **243** G6
 WUE GL12 .... **297** F8
Waterloo La *CIR* GL7 .... **254** D8
Waterloo Rd *CBRISNE* BS2 .... **364** E7
Waterloo St *CBRISNE* BS2 ..... **364** D7 🗗
 CHELTW GL51 .... **106** B3
The Waterloo *CIR* GL7 .... **249** K5
Waterloo Wy *TEWK* GL20 .... **13** K8
Watermans Ct VGL GL2 .... **156** D5 🗓
Water Meadow VGL GL2 .... **156** C7
Watermill Cl *WUE* GL12 .... **294** A7 🗓
Watermoor Cl *CHELTW* GL51 ...... **105** H2 🗓
Watermoor Ct *BWTH/CHD* GL3 .... **131** K5 🗓
Watermoor Rd *CIR* GL7 .... **249** K6
Watermoor Wy *CHEP* NP16 .... **288** A7 🗓
Watershed La *CLE* GL4 .... **159** H6
 LYD GL15 .... **233** J5
 NWNT GL18 .... **73** C7
 OLD/WMLY/WICK BS30 .... **369** J6
 VGL GL2 .... **128** B7
 VGL GL2 .... **210** D3
Wathen Rd *RDLND/MONT* BS6 ...... **364** D3
Watkins Yd
 HNLZ/SM/SNYPK/WT BS9 ...... **353** J6 🗓
Watledge Bank
 RSTROUD/NAIL GL6 .... **270** D1 🗓
Watledge Cl *TEWK* GL20 .... **33** J8 🗓
Watledge Rd *STROUD* GL5 .... **242** D8
Watley's End Rd *FRCTL/WBN* BS36.. **344** E7
Watson Av *BRSG/KWL/STAPK* BS4 .. **374** C5
Watson Gv *CLE* GL4 .... **159** H1 🗓
Watson's Rd
 OLD/WMLY/WICK BS30 .... **376** A3
Watters Cl *FRCTL/WBN* BS36 .... **345** K8
Watts Cl *BWTH/CHD* GL3 .... **131** J7
Wavell Cl *YATE/CS* BS37 .... **347** F2
Waverley La *RDLND/MONT* BS6 ..... **364** A5
 VGL GL2 .... **130** E4
 YATE/CS BS37 .... **346** D4
Waverley St *EVILLE/WHL* BS5 ..... **364** E5 🗓
Waylands
 OLD/WMLY/WICK BS30 .... **376** A3
Wayleaze *FRCTL/WBN* BS36 .... **345** K7
Wayside Cl *FRCTL/WBN* BS36 .... **345** H7
Weald Cl *GLE* GL4 .... **158** E1
Weavers Rd *CIR* GL7 .... **267** F6
 WUE GL12 .... **320** D3 🗓
Weavers Wy *CIR* GL7 .... **157** F4 🗓
 VGL GL2 .... **157** F4 🗓
Webb Rd *TET* GL8 .... **302** A5 🗓
Webbs Heath
 OLD/WMLY/WICK BS30 .... **367** K7
Webb St *EVILLE/WHL* BS5 .... **364** E6 🗓
Webbs Wood Rd *ALMDB* BS32 ...... **343** H8
Webley Rd *MTCHDN* GL17 .... **121** K8
Wedgewood Rd *MANG/FISH* BS16 .. **356** D5
Wedgwood Dr VGL GL2 .... **130** E1 🗓🗓
Wedmore Cl *KGWD/HNM* BS15 ...... **367** F7
Weedon Cl *CBRISNE* BS2 ...... **364** E4 🗓🗓
Weigh Bridge Ct *CHCAM* GL55 ..... **20** E2 🗓
Weight Rd *EVILLE/WHL* BS5 .... **365** G7 🗓🗓
Weir Bridge Cl *GLE* GL4 .... **131** G6
Weir La *CHPMW/MSHF* SN14 .... **371** K6
Welch Rd *CHELTW* GL51 .... **105** J2
Welland Ct *CHELTE/BC* GL52 .... **5** E1
Welland Dr *CHELTE/BC* GL52 .... **5** E1
Welland Lodge Rd *CHELTE/BC* GL52... **5** D1
Welland Rd VGL GL2 .... **157** F4 🗓
Wellbrook Rd *CHELTE/BC* GL52 ..... **83** F1
Well Cl *CHEP* NP16 .... **312** B2 🗓🗓
 TEWK GL20 .... **34** D5
Well Cross Rd *GLE* GL4 .... **158** B2
Well End *STROUD* GL5 .... **215** G6
Wellesley Cl *CHELT* GL50 .... **4** C2
Wellesley St *GL* GL1 .... **130** B8
Wellfield *TEWK* GL20 .... **34** A7 🗓
Well Hl *RSTROUD/NAIL* GL6 .... **243** J8
Welling Cl *DSLY* GL11 .... **267** F7
Wellington Av *RDLND/MONT* BS6 ... **364** C8
Wellington Crs *HORF/LLZ* BS7 ...... **354** C8
Wellington Dr
 HNLZ/SM/SNYPK/WT BS9 ...... **354** B8
 YATE/CS BS37 .... **346** D3
Wellington Hl *HORF/LLZ* BS7 ...... **354** C8
Wellington Hl West
 HNLZ/SM/SNYPK/WT BS9 ...... **354** A7

Wellington La *CHELT* GL50 .... **4** C2
 CHELTE/BC GL52 .... **4** C3
 RDLND/MONT BS6 .... **364** C5
Wellington Pde *GL* GL1 .... **3** D3 🗓
 CHELTE/BC GL52 .... **4** C2
 COTS GL54 .... **144** E3
 KGWD/HNM BS15 .... **366** D4 🗓
 MIM GL56 .... **70** B1
 YATE/CS BS37 .... **347** G2
Wellington Sq *CHELT* GL50 .... **4** C2
Wellington St *CHELT* GL50 .... **4** B4
 GL GL1 .... **2** C4
Wellington Wk
 HNBRY/STHM BS10 .... **354** A7
Well La *BAD* GL9 .... **350** E1
 COTS GL54 .... **88** C8
 COTS GL54 .... **92** C6
 MTCHDN GL17 .... **122** B7
Wellmeadow La *CLFD* GL16 .... **146** D8
Wellmeadow La *CLFD* GL16 .... **147** K7
Well Pl *CHELT* GL50 .... **106** B5
Wells Cl *CHELTW* GL51 .... **133** K1
Wells Gdns *BDWAY* WR12 .... **18** E6
Wellsprings Rd VGL GL2 .... **130** E3
Wells Rd *BRSG/KWL/STAPK* BS4 ... **374** A4
 GLE GL4 .... **130** C5
 HGRV/WHIT BS14 .... **374** A6
 RSTROUD/NAIL GL6 .... **216** E6
Wellstead Av *YATE/CS* BS37 .... **347** F5
Welsford Av *MANG/FISH* BS16 ...... **365** H2
Welsford Rd *MANG/FISH* BS16 ...... **365** G2
Welsh Back *CBRIS/FH* BS1 .... **364** B8
Welsh House La *NWNT* GL18 .... **50** E6
Welsh Wy *CIR* GL7 .... **220** A4
 CIR GL7 .... **221** K6
 CIR GL7 .... **222** B6
 CIR GL7 .... **225** F9
Welton Wk *KGWD/HNM* BS15 .... **366** C4 🗓
Welveland La *GLE* GL4 .... **131** C5
Welwyn Ms *CHELTW* GL51 .... **153** J1 🗓🗗
Wendover Gdns *CHELT* GL50 ...... **106** B5 🗓
The Wend *MTCHDN* GL17 .... **124** B4
Wenlock Rd *TEWK* GL20 .... **57** J1
Wenmore Cl *MANG/FISH* BS16 ...... **356** D5
Wentforth Dr *KGWD/HNM* BS15 .... **366** C4 🗓
Wentworth
 OLD/WMLY/WICK BS30 .... **367** G8 🗓
 YATE/CS BS37 .... **347** G5
Wentworth Cl *CHELTW* GL51 ...... **105** H3 🗓
 VGL GL2 .... **130** D1 🗓🗓
Wentworth Rd *HORF/LLZ* BS7 ...... **364** B3
Werth La *RTEWK/TIB* GL19 .... **56** A3
Wesley Av *KGWD/HNM* BS15 .... **375** J1
Wesley Cl *LYD* GL15 .... **233** H6
 MANG/FISH BS16 .... **366** D3 🗓
Wesley Hl *KGWD/HNM* BS15 .... **366** D5 🗓
Wesley La *OLD/WMLY/WICK* BS30... **376** C1
Wesley Rd *CIND* GL14 .... **151** F5
 HORF/LLZ BS7 .... **354** C2 🗓
 LYD GL15 .... **205** J5
 STNHO GL10 .... **240** E3
Wessex Av *HORF/LLZ* BS7 .... **354** D7
Wessex Dr *CHELTE/BC* GL52 .... **5** F4
Westacre Cl *HNBRY/STHM* BS10 ... **353** J4
Westal Pk *CHELTW* GL51 .... **106** B7
West Approach Dr *CHELTE/BC* GL52.. **4** C1
West Av *MTCHDN* GL17 .... **122** D6
Westbourne *EVE* WR11 .... **7** H1
Westbourne Dr *CHELTE/BC* GL52 ... **5** D3
 VGL GL2 .... **156** E7
Westbourne Rd
 EVILLE/WHL BS5 .... **365** F6 🗓🗓
 MANG/FISH BS16 .... **357** F6
West Broadway
 HNLZ/SM/SNYPK/WT BS9 ...... **354** B8
Westbrook Rd
 BRSG/KWL/STAPK BS4 .... **374** C6
Westbury Court Rd
 HNLZ/SM/SNYPK/WT BS9 ...... **353** H7
Westbury Hl
 HNLZ/SM/SNYPK/WT BS9 ...... **353** J7
Westbury La
 HNLZ/SM/SNYPK/WT BS9 ...... **352** E7
Westbury Rd *CHELTS* GL53 .... **134** E2
 GL GL1 .... **157** K3
 HNLZ/SM/SNYPK/WT BS9 ...... **353** J8
West Coombe
 HNLZ/SM/SNYPK/WT BS9 ...... **353** F8
Westcote Rd *GLE* GL4 .... **157** K5 🗓
Westcourt Dr
 OLD/WMLY/WICK BS30 .... **376** C2
West Cft
 HNLZ/SM/SNYPK/WT BS9 ...... **354** A7
West Dene
 HNLZ/SM/SNYPK/WT BS9 ...... **353** G8
Westdown Gdns *CHELTE/BC* GL52... **5** D4 🗓
West Dr *CHELT* GL50 .... **4** C2
Westend *DSLY* GL11 .... **266** B2
West End *CBRISNE* BS2 .... **364** B6
 CHNTN OX7 .... **119** F2
 COTS GL54 .... **169** G4
 RSTROUD/NAIL GL6 .... **243** H8

THNB/SVB BS35 .... **291** G8
West End La *THNB/SVB* BS35 .... **291** F8
West End La *BDWAY* WR12 .... **18** B7
 BWTH/CHD GL3 .... **131** K8
Westend Pde *GL* GL1 .... **2** A2 🗓
Westend Rd *WUE* GL12 .... **335** G2
Westend Ter *GL* GL1 .... **2** A2 🗓
Westering Cl *MANG/FISH* BS16 .. **367** G1 🗓
Westerleigh Cl *MANG/FISH* BS16 .. **357** F7 🗓
Westerleigh Rd
 MANG/FISH BS16 .... **356** E8 🗓
 MANG/FISH BS16 .... **357** G7
 MANG/FISH BS16 .... **358** D8
 YATE/CS BS37 .... **346** D8
 YATE/CS BS37 .... **358** D2
Westerley Cl *CIND* GL14 .... **151** F7
Western Av *CHEP* NP16 .... **312** A1
 FRCTL/WBN BS36 .... **345** G6
Western Hl Rd *TEWK* GL20 .... **36** E4
Western Rd *CHELT* GL50 .... **106** B5
 HORF/LLZ BS7 .... **354** C8
Western Wy *NWNT* GL18 .... **49** J3
Westfield *DSLY* GL11 .... **266** E4
Westfield Av *BWTH/CHD* GL3 .... **132** B8
 TEWK GL20 .... **34** D6
Westfield Cl *KGWD/HNM* BS15 ...... **375** J1
Westfield Cl *CIND* GL14 .... **151** F5
Westfield La *BRSTK/PCHW* BS34..... **355** J3
Westfield Rd *BWTH/CHD* GL3 .... **132** B8
 CIND GL14 .... **151** F5
 HNLZ/SM/SNYPK/WT BS9 ...... **353** J6
Westfields *WUE* GL12 .... **296** E7
Westfield Ter VGL GL2 .... **130** A1
Westfield Wy *ALMDB* BS32 .... **343** H4
Westgate St *GL* GL1 .... **2** C3
West Gv *RDLND/MONT* BS6 .... **364** D5
West Hay Gv *CIR* GL7 .... **276** B7
Westland Av
 OLD/WMLY/WICK BS30 .... **376** D2
Westland Rd VGL GL2 .... **156** D7
West La *CIR* GL7 .... **276** B7
West Leaze Pl *ALMDB* BS32 .... **343** J8
Westleigh Cl *HNBRY/STHM* BS10 **354** B5 🗓
 YATE/CS BS37 .... **346** E5
Westleigh Rd *HNBRY/STHM* BS10... **354** A5
West Littleton Rd
 CHPMW/MSHF SN14 .... **371** H4
West Market Pl *CIR* GL7 .... **249** J5 🗓
Westmarsh La *THNB/SVB* BS35....... **315** F1
Westmead Rd *EVILLE/WHL* BS5 ...... **366** B7
 VGL GL2 .... **131** F1
West Mill La *HGHW* SN6 .... **310** C6
Westminster Cl *CHELTS* GL53 ...... **5** D6 🗓
 HNLZ/SM/SNYPK/WT BS9 ...... **353** J7 🗓
Westminster Rd
 EVILLE/WHL BS5 .... **365** H6 🗓🗓
Weston Av *EVILLE/WHL* BS5 ... **365** H7 🗓🗓
Weston Cl
 HNLZ/SM/SNYPK/WT BS9 ...... **352** E7
Weston Crs *HORF/LLZ* BS7 .... **354** C8
Weston Rd *EVE* WR11 .... **6** D3
 GL GL1 .... **2** C5
Westons Brake *MANG/FISH* BS16 ... **357** G5
Westons Hill Dr *MANG/FISH* BS16 .. **357** G6
Westons Wy *KGWD/HNM* BS15 ...... **367** F7
Westover Cl
 HNLZ/SM/SNYPK/WT BS9 ...... **353** H5
Westover Ct *BWTH/CHD* GL3 .... **103** K7
Westover Dr
 HNLZ/SM/SNYPK/WT BS9 ...... **353** J6
Westover Gdns
 HNLZ/SM/SNYPK/WT BS9 ...... **353** H6 🗓
Westover Ri
 HNLZ/SM/SNYPK/WT BS9 ...... **353** J5
Westover Rd
 HNLZ/SM/SNYPK/WT BS9 ...... **353** J6
West Pde
 HNLZ/SM/SNYPK/WT BS9 ...... **352** E7
West Park Rd *MANG/FISH* BS16 ..... **366** E1
West Priory Cl
 HNLZ/SM/SNYPK/WT BS9 ...... **353** J7 🗓
West Rdg *FRCTL/WBN* BS36........... **345** H7
Westridge Rd *WUE* GL12 .... **296** E6 🗓
Westrip Pl *RSTROUD/NAIL* GL6 ...... **213** K6
West Rocke Av
 HNLZ/SM/SNYPK/WT BS9 ...... **353** F7
West St *CBRISNE* BS2 .... **364** D7 🗓
 CHNTN OX7 .... **119** F7
 KGWD/HNM BS15 .... **366** D6 🗓
 OLD/WMLY/WICK BS30 .... **376** D2
 SHPSTR CV36 .... **25** F7
 TET GL8 .... **302** B7
 WUE GL12 .... **333** G6
West Town Dr
 BRSG/KWL/STAPK BS4 .... **374** C5 🗓
West Town Gv
 BRSG/KWL/STAPK BS4 .... **374** C6
West Town La
 BRSG/KWL/STAPK BS4 .... **374** C5
 HGRV/WHIT BS14 .... **374** A6
West Town Pk
 BRSG/KWL/STAPK BS4 .... **374** C6
West Tynings
 RSTROUD/NAIL GL6 .... **270** C2 🗓

Westview *RTEWK/TIB* GL19 .... 79 G1
West Vw *CIND* GL14 .... 151 F7 ⑦
  NWNT CL18 .... 73 H6
  THNB/SVB BS35 .... 331 K2
Westward Rd *STROUD* GL5 .... 213 K8
West Wy *CIR* GL7 .... 249 J6
  CIR GL7 .... 285 G1
Westwick Rd *RTEWK/TIB* GL19 ...... 125 J2
Westwood Crs
  BRSG/KWL/STAPK BS4 .... 374 C1 ⑧
Westwood La *CHELTE/BC* GL52 .... 107 K3 ⑧
Westwood Rd
  BRSG/KWL/STAPK BS4 .... 374 C6
Wetherby Ct *FRCTL/WBN* BS36 ... 357 F5 ⑧
Wetherleigh Dr *VGL* GL2 .... 128 D1
Weyhouse La *STROUD* GL5 .... 243 F1 ⑦
Whaddon Av *CHELTE/BC* GL52 .... 5 E3
Whaddon Dr *CHELTE/BC* GL52 ...... 5 D3 ⑦
Whaddon Rd *CHELTE/BC* GL52 ...... 5 F3 ⑧
Whaddon Wy *GLE* GL4 .... 157 K5
Wharfdale Wy *STNHO* GL10 .... 212 E8
  VGL GL2 .... 156 D6
Wharfedale *THNB/SVB* BS35 .... 316 D6
The Wharfings *HCHW* SN6 .... 283 F8
Wharf La *CIR* GL7 .... 283 F8
  CIR GL7 .... 285 H2
Wharf Rd *MANG/FISH* BS16 .... 365 K2 ⑧
Wheatfield Ct *CHCAM* GL55 .... 9 F7
Wheatfield Dr *ALMDB* BS32 .... 343 H5
Wheat Hl *TET* GL8 .... 302 A6
Wheatland Dr *CHELTE/BC* GL51 ... 105 H2 ⑧
The Wheatridge (East) *GLE* GL4 ... 159 F2
The Wheatridge *GLE* GL4 .... 159 F2
Wheatsheaf Dr *CHELTE/BC* GL52 ... 82 D2
Wheatstone Rd *GL* GL1 .... 2 C6
Wheatway *GLE* GL4 .... 159 F3
Wheelers Wk *STROUD* GL5 .... 214 B5
Whelford Rd *CIR* GL7 .... 283 F7
Whimbrel Rd *VGL* GL2 .... 156 C5
Whimsey Rd *CIND* GL14 .... 150 D3
Whinchat Dr
  MANG/FISH BS16 .... 355 K8 ⑧
Whip La *RSTROUD/NAIL* GL6 .... 270 D1
Whippington Ct *CBRIS/FH* BS1 ...... 364 C7 ⑧
Whitby Rd
  BRSG/KWL/STAPK BS4 .... 374 B2 ⑧
Whitebeam Rd *VGL* GL2 .... 130 D1 ⑧
Whitechapel Rd *LYD* GL15 .... 205 F5 ⑧
Whitecourt *DSLY* GL11 .... 268 A5
Whitecroft *RSTROUD/NAIL* GL6 ... 270 D2
Whitecroft Rd *LYD* GL15 .... 205 C5
Whitecross Av
  HGRV/WHIT BS14 .... 374 B8 ⑧
White Cross Rd *LYD* GL15 .... 234 A4
Whitecross Sq *CHELTS* GL53 .... 4 C6
Whitefield Av *EVILLE/WHL* BS5 ... 366 A6
  KGWD/HNM BS15 .... 375 J1 ⑧
Whitefield Cl *STNHO* GL10 .... 212 E8
Whitefield Rd *EVILLE/WHL* BS5 ... 366 A4
Whitefields *CHELTE/BC* GL52 .... 82 D2
  YATE/CS BS37 .... 348 A5 ⑧
Whitefriars La *HGHW* SN6 .... 308 C3
Whitehall Av
  EVILLE/WHL BS5 .... 365 H6 ⑧
Whitehall Gdns
  EVILLE/WHL BS5 .... 365 H6 ⑧
Whitehall La *VGL* GL2 .... 99 H7
Whitehall Rd *EVILLE/WHL* BS5 ... 365 H6
White Hart La *COTS* GL54 .... 92 C6
White Hart St *CHELT* GL51 .... 4 A2 ⑧
Whitehill La *MTCHDN* GL17 .... 122 C6
White Horse La
  RSTROUD/NAIL GL6 .... 187 H6 ⑧
White Horse Rd *HCHW* SN6 .... 310 D6
Whitehouse La *NWNT* GL18 .... 72 B5
  TET GL8 .... 326 A6
Whitehouse Pk *STROUD* GL5 .... 214 A7
Whitehouse Rd *THNB/SVB* BS35 ... 328 E7
Whitehouse Wy *CHELTE/BC* GL52 ... 83 H3
Whitelands Rd *CIR* GL7 .... 250 A5
Whiteleaze *HNBRY/STHM* BS10 ... 354 A7 ⑧
White Lodge Rd *MANG/FISH* BS16 ... 367 J2
Whitemarsh Cl *CHELTW* GL51 ..... 105 H2 ⑦
Whites Hl *EVILLE/WHL* BS5 .... 366 A8
Whiteshill *MANG/FISH* BS16 .... 356 D3
White St *EVILLE/WHL* BS5 .... 364 D6
Whitethorn Dr *CHELTE/BC* GL52 ...... 5 F2
Whitewall La *THNB/SVB* BS35 ...... 317 F4
Whitewater Rd *TET* GL8 .... 323 J2
White Wy *CIR* GL7 .... 194 A5
  CIR GL7 .... 221 K8
Whiteway *DSLY* GL11 .... 267 C7
Whiteway Rd
  BRSG/KWL/STAPK BS4 .... 365 J8 ⑧
  DSLY GL11 .... 267 C7 ⑧
  EVILLE/WHL BS5 .... 366 A6
Whiteway Ms *EVILLE/WHL* BS5 ... 366 A6
Whiteway Rd *EVILLE/WHL* BS5 ... 366 A5
  GLE GL4 .... 158 D1
The Whiteway *CIR* GL7 .... 249 K1
Whiteway Vw *CIR* GL7 .... 249 H3
Whitewell Cl *GLE* GL4 .... 131 G7 ⑦
Whitewood Rd *EVILLE/WHL* BS5 ... 366 A5 ⑧
Whitfield Cl *KGWD/HNM* BS15 ... 366 D4 ⑧
Whitfield Rd *THNB/SVB* BS35 ...... 316 C8 ⑧

Whitfield St *GL* GL1 .... 2 C4 ⑦
Whitford Cl *EVE* WR11 .... 6 B2
Whitley Cl *YATE/CS* BS37 .... 346 E3
Whitley Md *BRSTK/PCHW* BS34 ... 355 J3
Whitlow La *CIND* GL14 .... 126 A5
Whitminster La *VGL* GL2 .... 210 E1
Whitmore Av
  BRSG/KWL/STAPK BS4 .... 375 F3
Whitmore Rd *COTS* GL54 .... 62 C7
The Whitmores *COTS* GL54 .... 115 H4 ⑧
Whitson St *CBRIS/FH* BS1 .... 364 B6 ⑬
Whittington Rd *CHELTW* GL51 ..... 105 H6
  MANG/FISH BS16 .... 356 C8
Whittington Wy *LYD* GL15 .... 205 H2 ⑦
Whittle Av *GLE* GL4 .... 157 K5
Whittle Cl *CHELTW* GL51 .... 105 C5 ⑧
Whittles La *VGL* GL2 .... 210 C2
Whittlestone Ct *COTS* GL54 .... 91 J6 ⑧
Whittlestone Hollow *COTS* GL54 ... 91 J6
Whittock Sq *HGRV/WHIT* BS14 ... 374 C7
Whittucks Cl *KGWD/HNM* BS15 ... 375 J2
Whittucks Rd *KGWD/HNM* BS15 ... 375 J1 ⑧
Whitwell Rd *HGRV/WHIT* BS14 ... 374 A6
Whitworth Ms *BWTH/CHD* GL3 ... 132 A8 ⑧
Whitworth Rd *CIR* GL7 .... 249 J7 ⑦
Whornes Orch *GLE* GL4 .... 159 H3
Whytes Cl
  HNLZ/SM/SNYPK/WT BS9 .... 353 J6
Wick Crs *BRSG/KWL/STAPK* BS4 ... 374 C3
The Wickets *HORF/LLZ* BS7 .... 354 D5
  KGWD/HNM BS15 .... 366 D4 ⑧
Wickfield La *CHELTE/BC* GL52 ...... 84 B2
Wickham Cl *YATE/CS* BS37 .... 348 B6
Wickham Gln *MANG/FISH* BS16 ... 365 H1
Wickham Hl *MANG/FISH* BS16 .... 365 H1
Wickham Vw *MANG/FISH* BS16 ... 365 H2 ⑧
Wick La *OLD/WMLY/WICK* BS30 ... 377 H5
  RTEWK/TIB GL19 .... 79 H2
Wickridge Cl *STROUD* GL5 .... 214 E6
Wick Rd *BRSG/KWL/STAPK* BS4 ... 374 C3
  MALM SN16 .... 306 C6
  THNB/SVB BS35 .... 328 E7
Wick St *RSTROUD/NAIL* GL6 .... 215 G2
Wickwar Rd *WUE* GL12 .... 320 C2
  YATE/CS BS37 .... 334 C6
  YATE/CS BS37 .... 335 J5
Wickwater La *CIR* GL7 .... 309 G2
Widcombe Cl *EVILLE/WHL* BS5 ... 366 A7 ⑧
Widden St *GL* GL1 .... 3 D4 ⑬
Wigmore Cl *GLE* GL4 .... 131 C8 ⑦
Wigton Crs *HNBRY/STHM* BS10 ... 354 A4
Wilcox Cl *KGWD/HNM* BS15 .... 366 C7
Wilder St *CBRISNE* BS2 .... 364 C6 ⑬
Wildlife Wk *BWTH/CHD* GL3 ...... 160 C2 ⑧
Wildmoorway La *CIR* GL7 .... 279 F7
Wilkes Av *BWTH/CHD* GL3 .... 131 J6
Wilkes Meadow *CLFD* GL16 .... 176 B3
Wilkinson Rd *CIR* GL7 .... 277 J1
Willcox Dr *CHELTE/BC* GL52 .... 83 H3
Willersey Rd *CHELTW* GL51 .... 105 J6
William Gough Cl *CHELTW* GL51 ... 105 H1 ⑧
William Mason Cl
  EVILLE/WHL BS5 .... 365 F7 ⑬
Williams Cl *OLD/WMLY/WICK* BS30 ... 376 A4
Williamson Rd *HORF/LLZ* BS7 .... 364 D3
Williams Orch *VGL* GL2 .... 128 D1
William St *CBRISNE* BS2 .... 364 D5
  CBRISNE BS2 .... 364 E8 ⑧
  EVILLE/WHL BS5 .... 365 G8 ⑩
  MANG/FISH BS16 .... 366 E3 ⑧
Willis Rd *KGWD/HNM* BS15 .... 367 F4
Willis Wk *TEWK* GL20 .... 34 D5
Willoughby Cl *THNB/SVB* BS35 ... 332 A2
Willoughby Rd *HORF/LLZ* BS7 .... 364 C1 ⑧
Willow Av *GLE* GL4 .... 3 F6
Willow Bank Rd *TEWK* GL20 .... 37 J8
Willow Bed Cl *MANG/FISH* BS16 ... 356 B8
Willowbrook Dr *CHELTW* GL51 ... 105 H2
Willow Cl *BRSTK/PCHW* BS34 .... 342 C7
  CHELTE/BC GL52 .... 83 H3
  DSLY GL11 .... 266 E3 ⑧
  EVE WR11 .... 14 D7
  OLD/WMLY/WICK BS30 .... 367 K6
  OLD/WMLY/WICK BS30 .... 368 D8
  WUE GL12 .... 319 J2
Willowcroft Cl *GLE* GL4 .... 159 F3 ⑧
Willow Gv *CIR* GL7 .... 278 E8
  MANG/FISH BS16 .... 366 C4 ⑧
Willow Hts *LYD* GL15 .... 234 B1
Willowherb Cl *CHELTE/BC* GL52 ... 107 J3 ⑧
Willowleaze *VGL* GL2 .... 131 F3
Willow Park Cl *CHELTE/BC* GL52 ... 83 F2 ⑧
  DSLY GL11 .... 266 E3 ⑧
Willow Rd *BDWAY* WR12 .... 18 E3
  CHELTS GL53 .... 135 J2 ⑧
  CHELTS GL53 .... 135 H1
  KGWD/HNM BS15 .... 375 H3 ⑧
  STNHO GL10 .... 212 E7
  STNHO GL10 .... 241 G2
The Willows *ALMDB* BS32 .... 343 H6
  MTCHDN GL17 .... 124 B4
  VGL GL2 .... 156 E5
  YATE/CS BS37 .... 347 F4 ⑧
Willow Wk *HNBRY/STHM* BS10 ... 353 K3
Willow Wy *FRCTL/WBN* BS36 .... 345 J8 ⑧
  GLE GL4 .... 3 F6

Willsbridge Hl
  OLD/WMLY/WICK BS30 .... 376 B4
Wills Dr *EVILLE/WHL* BS5 .... 364 E6
Willway St *CBRISNE* BS2 .... 364 D7 ⑩
Wilmot Ct
  OLD/WMLY/WICK BS30 .... 367 G8 ⑧
Wilshire Av *KGWD/HNM* BS15 ... 375 J1
Wilson Pl *CBRISNE* BS2 .... 364 D6 ⑧
Wilson Rd *CHELTW* GL51 .... 133 H5
Wilson St *CBRISNE* BS2 .... 364 D6
Wilton Cl *HNBRY/STHM* BS10 ..... 354 A6
Wilton Rd *GL* GL1 .... 129 K8
Wiltshire Av *YATE/CS* BS37 .... 347 J3
Wiltshire Pl *KGWD/HNM* BS15 ... 366 E3 ⑧
Wimbledon Rd *RDLND/MONT* BS6 ... 364 A1
Wimborne Cl *CHELTW* GL51 .... 105 J8
Winash Cl *HGRV/WHIT* BS14 .... 374 C7
Wincanton Cl *FRCTL/WBN* BS36 ... 357 F5 ⑧
Wincel Rd *COTS* GL54 .... 62 E8
Winchcombe Rd *EVE* WR11 .... 15 K5
  FRCTL/WBN BS36 .... 345 H6 ⑧
  GLE GL4 .... 158 A4 ⑧
Winchcombe St *CHELTE/BC* GL52 ... 4 C1 ⑬
  CHELTE/BC GL52 .... 4 C3 ⑬
Winchester Av
  BRSG/KWL/STAPK BS4 .... 374 C3 ⑧
Winchester Dr *GLE* GL4 .... 158 A3
Winchester Rd
  BRSG/KWL/STAPK BS4 .... 374 C3
Winchester Wy *CHELTW* GL51 ... 105 K8
Wincroft *OLD/WMLY/WICK* BS30 ... 376 D2
Windcliff Crs *AVONM* BS11 .... 352 A6
Windermere Cl *CHELTW* GL51 ..... 105 J7 ⑧
Windermere Rd
  BRSTK/PCHW BS34 .... 342 E6
  CHELTW GL51 .... 105 J7
  VGL GL2 .... 130 E2
Windermere Wy
  OLD/WMLY/WICK BS30 .... 367 K8
Windmill Fld *GLE* GL4 .... 131 F7
Windmill La *HNBRY/STHM* BS10 ... 353 F3
Windmill Rd *CIR* GL7 .... 276 B6
  STROUD GL5 .... 243 F7
Windrush Ct *THNB/SVB* BS35 ..... 316 C6
Windrush Rd *CHELTE/BC* GL52 ...... 5 E3 ⑧
  GLE GL4 .... 158 A4
Windrush Wy *COTS* GL54 .... 113 K4
  COTS GL54 .... 113 K4
Windsor Av *EVILLE/WHL* BS5 ...... 366 B8
Windsor Cl *BRSTK/PCHW* BS34 ... 355 J2 ⑧
Windsor Ct *MANG/FISH* BS16 ..... 356 E7
Windsor Crs *HNBRY/STHM* BS10 ... 352 E2
Windsor Dr *GL* GL1 .... 157 J4 ⑧
  LYD GL15 .... 206 B8
  YATE/CS BS37 .... 347 F3
Windsoredge La
  RSTROUD/NAIL GL6 .... 242 B8
Windsor Gv *EVILLE/WHL* BS5 ...... 365 F6 ⑰
Windsor La *DSLY* GL11 .... 268 A6
Windsor Pl *MANG/FISH* BS16 ...... 367 G1
Windsor Rd *DSLY* GL11 .... 267 F5
  OLD/WMLY/WICK BS30 .... 376 A4 ⑧
  RDLND/MONT BS6 .... 364 C4
  TET GL8 .... 302 B6
Windsor St *CHELTE/BC* GL52 .... 5 D2
  CHELTW GL51 .... 106 C1
Windyridge Gdns *CHELTW* GL51 ...... 4 A1
Windyridge Rd *CHELTW* GL51 .... 106 C1
Wineberry Cl *EVILLE/WHL* BS5 ... 365 H5
Wine St *CBRIS/FH* BS1 .... 364 B7
Winfield *NWNT* GL18 .... 73 H6
Winfield Rd
  OLD/WMLY/WICK BS30 .... 367 J7
Winkworth Pl *CBRISNE* BS2 .... 364 D5 ⑩
Winnycroft La *GLE* GL4 .... 158 E5
Winsbury Wy *ALMDB* BS32 .... 343 G6
Winscombe Cl *KEYN* BS31 .... 375 J8
Winsford St *EVILLE/WHL* BS5 ...... 364 E6 ⑬
Winsley Rd *GLE* GL4 .... 158 E2
  RDLND/MONT BS6 .... 364 B5 ⑧
Winstonian Rd *CHELTE/BC* GL52 ...... 5 D3
Winston Rd *BWTH/CHD* GL3 .... 131 K1
Winterbotham Rd *CHELTW* GL51 ... 105 H3
  DSLY GL11 .... 266 D1
Winterbourne Hl
  FRCTL/WBN BS36 .... 356 D1
Winterbourne Rd
  BRSTK/PCHW BS34 .... 343 J8
Winterspring La *WUE* GL12 .... 321 K3
Winterway *MIM* GL56 .... 44 C3
Wintles Cl *MTCHDN* GL17 .... 123 G5
Wintle's Hl *CIND* GL14 .... 153 J6
Wintles La *CIND* GL14 .... 125 G8
Winton Cl *CHELTW* GL51 .... 105 K7
Winton Rd *CHELTW* GL51 .... 106 A7
Wirewood Cl *CHEP* NP16 .... 288 B4
Wirewood Crs *CHEP* NP16 .... 288 C4
Wishford Cl *VGL* GL2 .... 131 G2
Wisloe Rd *VGL* GL2 .... 238 C4
Wistaria Av *YATE/CS* BS37 .... 347 J5 ⑧
Wistaria Rd *TET* GL8 .... 302 B6
Wisteria Wy *BWTH/CHD* GL3 ...... 103 H8
Wistley Rd *CHELTS* GL53 .... 135 G7
Witchell Rd *EVILLE/WHL* BS5 ..... 365 G7 ⑰
Witcombe *YATE/CS* BS37 .... 346 E7

Witcombe Cl KGWD/HNM BS15........ 366 E5
Witcombe Pl CHELTE/BC GL52 .... 4 C4 🔢
Witherlies Rd MANG/FISH BS16 ... 355 K8 🔢
The Withers CHELTE/BC GL52 .... 83 F2
Withington Cl
  OLD/WMLY/WICK BS30 .... 376 D4 🔢
Withleigh Rd
  BRSG/KWL/STAPK BS4 .... 374 A4
Withybridge Gdns CHELTW GL51 .... 80 E6
Withybridge La CHELTW GL51 .... 104 E1
Withyfield Rd CHELTE/BC GL52....... 83 G2
Withyholt Pk CHELTS GL53 .... 135 F1 🔢
Withymead Rd
  CHPMW/MSHF SN14 .... 372 B6
Withy Ms GLE GL4 .... 158 D1
Withypool CHELTW GL51 .... 133 J1 🔢
Withy Wy DSLY GL11 .... 266 D1
Witley Lodge Cl CHELTW GL51 .... 105 H8 🔢
Witpit La CIR GL7 .... 250 D7
Woburn Av GL GL1 .... 157 J5
Woburn Cl
  OLD/WMLY/WICK BS30 .... 376 A1 🔢
Woburn Rd EVILLE/WHL BS5 .... 365 F3
Woefuldane Bottom
  RSTROUD/NAIL GL6 .... 271 K1
Wolds End Cl CHCAM GL55.............. 20 E2
Wolferton Rd RDLND/MONT BS6 ... 364 D4
Wolford Rd MIM GL56 .... 47 H3
Wolfridge Gdns
  HNBRY/STHM BS10 .... 353 L2
Wolfridge La THNB/SVB BS35 .... 331 K2
Wolfridge Ride THNB/SVB BS35 .... 331 K2
Wolseley Rd HORF/LLZ BS7 .... 364 B3
  VGL GL2 .... 130 E4
Woodbine Cl GLE GL4 .... 159 C1 🔢
Woodbine Rd EVILLE/WHL BS5 .. 365 H6 🔢
Woodborough
  RSTROUD/NAIL GL6 .... 187 H7 🔢
Woodborough St
  EVILLE/WHL BS5 .... 365 F5 🔢
Woodbridge La COTS GL54 .... 166 A4
Woodchester KGWD/HNM BS15 .. 366 E3 🔢
  YATE/CS BS37 .... 347 G8
Woodchester Rd
  HNBRY/STHM BS10 .... 354 A7 🔢
Woodcock Cl GLE GL4 .... 158 E1
  STNHO GL10 .... 213 F5
Woodcock La STNHO GL10 .... 213 F6
Woodcote KGWD/HNM BS15 ...... 366 D8 🔢
  VGL GL2 .... 130 D1 🔢
Woodcote Rd MANG/FISH BS16 .... 366 B4
Woodcote Wk MANG/FISH BS16.... 366 B4
Woodcroft Av EVILLE/WHL BS5 .. 365 H5 🔢
Woodcroft Cl
  BRSG/KWL/STAPK BS4 .... 374 D2
  CHEP NP16 .... 288 C2
Woodcroft La CHEP NP16 .... 288 C2
Woodcroft Rd
  BRSG/KWL/STAPK BS4 .... 374 D2
Wood Edge Rd CLFD GL16 .... 176 A8
Woodend Cl GLE GL4 .... 131 C6
Woodend La BRKLY GL13 .... 292 D4
  CIND GL14 .... 209 F2
  DSLY GL11 .... 238 D8
  DSLY GL11 .... 238 A7
Woodend Rd FRCTL/WBN BS36 .... 345 H7
  MTCHDN GL17 .... 122 D8
Wood End St LED HR8 .... 29 G7
Wood End Wk
  HNLZ/SM/SNYPK/WT BS9 .... 352 E8
Woodfield Rd DSLY GL11 .... 266 C2
Woodgate Cl CIND GL14 .... 151 F5
  CLFD GL16 .... 176 A1
Woodgrove Rd
  HNBRY/STHM BS10 .... 353 F4
Woodhall Cl MANG/FISH BS16 ... 357 F8 🔢
Woodhouse Av ALMDB BS32........... 331 H7
Woodhouse Cl ALMDB BS32 .... 331 H7
  CIR GL7 .... 249 H8
Woodhouse Dr STROUD GL5 .... 214 D8
Woodhouse Gv HORF/LLZ BS7 .... 354 C8
Woodington Ct
  OLD/WMLY/WICK BS30 .... 376 A2 🔢
Woodland Av DSLY GL11 .... 266 E4 🔢
  KGWD/HNM BS15 .... 366 D4 🔢
Woodland Cl BDWAY WR12 .... 16 D5 🔢
  MANG/FISH BS16 .... 366 C4 🔢
Woodland Dr DSLY GL11 .... 266 E4 🔢
Woodland Gn GLE GL4 .... 159 G3
Woodland Gv
  HNLZ/SM/SNYPK/WT BS9 .... 353 F8
Woodland Pl LYD GL15 .... 206 C3
Woodland Ri LYD GL15 .... 177 H8
  LYD GL15 .... 234 B2
Woodland Rd CFTN/FAIL BS8........ 364 A7
  CLFD GL16 .... 147 F5
  LYD GL15 .... 177 H8
  LYD GL15 .... 204 E5
  MTCHDN GL17 .... 122 D8
  WUE GL12 .... 318 D2

Woodlands ALMDB BS32 .... 343 H3
  MANG/FISH BS16 .... 356 E8 🔢
  STNHO GL10 .... 240 E3
Woodlands Cl LYD GL15 .... 205 H5
Woodlands Dr STROUD GL5 .... 215 G6 🔢
Woodlands La ALMDB BS32 .... 343 G4
  BRKLY GL13 .... 263 C5
Woodlands Ml STROUD GL5 ...... 215 G6 🔢
Woodlands Reach CIND GL14 ...... 151 F6
Woodlands Ri MANG/FISH BS16 ... 356 D8
Woodlands Rd CHELT GL50 .... 134 A1
  CIR GL7 .... 249 H8
  WUE GL12 .... 319 J2
The Woodlands STROUD GL5 ...... 215 F6 🔢
Woodland Ter KGWD/HNM BS15 ... 366 D7
Woodland Vw CIR GL7 .... 192 E7 🔢
Woodland Wy KGWD/HNM BS15 ... 366 C4
Wood La CHPMW/MSHF SN14...... 363 H6
  EVE WR11 .... 14 D4
  NWNT GL18 .... 72 C7
  RSTROUD/NAIL GL6 .... 270 E2
  VGL GL2 .... 103 J4
  YATE/CS BS37 .... 336 E5
Woodlea CHPMW/MSHF SN14 ...... 373 K8
Woodleaze
  HNLZ/SM/SNYPK/WT BS9 .... 352 D8
Woodleigh THNB/SVB BS35 .... 316 C5
Woodleigh Fld VGL GL2 .... 100 E8 🔢
Woodleigh Gdns
  HGRV/WHIT BS14 .... 374 B8
Woodmancote DSLY GL11 .... 267 F6
  YATE/CS BS37 .... 347 F6
Woodmancote Rd
  RDLND/MONT BS6 .... 364 C5 🔢
Woodmancote V
  CHELTE/BC GL52 .... 83 H3 🔢
Woodmans Cl YATE/CS BS37 .... 347 K6
Woodmans Rd YATE/CS BS37 .... 347 K6
Woodmans V YATE/CS BS37 .... 348 A6 🔢
Woodmans Wy CHELTE/BC GL52 ...... 83 F3
Woodmead La
  OLD/WMLY/WICK BS30 .... 369 J5
Woodpecker Crs
  MANG/FISH BS16 .... 368 E2 🔢
Woodpecker Rd VGL GL2 .... 157 J1
Woodpeckers Cl
  RTEWK/TIB GL19 .... 77 G5 🔢
Wood Rd CLFD GL16 .... 176 B2
  KGWD/HNM BS15 .... 366 D6
Woodrow Wy VGL GL2 .... 157 C3
Woodruff Cl GLE GL4 .... 158 D1
Woodside LYD GL15 .... 232 A8
Woodside Av CIND GL14 .... 151 F7
Woodside Gv HNBRY/STHM BS10... 353 F3
Woodside La STNHO GL10 .... 241 F4
Woodside Rd
  BRSG/KWL/STAPK BS4 .... 365 J8
  FRCTL/WBN BS36 .... 345 K7
  KGWD/HNM BS15 .... 366 C6
  LYD GL15 .... 260 A2
  MANG/FISH BS16 .... 356 C7
Woodside St CIND GL14 .... 151 F6
Woods Orch GLE GL4 .... 158 A4
Woods Orchard Rd GLE GL4 .... 158 A4
Woodstock Av
  RDLND/MONT BS6 .... 364 A5 🔢
Woodstock Cl KGWD/HNM BS15 ... 367 F6 🔢
  TET GL8 .... 271 K5 🔢
Woodstock La TET GL8................... 271 K5
Woodstock Rd
  KGWD/HNM BS15 .... 367 F7 🔢
Woodstock Ter DSLY GL11 .... 268 C5
Wood St EVILLE/WHL BS5 .... 365 F4 🔢
  STROUD GL5 .... 215 F7 🔢
  TEWK GL20 .... 32 B5
Woodview Cl AVONM BS11 .... 352 A7
Woodview Rd DSLY GL11 .... 266 E2 🔢
Woodville Av CLFD GL16 .... 176 B2
Woodville Rd CIND GL14 .... 151 G6
  TEWK GL20 .... 57 J3 🔢
Woodville Rd West CIND GL14 ...... 151 F6
Woodward Cl TET GL8 .... 302 B5 🔢
Woodward Dr
  OLD/WMLY/WICK BS30 .... 376 A2
Woodwell Rd AVONM BS11 .... 352 A8
Woodyleaze Dr KGWD/HNM BS15 ... 366 C8
Woolaston Common LYD GL15 ..... 232 B7
Woolridge Hl RTEWK/TIB GL19 .... 100 E2
Woolstone La CHELTE/BC GL52.... 60 A5
Woolstrop Wy VGL GL2 .... 157 G3
Woolthorpe La VGL GL2 .... 181 G3
Wootton Crs
  BRSG/KWL/STAPK BS4 .... 365 J8
Wootton Pk HGRV/WHIT BS14 ...... 374 A5
Wootton Rd
  BRSG/KWL/STAPK BS4 .... 365 J8
Worcester Pde GL GL1 .... 2 C2
Worcester Rd CIND GL14 .... 151 G5
  KGWD/HNM BS15 .... 366 D5 🔢
  RTEWK/TIB GL19 .... 76 D3
Worcester St GL GL1 .... 2 C3
Worcester Wk CLFD GL16 .... 176 B3
Worchester Rd RTEWK/TIB GL19 ...... 54 A8

Worchestershire Way Link
  TEWK GL20 .... 32 A3
The Wordens STROUD GL5 .... 213 K6 🔢
Wordsworth Av CHELTW GL51 ..... 105 J5 🔢
Wordsworth Rd DSLY GL11 .... 267 G7 🔢
  HORF/LLZ BS7 .... 354 E7
Working La COTS GL54 .... 62 A5
Worldsend La BRKLY GL13 .... 262 E6
Worley Rdg RSTROUD/NAIL GL6 ... 270 C2
Wormwood Hl
  RSTROUD/NAIL GL6 .... 270 B5
Worrel's La MANG/FISH BS16 ...... 356 D8
Worsley St EVILLE/WHL BS5 ..... 365 H7 🔢
Worth Cl KGWD/HNM BS15 .... 367 F8 🔢
Worthing Rd BRSTK/PCHW BS34 ... 342 D6
The Worthys ALMDB BS32 .... 344 A8
Wortley Rd WUE GL12 .... 297 C8
Wotton Ct GLE GL4 .... 131 F5 🔢
Wotton Crs WUE GL12 .... 297 G8
Wotton Rd WUE GL12 .... 319 J1
  YATE/CS BS37 .... 346 A2
Wragg Castle La
  RSTROUD/NAIL GL6 .... 186 E8
Wraxall Rd KGWD/HNM BS15 ...... 367 G8
  OLD/WMLY/WICK BS30 .... 367 G8
Wrenbert Rd MANG/FISH BS16 .... 366 D1
Wren Cl GLE GL4 .... 130 D8
Wren Dr MANG/FISH BS16 .... 355 K8
Wren Ter VGL GL2 .... 103 F8
Wright Cl COTS GL54 .... 144 E1
Wright Rd COTS GL54 .... 144 E1
Wrington Cl BRSTK/PCHW BS34 ... 343 G7
Wroxham Dr
  BRSTK/PCHW BS34 .... 343 G6 🔢
Wychavon Wy PER WR10 .... 14 A2
  TEWK GL20 .... 38 E5
Wychbury Cl CHELTS GL53 .... 134 D1 🔢
Wychavon Wy EVE WR11 .... 37 K1
Wychwood KGWD/HNM BS15 .... 366 D8
Wyck Beck Rd HNBRY/STHM BS10.. 353 J2
Wycliffe Rd
  HNLZ/SM/SNYPK/WT BS9 .... 353 K7
Wycombe Gv
  BRSG/KWL/STAPK BS4 .... 374 C4 🔢
Wydelands MIM GL56 .... 44 E2
Wyebank Av CHEP NP16 .... 288 C5
Wyebank Crs CHEP NP16 .... 288 C6
Wyebank Pl CHEP NP16 .... 288 C6 🔢
Wyebank Ri CHEP NP16 .... 288 C6
Wyebank Rd CHEP NP16 .... 288 C6
Wyebank Vw CHEP NP16 .... 288 C6 🔢
Wyebank Wy CHEP NP16 .... 288 C6
Wye Ct THNB/SVB BS35 .... 316 C6
Wye Crs CHEP NP16 .... 288 A7
Wye Croft Cl HNBRY/STHM BS10 ... 354 B3
Wyedale Av
  HNLZ/SM/SNYPK/WT BS9 .... 352 D7
Wye Rd BWTH/CHD GL3 .... 160 D1
Wye Valley Wk CHEP NP16 .... 230 A6
  CHEP NP16 .... 258 A6
  CHEP NP16 .... 288 A3
  RWYE HR9 .... 120 E7
Wykis Ct KGWD/HNM BS15 .... 375 K1 🔢
Wyman's La CHELTW GL51 .... 82 B8
Wyman's Rd CHELTE/BC GL52 .... 5 E2
Wyndbrook La RTEWK/TIB GL19.... 30 E7
Wyndham Crs
  BRSG/KWL/STAPK BS4 .... 374 E3
Wynols Cl CLFD GL16................... 176 B3
Wynols Hill La CLFD GL16 .... 175 K3 🔢
Wynols Rd CLFD GL16 .... 176 B4 🔢
The Wynstones KGWD/HNM BS15 .. 366 C7
Wynyards Cl TEWK GL20 .... 33 J8 🔢
Wyvern Rd CHEP NP16 .... 312 D4

Y

The Yard EVE WR11........................ 15 K4
Yarlington Cl CHELTE/BC GL52 ..... 82 E2 🔢
Yarnolds CHELTW GL51.............. 133 H5
Yarrow Cl GLE GL4 .... 158 C2
Yartleton La MTCHDN GL17 .... 96 B7
Yate Rd YATE/CS BS37 .... 345 K2
Yate Rocks YATE/CS BS37 .... 335 H7
Yellow Hundred Cl DSLY GL11...... 267 F5
The Yetts CHEP NP16 .... 288 D7
Yew Tree Cl CHELTW GL51 .... 106 C1
Yewtree Cl DSLY GL11 .... 266 B3
Yew Tree Dr CHELTE/BC GL52 .... 60 B6 🔢
  KGWD/HNM BS15 .... 367 F3
Yew Tree Wy BWTH/CHD GL3 ..... 131 J1 🔢
  STROUD GL5 .... 243 C3
Yokehouse La RSTROUD/NAIL GL6 .. 215 H1
York Av HORF/LLZ BS7 .... 364 D2
York Cl BRSTK/PCHW BS34.......... 355 H2
  FRCTL/WBN BS36 .... 357 F5
  YATE/CS BS37 .... 347 G2
York Gdns FRCTL/WBN BS36 .... 345 F6
Yorkley La LYD GL15 .... 206 B5
Yorkley Wood Rd LYD GL15.......... 206 A5
York Pl CBRIS/FH BS1 .... 364 A8 🔢

York Rd *CIND* GL14 .... **151** G5
EVILLE/WHL BS5 .... **365** C5
GLE GL4 .... **130** E6
MANG/FISH BS16 .... **366** E2
RDLND/MONT BS6 .... **364** C5
TEWK GL20 .... **57** H2
York Rw *CHELTE/BC* GL52 .... **5** E1
York St *CBRISNE* BS2 .... **364** C6

CBRISNE BS2 .... **364** D4 **14**
CBRISNE BS2 .... **364** E4 **20**
CHELTE/BC GL52 .... **4** C3
EVILLE/WHL BS5 .... **365** G7 **18**
Youngs Ct *MANG/FISH* BS16 .... **357** H6 **1**
Youngs Orch *STROUD* GL5 .... **243** J5

Z

Zetland Rd *RDLND/MONT* BS6 .... **364** B4
Zinnia Cl *BWTH/CHD* GL3 .... **103** H7
Zion Hl *RSTROUD/NAIL* GL6 .... **214** B3
Zoons Rd *BWTH/CHD* GL3 .... **131** J6

Index - featured places

3-D Gallery
CBRISNE BS2 .... **364** A7
Abbey House Studio & Gallery
CHEP NP16 .... **258** A1
Abbeymead Primary School
GLE GL4 .... **159** H1
Abbotswood Infant School
YATE/CS BS37 .... **347** F8
Abbotswood Surgery
YATE/CS BS37 .... **347** F7
Air Balloon Hill Junior &
Infant School
EVILLE/WHL BS5 .... **366** A7
Airthrie School
CHELT GL50 .... **106** B5
Alderman Knight School
TEWK GL20 .... **34** B7
Allen School House
OLD/WMLY/WICK BS30 .... **376** B1
All Saints Exhibition Centre
CBRIS/FH BS1 .... **364** B8
Almondsbury Business Centre
ALMDB BS32 .... **343** H3
Almondsbury C of E VC
Primary School
ALMDB BS32 .... **342** E2
Almondsbury Surgery
ALMDB BS32 .... **342** E1
Almondsbury Town Football Club
ALMDB BS32 .... **342** E2
Alstone Trading Estate
CHELTW GL51 .... **106** A5
Amberley Parochial School
STROUD GL5 .... **242** E7
Amberley Ridge Special School
STROUD GL5 .... **242** E5
Anderson Gallery
BDWAY WR12 .... **18** E6
Andoversford Industrial Estate
COTS GL54 .... **137** K3
Andoversford Primary School
COTS GL54 .... **137** J3
Andoversford Sports Club
COTS GL54 .... **137** J3
Ann Edwards School
CIR GL7 .... **278** D8
The Archway School
STROUD GL5 .... **214** B6
Aretians RFC Clubhouse
BRSTK/PCHW BS34 .... **343** F7
Army Apprentices College
CHEP NP16 .... **312** D3
Arnoldsfield Trading Estate
WUE GL12 .... **335** J1
Art Gallery
CHELT GL50 .... **4** B5
Arthur Dye CP School
CHELTW GL51 .... **105** H2
Ashchurch Business Centre
TEWK GL20 .... **34** C6
Ashchurch County
Primary School
TEWK GL20 .... **34** E7
Ashleworth C of E
Primary School
RTEWK/TIB GL19 .... **77** G6
Ashley Down Junior School
HORF/LLZ BS7 .... **364** C1
Ashley Down OB Rugby Club
HORF/LLZ BS7 .... **355** F6
Ashley Trading Estate
RDLND/MONT BS6 .... **364** D4
Ashton Keynes C of E School
HCHW SN6 .... **308** C5
Ashton under Hill Primary School
EVE WR11 .... **14** D6
Ashville Industrial Estate
VGL GL2 .... **157** J1
Ashville Trading Estate
CHELTW GL51 .... **82** B8

Ashville Trading Estate
VGL GL2 .... **157** J1
Ashwicke Hall (School)
CHPMW/MSHF SN14 .... **381** H2
Avening School
TET GL8 .... **271** K5
Avlon Works
HNBRY/STHM BS10 .... **340** D3
Avon Business Park
MANG/FISH BS16 .... **366** A3
Avondale Business Centre
MANG/FISH BS16 .... **366** C4
Avon & Somerset Constabulary
CBRIS/FH BS1 .... **364** B7
Axiom Arts Centre
CHELTE/BC GL52 .... **4** C3
Aylburton C of E School
LYD GL15 .... **233** H5
Azure Gallery
HNLZ/SM/SNYPK/WT BS9 .... **353** H7
Badminton Road Trading Estate
YATE/CS BS37 .... **346** E5
Badocks Wood Primary School
HNBRY/STHM BS10 .... **354** A6
Baileys Court Primary School
ALMDB BS32 .... **343** K8
Balaclava Industrial Estate
MANG/FISH BS16 .... **365** K3
Balcarras School
CHELTS GL53 .... **135** J1
Bank Leaze Primary School
AVONM BS11 .... **352** D4
Bank Yard Industrial Estate
WUE GL12 .... **296** E7
Bannerman Road
Primary School
EVILLE/WHL BS5 .... **365** F5
Barley Close Primary School
MANG/FISH BS16 .... **357** G8
The Barn Business Centre
COTS GL54 .... **144** E6
Barn Close Surgery
BDWAY WR12 .... **18** D6
Barnwood Business Centre
GLE GL4 .... **131** H5
Barnwood C of E Primary School
GLE GL4 .... **131** F5
Barrett Industrial Estate
GL GL1 .... **2** B1
Barrs Court Primary School
OLD/WMLY/WICK BS30 .... **376** A1
Bartongate Surgery
GL GL1 .... **3** D4
Barton Hill Primary School
EVILLE/WHL BS5 .... **365** F8
Barton Hill Trading Estate
EVILLE/WHL BS5 .... **365** F8
Battledown Industrial Estate
CHELTE/BC GL52 .... **5** E5
Beachley Road Doctors Surgery
CHEP NP16 .... **288** C6
The Beacon Medical Practice
RSTROUD/NAIL GL6 .... **187** G7
Beacon Rise Junior School
KGWD/HNM BS15 .... **366** D8
Beaufort Community School
GL GL1 .... **157** H4
Beeches Trading Estate
YATE/CS BS37 .... **346** C4
Beech Green CP School
VGL GL2 .... **157** F5
Beechwood Shopping Centre
CHELTE/BC GL52 .... **4** C4
Beehive Trading Estate
EVILLE/WHL BS5 .... **365** J7
Begbrook Primary School
MANG/FISH BS16 .... **355** K8
Bells Hotel & the Royal
Forest of Dean Golf Club
CLFD GL16 .... **175** K4

Benhall Infant School
CHELTW GL51 .... **105** H7
Berkeley Association
Football Club
BRKLY GL13 .... **264** B2
Berkeley Castle
BRKLY GL13 .... **264** B4
Berkeley Hospital
BRKLY GL13 .... **264** A3
Berkeley Leisure Centre
BRKLY GL13 .... **236** A7
Berkeley Primary School
BRKLY GL13 .... **264** A3
Berkeley Vale Community School
BRKLY GL13 .... **236** A7
Berkhampstead School
CHELTE/BC GL52 .... **5** D3
Berry Hill RFC
CLFD GL16 .... **147** K8
Bettridge School
CHELTW GL51 .... **106** A8
Bibury C of E Primary School
CIR GL7 .... **225** H4
Birdlip School
BWTH/CHD GL3 .... **161** K5
Bishop Road Primary School
HORF/LLZ BS7 .... **364** B2
Bishops Cleeve Primary School
CHELTE/BC GL52 .... **83** F3
Bishops Cleeve Sports Centre
CHELTE/BC GL52 .... **83** G4
Bishopston House Clinic
HORF/LLZ BS7 .... **364** C2
Bisley Blue Coat School
RSTROUD/NAIL GL6 .... **216** E6
Blackberry Hill Hospital
MANG/FISH BS16 .... **365** K1
Blackhorse CP School
MANG/FISH BS16 .... **357** G6
Blaise Hamlet (NT)
HNBRY/STHM BS10 .... **353** F4
Blakeney CP School
LYD GL15 .... **207** H4
Bledington County
Primary School
CHNTN OX7 .... **118** D4
Blockley C of E School
MIM GL56 .... **44** B3
Blue Coat Church of
England Primary School
WUE GL12 .... **297** F7
Bonds Mill Trading Estate
STNHO GL10 .... **212** C7
Bonville Business Centre
BRSG/KWL/STAPK BS4 .... **374** E4
Bourton Industrial Estate
COTS GL54 .... **115** H7
Bourton on the Water
County Primary School
COTS GL54 .... **115** H7
Bowden Hall (Hotel)
GL GL1 .... **2** C3
Bowden Hall (Hotel)
GLE GL4 .... **159** J3
Bowling Club
CHELT GL50 .... **4** A5
Bowling Hill Business Park
YATE/CS BS37 .... **347** J5
Bownham Park School
STROUD GL5 .... **243** F4
Bradgate Surgery
HNBRY/STHM BS10 .... **353** J3
Bream Sports Club
LYD GL15 .... **204** E6
Bredon Hancocks Endowed
First School
TEWK GL20 .... **13** J7
Bredon School
TEWK GL20 .... **32** B5

Brentry Hospital
HNBRY/STHM BS10 .... **353** K4
Brentry Primary School
HNBRY/STHM BS10 .... **353** K3
Bretforton First School
EVE WR11 .... **6** C2
Briarwood School
MANG/FISH BS16 .... **366** B3
Brickhampton Court Golf Club
BWTH/CHD GL3 .... **103** K6
Brickwell Swimming Pools
RSTROUD/NAIL GL6 .... **244** B7
Bridge House Gallery
CIR GL7 .... **285** F2
Brimscombe C of E
Primary School
STROUD GL5 .... **243** H5
Brimscombe Mills Estate
STROUD GL5 .... **243** H5
Brimscombe Port Business Park
STROUD GL5 .... **243** H5
Brimsham Green School
YATE/CS BS37 .... **347** F2
Brislington Retail Park
BRSG/KWL/STAPK BS4 .... **374** D5
Brislington School
BRSG/KWL/STAPK BS4 .... **374** E6
Brislington Trading Estate
BRSG/KWL/STAPK BS4 .... **374** E4
Bristol Business Park
MANG/FISH BS16 .... **355** K5
Bristol Cathedral
CBRIS BS1 .... **364** A8
Bristol Cathedral School
CBRIS/FH BS1 .... **364** A8
Bristol City Council
AVONM BS11 .... **352** C5
Bristol City Council
AVONM BS11 .... **352** C7
Bristol City Council
BRSG/KWL/STAPK BS4 .... **374** E3
Bristol City Council
BRSG/KWL/STAPK BS4 .... **374** B2
Bristol City Council
CBRIS/FH BS1 .... **364** A8
Bristol City Council
CBRISNE BS2 .... **364** D5
Bristol City Council
EVILLE/WHL BS5 .... **365** F4
Bristol City Council
HGRV/WHIT BS14 .... **374** B6
Bristol City Council
HNBRY/STHM BS10 .... **353** K6
Bristol City Council
HNBRY/STHM BS10 .... **353** K3
Bristol City Council
HNBRY/STHM BS10 .... **354** B4
Bristol City Council
HNBRY/STHM BS10 .... **354** C8
Bristol City Council
HORF/LLZ BS7 .... **354** D5
Bristol Civil Service Sports Club
HORF/LLZ BS7 .... **354** D8
Bristol County Court
CBRISNE BS2 .... **364** B7
Bristol County Sports Club
CBRIS/FH BS1 .... **364** A7
Bristol Crown Court
CBRIS/FH BS1 .... **364** B7
Bristol Dental Hospital
CBRIS/FH BS1 .... **364** B7
Bristol Harlequins RFC
BRSG/KWL/STAPK BS4 .... **375** F4
Bristol Ice Rink
CBRIS/FH BS1 .... **364** A8
Bristol North Baths
HORF/LLZ BS7 .... **364** B3
Bristol Old Vic (New Vic Theatre
& Theatre Royal)
CBRIS/FH BS1 .... **364** B8
Bristol Rovers Football Club
BRSG/KWL/STAPK BS4 .... **374** E5
Bristol Royal Hospital for
Sick Children
CFTN/FAIL BS8 .... **364** A7
Bristol Royal Infirmary
CBRISNE BS2 .... **364** B6
Bristol University
CFTN/FAIL BS8 .... **364** A7
The British School
WUE GL12 .... **297** G8
Broadfield House Glass Museum
CIR GL7 .... **249** J6

Broadlands School
KEYN BS31 .... **375** J8
Broadmead Lane
Industrial Estate
KEYN BS31 .... **376** B7
Broadwalk Shopping Centre
BRSG/KWL/STAPK BS4 .... **374** A4
Broadway County Infant School
YATE/CS BS37 .... **347** H4
Broadway Dental Health Centre
BDWAY WR12 .... **18** D6
Broadway Primary School
BDWAY WR12 .... **18** E5
Broadway Trading Estate
CIR GL7 .... **308** E1
Broadway United Football Club
BDWAY WR12 .... **18** B6
Brockeridge Infant School
FRCTL/WBN BS36 .... **345** J7
Brockworth
Comprehensive School
BWTH/CHD GL3 .... **132** D8
Brockworth County
Primary Infant School
BWTH/CHD GL3 .... **132** C8
Bromesberrow C of E School
LED HR8 .... **29** J5
Bromley Heath Infant School
MANG/FISH BS16 .... **356** E6
Bromley Heath Junior School
MANG/FISH BS16 .... **356** E6
Bromsberrow Heath
Business Park
LED HR8 .... **29** F8
Brookfield School
CHELTW GL51 .... **106** A7
Brooklea Clinic
BRSG/KWL/STAPK BS4 .... **374** D1
Brookside Business Centre
TEWK GL20 .... **34** A7
Broomhill Infant School
BRSG/KWL/STAPK BS4 .... **374** E3
Broomhill JM School
BRSG/KWL/STAPK BS4 .... **374** E3
Brunston Surgery
CLFD GL16 .... **175** J5
B Tech Business Park
CIR GL7 .... **249** K8
Burnbush School
HGRV/WHIT BS14 .... **374** C8
Bush Industrial Estate
EVILLE/WHL BS5 .... **365** H6
Business Park
VGL GL2 .... **2** A4
Bussage C of E Primary School
RSTROUD/NAIL GL6 .... **244** B2
CAB & Guildhall
CBRIS/FH BS1 .... **364** B7
Cabot Primary School
CBRISNE BS2 .... **364** D6
Cadbury Heath CP School
OLD/WMLY/WICK BS30 .... **367** H8
Cadbury Heath Health Centre
OLD/WMLY/WICK BS30 .... **376** B1
Cainscross Parish Council
STROUD GL5 .... **213** K8
Callicroft Infant School
BRSTK/PCHW BS34 .... **342** D6
Callicroft Junior School
BRSTK/PCHW BS34 .... **342** C6
Callowell CP School
STROUD GL5 .... **214** C5
Calton Junior School
GL GL1 .... **130** A8
Cam Everlands CP School
DSLY GL11 .... **266** E2
Cam Hopton School
DSLY GL11 .... **266** E2
Cam House School
DSLY GL11 .... **267** G4
Cam Sports Club
DSLY GL11 .... **266** E2
The Card Gallery
YATE/CS BS37 .... **347** K5
Carlyle Business Centre
CBRISNE BS2 .... **364** E8
Carrant Brook Junior School
TEWK GL20 .... **34** D5
Carrick Business Park
BRSG/KWL/STAPK BS4 .... **374** E5
Cascade Swimming Pool
TEWK GL20 .... **33** H8
Cashes Green CP School
RSTROUD/NAIL GL6 .... **213** K6

Castle Business Centre
THNB/SVB BS35 .... **316** B5
Castle Hill CP School
BWTH/CHD GL3 .... **160** C2
The Castle School
THNB/SVB BS35 .... **316** B4
Cattle Market Industrial Estate
GL GL1 .... **2** C1
Cedars Health Clinic
GL GL1 .... **2** C4
Central Technology College
GLE GL4 .... **158** D1
Central Trading Estate
BRSG/KWL/STAPK BS4 .... **374** A2
Central Trading Estate
VGL GL2 .... **157** G3
Centurion Industrial Estate
VGL GL2 .... **157** H1
Chalford Hill County
Primary School
RSTROUD/NAIL GL6 .... **244** D4
Charborough Road CP School
BRSTK/PCHW BS34 .... **354** D4
Charfield CP School
WUE GL12 .... **319** H1
Charles Street Industrial Estate
GL GL1 .... **3** D4
Charlotte Keel Health Clinic
EVILLE/WHL BS5 .... **364** E5
The Charlton Kings Clinic
CHELTE/BC GL52 .... **5** E6
Charlton Kings County
Infants School
CHELTS GL53 .... **107** H8
Charlton Kings Junior School
CHELTS GL53 .... **135** H1
Cheltenham Art Gallery &
Museum
CHELT GL50 .... **4** A3
Cheltenham Borough Council
CHELTW GL51 .... **106** A2
Cheltenham Bournside School & Sixth
Form Centre
CHELTW GL51 .... **106** A8
Cheltenham College
CHELTS GL53 .... **4** C6
Cheltenham College
Junior School
CHELTS GL53 .... **4** B6
Cheltenham Cricket Club
CHELTE/BC GL52 .... **5** D4
Cheltenham General Hospital
CHELTS GL53 .... **4** C5
Cheltenham & Gloucester
College of Higher Education
CHELT GL50 .... **106** C8
Cheltenham & Gloucester
College of Higher Education
CHELTE/BC GL52 .... **5** D1
Cheltenham Kingsmead School
CHELTW GL51 .... **105** K2
Cheltenham Ladies College
CHELT GL50 .... **4** A4
Cheltenham North Rugby Club
CHELTE/BC GL52 .... **82** C2
Cheltenham Race Course
CHELTE/BC GL52 .... **83** G8
Cheltenham Retail Park
CHELTW GL51 .... **105** K1
Cheltenham Road Surgery
GL GL1 .... **3** F2
Cheltenham Saracens Sports Club
CHELT GL50 .... **4** B2
Cheltenham Saracens Sports Club
CHELTW GL51 .... **106** A3
Cheltenham Synagogue
CHELT GL50 .... **4** B4
Cheltenham Theatre & Arts Club
CHELT GL50 .... **4** C5
Cheltenham Town
Association Football Club
CHELTE/BC GL52 .... **5** D2
Cheltenham Tutorial College
CHELT GL50 .... **4** B3
Chepstow Castle
CHEP NP16 .... **288** A5
Chepstow County Court
CHEP NP16 .... **288** B6
Chepstow Museum
CHEP NP16 .... **288** A5
Cherry Garden Primary School
OLD/WMLY/WICK BS30 .... **376** C4
Chester Park Primary School
MANG/FISH BS16 .... **366** A3

Chesterton County
Primary School
CIR GL7 .... **249** J8
Childswickham School
BDWAY WR12 .... **17** K4
Chipping Campden School
CHCAM GL55 .... **20** E2
Chipping Edge Estate
YATE/CS BS37 .... **347** K5
Chipping Sodbury Library
YATE/CS BS37 .... **347** K5
Chipping Sodbury School
YATE/CS BS37 .... **347** K6
The Chipping Surgery
WUE GL12 .... **296** E7
Chosen Hill Former Pupils Rugby
Football Club
BWTH/CHD GL3 .... **132** B1
Chosen Hill School
BWTH/CHD GL3 .... **132** C1
Christ Church C of E School
RSTROUD/NAIL GL6 .... **244** C4
Christ Church C of E VC
Infant School
MANG/FISH BS16 .... **366** D1
Christchurch Junior School
MANG/FISH BS16 .... **366** D1
Christchurch School
CHELTW GL51 .... **106** B5
Christ the King RC School
THNB/SVB BS35 .... **316** C5
Churcham School
VGL GL2 .... **127** F4
Churchdown School
BWTH/CHD GL3 .... **131** K1
Churchdown Village
County Junior School
BWTH/CHD GL3 .... **132** A2
Churchdown Village
Infant School
BWTH/CHD GL3 .... **132** A1
Churchill Industrial Estate
CHELTS GL53 .... **106** D8
Church of England School
CLFD GL16 .... **203** J2
Church Street Gallery
COTS GL54 .... **92** B6
Cinemas
CBRISNE BS2 .... **364** B6
Cirencester Business Estate
CIR GL7 .... **250** A8
Cirencester College
CIR GL7 .... **249** G6
Cirencester
Comprehensive School
CIR GL7 .... **249** F6
Cirencester County
Junior School
CIR GL7 .... **249** K6
Cirencester Golf Club
CIR GL7 .... **221** H8
Cirencester Hospital
CIR GL7 .... **249** H7
Cirencester Kingshill School
CIR GL7 .... **250** B5
Cirencester Polo Club
CIR GL7 .... **249** G6
Cirencester Rugby Union Club
CIR GL7 .... **249** J4
Cirencester Town Council
CIR GL7 .... **249** J5
Cirencester Town Football Club
CIR GL7 .... **249** G7
City Business Park
CBRIS/FH BS1 .... **364** C7
City Business Park
EVILLE/WHL BS5 .... **364** E7
City Council Offices
GL GL1 .... **2** B3
City of Bristol College
HORF/LLZ BS7 .... **364** D2
Civic Centre
KGWD/HNM BS15 .... **366** E6
Civil Service Sports Club
CHELTW GL51 .... **105** K1
Civil Sports Club
GL GL1 .... **3** D1
Claremont Special School
RDLND/MONT BS6 .... **364** A1
Cleeve School
CHELTE/BC GL52 .... **83** G4
Cleeve View Infant School
CHELTW GL51 .... **4** A1

Clifton Rugby Club
HNBRY/STHM BS10 .... **353** H1
Close Farm Surgery
OLD/WMLY/WICK BS30 .... **376** E1
Club House
TEWK GL20 .... **57** F3
Coalway County Junior &
Infant School
CLFD GL16 .... **176** B5
Coberley School
CHELTS GL53 .... **163** G1
Cold Aston C of E Primary School
COTS GL54 .... **141** K2
Coleford County Primary School
CLFD GL16 .... **147** K8
Coleford Health Centre
CLFD GL16 .... **175** K5
Coleford Road Surgery
CHEP NP16 .... **288** B4
College House
MANG/FISH BS16 .... **366** A1
College of Art & Technology
GL GL1 .... **2** C4
College of St Mathias
C of E (A) Infant School
MANG/FISH BS16 .... **366** A1
College Pharmacy
CHELT GL50 .... **4** B6
The College Yard Surgery
GL GL1 .... **2** B2
Coln Gallery
CIR GL7 .... **249** J5
Coln Gallery
CIR GL7 .... **254** E7
Coln House Special School
CIR GL7 .... **254** D8
Colston Hall
CBRIS/FH BS1 .... **364** A7
Colstons Collegiate
Lower School
MANG/FISH BS16 .... **365** H1
Colstons Girls School
RDLND/MONT BS6 .... **364** C4
Colstons Primary School
RDLND/MONT BS6 .... **364** A5
Colstons School
MANG/FISH BS16 .... **365** H2
Commercial House Station Road
Business Park
TEWK GL20 .... **33** J8
Community Health Authority
KEYN BS31 .... **375** K8
Community Services Clinic
TEWK GL20 .... **33** J8
Coney Hill Infant School
GLE GL4 .... **130** E7
Coniston Primary School
BRSTK/PCHW BS34 .... **342** D5
Connoisseur Gallery
TET GL8 .... **302** C7
Conygre Medical Centre
BRSTK/PCHW BS34 .... **354** E3
Copse Surgery
RTEWK/TIB GL19 .... **53** H7
Corbett House Clinic
EVILLE/WHL BS5 .... **365** F7
Corinium Business Park
CIND GL14 .... **150** D3
Corinium Museum
CIR GL7 .... **249** J5
Coroners Court
CBRISNE BS2 .... **364** C6
Cossham Memorial Hospital
KGWD/HNM BS15 .... **366** C4
Cotham Grammar School
RDLND/MONT BS6 .... **364** A5
Cotham Road Surgery
RDLND/MONT BS6 .... **364** A6
Cotswold Bowl (Cheltenham)
CHELTW GL51 .... **106** B1
Cotswold Chine Home School
RSTROUD/NAIL GL6 .... **271** F1
Cotswold District Council
CIR GL7 .... **249** J6
Cotswold Edge Business Centre
VGL GL2 .... **2** A5
Cotswold Edge Golf Club
WUE GL12 .... **297** K3
Cotswold Motor Museum & Toy
Collection
COTS GL54 .... **115** C8
Cotswold Nuffield Hospital
CHELTW GL51 .... **106** A6

Cotswold School
COTS GL54 .... **115** H7
Cotswold Sports Centre
CIR GL7 .... **249** H6
The Cotswold
Teddy Bear Museum
BDWAY WR12 .... **18** E6
Council Offices
GLE GL4 .... **158** E3
Council Offices
MIM GL56 .... **46** A8
Council Offices
TEWK GL20 .... **57** G1
County Court & District Registry
CHELTE/BC GL52 .... **4** C4
County Police Court
CHCAM GL55 .... **20** E3
Courtney Primary School
KGWD/HNM BS15 .... **367** F7
Courtside Surgery
YATE/CS BS37 .... **347** G5
Courtyard Shopping Centre
CHELT GL50 .... **4** A5
Cowdy Gallery
NWNT GL18 .... **73** J6
The Craft Gallery
HORF/LLZ BS7 .... **354** D5
Cribbs Causeway
Shopping Centre
BRSTK/PCHW BS34 .... **342** A8
Cricklade Hotel & Country Club
HGHW SN6 .... **310** B7
Cricklade Leisure Centre
HGHW SN6 .... **310** C6
Cricklade Town Council
HGHW SN6 .... **310** D6
Croft Primary School
RSTROUD/NAIL GL6 .... **187** G6
Crofts End Industrial Estate
EVILLE/WHL BS5 .... **365** J5
Crofts End Trading Estate
EVILLE/WHL BS5 .... **365** J5
Crooks Industrial Estate
CHELTS GL53 .... **106** D8
Crossways Junior & Infant School
THNB/SVB BS35 .... **316** D5
Crudwell C of E Primary School
MALM SN16 .... **305** F8
The Crypt School
GL GL1 .... **157** K2
Culverhay Surgery
WUE GL12 .... **297** F7
Culverhill School
YATE/CS BS37 .... **347** F7
Custom House
CBRIS/FH BS1 .... **364** B8
Cutlers Brook Junior School
CBRISNE BS2 .... **364** E4
Daniels Industrial Estate
STROUD GL5 .... **242** B1
Darcy Galleries
CHELT GL50 .... **4** A6
Dean Close Junior School
CHELTW GL51 .... **106** A6
Dean Close School
CHELTW GL51 .... **105** K6
Dean Heritage Museum
CIND GL14 .... **179** G4
Deerhurst C of E Primary School
RTEWK/TIB GL19 .... **79** G1
Deers Wood Primary School
KGWD/HNM BS15 .... **367** G4
The Dell Primary School
CHEP NP16 .... **288** A5
Dene Magna Community School
MTCHDN GL17 .... **123** H6
Denmark Road High
School for Girls
GL GL1 .... **3** D2
The Diane Breen Gallery
CIR GL7 .... **225** H4
Didbrook CP School
COTS GL54 .... **64** A3
Dilke Memorial Hospital
CIND GL14 .... **150** C8
Dinglewell Primary School
GLE GL4 .... **131** H7
Dixon Business Centre
BRSG/KWL/STAPK BS4 .... **374** E4
Docks Industrial Estate
AVONM BS11 .... **340** A6
The Doctors Surgery
EVILLE/WHL BS5 .... **365** F5

Dodington Parish Council
  YATE/CS BS37 .... **347** J6
Dodington Park
  YATE/CS BS37 .... **360** E2
Dormer House PNEU School
  MIM GL56 .... **46** A8
Down Ampney C of E
  Primary School
  CIR GL7 .... **280** E7
Downend Cricket Club
  MANG/FISH BS16 .... **356** D8
Downend School
  MANG/FISH BS16 .... **366** E1
Downend Surgery
  MANG/FISH BS16 .... **366** D1
Dr Bells C of E School
  MANG/FISH BS16 .... **366** A2
Drybrook Primary School
  MTCHDN GL17 .... **122** C7
Drybrook Rugby Football Club
  MTCHDN GL17 .... **122** D6
Drybrook Surgery
  MTCHDN GL17 .... **122** C7
Dunalley County Primary School
  CHELT GL50 .... **4** C2
Dunalley Street School
  CHELT GL50 .... **4** B3
Dunmail Primary School
  HNBRY/STHM BS10 .... **354** A4
Dursley C of E Primary School
  DSLY GL11 .... **267** G6
Dursley Day Hospital
  DSLY GL11 .... **266** B5
Dursley Magistrates Court
  DSLY GL11 .... **266** D3
Dursley Town Council
  DSLY GL11 .... **267** F5
Eagles Wood Business Park
  ALMDB BS32 .... **343** G3
Eastbrook Road Trading Estate
  GLE GL4 .... **130** E6
Eastcombe CP School
  RSTROUD/NAIL GL6 .... **244** B1
Eastern Avenue Retail Park
  GLE GL4 .... **3** F5
East Gloucestershire NHS Trust
  CHELTW GL51 .... **105** J4
Eastington CP School
  STNHO GL10 .... **212** A6
Eastington Trading Estate
  STNHO GL10 .... **211** K5
Easton Business Centre
  EVILLE/WHL BS5 .... **365** F6
Easton CEVA Primary School
  EVILLE/WHL BS5 .... **364** E6
Easton Leisure Centre
  EVILLE/WHL BS5 .... **364** E6
Eastpark Trading Estate
  EVILLE/WHL BS5 .... **365** H5
Eastville Health Centre
  EVILLE/WHL BS5 .... **365** F4
Ebley Industrial Estate
  STROUD GL5 .... **213** K8
Eight Bells Gallery
  TET GL8 .... **302** C7
Eldersfield Lawn School
  RTEWK/TIB GL19 .... **55** F4
Ellwood County Primary School
  CLFD GL16 .... **204** B1
Ellwood Football Club
  CLFD GL16 .... **204** C1
Elmbridge Junior School
  VGL GL2 .... **130** E4
Elmbridge Rugby Club
  VGL GL2 .... **131** F3
Elmfield Junior School
  CHELTW GL51 .... **4** A1
Elm Park School
  FRCTL/WBN BS36 .... **344** E8
The Elms Day Hospital
  THNB/SVB BS35 .... **316** B5
Embleton Junior School
  HNBRY/STHM BS10 .... **353** K5
English Bicknor C of E Primary
  CLFD GL16 .... **148** A2
English Estates Workshops
  CIND GL14 .... **150** D5
Evergreen Industrial Estate
  CIR GL7 .... **308** D1
Everyman Theatre
  CHELT GL50 .... **4** B4
Exhibition Centre
  CBRIS/FH BS1 .... **364** A8

Explore @ Bristol
  CBRIS/FH BS1 .... **364** A8
The Eye Clinic
  CBRIS/FH BS1 .... **364** C7
Fairfield Grammar School
  RDLND/MONT BS6 .... **364** D4
Fairford C of E Primary School
  CIR GL7 .... **254** E6
Fairford Football Club
  CIR GL7 .... **255** G7
Fairford Hospital
  CIR GL7 .... **254** E7
Fairway Industrial Centre
  BRSTK/PCHW BS34 .... **354** D3
Falconride Primary School
  KGWD/HNM BS15 .... **366** E5
The Family Practice
  RDLND/MONT BS6 .... **364** A6
Family & Youth Court
  CBRIS/FH BS1 .... **364** B7
Farmors School
  CIR GL7 .... **254** E6
Feathers Gallery
  BDWAY WR12 .... **18** D7
Federated Primary Schools of
  Ebrington & St James
  CHCAM GL55 .... **20** E4
Field Court C of E Junior &
  Infant School
  VGL GL2 .... **157** F6
Filand School
  MALM SN16 .... **327** K8
Filton Avenue Junior School
  HORF/LLZ BS7 .... **354** E7
Filton Clinic
  HORF/LLZ BS7 .... **354** E4
Filton College
  BRSTK/PCHW BS34 .... **354** E2
Filton High School
  BRSTK/PCHW BS34 .... **355** H3
Filton Hill CP School
  BRSTK/PCHW BS34 .... **355** F2
Filton Park School
  BRSTK/PCHW BS34 .... **354** D4
Filton Recreation Centre
  BRSTK/PCHW BS34 .... **354** E4
Filton Shield Road School
  HORF/LLZ BS7 .... **354** E5
Filton Town Council
  BRSTK/PCHW BS34 .... **354** E4
Finlay Primary School
  GLE GL4 .... **130** C8
Fire Service Technical College
  MIM GL56 .... **46** D8
Fire Station
  CBRIS/FH BS1 .... **364** C8
Fishponds Health Centre
  MANG/FISH BS16 .... **366** B2
The Florence Brown School
  CBRISNE BS2 .... **364** D7
Flower Gallery
  FRCTL/WBN BS36 .... **344** D8
Folk House
  CBRIS/FH BS1 .... **364** A7
Fonthill Junior School
  HNBRY/STHM BS10 .... **354** C4
Forest Health Care
  CIND GL14 .... **151** F6
Forest Hills Golf Club
  CLFD GL16 .... **176** A2
Forest of Dean District Council
  CIND GL14 .... **151** F5
Forest of Dean District Council
  CLFD GL16 .... **175** J4
Forest View Primary School
  CIND GL14 .... **151** G5
Forest View Upper School
  CIND GL14 .... **151** G5
Fosse Cross Industrial Estate
  CIR GL7 .... **195** F7
Fosse Way Business Centre
  MIM GL56 .... **46** A8
Foster Almshouses
  CBRIS/FH BS1 .... **364** B7
Foxmoor CP School
  STROUD GL5 .... **213** K7
Frampton Cotterell C of E
  School
  FRCTL/WBN BS36 .... **345** G6
Frampton on Severn C of E
  School
  VGL GL2 .... **182** D8
Francis Woodcock Estate
  GL GL1 .... **3** E5

Frenchay C of E School
  MANG/FISH BS16 .... **356** B7
Frenchay Health Authority
  MANG/FISH BS16 .... **366** C1
Frenchay Hospital
  MANG/FISH BS16 .... **356** B6
Frenchay Village Museum
  MANG/FISH BS16 .... **355** K7
The Friends of Gloucester
  Cathedral
  GL GL1 .... **2** C3
Frithwood Surgery
  RSTROUD/NAIL GL6 .... **244** B2
Frome Bank Junior School
  YATE/CS BS37 .... **347** F3
Fromeside Clinic
  MANG/FISH BS16 .... **365** K1
The Gallaries Shopping Centre
  CBRIS/FH BS1 .... **364** C7
The Gallery
  CIR GL7 .... **249** J6
Gastrells CP School
  STROUD GL5 .... **242** C2
Gas Works
  HNBRY/STHM BS10 .... **340** D6
Georgian House
  CBRIS/FH BS1 .... **364** A8
Glebe Infant School
  NWNT GL18 .... **73** H5
Glenfall CP School
  CHELTE/BC GL52 .... **107** J8
Glenfrome Primary School
  EVILLE/WHL BS5 .... **365** G2
Glevum Industrial Estate
  GL GL1 .... **3** E6
Glevum Shopping Centre
  GLE GL4 .... **159** F2
Gloucester City
  Association Football Club
  VGL GL2 .... **129** H6
Gloucester City Council
  GL GL1 .... **2** C1
Gloucester County Constabulary
  GL GL1 .... **3** E5
Gloucester County Constabulary
  STNHO GL10 .... **213** F7
Gloucester County Council
  CHELT GL50 .... **106** B6
Gloucester County Council
  GLE GL4 .... **3** E6
Gloucester County Council
  VGL GL2 .... **211** K4
Gloucester Crown &
  County Court
  GL GL1 .... **2** B4
Gloucester Folk Museum
  GL GL1 .... **2** B3
Gloucester Retail Park
  GLE GL4 .... **130** E5
Gloucester Road Primary School
  CHELTW GL51 .... **106** B4
Gloucester Rugby Football Club
  GL GL1 .... **2** C2
Gloucestershire
  Aviation Museum
  BWTH/CHD GL3 .... **104** A6
Gloucestershire College of
  Arts & Technology
  GL GL1 .... **2** C4
Gloucestershire
  Community Health Centre
  GL GL1 .... **3** D3
Gloucestershire County Council
  CHELTS GL53 .... **4** C5
Gloucestershire County Council
  CHELTW GL51 .... **104** D7
Gloucestershire County Council
  CIR GL7 .... **249** K8
Gloucestershire County Council
  CLFD GL16 .... **175** J4
Gloucestershire County Council
  COTS GL54 .... **115** J7
Gloucestershire County Council
  GL GL1 .... **157** H3
Gloucestershire County Council
  KGWD/HNM BS15 .... **366** E6
Gloucestershire County Council
  STROUD GL5 .... **214** D7
Gloucestershire County
  Cricket Club
  HORF/LLZ BS7 .... **364** C3
Gloucestershire County
  Library Arts & Museums Service
  CHELT GL50 .... **4** A3

Gloucestershire Health Authority
  GL GL1 .... 2 B4
Gloucestershire Islamic Secondary
  School for Girls
  GL GL1 .... 3 D4
Gloucestershire Royal Hospital
  GL GL1 .... 3 E3
Gloucester Sports Club
  GL GL1 .... 2 B5
Glynne Wickham Studio Theatre
  CFTN/FAIL BS8 .... 364 A7
The Golf Club
  DSLY GL11 .... 266 D5
Golf Course
  HCHW SN6 .... 310 B6
Goodridge Industrial Estate
  VGL GL2 .... 157 G2
Goodridge Trading Estate
  VGL GL2 .... 157 G3
Gordon League Rugby
  Football Club
  VGL GL2 .... 129 H7
Grange Infant School
  GL GL1 .... 157 J4
Grange Junior School
  GL GL1 .... 157 J3
Greatfield Park Primary School
  CHELTW GL51 .... 133 K1
Great Rissington CP School
  COTS GL54 .... 144 E7
Great Western Business Park
  YATE/CS BS37 .... 346 D3
The Great Western
  Railway Museum
  CLFD GL16 .... 175 K4
Gretton School
  COTS GL54 .... 62 A5
Greyholme Surgery
  CHELTE/BC GL52 .... 83 F2
Greystones Gallery
  CIR GL7 .... 285 G2
Grimsby Park School
  OLD/WMLY/WICK BS30 .... 367 H7
Grove Industrial Estate
  BRSTK/PCHW BS34 .... 343 F7
Hadwen Practice
  GLE GL4 .... 159 G2
Hambrook CP School
  MANG/FISH BS16 .... 356 D3
Hambrook Sports Club
  MANG/FISH BS16 .... 356 D3
Hampton Street
  Industrial Estate
  TET GL8 .... 302 A5
Hanham Abbots Junior School
  KCWD/HNM BS15 .... 375 H2
Hanham Business Park
  KCWD/HNM BS15 .... 375 G1
Hanham C of E Primary School
  KCWD/HNM BS15 .... 375 G2
Hanham High School
  KCWD/HNM BS15 .... 375 H2
Hanham Surgery
  KCWD/HNM BS15 .... 375 J2
Hannah More Primary School
  CBRISNE BS2 .... 364 D8
Hardwicke Parochial
  Primary School
  VGL GL2 .... 156 E8
Haresfield C of E Primary School
  STNHO GL10 .... 185 H5
Harewood Junior & Infant School
  GL GL1 .... 157 J5
Harlequin Gallery
  CHELTE/BC GL52 .... 4 C3
Hartpury College
  RTEWK/TIB GL19 .... 100 B4
Harveys Wine Museum
  CBRIS/FH BS1 .... 364 A8
Hatherley Infant School
  GL GL1 .... 3 E6
Hatherop Castle School
  CIR GL7 .... 226 E7
Hatherop C of E School
  CIR GL7 .... 227 F7
Hawkesbury Upton
  Primary School
  BAD GL9 .... 337 K3
Hayward Road Industrial Estate
  MANG/FISH BS16 .... 366 D3
Heath House Priory Hospital
  HORF/LLZ BS7 .... 365 F2
Heathville Road Surgery
  GL GL1 .... 3 D3

Hempsted School
  VGL GL2 .... 129 G7
Henbury Court Junior &
  Primary School
  HNBRY/STHM BS10 .... 353 H3
Henbury Manor School
  HNBRY/STHM BS10 .... 353 G4
Henbury Old Boys AFC
  HNBRY/STHM BS10 .... 353 H4
Henbury School
  HNBRY/STHM BS10 .... 353 G3
The Henbury Surgery
  HNBRY/STHM BS10 .... 353 H3
Henbury Swimming Pool
  HNBRY/STHM BS10 .... 353 H4
Henfield Business Park
  FRCTL/WBN BS36 .... 357 K4
Hengrove School
  HGRV/WHIT BS14 .... 374 A7
Henleaze Infant School
  RDLND/MONT BS6 .... 364 A1
The Herd A F C Club House
  CIR GL7 .... 249 H7
The Heron Primary School
  GLE GL4 .... 159 F1
The Heywood School
  CIND GL14 .... 151 G4
Heywood Sports Centre
  CIND GL14 .... 151 G4
Highcroft Junior School
  FRCTL/WBN BS36 .... 345 J6
Highnam Business Centre
  VGL GL2 .... 128 C1
Highnam School
  VGL GL2 .... 128 D1
The High Street Medical Centre
  STNHO GL10 .... 212 E6
Hillesley C of E Va Primary School
  WUE GL12 .... 321 J6
Hillfields Park Primary School
  MANG/FISH BS16 .... 366 C3
Hillview County Primary School
  BWTH/CHD GL3 .... 131 H6
The Hindu Temple
  EVILLE/WHL BS5 .... 365 G6
Hippodrome Theatre
  CBRIS/FH BS1 .... 364 A8
H & L Estate
  STROUD GL5 .... 214 A8
H & L Trading Estate
  STROUD GL5 .... 214 A8
HM Young Offender Institute
  WUE GL12 .... 293 K7
Hollywood Bowl
  CBRISNE BS2 .... 374 B1
Holst Birthplace Museum
  CHELTE/BC GL52 .... 4 C3
Holts Health Centre
  NWNT GL18 .... 73 J6
Holy Apostles C of E School
  CHELTE/BC GL52 .... 5 E4
Holy Family RC Primary School
  BRSTK/PCHW BS34 .... 343 F6
Holymead Infant School
  BRSG/KWL/STAPK BS4 .... 374 C4
Holymead School
  BRSG/KWL/STAPK BS4 .... 374 C3
Holy Trinity Primary School
  ALMDB BS32 .... 343 G4
Holy Trinity School
  CHELTE/BC GL52 .... 4 C3
Homedowns Business Park
  TEWK GL20 .... 58 D1
Homeopathic Hospital
  CFTN/FAIL BS8 .... 364 A6
Honeybourne Airfield
  Industrial Estate
  EVE WR11 .... 7 H5
Honeybourne First School
  EVE WR11 .... 7 G2
Hopelands School
  STNHO GL10 .... 213 F7
Hopes Hill Primary School
  MTCHDN GL17 .... 124 D5
Horcott Industrial Estate
  CIR GL7 .... 282 D1
Horcott Road Industrial Estate
  CIR GL7 .... 254 E8
Horfield C of E School
  HNBRY/STHM BS10 .... 354 B7
Horfield Health Centre
  HORF/LLZ BS7 .... 354 E8
Horfield Sports Centre
  HORF/LLZ BS7 .... 354 D7

Horsley School
  RSTROUD/NAIL GL6 .... 270 B5
Horton Primary School
  YATE/CS BS37 .... 349 G1
Hotspots Indoor Sports Centre
  BRSG/KWL/STAPK BS4 .... 374 E4
Ilmington School
  SHPSTR CV36 .... 11 F2
Inchbrook Trading Estate
  STROUD GL5 .... 242 C7
Innsworth County
  Primary School
  VGL GL2 .... 103 F8
Innsworth Technology Park
  VGL GL2 .... 102 E7
Iron Acton C of E School
  YATE/CS BS37 .... 346 A2
Jama Al-karim Mosque
  GL GL1 .... 3 D4
JHP Business Centre
  CIR GL7 .... 249 K6
John Blockley Gallery
  COTS GL54 .... 92 C6
John Cabot City
  Technology College
  KCWD/HNM BS15 .... 366 C7
The John Milton Health Clinic
  HNBRY/STHM BS10 .... 353 J3
The John M Museum
  TEWK GL20 .... 57 H1
Jorrocks Estate
  YATE/CS BS37 .... 358 E2
Joys Green CP School
  MTCHDN GL17 .... 148 E1
Jubilee Public Baths
  BRSG/KWL/STAPK BS4 .... 374 A4
Katerine Lady Berkeley School
  WUE GL12 .... 296 D8
Kemble County Primary School
  CIR GL7 .... 276 B7
Kennedy Way Surgery
  YATE/CS BS37 .... 347 G5
Kensington Business Centre
  CHELT GL50 .... 4 B5
Keynsham Rugby Club
  KEYN BS31 .... 375 J7
Keynsham Town Football Club
  KEYN BS31 .... 375 J7
King Edmund Community School
  YATE/CS BS37 .... 347 G5
Kingfisher Business Park
  STROUD GL5 .... 243 G4
Kingham County Primary School
  CHNTN OX7 .... 119 G1
Kingham Hill School
  CHNTN OX7 .... 95 H5
Kings Business Park
  CBRISNE BS2 .... 365 G8
Kings Chase Shopping Centre
  KCWD/HNM BS15 .... 366 D6
Kings Court Primary School
  YATE/CS BS37 .... 347 G5
Kingsditch Retail Park
  CHELTW GL51 .... 106 A1
Kingsdown Sports Centre
  RDLND/MONT BS6 .... 364 A6
Kingsfield School
  KCWD/HNM BS15 .... 367 G6
Kingsholm C of E Primary School
  GL GL1 .... 3 D2
Kings School
  GL GL1 .... 2 C3
Kings Stanley C of E
  Primary School
  STNHO GL10 .... 241 G2
Kings Stanley County
  Infant School
  STNHO GL10 .... 241 G3
Kings Theatre
  GL GL1 .... 2 C4
Kingsweston School
  AVONM BS11 .... 352 C6
Kingswood Borough Council
  MANG/FISH BS16 .... 366 D2
Kingswood County
  Primary School
  WUE GL12 .... 320 C1
Kingswood District Council
  KCWD/HNM BS15 .... 366 D7
Kingswood Health Centre
  KCWD/HNM BS15 .... 366 E6
Kingswood Leisure Centre
  MANG/FISH BS16 .... 366 D3

Kirtlands Preparatory School
BDWAY WR12 .... 18 E6
Knightsbridge Business Centre
CHELTW GL51 .... 80 C4
Ladygrove Business Park
MTCHDN GL17 .... 123 J5
Lakers School
CLFD GL16 .... 176 A1
Lakeside Primary School
CHELTW GL51 .... 105 J7
The Lake Surgery
HNBRY/STHM BS10 .... 353 K7
Lansdown Industrial Estate
CHELTW GL51 .... 106 A5
Larkfield Infant School
VGL GL2 .... 103 G8
Lawnwood Road Industrial
Estate
EVILLE/WHL BS5 .... 365 F6
Lawrence Hill Health Centre
CBRISNE BS2 .... 364 E7
Lawrence Hill Industrial Estate
EVILLE/WHL BS5 .... 365 G6
Lawrence Hill Industrial Park
EVILLE/WHL BS5 .... 365 F6
Lawrence Weston School
AVONM BS11 .... 352 D5
Leckhampton Industrial Estate
CHELTS GL53 .... 134 D3
Leckhampton Primary School
CHELTS GL53 .... 134 C2
Leckhampton Surgery
CHELTS GL53 .... 106 C8
Leconfield Cheltenham College
CHELTS GL53 .... 4 B5
Leighterton County
Primary School
TET GL8 .... 323 J3
Leisure Centre
CLFD GL16 .... 148 A8
Leisure Centre
GL GL1 .... 3 D4
Leonard Stanley C of E
Primary School
STNHO GL10 .... 241 F2
Library; Museum & Art Gallery
CHELT GL50 .... 4 B3
Liddington Industrial Estate
CHELTS GL53 .... 134 D1
Linden Primary School
GL GL1 .... 129 K8
Linear Business Park
CIND GL14 .... 150 E7
Little Dean Hall
CIND GL14 .... 151 J7
Littledean Primary School
CIND GL14 .... 151 J6
Little Stoke Junior School
BRSTK/PCHW BS34 .... 343 H8
Llanthony Industrial Estate
VGL GL2 .... 2 A5
Llanthony Secunda Priory
VGL GL2 .... 2 A5
Lockleaze School
HORF/LLZ BS7 .... 355 G6
Lodge Causeway Trading Estate
MANG/FISH BS16 .... 365 K3
London Road Medical Practice
GL GL1 .... 3 E3
Longborough C of E
Primary School
MIM GL56 .... 68 E6
Longford Special School
VGL GL2 .... 130 D1
Longhope C of E Primary School
MTCHDN GL17 .... 124 A2
Longhope Industrial Estate
MTCHDN GL17 .... 124 B3
Longlevens Primary School
VGL GL2 .... 130 E2
Longlevens Primary School
VGL GL2 .... 131 F2
Longlevens RFC
VGL GL2 .... 130 D1
Longlevens Surgery
VGL GL2 .... 130 E2
Longney C of E Primary School
VGL GL2 .... 183 G1
Longwell Green CP School
OLD/WMLY/WICK BS30 .... 376 A3
Lonsdale Business Centre
KGWD/HNM BS15 .... 366 C4
Lord Chancellors Department
CBRIS/FH BS1 .... 364 B7

Love Lane Industrial Estate
CIR GL7 .... 249 K8
Love Lane Trading Estate
CIR GL7 .... 249 K8
Lydbrook County Primary School
MTCHDN GL17 .... 148 E3
Lydbrook Health Centre
MTCHDN GL17 .... 148 E2
Lydney C of E School
LYD GL15 .... 234 A3
Lydney Cricket Club
LYD GL15 .... 234 A3
Lydney & District Hospital
LYD GL15 .... 233 K3
Lydney Golf Club
LYD GL15 .... 234 C4
Lydney Health Centre
LYD GL15 .... 234 B3
Lydney Industrial Estate
LYD GL15 .... 234 D6
Lydney Rugby Football Club
LYD GL15 .... 234 B3
Lydney Yacht Club
LYD GL15 .... 234 E6
Lyneham Golf Club
CHNTN OX7 .... 119 J8
Lyntony House Reading School
HORF/LLZ BS7 .... 364 B3
Lynworth Primary School
CHELTE/BC GL52 .... 5 E2
Madleaze Trading Estate
GL GL1 .... 2 A5
Maidenhill School
STNHO GL10 .... 213 F5
The Mall
BRSTK/PCHW BS34 .... 342 B8
Malvern View Business Park
CHELTE/BC GL52 .... 82 D2
Mangotsfield School
MANG/FISH BS16 .... 367 H2
Mangotsfield United
Football Club
MANG/FISH BS16 .... 367 H1
Manor Brook School
THNB/SVB BS35 .... 316 C3
Manor C of E School
FRCTL/WBN BS36 .... 345 J8
Manor Park Business Centre
CHELTW GL51 .... 106 A1
Market
GL GL1 .... 2 C4
Marling School
STROUD GL5 .... 214 B7
Marlwood School
THNB/SVB BS35 .... 331 K1
Marshfield Primary School
CHPMW/MSHF SN14 .... 372 A6
Martor Industrial Estate
CHPMW/MSHF SN14 .... 372 A4
Marybrook Medical Centre
BRKLY GL13 .... 264 A2
Matson Rugby Club House
GLE GL4 .... 158 E3
May Park Primary School
EVILLE/WHL BS5 .... 365 G4
Mead Lane Industrial Estate
LYD GL15 .... 233 K6
The Meadows Primary School
OLD/WMLY/WICK BS30 .... 376 E6
Mead Park Industrial Estate
CHELTS GL53 .... 106 D8
Medical Surgery
CIND GL14 .... 153 H6
Meteor Business Park
BWTH/CHD GL3 .... 104 A5
Meysey Hampton C of E School
CIR GL7 .... 281 H2
Midland Way Business Park
THNB/SVB BS35 .... 316 B6
The Milestone School
VGL GL2 .... 130 D1
Millcot Gallery
TEWK GL20 .... 33 G8
Millpond Primary School
EVILLE/WHL BS5 .... 364 E5
Minchinhampton Golf Club
TET GL8 .... 272 B4
Minsterworth School
VGL GL2 .... 127 K7
Minto Road Industrial Centre
RDLND/MONT BS6 .... 364 D4
Miserden C of E Primary School
RSTROUD/NAIL GL6 .... 190 A8

Mitcheldean Endowed
Primary School
MTCHDN GL17 .... 123 G5
Mitcheldean Surgery
MTCHDN GL17 .... 123 G4
Mitton Manor Primary School
TEWK GL20 .... 33 K6
The Moat Infant School
GLE GL4 .... 158 D2
Monk Meadow Dock
VGL GL2 .... 2 A6
Monkscroft Junior &
Infant School
CHELTW GL51 .... 105 J5
Monks Park School
HORF/LLZ BS7 .... 354 D5
Monks Park Surgery
HORF/LLZ BS7 .... 354 D6
Monmouthshire County Council
CHEP NP16 .... 288 A6
Montpelier Health Centre
RDLND/MONT BS6 .... 364 C5
Montpellier Gallery
CHELT GL50 .... 4 A4
Moore Cottage Hospital
COTS GL54 .... 115 H8
Moore Health Centre
COTS GL54 .... 115 H7
Morelands Trading Estate
GL GL1 .... 2 B5
Moreton-in-Marsh Hospital
MIM GL56 .... 45 K8
Moreton Wanderers
Football Club
MIM GL56 .... 70 B1
Mosque Centre
CHELT GL50 .... 4 A3
Mount Zion School
RDLND/MONT BS6 .... 364 B5
Much Marcle C of E
Primary School
LED HR8 .... 26 A7
Museum; Library & Art Gallery
GL GL1 .... 2 C4
Museum of Advertising &
Packaging
GL GL1 .... 2 B4
Naas House
LYD GL15 .... 234 D6
Nailsworth Mills Estate
RSTROUD/NAIL GL6 .... 270 E2
National Star Centre College
CHELTS GL53 .... 134 C8
National Waterways Museum
GL GL1 .... 2 B4
Naunton Downs Golf Club
COTS GL54 .... 113 G3
Naunton Park Primary School
CHELTS GL53 .... 106 E8
Newbridge Industrial Estate
BRSG/KWL/STAPK BS4 .... 365 H8
Newent Community School
NWNT GL18 .... 73 H7
Newent Sports Centre
NWNT GL18 .... 73 H6
Newent Town Associated
Football Club
NWNT GL18 .... 74 B6
Newent Town Council
NWNT GL18 .... 73 H6
New Fosseway School
HGRV/WHIT BS14 .... 374 A7
Newnham C of E School
CIND GL14 .... 180 C1
Newnham Surgery
CIND GL14 .... 180 B2
The New Olympus Theatre
GL GL1 .... 3 D5
New Siblands School
THNB/SVB BS35 .... 316 D5
Newtown Trading Estate
TEWK GL20 .... 34 B7
Northavon Business Centre
YATE/CS BS37 .... 346 E3
North Avon Magistrates Court
YATE/CS BS37 .... 347 G5
North Bristol Rugby
Football Club
ALMDB BS32 .... 342 E3
North Cerney Primary School
CIR GL7 .... 221 J1
North Nibley C of E
Primary School
DSLY GL11 .... 296 B1

Northridge Business Centre
YATE/CS BS37 .... **346** E4

North Road CP School
YATE/CS BS37 .... **346** D2

North Star Business Park
VGL GL2 .... **157** H3

Northville Family Practice
HORF/LLZ BS7 .... **355** F5

Northway County Infant School
TEWK GL20 .... **34** D5

Northway Trading Estate
TEWK GL20 .... **34** D7

Northwick Business Centre
MIM CL56 .... **21** J8

Norton C of E School
VGL GL2 .... **102** E2

Oakdene School
CIND GL14 .... **151** F6

Oakfield Business Park
KGWD/HNM BS15 .... **366** D7

Oak Hill Primary School
TEWK GL20 .... **37** K7

Oakridge Parochial School
RSTROUD/NAIL GL6 .... **245** G3

Oatley Trading Estate
KGWD/HNM BS15 .... **366** D5

Odeon Cinema
CHELTE/BC GL52 .... **4** C3

Offas Mead CP School
CHEP NP16 .... **288** C6

Oldbury Court Infant School
MANG/FISH BS16 .... **356** C7

Oldbury Court Jm School
MANG/FISH BS16 .... **356** C7

Oldbury-on-Severn C of E School
THNB/SVB BS35 .... **315** F1

Old Coalyard Farm Estate
COTS GL54 .... **169** F4

Old Cryptians RFC
GLE GL4 .... **158** A2

The Old Estate Sawmill
Workshops
CIR GL7 .... **227** F7

Old Inchbrook School
RSTROUD/NAIL GL6 .... **242** C8

Oldland Surgery
OLD/WMLY/WICK BS30 .... **376** D3

The Old Mill Museum
COTS GL54 .... **115** G4

Old Print Gallery
BDWAY WR12 .... **18** D7

Old Quarries Industrial Estate
TET GL8 .... **302** C8

Old Sodbury County
Primary School
YATE/CS BS37 .... **349** F6

Olveston & Elberton
Primary School
THNB/SVB BS35 .... **330** E3

Optimax Laser Eye Clinic
CBRIS/FH BS1 .... **364** B8

The Orchard Medical Centre
DSLY GL11 .... **266** D1

The Orchard Medical Centre
KGWD/HNM BS15 .... **366** D6

Our Lady of Lourdes RC School
KGWD/HNM BS15 .... **366** E7

Our Lady of the Rosary
RC Primary School
AVONM BS11 .... **352** C6

Overndale School
YATE/CS BS37 .... **348** E7

Overton Park Surgery
CHELT GL50 .... **4** A4

Oxstalls Community School
GL GL1 .... **3** E1

The Palace Theatre
CIND GL14 .... **151** F6

Parkend School
LYD GL15 .... **205** J2

The Park Primary School
STNHO GL10 .... **212** E7

The Park School
KGWD/HNM BS15 .... **366** E6

Park Surgery
CIR GL7 .... **249** H6

Parkwall CP School
OLD/WMLY/WICK BS30 .... **376** B2

Parkway Trading Estate
CBRISNE BS2 .... **364** E4

Parliament School
STROUD GL5 .... **215** H7

Parnall Road Industrial Estate
MANG/FISH BS16 .... **366** A3

Parton Manor Infant School
BWTH/CHD GL3 .... **103** K8

Parton Manor Junior School
BWTH/CHD GL3 .... **103** K8

Patchway C of E Primary School
BRSTK/PCHW BS34 .... **343** C5

Patchway Health Clinic
BRSTK/PCHW BS34 .... **342** E6

Patchway High School
ALMDB BS32 .... **343** F5

Patchway Town Council
BRSTK/PCHW BS34 .... **342** D6

Patchway Trading Estate
BRSTK/PCHW BS34 .... **342** B6

Pates Grammar School
CHELTW GL51 .... **105** J3

Pauntley C of E Primary School
NWNT GL18 .... **51** F7

Pavilion Business Park
CIND GL14 .... **150** D3

Pembroke Junior &
Infant School
CHEP NP16 .... **288** A8

Pendock C of E School
RTEWK/TIB GL19 .... **31** G7

Pen Park School
HNBRY/STHM BS10 .... **354** B4

Petherton Road Infant School
HGRV/WHIT BS14 .... **374** A7

Philblack Works
HNBRY/STHM BS10 .... **340** B6

Phoenix NHS Trust
KGWD/HNM BS15 .... **375** H2

Phoenix Surgery
CIR GL7 .... **249** H7

Phoenix Surgery
CIR GL7 .... **278** D7

Phoenix Trading Estate
STROUD GL5 .... **243** G3

Pillowell CP School
LYD GL15 .... **205** K5

Pilning CP School
THNB/SVB BS35 .... **329** C8

Pittville Comprehensive School
CHELTE/BC GL52 .... **5** D1

Pittville Sports Centre
CHELTW GL51 .... **4** A1

Playhouse Theatre
CHELT GL50 .... **4** B4

Plump Hill County Primary School
MTCHDN GL17 .... **123** H8

Police Station, Magistrates
Courts & Register Office
CHELT GL50 .... **4** A4

Portrait Gallery
HORF/LLZ BS7 .... **354** D5

Portway School
AVONM BS11 .... **352** A7

Powells C of E School
CIR GL7 .... **249** H5

Prices Mill Surgery
RSTROUD/NAIL GL6 .... **270** D3

Prim School
THNB/SVB BS35 .... **316** B6

Prinknash Abbey
GLE GL4 .... **159** K6

Prior Park Preparatory School
HGHW SN6 .... **310** E7

Priory Doctors Surgery
BRSG/KWL/STAPK BS4 .... **374** A4

Priory Industrial Estate
TET GL8 .... **302** C6

Priory Ruins
GL GL1 .... **2** C4

The Priory Surgery
BRSG/KWL/STAPK BS4 .... **374** A4

Pucklechurch C of E
Primary School
MANG/FISH BS16 .... **358** E8

Quakers Friars
CBRIS/FH BS1 .... **364** C7

Quedgeley Trading Estate East
STNHO GL10 .... **212** E1

Quedgeley Trading Estate West
VGL GL2 .... **184** E1

Queen Margaret County School
TEWK GL20 .... **57** H2

Querns Business Centre
CIR GL7 .... **249** J7

Querns School
CIR GL7 .... **249** J6

Randwick C of E Primary School
RSTROUD/NAIL GL6 .... **213** K4

Rangeworthy C of E
Primary School
YATE/CS BS37 .... **334** B5

Raysfield Infant School
YATE/CS BS37 .... **347** H6

Raysfield Junior School
YATE/CS BS37 .... **347** H6

Redbrook C of E Primary School
MONM NP25 .... **174** B6

Redcliffe College
GL GL1 .... **3** E3

Redfield Edge Primary School
OLD/WMLY/WICK BS30 .... **376** E2

Redfield Leisure Centre
EVILLE/WHL BS5 .... **365** G7

Redland High Junior School
RDLND/MONT BS6 .... **364** A4

Redland High School
RDLND/MONT BS6 .... **364** A4

Red Maids Junior School
HNLZ/SM/SNYPK/WT BS9 .... **353** J8

Red Maids School
HNLZ/SM/SNYPK/WT BS9 .... **353** J8

Redmarley C of E Primary School
RTEWK/TIB GL19 .... **51** K3

Rednock Comprehensive School
DSLY GL11 .... **266** E4

Redwick & Northwick
C of E VC School
THNB/SVB BS35 .... **329** F4

Regent Arcade Shopping Centre
CHELT GL50 .... **4** B4

Regent Gallery
CHELT GL50 .... **4** B4

Regent Street Doctors Surgery
STNHO GL10 .... **212** E7

Regimental Museum
GL GL1 .... **2** B4

Register Office
CBRIS/FH BS1 .... **364** C7

Rendcomb College
CIR GL7 .... **193** H6

Ribston Hall Girls High School
GL GL1 .... **158** A1

Richard Hagen Gallery
BDWAY WR12 .... **18** D7

The Richard Pate School
CHELTS GL53 .... **134** E3

The Ridge Junior School
YATE/CS BS37 .... **347** H4

Ridgeway Industrial Centre
EVILLE/WHL BS5 .... **365** J4

Riding School
CIR GL7 .... **309** K2

Ridings High School
FRCTL/WBN BS36 .... **344** D8

Rigestate Industrial Estate
BRKLY GL13 .... **264** A1

Riverside Business Park
EVILLE/WHL BS5 .... **365** H8

Riverside Leisure Centre
CBRISNE BS2 .... **364** D6

Riverside Sports & Leisure Club
GL GL1 .... **2** B2

Riverside Surgery
BRSG/KWL/STAPK BS4 .... **374** E3

Rodborough CP School
STROUD GL5 .... **214** D8

Rodford CP School
YATE/CS BS37 .... **347** F7

Rodford Infant School
YATE/CS BS37 .... **346** E7

Rodmarton School
CIR GL7 .... **274** C6

Romney Avenue Junior
Mixed School
HORF/LLZ BS7 .... **355** F8

Romney House Surgery
TET GL8 .... **302** B7

Rosary RC Primary School
STROUD GL5 .... **214** D7

Rosebank Surgery
GL GL1 .... **2** C6

Rose Green Sports &
Leisure Centre
EVILLE/WHL BS5 .... **365** H5

Rose Hill School
WUE GL12 .... **321** H4

Roses Theatre
TEWK GL20 .... **33** H7

Rothdean Trading Estate
CIND GL14 .... **150** E6

Rowanfield Infant School
CHELTW GL51 .... **105** K3

Rowanfield Primary School
CHELTW GL51 .... **105** K4

Rowcroft Medical Centre
STROUD GL5 .... **214** D7

Royal Crescent Surgery
CHELT GL50 .... **4** B4

Rruardean C of E Primary School
MTCHDN GL17 .... **121** H7

Russell Town Avenue
Industrial Centre
EVILLE/WHL BS5 .... **365** G7

Ryeford Industrial Estate
STNHO GL10 .... **213** H8

St Andrews C of E VC
Primary School
WUE GL12 .... **318** C5

St Andrews School
COTS GL54 .... **195** F3

St Annes C of E Primary School
OLD/WMLY/WICK BS30 .... **376** D3

St Annes Junior Mixed School
BRSG/KWL/STAPK BS4 .... **374** C1

St Annes Park JMI School
BRSG/KWL/STAPK BS4 .... **374** D1

St Apollonias Surgery
KEYN BS31 .... **375** K8

St Augustine of Canterbury
RC Primary School
MANG/FISH BS16 .... **356** E7

St Barnabas C of E VC
Junior Mixed Infant School
RDLND/MONT BS6 .... **364** D5

St Bedes RC School
AVONM BS11 .... **352** C4

St Benedicts Catholic
High School
CHELTW GL51 .... **106** A3

St Bernadette RC School
HGRV/WHIT BS14 .... **374** B8

St Bernadettes RC Primary School
HGRV/WHIT BS14 .... **374** A8

St Bernards RC Primary School
AVONM BS11 .... **352** A8

St Bonaventures RC School
RDLND/MONT BS6 .... **364** A2

St Brendans Sixth Form College
BRSG/KWL/STAPK BS4 .... **374** E5

St Briavals Castle
LYD GL15 .... **203** F8

St Briavels Primary School
LYD GL15 .... **231** F1

St Briavels Surgery
LYD GL15 .... **231** G1

Saintbridge Sports Centre
GLE GL4 .... **158** D1

St Catherines Surgery
CHELTW GL51 .... **4** A2

St Davids Primary School
MIM GL56 .... **70** A1

St Dominics RC Primary School
STROUD GL5 .... **242** C8

St Edwards Junior School
CHELTE/BC GL52 .... **5** F5

St Edwards School
CHELTE/BC GL52 .... **5** E6

St Gabriels Business Park
EVILLE/WHL BS5 .... **365** F6

St George Health Centre
KGWD/HNM BS15 .... **366** A6

St Georges Business Park
CHELTW GL51 .... **106** A4

St George School
EVILLE/WHL BS5 .... **365** F6

St Gloucester Council
THNB/SVB BS35 .... **316** A5

St Gregorys RC School
CHELT GL50 .... **4** A3

St Helens C of E Primary School
THNB/SVB BS35 .... **332** A2

St James C of E Junior School
GL GL1 .... **3** E5

St James C of E Primary School
CHCAM GL55 .... **20** E3

St James Health Centre
VGL GL2 .... **157** F5

St James School
CHELT GL50 .... **106** B8

St James Trading Estate
GL GL1 .... **3** E5

St Johns Mead C of E VC
Primary School
YATE/CS BS37 .... **347** K5

St Johns on the Hill School
CHEP NP16 .... **288** B4

St Johns Primary School
CHELTE/BC GL52 .... **4** C4

St Johns School
CLFD GL16 .... **175** J4

St Josephs RC School
MANG/FISH BS16 .... **366** B3

St Laurence C of E School
CIR GL7 .... **285** H3

St Marks C of E Junior School
CHELTW GL51 .... **105** H7

St Martins Surgery
BRSG/KWL/STAPK BS4 .... **374** A5

St Mary De Crypt
School & Church
GL GL1 .... **2** C4

St Marys C of E Primary School
TET GL8 .... **302** B6

St Marys C of E Primary School
YATE/CS BS37 .... **347** G4

St Marys C of E School
THNB/SVB BS35 .... **316** A4

St Marys RC Primary School
BDWAY WR12 .... **18** D6

St Marys RC Primary School
BWTH/CHD GL3 .... **103** H8

St Marys Roman Catholic
Junior & Infant School
CHEP NP16 .... **288** A7

St Marys Rugby Club
ALMDB BS32 .... **343** K4

St Matthews School
STROUD GL5 .... **214** A7

St Michael on the Mount
C of E Primary School
CFTN/FAIL BS8 .... **364** A4

St Michaels C of E VC
Primary School
FRCTL/WBN BS36 .... **344** E8

St Michaels Hill Clinic
CBRIS/FH BS1 .... **364** B7

St Michaels Hospital
CBRISNE BS2 .... **364** A6

St Michaels Primary School
BRSTK/PCHW BS34 .... **355** J1

St Michaels Surgery
GL GL1 .... **2** C4

St Nicholas Market
CBRIS/FH BS1 .... **364** B7

St Oswald's Priory
GL GL1 .... **2** C2

St Patricks RC School
EVILLE/WHL BS5 .... **365** H7

St Pauls C of E Primary School
GL GL1 .... **2** C5

St Pauls RC Primary School
YATE/CS BS37 .... **347** G6

St Peter & St Paul School
RDLND/MONT BS6 .... **364** A6

St Peters Infant School
GL GL1 .... **3** F3

St Peters RC Secondary School
GLE GL4 .... **158** A5

St Peters Road Surgery
CIR GL7 .... **249** J6

St Roses Special School
STROUD GL5 .... **214** D7

St Sampsons Church of
England Junior School
HGHW SN6 .... **310** D6

St Sampsons County
Infants School
HGHW SN6 .... **310** D6

St Stephens Business Centre
OLD/WMLY/WICK BS30 .... **376** D1

St Stephens C of E VC
Junior School
KGWD/HNM BS15 .... **366** D4

St Teresas RC School
HORF/LLZ BS7 .... **354** C5

St Thomas More Primary School
CHELTW GL51 .... **105** H4

St Thomas More RC School
HORF/LLZ BS7 .... **364** E3

St Ursulas High School
HNLZ/SM/SNYPK/WT BS9 .... **353** J8

St Vincents Trading Estate
CBRISNE BS2 .... **365** G8

St Whites School
CIND GL14 .... **151** F8

Salmon Springs Trading Estate
STROUD GL5 .... **214** D5

Sampson House Business Park
HNBRY/STHM BS10 .... **341** F7

Samuel Whites Infant School
KGWD/HNM BS15 .... **375** H1

Sandford Park Lido
CHELTS GL53 .... **4** C5

Sandford Park Trading Estate
CHELTS GL53 .... **4** C5

Sandford School
CHELTS GL53 .... **4** C6

Sandpits Clinic
DSLY GL11 .... **266** D3

Sapperton C of E Primary School
CIR GL7 .... **246** D3

Saracens Rugby Club
HNBRY/STHM BS10 .... **353** H1

Satellite Business Park
EVILLE/WHL BS5 .... **365** H8

Saul C of E Primary School
VGL GL2 .... **182** D7

Sea Mills Infant School
HNLZ/SM/SNYPK/WT BS9 .... **352** E7

Sedbury Trading Estate
CHEP NP16 .... **288** D6

Sedgeberrow C of E First School
EVE WR11 .... **15** J5

Seeba Gallery
CIR GL7 .... **285** G2

Sefton Park School
HORF/LLZ BS7 .... **364** D3

Severn Banks Primary School
LYD GL15 .... **234** C3

Severn Beach CP School
THNB/SVB BS35 .... **328** C8

Severn Sailing Club
TEWK GL20 .... **13** K7

Severnside Trading Estate
VGL GL2 .... **129** H5

Severnside Works
HNBRY/STHM BS10 .... **340** C4

Severn Vale Secondary School
VGL GL2 .... **156** E5

Shaftesbury Industrial Estate
CHELTW GL51 .... **82** A8

Shambles Museum
NWNT GL18 .... **73** J6

Sharpness Primary School
BRKLY GL13 .... **235** K6

Sheepscombe County
Primary School
RSTROUD/NAIL GL6 .... **188** C5

Sheilding Schools
THNB/SVB BS35 .... **316** A5

Shire Hall
GL GL1 .... **2** B3

Shirehampton Baths
AVONM BS11 .... **352** A8

Shirehampton Cricket Club
AVONM BS11 .... **352** B7

Shirehampton Health Centre
AVONM BS11 .... **352** A8

Showcase Cinema Bristol
CBRISNE BS2 .... **374** B1

The Shrubberies School
STNHO GL10 .... **212** E6

Shurdington Primary School
CHELTW GL51 .... **133** H5

Siddington C of E School
CIR GL7 .... **277** K2

Sikh Temple
EVILLE/WHL BS5 .... **365** G4

Silverhill School
FRCTL/WBN BS36 .... **344** E7

Simplex Trading Estate
OLD/WMLY/WICK BS30 .... **376** E2

Sir Bernard Lovell School
OLD/WMLY/WICK BS30 .... **376** D2

Sir Thomas Richs
Grammar School
VGL GL2 .... **131** F3

Sir William Romneys School
TET GL8 .... **302** C5

Sixways Clinic
CHELTE/BC GL52 .... **5** E6

Slimbridge CP School
VGL GL2 .... **238** C4

Soaphouse Industrial Estate
EVILLE/WHL BS5 .... **365** J6

Soudley CP School
CIND GL14 .... **179** G4

Soundwell College
KGWD/HNM BS15 .... **366** E4

South Gloucestershire Council
BRSTK/PCHW BS34 .... **342** D5

South Gloucestershire Council
BRSTK/PCHW BS34 .... **355** F3

South Gloucestershire Council
MANG/FISH BS16 .... **357** H8

South Gloucestershire Council
THNB/SVB BS35 .... **341** F1

South Gloucestershire Council
YATE/CS BS37 .... **346** E2

South Gloucestershire Council
YATE/CS BS37 .... **347** H5

South Gloucestershire
Magistrates Court
STROUD GL5 .... 214 E7
Southmead Health Centre
HNBRY/STHM BS10 .... 354 A4
Southmead Health Services
NHS Trust
HNBRY/STHM BS10 .... 354 C6
Southrop C of E Primary School
CIR GL7 .... 256 E2
South View Business Centre
MANG/FISH BS16 .... 366 E1
South View Business Park
MANG/FISH BS16 .... 366 E1
Spartans Rugby Club
GL GL1 .... 2 B2
Speedwell School
EVILLE/WHL BS5 .... 366 A5
Speedwell Swimming Baths
EVILLE/WHL BS5 .... 365 K5
Springfield Business Centre
STNHO GL10 .... 212 C6
Springfield School
RDLND/MONT BS6 .... 364 C4
Springhill Industrial Estate
BDWAY WR12 .... 42 E2
Spring Mill Industrial Estate
RSTROUD/NAIL GL6 .... 271 F3
Springwater Park Trading Estate
EVILLE/WHL BS5 .... 365 J7
Stanbridge CP School
MANG/FISH BS16 .... 357 F8
Standish Hospital
STNHO GL10 .... 213 H4
Staple Hill Primary School
MANG/FISH BS16 .... 366 D2
Station Approach
Industrial Estate
BAD GL9 .... 351 G7
Station Road Industrial
Estate South
STROUD GL5 .... 242 C5
Station Road Trading Estate
STROUD GL5 .... 242 C5
Station Street Business Park
CIND GL14 .... 150 E6
Station Yard Industrial Estate
CHEP NP16 .... 288 B6
Staunton & Corse C of E
Aided School
RTEWK/TIB GL19 .... 53 H7
Staunton Court Business Park
RTEWK/TIB GL19 .... 53 F7
Steadings Business
Centre Maisemore Court
VGL GL2 .... 101 G6
Steam Mills School
CIND GL14 .... 150 D2
Stenders Business Centre
MTCHDN GL17 .... 123 F5
Stenders Business Park
MTCHDN GL17 .... 123 F4
Steps Gallery
CBRIS/FH BS1 .... 364 A7
Stock Exchange
CBRIS/FH BS1 .... 364 B8
Stoke Gifford Medical Centre
BRSTK/PCHW BS34 .... 355 J2
Stoke Lodge Infant School
BRSTK/PCHW BS34 .... 343 G6
Stokes Medical Centre
BRSTK/PCHW BS34 .... 343 G7
Stoke View Business Park
MANG/FISH BS16 .... 365 K2
Stonebury Day Hospital
LYD GL15 .... 233 K3
Stone Cricket Club
BRKLY GL13 .... 264 D8
Stonehill Business Centre
OLD/WMLY/WICK BS30 .... 375 K2
Stonehouse Health Clinic
STNHO GL10 .... 213 F7
Stone with Woodford
C of E Primary School
BRKLY GL13 .... 294 A2
Stover Trading Estate
YATE/CS BS37 .... 346 D5
Stow on the Wold
Primary School
COTS GL54 .... 92 D6
Stratton C of E Primary School
CIR GL7 .... 249 G2
Stroud College
RSTROUD/NAIL GL6 .... 270 B2
Stroud College
YATE/CS BS37 .... 347 G5
Stroud College of
Further Education
STROUD GL5 .... 214 C6

Stroud District Council
STROUD GL5 .... 213 K8
Stroud General Hospital
STROUD GL5 .... 215 F8
Stroud High School
STROUD GL5 .... 214 B7
Stroud Maternity Hospital
STROUD GL5 .... 215 F8
Stroud Rugby Club
STROUD GL5 .... 214 C8
Stroud Town Council
STROUD GL5 .... 214 E7
Stroud Valley Primary School
STROUD GL5 .... 214 E8
Stuckleys Pine Gallery
HORF/LLZ BS7 .... 364 C1
The Studio Gallery
WUE GL12 .... 297 F7
Sudbrook Trading Estate
GL GL1 .... 2 B5
Sudeley Castle
COTS GL54 .... 86 A2
Summerhill Infant School
EVILLE/WHL BS5 .... 365 J6
Sunday School
WUE GL12 .... 320 D2
Sun Life Sports Club
HNBRY/STHM BS10 .... 353 H2
Sussex Place Surgery
RDLND/MONT BS6 .... 364 D4
Swell Primary School
COTS GL54 .... 91 J7
Swimming Pool
CHCAM GL55 .... 20 E5
Swimming Pool
LYD GL15 .... 233 K5
Swindon Village Primary School
CHELTW GL51 .... 82 B7
Taits Hill Industrial Estate
DSLY GL11 .... 266 A2
Temple County Primary School
KEYN BS31 .... 376 A8
Temple Guiting School
COTS GL54 .... 88 B2
Temple Industrial Estate
CHELTE/BC GL52 .... 5 D2
The Temple
MTCHDN GL17 .... 124 B4
Temple Trading Estate
CBRISNE BS2 .... 374 A1
Ten Pin Alley
GL GL1 .... 2 B4
Tetbury Gallery
TET GL8 .... 302 C7
Tetbury Industrial Estate
TET GL8 .... 302 D6
Tewkesbury Abbey School
TEWK GL20 .... 33 H8
Tewkesbury Business Centre
TEWK GL20 .... 34 B6
Tewkesbury C of E School
TEWK GL20 .... 33 J8
Tewkesbury Cottage Hospital
TEWK GL20 .... 33 H8
Tewkesbury Grant Maintained
Comprehensive School
TEWK GL20 .... 34 B7
Tewkesbury Museum
TEWK GL20 .... 33 H8
Tewkesbury Rugby Football Club
TEWK GL20 .... 57 H1
Tewkesbury Squash Club
TEWK GL20 .... 34 A7
Thomas Keble School
RSTROUD/NAIL GL6 .... 244 C1
Thornbury Health Centre
THNB/SVB BS35 .... 316 C5
Thornbury Hospital
THNB/SVB BS35 .... 316 C5
Thornbury Leisure Centre
THNB/SVB BS35 .... 316 B7
Thornwell Junior School
CHEP NP16 .... 312 B1
Thrupp Primary School
STROUD GL5 .... 243 C3
Tibberton Primary School
VGL GL2 .... 99 G5
Tirlebrook CP School
TEWK GL20 .... 34 A8
Tockington Manor School
ALMDB BS32 .... 331 G4
Toddington Primary School
COTS GL54 .... 63 C1
Toll House Clinic
YATE/CS BS37 .... 348 A5
Tortworth Vc Primary School
WUE GL12 .... 294 E7
Towncrest Sports Club
TEWK GL20 .... 33 J8

Transport Museum
GL GL1 .... 2 B3
Tredworth Infant School
GL GL1 .... 3 D6
Tredworth Junior School
GL GL1 .... 3 D6
Trinity C of E School
BAD GL9 .... 351 G8
TT Trading Estate
YATE/CS BS37 .... 348 A5
Tuffley Primary School
CLE GL4 .... 158 A5
Tuffley Trading Estate
VGL GL2 .... 157 H2
Tufthorn Industrial Estate
CLFD GL16 .... 176 A6
Tutshill Church of
England School
CHEP NP16 .... 288 B3
Twigworth C of E School
VGL GL2 .... 102 B7
Two Mile Hill Junior &
Infant School
KGWD/HNM BS15 .... 366 B6
Twyford House Cricket Club
AVONM BS11 .... 352 B7
Twyning CP School
TEWK GL20 .... 12 E8
The Tynings CP School
MANG/FISH BS16 .... 366 E2
Uley C of E Primary School
DSLY GL11 .... 268 C5
United Bristol Healthcare
NHS Trust
CBRISNE BS2 .... 364 B7
University of Bristol
CFTN/FAIL BS8 .... 364 A6
University of Bristol
Childrens Hospital
CFTN/FAIL BS8 .... 364 A7
University of the
West of England
CBRIS/FH BS1 .... 364 B8
University of the
West of England
MANG/FISH BS16 .... 365 J1
University of the
West of England Bristol
MANG/FISH BS16 .... 355 H5
University of the
West of England Bristol
MANG/FISH BS16 .... 366 A1
Uplands CP School
STROUD GL5 .... 214 E6
Upper Horfield Primary School
HORF/LLZ BS7 .... 354 E6
Upton St Leonards
C of E (C) School
GLE GL4 .... 159 H3
Upton St Leonards
Primary School
GLE GL4 .... 159 G4
Venture Business Centre
GL GL1 .... 2 B5
Wadehurst Industrial Park
CBRISNE BS2 .... 364 E7
Wallis Estate
CBRISNE BS2 .... 364 D3
Wallsworth Hall
VGL GL2 .... 102 C4
Walmore Hill Primary School
CIND GL14 .... 154 D4
Walton House Gallery
COTS GL54 .... 92 B6
Warden Hill Primary School
CHELTW GL51 .... 134 A1
Ward Industrial Estate
LYD GL15 .... 234 A6
Warmley C of E School
OLD/WMLY/WICK BS30 .... 367 J8
Watermoor C of E
Controlled Primary School
CIR GL7 .... 249 K7
Watershed Arts Complex
CBRIS/FH BS1 .... 364 B8
Watledge Surgery
TEWK GL20 .... 33 J8
Wellesley CP School
YATE/CS BS37 .... 347 F8
Westbury Bazaar & Gallery
HNLZ/SM/SNYPK/WT BS9 .... 353 J7
Westbury on Severn
C of E Primary School
CIND GL14 .... 153 H5
Westbury-on-Trym
C of E Primary School
HNLZ/SM/SNYPK/WT BS9 .... 353 J7
Westbury on Trym Practice
HNLZ/SM/SNYPK/WT BS9 .... 353 H8

Westbury Surgery
CIND GL14 .... **153** G5
Westlands School
CHELTW GL51 .... **106** A7
Westonbirt School
TET GL8 .... **325** G6
Weston House Group Practice
CHELTW GL51 .... **4** A2
Weston Park Primary School
AVONM BS11 .... **352** B6
Westpoint Trading Estate
KGWD/HNM BS15 .... **366** D7
West Town Lane Infant School
BRSG/KWL/STAPK BS4 .... **374** B5
West Town Lane Junior School
BRSG/KWL/STAPK BS4 .... **374** B5
West Walk Surgery
YATE/CS BS37 .... **347** G5
Westwing School
THNB/SVB BS35 .... **315** J6
Whaddon Primary School
CHELTE/BC GL52 .... **5** F3
Whimsey Industrial Estate
CIND GL14 .... **150** D4
Whitecross Business Park
LYD GL15 .... **234** A4
Whitecross School
LYD GL15 .... **233** K4
Whitefield Fishponds School
MANG/FISH BS16 .... **365** K2
Whitehall Primary &
Infant School
EVILLE/WHL BS5 .... **365** H5
Whitehall Trading Estate
EVILLE/WHL BS5 .... **365** G6
White Knight Gallery
CHELT GL50 .... **4** A6
Whiteshill Primary School
RSTROUD/NAIL GL6 .... **214** B3
Whitminster Endowed
Primary School
VGL GL2 .... **211** J1

Whitminster Sports Club
VGL GL2 .... **211** J1
Wick School
OLD/WMLY/WICK BS30 .... **368** D8
Wick Surgery
OLD/WMLY/WICK BS30 .... **369** F8
Wickwar Primary School
WUE GL12 .... **335** K1
Wickwar Trading Estate
WUE GL12 .... **319** K7
Wicliffe Industrial Centre
STROUD GL5 .... **214** C8
Widden Infant School
GL GL1 .... **3** D4
Widden Junior School
GL GL1 .... **3** D4
Wildscreen @ Bristol
CBRIS/FH BS1 .... **364** A8
Willersey Industrial Estate
BDWAY WR12 .... **18** E1
Willersey School
BDWAY WR12 .... **19** F2
Willow Green Infant School
CBRISNE BS2 .... **364** E4
Willow Tree Surgery
CLFD GL16 .... **175** K4
Wilverley Trading Estate
BRSG/KWL/STAPK BS4 .... **374** D5
Winchcombe Business Centre
COTS GL54 .... **62** E6
Winchcombe C of E
Infant School
COTS GL54 .... **85** J1
Winchcombe Junior School
COTS GL54 .... **85** J1
Winchcombe School
COTS GL54 .... **62** E7
Winfield Hospital
VGL GL2 .... **130** A1
Withington C of E School
COTS GL54 .... **165** K2

Withington Primary School
COTS GL54 .... **166** A2
Woodchester Endowed
Primary School
STROUD GL5 .... **242** C4
Woodfield Infants School
DSLY GL11 .... **266** C1
Woodmancote CP School
CHELTE/BC GL52 .... **83** H2
Wood Road Industrial Centre
KGWD/HNM BS15 .... **366** D6
Woodside County
Primary School
MTCHDN GL17 .... **149** K1
Woodstock Special School
KGWD/HNM BS15 .... **366** E7
Wotton Sports Centre
WUE GL12 .... **296** D8
Wotton Under Ege
Town Council
WUE GL12 .... **296** E7
Wycliffe College
STNHO GL10 .... **213** F7
Wyedean School
CHEP NP16 .... **288** C6
Wynstones School
GLE GL4 .... **158** A6
Yate Leisure Centre
YATE/CS BS37 .... **347** G4
Yate Town Council
YATE/CS BS37 .... **347** G4
Yate Town Football Club
YATE/CS BS37 .... **346** D3
Yorkley County School
LYD GL15 .... **206** B3
Yorkley Health Centre
LYD GL15 .... **206** B3

Page 4

A2
1 Aldridge Cl
2 Bullingham Ct
3 Carlton Pl
4 Marsh Cl
5 Midwinter Av
6 Russell Pl
7 Russell St
8 Vine Cl
9 White Hart St

B3
1 Ambrose Cl
2 Baynham Wy
3 Chester Wk
4 Church St
5 Jenner Wk
6 Oxford Pas
7 Rose And Crown Pas
8 Royal Oak Ms
9 St George's Pl

B5
1 Bath Ville Ms
2 Belmore Pl
3 Calderwood Ct
4 Cedar Court Rd
5 Eaton Pl
6 Glensanda Ct
7 Montpellier Dr
8 Montpellier Retreat
9 Paragon Ter
10 Trafalgar St
11 Vittoria Wk

C3
1 Albert Pl
2 Albion Pl
3 Back Albert Pl
4 Berkeley Av
5 Clarence St
6 Columbia St
7 Gloucester Pl
8 Jersey St
9 North Pl
10 Portland Pl
11 Portland Sq
12 Trinity La
13 Warwick St
14 Winchcombe St

C4
1 Albion St
2 Barratt's Mill La
3 Berkeley Ct
4 Berkeley Pl
5 Grosvenor Pl South
6 Grosvenor St
7 Grosvenor Ter
8 Hewlett Pl
9 Highbury La
10 St Anne's Rd
11 St James St
12 Tom Price Cl
13 Vernon Pl
14 Winchcombe St
15 Witcombe Pl

C5
1 Corpus St
2 Keynshambury Rd
3 Mitre St
4 Olio La
5 Orrisdale Ter
6 St Luke's Pl
7 Sandford St

Page 5

E6
1 Cirencester Rd
2 Hamilton St
3 Langton Grove Rd
4 Langton Pl
5 Oakland St
6 Overbury St

Page 33

H8
1 Compton's Alley
2 East St
3 Nelson St
4 Post Office La
5 Quay St
6 Saffron Rd
7 Shakespeare St
8 Smiths Ct
9 Smith's La

J8
1 Back Of Mount Pleasant
2 Barton Ms
3 Chance St
4 Link Rd
5 Orchard Ct
6 Watledge Cl
7 Wynyards Cl

Page 34

D5
1 The Apple Orch
2 Bevan Gdns
3 Cromers Cl
4 George Dowty Dr
5 Monkey Meadow
6 The Pear Orch
7 Redwood Ct
8 Wheatstone Cl

Page 82

E3
1 Charlecote Cnr
2 Clematis Ct
3 Delphinium Dr
4 Gatcombe Cl
5 Lavender Ms
6 Littlecote Cl
7 Marlborough Ct
8 Middlehay Ct

Page 83

H3
1 Anderson Cl
2 Coombe Meade
3 Drapers Ct
4 East Gable
5 Hawthorn Av
6 Kempsford Acre
7 Lyndhurst Cl
8 Peakstile Piece
9 Thatchers End
10 Woodmancote V

Page 105

F8
1 Dumbleton Gv

H1
1 Cornmeadow Dr
2 Fulbrook Cl
3 Hallmead Cl
4 Harvest Gv
5 Rye Av
6 William Cough Cl

H3
1 Beale Rd
2 Dunster Cl
3 Oldbury Cl
4 Stanley Pl
5 Tiverton Cl
6 Wentworth Cl

H6
1 Postlip Wy

H8
1 Aylton Cl
2 The Hawthornes
3 Holmer Crs
4 Montgomery Rd
5 Witley Lodge Cl

J4
1 Amberley Rd
2 St Aidans Cl
3 Seacome Rd

J7
1 Harrington Dr
2 Hatherley Brake
3 Ullswater Rd
4 Windermere Cl

K1
1 Attwood Cl
2 Patterdale Cl
3 Summerfield Cl

K3
1 Brooklyn Cl
2 Tanner's La

K6
1 Church Rd
2 Finstock Cl
3 Granley Cl
4 Greville Ct
5 Lansdown Castle Dr

K7
1 Bronte Cl
2 Browning Ms
3 Chapman Wy
4 Deacon Cl
5 Deans Ct
6 Grasmere Rd
7 Manse Gdns
8 Rolleston Wy

K8
1 Dover Hay
2 Warden Hill Cl

Page 106

A1
1 Kingsville Rd
2 Upperfield Rd

A2
1 Frank Brookes Rd
2 O'brien Rd
3 St Peter's Sq

A3
1 Merriville Gdns
2 Penharva Cl

A4
1 Clevedon Sq

A5
1 Libertus Ct
2 Stow Cl

A6
1 Glencairn Ct
2 Lansdown Cl
3 Lansdown Lodge Dr
4 Skillicorne Ms

B1
1 Stanwick Crs

B2
1 Compton Rd
2 Richards Rd

B3
1 Addis Rd
2 Cobham Ct

B4
1 Millbrook Gdns
2 Old Millbrook Ter
3 Queen's Retreat
4 St George's Cl
5 Sterling Ct

B5
1 Wendover Gdns

B6
1 Thorncliffe Dr
2 Tivoli Wk

B7
1 Bakehouse La

B8
1 Ellesmere Cl
2 Kenelm Gdns
3 Merestones Dr

C1
1 Fortina Cl

C2
1 Elmfield Rd
2 Thomond Cl

C3
1 Aldridge Cl
2 Bullingham Ct
3 Carlton Pl
4 Marsh Cl
5 Midwinter Av
6 Russell Pl
7 Russell St
8 Vine Cl
9 White Hart St

C4
1 Devonshire St
2 Hereford Pl
3 Knapp La

C5
1 Fauconberg Rd
2 Overton Park Rd

C6
1 Lansdown Wk
2 Parabola Rd
3 Queens La

C7
1 Andover Wk
2 Brandon Pl
3 Sadlers La
4 St James' Pl
5 Tivoli Ms

C8
1 Brooksdale La
2 Kenelm Dr
3 Pickering Cl
4 Pickering Rd
5 Upper Norwood Cl

D1
1 Pentathlon Wy

D3
1 Dunalley Pde
2 Hungerford St
3 Malthouse La
4 New Rutland Ct
5 St Paul's La
6 St Paul's Pde
7 St Paul's St North

D4
1 Ambrose Pl
2 Baynham Wy
3 Chester Wk
4 Church St
5 Jenner Wk
6 Oxford Pas
7 Rose And Crown Pas
8 Royal Oak Ms
9 St George's Pl

D5
1 Clarence Pde
2 Clarence St
3 College Pl
4 County Court Rd
5 High St
6 Imperial Circ
7 Imperial Sq
8 Oriel Rd
9 Ormond St
10 Post Office La
11 Promenade
12 Queen's Circ
13 Regent St
14 Rodney Rd
15 Royal Well Pl
16 Royal Well Rd

D6
1 Bath Ville Ms
2 Belmore Pl
3 Calderwood Ct
4 Cedar Court Rd
5 Eaton Pl
6 Glensanda Ct
7 Montpellier Dr
8 Montpellier Retreat
9 Paragon Ter
10 Trafalgar St
11 Vittoria Wk

D7
1 Bath Ter
2 Bethesda St
3 Chapel La
4 Clare St
5 Exmouth Ct
6 Gratton St
7 Victoria Retreat

D8
1 Badminton Cl
2 Fairfield Park Rd
3 Fairfield St
4 Fairhaven Rd
5 Fairhaven St
6 Maida Vale Rd
7 Mornington Dr

E1
1 Cleevelands Cl
2 Thoresby

E2
1 The Gardens
2 Huntsfield Cl

E3
1 Evesham Cl

E4
1 Albert Pl
2 Albion Pl
3 Back Albert Pl
4 Berkeley Av
5 Clarence St
6 Columbia St
7 Gloucester Pl
8 Jersey St
9 North Pl
10 Portland Pl
11 Portland Sq
12 Trinity La
13 Warwick Pl
14 Winchcombe St

E5
1 Albion St
2 Barratt's Mill La
3 Berkeley Ct
4 Berkeley Pl
5 Grosvenor Pl South
6 Grosvenor St
7 Grosvenor Ter
8 Hewlett Pl
9 Highbury La
10 St Anne's Rd
11 St James St
12 Tom Price Cl
13 Vernon Pl
14 Winchcombe Pl
15 Witcombe Pl

E6
1 Corpus St
2 Keynshambury Rd
3 Mitre St
4 Olio La
5 Orrisdale Ter
6 St Luke's Pl
7 Sandford St

E8
1 Verney Cl
2 The Verneys

Page 107

F4
1 All Saints' Villas Rd
2 Fairview Cl
3 Glenfall St
4 Pittville Circ
5 Pittville Circus Rd
6 St Anne's Cl
7 Whaddon Dr

G5
1 Eldon Av
2 Richmond Dr

G7
1 Cirencester Rd
2 Hamilton St
3 Langton Grove Rd
4 Langton Pl
5 Oakland St
6 Overbury St

H4
1 Hill View Rd
2 Isbourne Rd
3 Ladysmith Rd
4 Salamanca Rd
5 Whaddon Rd

J3
1 Corfe Cl
2 Honeysuckle Cl
3 Ivy Bank
4 Willowherb Cl

K3
1 Cleeve Cloud La
2 Westwood La

Page 129

K4
1 Archdeacon Ct
2 Barbican Ct
3 Barbican Wy
4 Barrack Sq
5 Bearland
6 Berkeley St
7 Longsmith St
8 Lower Quay St
9 Mount St
10 Priory Rd
11 Quay St
12 Upper Quay St

Page 130

A1
1 The Limes
2 Rivermead Cl

A2
1 Kingsholm Sq

A3
1 Dean's Ter
2 Priory Rd
3 Secret La

A4
1 Bull La
2 Cross Keys La
3 Hare La
4 Market Pde
5 New Inn La
6 St Mary's St
7 Spread Eagle Rd
8 Station Rd

A5
1 Bell La
2 Brunswick Sq
3 Hampden Wy
4 Parliament St
5 St Michael's Sq
6 Southgate St
7 Whitefield St

A6
1 Farm St

A7
1 Goodwin Ct
2 Stanley Ter
3 Sydenham Ter

B1
1 Fircroft Rd
2 Stamp's Meadow
3 Taurus Cl
4 Teasel Cl
5 Tewkesbury Rd

B4
1 Claremont Rd
2 George St
3 Newland St
4 Wellington Pde

B5
1 Albert St
2 Bedford St
3 Cambridge St
4 Charles St
5 Eastgate St
6 King's Barton St
7 Napier St
8 Nettleton Rd
9 Prince St
10 Raglan St
11 St Kilda Pde
12 Snope St
13 Widden St

B6
1 Daventry Ter
2 Old Rw
3 Thomas St
4 Vauxhall Ter

B8
1 Carmarthen St
2 Dainty St
3 Dora Wk
4 Ducie St
5 Faraday Ct
6 The Laurels
7 Llandilo St
8 Massey Pde
9 Melbourne St West
10 Morpeth St
11 Paul St
12 Percy St

C1
1 Stevans Cl

C5
1 Alington Cl
2 Great Western Ct
3 Magdala Rd
4 Millbrook Cl

C6
1 Herbert St
2 Hethersett Rd

C7
1 Collingbourne Rd
2 The Conifers

D1
1 Alders Gn
2 Ashmead
3 Ferndale Cl
4 Firethorne Cl
5 Foxcote
6 Hornbeam Ms
7 Longland Ce
8 Oxstalls Wy
9 The Tulworths
10 Wentworth Cl
11 Whitebeam Cl
12 Woodcote

D2
1 The Hedgerow
2 Longland Ct
3 Oxstalls Dr

D4
1 Bradford Rd
2 Kencourt Cl

D5
1 Armscroft Gdns
2 Etheridge Pl

D7
1 Fairford Wy
2 Stonehenge Rd

D8
1 Old Painswick Rd

E1
1 Dane Cl
2 Gifford Cl
3 Gilbert Rd
4 Langdale Gdns
5 Lea Crs
6 Malet Cl
7 Manley Gdns
8 Mortimer Rd
9 Mowberry Cl
10 Saxon Cl
11 Wedgwood Dr

E5
1 Armscroft Cl

E7
1 Coney Hill Pde
2 Druids Cl

E8
1 Ashgrove Wy
2 Church Wy

Page 131

F5
1 Hammond Wy
2 Wotton Ct

F7
1 Blake Hill Wy
2 Dodington Cl
3 Little Hd
4 Snowshill Cl
5 Ullenwood Rd

G2
1 Maple Ct

H1
1 Hawthorn Dr

J5
1 Deer Park Rd

K1
1 Tall Elms Cl
2 Watermoor Ct

Page 133

J1
1 Arlingham
2 Ashcot Ms
3 Aysgarth Av
4 Beechmore Dr
5 Calverley Ms
6 Chasely Crs
7 Glyndthorpe Gv
8 Larchmere Gv
9 Meadow La
10 Pyrton Ms
11 Rowan Wy
12 Selworthy
13 Sevelm
14 Silverwood Wy
15 Swarescombe Dr
16 Thornhaugh Ms
17 Welwyn Ms
18 Withypool

K1
1 Amaranth Wy
2 Barwick Rd
3 Cheriton Cl
4 Croft Thorne Cl
5 Crythan Wk
6 Ferndales Cl
7 Genista Wy
8 Glebe Farm Ct
9 Glenlea Gv
10 Greatfield La
11 The Greenings
12 Hawcombe Ms
13 Rothermere Cl

Page 157

K5
1 Bateman Cl
2 Enborne Cl
3 Harwell Cl
4 Headlam Cl
5 Linsley Wy
6 Westcote Rd

Page 158

E2
1 Brindle Cl
2 Drayton Cl
3 George Whitefield Cl
4 Prinknash Cl
5 Prinknash Rd
6 Timmis Cl

Page 159

G1
1 Brierley Cl
2 Broadwell Cl
3 Chaceley Cl
4 Cranham Cl
5 Edgeworth Cl
6 Longhope Cl
7 Oakridge Cl
8 Peacock Cl
9 Ruspidge Cl
10 Snowdrop Cl
11 Sudgrove Pk
12 Verbena Cl
13 Woodbine Cl

G2
1 Alderton Cl
2 Apple Tree Cl
3 Birdwood Cl
4 Blackberry Cl
5 Combrook Cl
6 Deerhurst Cl
7 Grayling Cl
8 Monarch Cl
9 Plum Tree Cl
10 Rendcomb Cl
11 Staunton Cl
12 Tarlton Cl

Page 213

F6
1 Blackbird Ct
2 Cedar Gdns
3 Chaffinch Ct
4 Coates Gdns
5 Glen Ct
6 Goldcrest Ct
7 Greenstreet
8 Magpie Ct
9 Partridge Ct
10 Pheasant Mead
11 Sherbourne Cl
12 Starling Ct

Page 214

E6
1 Birches Cl
2 The Circle
3 The Square
4 Upper Springfield Rd

1 Bedford St
2 Fawkes Pl
3 Gloucester St
4 John St
5 Kendrick St
6 King St
7 Lime Gv
8 Locking Hl
9 Parliment Ct
10 Russell St
11 Ryeleaze Cl
12 Ryeleaze Rd
13 The Shambles
14 Streamside
15 Swan St
16 Threadneedle St

Page 249

H6
1 Hammond Wy

H7
1 Beaufort Ct
2 Garden Cl
3 Crantley Crs
4 Limes Cl
5 Martin Cl
6 St Michaels Rd
7 Whitworth Rd

Page 288

A6
1 Bank Sq
2 Beaufort Pl
3 Garden City Wy
4 Hardwick Av
5 High Vw
6 Middle St
7 Oxford St
8 Regent Wy
9 River Vw
10 Thomas St
11 Upper Nelson St

Page 312

B2
1 Bishops Cl
2 Cidermill Cl
3 Fountain Wy
4 Lady Margaret Ct
5 Lewis Wy
6 Lord Eldon Dr
7 Preston Cl
8 Rougemont Gv
9 Summerhouse La
10 Thorn Tree Dr
11 Well Cl

Page 343

H5
1 Shellmor Cl

J7
1 The Bluebells
2 Pimpernel Mead
3 Teasel Mead

Page 345

K7
1 Fire Engine La
2 Larkfield
3 Oakleaze
4 Orchard Rd
5 Rose Oak La
6 Rose Oak Gdns

Page 347

F3
1 Chichester Wy

F5
1 Blakeney Mills
2 Village Cl

G5
1 Painswick Dr
2 Stinchcombe
3 Thorns Farm

J1
1 Rectory Cl

J5
1 Cherry Rd
2 Chestnut Dr
3 Meadow Rd
4 The Parade
5 River Rd
6 Streamside Rd
7 Wistaria Av

Page 352

E6
1 Bilberry Cl
2 Cranberry Wk
3 Drayton Rd
4 Mulberry Wk

Page 353

H5
1 Standish Cl

J7
1 Cote Lea Pk
2 East Hill Eastfield Rd
3 Priory Dene
4 Southfield Cl
5 Westminster Cl
6 West Priory Cl

Page 354

A5
1 Danbury Wk
2 Trowbridge Wk

B4
1 Avondown Cl
2 Caldbeck Cl
3 Easedale Cl

B7
1 Cordwell Wk
2 Reed Cl

D6
1 St Aldwyn's Cl

E7
1 Masefield Wy
2 Rose Mead
3 Shearmore Cl
4 Taunton Wk

Page 355

K1
1 Bakers Gnd
2 Court Av
3 Couzens Pl
4 Somerset Crs

Page 356

D6
1 Bromley Heath Rd
2 Pilgrims Wy
3 Quaker's Cl
4 Scantleberry Cl

E1
1 Burghley Ct

E6
1 Sandholme Cl
2 Sandringham Pk

Page 364

A1
1 Longleat Cl
2 St Margaret's Dr
3 Tennessee Gv
4 Twickenham Rd

A2
1 Fairhaven Rd
2 Good Shepherd Cl
3 Malmesbury Gv
4 Maplemeade

A3
1 Metford Gv

A4
1 Ermleet Rd
2 Glentworth Rd

A5
1 Courtside Ms
2 Kenilworth Rd
3 Woodstock Rd

A6
1 Clarence Pl
2 Highbury Vis
3 Osborne Vis
4 Southwell St
5 Tyndalls Park Ms

A7
1 Berkeley Av
2 Berkeley Sq
3 Lodge Pl
4 Lodge St
5 Old Park Hl
6 Park La
7 Park Street Av
8 Royal Fort Rd
9 There-and-back-again La

A8
1 Bigwood La
2 Brandon Steep
3 Charlotte St South
4 College La
5 Culver St
6 Denmark Av
7 Frogmore St
8 Gaunt's La
9 Hobb's La
10 Lower College St
11 Lower Lamb St
12 Orchard Av
13 Orchard St
14 Orchard St
15 Partition St
16 Unity St
17 Upper Wells St
18 York Pl

B1
1 Brookland Rd
2 Lansdown Ter

B2
1 Dulverton Rd
2 Egerton Brow

B3
1 Brookfield La
2 Kersteman Rd
3 Pine Grove Pl
4 Raglan Pl

B4
1 Brookfield La
2 Brookfield Rd
3 Cotham Brow
4 Edgecumbe Rd
5 Purton Rd

B5
1 Arley Cottages
2 Arley Pk
3 Elmgrove Pk
4 Fremantle La
5 Fremantle Rd
6 St Matthew's Av
7 Southfield Rd
8 Victoria Gdns
9 Winsley Rd

B6
1 Barton St
2 Cherry La
3 Clevedon Ter
4 Cottage Pl
5 Earl St
6 Henrietta St
7 Hillgrove St North
8 King Sq
9 King Square Av
10 Lower Gay St
11 Marlborough Hill Pl
12 Montague Hl
13 Montague Hill South
14 Montague St
15 Princes Rw
16 Spring Hl
17 Terrell St
18 Whitson St

B7
1 All Saints' St
2 Bell La
3 Blackfriars
4 Bridewell St
5 Cannon St
6 Christmas St
7 Fiennes Ct
8 High St
9 Host St
10 Lewins Mead
11 Nelson St
12 Newmarket Av
13 Pithay
14 Pithay Ct
15 Quay St
16 St Stephen's St
17 Silver St
18 Union St

B8
1 All Saints' La
2 Assembly Rooms La
3 Bridge St
4 Broad Quay
5 Clare St
6 Coronation Pl
7 Crow La
8 High St
9 King William Av
10 Marsh St
11 Middle Av
12 Queen Square Av
13 Rackhay
14 St Stephen's Av
15 Telephone Av

C1
1 Tennyson Rd
2 Willoughby Rd

C2
1 Morley Sq
2 Seymour Av
3 Wesley Rd

C3
1 Denmark St
2 Princes' Pl
3 Rutland Rd
4 Surrey Rd

C4
1 Cheltenham La
2 Chesterfield Av
3 Norfolk Av
4 St Andrew's Rd

C5
1 Armidale Av
2 Barnabas St
3 Bath Buildings
4 Dalrymple Rd
5 Drummond Rd
6 Norrisville Rd
7 Woodmancote Rd

C6
1 Backfields
2 Backfields La
3 Brunswick Sq
4 Chapter St
5 Cumberland St
6 Dalton Sq
7 Gloucester St
8 Hillgrove St
9 Little Bishop St
10 Norfolk Av
11 Pembroke St
12 Portland Sq
13 Thomas St
14 Wilder St

C7
1 Callowhill Ct
2 George Whitefield Ct
3 Hanover Ct
4 Marybush La
5 Meadow St
6 Merchant St
7 Old King Street Ct
8 Philadelphia Ct
9 Quakers' Friars
10 Wellington Ct
11 Whippington Ct

C8
1 Church St
2 Ferry St
3 Long Rw
4 Narrow Pln
5 St Thomas St East
6 Three Queens' La
7 Tower St

D1
1 Draycott Rd
2 Uphill Rd

D3
1 Hopetoun Av
2 Osborne Av
3 St Bartholomew's Rd

D4
1 Ashley Court Rd
2 Ashley Grove Rd
3 Ashley Pde
4 Cumberland Gv
5 Fairlawn Rd
6 Falkland Rd
7 Milverton Gdns
8 Old Ashley Hl
9 Richmond Av
10 Richmond Rd
11 St Andrew's Ter
12 St Werburgh's Rd
13 Sommerville Rd South
14 York St

D5
1 Albany Rd
2 Albert Pk
3 Ashfield Pl
4 Brook La
5 Cairns' Crs
6 Corey Cl
7 Franklyn La
8 London Rd
9 Tudor Rd
10 Winkworth Pl

D6
1 Beggarswell Cl
2 Charlotte St
3 Cheapside
4 East St
5 Elton St
6 Eugene St
7 Frome St
8 Wilson St

D7
1 Asher La
2 David St
3 Eyer's La
4 Gloucester La
5 Hawkins St
6 Redcross St
7 St Matthias Pk
8 Tucker St
9 Waterloo St
10 Willway St

D8
1 Broad Pln
2 Louisa St
3 Midland St
4 New Kingsley Rd
5 New Thomas St
6 Providence Pl
7 Straight St

E4
1 Boucher Pl
2 Boyce Dr
3 Cleave St
4 Dorset Gv
5 Durham Rd
6 Hereford Rd
7 John St
8 Lancaster Rd
9 Lynmouth Rd
10 Merstham Rd
11 Norman Rd
12 Ryland Pl
13 Seddon Rd
14 Stafford Rd
15 Tewkesbury Rd
16 Treefield Pl
17 Trentham Cl
18 Warminster Rd
19 Weedon Cl
20 York St

E5
1 Ashley Grove Rd
2 Baptist St
3 Barker Wk
4 Bean St
5 Blenheim St
6 Byron St
7 Conduit Pl
8 Dermot St
9 Gable Rd
10 Highett Dr
11 Kensington Pk
12 Lower Ashley Rd
13 Newfoundland Rd
14 Oxford Pl
15 Pennywell Rd
16 Rosebery Av
17 Summers Rd
18 Waverley St

E6
1 Armoury Sq
2 Ashman Cl
3 Bates Cl
4 Beaufort St
5 Beaumont St
6 Beaumont Ter
7 Clark St
8 Durbin Wk
9 Hamilton Rd
10 Harleston St
11 Perry St
12 Robinson Dr
13 St Gabriel's Rd
14 Webb St
15 Winsford St

E8
1 Barton V
2 Dings Wk
3 Freestone Rd
4 Queen Victoria St
5 William St

Page 365

F1
1 Haydon Gdns

F3
1 Bridge Rd
2 Kirtlington Rd
3 Tackley Rd

F4
1 Chester St
2 Clare Rd
3 Robert St
4 Wood St

F5
1 Chapel Rd
2 Church Av
3 Graham Rd
4 Greenbank Av West
5 Henrietta St
6 Lawrence Av
7 Moorhill St
8 Normanby Rd
9 Northcote St
10 St Mark's Ter
11 St Nicholas Pk
12 Warwick Av
13 Warwick Rd
14 Woodborough St

F6
1 Abraham Cl
2 Adelaide Pl
3 All Hallows Rd
4 Brighton Pl
5 Cattybrook St
6 Clayton St
7 Combfactory La
8 Eastbourne Rd
9 Elmgrove Av
10 Luxton St
11 Owen St
12 Pountney Dr
13 Thomson Rd
14 Tyndall Rd
15 Vining Wk
16 Westbourne Rd
17 Windsor Gv

F7
1 Arthur Skemp Cl
2 Atchley St
3 Bright St
4 Charlton St
5 Church St
6 Earl Russell Wy
7 Ernest Barker Cl
8 Morton St
9 Payne Dr
10 Robert St
11 St Luke St
12 Strawbridge Rd
13 William Mason Cl

F8
1 Beaconsfield St
2 Bradhurst St
3 Canterbury St
4 Cookworthy Cl
5 Fripp Cl
6 Goulter St
7 Holmes St
8 Maze St
9 Napier St
10 Parkers Barton
11 Victor St

G1
1 Baileys Mead Rd
2 Heath House La
3 Little Parr Cl

G2
1 Croft Av
2 Rowland Av

G3
1 Chisbury St
2 Coleridge Rd
3 Freemantle Gdns
4 Freemantle Rd
5 Muller Rd

G4
1 Apsley St
2 Argyle St
3 Bay Gdns
4 Berkeley Gv
5 Boswell St
6 Caraway Gdns
7 Coombe Rd
8 Coriander Wk
9 East Park Dr
10 Fountaine Ct
11 Freeland Buildings
12 Juniper Ct
13 St Leonard's St

G5
1 Cartledge Rd
2 Colwyn Rd
3 Leonards Av
4 Prudham St
5 Seaton Rd

G6
1 Albion St
2 Alfred St
3 Arthur St
4 Clare St
5 Edward St
6 George St
7 Ida Rd
8 Lillian St
9 Samuel St
10 William St

G7
1 Beam St
2 Brook St
3 Brunswick St
4 Byron St
5 Cambridge St
6 Cowper St
7 Hanover St
8 Howett Rd
9 Lancaster St
10 Matthew's Rd
11 Milton Pk
12 Morse Rd
13 Osprey Rd
14 Oxford St
15 Verrier Rd
16 Weight Rd
17 Witchell Rd
18 York St

G8
1 Barton Ct
2 Ford St
3 Great Western La
4 Kings Park Av

H1
1 Lynn Rd
2 Rockland Gv
3 Stapleton Rd

H2
1 Fry's Cl
2 Wickham Vw

H3
1 Gloster Av
2 Herbert Crs
3 Queen St
4 Shamrock Rd

H4
1 Berkeley Gv
2 Bridge St
3 Crabtree Wk
4 Edward St

H5
1 Camelford Rd
2 Camerton Rd
3 Turley Rd
4 Woodcroft Av

H6
1 Altringham Rd
2 Bourneville Rd
3 Charterhouse Rd
4 Congleton Rd
5 Hammersmith Rd
6 Mary St
7 Neath Rd
8 Oakleigh Av
9 Poets' Cl
10 Stretford Rd
11 Tintern Av
12 Trelawney Rd
13 Westminster Rd
14 Whitehall Gdns
15 Woodbine St

H7
1 Barnes St
2 Beaufort Cl
3 Ebenezer St
4 Gladstone St
5 Handel Av
6 Lewin St
7 Orchard Sq
8 Parkfield Av
9 Seneca St
10 Speedwell Av
11 Terrell Gdns
12 Weston Av
13 Worsley St

J1
1 Blackberry Av
2 Cromwells Hide
3 Frome Ct
4 Glenside Pk
5 Kite Hay Cl
6 Lark's Fld
7 Pennyroyal Gv
8 Spires Vw

J2
1 Foxglove Cl
2 Honey Suckle La
3 Lower Grove Rd
4 Rosebay Mead

J3
1 Huyton Rd
2 Knowsley St
3 Marlborough Av
4 Marlborough St
5 Ridgeway Pde

J5
1 Arley Ter
2 Bowden Rd
3 Chester Rd
4 Thurstons Barton

J6
1 Hudd's Vale Rd
2 Oakland Rd
3 Snowberry Wk

J7
1 Bennett Rd
2 Burgess Green Cl
3 Pilgrims Whf

J8
1 Holy Well Cl
2 Roegate Dr
3 Whiteway Cl

K2
1 Adelaide Pl
2 Albert Ter
3 Featherstone Rd
4 Langdale Rd
5 Wharf Rd

K3
1 Balaclava Rd
2 Drummond Rd
3 Haldock Av
4 Lodore Rd
5 Midland Ter
6 Stoke View Rd

K4
1 Irena Rd
2 Madeline Rd

K5
1 Dragon Wk
2 Emra Cl
3 Fernhurst Rd
4 Whitewood Rd

K6
1 Albert Gv
2 Bruton Cl
3 Orchard Rd
4 Park St

K7
1 Summerhill Ter

K8
1 Angels Gnd
2 Avonside Wy
3 Barton Cl
4 Celia Ter
5 Cousins Ms
6 Coventry Wk
7 Crew's Hole Rd
8 Elizabeths Ms
9 Quayside La
10 Riverside Wk
11 St Georges Av

Page 366

A1
1 Claverham Rd
2 College Rd
3 Guinea St

A2
1 Hinton Rd
2 Hockey's La

A3
1 Acton Rd
2 Ivy La
3 Justice Rd
4 Poplar Pl

A4
1 Dean's Dr

A5
1 Ponting Cl
2 Thomas Pring Wk

A6
1 Kensington Rd

A7
1 Cassey Bottom La
2 Kennion Rd
3 Marling Rd
4 Parslow Barton
5 Staple Grove Crs
6 Widcombe Cl

A8
1 Dundridge Gdns
2 Gunter's Hl
3 Harcourt Av
4 Maybec Gdns
5 Petersway Gdns
6 Valma Rocks

B1
1 Cunningham Gdns

B2
1 Bridges Ct
2 Chasefield La
3 Daws Ct
4 Parkhurst Av
5 Vicars Cl

B3
1 Filwood Ct
2 William St

B4
1 Forest Wk
2 Lyncombe Wk

B5
1 Beaufort Rd
2 Claymore Cresent
3 Duncombe Rd
4 Launceston Rd
5 Prospect Av

B6
1 Monks Av
2 St Michaels Ct
3 Two Mile St

B7
1 Battens Av
2 Meg Thatchers Cl
3 Sheldare Barton
4 Thatchers Cl

B8
1 Beverley Cl
2 Clyde Cobs
3 Old Farm La
4 St Aidan's Cl

C1
1 Pemberton Ct

C2
1 Edgeware Rd

C3
1 Acacia Cl
2 The Chase
3 Glendale
4 Glenwood
5 The Greenway
6 Market Sq
7 Quadrant East
8 The Rosery

C4
1 Coulson Wk
2 Henshaw Cl
3 Welton Wk
4 Wentforth Dr
5 Willow Gv
6 Woodland Cl

C5
1 Dalkeith Av
2 Lodgeside Av
3 Seymour Rd
4 Soundwell Rd

C6
1 Barcroft Cl
2 Beverstone
3 Grantham La

C7
1 Trevethin Cl

C8
1 Magpie Bottom La

D1
1 Christchurch Cl
2 Christchurch La
3 Downend Park Rd
4 Nelson Rd
5 Tyler's La

D2
1 Alexandra Cl
2 Kensington Rd
3 Nelson Rd
4 North Vw
5 Pendennis Av

D3
1 Beazer Cl
2 Colston Cl
3 Leicester Sq
4 Portland Pl
5 Wesley Cl

D4
1 Norman Gv
2 Wellington Rd
3 Whitfield Cl
4 The Wickets
5 Woodland Av

D5
1 Brighton Pl
2 Chesham Wy
3 Gladstone Rd
4 Hampton St
5 Kennington Av
6 Kimberley Rd
7 Morley Ter
8 Wesley Hl
9 Worcester Rd

D6
1 Bank Rd
2 Ellesmere Rd
3 Halls Rd
4 Parklands
5 West St

D7
1 Abbotswood

D8
1 Dundry Cl
2 Woodcote
3 Woodend

E1
1 Clarence Gdns
2 Heathcote Rd

E2
1 Byron Pl
2 Eastleigh Cl
3 Fiennes Cl
4 Irving Cl
5 James Cl
6 Saunders Rd
7 Shipman Cl
8 Teewell Cl

E3
1 Gladstone Dr
2 Gloucester Rd
3 St Stephens Cl
4 Wiltshire Pl
5 Woodchester

E4
1 Blackthorn Wk
2 Deerhurst
3 Frys Hl
4 Pembroke Wk
5 Tyndale Wk

E5
1 Collingwood Av
2 Frys Hl
3 Holly Crs
4 Runnymede

E6
1 Macrae Cs
2 Staynes Crs

E7
1 Bellevue Cl
2 Berkeley Rd

E8
1 Elmfield Cl
2 Cranny's La
3 High Elm
4 Kemble Cl

Page 367

F4
1 Cranham Cl
2 Elmore
3 Fairford Cl
4 Peartree La

F7
1 Brake Cl
2 Bredon Cl
3 Gee Moors
4 Kingsleigh Ct
5 Kingsleigh Gdns
6 Ladd Cl
7 Norton Cl
8 Penard Wy
9 Shilton Cl
10 Woodstock Rd

G5
1 Greenways
2 Perrott Rd

D3
1 Brookfield Wk
2 Chequers Cl
3 The Clamp
4 The Croft

D4
1 Lodge Dr
2 Oaklands Dr
3 Withington Cl

E2
1 Batley Ct
2 Lovell Av
3 North Cft

Page 374

A5
1 Newlyn Wk
2 St Martin's Gdns
3 St Martin's Wk
4 Shapcott Cl

A7
1 Elderwood Rd

B4
1 Tozers Hl

C5
1 Adams Hay
2 Bartonia Cv
3 Ellesmere Rd
4 Craveney Cl
5 Hammond Cl
6 Homemead Dr
7 Prestwick Cl
8 West Town Dr

C8
1 Burgis Rd
2 Dutton Cl
3 Dutton Wk

D8
1 Beale Cl
2 Cornish Cv
3 Harrington Cv
4 Harrington Wk
5 Meardon Rd
6 Puxley Cl
7 Thompson Rd

E1
1 Abbey Ct
2 Chelmsford Wk
3 Davies Dr
4 Stockwood Ms

E3
1 Millbrook Av
2 St Helier Av

E8
1 Cogsall Rd
2 Holsom Rd
3 Swane Rd

Page 376

A2
1 Alwins Ct
2 Bramley Ct
3 Britten Ct
4 Drummond Ct
5 Dudley Ct
6 Frampton Ct
7 Godfrey Ct
8 Greve Ct
9 Harris Ct
10 Hicks Ct
11 Laphams Ct
12 Logus Ct
13 Lynch Ct
14 Miles Ct
15 Park Farm Ct
16 Pippin Ct
17 Press Moor Dr
18 Stibbs Ct
19 Tindell Ct
20 Turners Ct
21 Woodington Ct

B1
1 Betjeman Ct
2 Churchill Cl
3 Coronation Cl
4 Dylan Thomas Ct
5 Earlstone Crs
6 Henry Williamson Ct
7 Laurie Lee Ct

B2
1 Chesters
2 Harptree Ct
3 Haskins Ct
4 Horwood Ct
5 Little Dowles
6 Marygold Leaze
7 Stokes Ct
8 Tapsters
9 The Warns

B3
1 Bakersfield
2 Beaumont Cl
3 Fairoaks
4 Penngrove
5 Redwood Cl
6 Rutherford Cl
7 Springville Cl

C3
1 Handford Wy
2 Rawens Wd
3 Stockton Cl

Notes

Notes

Notes

Notes

Notes